DESIGN AND IMPLEMENTATION OF OPTIMIZATION SOFTWARE

NATO ADVANCED STUDY INSTITUTES SERIES

Proceedings of the Advanced Study Institute Programme, which aims at the dissemination of advanced knowledge and the formation of contacts among scientists from different countries.

The series is published by an international board of publishers in conjunction with NATO Scientific Affairs Division

A	Life Sciences	Plenum Publishing Corporation
B	Physics	London and New York
C	Mathematical and Physical Sciences	D. Reidel Publishing Company Dordrecht and Boston
D	Behavioural and Social Sciences	Sijthoff & Noordhoff International Publishers B.V.
E	Applied Science	Alphen aan den Rijn, The Netherlands and Winchester, Mass., USA

Series E: Applied Science — No. 28

DESIGN AND IMPLEMENTATION OF OPTIMIZATION SOFTWARE

edited by

HARVEY J. GREENBERG
Department of Energy, Washington, D.C., U.S.A.

SIJTHOFF & NOORDHOFF   1978
Alphen aan den Rijn — The Netherlands

Proceedings of the NATO Advanced Study Institute on Design and Implementation of Optimization Software
Urbino, Italy
20 June — 2 July, 1977

ISBN-13:978-94-009-9937-4   e-ISBN-13:978-94-009-9935-0
DOI: 10.1007/978-94-009-9935-0

NATO ADVANCED STUDY INSTITUTE ON

DESIGN AND IMPLEMENTATION OF OPTIMIZATION SOFTWARE

SOGESTA, Urbino, Italy, 20 June - 2 July, 1977

Director   : F.A. Lootsma, Department of Mathematics,
            University of Technology, Delft, Netherlands

Co-director: H.J. Greenberg, Department of Energy,
            Washington, D.C. 20461, U.S.A.

Scientific Contents of the Advanced Study Institute

The Advanced Study Institute has been organized by the
Committee on Algorithms (COAL) established by the Mathematical
Programming Society to concern itself with recommendations and
actions on optimization algorithms and testing methodologies.
The ASI was intended to bring together optimization specialists,
computer scientists, representatives of computer manufacturers,
representatives of software houses, and members from user organizations, in order to promote the professional development of
optimization software.

The scientific program started with a series of introductory
lectures on the development of mathematical programming systems
(W. Orchard-Hays), linear algebra (T.J. Dekker), matricial packing (H.J. Greenberg), and solution strategies for linear programming (H.J. Greenberg). Thereafter, much attention was given to
related software for networks (F. Glover), integer programming
(E.L. Johnson), and LP driven nonlinear programming (E.M.L. Beale).
Finally, there was a large section devoted to nonlinear-program-
ming software: unconstrained minimization (P.E. Gill), reduced-
gradient methods (J. Abadie and L.S. Lasdon), penalty-function
methods (F.A. Lootsma), global optimization (L.C.W. Dixon), and
geometric programming (M.J. Rijckaert). Several contributions
were presented by participants: matrix and report generators
(J.M. Anthonisse), MPSX and the Extended Control Language (M.
Benichou), quadratic programming (R. Benveniste), unconstrained
optimization (J.S. Kowalik), mathematical programming in optimal
control (D. Kraft), optimal design of community energy systems
(M. Minkoff), and black-box heuristics for combinatorial optimization (G.L. Nemhauser). The scientific program was much enlivened
by two COAL sessions where guidelines for reporting computational
experiments in mathematical programming (R.S. Dembo) and guidelines for the documentation of test problems in nonlinear programming (J.C.P. Bus) were discussed.

Lecturers

J. Abadie, Electricité de France, Paris, France.
E.M.L. Beale, Scientific Control Systems, Milton Keynes, England.
T.J. Dekker, University of Amsterdam, Netherlands.
L.C.W. Dixon, Numerical Optimization Centre, Hatfield, England.
P.E. Gill, National Physical Laboratory, Teddington, England.
F. Glover, University of Texas, Austin, Texas, U.S.A.
H.J. Greenberg, Department of Energy, Washington, U.S.A.
E.L. Johnson, IBM Research, Yorktown Heights, U.S.A.
L.S. Lasdon, University of Texas, Austin, Texas, U.S.A.
F.A. Lootsma, University of Technology, Delft, Netherlands.
W. Orchard-Hays, Nat. Bureau of Economic Research, Cambridge,
Mass., U.S.A.
M.J. Rijckaert, University of Louvain, Belgium.

Contributors

J.M. Anthonisse, Mathematical Centre, Amsterdam, Netherlands.
M. Benichou, IBM Program Product Centre, Paris, France.
R. Benveniste, Imperial College, London, England.
J.S. Kowalik, Washington State University, Pullman, U.S.A.
D. Kraft, DFVLR, Oberpfaffenhofen, Germany.
M. Minkoff, Argonne National Laboratory, Argonne, Illinois, U.S.A.
G.L. Nemhauser, CORE, Louvain, Belgium.

Committee on Algorithms (COAL)

J.M. Mulvey (chairman), Harvard University, Boston, U.S.A.
J.C.P. Bus (co-chairman), Mathematical Centre, Amsterdam, Nether-
lands.
Karla L. Hoffman (editor of newsletter), Nat. Bureau of Standards,
Washington, U.S.A.
M. Benichou, IBM Program Product Centre, Paris, France.
H.P. Crowder, IBM Research, Yorktown Heights, U.S.A.
R.S. Dembo, Yale University, Newhaven, U.S.A.
P.E. Gill, National Physical Laboratory, Teddington, England.
R.H.F. Jackson, Nat. Bureau of Standards, Washington, U.S.A.
L.S. Lasdon, University of Austin, Texas, U.S.A.
Melanie Lenard, Illinois Institute of Technology, Chicago, U.S.A.
F.A. Lootsma, University of Technology, Delft, Netherlands.
R.P. O'Neill, Department of Energy, Washington, U.S.A.
Susan Powell, London School of Economics, London, England.

Local Organization

J.M. Anthonisse, Mathematical Centre, Amsterdam, Netherlands.
J.C.P. Bus, Mathematical Centre, Amsterdam, Netherlands.
E. Catani, SOGESTA, Urbino, Italy.
O.B. de Gans, University of Technology, Delft, Netherlands.
J.E. Taylor, SOGESTA, Urbino, Italy.
C. de Wit, University of Technology, Delft, Netherlands.

Secretarial Staff

Clara Bottazzi, SOGESTA, Urbino, Italy.
Graziella Massi, SOGESTA, Urbino, Italy.
Valeria Rossi, SOGESTA, Urbino, Italy.
Annelies Rouwenhorst, University of Technology, Delft, Netherlands.
Ans Stephan, University of Technology, Delft, Netherlands.

Proceedings

H.J. Greenberg (editor), Department of Energy, Washington, U.S.A.
Anita B. Knapp (typing and lay-out), Fairfield, Conn., U.S.A.

TABLE OF CONTENTS

X

PREFACE

This proceedings contains tutorials presented at the NATO
Advanced Study Institute on Design and Implementation of Optimization Software (Urbino, Italy, 20 June - 2 July, 1977) organized
by the Committee on Algorithms (COAL) of the Mathematical Programming Society. The authors are to be congratulated on their clear
expositions plus their prompt cooperation. We were especially
fortunate to have had two of the first pioneers in designing
mathematical programming systems: W. Orchard-Hays and E.M.L. Beale.

Surveying the contents the reader will find that the papers
fall into three categories which we can roughly designate by:
linear programming, extensions of linear programming, and nonlinear programming.

In the first category on linear programming, the three background papers by W. Orchard-Hays capture a historical perspective
through the scope of modern systems, while T.J. Dekker's paper
provides background in numerical methods used in optimization
software. One area neglected by most previous mathematical programming symposia is the information structure employed to manipulate large volumes of data. The tutorial on matricial packing
by H.J. Greenberg includes modern structures, including recent
suggestions by J. Kalan and D. Rarick; another tutorial on pivot
selection describes the vast range of tactics that have evolved,
aimed at reducing computational effort with the strategy of the
simplex method. An important development in computer technology
is the interactive system environment, and the design of optimization software is entering a new plateau by concentrating on
user interfaces. One of the new ideas, presented by R. O'Neill,
is that of diagnostic analysis of a linear program's solution;
his PERUSE system enables analysts to query the solution file
interactively with a powerful, but simple, language.

Thereafter we enter the second category of papers, which are
concerned with network problems and other areas closely related to
linear programming. Special consideration for network problems
is appropriate because the class of problems is large. F. Glover

and D. Klingman have shown how dramatically the computing costs are reduced by their vast experiences in modeling "netforms" and by their associated software. An important extension of linear programming is the allowance of integer restrictions. E.L. Johnson has described how users may become more sophisticated in modeling an integer program, aimed at helping the optimizer to terminate quicker; his second paper, with S. Powell, surveys integer-programming codes. As we move towards nonlinear programs, we pay special attention to an early extension of linear programs, namely quadratic objective functions; E.M.L. Beale and R. Benveniste have described solution techniques which pertain to the capability in SCICONIC. In another paper, Beale describes how an LP-driven system, such as SCICONIC, can be used to solve nonlinear programs. In cases where there is a large volume of data and manageable functional forms, such as when a large portion of the problem is linear or quadratic, using an MPS holds many benefits, and the computational overhead associated with recursion may then be relatively negligible. Beale's approach is complementary to the library approach, which builds subroutines, letting the user build his own algorithm, tailored to his problem.

The third category of papers on nonlinear programming traditionally starts with a contribution on optimization without constraints. P.E. Gill and W. Murray have provided us with an insightful tutorial on unconstrained minimization. Much of their material is based on their own research. Both, J. Abadie as well as L.S. Lasdon and A.D. Waren refer to Gill and Murray's exposition in their complementary papers on designing optimization software based on the generalized reduced gradient method; since the mid sixties this method has always attracted considerable attention because of its performance as reported by Abadie and his colleagues at Electricité de France. F.A. Lootsma describes the design and use of minifun, a nonlinear programming code based on penalty functions and written in ALGOL 60; it is a blueprint from which various other ALGOL 60 and FORTRAN codes have been derived. Conjugate gradient algorithms comprise an important class of nonlinear programming solution strategies; J.S. Kowalik consented to describe an acceleration scheme he invented, and an abstract of his presentation is included. L.C.W. Dixon reports his own research into methodologies that seek global optima in the absence of convexity; this difficulty is compounded in multi-variable problems, and Dixon's paper reflects new insights with sample problems he has solved. M.J. Rijckaert's paper on geometric programming returns us to address a special problem class. The data handling problems can be solved with LP technology since the exponent matrix and other coefficients can be accounted for in a matricial structure. Useful properties, such as sparsity, can be recognized and advantageously exploited. Therefore, of primary interest is the basic optimization strategy to be employed in a design, and Rijckaert's paper addresses this aspect.

The book ends with a number of discussion papers written by members of the Committee on Algorithms. The European chairman of COAL, J.C.P. Bus, proferred an approach to classification and documentation of test problems. This important topic has been of primary interest to COAL since its inception, and Bus has advanced our state of knowledge. On a closely allied topic, namely how to design experiments and report their implications for evaluating optimization software, COAL members, H.P. Crowder, R.S. Dembo and J.M. Mulvey (North American Chairman), present guidelines for so doing. These two papers were discussed, along with related topics, at a COAL panel discussion. A transcription edited by R.H.F. Jackson is included in this proceedings.

Now that we have introduced the contents and central theme of this proceedings it is befitting to acknowledge the work expended by so many. The A.S.I. could not have succeeded without the help of staff who assisted in the planning and operations. First, Dr. Tilo Kester (member of NATO's Scientific Affairs Division in Brussels) has given us considerable guidance during the period that we set up the program of the A.S.I. Annelies Rouwenhorst (University of Technology, Delft) assisted us cheerfully from the beginning of our preparations in 1975 until the very last moment that we completed this proceedings, and Ans Stephan (University of Technology, Delft) accurately processed all the registrations when Annelies was in New-Zealand (December 1976 - June 1977). John Taylor (SOGESTA, Urbino) smoothly coordinated our activities on the conference site, and Enrico Catani (SOGESTA, Urbino) beautifully organized our social program. Clara Bottazzi (accounts), Valeria Rossi (travel arrangements) and Graziella Massi (interpretation) were permanently present in the A.S.I.'s office to help participants in a charming and efficient manner. Dr. Riccione (Computer Manager, SOGESTA, Urbino) assisted us attentively in testing and running the optimization software of the lecturers. Last, but certainly not least, Anita Knapp produced this proceedings. Anita not only typed the entire book, she also proofread and identified instances where a paper could be improved. Authors generally appreciated this and revised their papers accordingly. It is a pleasure for us to acknowledge the quality of her work.

September 1978

H.J. Greenberg, Co-director of the A.S.I.
Editor of the Proceedings

F.A. Lootsma , Director of the A.S.I.

We all, members of the Summer School, were deeply moved by the sad message that Haje Willemse, one of the participants, passed away in the Ancona hospital, a few days after the end of the Summer School. He became seriously ill on Thursday, June 30. In the Urbino Hospital his condition improved over the weekend, but on Monday there was a rapid deterioration necessitating a further treatment in Ancona. On Thursday, July 7, he died due to a cerebral hemmorhage.

Born in 1947, Haje graduated in 1972 from the University of Technology, Twente (Netherlands). In 1975, after some years in a computer consulting firm, he joined the department of Econometrics of the University of Groningen (Netherlands). He worked on inventory control problems, stochastic programming, dynamic programming and conjugate duality. He was a promising staff member of the Operations Research group, and his death is a loss which is deeply felt.

His wife, Marie-France, went back to work at the University with admirable courage. We all wish her the strength to carry her grief and to find her way to a new life.

F.A. Lootsma

HISTORY OF MATHEMATICAL PROGRAMMING SYSTEMS

Wm. Orchard-Hays

International Institute for Applied Systems Analysis,
Laxenburg, Austria

OVERVIEW OF AN ERA

One cannot clearly comprehend the development of mathematical
programming software without reference to the development of the
computing field itself. There are two main reasons, one specific
and one general. First, mathematical programming and computing
have been contemporary in an almost uniquely exact sense. Their
histories parallel each other year by year in a remarkable way.
Furthermore, mathematical programming simply could not have developed without computers. Although the converse is obviously not
true, still linear programming was one of the important and de-
manding applications for computers from the outset. I will not
try to trace early encouragement for the development of computers
which emanated from influential agencies of the U.S. government
and other quarters concerned with the application of LP and similar techniques. I have heard this story from unimpeachable
sources but it antedates my personal experience and I might claim
too much credit for our field. I am aware of later influences on
computer technology for which we perhaps have not received sufficient credit. I will point out two or three of these along the
way.

The second and more general reason for relating the two histories closely is based on the lessons of history itself. It is
easy to find fault with the way things have developed in the past,
whether political, cultural or technological. I predict that some
of you will be tempted to ask during this two weeks, "But why did
you do it that way, who not this way?" While it may be possible
and even interesting to answer such questions--and I will try to
anticipate some--it is largely futile to dwell on what may be

considered past mistakes. The quarter century from the late 1940s to the early 1970s constituted an era, one of the most dynamic in the history of mankind. Among the many technological developments of that period--and indeed of any period--the computing field has been the most virulent and astounding. At the beginning of such an era, it is unpredictable just how things will evolve and there is--or appears to be--a plasticity which might permit basic forms to emerge in any of several ways. But as the pace and intensity of activity increase, commitments are made which determine the forms for the future. These cannot thereafter be changed in a significant way. If you doubt that, I call your attention to any of the other far-reaching technologies of the past hundred years. The basic form of the electric power industry was determined while Edison was still alive, the telephone system in the U.S. is still called the Bell system, automobiles today are scarcely different from the 1939 models, and commercial aircraft assumed their essential characteristics in the 1950s. Similarly, the nature of the computing industry, profession, and technology has by now been determined--all their essential features have existed for perhaps five years. One hopes that some of the more recent developments will be applied more widely and effectively but the technology that now exists is pretty much what will exist, leaving aside a few finishing touches to areas already well developed, such as minicomputers and networks.

I realize that we are still too close to the end of the period of development for my statement to stand unchallenged; there are still lingering hopes that things can somehow be different from what they are. I will not push the point further but I would like to suggest that we at the beginning of a new era with even greater challenges. The past twenty-five years have given us an enormous set of capabilities. It has been great fun creating them--in spite of some disappointments--but the time has come to apply them more seriously and expertly to the many critical problems facing the world. No one can foresee how that will come out but the challenge is worthy of the best efforts of any generation.

So let us now see what has been. It may be useful to first place computing within the framework of modern technological history. The electronic digital computer was the outgrowth of several lines of development, some quite old, which began to coalesce after WW II. These are shown at the top of Figure 1. The concept of a computer goes back at least to Babbage in the first third of the XIX century. He even had a programmer, and a female at that--Lady Lovelace, the estranged daughter of Lord Byron. But his proposed technology was purely mechanical and, in spite of monumental efforts at detailed design--he greatly advanced the art of mechanical drawing--no one could shape metal to his required tolerances. Mechanical calculators had existed since Fermat's time and continued to develop until about twenty years ago when an

elegant little hand model was produced in Lichtenstein. During
WW II, IBM, which was already a big company in the tabulating and
office equipment field, essentially built Babbage's machine. It
was called Mark I and is, or was, in a kind of museum at Harvard
University. It was a monster and hardly of practical value. The
key to computers, of course, was electronics which burgeoned during
the war in connection with RADAR, LORAN and fire-control devices.
It is no accident that the development of computers was initially
fostered by the military.

The first electronic computers were one-of-a-kind, laboratory
creations in universities and research centers. Two new ideas were
needed, however, to make them practical. The first was von Neumann's
notion of an internally stored program--that is, the data and program should be in a common storage. Previously, from Babbage's
time, the two had been regarded as different sorts of things. The
other requirement was some kind of fast and reliable storage medium. It would take too long to recount all the wierd contrivances
that were invented for memory units--one of the weirdest and yet
most successful until then was the William's tube. This was used
in the IBM 701 and also in the first very large computer (for its
day), the NORC, built by IBM for Naval Ordnance. The first commercial machine, the UNIVAC-I, used memory tanks. But it was the
invention of the ferrite core memory that permitted the large-
scale development of computers. (There are some good stories about
these devices too, which are best told over cocktails.) Good magnetic drums of limited size already existed and also magnetic tapes
although it took several years to make tapes reliable. Even as late
as 1971, we were keeping card decks around because we still didn't
fully trust tapes and disks, though by then they had extremely low
failure rates.

Note that the whole history of electronic computers to the
present is represented by a very short line on a scale covering
only about two centuries. I sometimes point out that I had lived
nearly half a lifetime before getting into computing and yet my
career has spanned almost its entire history. Still it is a mistake to think that computers have developed extraordinarily fast.
It has been nearly thirty years since the first beginnings. Most
of the other modern technologies fully developed within forty to
forty-five years. A more remarkable feature is the scope and
depth of its penetration into other human activities. Electricity,
the telephone, the automobile have had perhaps a broader effect on
peoples' lives--at least visibly--but they have not interacted so
deeply with intellectual pursuits. The computer created a new
kind of activity, blending mental and mechanistic realms.

Turning now to the technical, professional and organizational
patterns which evolved as a necessary part of the field, it is convenient to take 5-year periods starting in 1950. Rather oddly,

such stereotyped periods seem to fit the facts although, for some purposes, the end of 1947 is a better time zero. I started in computing in 1951--at the RAND Corporation in Santa Monica, California. The technology was so meager that I mastered most of it and even made some contribution within two years. We didn't have a computer but a collection of tabulating equipment plus a couple of IBM's card-programmed-calculators (CPC) which consisted of a tabulator, an electronic calculator, and a bank of 16 mechanical storage registers, essentially ten-decade counters, all strung together with cables. The last component was called an icebox since it was almost exactly the size and shape of a Coco Cola box. All work was done with punched cards in the style and custom of a tabulating shop. Let me illustrate how precedents are set by almost incidental choices and how difficult it is to change conventions once they have become established.

Did you ever wonder why standard MPS input formats put the column identifier first and the row second? In mathematics, FORTRAN and almost any other notation, one gives the row first and then the column. Well, in tabulating they had the concept of sort fields on a card with the major key first, followed by any intermediate fields, and the minor key on the right, all followed by the data fields. Incidentally, the card number was in the last eight columns on the right, a custom which still persists even on disk files. When I first started working with George Dantzig on developing practical LP computing techniques in late 1952, we began on the CPC (which by then had five iceboxes with 80 registers). I had had the notion of sort fields drilled into me for two years and, since we handled everything by columns, with row indices within columns, obviously the column index was the major sort field and went on the left. Some years later we went to alphanumeric column identifiers and, later still, to alphanumeric row names, but the old order was maintained. By the time I was designing MPS/360, several large oil companies, the major users, believed there was something fundamental in this arrangement and were developing matrix generators and data management systems based on it--the most notable outcome being the MARVEL processor which was a marvel mainly for its inefficiency.

In designing the LP/600 MPS (GE 600 line) and OPTIMA system (CDC 6000 line), we attempted to correct this mistake and specified row first and column second. Surprisingly, many practitioners didn't like it. But we went further. The LP/600 and OPTIMA input processors were very elaborate and did not require one to specify everything in strict row, column, righthand-side, range, and bound sections. One could specify elements in any convenient order. Surely, mathematicians would like this. Of course, it required sorting and the resulting input speed seemed slow compared with the stereotyped IBM scheme in which the input file is carefully arranged in exact sequence and the input program goes zip-zip. We had to provide an alternate input program to accept MPS/360 format for compatibility (after all, we were trying to entice away IBM customers) and it executed very quickly also. Consequently, users preferred the faster input and used MPS/360 format ignoring all the improvements we had provided for model formulation. The MPS/360 input formats thereafter became a de facto industry standard and still remain so--with column first, row second, and strict sequence by sections. Only by going to true matrix generators, apparently, can we ever break the pattern and, even, then, one often finds himself using the generator in much the same way.

In Figure 2, I have tried to summarize the major developments in computing and math programming software as they appear to me in retrospect. The first five years from 1950 were devoted to creation of basic tools and techniques, and also saw the establishment of the first professional societies in the field. (I have often been surprised that this should have happened so soon.) Though I have played active roles in some of these socities at various times, it is by no means clear how beneficial they have been in furthering the field. Certainly they have provided a meeting ground and perhaps that is the most important thing that can be hoped. There have been polarizations within the various societies, and among them, which have fostered either competition or indifference rather than cooperation. But politics seem to be the same no matter what the field. One must also take into account the strong economic pressures which have existed; I have tried to indicate some of these. Much of the practical development of math programming, and of other areas too, has been made by small or only barely medium-sized companies to which success was a life-and-death matter. Many have fallen by the wayside including some of the largest independent consulting and computer service companies. Most of these were founded and run by technicians rather than business men. The strains which this put on peoples' lives--particularly during the whole miserable decade of the 1960s--resulted in many hoped-for capabilities turning out rather different than expected. Even IBM got into deeper water with its 360 line and the software for it than they anticipated. Nevertheless, the 1960s brought to fruition the essential features of the field as it exists. A much more orderly industry--in hardware, software, and consulting-- emerged in the early 1970s even though some of the old charisma and fun was gone. The commercial, industrial, engineering, and administrative applications are now pretty well standardized and set in their molds. My own personal hope is that this is not yet true of scientific and planning applications because this area still needs much improvement and it is here that mathematical programming primarily applies. So you need for feel that there is nothing left to do. But, in my judgment, the greatest progress will not be made now in algorithms or optimizing procedures but in data management and man-machine interplay. And this will require not only incisive and logical thinking but also a good deal of persuasion and retraining. Unfortunately, academicians are the hardest people of all to retrain.

EVOLUTION OF THE SIMPLEX ALGORITHM

Linear programming refers to the scheduling of a set of interdependent activities so as to account for the consumption and/or
production of a set of commodities, in such a way as to maximize or
minimize a linear function associated with the activities. The
recognizable beginnings of LP arose in about 1947 in connection
with planning and scheduling problems under study at the Pentagon
by the U.S. Air Force. Earlier work of a similar nature in connection with planned economies had been done as early as 1939 by
Academician L.V. Kantorovich of the Soviet Union but his work had
gone largely unnoticed. He finally did obtain recognition and in
1976, he and T.C. Koopmans jointly received a Nobel Prize. For
early developments in the field, one should obtain a copy of the
Cowles Commission Monograph No. 13, "Activity Analysis of Production and Allocation," edited by Koopmans and published by John
Wiley and Sons in 1951, reprinted several times.

The central mathematical problem of LP is the optimization of
a linear form subject to linear inequality constraints. Prof.
George B. Dantzig was working at the Air Force at the time of the
studies mentioned above and in 1974-8, he developed his now-famous
simplex method for solving this problem. Surprising as it may seem,
there appear to have been no formalized methods for handling systems of linear inequalities prior to that time although systems of
linear equations had been solved at least since Gauss' time. The
importance of Dantzig's algorithm was quickly recognized although it
was several years before all details were worked out and implemented
in a general procedure.

In later lectures, it will be necessary to go into various details of the simplex algorithm in greater depth, but for the present
discussion, my purpose is only to indicate the nature of the problems we faced in the early 1950s in attempting to computerize it.
Most of the basic mathematical and computer science difficulties
were resolved before the end of the 1950s, although the handling of
overlapped I/O--that is, transmission of data to and from auxiliary
storage while computations are in progress-came a little later. I
worked at great length on such techniques from 1959 when computers
with this capability became available.

Incidentally, some useful schemes which evolved in the early
years had to be abandoned due to changes in computers. For example,
I designed and used what amounted to a link-loader in about 1955 on
the IBM 701. This had to be abandoned on the 704 due to timing
differences and, to this day, it has not been possible to recreate
it with the same simplicity. It takes several years to perfect a
technology even after the concepts are understood and many details
of technique known.

Most actual LP computations up to 1952 had been done at the Air Force installation using a punched-card calculator. That year, Dantzig moved to RAND with the intention of developing more practical methods in a less hectic environment. No one, at that time, had a clear idea of the difficulties to be encountered but it was evident that the practical application of LP would require significant improvements in computing. A small code existed for the Bureau of Standards' SEAC which took 15 minutes to solve a trivial problem of 10 constraints in 20 variables. An LP program was attempted for the UNIVAC-I but it apparently never solved any real problems. A program was planned by IBM for the 701, their first stored-program, scientific computer. It was to resolve ties in pivoting by a mathematically rigorous but cumbersome method to prevent cycling of the algorithm, probably the only time this was ever done. The program was completed (by Kurt Eismann)--whether for the 701 or 704, I have now forgotten--but evidently saw little practical use.

The immediate goal was, somewhat vaguely, to handle 100-order models, i.e., 100 constraints in some presumably larger number of variables. It is doubtful whether a 100-order matrix had ever been inverted by then, except for Leontif models which can be inverted by taking a few terms of a series expansion, i.e., by matrix multiplications. Larger, faster computers were on the way but it was inconceivable that hardware improvements alone could make computations with even modest model sizes really practical. My first attempt on the CPC used the revised simplex method with explicit inverse which was currently in vogue for hand calculations. Dantzig took one look at the cards chunking through the hopper for one update of the tableau and decided that it would never do. This prompted him to recall an old suggestion by Alex Ordan and we developed the produce form of inverse. When I implemented this on the CPC, it still took eight hours of hard work pushing card decks through the hopper to solve a small problem (maximum size possible was about 45 by 70) but it was clearly a significant improvement and showed promise of being a practical method on a real computer.

An interesting vignette related to the latter CPC setup (the things were not programmed in a modern sense) was the handling of the backward transformation, that is post-multiplication of a row by the basis inverse. This became know as BTRAN and the forward transformation as FTRAN. At the end of an iteration, one has an updated column, the transformation of the incoming basis vector A_s by the basis inverse, B^{-1}, i.e., $\bar{A}_s = B^{-1}A_s$. If the pivot row has index r, then $\bar{A}_s^r$ is the pivot element. One then creates an update column called an eta-column by replacing the pivot element by its reciprocal and multiplying all other elements of $\bar{A}_s$ by the negative of that reciprocal. These eta-columns may then be used in a cumulative way to update a column on succeeding iterations. At the end of each iteration, I punched out the eta-column and added these cards to the deck of prior eta-columns already produced. Hence one could literally see the growth of the eta-file, as well as feel it in one's hands. The problem was that this growing deck was set up to transform columns but the first thing to do on the next iteration was to transform a row which requires application of the same values in a different way and in <u>precisely reverse order</u>. (FTRAN is a series of linear vector forms, BTRAN is a series of inner products.) So I used the first 40 columns of the card for the FTRAN deck and the last 40 columns in mirror-image form from the BTRAN deck. Hence, one ran the deck face up for BRTAN and face down for FTRAN. It worked beautifully. I later did the same thing with the 701 backward-reading tapes but on later computers, we had to have an awkward read-backward sequence for a tape which could only be read forward and then backspaced two records. On the 701, the numbers actually came in from tape in reverse order which was precisely what one wanted.

A related problem that plagued us in later years was that the builders of basic software had the strange idea that a file should not be open for both reading and writing at the same time. Even to this day, the complexity of arranging it on some systems is almost unbelievable. Why anyone ever had such a silly idea baffles me. There have been a number of such differences of opinion between basic and application software people.

On the CPC, I had used floating decimal arithmetic with 8-digit mantissa and had no trouble with roundoff on such small problems. I got the notion somehow that I could get by with fixed-point arithmetic on the 701, partly, I suppose, because 36 bits sounded like a lot, and partly because there was no floating-point arithmetic on the machine and the subroutines to simulate it were slow. I quickly discovered the notorious propensity of matrix operations to generate noise. A tiny test problem wouldn't run a dozen iterations without failing tolerance tests. I rebuilt the program to use double-precision floating point for all computations except BTRAN and there I used double-precision fixed-point with some attitional tricks. This was to try to retain some speed, BTRAN being the most time-consuming operation and we had not yet invented multiple and partial pricing.

The maximum size problem on the 701 was 100 rows, or that is what I intended. Alan Manne was working on his gasoline blending model and evidently thought I meant 100 constraints, in addition to the objective function. He insisted he could not get below 100 constraints so I rebuilt the programs again to get in that extra row. We also implemented the parametric RHS algorithm in connection with that model. One night we ran for ten hours solid with scarcely an error—a remarkable performance for the 701—and got essentially all the cases he wanted, although we later ran some parametric studies. This was in 1954 and was the first big success.

I should mention, I suppose, that essentially all LP models are sparse (the few exceptions are almost irrelevant) and we took advantage of that from the outset. I don't recall ever giving much thought to storing only the nonzero values of a column with their row indices, the columns being demarked by a header. It just seemed the sensible thing to do. However, a variety of schemes had to be devised for packing indexed values. The first thing one does in designing a system for a new computer is to decide how to store the matrix, the eta-columns and the full working columns, plus the representation of the basic indices. These are absolutely explicit to the make and type of computer--there is no such thing as transferability. (Even with FORTRAN, one does it differently on different machines.) All the large LP codes and later MPSs have been programmed in assembly language with only a couple of exceptions. Bonner and Moore's FMPS was originally in FORTRAN (the acronym meant FORTRAN MPS) but it has been rebuilt several times with various parts in assembly language and the acronym is now said to mean Functional MPS. Some other systems have used a higher-level language framework or envelope, which has certain advantages. Burrough's bit computers use an extended ALGOL as their basic programming language but much of this is in the hardware or basic software. Useful FORTRAN codes have existed and still do, but that comes a little later.

By 1956, I had built five successive LP codes for the 701--plus a sixth with some experimental procedures--and two of these saw considerable use. We also built a code for RAND's in-house built JOHN-NIAC computer. It had several interesting features but the most important was that it incorporated Markowitz' inversion scheme, or at least my interpretation of it. This was really a form of LU decomposition although the term was not coined until a decade later. It was remarkably efficient and maintained the sparsity of the basis to within a few percent in the inverse, which was a double product form connected with a permutation in the middle. The pivot agenda was prescheduled using logical operation on an incidence matrix represents with bits. Unfortunately, the problem of a pivot accidentally going to zero was not satisfactorily resolved. Furthermore, problem size was limited to 128 rows and, although the handling of the incidence matrix was completely satisfactory in other respects for this problem size, it was clear that it would be impractical for large models. (A million bits is even a lot of data.) Hence this important area of development was abandoned for many years until slow inversion speeds on large models forced a return to it. Harry Markowitz was an economist at RAND in the 1950s but later was better known for his development of SIMSCRIPT.

In 1955, IBM offered to provide some machine time, system programming assistance and general support for development of an enhanced package of programs for their then new 704 computer. The goal was to go to 256 rows with increased execution speed. Hal

Judd, formerly at RAND but then with IBM, was assigned to the project. Leloa Cutler, who had been working with me on the 701 and JOHNNIAC, continued on this project. The 704 had index registers and automatic subroutine linkage but still no floating-point operations. Miss Cutler and I had engaged in a contest between ourselves to see who could program the most efficient floating-point subroutines for the 701. We had then merged the best results of both our efforts and had probably as flexible, robust, and efficient a package of these subroutines as was possible on that equipment. These were converted to the 704 and used essentially without change until floating-point was available in hardware. I always thought that it was no coincidence that the floating-point formats on the later 7090 were identical with ours, that the hardware implementation worked exactly like our subroutines and that numerical results were identical.

The 704 package was completed in the fall of 1956 and released through the SHARE library as RSLP1. These became the backbone of several later developments and the structure of the programs is still reflected to some extent in current MPSs. Many of the acronyms we used became practically standard terminology.

Dantzig has worked out the details of bounded variables and I started an experimental version of RSLP1 incorporating these. I left RAND in late 1956 before this was completed but Miss Cutler later finished it. It was eventually released in late 1959, almost too late to see any use since the 704 was being replaced by then. Unfortunately, bounded variables were not incorporated in the next generation or two of LP packages and did not become widely used until the mid-1960s.

Summary of Developments Through 1956

Let me summarize what had been accomplished by the end of 1956.

1. Packing schemes for sparse matrices, including efficient code sequences for unpacking and doing the necessary arithmetic, were standard practice.

2. The product form of inverse had been more or less perfected, taking advantage of sparse bases and greatly simplifying maintenance of the basis inverse. In fact, matrix operations were not used at all, most computations being in terms of linear column-vector forms and the remainder in terms of inner products between a packed and an unpacked vector.

3. The first sophisticated sparse matrix inversion scheme had been implemented and used. The JOHNNIAC code was actually

used by at least one or two projects, one in an oil
company, for over ten years.

4. The problem of finding an initial feasible solution--Phase
   1 of the simplex method--had been solved although refinements continued to be made for more than a decade. Out of
   this grew many techniques using the fast and definite logical operations of computers instead of vague "large number"
   and weighting schemes depending on arithmetic. (Oddly,
   many academicians still seem not to recognize the value of
   this and continue to use ambiguous weighting schemes.)

5. Heuristic tie-breaking rules, efficiently implemented with
   more logic than arithmetic, had been proved to be fully
   satisfactory in avoiding cycling of the algorithm, which had
   been one of the troublesome theoretical problems originally.
   I have seen only two or three cases of genuine cycling in
   my entire career but it can happen.

6. We had learned how to maintain sufficient numerical precision for most problems up to 250 rows. The use of double-
   precision floating-point arithmetic and a system of tolerances and checks gave reliable results. With further
   refinements, this approach later proved adequate for models
   up to a few thousand rows. (It has perhaps been forgotten
   that the use of floating-point arithmetic was a contro-
   versial technique in the 1950s. Many people felt it hid
   accumulated error and that results could not be trusted.
   At least two or three computerized techniques were developed
   to attempt to complete error analysis throughout a lengthy
   computation. For most purposes, this is now seen as non-
   sense. A separate controversy developed over the use of
   double-precision with its additional requirements for storage and execution time. This has more or less died out
   due to practical considerations but there are still differences of opinion.)

7. The problem of storing the high volume of code and intermediate data had been overcome by detailed analyses of the
   time phasing of various steps of the simplex algorithm,
   plus the development of sequential data transmission schemes
   and program segmentation techniques. LP systems were fore-
   runners in the use of program overlay and binding methods
   and later overlapped I/O for LP was perhaps the most efficient in the industry. Though now less important, these
   schemes were critical to the development of large-scale
   systems in the 1960s. (The JOHNNIAC code had a particularly neat and efficient overlay scheme based, however, on
   unique features of that machine.)

8. Subroutinization of the revised simplex method with product form of inverse, and related procedures, was first worked out in 1953-4 when I was developing the first 701 program at RAND. The stage which was reached in the RSLP1 package has remained the basic structure even to the present. It is not far-fetched to regard this as the beginning of both algorithm engineering and application system design.

9. Both the parametric RHS algorithm, which I developed at RAND and as part of my master's dissertation, and the parametric OBJ algorithm, developed in the East by Saul Gass and Tom Saaty, had become standard LP procedures. Other related procedures were also in use and, in general, virtually all aspects of primal and dual pricing and pivoting theory had been implemented at least experimentally.

10. Some progess had been made in standardizing input and output formats though much remained to be done. At least one matrix generator and an elaborate pre-checking routine for LP input had been programmed. This was done by the GE Hanford Atomic Products Operations who used the 701 code for extensive LP work. This seems to have been the first realization that massive LP input had to have extensive computer processing itself. Several similar pre-processors were programmed in various places during the next few years.

11. Confidence had been gained that LP was a practical methodology and that massive calculations could be effectively carried out and controlled on a computer.

12. The scope of supporting software required for a major algorithm was beginning to be understood. This gradually unfolded into an astounding revelation which almost no one had foreseen. It took another fifteen years to create adequate software systems for this one application area.

I have talked so far mostly about work in which I was personally involved. Certainly, LP was being studied and experimented with in many places. The excellent little text by Charnes and Cooper should be mentioned, although it was not directly related to any software development. Unfortunately, their notation and Dantzig's were not identical so that two basic notations evolved. Much of the early work in LP was restricted to the transportation problem. This was represented at RAND by Ford and Fulkerson, out of whose work extensive network methods evolved. Elsewhere, a number of LP codes for the IBM 650 were successfully used. (The 650 was a rather curious computer which was popular for several years.) No doubt codes were attempted for other machines but they seem not to have had any permanent influence, with the possible exception of one for the IBM 702 at Esso Research. Bonner and Moore were very active in the field from the mid-1950s and wrote their own programs but their better-known software was a later development. There was some activity in Europe, notably in England and France. I am not familiar with that history before 1961 but somewhere in the interim, Beale emerged as a leader in the field in England and Pigot in France. A considerable amount of software has been built in France and currently this seems to be the locale for much of IBM's continuing development.

It should perhaps be mentioned also that other aspects of math programming were pursued at RAND in the 1950s, such as programming under uncertainty and decomposition methods. The first still has not been successfully handled although there has been a continuing interest in it in certain places, mainly universities. Decomposition, of course, later attracted wide interest and much effort has been devoted to it but I would say it is stil not in a satisfactory state and I doubt now it ever will be. Perhaps I can say more about this in a later lecture.

THE DEVELOPMENT OF SYSTEMS

At the end of 1956, I moved to Washington, D.C., to join CEIR, Inc. who pioneered in the field of computer services and consulting centers. There were certainly other such organizations, including IBM's old Service Bureau Corporation, but CEIR played a uniquely catalytic role, and particularly in the application of LP and its extensions. For several years, CEIR became the focal point for the continuing development of large LP packages and sytems. These were confined to IBM computers since that is what we used and there was no development of the same scope on other makes, either by the manufacturers or the users. Indeed, IBM itself contributed essentially nothing more until 1963.

I should make it clear that activity at RAND didn't stop but it took a somewhat different course. Philip Wolfe moved to RAND and initiated development of a line of FORTRAN programs for LP. Although not competitive with the large LP packages, they were highly useful for some purposes and saw wide use for many years---some may still be in use. However, Wolfe is better remembered for his resumed collaboration with Dantzig (they had worked together before Dantzig came to RAND) and their publication of the Dantzig-Wolfe Decomposition principle. The careers of both men are still continuing, of course, and I shall not presume to try to follow their paths further.

Although CEIR had great plans for computer service centers,

their immediate backing was by the Air Force and later the Department of Defense for a series of studies in which LP was to be the main analytical tool. The models were derived from Leontief matrices and had particularly nice solution characteristics but they were large for the time. By then, 8K words of core were available for the 704. (The 701 had 2K words and the early 704s only 4K.) The RSLP1 package was enhanced to handle 512 rows and was used extensively for nearly maximum size problems at CEIR.

In the meantime, RSLP1 began to be used elsewhere in regular production work, primarily in computing centers in the petroleum industry. LP was just the right methodology for many of their problems and they were uniquely prepared to utilize it with data accumulated for decades, much computerized already. The great period of expansion in the use of LP, and the willingness a few years later for computer manufacturers to finance large MPSs, can be credited almost solely to the great petroleum companies and the vast sums they spent on computing departments.

However, the operation of RSLP1 was untenably awarkward. Each major algorithmic program existed as a deck of punched cards in absolute format whose loading had to be hand initiated[1] for each major LP procedure. While this had served fairly well as a developmental tools in the hands of LP analysts and computer specialists, it would not do in an organized, well managed computer shop. CEIR, with the joint sponsorship of Richfield Oil Corporation, Standard Oil of California, and Socony-Mobile Oil Company, undertook to systematize these programs, producing the first LP system known as SCROL. It was scarcely a system in the current sense but it was contained on magnetic tape which was self-transferable to magnetic drum and had provisions for calling different algorithms by means of punched cards with simple formats. These cards, called "agendum cards" since a deck of them specified the agenda for a run, were read through a standard card reader but all actual programs for execution were read from tape or drum. The agenda was strictly by card sequence except that the basis reinversion program could be called by other algorithms on demand, automatically. To save space, the

---

1. The initial load deck for executing RSLP1 was complicated and varied according to the nature of the run. All the standard subroutines were loaded to drum once by a special editing program which created a table of drum locations. Subroutines were called into main memory on demand by the algorithm control routine, using a kind of executive loader which referenced the table. The control routine was also stored on drum (one at a time for each algorithm) to facilitate picking up form the last check-point in case of system malfunction. Other controls were actuated by physical switches. The whole arrangement was a computer operator's nightmare. Nevertheless, the package was a kind of embryonic system.

supervisory program itself did a vanishing act, appearing in main memory auxiliary storage when required. If a drum was used, the system could be restarted instantly by pushing a button to load the initialization program from drum. In spite of its relative crudeness, SCROL was heavily used in production work and prepared for users for the LP/90 system which raised LP to a standard production technology. A version of SCROL for a 32K core was prepared for Esso Research as a condition for their participation in LP/90.

It may be of interest in passing to note that SCROL permitted only 5-character symbols for columns and still used sequence numbers for rows. The objective row had to be first and output formats formats were still crude and poorly organized. Also, SCROL project badly overran both time and cost estimates, primarily because the increased difficulty of creating and maintaining a systen of programs, rather than a set of individual programs, was completely underestimated. This experience led to heavy emphasis on system design in creating LP/90. Although needed, this emphasis tended to overshadow further development in algorithms and an LP discipline. As a result, LP/90 and several descendent systems failed to include such features as bounded variables or a Markowitz inversion method, even though they had been successfully implemented previously.

In 1958-9, users of IBM 704s and others were looking forward to the new second-generation computer from IBM, the 7090, which became the most widely used scientific computer of the early 1960s. Software preparation for the 7090 went on for a period of years, first by the SHARE organization and later by IBM. In particular, the first large effort at a multi-phase operating system, called SPS (SHARE, Operating System), dominated software work for the 7090 until 1961 or so. From the point of view of most users, it was a fiasco and thereafter IBM insisted on providing its own basic software. The resulting confusion influenced the development of LP systems for several years and led to some hearty disagreements regarding the proper functions of operating systems versus application systems. Operating system designers and computer center managers contended that the standard operating system should maintain control of the equipment at all times and that application programmers and users were not to have hands-on access to the computer under any circumstances. The applications people, while not necessarily disagreeing in principle, contended that operating systems had not yet achieved anywhere near the scope and sophistication required to make this practical. Furthermore, the operating system preempted so much of the fixed amountof storage space, transmission capacity, and computing time, as to effectively prohibit large applications. The operating system people finally won out in the last half of the decade but only after both hardware and software had improved markedly.

Several large users formed a consortium and asked CEIR to develop a new system for the 7090. The sponsors were Esso Research and Engineering, Gulf Research (Gulf Oil Company), Shell Oil Company), Socony-Mobile Oil Company, Texaco Inc., and Union Carbide Corporation. This list is sufficient in itself to indicate the stature which LP had attained as a planning and management tool. Incidentally, several such firms were already clients of CEIR and the system development team was familiar with some of their applications.[1] This was a gread advantage in anticipating user's requirements; it was lost later when the computer manufacturers financed systems and insisted on insulating the developers from the clients.

The design goals included the ability to handle 1000-order models with several thousand variables, to achieve sufficient numerical precision to assure reliable convergence of the algorithms, to improve computing speed several-fold, to provide a fairly complete set of algorithms and procedures for post-optimal analyses, and to implement a convenient and reliable system control mechanism for the user, following the idea of a deck of agendum cards. All these goals were reached or exceeded by 1961-2.

In order to have a practical vehicle for building, modifying, distributing, and maintaining the application system, we first designed and built our own special operating system. It was a dual system. The first part contained a specialized assembler, a linkage-editor, and several related features which permitted fast updates to the system. These parts, plus a copy of the operating monitor, were on the front of a library of source code. This maintenance half was self-loading and treated the source code following much as an input file in a data processing system. This master system reproduced itself with updates from another file and at the same time created a fully linked operating system ready to run with its own operating monitor. The importance of this scheme was that it permitted quick, convenient and reliable updates to the LP/90 system ready for immediate testing, during a period of intense development and application to live industrial problems. LP/90 was updated in ten to twenty minutes more than once a day, on the average, for a period of two to three years. Without this facility, the perfection of the LP system would not have been possible. This may not strike current listeners as a particularly startling achievement. However, whole working days, often two or three, had been wasted in attempting to update SCROL, and as late as 1964-5 a derivative system of LP/90, maintained with a standard operating system, could consume a whole shift of computer time for a major system update, and it was not always successful then.

---

1. Eli Hellerman was active in the LP work at CEIR throughout the company's pertinent history and his contributions were invaluable. He originated several supporting procedures and later greatly enhanced inversion routines.

Not all interested parties understood these difficulties even on the LP/90 project and there was some dissension over its stand-alone nature, i.e., its incompatibility with standard operation systems. However, at least two more LP systems were constructed in the same way, due to continuing inadequacies of operating systems.

With LP/90, several computing centers ran many hours of computing time per day on LP problems on a scheduled and semi-automatic basis. In at least one case, early telecommunications links were used to transmit input across the U.S. with results being sent back the next morning. LP/90 became, in effect, the industry standard and also saw use in Europe and other parts of the world. It was perhaps a significant development that a system as complex as LP/90 could be maintained by a small group, distributed through an agency, and utilized by a great variety of users in many places with no direct communication.

LP/90 was a major source of income to CEIR but was finally distributed through the SHARE library at the insistence of the other sponsors. CEIR spent far more on the system than the sponsors paid but they had become somewhat alarmed about the possible anti-trust action and also about taking over a methodology which had originally been developed with Air Force funding. Such things may sound far-fetched but lawyers worry about them.

David M. Smith from Esso joined my group at CEIR in 1961 and added many refinements to LP/90. He and I worked together for several years and he deserves much of the credit for future developments and enhancements made to MPSs in the 1960s. David M. Carstens, who has previously built an LP package for the 7070 computer, also joined me and was responsible for many system and algorithm innovations. He is currently in charge of Burrough's math programming work and has brought together features and capabilities from a number of systems there.

LP/90 continued to be enhanced and was upgraded to a version called LP/90/94 for use on the successor IBM 7094. Other manufacturers of computers began to realize that they were missing a market and to sponsor LP systems. A very fast LP code was produced for the UNIVAC 1107 for up to 2000 rows but evidently ran into difficulty later. Improved implementations of special features of the simplex algorithm were produced in Europe. LP/90/94 was extended for Dantzig-Wolfe decomposition by Martin Beale and his associates at CEIR, UK, which later became Scicon, Ltd.

In 1963 or therabouts, a series of business upheavals, realignments and policy changes began to occur. It is difficult to say what the overall effect on the development of the math programming field was but certainly it was substantial. However, that is not properly a part of this history except as particular relocations must be explained.

Dave Smith and I, with some associates, left CEIR and formed a small company, familiarly known as O-H&C (Orchard-Hays & Co.), which was later absorbed by Computer Applications, Inc. The latter company, after growing to substantial size, became involved in fantastic projects of a different kind which led to its complete collapse in 1968, and O-H&C with it. The excellent CEIR group in England was taken over by British Petroleum and the parent CEIR was eventually taken over by Control Data Corporation and effectively ceased to exist. However, it was the decision of the major computer manufacturers (UNIVAC excepted) to sponsor their own math programming systems that is perhaps of most importance here.

In 1962, IBM was beginning to market its 7040/44 line, related to but not identical with the 7090/94 line. LP/90 would not operate on the 7040 which left their potential users with no LP system. Contract negotiations were under way with CEIR to convert LP/90 when O-H&C was formed. We bought the rights to this contract and two others when we left. (One was a consulting arrangement with Honeywell to design and review their ALPS package, the other to complete a successor to LP/90 known as LP/94, not the same as LP/90/94 previously mentioned.) The first 7040 system was known officially as IBLP40-I, usually called LP-I. It ran successfully but the maintenance half remained on the 7090. This led to intolerable problems in the field and IBM contracted for two successor-systems, LP-II and LP-III. In reality, they were two stages of the same system, only LP-III ever seeing any real use. The main condition for these systems was that they should be maintained and operate under their 7040/44 operating system called IBSYS. This was finally accomplished, with incredible difficulty, and the efficiency of the system for LP was surprisingly good. However, maintenance was a nightmare. No major LP system was produced thereafter to run on a stand-alone basis although one more had its own system compiler-maintenance package running under an operating system. The LP/94 system mentioned above had the most elaborate stand-alone system ever built for math programming work. Commercially, it was a failure but in many ways it was the first comprehensive MPS, besides incorporating several innovative system programming features which have reappeared in several places since. Carstens produced probably the fastest re-inversion program not based on triangularization techniques which ever appeared. It was tape oriented and I still don't know how he did it.

LP-III incorporated improved system control features and also four special algorithms. The first was for what we then called group problems which were GUB (generalized upper bounds) problems before the GUB algorithm was developed. The second was a special case of the first, namely transportation problems. The performance of the first was poor but the second was intolerably bad and didn't even

produce integer answers in all cases. Both were based on the Dantzig-Wolfe (D-W) decomposition principle which I thereafter refused
to use in any way. The third algorithm was a re-implementation of
the Dzielinski-Gomory algorithm for discrete production resource
allocation. This algorithm could be regarded at best as a development effort although it was hoped it would be used commerically.
Mead Paper Co. did actually use it for a while but, mainly for other
reasons, the project was given up.

The fourth algorithm was a replacement for the transportation
algorithm based on a partitioning decomposition scheme and parametric techniques. This worked quite well but problem size was limited in that implementation. A generalization of the approach re-
sulted in the block-product-form decomposition algorithm which I
later implemented twice, the first time with the help of Carstens
who straightened out some subtle logic which I had got wrong.

In 1964, IBM mounted a project to design, with the help of several consultants, a comprehensive MPS for their forthcoming System/
360 line. I was the chief designer of the algorithms, with help
from Smith, and I completed the set of parametric algorithms. IBM
rejected some of our suggestions for data management and instead accepted the MARVEL design, which I still think was a bad mistake for
everyone and the whole field. I don't know where the inversion algorithm in MPS/360 came from—IBM considered it confidential. Smith
and I had not yet worked out a good inversion scheme and Carstens'
method did not seem right for a disk-oriented system even if we had
understood it better.

O-H&C had hoped to get the implementation contract for MPS/360
but, probably due to disappointment with delays in MPS-III, IBM decided to do it in-house. Most of it came out as designed although
the I/O drivers were a mess. This was evidently because even an IBM
in-house group had to wait for standard OS/360 routines and in the
meantime used gerry-rigged codes, some of which remained. I don't
know just when IBM claimed MPS/360 was available but in later work
in 1969, I found they were still making fairly important corrections
and that a few bad bugs of a subtle nature still remained. The magnitude and complexity of such systems simply require years of field
testing to perfect. The only way this can be avoided is to carefully modify an existing system, an approach I have since used several times.

In 1965, General Electric contracted with O-H&C for the design
and implementation of a similar system—that is, equal to or better
than MPS/360—for their 635 computer. The GE 635 was in some ways
more like the IBM 7094 than was IBM's new 360 and they hoped to capture a good share of the 7090 market. The design of LP/600, as this
MPS was called, was very comprehensive and Tom Wooster, who was assigned to the project by GE, worked closely with us to ensure that

all features were checked for consistency and usefulness, that good
user documentation was produced, and that live problems were used
for testing. The best matrix generator produced until that time
and an equally good report writer were designed and implemented with
the best programming techniques we could devise. Unfortunately, the
operating system was far from check out and even the computer still
had some flaws in it. To make matters worse, GE was under great pres-
sure to complete their COBOL compiler and we were unable to get sufficient machine time. The project was moved across country twice.
The other difficulties which eventually forced GE to retire from the
computer field were already having an effect. Although the system
was completed eventually, it saw nowhere near the usage that had been
hoped. When Honeywell took over the GE activities, they inherited
LP/600 and I understand further work was done on it. However, I have
completely lost track of the system. It was a great disappointment
since it represented a culmination to almost fifteen years of con-
tinual improvement in LP system design and had shown promise of providing a new plateau of capability. Dave Smith designed a GUB algorithm for it, based on Dantzig and Van Slyke's work, and Carstens
and I implemented the block-product-form decomposition algorithm.
Numerous other advanced features were incorporated.

In 1966, Control Data contracted with O-H&C for yet another
system of similar scope. CDC insisted they wanted everything we
could produce and a little more. We took them at their word and
the resulting OPTIMA system was undoubtedly the most elaborate of
its kind ever produced. Not only did it include essentially all the
features of LP/600, plus both RHS and OBJ parametric extensions to
the decomposition algorithm, but it had extremely flexible internal
software. CDC was almost apologetic about their assembler at the
time of contract negotiations but we took what they had and built an
LP/90-style system compiler with greatly enhanced capability. For
nearly two years, update and test decks were transmitted five days
a week by wire from Maryland to Palo Alto, processed by an operating
staff we kept out there, and the results flown back overnight to be
on our desks in Maryland by 9:00 AM the next morning. Only occasionally did this fail, due to delays in flights. The 6400 computer
we used was a fully shaken-down piece of equipment and the SCOPE operating system was a delight to use.[1] So what could go wrong? Well,
just about everything one can imagine, at least from the standpoint
of business relations and cooperation between technical managements.
It is a complicated story which does not belong here but the upshot
was that OPTIMA, although completed, saw very little use in its
original form and no credit accrued to any of the original parties
involved, let alone general benefit to the field. However, CDC's

---

1. Later versions of SCOPE were not so delightful. In recent
years, in computing as elsewhere, improvements often turn out as
retrogressions.

current series of APEX systems are based to some extent on OPITMA. (The name comes from OPTIMA's control program.) So the effort was not completely in vain except for decomposition.

During the 1960s, CDC had also produced several efficient LP systems for their smaller lines (as had GE) either internally or using European consultants. The Ophelie system produced in France was marketed in the U.S. by CDC; it was perhaps the fastest implementation of the simplex algorithm ever programmed but, as a system, it was completely inflexible. IBM also produced or had produced LP packages for their smaller lines. Haverly Systems Associates has produced widely used LP systems for nearly all the major makes of computers. Their wide acceptance seems to be based largely on superior matrix and report generation capabilities, at least for modest-sized models. Bonner and Moore have built a series of their Gamma matrix generator-report writer packages, in addition to FMPS. UNIVAC as a company seems to have done very little but Beale and his associates in England built UMPIRE for the UNIVAC which has some novel features in addition to being a good workhorse. The universities have produced almost nothing of any value with the exception of Stanford which has its own in-house computer system with various capabilities for math programming. Dantzig's presence there must help a great deal.

Following the series of business disasters which I and my associates were involved in, Management Science Systems, Inc. was formed in 1968 by some of them and I was brought in as chairman and chief technical officer; later I also served as president after another series of business misfortunes and other troubles. We undertook to add GUB capability to MPS/360 for Standard Oil of Indiana which was successfully done. However, having gotten that far into MPS/360, we realized that other enhancements could be made and that GUB could also be generalized. Furthermore, Dave Smith had returned to Esso Research and, partly under his guidance but also due to other requirements within the complex of the huge parent company, the concept of a comprehensive data management subsystem—rather than separate matrix and report generators—was emerging. A contract was concluded and, with other clients interested both in the data handling and in the GUB extensions, development of the MPS-II system was undertaken. Dennis Rarick was brought in and he produced the fastest inversion routine yet implemented, at least until the last year or so. The system was substantially completed by 1971 although Rarick made important additions later.[1] It has been very successful in several industries besides petroleum, such as paper, glass, and breweries. During this same period, IBM produced their MPSX, upward

---

1. The data management subsystem is known as DATAFORM and was largely the work of Helen A. Patton who had been at GE during development of LP/600.

compatible from MPS/360. This brings us to the end of 1971. One
more set of developments will complete the story.

INTERACTIVE SYSTEMS AND NETWORKS

In late 1971, I left Management Science Systems, having had
quite enough of small software and consulting companies and, no doubt
as a consequence, with my relations with the rest of the management
deteriorating. Actually, I did further work for them through 1974
but on a contract basis. If anyone is tempted to go into business
for himself in this field, let me dissuade him. If you can invent
some small speciality useful to local business men or merchants, or
produce special programs to order on a subcontract basis, then it
may be possible to succeed, but working in big systems is simply
out of a small company's league. The only remaining successful
small company of which I am aware is Haverly's. The rest either
disappeared or are subsidiaries of large corporations. Management
Science Systems has recently gone under (though parts of it will
survive) even though they had one of the finest products in the
field. Excellence alone does not assure financial success.

However, an area had been developing which I had long ignored--
at times against the advice of associates--namely, interactive systems and networks. The National Bureau of Economic Research, Inc.
(NBER), the oldest of U.S. nonprofit corporations, had established
a computer research center in Cambridge, Massachusetts, to develop
software for economics and business management. They are financed
largely through National Science Foundation grants to provide software to universities and research organizations with scope and power
as good as or better than commercially available systems. Their
computer work is done and made available exclusively through a network and they seem pretty much committed to the big IBM/370 interactive systems.

NBER asked me to design and implement an MPS for an interactive
host which was to include substantially all the features of the big
commercial MPSs but to be slanted toward interactive use. I undertook to do so, starting in January 1972, on a half-time basis and
later on a slightly less than full-time basis, since I carried on
certain other activities as well.

First, I had to get used to working with an interactive facility
since all my previous experience had been on batch systems although
I was used to working remotely for several years. This didn't take
long and a whole new world of possibilities soon opened up to my
view. I found I could get as much done in a day as previously in a
week or two, or even a better ratio when one gets into heavy debugging. I was so excited about it that I undertook two other projects
of smaller scope concurrently, often working at home with a portable

terminal hooked to my telephone with an acoustic coupler. The advantages of a continuous train of thought and instant response from a computer were astounding.

The NBER project was never heavily manned. William D. Northop was already there and was familiar with the hosts systems (we changed computer centers twice). He was also working on integer programming with Jeremy Shapiro and so was not a stranger to LP. Later, we brought Michael J. Harrison over from England where he had been involved with LP system design for ICL. None of us worked full-time on the project though there were periods of intense activity. We had only an insignificant amount of other assistance. The system we created is called SESAME and, as far as the algorithms go, it is very similar to MPS-III. I essentially knew those programs by heart and more or less reproduced them. There are some notable exceptions: Harrison programmed the inversion routine (a Hellerman-Rarick type) and the parametric algorithms from scratch with help from me in the design. The rest of the system, however, though functionally similar to other MPSs is a completely new re-implementation, taking advantage of the VM/CMS interactive host system's capabilities. The traditional style of problem files were completely replaced with a tree-structured file which had been used in earlier forms in LP/600 and OPTIMA and is the heart of the DATAFORM extension to MPS-III. The system was essentially completed by late 1974 and fully tested by March 1975. It has been operating successfully without any substantial change since then.

Although SESAME accepts MPS/360 style input, a somewhat more flexible free-form input was provided from the outset. However, this proved inadequate for interactive use for all but the smallest models. It became clear that a data management subsystem was badly needed. In late summer of 1974, I started work on one, working completely alone. I started with the DATAFORM design and stayed fairly close to external specifications, but the implementation is completely different. DATAFORM is about two-thirds in FORTRAN and uses a compiler. That is reasonable for a batch system but a separate compilation phase is a terrible nuisance with an interactive system. The extension to SESAME is called DATAMAT and it is 100 percent assembler language with no compiler but completely interpretive execution. With the exception of the report writing verbs, it was substantially complete by April 1975 but not thoroughly tested. Although it was used on three or four projects at NBER, no further work was done until this year since I moved to IIASA in May 1975 and suitable equipment was not available. SESAME/DATAMAT was installed at the CNUCE center in Pisa and also in Brussels in the spring of 1975 but European telephone service is not reliable on a dial-up basis. IBM installed VM/CMS in Vienna in January, this year, and I have completed and enhanced DATAMAT there. We now have a leased line to Pisa also so that the use of the system is expected to be substantial. I am using it as a main vehicle for IIASA's modelling work for the Energy Program.

24

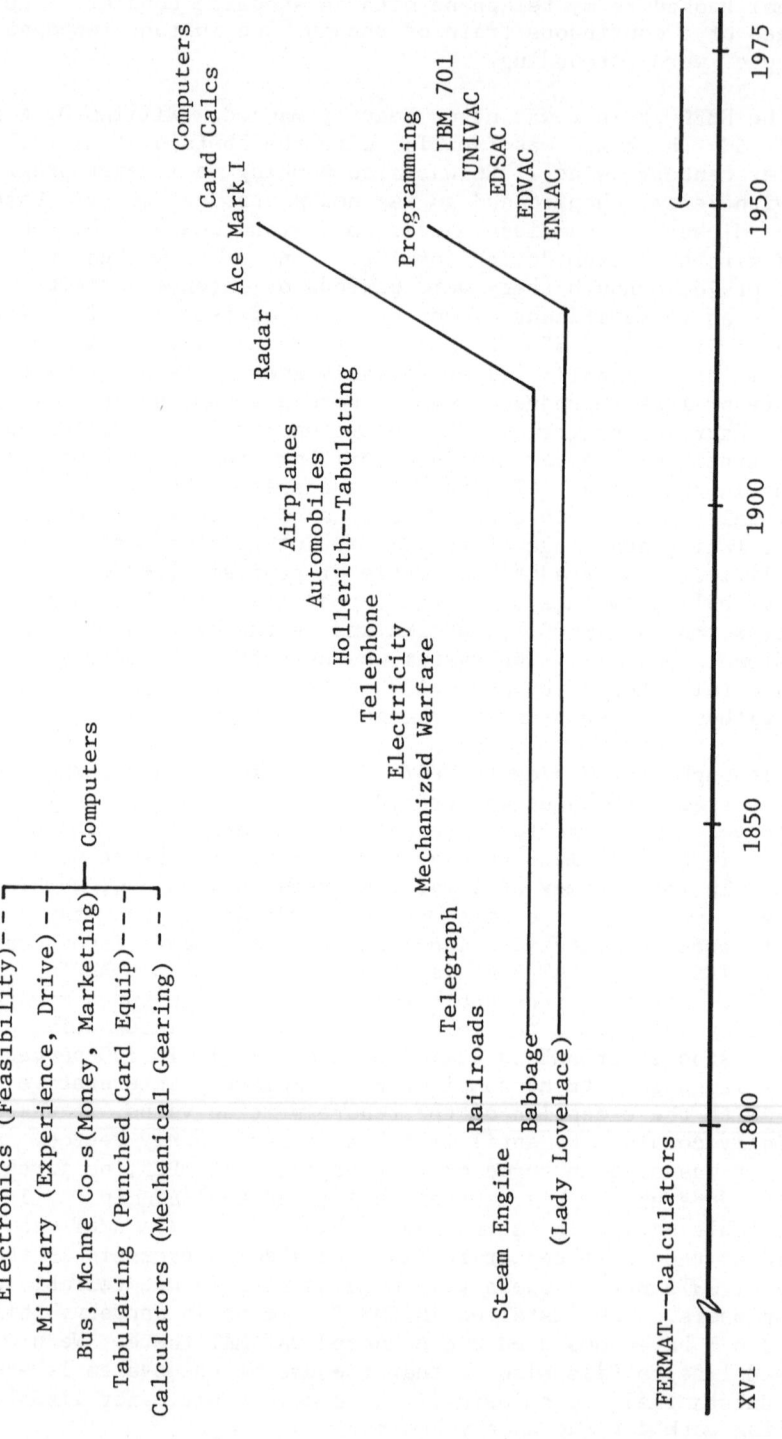

1. DEVELOPMENT OF COMPUTERS

2. DEVELOPMENT OF PROGRAMMING

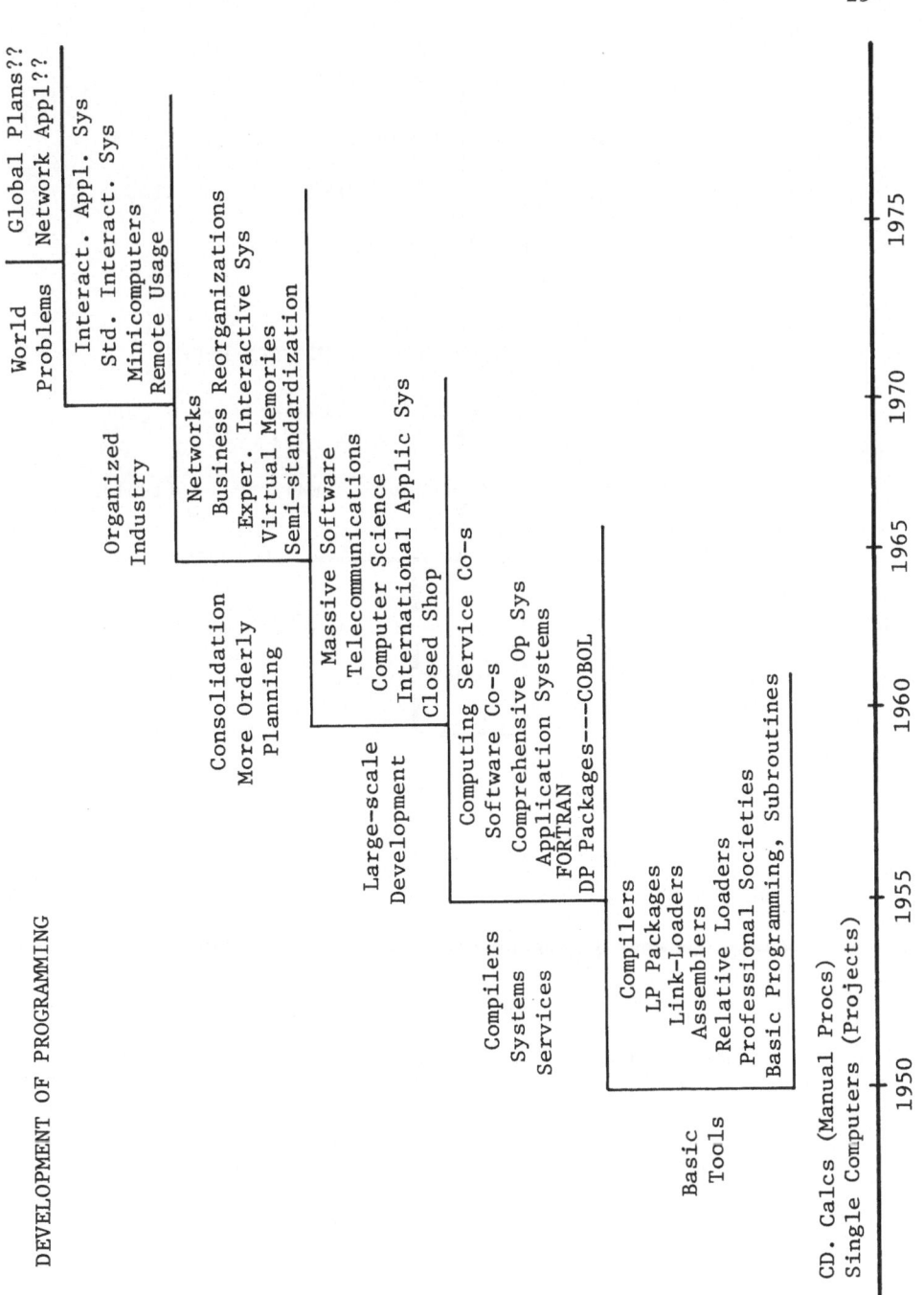

CD. Calcs (Manual Procs)
Single Computers (Projects)

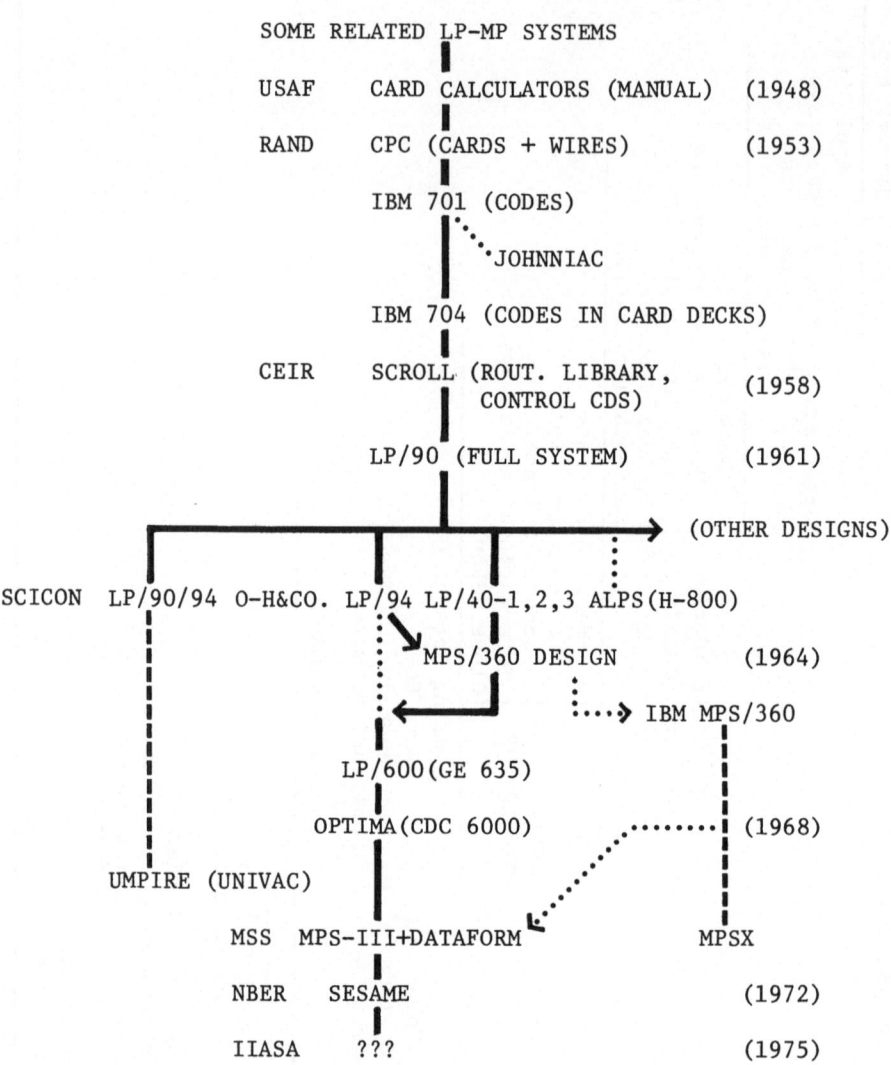

SOME RELATED LP-MP SYSTEMS

USAF   CARD CALCULATORS (MANUAL)   (1948)

RAND   CPC (CARDS + WIRES)   (1953)

         IBM 701 (CODES)

                      JOHNNIAC

         IBM 704 (CODES IN CARD DECKS)

CEIR   SCROLL (ROUT. LIBRARY,   (1958)
              CONTROL CDS)

         LP/90 (FULL SYSTEM)   (1961)

                                        (OTHER DESIGNS)

SCICON LP/90/94 O-H&CO. LP/94 LP/40-1,2,3 ALPS(H-800)

                      MPS/360 DESIGN   (1964)

                              IBM MPS/360

         LP/600(GE 635)

         OPTIMA(CDC 6000)   (1968)

UMPIRE (UNIVAC)

     MSS MPS-III+DATAFORM   MPSX

     NBER   SESAME   (1972)

     IIASA   ???   (1975)

3.   EXAMPLE OF EVOLUTION OF APPLICATION SYSTEMS

SCOPE OF MATHEMATICAL PROGRAMMING SOFTWARE

Wm. Orchard-Hays

International Institute for Applied Systems Analysis,
Laxenburg, Austria

I take the phrase "scope of current math programming software" to refer to the big, commercial MPSs plus a couple of related systems. It just happens to be true that these MPSs--even those with which I have had nothing to do--are all based to some extent on my work and that of my former associates and hence I suppose I might be accused of defining terms to my own advantage. That is not my intent, and, in fact, it was some time before I would accept the grandiose term "mathematical programming systems" since they are for linear programming and its extensions, and not general to the whole field of math programming. Some might then argue that my viewpoint is too narrow. This is an old contention and perhaps deserves a few preliminary remarks. Some of my former colleagues at Management Science Systems thought is was a mistake to become known as merely linear programming specialists and frittered away considerable time, money, and momentum in trying to prove they were something more, largely in vain. If one is going to make a business of building and marketing software, then the product must be definable, manageable, and reliable--as well as useful, of course. A small organization will have its hands full taking care of all aspects of one or two major products, without pretending that its capability extends to a whole scientific discipline. Nevertheless, the field of mathematical programming is certainly much broader than the theory and techniques embodied in the so-called MPSs.

The difficulty in attempting a broader view is twofold: first, one cannot circumscribe the field and, second, software in a broader context quickly becomes very amorphous. Linear programming was originally regarded as a tool of operations research and management science (a later term). Today, systems analysis is regarded as a more general term and its subject matter as an extension and outgrowth of operations research, with mathematical programming as one of its broad areas of theory and approach to problem solving. Actually, system analysis is not even regarded as being concerned with problem solving in the usual sense but in studying broader issues to assist policy makers. Still, when one gets right down to it, standard forms of statistical analyses, one or two definable econometric modelling techniques, certain simulation methods, and linear programming with a few extensions are about the only well-defined tools with more or less standardized software available. Among these, only the last seems to belong to mathematical programming. Such things as critical path methods may be regarded as part of management science but outside our field.

It is true that there is an extensive literature in math programming and that one can find numerous references to such things as network problems, queuing theory, nonlinear programming, decomposition methods, fixed-point algorithms, and several other techniques, even including control theory. Also, there are program packages available from several sources for many of these. But it would be a hopeless task to attempt a meaningful survey of such an ill-defined and unstandardized collection. If you are interested in these things, then you should belong to the Mathematical Programming Society and take its journal--I hope many of you already do. Further, if you have access to a computing center-- and if you don't, it is not clear what you are doing here--you will find various lists of systems, programs, and packages which are available. Unfortunately, what you see is not always what you get, and what you get is not always what you want.

There is a further difficulty in circumscribing the meaning of the word "software." Are all computer programs to be regarded as software? Some would go even further and include all the literature, procedures, standard operating practices, etc. connected with the use of actual computer hardware. The effect of such broad definitions is often not to make the term general but meaningless. To me at least, "software" implies a system of programs, maintained and formalized, with usage and symbology defined in printed manuals, and which has a continuing life independent of any particular project. It is hard to find much in the math programming field which fits this definition outside of the MPSs. If you still think I am defining terms to my advantage, I am sorry.

How many MPSs are there in fairly current use? Not many. Several systems have already passed into the domain of history. The best-known and most widely-used system is no doubt MPSX or possibly, by now, MPSX/379. The differences between the two are signigicant but not revolutionary, about the same as the differences between the earlier MPS/360 and MPSX, not necessarily in the same direction in all cases. MPSX/370 is large—I counted 51 procedures —but it is not the largest. That nonor appears to go to MSP-III in which I found 76 procedures as of 1974 although perhaps 10 or 12 of these should be discounted as not being of general interest.[1] It may be that Burroughs' TEMPO systems are the largest in fact, but the comparison is not strictly valid since it is a set of systems. Most of the manufacturers play this game now, mostly a result of the unbundling of hardware/software a few years ago but also partly for better organization. IBM's mixed integer system is called MIP/370 and is a separate program product.

None of the above three systems appear to be the fastest. MPSX and MPS-III were about even, each one being faster in some respects. I have no comparison of either with MPSX/370 and no information of this kind for TEMPO. I have been told very recently by someone familiar with running large LP problems on different systems that APEX-III is three times faster on a CDC 7600 than MPSX (I presume he meant MPSX/370) running on an IBM 370/168. I told him one would have to examine the comparison very carefully but a factor of 3, though large, is not unbelievable—certainly more believable than factors claimed for OPHELIE a few years ago which were as much as 20 times then-current systems. CDC has always emphasized the speed of their big computers. It is possible that the OPTIMA system which my staff and I built for CDC in the 1960s would still rate as the largest and most comprehensive. However, it was not extremely fast which was the main point of contention between CDC and my company—had it been as fast as they expected, all other differences could probably have been settled quickly. The APEX series retains several external features of OPTIMA, and probably internal ones as well, but most of the comprehensive features of OPTIMA were stripped away and much faster algorithmic procedures installed. It is quite clear that IBM and CDC are the keenest competitors in the field and they have responded to each other's features so much that MPSX/370 and APEX-III can be compared as being alike though, in fact, they are not at all. But it is clear that APEX is currently very fast. The WHIZARD optimizer created by Dennis Rarick at Management Science Systems should also be very fast for somewhat different reasons but I have no explicit figures. It is not really a system in itself but requires an MPS for support.

Four current systems have already been mentioned: MPS-III and MPSX, both for IBM computers, TEMPO for Burroughs computers, and APEX for CDC computers. There are about as many more although I can count five if I try. As I mentioned in the session on history,

---

1. The most comprehensive system of all is no doubt (as they claim) LP6000, Honeywell's updated version of the GE LP/600 system which was the major effort of my staff during the mid-1960s. A new manual appeared in 1973.

Honeywell inherited LP/600 from General Electric. They added MIP
and upgraded it to LP6000 with activity at least as late as 1973,
but I have had no contact with it for many years. It is poten-
tially a very fine system. That leaves only two manufacturer of
large processors: UNIVAC and ICL. UNIVAC apparently had bad experience with a system built for them in the early 1960s and never
seem to have had one of their own since, although they are now
active as will be explained in a moment. Martin Beale and his associates at Scicon built the UMPIRE system for a UNIVAC, as a proprietary product. UMPIRE is interesting in that it shows clearly
its lineage from LP/90 without the influence of the other big systems of the 1960s which all other systems show. UMPIRE has fewer
procedures than the systems already mentioned but it still a substantial contender. Its style is quite different with heavy emphasis on solution strategy controls.

I am unclear as to just what capabilities ICL provides for LP.
They have worked in the field for some time or at least they were
designing a system as early as 1971. I have heard of their software from as unlikely places as Moscow and Cairo but really have
no details. There may well be others here who are more familiar
with it and I will not attempt to cover ICL. M.J. Harrison was
with their group before he joined me at NBER and he was a very
valuable addition to the SESAME team. SESAME is one of the two remaining systems. The other is FMPS, a product of Bonner and Moore
Associates, Inc., at least originally. In some sense, FMPS has
become the "standard alternate," that is, if a manufacturer does
not want to build an MPS but only to provide one, the most common
choice is FMPS. That is because it is basically FORTRAN although
I believe it never remains all FORTRAN in any delivered version.
To what extent FMPS differs in its various manifestations is unclear to me. This is the system offered by UNIVAC but whether it
is now more a Bonner and Moore product or a UNIVAC product, I do
not know. Again, perhaps someone else here can tell us. Bonner
and Moore also produced the Gamma series of matrix-generators/re-
port-writers which has been adopted by different manufacturers.

One other set of systems must be mentioned: Haverly Systems,
Inc.'s PDS/MaGen. I am not familiar with Haverly's full current
line of software but his matrix-generator/report-writer system is
the most widely used in the industry. He even has his own users
groups on both sides of the Atlantic and has probably come closer
to establishing standards in data management for the MPS than anyone else. Although at one time he did produce optimizers, it is
my understanding that he does not produce a complete MPS--unless
it is for smaller or less known machines--but some MPSs from the
manufacturers have special provisions for interfacing with PDS/
MaGen. It is the main data subsystem for APEX and is available
with TEMPO although Burroughs also has a system called MODELER
which is, in some ways, more like DATAFORM and DATAMAT.

A total of ten families of systems have been mentioned. However, it will be sufficient to consider only seven: MPSX/370, APEX-III, TEMPO, MPS-III, FMPS, UMPIRE, and SESAME. I do not have equally up-to-date information on them all and, for FMPS, what I have may even be obsolete. Not all are equally available or on the same basis but all can be considered as current systems more or less generally available. The first three are built, maintained and made available by computer manufacturers except for the uses of Gamma and PDS/MaGen noted above. The next three started as proprietary products of small independent companies but various other arrangements have been made. The last system, SESAME, differs from the others in two respects: first, it was designed from the beginning for interactive use only, and second, it was financed from public funds and is, in theory, available to anyone with a demonstrable, noncommercial need to use it. In practice, it is not quite so easily available except via a network. This is not due to anyone trying to make money out of it but to practical realities like maintenance, documentation, and such things. Also, NBER is mote aligned with the academic world than the commercial world and do not engage in the kind of marketing activities necessary to promore use of a system. This is a major dilemma which our field faces. Only the major manufacturers have the financial and organizational muscle to really handle big systems but their interests do not necessarily coincide with progress in the field and, in any event, the field tends to be at their mercy. I had great hopes that government or international agency funding would overcome this but commercialization is anathema to them. Without commercialization, the necessary discipline is missing. This issue is much broader than math programming--one might almost say it is the major ideological problem of our time.

In discussing these sytems, the emphasis will be on capabilities but excluding speed. There are two reasons for this exception. First, timing comparisons are extremely difficult to make and even harder to interpret and they lead to arguments which we will do better to avoid. Second, I don't really care and believe you shouldn't either. I was once known for overemphasizing efficiency and don't mean to minimize its importance. If you are building a system, you neglect it at great peril. But today's big computers and their large application systems are very fast and handle enormous problems, faster and bigger than human beings can make use of effectively. In my opinion, this is the time for improved flexibility and comprehensiveness and not for electronic horse races.

One other term deserves a few remakrs before looking at comparative charts, namely, flexibility. What does it really mean? There are many opinions but they seem to fall into three major cases.

(1) Flexibility and power in data management. All current

systems make some provision for this but both the builders
and users of systems need to learn a great deal more.
Rather strangely, IBM has done the least here.

(2) Flexibility in linkages so that parts of the system can
be used as subroutines or, conversely, the system can
use alien subroutines. The first major attempts at this
were probably in FMPS and OPTIMA, using quite different
approaches. (Perhaps the old FORTRAN packages started
at RAND should be credited with being first here.) MPS/
360 and MPSX had almost no provision for this. In MPSX/
370, PL/I is used as a vehicle both for data management
and linkage flexibility. APEX, UMPIRE and FMPS utilize
FORTRAN. I have always had serious reservations about
the practicability of making available pieces of highly
integrated, balanced systems. It can certainly be done
but the user must become a system builder.

(3) Flexibility in actual algorithmic processes, that is, below the level of simply calling system parts but the
ability to modify the internal workings of major subroutines and their interfacing with data. The chief pro-
ponent of this was Prof. George Dantzig himself, with his
MPL. There has been a joint project between NBER and
Stanford to develop such a system, the purpose being to
permit experimenting with algorithms. This is in addition to implementation efforts at Stanford for MPL. I
usually have better sense than to differ with George
Dantzig but this is one case where we differ strongly.
It would take too long to explain all the reasons why.
Nevertheless, the MPL concept may have some beneficial
influence on the other two levels of flexibility and may
also be useful pedagogically so that in the long term
the benefits will be substantial. But as a practical
method of solving real problems, I think this level of
flexibility is entirely too deep.

Let us now turn to a comparison of the procedural and control
capabilities of the seven systems. Above, certain procedure counts
were mentioned. These are misleading. IBM separates their control
languages from the procedures even to the extent of issuing separate
users manuals. CDC uses the term "verb" which was introduced in
LP/600 and OPTIMA. Others speal of "commands" which, like "verb,"
include both control and procedure call statements. By and large,
it seems preferable to consider the control language as a single
formalism even though the execution of different statements will
involve quite different sorts of actions internally. Basically,
one must deal with a command language which consists of statements;
statements will either be assignment statements or involve use of
a verb of some kind. So far as I know, all computing languages are

of this nature though sometimes they are made to look fancy. Procedures are elaborate substructures which must be called from the command language whether the word CALL is used or not. But in using a system, some commands which have very simple executions are almost as important. In any event, comparisons will be made on the basis of the entire command language and not merely by procedures.

One final preliminary remark: the definitions and pricing of different options differ markedly among the systems. No attempt will be made to reproduce these distinctions accurately. For example, IBM provides MIP as MIP/370 and does not regard it as part of MPSX/370. TEMPO is separated into a number of parts. The purpose of such sorts of arrangements is to charge the user more money, and its discussion does not belong here.

Anyone who has written a users manual has faced the problem of classifying commands; if he has done it more than once, he has come up with a different scheme each time. It seems impossible to devise a scheme which fits equally across all systems and it is certainly impossible to indicate all features. The scheme below more or less follows traditional groupings but it must be realized that no class is independent of all others.

It should perhaps also be mentioned that the external specifications for OPHELIE-II included a control language with most of the best features of the systems shown. It amounted to a freeform subset of FORTRAN statements and also utilized longer forms with almost English- or French-like quality. I am unaware of the actual performance or current status of it.

In addition to the above more-or-less standard capabilities, various systems have numerous other control devices for such things as file declarations, mode or algorithm settings, defining the source of lists and sets, and so on. It is almost impossible to make across-the-board comparisons since they depend on the operating systems, operational styles, various customs and traditions among different manufacturers, etc. One of the great advantages of an interactive facility such as VM/CMS under which SESAME runs is that most of these things are simple, direct and/or automatic. By contrast, the MPSX/370 manual devotes 20 pages explicitly to files, plus several procedures whose only function is file control, plus numerous parameters and comments connected with files.

There is almost equal variability in the mechanism for printing various values, accessing LP results, interspersing messages and time indicators, etc. In MPSX, MPS-III and to a lesser extent in APEX, many of these functions require the use of procedures, not merely local command language execution. In SESAME, the data management subsystem DATAMAT can be used, either with a pre-planned program or ad hoc, for elaborate calculations on models or results,

Program Control

(MSP-III is identical to MPSX for this set of commands. An interactive version also exists which is more similar to SESAME. TEMPO also has an interactive version, again with some similarity to SESAME. In general, handling of demands is different with interactive use although a part of this capability is always necessary.

	MPSX/370	APEX-III	TEMPO	UMPIRE	FMPS	SESAME
Alternate method	PL/I	FORTRAN	Int'act	FORTRAN		Interactive
Standard method Compile phase	Cont.Lang yes	Cont.lang yes	Cont.lang yes	Seq.card no (?)	Cont.lang yes	RUN file no
Initialization	INITIALIZ	(auto)+ INITIAL	(auto)+ RESET	(auto)	(auto)	(auto)
Uncond. branch	GOTO	BRANCH	GOTO	*	GOTO	GOTO,SKIP
Conditional branch	IF, TALLY	via TEST	IF		IF	IF,TALLY
Subsequence Return	EXEC STEP	PERFORM§ NEXT	PERFORM RETURN NEXT			
Demand stack Action	yes CONTINUE STEP comm.seq	(priority) predefnd comm.seq	yes RETURN NEXT comm.seq	(internl calls used)	(inter'pt) comm.seq RETURN EXIT(next)	yes predefnd CONT STEP
Switch	MVADR (to any)	BRANCH PERFORM	assign't state.		ASSIGN	SWITCH
Macros Substit.args	yes no	no	yes(lib) no		no	(multiple RUN files)
CR settings	Arith. state MOVE	SET STEP SELECT	Assign state.	via args on Agendum cds.	Arith., assign. states.	Arith. state. MOVE
Local arithmetic	yes	no	yes+ 1-dim. arrays		yes	with user CR cells only
Predefined LP sequences	yes	yes	no	yes	no(?)	trivial to create

* UMPIRE uses the LP/90 concept of "agendum cards" to which much of this group does not apply. However, it has numerous strategy control settings, particularly for MIP.

§ The handling of subsequences and demands in APEX is different in style from the other systems. Neither APEX nor FMPS have a demand stack in the usual sense. The most elaborate demand scheme is probably in LP6000.

available at a terminal. The latter action is direct and requires no pre-planning, programming or other procedure execution. Some of this will be discussed further in the session on anatomy of an MPS.

It appears that all systems provide a means for defining a title line for output and, as far as I can determine, this is one thing that is absolutely standard. The verb (command) used is TITLE followed by an enquoted string. TEMPO has added a frill to this: either single quotes can be nested within double quotes, or vice versa. Some systems, such as SESAME, absolutely preempt the single quote for delimiting a string of characters (except in FOR-MAT statements in DATAMAT).

For illustration, MPSX/370's so-called control procedures are shown briefly.

READ	Reads card images to CR cells.
WRITE	Writes CL or CR values to standard output files.
TYPE	Displays CL or CR values on operator's console.
COMMUN	Types a message at operator's console and waits for reply.
BCD	Converts an integer value from CL value to 8-character form.
TIME	Stores current elapsed time in a CL variable.
FREECORE	Release SETUP's core allocation. Common to several systems.
EXIT	Terminate MPSX/370. All systems have such a verb which generally requires considerable terminal action before returning to op/sys.

The only system that I know of which has a general decomposition capability is LP6000. The algorithm is the block-product one which I developed with some help from Carstens, and which we first implemented in LP/600. He worked on it later for that system and reported some good timing figures. Honeywell recommends that it be used when there are more than two subproblems. S.T. Katz and I implemented it in OPTIMA but so far as I know it never saw use in that system. Carstens implemented it for the TEMPO set but they have recently withdrawn it because no one was using it and provided a network algorithm instead. This is the only network option in a standard system that I am aware of. In this connection, mention should be made of the work done recently at the University of Texas' Center for Cybernetics Studies by F.D. Glover, D. Klingman, and J. Stultz. They have made extensive experiments, developed a number of programs, and documented them. Although I have no personal experience with them, they appear to be the best piece of work for practical use to have come out of a university. As I have mentioned before, by and large, the universities have produced very little in the way of systems or integrated packages. The work of Glover, Klingman, et al. appears to be an exception.

The National Physical Laboratory in Teddington, England has a Numerical Optimization Software Library. This is apparently the work of Drs. Philip E. Gill and Walter Murray. Their viewpoint is entirely different from that of the designers of the MPSs discussed here but is directed toward more general consideration of optimization and mathematical programming theory. Work has gone on and still goes on in many places on nonlinear programming methods.

PROCEDURE CLASS Function	MPSX/370	APEX-III	TEMPO	MPS-III	UMPIRE	FMPS	SESAME
USER FILE PROCES'NG							
Editing	(OS utils)	(?)	(?)	ALTER prgm	CORRECT,REVISE	(?)	CMS Edit
MPS/360 input (Some also accept other formats)	CONVERT	INPUT (one-stage)	INPUT	CONVERT (MPS/360 + extensions)	MPSCON, then (UMPIRE)INPUT	INPUT (one-stage)	(MPS/360, MPS-III SESAME formats)
Revision (SAVERHS also in TEMPO,MPS-III)	REVISE SAVERHS	REVISE (direct to matrix)	REVISE INTERPolate (separable)	REVISE, also DATAFORM and various tran	(none in usual sense PRESOL)	REVISE (direct to matrix)	(Only with DATAMAT, minor with BROWSE)
File maintenance and conversion	COPY,COPYOLD EX/IMPORT	n/a	COPY	(extensive set)	n/a	n/a	PURGE, COMPREST
Listing, display reconversion to card image	PROBLEMS BCDOUT	LIST EQLIST	BCDOUT	PROBLEMS BCDOUT LISTFILE (DEGROUP)	ATOI	OUTPUT (very flexible)	BROWSE CARDOUT Anything with DATAMAT
WORK MATRIX SETUP							
Initial Changes	SETUP REDUCE FLAGS MODIFY SCALE SAVERHS	(SELECT SETINDirect REDUCE	SETUP PRESOLVE SAVERHS	SETUP,READY FLAGS AXE1,2,3 BNDFIX EDITW (indirs) GROUPER (GUB) GUIDE (GUB) SEMIFLAG SAVERHS	n/a FLAG NEWRHS	n/a	SETUP FIXVALUE (indirects) Numerous selections available in SETUP
WORK MATRIX ACCESS OR DISPLAY AND REFORMING							
(Note: DEGROUP in MPS-III reforms in a DATAFORM file; many paths)	INQUIRE(PL/I) PICTURE BCDOUT RECREATE TRACE	(see above RECREATE	PICTURE CREATE	MATDMP PICTURE WFTOPB TRACE	PICTURE (ATOI)	(see above)	MATDMP

PROCEDURE CLASS / Function	MPSX/370	APEX-III	TEMPO	MSP-III	UMPIRE	FMPS	SESAME
SIMPLEX SOLUTION ALGORITHMS, EXTENDED							
Fast feasibility	CRASH	CRASH	CRASH	CRASH	--	CRASH	--
Main algorithm(s)	PRIMAL	PRIMAL DEVEX	PRIMAL	PRIMAL, VARIFORM	NORMAL, CMPSIT	OPTIMIZE	ITERATE
GUB (+SOS)	--	--	GUB ext.	VARIFORM	NORMAL(SOS)	--	ITERATE
Dual algorithm	DUAL	--	DUAL	DUAL	--	--	ITERATE (incl. GUB)
Separable (delta) (lambda)	PRIMAL	--	GUB ext.	PRIMAL VARIFORM	(SOS/GUB)	--	ITERATE
Reinversion (all auto)	INVERT	SOLN	INVERT	INVERT GENINV	(Auto, no call)	INVERT	INVERT
Recover from singularity, etc.	RETRIEVE FORCE	--	--	RETRIEVE	--	--	--
Integer programs	MIP/370	MIP option	MIP option	MISTIC	INTEGR	--	--
Parametrics	PARARHS " OBJ " RIM " COL " ROW	PARARHS opt PARAOBJ	PARARHS " COS " RIM " COL " ROW	PARARHS " OBJ " RIM " COL " ROW	PARARHS " OBJ	PARARHS " OBJ	RIMPARAS (RHS, OBJ, RIM) STRPARAS (COL, ROW)
Solution check	CHECK	(?)	10^{-3}, no demand	FULLY automatic	(?)	ERRORS	Fully automatic
Demand handling	yes	no	no	yes	(?)	no	yes
Ranging (styles, extents vary)	RANGE	RANGE	RANGE	RANGE	BRANGE CRANGE	RANGE	VARY

Comments   There is a high degree of variability in the way the various algorithms and supporting techniques are handled among the systems. TEMPO, for example, if presented with an all-logical basis, will automatically invoke PRESOLVE, CRASH, and PRIMAL. In SESAME, primal, dual, GUB and separable are all integrated into one procedure, ITERATE. MPS-III has, in general, a double set of algorithms, one essentially like MPS/360 and the other built around VARIFORM and GENINV (generalized invert). APEX-III and UMPIRE allow the user much less control, not as an option or using command macros, but as a policy. The inversion schemes also differ and some are considered proprietary. Only MPS/370, MPS-III and SE-SAME have what this writer considers adequate error control handling. The VARY procedure in SESAME is primarily interactive although it can be run automatically. It answers individual questions fully rather than producing wholesale output.

PROCEDURE CLASS Function	MPSX/370	APEX-III	TEMPO	MPS-III	UMPIRE	FMPS	SESAME
RESULTS OUTPUT AND ACCESSING							
Any LP Solution	SOLUTION	OUTPUT	SOLOUT	SOLUTION	UNRAVL PRNTDJ	SOLUTION	SOLUTION
Tableau (col)	TRANCOL	--	TRANCOL	TRANCOL	--	--	TABLEAU (print
(row)	TRANROW	--	TRANROW	TRANROW	--	--	or enfile)
Selected values	SELECT	GETROW GETCOL	--	--	--	GET	--
System, CR status	STATUS	CPRINT	STATUS	STAT, STATUS	--	CONDITIONS	STATUS, MPFILES
CHECKPOINT AND RESTART PROCEDURES							
Complete save/restrt	--	SAVE/RESTART	--	--	GETOFF/RESTRT	SAVE/RESTORE	--
Minimum basis infor	SAVE/RESTORE	--	SAVE/LOAD	SAVE/RESTORE PRESERVE/RESET	--	--	SAVE/RESTORE
Basis, card image	PUNCH/INSERT	BASISOUT/IN	BASOUT/BASIN	MAPOUT/MAPIN	--	BASISOUT/IN	MAPOUT/MAPIN
GENERAL BIT MAPS FOR SET OPERATIONS *							
Card image--internl	--	--	--	GMAPOUT/IN	--	--	MAPOUT/MAPIN
Generation	--	--	--	GMAPGEN	--	--	MAPGEN
Boolean opers	--	--	--	GMAPOP	--	--	BOOL
DATA MANAGEMENT							
Matrix generation	--	**PDS**/MaGen	Gamma MODELER	DATAFORM	FORTRAN based MGG	Gamma	DATAMAT
Report Generation	ANALYZE SETREP REPORT	**PDS**/MaGen	Gamma	DATAFORM	REPORT REPTEL (term)	Gamma	DATAMAT
General purpose	[PL/I (?)]	--	MODELER	DATAFORM	--	--	DATAMAT

* It is difficult to understand why this extremely powerful and flexible method of set selection for PL identifiers has not been adopted by other system designers. All systems permit some kind of list specification or masking capability for this purpose and in some circumstances these are preferable but they do not have the scope of bit maps

Some systems of programs even exist but, from what I hear through the grapevine, none are really very satisfactory although one can read claims of practical applications. I have looked at this from time to time myself. Aside from mathematical and numerical difficulties, the system and human interfacing problems are enormous. This was the main trouble with decomposition methods and nonlinear programming in any kind of general sense seems to be even much worse.

Some systems have experimental procedures and algorithms which are not announced or made generally available. I know this to be true of MPS-III and SESAME and I believe it is also the case with UMPIRE. I have twice implemented a quadratic algorithm for a special class of problems. One version, in a small commercially-used code, has been very successful. The other version is in SESAME and, although it shows promise, it is not yet polished enough for general use. It has solved a problem with approximately 1300 rows and 2600 columns but not without close attention. I have also implemented a MIP algorithm which, at least on one problem, performed fantastically well but there are many loose ends which prohibit its general distribution.

It would seem that one should say something about the size of models which can be solved but this is almost as difficult as giving reliable running time estimates. Generally speaking, a model with 1000 rows is not considered very large in the big systems running on a reasonable-sized computer. In practice, many models fall in the range of 300 to 700 rows and there seems to be another group in the 1200 to 1500 range. The systems all accept up to 4000 rows and many permit more. This is apart from GUB problems which can be much larger in the general formulation. I would approach the solution of any problem with more than 2000 rows very carefully but models up to 4000 or 5000 general rows have been solved. I don't know what the largest one ever solved is. Several years ago, MPS-III solved a problem quite efficiently with about 1000 general rows, 45000 GUB constraints and 280,000 columns. That is the largest I have ever tackled. The most restrictive of the big systems for problem size is evidently APEX-III. Its limits are 8190 rows (surely enough), 32760 columns (quite small) and 32760 unique nonzero elements. This last restriction is no doubt imposed by the use of super-sparsity techniques in core. This probably accounts for their excellent speed, but I am surprised at such a low limit.

In closing, it may be worth mentioning that I built a small LP package at IIASA for the PDP-11/45. It is all FORTRAN-IV and all in-core. It is limited to 100 rows and 250 columns but performs well. It includes PARAOBJ and PARARHS and accepts standard MPS/360 input. It can also produce a full tabular form of the input. There is also a pair of companion programs which are subsets of DATAMAT with some changes. One is for table generation and maintenance and the other for matrix generation. They would be combined if I had about 2000 bytes of additional core available, and this would be much better. The matrix generator is a little slow but acceptable. It can produce fairly large models since it must output the cards sequentially for MPS/360 format and hence gets rid of them as it goes. This sequential style is somewhat of a nuisance however, just as in most matrix generators which must conform to this restriction.

There is a larger version of the LP package for the CDC CYBER-74. It certainly does not compete with APEX but it was fairly easy to produce from the PDP version at a time when it was not clear that APEX was available to us. A friend of mine in the U.S. was also converting the LP package to run on another mini-computer but I haven't heard how he made out. It turns out that, in many research centers, there are quite a number of small models--such as pilot versions--and a mini-computer can be very useful if it is available in-house at all hours. We use the UNIX operating system, developed at Bell Labs, on the PDP and it is the finest operating system I have ever seen. I wish some big computers had something as good.

ANATOMY OF A MATHEMATICAL PROGRAMMING SYSTEM

Wm. Orchard-Hays

International Institute for Applied Systems Analysis,
Laxenburg, Austria

SETTING THE PERSPECTIVE

When I agreed to present this subject, I realized it was a nearly impossible task. One could easily devote a semester to it and at least a month would be required to treat it in depth. Perhaps in a full week, the main aspects could be covered, provided we did not all become exhausted before we got to the end. But in three 45-minute sessions, only the outline can be drawn with perhaps one or two more detailed discussions for illustration.

The first difficulty is the dimensionality. Any two-dimensional view is not only incomplete but actually misleading. If I show you a kind of organization chart--as I will--depicting the way routines are linked, then the collections of data are missing. If I show you data flow, you have to imagine something making it happen. If I try to put both together--as I will--the diagram gets very messy, has the appearance of an old car after it has been squashed by a press, and still only shows typical connections.

The second difficulty, at least for some people, is that one needs to take an anthropomorphic view of the components of a system.[1] A routine is not just a mathematically described function or a list of instructions in some tedious programming language. A routine in a system serves a dynamic function, has a responsibility

---

1. Reference 1 should be read for a fuller discussion of this viewpoint.

for certain actions or checks, must cooperate with superiors, peers, and inferiors in an organized scheme of management, and is imbued with a personality. You may think this is a little silly, but I will counter that you will never understand systems otherwise. Let me give a very rough analogy. There are some people who will never be good automobile drivers because they always regard the car as a machine which they must operate in a dangerous environment. A good driver becomes a part of the car so that driver and car together become almost a single living thing. This is much the way one must view a system. You must get down into it and look around with an appreciation of the coordination of its many parts. If you notice a result coming out somewhere that doesn't seem right, you had better investigate, just as when your car makes a new noise, you had better find out why, or when you feel an unnatural sensation in your body, you had better consider what might have caused it.

The third difficulty is whether to start from the inside and work out or from the outside and work in. In spite of some current theory about structured programming, I prefer to start from the inside. If that doesn't work, the outside doesn't matter. However, we will in fact have to take different views, some from inside and some from outside.

The core of an MPS, of course, is the simplex algorithm and the inversion routine. These are not simple entities and a full delineation of their structures would take the next couple of hours. Nevertheless, this is perhaps a good place to start. I will assume a checked out system, running on an essentially error-free machine.

First, let us outline the steps of the simplex algorithm.[1] In its original form it had only four steps with two tests between, plus the overall condition of whether it is looking for a feasible solution (Phase 1) or an optimal solution (Phase 2). It will be convenient to define three subsets of the row indices $i=1,\ldots,m$:

> $i \in F$ if row i is a functional,
> $i \in P$ if β_i is nonnegative,
> $i \in M$ if β_i is negative.

For simplicity, we will assume for the present that row 1 is the objective function. Then the original simplex method is as follows:

> Step I: Scan all β_i, $i=1,\ldots,m$. If no i is in set M, status is Phase 2, otherwise Phase 1.
>
> Step II: For $j=1,\ldots,n$, set
> $$d_j = \alpha_j^1 \text{ if in Phase 2}$$

---

1. Notation is defined in Reference 2. It will be presumed that this has been read.

$$= \sum_{i \varepsilon M} \alpha_j^i \text{ if in Phase 1}$$

Select j=s by

$$d_s = \min_j d_j \text{ if any } d_j < 0$$

s = 0 otherwise

Test I: If s = 0, then, if Phase 1, NO FEASIBLE SOLUTION
if Phase 2, OPTIMAL SOLUTION (at hand)

Else, proceed.

Step III: For i=1,...,m

$0_i = + \infty$ if $i \varepsilon F$, if $\alpha_s^i = 0$, or if β_i and α_s^i have

different signs.

$$= \beta_i / \alpha_s^i \text{ otherwise}$$

Select i=r by

$$0_r = \min_i 0_i \text{ if any } \theta_i$$

r = 0 otherwise

Test II: If r = 0, then, if Phase 2, UNBOUNDED SOLUTION (available).

Else, proceed.

Step IV: Update the entire tableau including β, using α_s^r as the print element. Record s as the identifying index for the r-th basis column. Then return to Step I.

Simplicity itself! However, a few questions arise.

1. Q. Where are the tableau, its limits m and n and the β columns?
   A. The input routine put them somewhere.
   Q. What input routine and how do we know where?
   A. That has to be worked out.
   Q. Ummm.
2. Q. What do we do if s=0 or r=0?

A. Print the results.
Q. With what and in what format?
A. That has to be worked out.
Q. Ummm.
3. Q. In Test II, what if r=0 in Phase 1?
A. Such a condition is obviously impossible.
Q. What if it occurs anyway?
A. How can it?
Q. I don't know but it will.
4. Q. How should we record the phase?
A. Why not use the cardinality of the set M?
Q. OK but then it must be counted each time in Step I.
A. Sure. Why not add up the sum of infeasibilities too?

This is about where I started after I first talked with Dantzig in 1952, except Phase I was much more complicated until the time of LP/90.[1] It would take much too much time to trace all the increasing circles of evolution, so let us jump right to the revised simplex method with product form of inverse, upper bounds, and multiple and partial pricing. Then we will have a better idea of how many things have to be "worked out."

We will need to be a little more precise about indices. We will let i=1,...,m run through logicals, j=1,...,n run through structurals and h=1,...,m run through the rows of a column. We also need two more subsets of row indices, two subsets of combined row and column indices or flags, a set of basis identifiers, and indeed several pages of notation. If we tried to continue at this level of detail, it is clear we should never get through. I will have to assume you have read the list of notation in Reference 2 as I will utilize it when necessary. However, let us look at the simplex algorithm with all its "bells and whistles" in a more aggregated form. (See Figure 1.)

First, Step I above gets elaborated considerably and is usually put in a subroutine called CKFEAS (or CKFEZ). It is its responsibility to check the feasibility of the current solution vector, add up the sum of primal infeasibilities and record both their number and sum, and set flags in a list somewhere as to the status of each element. In addition to being negative, a variable can be infeasible because it is above its upper bound, including the case of a positive value for a zero-valued logical, i.e., an equality row which is not yet satisfied.

Before CKFEAS can be executed for the first time, however, many other things have to be done. If we are restarting from an advanced

---

1. Dantzig himself was unsure of how Phase I should be carried out in 1952.

basis, the inversion routine, INVERT, must be executed first. The decision to call INVERT is usually made within the control routine for an algorithm since there are many reasons why it may be necessary. So another procedure of equal or greater complexity may be called before the simplex algorithm really gets started. We will call the simplex control routine ITERATE. Its main functions are to make tests, decisions, and calls to subroutines or other procedures. ITERATE and similar control routines are the boss within their scope of authority but this authority is delegated by the application system control routine which in turn is authorized to execute by the host system. When ITERATE calls INVERT, it essentially relinquishes its authority with an implied priority to regain it provided no difficulties are encountered elsewhere, or the system control routine does not override for some reason.

Whether or not INVERT is required, another routine usually called FIXVEC must be executed. This routine is a subroutine common to essentially all algorithms and even to the output prodecure. It is one of the most complicated routines in the whole simplex library. It must determine the status of the solution vector, i.e, whether anything has happened which rendered it invalid, and unless everything is clearly OK, it recomputes a fresh solution vector. To do this, it must obtain the current RHS column from the matrix work file, subtract all columns whose variable (X_j or u_i) has a non-zero lower bound or which is at a finite upperbound times the appropriate value, take into account a composite RHS or objective function, and transform the result by the inverse of the current basis. Thus FIXVEC may call FTRAN at a second-order level. FIXVEC also checks up on proper definition of the RHS column, the OBJ (objective function) row, and any parametric columns, rows and values. FIXVEC can set error returns which inhibit continuing with ITERATE, as for example, when the user has overlooked some definition. If generalized uper bounding (GUB) is implemented in the same procedure (as in MPS-III or SESAME, for example), then another subroutine of equal or greater complexity, usually called GUBSTART, must be executed after FIXVEC. In fact, FIXVEC and GUBSTART can play a little iterative game between themselves before allowing ITERATE to continue. Hence, ITERATE does not have absolute authority even within his realm.

Step II of the original simplex method breaks into a number of parts with the product form of inverse. First, a routine called PIFORMS (or FORMPI) generates a pricing form which is a row consisting of plus and minus ones and zeroes. (Sometimes these are replaced with scaling values based on various rules.) PIFORMS is usually generalized to produce two forms when they are required, as for the dual algorithm or composite OBJ feature. Although PIFORMS could be generalized for all such pruposes, the logic becomes too complicated and separate routines for the parametric algorithms and similar purposes are usually created. PIFORMS relies on the

results of CKFEAS, plus various switches and values set either by
ITERATE or the control routine, to decide what form or forms to
generate. Then, either PIFORMS calls BTRAN or ITERATE calls it on
return to transform the form or forms by the basis inverse. BTRAN
is usually programmed to handle up to three forms simultaneously.
The transformed primary form is the pricing vector traditionally
called π.

Next, ITERATE calls another large and complicated subroutine
named PRICE which amounts to a sub-algorithm. It is the function
of PRICE to find as many candidate columns as possible--up to a
specified limit--to bring into the basis. By PRICE's rules, each
column which it selects would give an improved solution if put in
the basis. However, many further tests are made before any are
actually introduced. The elaboration of PRICE routines has led to
such complexity as to almost defy description unless one can read
the code. If GUB or other special sets are used, or if two or more
algorithms are combined, the intricacy is enormous. We cannot take
the time now to go into such things; all I can suggest is that, if
there is sufficient interest, we could have a special session.

When PRICE returns control to ITERATE, it may be that no col-
ums have been selected at all. In this case, ITERATE must investigate the situation, for example to determine the phase, whether any
special conditions have been set which may have inhibited PRICE from
finding anything, etc. These tests must be thorough and rigorous
since the termination of the algorithm depends on them. If a model
is declared infeasible when it is not , or optimal before optimality
is attained, the credibility of the system is badly compromised.
These same remarks apply with equal force to other tests which appear subsequently in relation to terminations.

If PRICE produced one or more candidates, ITERATE calls FTRAN
to transform them by the inverse of the basis. FTRAN is usually
programmed to handle several columns simultaneously. The maximum
number of candidates is typically seven or nine although some systems have permitted as many as twenty. In fact, the number to be
sought is often adjusted dynamically depending on how many of a set
have actually been used during some number of preceding iterations.
The reason for this is that FTRAN is a very time-consuming operation. Indeed, before additional refinements were introduced in the
last few years, it was found that for many models up to 55 percent
of total execution time was spent in FTRAN. The other expensive
operation in time is BTRAN but it usually transforms only one row
and does not require the delicate tolerance tests which FTRAN does.
Neither BTRAN nor FTRAN are very large routines but they have to be
programmed very carefully, using all the time-saving tricks of assembler language which one can devise. For example, floating-point
numbers are tested with logical bit-masking operations rather than

arithmetic. So-called higher level languages have no equivalent capability.

The remainder of the algorithm is usually called a minor iteration since the part described thus far, starting with PIFORMS, is not executed again until the set produced by PRICE is exhausted. When the preceding part is used, this is called a major iteration. (The term grand iteration is usually applied to a super-algorithm which uses the simplex algorithm as a sub-procedure, the term referring to a complete simplex reoptimization.)

It will be helpful now to refer to the chart in Figure 2. The first step of a minor iteration is a subroutine called TRUDJ which has often been implemented in-line in ITERATE. Its function is to recompute the d_j values for the set produced by PRICE. At first glance, this would appear to be redundant. However, there are three reasons for it.

1. The code is needed anyway for succeeding minor iterations.

2. PRICE sometimes uses weighted values, either set up by PIFORMS or according to some selection variant.

3. In any event, the d_j from PRICE are computed by inner products. The transformed columns from FTRAN are computed by linear forms with very careful tolerance testing and are more accurate. At any rate, it is the values computed in the latter way which are used for the eta-vectors and all succeeding transformations.

Consequently TRUDJ may reject candidates produced by PRICE.

Here a delicate question arises: What shall we do if TRDUJ rejects all PRICE's candidates? If we go back to PRICE he may select the same columns again so these two guys would argue endlessly (i.e., a large program loop). The real trouble, of course, is that we have an ill-conditioned basis so that numbers cannot be computed in two ways accurately enough to match. Calling INVERT might help but this is rather drastic and we may have just done INVERT anyway. The traditional solution is what is called a reject list, which has a limited length, typically room for 8 entries which PRICE honors. The identifiers for the columns PRICE selected are put in this list or as many as it will hold. Then PRICE is called again, in the hope that he finds something else. This is repeated until either PRICE and TRUDJ agree on at least one candidate or the list fills up. If the list fills, we give up, declaring the model either infeasible or optimal, perhaps with a warning that this is a presumed result. On the other hand, if at least one candidate can be agreed on and it makes it all the way through an iteration, the reject list is cleared.

I have no idea of how often the reject list gets used but it occurs sometimes because, without it, false results are obtained in rare cases. If you think this heuristic gimmick is too crude to be in a sophisticated mathematical programming system, I challenge you to invent something better. If it is practical, I will gladly adopt it. When one is dealing with numbers obtained with thousands of multiplications and additions, he must be prepared to deal with logically impossible situations--they are sure to happen, most likely on an important run for an important user.

If TRUDJ rejects all remaining candidates on a minor iteration, we have no problem; a major iteration is made. There are other reasons why PRICE may obtain no candidates or he and TRUDJ may disagree. For example, if pi-weighting is in use (a very old gimmick which still seems to be useful occasionally), then this option is simply cancelled and PRICE called again. The reject list is a last resort.

Assuming candidates still available, PIVOT (originally called CHUZR for "choose r") is called. PIVOT calculates the θ value for each candidate column and the index i=r on which this occurs or, if the variable should only change bound, it sets r=0. PIVOT has continually grown in complexity over the years. I once calculated that there are nearly 150 different cases which it must take into account. If GUB is in use, the complexity is much greater. The PIVOT calculations are perhaps the most critical of all. It is his responsibility to see that improvements in feasibility are made or to maintain feasibility if it exists. Any error her causes the algorithm to retrogress or to get into a false cycle. Since, due to tolerance problems, PIVOT cannot always do an absolutely perfect job, CKFEAS will switch back to Phase 1 if a feasible solution goes slightly infeasible. This is most likely to happen when the solution is very close to optimal since PRICE is straining to find any worthwhile candidate. I have not seen a checked-out PIVOT allow a gross infeasibility to creep back in for many years but in very rare cases it is possible to get into a 2-step cycle with a tiny infeasibility right at termination. To my knowledge, no system protects against this except by limiting total number of iterations or total execution time. There are degrees of impossibility.

The multiple-pricing technique, selecting a set of candidates, creates another problem at this point. Which one of the set shall we actually use? It was David M. Smith who set about answering this question. He invented another subroutine called SELECT which uses a set of priority sifting rules to find the candidate which will give the ostensibly greatest improvement in the solution. This is not necessarily the one which makes the largest change in the functional. Other considerations come into play such as reducing the number of infeasibilities, eliminating a zero-valued logical still in the basis, the possibility that none of the candidates make a nonzero change on a minor iteration, and others. If the solution is feasible, and any candidate leads to an unbounded solution, this takes priority since there is no point in proceeding further; one unbounded solution is as good as another. It is here also that the possibility that PIVOT could find no limiting value for any candidate when the solution is infeasible must be guarded against. This is an extremely rare phenomenon but it has happened, again due to arithmetic troubles. If GUB is in use, other conditions must be checked and separable programming creates additional problems. Hence, it is conceivable that SELECT may also reject all candidates, just as TRUDJ. Similar logic is used to resolve the problem.

If SELECT chooses a candidate, then all decisions have finally been made and UPDATE is called to complete the iteration. One of the advantages of the product form of inverse was supposed to be making updating easier so UPDATE should be simple, right? Not so. UPDATE is busier than a circus juggler with only a short time to do his act. Everybody has been leaving flags and bits and numbers laying around all over the place and UPDATE must collect all this information, make some sense out of it, carefully update all the records, update the solution vector, and probably create an eta-vector which he then calls upon WRETA to pack up and add to the eta-file. If GUB is in use, he may have to make some additional eta-vectors which he invents from indices or from a recursive updating process. He must also make some check on the range of numbers produced by division in case they go wild. Finally, he must update the remaining candidate columns, essentially one step of FTRAN. This is done in-line with highly tricky code to make it as fast as possible. Speed is of the essence. (In timing tests, this was almost the only local code sequence outside of FTRAN and BRTAN which could be identified clearly. Arithmetic is expensive.)

Having done all this, we ought to produce a log of what has happened in case the user likes to read run logs. There are also some possible instructions from our superiors which we had better check. However, for our information to be up-to-date, we must call on CKFEAS again to find out how many infeasibilities are left, and some other information. We would need to do it anyway before starting the next minor iteration. Before we call CKFEAS though, we should remember the previous status in case the solution has just gone feasible. If it has, we want to print a caption and perhaps we were instructed to return to the system control routine when this occurred.

LOGLINE is named for its function of producing log lines but that is not its only function. In fact, log lines may not be wanted or only every so many iterations. Such a number is called a _frequency_ and a great variety are used. LOGLINE is a convenient place to put a lot of such stuff so that, even if it doesn't output a log line, it may return with some demand set, for example, the conditions for a user-specified break may have been met. LOGLINE also computes an up-to-date value for the functional since it is not automatically produced anywhere in all circumstances.

Assuming nothing special has happened, control goes back to TRUDJ to start another minor iteration. If that is not possible, then control goes on back to PIFORMS to start another major iteration.

Two more subroutines complete the set under ITERATE's supervision. The first is usually called INVTCTRL (invert control) and is executed at the start of a major iteration. If reinversion is done on a frequency, this could be caught in LOGLINE but there are other criteria more commonly used. One has to do with changes in the in-core status of the eta-file and the other is based on a clock. All these conditions, or the one in effect, are tested in INVTCTRL. It is placed at the start of a major iteration so as not to interfere with the completion of the minor iterations in progress and also to minimize its execution time.[1] INVTCTRL is used by all algorithms.

The last subroutine, CHECK, is probably the largest of all and combines many of the features of both FIXVEC and PRICE plus quite a bit of printing gear. CHECK does a complete primal and dual check on the existing solution and if residues are not within specified tolerances, it prints messages and sets demands appropriately. Different system designers have different policies regarding the use of CHECK. My own is to always call CHECK after INVERT unless instructed otherwise, to call CHECK at every termination, including just going feasible, and to honor a beginning and ending iteration number which may be specified for debugging either the system or a model. I regard it as inexcusable for any system to declare a termination without first doing a complete check. If trouble is found, the INVERT is called and another check performed. If there is still trouble, a demand is set which will terminate calculations unless overridden by the user.

In some systems, the primal and dual checks are separated and one may be performed more frequently than the other. In some programming languages, it is more efficient to make two subroutines but they should be used together. One wants to catch unrecoverable errors as soon as practicable no matter how they are found.

The checking tolerances are settable by the user so that if

---

1. In MPS/360 and derivative systems, only BTRAN and FTRAN time is clocked so it only makes sense to put INVTCTRL at the start of a major iteration.

some models have a propensity to generate noise slightly above
standard settings, the user can override. However, playing with
tolerances in a system is dangerous.

Well, the simplex algorithm doesn't look so simple now, does
it? We could ask innumerable questions. Where is all this data,
where are tolerances, frequencies, and other instructions kept and
how do they get there? What is a demand? How is the system linked
together, how are common subroutines used in various procedures?
And so on, and so on.

We will not have time to examine other procedures at such great
length. There are others with more overall logic though perhaps
none with quite as much total volume of code, unless one includes
data management subsystems which can be enormous. However, I hope
this excursion through the revised, extended, composite, super-
duper simplex algorithm has given you some feel for the nature of
MPSs and a point of view which will enable us to examine the total
system in a more aggregated way.

We will go back outside at this point and look at the major
parts of a system. The algorithmic routines account for no more
than perhaps 20 percent of the total code.

THE VARIOUS SUBSYSTEMS

When one speaks of subsystems, the breakdown depends somewhat
on the viewpoint. That is, most subsystems are not really separable
modules which could work independently but functionally similar
items which may thread through the entire system. There are exceptions. A data management subsystem could be separated more or less
cleanly, and the overall system control might be used for other applications. But, in general, subsystems in the present context are
analogous to the elaborate diagrams of the human body one finds in
an encyclopedia: a red one for the blood system, a blue one for
the nerve system, a yellow one for the muscular system, and some
other color for the bone structure. None of these subsystems exist
in isolation nor do they function without reference to each other.
Still, the viewpoint is useful.

As a first cut, we can distinguish four major subsystems:

1.   The heirarchy of routines; their purposes and responsibil-
     ities. This is most easily depicted as an organization
     chart.

2.   Categories of data sets; their relationships and access
      methods. This is rather imperfectly represented by flow
     diagrams and lists of parameters and pointers.

3. User controls; man-machine interfacing and activation. This is difficult to depict but can be indicated by control statements.

4. Execution controls; storage allocation and operating system conventions. This would require a set of programmers' flow charts to be depicted thoroughly. However, it can be "talked through" with less detail.

Before proceeding, three observations may be helpful. First, an hierarchical diagram of routines is often regarded as the best overall way to depict a system. This is almost as much a mistake as thinking a manufacturing company's organization chart depicts the factories, shipping and receiving docks, sales and accounting departments, etc. In fact, an organization chart is almost a complete abstraction. It shows lines of authority but not how the whole complex really works or what it is doing. In a software system, the hierarchy of routines does have somewhat more relevancy to operational facts but it is still only a partial picture.

Second, there is something akin to a duality relationship between executive control of routines and what they do with sets of data, just as there is between a manufacturing operation and the technology for the material it processes. The operation tends to be decentralized and may be modified or extended from time to time. However, the technology tends to become more and more refined and standardized and is a strong centralizing force. Pursuing this idea would lead us far afield but it is a point worth keeping in mind. In particular, it is much easier to change routines and re-structure procedures than to alter the basic data structures on which they operate or the fundamental assumptions on which they are based.

Third, the actual construction and linkage of routines is a completely different subject. If you look at the assembly listings for a system, you will find a great many lines of code which seem to have nothing to do with the application at all. In fact, they don't. They reflect the whole vast technology of computer programming and the conventions of the particular programming language, assembler or compiler, type of computer, and the system programmer's style. To really find your way around in the actual program, you have to be familiar with these things which takes considerable experience. So, if you are not already a system programmer, don't expect to be able to leave here and go read code. The number of people who can really do that is surprisingly small. There may be less then ten people in the world who have an extensive knowledge of the actual code for any one MPS. I hope you won't think me immodest if I claim to be familiar with more parts of more MPSs than anyone else alive. But I am completely unfamiliar with some of them and, even in systems which I know intimately, there are some routines which I can follow only with the greatest difficulty. Obviously, this has strong implications for maintenance and extensions. A subtle bug can consume days of a programmer's time and not many such people are available. Also, it is gruelling work. After eight hours on a tough system problem, I am exhausted, mentally if not physically.

The Data Subsystem

It will probably be least confusing to start with the data subsystem. First, we will at least know what we are trying to operate on and, second, just like the simplex algorithm, the collections of data are not as simple as might be supposed. To begin with, some sort of communication region is essential in order that all routines can work in a coordinated manner. There are from 150 to 250 routines in a big system, or possibly more. It is completely impractical to have every call to a routine include all possible arguments that might be required. I recently built a small LP package completely in FORTRAN. (That may surprise those of you who know me but there were special reasons.) Even though I used COMMON blocks, the limitations of FORTRAN forced me to use long argument lists on many calls. The biggest trouble I had in checking out was in getting the confounded things straight. Furthermore, argument lists take space in core and processing them takes time. A call to a subroutine is bad enough anyway; registers have to be saved, base registers have to be set up, etc. The first page of code for a routine is typically merely the linkage and the next half page or more is for initialization. This is hidden to the FORTRAN programmer and, even in assembler language, use of macros makes it very easy to write, but it is there all the same. Even the exit from a subroutine can be elaborate. I have used a communication region from the first package I ever built and, so far as I know, all the big MPSs still do. We call it the CR.

Over the years, CRs grew very large. Although all parts were used, they were not all used at all times. Not only is it somewhat of a nuisance to have a large fixed block which is always there, but it is difficult to change and time consuming when assembling routines to have to call in all the definitions. In a very real sense, the CR is the actual core of the system. It is typically defined by relative offsets, like a template or, in 360 jargon, DSECTS (definitional sections). Once it is defined and many routines are assembled, any change in the CR requires reassembly of everything. Consequently, in the design of OPTIMA and again in SESAME, we broke the CR into parts with only the truly universal parameters remaining in the CR proper and the others put in blocks which pertain only to subsets of procedures. I don't know to what extent this has been done by others but it is to be recommended. However, if it wasn't done in the initial design, it may be an impracticle undertaking.

In somewhat the same way, not all the data files are in the same category. One can distinguish five levels of files, not counting program libraries in any form and irrespective of such distinctions as input files and output files. These levels have to do with the degree of permanency and human manipulation. (See Figure 3.) At level 1 or the top level, on the input side the files essentially consist of punched card images, whether or not they were ever literally holes in cardboard. On the output side, level 1 files may be card images, actual punched cards, or listings. A listing is as much a file as a card deck. The main characteristic of level 1 files is that they are, or could be, prepared, manipulated or read by human beings. They are also inefficient but necessary. After all, a computer is not intended to run for its own sake but to serve users. Unfortunately, however, in many systems, the only way to interface with another system or package is through level 1 files, i.e., card or line images. This is a widely used technique but can be grossly inefficient both in programming effort and processing time. For example, if the MPS does not include matrix generation capability, they typically a matrix generator is written separately, usually in FORTRAN, which produces MPS/360 card-image input. A matrix generator should feed directly into level 2.

Level 2 consists of what I call user files. (See Figure 4.) On the input side, the level has a models file. In MPS/360 or MPSX terminology, this is the problem file; I have no objection to the name but I do to the structure those systems use but let's not pursue that right now. On the output side is a results file; this is where one puts the solution output when it is intended for further use and not for reading. Many systems have not had such a feature but it is essential for a data management subsystem such as DATAFORM or DATAMAT or for any report writing capability which can handle cross-case summaries. There are other important uses for this file such as grand iterative schemes or data base management. Level 2 also has intermediate files, such as save files. Combining these with the problem file in MPS/360 was an error in design in my opinion. Of course, in 1964, we hadn't yet got used to disks and thought in terms of tapes, with a limited number of tape drives.

Level 2 files are under the user's control as far as contents and use are concerned but not with respect to detailed format which the user is unaware of except in a gross sense. However, they clearly belong to the user and may be relatively permanent. In particular, they are retained from run to run or session to session. The user cannot manipulate them directly but only through system commands; i.e., control statements.

The main file at level 3 is the work matrix although some systems provide for two forms. In SESAME there is also an output file at this level for use by special user-written procedures. So far, this feature has not been taken advantage of but there was a similar arrangement in an extension to MPS-III. Some of Rarick's innovations may also use such a file. The purpose is to provide the essential output information from a solution in a highly packed form for fast processing down-stream.

In SESAME, there is another file which may be considered to be at this level although it has the structure of a level 2 file and is under the user's control. We call this the MAPSFILE and it is used for basis saves and general bit maps. This file is very dynamic and tends to get filled with dead space. Hence, there is another form called the USERMAPS file and a procedure for copying back and forth between the two. Thus the user, at the end of a session, can save his good maps on USERMAPS and discard MAPSFILE.

The level 3 files are indirectly under the user's control but only to the extent of causing their creation and invoking them. They are not retained from run to run or session to session (MAPSFILE may be). They really do not belong to the user, he just borrows them.

The distinction between levels 3, 4, and 5 is very slight. The chief file at level 4 is the eta-file. The user has almost no control of this although by using an INVERT command he can cause a new one to be created. Generally, however, creation and use of level 4 files are automatic and the user may not know their structure even in principle. They are retained over some number of iterations or set of procedures and then are either recreated or discarded.

Level 5, if one wishes to go that far, are strictly scratch files necessary for temporary storage for some program. The user may not even know they exist. The scratch files used by an assembler or compiler are of this nature.

In addition to the characteristics already noted, there is another kind of distinction relevant to the present discussion. Let me use the term level 3 to mean levels 3, 4, and 5 collectively. Then, levels 1, 2, and 3 take completely different kinds of processing routines and low-level I/O interfacings. At the very lowest level, the I/O drivers, which almost belong to the host operating system, may be alike but upwards the routines diverge into different styles. Thus, the breakdown of the data subsystem implies sub-sub-systems in the complex routines.

The processing routines for the level 1 files must conform to a number of conventions for the host system and also human interfacing with the MPS control. Level 2 files have taken several forms. My own current design here is to use tree-files. This technique dates back to LP/600 when a very clever system programmer named Jim Welch utilized them for several purposes. In an interactive system, such files are necessary for full flexibility in browsing at the terminal and data management schemes such as DATA-FORM and DATAMAT rely on them almost completely. Efficiency here is not so much in lightening fast file passing and arithmetic but in the ability to get at anything at any time and to extend, modify or purge as required.

The requirements for level 3 files are what they have traditionally been for LP work: highly packed, fast file passing, clever arrangement of information to permit fast unpacking and use in arithmetic or logic, and highly specialized processing routines. It should be noted that levels 2 and 3 are seldom required at the same time. The SETUP procedure which creates the work matrix must read the models file, and the SOLUTION procedure which computes, formats, and prints or enfiles results (plus a few other procedures of a similar type) require files at all levels simultaneously but they are the exception. Hence the CR proper should not contain information specific to file levels except for primary pointers necessary for dynamic core allocation.

In the next section, we will turn to the heirarchical subsystem of routines. It will be easier to discuss the nature of the CR and other in-core data blocks from that point of view.

The Heirarchy of Routines

A diagram of the heirarchy of routines looks like a human organization chart showing line and staff functions. The MPS is only a sub-hierarchy, like the manufacturing division of a huge enterprise. The top of the pyramid is a computer system with its basic control program, often called an operating monitor in batch systems. At this level, it is hard to separate the hardware and software. It would be like separating bone and marrow. The basic control program actually oversees everything the computer facility does and is the big boss in the specialized world created by a computer. For the most part, we need not be concerned with how it functions--it is given. However, it does respond to requests and some of these need to be understood by the user even though most of them are for the computer operators. In a truly interactive system such as IBM's VM/CMS facility, the user interacts with the control program rather intimately, or may do so, but in a stereotyped way. This is quite in contrast to the operating monitor in traditional operating systems, such as OS/360, which is insulated from any real contact with human users. However, this difference is important mainly when one is building a system and debugging it. From the user's viewpoint, it is the conversational monitor in an interactive system which makes the difference. There is no real equivalent in a batch system. For example, a remote job entry station (RJE) or IBM's TSO (time sharing option) for OS/360 are not

truly interactive even though one may enter commands through a
terminal.

However, the line between the control program and a conversational monitor is also fuzzy and, for many commands or requests,
the user is scarcely aware which one is responding. A better concept is that of levels of environment which is appropriate to both
batch and interactive facilities. As one goes to lower echelons
in the pyramid or inverted tree, it becomes more and more important
to be aware of which environment one is in. If one is dealing with
the operating vice-president for manufacturing, he need not be too
explicit about whether something is made in a foundry or a machine
shop. If one is concerned with what is being done in a machine
shop, he had better be able to tell it from a foundry.

A modern computer is able to process several jobs concurrently
and a main function of the basic control program is to schedule
these, both in the large and small time slices, and to keep everything straight. It is really unnecessary for us to consider this
except as there may be competing demands for hardware facilities
and execution time. A computer seems to run fast sometimes and
slow at other times. Two o'clock on a Wednesday afternoon is probably a bad time to expect fast response, while at 7:00 PM on Fri-
day--if the computer is up--you will probably get lightening fast
execution. But the same organizational structure is in effect for
your job at both times.

A large application system requires its own control program
which we will call EXECUTOR to distinguish it from the basic control program or operating monitor. In Figure 5 which I am using
for an example, this is labelled SESAME EXECUTIVE CONTROL PACKAGE
but this is only its name in this particular system. In OPTIMA it
was called APEX, in MPS/360 and MPS-III it is called EXECUTOR. The
name is really unimportant except that some noun must be assigned
to invoke it, that is, to request the operating monitor to load it
to core and initiate execution. The request name and the EXECU-
TOR's actual name need not be the same and the mechanisms for invoking an application will differ among various computing facilities.

EXECUTOR is not a single routine any more than the basic operating monitor is. Just as an operating vice-president will have
his own staff which may rival the president's in size and scope,
so EXECUTOR has a number of subroutines which it keeps close to
itself and which almost rival those of the operating monitor. However, most of them do not perform staff functions but rather provide universal facilities which need to be standardized and cen-
tralized. For example, a general statement-parsing routine and a
general print-formatting routine are usually part of the EXECUTOR
package, as well as the I/O drivers which must interact with the

host. One does not want these replicated in special versions for each procedure. Incidentally, in designing SESAME, I did a comprehensive clean-up in this area. In both MPS/360 and MPS-III, for example, there was a terrible proliferation of special I/O routines. Almost each file had its own separate read routine and write routine. Such complication is unnecessary and a horror to maintain.

The operating monitor can have several jobs in execution concurrently. This capability is not available to the application system, except for overlapped I/O. Even this has disappeared in interactive facilities with respect to any one job. The overlapping is with respect to all jobs. Otherwise, however, EXECUTOR can cause the loading and execution of any one of many procedures. The number of procedures is typically between 30 and 50. Some of these have options which give almost the effect of multiple procedures. The procedures constitute the next echelon.

The simplex algorithm we went through earlier is such a procedure. From the viewpoint of construction, a procedure is a pre-linked module which is loaded as a unit. All procedures overlay the same section of assigned main storage, at least in theory. In operating systems with multiple variable tasks, one cannot exactly predetermine where any module will be loaded, a characteristic that has caused a great deal of trouble in several MPSs. The EXECUTOR package is another such module which resides in a different section and remains there throughout execution of the MPS. In reality, some loading and binding schemes are considerably more complicated than this and large procedures often utilize overlay structures themselves. VM/CMS has considerably less flexibility in this respect then OS/360, so in SESAME each procedure is actually a completely pre-bound, absolutized module. This really works much better than more complex arrangements but that is because VM/CMS uses virtual core. In real core, loading is highly dynamic but is accounted for by relocation registers fundamental to a virtual machine. This is probably one reason that virtual machines are not as inefficient as it was feared they might be. The extra level of abstraction greatly simplifies linking, binding and I/O procedures. The entire SESAME system can be pre-bound in less than a minute of elapsed time, probably less in both elapsed and CPU time than link-editing one large procedure under OS/360. Another advantage of virtual core is that plenty is available. I typically run SESAME in between a half megabyte and a full megabyte. In theory, one can go to 16 megabytes though in practice the real machine may not be able to handle it. I have never tried it.

The next lower echelon consists of major subroutines. That is, if we consider ITERATE to be the control program for the simplex method, then subroutines such as PRICE and PIVOT constitute the next lower level. There is only one copy of a procedure in the executable library but there are as many copies of subroutines as there are procedures which use them, except for the universal routines in the EXECUTOR module. Procedures are constructed from a library of assembled routines or TEXT decks (sometimes with one preliminary step of link-editing). There, of course, only one copy of each routine exists. If one is changed, however, all procedures using it must be re-linked. This is another advantage to the absolutized modules used under VM/CMS. If a widely used subroutine is changed, it is no great difficulty to simply rebind the entire system. Under OS/360 this was very expensive and it was hard to keep track of which procedures used which routines. As an historical footnote, in OPTIMA the final binding was done at load time of the system and it was possible to load alternate versions of routines and either absolute or relative patches. This was also possible in the LP/94 system circa 1963. Modern operating systems simply do not allow this degree of flexibility, an example of the standardizing and centralizing tendency in the evolution of technology which I remarked on earlier. At one time, Chevrolets and Fords were quite different; now you have to look at the name-plate to tell which is which.

A procedure may include sub-procedures. Thus in MPS-III and SESAME, the primal and dual algorithms are combined. This is arranged by having a subroutine to ITERATE which outranks the other subroutines. It is shown at ITERDUAL. The routine utilizes many of the other simplex subroutines in the same manner that ITERATE does for the primal algorithm. However, when the dual algorithm completes execution, it returns to ITERATE which continues in normal fashion. If the dual algorithm was successful, the solution will be immediately optimal. If not, the primal algorithm continues.

We now need to look at a broader spectrum of procedures and it is more meaningful to combine this with the data subsystem. So we will now look at the messy diagram I promised you.

Incidentally, although I am using the SESAME system for illustration, essentially the same structure applies to MPS/360, MPS-III and the original MPSX. I am not familiar with the new MPSX internal structure. One can use PL/1 as an executive control for the latter system and it also includes a new LUD inversion routine developed by IBM-France. The latter is reportedly a very fine piece of work. For some reason, they have dropped GUB which I cannot understand. I only guess that it was based on an analysis of sales; if so, then this does not bode well for progress in the field. As to the use of PL/1, I view this development with apprehension. It is true that the internal programming of the old MPS/360 EXECUTOR was a terrible pirce of work but it did provide a new plateau of capability. No doubt it should have been rebuilt with more flexible capability. However, if we are not careful, it will soon be necessary to use PL/1 to run an LP problem. IBM has never given up on trying to foist this terrible language on the industry. Of

course, there are those who disagree with me, including one of my
current co-workers.

The Interleaved System of Files and Procedures

The interleaved system of most of the files and procedures in
SESAME is shown in Figure 6. It is difficult to comment much further on it since the diagram shows the main relationships. In a
batch system, most of these same relationships exist except that
the keyboard is replaced with a job control language (JCL) deck and
the display unit with a run log. One procedure shown, BROWSE, is
unique to an interactive system. It permits one to look through
the models file and results file in a browsing fashion. Single
numerical changes to a model can even be made. The VARY procedure,
which corresponds to the RANGE procedure in other systems, can be
used for interactive investigation of ranges or it can be programmed by means of a card-image file to produce selected ranging information. These differences, which may appear small with respect
to the whole system, are nevertheless significant.

The Subsystem of User Controls: General Concepts and the CR

At this point, I am confronted with a difficult choice in the
style of presentation. The SESAME system has been used for illustration and, up to now, this has been as good as any. In fact, if
you are not interested in interactive systems in general or SESAME
in particular, you can regard it as a general, abstract system designed for illustration. However, in turning to user controls and
human interfacing, the difference between a batch and an interactive system is so great that it makes a qualitative change. In
fairness, since batch systems are much more common and extensively
used, one of them should be chosen and, by the same argument, it
should probably be MPSX. But this would lead to a whole set of
complications in notation and terminology which would be time-consuming to explain and would add little to the subject under discussion. If you are not used to running jobs with a batch system,
you will have to consult with someone who is, in your own center;
if you are, you already know that I am talking about.

The OS/360 operating system, for example, is very powerful
with a wealth of capabilities but its JCL is one of the ugliest,
most error-prone communications media ever devised. In fact, it
is essentially unusable in an ad hoc fashion. A form of control
language procedure, called a PROC, is almost always used in practice. These can be catalogued and invoked by a single call card
which can be and usually is followed by values for substitutable
symbolic arguments in a notoriously intricate scheme. If one turns
to one of the CDC operating systems, the command language certainly
looks better than IBM's JCL, but it turns out that things do not

always work exactly as one would expect and a lot of tricks must be used to accomplish one's purpose. The only practical modus operandi is to have programmer's aides or computer center user-assistance personnel who know about these things. These have become specialities which most people don't have the time or inclination to learn. I suspect that, unfortunately, most complaints about MPSs are really complaints about the operating system but, of course, the user doesn't understand some of these fine distinctions.

With a truly interactive system much as VM/CMS, on the other hand, almost all these problems disappear. It is entirely feasible, and expected, that the user will become familiar with the various levels of command languages and use them effectively. Hence, I will proceed to use SESAME for illustration and hope you will be understanding about it. Actually, all systems provide a comparable set of capabilities and the format of the actual SESAME commands are readily translatable into the particular system you may be interested in.

The equivalent of submitting a run deck is logging in. This presupposes that you have an authorized identification code, called a userid, and know the password. The login immediately places you in the environment of either the basic control program or the conversational monitor. In VM/CMS, the first is known as CP and the second as CMS. Each environment has a repertoire of commands but many CP commands are passed up automatically by CMS so that the user need not be too concerned about which is which. In whichever environment you are placed—this is determined by the way the userid was defined—the difference is trivial. It only takes a type-in of 5 characters to get from CP to CMS at this point. One can always get back to CP by using the attention key.

There is a special file called a PROFILE EXEC which is one of the first things set up when a new userid is first used. An EXEC file is a sequence of CMS commands with substitutable arguments and other special control devices which we need not go into here. The PROFILE EXEC is special because it is executed automatically when you first enter CMS. (I am oversimplifying; the PROFILE can be avoided if there is some reason to do so.) Between the definition of the userid and the PROFILE, your virtual machine is already set up although you may chage its definition later if you wish, within limits. The important thing here, however, is that you now have access to your whole set of files. We have not had to use any DD-cards, ATTACH cards, REQUEST cards or other such annoying things. CMS does provide a simplified form of DD-card, called a FORMAT command, which may have to be used if you are reading or writing a tape or some disk file which was written or is to be read by a batch facility but even this can be made painless by creating appropriate EXEC files.

This is about as much as we need to know about the operating system for present purposes. However, a very important feature of CMS is a context editor. This enables one to create card-image files of any kind interactively. Operationally, it is at the same echelon as SESAME so the two cannot be used simultaneously. It is made available by the CMS command EDIT. It is a very good editor although I know of a better one. If one is available to you, I strongly recommend the use of a conversational editor for creating and modifying card-image files, regardless of whether they are intended for use in a batch or interactive system. Key-punching decks of cards and modifying files with alter decks is too much work and too subject to error. Some of the things one can do with a good conversational, context editor are fantastic. At IIASA we have converted entire systems of programs from one type of computer to another in this way. (Not assembler language programs.)

Let us suppose we have an LP model already in MPS/360 input format, either on tape or in a deck of punched cards. No matter whether one is using a batch or an interactive system, the input file must be transmitted to the actual computer somehow. If you have an RJE, then the deck can be transmitted. If you have machine-machine communication of some kind, you may be able to transmit the file from one system to another—we do this regularly from IIASA. Otherwise, a physical tape reel must be transported to the computer center, given an identification and then mounted on an actual tape drive when we are ready to run. Let us suppose that the input file has been read into our virtual machine somehow and has been enfiled as PROBLEM1 DATA. The first word is the file name, the second is the file type. In VM/CMS, there is a third part called the mode which indicates which minidisk the file resides on but this can often be ignored. In fact, SESAME will find an input file on any minidisk which has been accessed.

To invoke SESAME, we need only type the CMS command "SESAME." This causes a SESAME EXEC to be executed. The purpose of this EXEC is to notify us if there is urgent mail regarding the system and also to obtain a scratch minidisk for levels 3 and 4 (including 5) files. If this is not possible, a message will be displayed at the terminal asking if we want to proceed using our main minidisk for scratch files. If we respond "yes", we will receive a reminder to erase them when SESAME has finished execution. They are given a distinctive mode identification so they can all be erased with one CMS command. Actually, it makes little difference whether we do or not unless we are short of disk space. They will be overwritten on the next invocation of SESAME anyway. In a batch system, all this is unnecessary; scratch files are simply dropped at the end of the job.

The SESAME EXEC in turn invokes the SESAME MODULE which is our EXECUTOR. We are now in a different environment—the MPS command environment—and cannot issue CMS commands. Actually, SESAME, like many interactive control programs, permits execution of a limited set of CMS commands by preceding the CMS command line with the

SESAME command verb CMS. One can also use the attention key to
temporarily enter the CP environment. Such facilities do not exist
in batch systems so we will not pursue them here but they are extremely convenient. They help provide true man-machine interaction.

Once in the MPS environment, and ignoring the above interactive
capabilities, all user controls are implemented by means of commands
--either typed or coming from a card-image file. In batch systems,
this file often goes through a compilation phase but this is more or
less transparent to the user. With current computer speeds and capacities, a compilation phase is more a nuisance than anything
else--I have completely abandoned the use of compilation phases
with an interactive system. Interpretive execution is sufficiently
efficient and is more flexible--in some uses essential. Much more
could be said about this if we were discussing interactive systems.

Commands in the MPS environment can be placed in five major
classes although they may be grouped in other ways in different
systems. The first class consists of references to the CR--for
assignments, local calculations or manipulations, and display.
Hence we need first to discuss the classes of CR cells which the
user may set or otherwise manipulate. There are other classes of
cells which are for internal use only. Some of these will be discussed in the next section.

User-accessible CR cells are the primary method of specifying
arguments and parameters to the MPS and of controlling the algorithms and even the system. CR cells have symbolic names and, in
many systems though not all, these names have a distinctive first
letter. In MPS/360 and derivative systems, the letter X is used
for this purpose. In SESAME, the dollar sign ($) is used which I
like better since X is a useful mnemonic character for other purposes. The dollar sign is often treated conventionally in computing practice as an extra letter rather than as a special character
and hence is particularly suitable for CR names. The reason
for a special first letter is partly to avoid duplicate symbols
and partly to simplify both syntax and internal analysis of
statements, but the visual mnemonic value is also useful.

One can distinguish at least seven classes of user-accessible
CR cells, not counting a few special or conventional ones which the
user controls indirectly. There is also a concept of type which,
in byte-oriented machines, may be designated as follows:

type	form of contents	
H	half-word integer	(2 bytes)
F	full-word integer	(4 bytes)
E	full-word floating	(4 bytes
D	double-word floating	(8 bytes)
C	characters (symbol)	(8 bytes)

Single-byte flags may also be used in some systems but they are rather a nuisance to implement. In fact, types E and F are also a nuisance but, for a few integers, type H has insufficient range and, for certain floating values--notably tolerances--type E is traditional. Those of us who design systems cannot seem to get over our old habit of saving every bit possible, a holdover from the days when 4K words was considered a big memory. The MPS automatically uses the correct length since the length of each cell and its access restrictions are built into the internal definitions.

The members of the seven classes used in SESAME are listed below, showing their type and purpose. This list is typical although no two systems will have identical collections of CR cells.

Class 1: Model Parameters

$MODEL	C	Name of model in level 2 files.	(required)
$OBJ	C	Row name of objective function.	(required)
$COBJ	C	Row name of change vector to $OBJ.	
$RHS	C	Name of right-hand-side (RHS) to be used	(required)
$CRHS	C	Name of change column to $RHS.	
$BOUND	C	Name of bound set to be used.	
$RANGE	C	Name of range set to be used.	
$BCOL	C	Name of base column for parametric column algorithm	
$CCOL	C	Name of change column to $BCOL.	
$BROW	C	Name of base row for parametric row algorithm.	
$CROW	C	Name of change row to $BROW.	
$PARAMAX	D	Upper limit for parameter in any parametric algorithm	
$OLDMOD	C	name of "old model."	(default=1.0)

Class 2: Files and Partitions

$DDMODEL	C	Name of level 2 models file.
$DDMAPS	C	Name of level 2 file for user's maps and saves. (Name of working maps file is not settable.)
$DDRESLT	C	Name of level 2 results file (solutions and tableaux)
$INFILE	C	Name of card-image input file.
$DECKNM	C	Name of card-image input or output deck. (Output files are arguments to procedures.)
$DDOLDMD	C	Name of level 2 "old models" file.

  (Different systems have different default conventions for these.)

Class 3: Computed Values

$FUNCT	D	Current value of functional (possibly composite).
$ITERNO	H	Current iteration number
$KINFS	H	Current number of primal infeasibilities.

$KDINFS	H Current number of dual infeasibilities. (Conventional above 32K)
$KGINFS	H Current number of GUB infeasibilities.
$MSIZE	F Number of rows. (F type for compatibility with $NSIZE.)
$NSIZE	F Number of columns.
$PHI	D Value of multiplier for $COBJ (also settable).
$PSI	D Value of multiplier for $CCOL or $CROW (also settable).
$THETA	D Value of multiplier for $CRHS (also settable).
$SINFS	E Sum of magnitudes of current primal infeasibilities.

Class 4: Algorithm Controls, Frequencies and Switches

$CHECKSW	H Switch for solution check after INVERT.
$COMPSW	H Compound switch for parametric forms
$CYCLING	H Number of improvements to find in partial pricing.
$DETAIL	H Used variously for debugging.
$DZPCT	E Percentage gain for minor to be used. (SELECT)
$FBREAK 1,2	H Two independent break frequencies for algorithms.
$FGUBPR	H Pricing frequency for GUB sets.
$FINVERT	H Frequency for demanding INVERT. (Default is use clock)
$FLOG	H Frequency for producing log lines.
$FSCALE	D Scale for infeasibility form. (Default=1.0)
$FSEMIFL	H Frequency for pricing beyond special marker.
$INTSW	H Switch for treating special column types as fixed integers.
$PRICING	H Maximum multiplicity for pricing.
$PRSETSW	H Switch for honoring special pricing set markers.
$RXFSW	H Switch for setting special decomposition row types.
$SEPSW	H Switch for treating special GUB sets as separable programming.
$STRTVEC	C Name of first column of a set not to be priced.
$STOPVEC	C Name of last column of a set not to be priced.
$XCLUDSW	H Switch to honor $STRTVEC, $STOPVEC or not.
$XFSW	H Switch for setting special settable row types.
$ZOSW	H Switch for honoring special zero/one variables.
$ZSCALE	D Scale for functional. Default=1.0 for minimizing, -1.0 for maximizing. Also settable by argument to SETUP.

(Class 4 and default settings will differ among systems.)

Class 5: Tolerances (Default values are typical.)   (Default)

$TOLBETA	E Tolerance for primal infeasibility	1E-7
$TOLCHK	E Tolerance for reporting check error.	1E-7
$TOLDJ	E Tolerance for dual infeasibility	1E-7

$TOLERR	E Tolerance for check error demand	1E-5
$TOLSING	H Maximum number of basic vector drops in INVERT before SINGULAR demand is set.	5

(Pivot tolerances are not settable in SESAME   (5E-9)
are in some systems; there is usually more than
one. Same is true of relative tolerances for cancellation which is typically about 1E-10 but is
often handled non-numerically.)

Class 6: <u>Core Allocation</u>

$COREMAX	F Maximum amount of main storage to be used for data.	
$FRECORE	F Amount of main storage to be left available for <u>ad hoc</u> use.	
$STMCORE	F Amount of main storage to be used for level 2 file buffers.	

(These or similar parameters will vary widely in different
systems.)

Class 7: <u>Scratch Cells for User's Convenience</u>

$CHARn	C n=0,1,...,9 is typical.	
$REALn	D	
$INTn	H	

Almost all the CR cells have default values, often zero or
null. The entire CR is considerably larger and, if internal blocks
for sets of procedures are included, very much larger. However,
the above-listed user-accessible cells indicates the great variety
of controls available. Utilizing all these effectively is an art
in itself. Systems may contain elaborate features which have never
been thoroughly experimented with. This is particularly true of
pricing techniques and gimmicks. These have often been invented due
to slow convergence on some particular class of problems. If some
improvement was achieved, the feature was retained but may never
again have been exercised aside from checking out a new version of
the system. Also, a few of the cells listed above were designed
for intended extensions to the system, such as decomposition, which
were never implemented although the pertinent routines which do
exist honor the settings. Most systems have such loose ends in
them. The $DETAIL switch is somewhat different. It was used ex-
tensively in checking out SESAME as in several prior systems and
was retained for future use. Some systems have had such a feature
which was excised before public release. Such remnants could be
found in MPS/360.

Returning now to the classes of MPS commands, the first class
is for CR references. SESAME has only four such commands and they

are not very elaborate. (If you will pardon an excuse, SESAME was originally intended to operate under a more elaborate control language which, through no fault of the SESAME team, was not produced during the project. The existing arrangement was an expediency which was later enhanced somewhat. In spite of that, SESAME has about as much capability in this respect as other systems.) The four CR commands are as follows:

Assignment phrases

These are phrases of the form $name = value and one or more may be written on a line. The equals sign is mandatory and, with the dollar sign, indicates a CR assignment. These phrases may also be used freely on procedure calls, intermixed with other arguments.

PRINT command

This is of the form
    PRINT $name, $name, ...
The contents of the named cells are displayed at the terminal and printed on the run log. Some systems treat these two dispositions as different things. i.e., they go to two different print files.

CALC command

A limited arithmetic capability is provided. A CACL statement may take either of the following forms:

    CALC $name1 = $name2
    CALC $name1 = $name2 op operand2
    where op is + - * or / (add, subtract, multiply,
        divide) operand2 is another $name3 or a constant.
The CALC command is used primarily in RUN files which are automated strings of commands, equivalent to traditional MPS program files. In conjunction with the IF command, sufficient capability for most purposes is provided. By utilizing DATAMAT, complete capability is available.

MOVE command

The MOVE command is equivalent to the first form of CALC but for symbolic operands.

Going back to the example we started some time ago, the first thing we must do is set at least $INFILE, $DECKNM and $MODEL. If the name on the NAME card of our input file is CASEA and we want to call the model PR1.A in our models file, this is all accomplished

with the single statement
```
        $INFILE=PROBLEM1, $DECKNM=CASEA, $MODEL=PR1.A
```

Other Classes of MPS Commands

The other four classes of MPS commands in the breakdown previously indicated provide for the following functions:

Disposition of printed output
Procedure calls
Demand stack manipulation
Program flow-control

We proceed to discuss these in the order indicated. This order provides prerequisite information from one class to the next and should simplify both the discussion and the understanding.

One expects to get a considerable volume of printed output from an LP run although this can be controlled and one need only get a bare minimum if that is desirable. It is common practice to have two output files, one for log information and one for the main printed output. The default is usually to have these interspersed on one output file. In an interactive system, the log output is the terminal, whereas in a batch system, the log output file can be defined separately but the default is the drandard system print file. When one is using a system remotely, whether interactive or batch, an additional difficulty arises. The disposition of output is usually predefined for spooling to some remote station. If this remote station does not exist, or no telecommunication link is available, or no one actives it, the spooled output remains in the spooling system until some time limit (fry two days a week) has expired and is then discarded. Another possibility, now. is that the output is printed at the computer center which may be hundreds of kilometers from the user.

Various devices are used to control these problems. The way they are handled in SESAME is as follows. A TITLE command is provided for defining a title line for printed output, as is usual in MPSs. However, the TITLE command performs another function. If no TITLE command is used, all output--whether log or formal printouts--is to the terminal. Once a title command is issued, the output print file is activated and only log and error information comes to the terminal. However, this can be further controlled. (Card-image files never go a punch--whether virtual or from SESAME but may do so from either DATA or CMS).

The terminal output is designed in on-line and the output print file as off-line. In batch system, some similiar pair of designations will be used. Superimposed on this is the concept of three classes of output: LOG, REPORT and ERROR. The definitions

of these classes are built into the routines, i.e., in code, and
are not subject to change by the user. However, their disposition
is controllable. The standard dispositions (after a TITLE command)
are:

    LOG   both on- and off-line
    REPORT   off-line only
    ERROR   both on- and off-line

By using the MPS command MSGCLASS, these classes can be set to any
desired disposition except that ERROR class cannot be set to off-
line only. The format of the MSGCLASS command is:

    MSGCLASS class = disposition

where "class" is as above and "disposition" may be ONLINE, OFFLINE
or BOTH. Both class and disposition may be abbreviated down to two
characters.

For the next class of commands, there is only one procedure
call command, namely

    CALL procedure-name arguments CR-phrases

where the arguments will vary in syntax from procedure to procedure.
The CR phrases are as defined previously and may be interspersed
among the arguments in any order. Occasionally one wishes to reference a CR cell as an argument rather than assigning it a value.
If a $name occurs without an equals sign following or as the right
member of a phrase, it is interpreted as a reference. All procedures are called in this manner except those which are called as a
result of some demand being set in a prior procedure execution.

The commands for manipulating the demand stack are more complicated and they differ somewhat between interactive and batch
systems. The demand stack is the primary means of controlling foreseeable off-normal conditions in a batch system and evolved into a
highly complex mechanism in several systems. A batch MPS is programmed almost as much through demand command sequences as through
the normal program. At first glance, it might seem that a
demand stack would be unnecessary with an interactive system
but this is not so although it is less complicated. Perhaps an
explanation of SESAME's demand stack handling will be sufficient
although this will omit certain considerations which arise in a
batch system. A full discussion of this machanism in batch
systems would consume more time than we can take here. Let me
only say that a batch demand stack is two-dimensional whereas in
SESAME it is only one-dimensional although typed-in commands
give somewhat a two-dimensional effect. Let us proceed to see what
all this means.

Procedures do not always return in the usual manner but may
instead return and set a demand. A demand is a way of indicating
that some special condition exists and that action should be taken
accordingly. Generally, the procedure that set the demand is re-
invoked once action on the demand is complete but in some cases

this may be impossible or undesirable. Some demands result from unsatisfied prerequisites or errors during execution of a procedure. Others indicate conditions that have occurred during one of iterative algorithms.

A demand is identified by its demand-name and is classified as prespecified, unspecified, or switchable. Prespecified demands are set when one procedure requires the execution of another, as when ITERATE requires execution of INVERT. These demands automatically call the procedure that is required and then re-invoke the procedure that originally set them, with the same arguments.

Unspecified demands cause a prompt at the terminal of the form
    demand-name DEMAND AT LEVEL n.   WHAT NOW?
(The level is discussed below.) In a batch system, the equivalent would probably be to abort the run at this point. Typical demands of this kind are:

USERERR	The user has left some required parameter undefined
MAJERR	An unrecoverable condition has been encountered
COMPERR	Computational error, such as numbers out of range
DONFS	The model has no feasible solution
DOUNB	An unbounded solution has been found

In a batch system, the last two would be switchable; in fact, all demands are switchable in most batch systems with prespecified demands having default action sequences.

SESAME has four switchable demands and these are typically found in batch systems as well. They may be set to the following predefined actions:

STOP   Equivalent to unspecified (abort in a batch MPS)

CONT   Causes the procedure that set the demand to be re-invoked immediately after the demand is cancelled.

STEP   Automatically cancels the demand as soon as it is set. It is equivalent to the STEP command described below. In a batch demand stack, STEP is more elaborate and is somewhat like a "knight's move."

The four switchable demands are:

DOFEAS   A feasible solution has been found. Default is CONT

SINGULAR   Too many basis vector drops in INVERT ($TOLSING). Default is STOP

BREAK.1)   The specified frequency in $FBREAK1 or 2 has been
BREAK.2)   reached. Default is STOP

Demands are switched with the command
    SWITCH   demand-name = setting

Every time a CALL command is used, the command is put in a LIFO stack (the demand stack). In SESAME, this stack has five levels, numbered 0 to 4. This is fairly typical. The stack is empty initially. The first CALL is <u>pushed</u> onto the stack at level 0. When this procedure returns, it remains on the stack but, if no demand was set, as soon as another CALL is issued, the first one is <u>popped</u> from the stack, and the second pushed on at level 0.

Suppose now that some procedure returns with an unspecified demand set. The following prompt is given:
demand-name DEMAND AT LEVEL 0. WHAT NOW?
Several options are now available.

1. Execute any command except CALL or the stack controls (see below). There is no effect on the stack and the options are unchanged.

2. Issue the stack control command CONTINUE to re-invoke the procedure (at level 0) that just set the demand.

3. Issue any of the stack control commands CANCEL, UPSTACK or STEP to cancel the demand (These differ at other levels than 0.)

4. Issue another CALL. It is pushed on the stack at level 1, while the original CALL remains at level 0.

What happens next depends on how the second procedure returns. If it sets no demand, a prompt is displayed
AT LEVEL 1. NEXT?
If the second procedure sets a demand, the prompt is
demand-name DEMAND AT LEVEL 1. WHAT NOW?
Prespecified demands that may occur in such a sequence are interleaved in the stack but cause no difficulty unless an automatically called procedure sets another demand. If an attempt is made to push a command onto the stack when it is full, the following prompt is displayed
DEMAND STACK FULL. WHAT NOW?
Some command other than CALL must be issued. This condition is usually due to misuse of the stack.

The stack control commands noted in 3. above have the following meanings when used at a level above 0.

CANCEL   Pops all commands from the stack and cancels all demands.

UPSTACK   Pops only the last command from the stack and waits for another command to be issued.

STEP   Pops only the last command from the stack and then re-invokes the prior command. If this returns without a demand, the command prior to that, if any, is re-invoked without comment or stopping.

Note that CONTINUE always re-invokes the last command entered. Any stack control command or CALL cancels the last demand set.

The final class of commands is for use only with a RUN file in SESAME but, in batch systems, the control program is the equivalent of a RUN file and so these commands are general. SESAME obviously has to have a command to initiate execution from a file and we include it for completeness. A RUN file is simply a card-image file containing MPS commands in decks which start with a NAME card and end with an ENDATA card, just like input files. The file type is DATA but the file name is arbitrary. The file must be on a mini-disk which has been accessed. (With CP and CMS commands.)

RUN   filename   deckname

Execution starts with the first line after the NAME card and continues until either a QUIT or RETURN command is encountered, the ENDATA card is encountered or some procedure returns with an unspecified demand set. In all these cases, the RUN file is closed and control reverts to the terminal, except that a RETURN command terminate SESAME and returns to CMS.

The additional commands which may be used in a RUN file follow.

GOTO   label

where a label has a stereotyped form which will differ among systems. In SESAME, labels consist of a period followed by one or two alphanumeric characters. For GOTO to work, there must be a line in the deck containing only a label starting in column 1. Execution resumes at the line following the label line which may be before or after the GOTO command.

      n   Skip the next n cards where n is an integer.
SKIP -n   Go back n cards where n is an integer.
   TOP   Restart at the first line after the NAME card.

```
                      GOTO label
IF  $name  op  number,  n  (or-n)
                      TOP
```

where "op" is any of the relational operators and "number" is a numerical literal. If the condition is satisfied, either the GOTO or one of the forms of SKIP is executed. Otherwise execution proceeds to the next line. The operators are:

        <EQ>, <NE>, <LT>, <LE>, <GT>, <GE>

with obvious meaning. The syntax will differ among systems.

    QUIT

        Close the RUN file and return to the terminal.

If QUIT is issued from the terminal, SESAME is terminated and control returns to CMS. The command RETURN has this action no matter
where issued. Similar schemes are used in various systems. Terminating the MPS is usually not a simple action but involves closing
files and generally cleaning up.

    Most MPSs permit comment cards to be interspersed in a control
program. Comments are usually indicated by an asterisk in column 1.
Whether and when these are printed depend on system conventions.
Additionally, SESAME has three special card forms to implement interactive response sequences where the user responds to simple "yes/
no" questions or intersperses MPS commands from the terminal during
execution of a RUN file.

STORAGE ALLOCATION AND EXECUTION CONTROLS

    A presentation of the anatomy of an MPS would be incomplete
without some discussion of storage allocation and internal execution
controls. Several comments have already been made but not in an
organized way. This dimension of MPS technology need not be standardized since it is mostly below the threshhold of user visibility.
System builders deem this area to be their business and no one
else's. Obviously, I cannot claim to know how all systems are put
together. All I can do is outline how the systems I do know, or at
least one or two of them, have been constructed.

    This area has been the subject of rather heated controversies
at various times over the years. I have even argued at length with
myself about it. From time to time it appears that some new and
greatly improved scheme is almost within reach. The latest such
experience for me was in assessing the use of virtual core. It was
urged on me that I should regard core as unlimited for all practical purposes. It sounded good but it didn't work out.

    The fact is that, leaving aside improvements in assemblers and
the general maturing of the programmer's art, current systems that
I am familiar with are very much like what they always have been.
I have a diagram of core allocation and a chart of updating and
maintenance procedures which are nearly ten years old, in reference
if not in actual paper, and they are still applicable, in fact both
ways in time. Either we did a remarkably good job back in the
1950s, or we haven't gotten much smarter, or the nature of the

problem dictates the answer. I am inclined to believe the last
with the additional comment that we were lucky in hitting on essentially the right answer in the first place.

Like Caesar's Gaul, all core is divided into three parts. The
first part contains programs, the second part contains data, and
the third part contains all the operating system records specific
to the job. The boundaries between them have not always been firm
and, ideally, they should adjust dynamically to changing needs.
The most elaborate provision for this ever implemented was undoubtedly in OPTIMA. It proved to be partly counterproductive and
we eventually short-circuited some of the elaborate storage management gear. It turns out that the system almost always does the
same things anyhow. By contrast, SESAME has absolutely fixed
boundaries between CMS (which is a fourth part), SESAME programs,
and the data. The operating system records in high core fluctuate
somewhat but this area is relatively small. Between it and the
data, some space is left for ad hoc use. Inadequacies in the CMS
dynamic loader originally forced us to this rigid overall breakdown but I now believe it worked out for the best.

The handling of program storage has already been partly described so let us look at the data area. This is usually the
largest and has the most dynamic allocation requirements. It is
also subdivided into the most parts for the algorithms and the
term core allocation usually refers specifically to it, or more
particularly, to the allocation for the algorithms. All the simplex algorithms, including solution output procedures and some
others, require a specific set of subdivisions. This is commonly
referred to as setup core since it is allocated by the procedure
SETUP. All other allocation schemes, which vary by procedure, are
called not setup core.

There are two approaches to core management. One is to use
the capabilities of the operating system for obtaining and releasing specific pieces. The other is to take over all the core one
can get and do all the management within the MPS. Which one is
preferable depends on several circumstances but the first is the
most common. (Older systems like LP/90, of course, managed the
whole machine but that is no longer possible.) In SESAME, the
first method is used except for DATAMAT which uses the second. The
same is true in MPS-III and DATAFORM. MPS/360 and I am fairly sure
MPSX use the first scheme.

It must be realized that, apart from the CR and a few local or
temporary blocks, no dimensions are known when the system is constructed, or even reasonable limits. One cannot just declare arrays as in FORTRAN. One must start with a large, contiguous block
of core and carve it up as required for the model being processed.
The most fundamental dimension is the number of rows, the second

the number of columns, and the third the number of nonzero elements. The use of GUB introduces some additional considerations but these are not so fundamental. The use of a mixed integer algorithm (MIP), however, compounds the requirements. Decomposition is even worse, but we will not have time to consider these. In fact, their requirements are much less standardized.

Determining the optimal allocation within a fixed size for a large model is a difficult problem, in fact it is a quite nonlinear programming problem. If one took an ivory tower view, we would be unable to solve an LP problem because we would have to first solve a nonlinear programming problem to allocate space for the LP. Naturally, that is not the way it is done. As usual, reasonable, heuristic rules are applied in a somewhat recursive fashion to obtain an acceptably good allocation. Some systems will report whether they "think" the core available is sufficient for efficient solution and recommend an additional amount for the next time. Of course, it is possible that there is insufficient core to even make a feasible allocation. In such a case, SETUP will return with a MAJERR demand.

Returning to our earlier example, we had put in the CR the name of the input file, the deck name, and the name to be given the model in a level 2 file. We can suppose the level 2 file name is by default. (In SESAME, this would be MODELS; in MPS/360 et al., it would be PROBFILE.) The EXECUTOR module is in core and in execution, ready for the next MPS command. (It initialized the CR to default conditions before accepting any command.) There are several things we might do, such as issue a TITLE command, but let us suppose we are ready to process our model. The next command, then, would be

```
CALL CONVERT    MPS360 JLIST
```

The MPS360 argument indicates that the input format is that MPS/360 or MPS-III, either of which is acceptable. Such an argument is needed in any system that accepts more than one style of input. The JLIST argument indicates that we want a listing of all row and column names with their assigned index number—call a J-no.—and a count of the nonzero elements in each row and each column. Nearly all further internal references to rows and columns will be by J-no. and they may appear externally in several places. Full row and column identifiers are too cumbersome.

The above command is pushed on the demand stack, the CONVERT module is loaded, and control passed to it. CONVERT examines the arguments, looks in the CR for the other information it needs, and sets its internal parameters accordingly. All that is in core at this point is EXECUTOR, the CR, and the CONVERT module which is in execution. (We are ignoring the operating system, here CMS, and its job records in high core.) Before it can proceed, CONVERT needs buffers for the level 2 file, probably working space (it is going to process a lot of information), and possibly buffer space for the input file. I cannot be more precise without referring to a specific system. I don't suppose I or any of my staffs have ever programmed CONVERT twice in exactly the same way, not to speak of how other groups have done it. This process requires an intimate grafting of MPS technology onto computer technology, or vice versa if you prefer. CONVERT is a pure data processing procedure and a fairly complex one at that. All we can do is list its major actions.

1. If core had previously been set up, it is released. CONVERT or its subroutines then allocate core for their own purposes.

2. The input deck is read and checked for conformity to the rules of the format in use. CONVERT will (or certainly should) try to process the entire input deck and report all errors it finds. Certain errors may be so severe that this is impossible, for example if a ROWS section does not appear first. If CONVERT does not report any errors, this does not mean the model is correct but only that the input has no errors of syntax.

3. If the named level 2 file already exists, the new model is added to it or replaces an old one of the same name. Otherwise, the level 2 file is created. A great many difficulties are possible in this connection, again specific to the system. The level 2 model created is formatted explicitly for processing by other procedures in the same system and it is usually entirely unsuitable for use by any other system. There is upward compatibility from MPS/360 to MPS-III and MPSX, and partially between the latter two, but these are the only instances I know of.

4. Some values may be put in the CR, such as $MSIZE and $N-SIZE, but most such information is incorporated in the header of the model in the level 2 file. In general, this version of the model retains full information but much of it in compact, encoded form.

5. Appropriate information is sent to the output print files, such as the JLIST or any error messages.

6. Any core allocations are released.

Assuming CONVERT returns with no demand set, the next thing to do is SETUP. (In SESAME, I frequently use BROWSE at this point to check on certain model statistics and values but my interest is more in the system than in the LP model per se.) At some point, we will

have to specify the OBJ and RHS. If we do it now, it will save a
pass of the work matrix by ITERATE to identify the J-nos. which
SETUP can do. This is a refinement which does not occur in all
systems. Perhaps it deserves a short explanation.

Obviously, the row and column identifiers must be kept in symbolic form on the level 2 file but this is too much information for
the work matrix. A model with 1000 rows and 2000 columns has 24,
000 bytes of such information. It is never needed until output
time when the level 2 file can be read since other information is
needed from it anyway. There are a few exceptions, however. Any
rows to be used for the OBJ must be identified and also the RHS.
We handled this in SESAME with the convention that any free rows
and all RHS columns retain their symbolic identifiers on the work
matrix. This takes care of nearly all situations except for the
structural parametric algorithms which must refer to the level 2
files. FIXVEC has an option for reading this file if necessary,
contributing further to its complexity.

We now issue the following command

CALL SETUP $OBJ=rowid, $RHS=rhsid, PRINT

The PRINT argument causes SETUP to produce a summary of core allocation in case we want to peruse it. Even a user not interested
in the computer science aspects of LP should do this a few times to
get a feel for the amount of space required and how it is used.
Let us now examine the core allocation for data which SETUP makes.
Again, SESAME will be used but both MPS/360 and MPS-III have similar
layouts, actually subsets plus a few differences. A certain number
of subdivisions are completely determined by $MSIZE and they, to-
gether with the bit maps determined by both $MSIZE and $NSIZE, are
allocated first.

Figure 7 shows the overall partitioning of core in MPS/360 and
OPTIMA and this applies generally to MPS-III and MPSX as well. We
now want to look more closely at the data area between the cross-
hatched spaces. This is shown in Figure 8 for SESAME which has a
minor rearrangement, for example, the bit maps are first. A bit
map is a contiguous string of m+n bits, padded out to an integral
number of double words. I have used bit maps for at least fifteen
years, in fact for twenty for some purposes, but other designers
declined to do so for a long time. The bits represent all the rows
(really the logical columns) followed by all the structural columns
and the map defines a set, 1-values denoting inclusion and 0-values
exclusion. There are two primary maps, one to indicate the simplex
basis and one to indicate variables at upper bound. (Bounds on
logicals represent ranges.) The first is called the B-map and the
second the K-map. Since only three combinations for a corresponding
pair of bits from the two maps are needed, the fourth combination--

i.e., 1,1 is often used for a special purpose such as denoting the
balance variable in a GUB set which is neither basic nor at a limit.
In recent years, it has been found expedient to leave a gap between the row and column subsets so that rows can be added without
changing total length. The J-nos. must then have a corresponding
break in sequence since they point at bits. A basis save is an
enfiling of these two maps which is more efficient than a list of
indices for most purposes and model dimensions. In MPS-III, SESAME
and possibly other current systems, there is a further concept of
general maps. The two systems just named have an extensive repertoire of procedures which provide for generating maps and performing boolean operations with entire maps as operands. This can be
a very useful technique.

The subdivisions following the maps are called _regions_ and
they are m words long, usually with a header. In particular, it
has long been found useful to define a zero
gions, both to simplify indexing (which starts from 0 and not 1 in
assembler language) and to provide space for temporary information
associated with the region. The alpha regions have larger headers
and, with GUB, either header extensions or trailers which are used
for additional information when the model has GUB sets. A word
for most regions is 8 bytes but there are exceptions. There are
also two or three packed vector regions (whose required length are
determined by CONVERT) and possibly another special region for GUB.
SETUP can allocate space for all these down to and including the
first two alpha regions (which are always required) in a completely
deterministic way. The difficulty arises in allocating the remaining space between additional alpha regions, eta-file buffers, and
work matrix buffers. Space must also be left available for subsequent use for model file buffers and ad hoc use. In fact, SETUP
itself needs this.

The handling of eta-file and work matrix buffers and all the
routines associated with them has undoubtedly consumed more time
than any other part of MPS design and implementation. These difficulties started with my first 701 code in 1953 and probably
reached a zenith in MPS-III. However, even in SESAME which does
not have to deal with overlapped I/O, we devoted a great deal of
effort to this area. The difficulties are not caused by any fundamental problem of the simplex method although the product form of
inverse does contribute to them. (LUD methods can only further increase the complexity even though they might improve performance.)
To oversimplify, the problem is how to make most efficient use of
limited space where efficiency is measured in processing time. It
is no use saying that one can trade space for time or vice versa
since there may not be enough of either.

Almost every combination of space allocation imaginable has
been tried. At one time, a pool of buffers was thought to be a

good idea but in practice it has worked out better to keep the eta-
file and work matrix buffers distinct. INVERT and possibly other
procedures must also use this space without changing setup core
but the requirements are different. This increases the complexity
of INVERT which is already very complicated in modern versions.
Rarick achieved the fantastic speeds in his INVERT procedures at
least in part through very clever and intricite dynamic allocation
schemes. I have seen him poring over memory dumps in hex which
were literally hundreds of pages long and I have done my share of
this too. In checking out INVERT in LP/90 on its first really big
problem, we actually papered a wall with regionalized dumps devised
for the purpose in order to see what was going on. It took the
better part of a week to begin to get enough clues to see the problem. If you have never been involved with massive sequential problems of this kind, you can hardly imagine how hard they are.

In recent years, with the availability of multiple-megabyte
core and using advanced matrix packing schemes, completely in-core
packages have been developed. This can avoid sequential buffering
problems and the use of intermediate auxiliary storage, thus leading to very high processing speeds. However, they are also intricate, expensive to develop, require a truly big computer, and tend
to be tailored to the requirements of a particular big user. But
if the possibility of some problems going out of core must be ad-
mitted, then some form of buffers must be used. Although we have
this capability in SESAME, in practice many problems really stay
in core since virtual core can be quite large. As soon as auxiliary storage is needed for the eta-file, for example, INVERT is
executed which reduces the required space. This has been happening
in MPS/360 and its derivative systems and, I am sure, in others for
several years. No doubt, the last word has not been said in this
area but I am afraid our own schedule demands that we move on now.

DATA MANAGEMENT SUBSYSTEMS

We will spend the remainder of the time on data management subsystems. I was asked to cover this area and I also believe it is
the most important one for development now and in the foreseeable
future. It far outweights, in my opinion, any algorithmic developments and may indeed be a necessary prerequisite for effective progress. A whole week wouldn't be enough time so I can do little more
than try to indicate the nature of the subject. There will be no
attempt at a broad survey or even many indications of the comparative capabilities of existing systems. Most of my recent efforts
have been in this area and I admit to my bias without apology. I
also recognize that no one, myself included, knows nearly as much
as we should about this subject. More importantly, however, I am
convinced that the truly useful application of what is now called
systems analysis to important and critical problems is dependent

on a much wider understanding and use of man-machine interaction, and that means data management in the context of interactive systems, probably extended by telecommunication networks.

Let me begin with a very brief historical recap. As mentioned in the history of MP software, at least one matrix generator and pre-processor was built as early as the mid-1950s. There were two report generators written for use with LP/90--one by Esso and one by Eli Hellerman at CEIR. Although awkward to use and limited in scope, they were useful. As early as 1960-1, a committee was formed to develop, recommend, and possibly implement a general-purpose matrix generation scheme. In spite of several useful ideas already known or developed by this group, its effort came to nought over what is most succinctly described as bickering. CEIR's report generator was carried forward in the LP/40 systems but, for MPS/360, the more comprehensive but ill-conceived MARVEL processor was selected. A few years later, when MARVEL was in disrepute, IBM produced a report generator that was esentially a re-hash of the old LP/90 scheme.

In the meantime, we had devoted considerable effort to this area for LP/94 but that system came to nought. In designing LP/600, we did three things: generalized the standard input formats (rejected by most users), designed and implemented an elaborate matrix generator which accommodated different opinions and formulation styles, and produced a much enhanced report generator. These were re-implemented with some changes in OPTIMA. Apart from the ill-fated history of these systems, it was realized already that separate matrix and report generators, no matter how well done, simply did not solve the entire data management problem and even complicated the use of an MPS in some ways.

During the 1960s, Larry Haverly developed his series of processors known as MAGEN, beginning with the old IBM 1401 and eventually covering most standard computers. He used simple, clearly defined concepts and at least partially solved the problem of comprehensiveness. That is, he made fairly practical provision for carrying information from the matrix-generation phase around the optimizer system to the report-generation phase. We did some of this in LP/600 and OPTIMA but never very satisfactorily. I applaud Haverly's success and willingly grant that he has provided a useful service to the field but many years ago I concluded that his methods would run into trouble with larger models and more intricate formulation requirements. He has made heroic efforts to stay abreast of increased capability in hardware and basic software but the weakness that I foresaw is beginning to show in places.[1]

---

1. At the same time, the external handling of tables in MaGen, and partly in Gamma is superior to that in DATAFORM and DATAMAT.

During this period, Bonner and Moore began their Gamma series which, though standard subsystems for some MPSs (with various modifications) show pretty much the same characteristics and inadequacies as the others mentioned above. Although providing Gamma, Burroughs now has the more comprehensive MODELER.

The reasons for the development of the DATAFORM extension to MPS-III were an outgrowth of these experiences, as already mentioned in the session on history and its design was not simply based on system programming experience with MPSs but also on extensive user experience by Esso. DATAFORM proved to be powerful and comprehensive but there were two drawbacks. First, it was 65 to 70 percent in FORTRAN. This was somewhat against my better judgment but there were reasons which seemed overriding at the time and the decision was not entirely in my hands anyway. Partly, though not completely for this reason, it proved slow in execution on certain big and important projects, not only at Esso but elsewhere. In fact, internal improvements were later made which increased processing speed significantly. Many users have been very pleased with it but some momentum was lost in its application. This was true even at Esso. Second, it turns out that a language and processor like DATAFORM is not really suitable for ad hoc use by a novice but requires determined and careful planning by knowledgeable practitioners. Once the initial effort has been made, then the resulting capabilities can be used with marvelous flexibility and power. It is very much like a data base system--which, in fact, it is a special case of--which provides only the potentiality for, and not the realization of, any particular data management system. In other words, a subsystem like DATAFORM is a system for building data systems but not itself a data system. It plays a role very much analogous to that of assemblers, compilers and linkage editors for computer programming. Nevertheless, I adopted the external specifications of DATAFORM for my DATAMAT extension to SESAME since I am convinced this is exactly the correct way to proceed. If anything, this is even more true for interactive systems.

Besides these more or less general and formalized efforts, there have been innumerable ad hoc and in-house matrix and report generators written--no one knows how many or where. Consequently, it is simply not true that this area has not received substantial effort. In LP/600, OPTIMA, MPS-III and SESAME, to my knowledge-- and it is no doubt true of other systems--the data management routines have represented from a third to a half of the total effort. This does not include the traditional, standard procedures such as CONVERT and solution output. In spite of this, there is almost no degree of standardization and, what is worse, available systems are often not used when they are available in-house or in the MPS being used.

Clearly something is wrong. I think I know what it is but I

don't know how to say it succinctly. Nevertheless, let me try.
The problem is not primarily one of technological know-how or capability but of technical management, plus the fact that the enormous growth of the field no longer permits a well-focused effort
to come to fruition and then be disseminated widely as a de facto
accomplishment. In the session on history, I said that at the beginning of an era, commitments are made which determine forms for
the future. But there is a corollary to this: When commitments
are not made and forms not determined early in an era, they are
likely to remain forever amorphous. I think this has happened not
only with data management systems for math programming software
but in the whole style and technique of applying computers in the
academic world. Our field is much closer to the academic world
than the industrial and commercial world even though the latter
provided the problems and the resources for its growth. If we were
concerned with payrolls, bank statements, utility bills, or internal revenue records, we would have much less trouble with data
management. But the data in our field, and the processes applied
to it as well, are only partly based on manifest facts and only
partly subject to definitive conventions. Partly for this reason,
partly due to professional competition, and partly because of the
urgency of today's problems, senior analysts with managerial responsibility often just do not allow sufficient time--let alone
manpower--to do a job in a thorough and well-planned way. They are
interested in getting some computer output that satisfies their immediate need as fast as possible. The bright new programmer who
can write a quick and dirty FORTRAN routine to provide this for the
one case at hand, is enhanced in stature, to the detriment of the
project as a whole and to his own professional growth. One sees
this over and over again. Sometimes, we oldtimers even play the
game.

    Well, enough of philosophizing. Let me quickly present the
salient features of DATAMAT which I am using as the main vehicle
for coordinating the computerization of the modelling effort in
IIASA's Energy Program. The models are of various kinds, only the
central one and a couple of others being LP models. So an MPS data
management subsystem can be useful for more than generating LP matrices and writing LP reports. Properly designed and used, such a
system is also useful for specialized data base maintenance, grand
iterative schemes, on-line browsing, interfacing different systems,
and similar nice things.

    I will only discuss the language and capabilities and not the
processing programs. DATAMAT runs as a SESAME procedure and hence
has access to the CR and all SESAME level 2 files. It can be manually operated from the terminal, automatically from a file--file
type is DATARUN--or a combination. It is considerably more flexible
in this respect than DATAFORM since there is no compilation phase.
Commands are executed immediately on entry in symbolic form.

The DATAMAT language combines characteristics from several types of languages used in computing. Fundamentally, it is a command language but includes assignment statements which essentially follow FORTRAN rules. However, they do not quite look like FORTRAN for reasons to be explained presently. Both aspects are combined in matrix generation statements. Some commands look like assembler directives and the report writing capability uses FORTRAN's FORMAT statement with only slight modification.

The language provides approximately 60 verbs, i.e., commands. Every statement except an assignment statement must start with a verb. Assignment statements may be arithmetic, logical or symbolic and, in fact, may combine aspects of all three. This is really the essence of MPS data management: a combination of arithmetic and symbology in simultaneous execution. I think mathematicians often fail to realize that, when they define models in mathematical-like expressions, only part of these expressions are mathematical in the usual sense. In part, they mean to generate symbols over all combinations shown. This is particularly true of the acronym-like schemes commonly used for indexing.

Almost all types of commands may be intermixed as desired although a few precedence relationships exist. For example, a macro capability is provided. A macro is a DATAMAT program with substitutable arguments, really used like a subroutine rather than a macro. They reside on another file with file type DATAMAC. If such a library of macros is to be used, this must be declared with the first or second command issued. The only command which may-- and must if used--precede it is a declaration of real subroutines to be used. In theory, these may be FORTRAN, PL/1 or Assembler Language subroutines; in practice, FORTRAN and PL/1 routines present a problem because of the huge library they usually haul in with them. There is a further difficulty that FORTRAN always wants to be the main program, not just a subprogram. However, I use Assembler Language routines fairly extensively, for example, for graphic output and random number generation. These routines are called either with a CALL verb or implicitly by reference, essentially as in FORTRAN.

DATAMAT, like most data subsystems, relies heavily on the use of tables; it is even fair to say that, in many applications, it is table driven. A table is a two-dimensional array with four parts:

(i) The table header which includes its name, type and dimensions, say m rows and n columns.

(ii) A <u>head</u> which consists of n symbols with up to 8 characters each which are the table's column names.

(iii) A <u>stub</u> which consists of m symbols up to 8 characters each which are the table's row names.

(iv) A <u>body</u> consisting of m*n elements, each 8 bytes.

Three types of tables are used:

G-tables with numeric body elements (REAL*8).
M-tables with symbolic body elements.
H-tables where each row is one or more strings of text.

The H-tables have a different form of head, encoded into a single double word, which defines the layout of the rows. A row may have up to eight character strings, each up to 64 characters, and addressable by 8-byte actions. Any type may be a head-only table (m=0) and G- and M-tables may be stub only tables (n=0) or null tables (m=n=0). A FORTRAN-type array is also provided which may be either REAL*4 or REAL*8. These have only a header and a body. They are used as arguments to real subroutines and are also useful for automatic indexing purposes.

There are no declaration statements in the FORTRAN sense. Rather, each symbolic referent is identified by a prefix which consists of a letter followed by a colon. The colon is absolutely preempted for this purpose and most of the commonly available special characters are used with special meaning. The arithmetic operators, equals sign, comma and parentheses are used in standard fashion. A pair of vertical bars is used for absolute value but otherwise rank as parentheses with which they may be nested. Other special characters are used with nonstandard meanings, except the period used in numbers. Self-defining numeric literals are as in FORTRAN, but with slightly more flexibility between integers and reals.

All 26 letters are in use for prefixes; they are shown in Figure 9. This list in itself indicates much of the scope of the language. Both LP model elements and all the great variety of LP results which exist in SESAME level 2 files may be referenced. Bit maps may be referenced as units for selection purposes. There are five types of local variables in addition to tables and arrays:

I:name	refers to an interger variable
E:name	refers to a REAL*8 variable
N:name	refers to an 8-byte symbolic variable
O:letter	refers to one of 26 pre-defined 0-1 switches which may be used either as arithmetic or logical variables
Q:name	refers to a T/F (true, false) variable. These are limited to a maximum of 7 with a maximum of 7 character names.

All such variables except O-switches are defined by their first appearance as the left member of an assignment statement. Tables and local variables may be referenced indirectly by double prefixing and use of an N-variable. For example, E:N:name refers to the E-variable whose name is the current value of N:name. Figures 13 and 14 show the real and symbolic functions.

Another level 2 file called a TABLES file is used. Tables may be enfiled and recalled either selectively or en masse. A table may be erased in the file but only one at a time to prevent catastrophic errors. Tables may be defined in-line, generated, or read in from a card-image file. The latter method also permits addition or deletion of rows or selective updating of body values in core.

All types of tables and arrays may be referenced with automatic indexing of their elements. Additionally, tables may have their elements referenced with automatic name-matching. The tables need not be conformable for name-matching and so generalized table operations can be created. For automatic indexing, if the tables involved are not conformable, the shorter dimension rules. Examples of table and array referencing are shown in Figure 10.

Figures 11 and 12 list the verbs with a brief indication of their functions. The largest set is the matrix generation repertoire but many of these are variations on the same theme. They permit one to generate a model in almost any sequence desired--by rows, by columns, by submatrices, etc. The use of automatic indexing and name-matching in these verbs allows one command to generate a whole submodel.

I hope you will agree that such a language opens up important new capabilities in math programming work but, even if you do, I would be remiss if I dind't point out that using such a powerful language is not easy. Once one has built a data system with it, then he can do surprising things but the initial planning of table organization, symbology, and procedural use takes a great deal of thought.

REFERENCES

1. Orchard-Hays, W., "Software Systems Viewed as an Analogy to Industrial Organization," IIASA Research Memorandum RM-75-50, September 1975.

2. Orchard-Hays, W., "Some Additional Views on the Simplex Method and the Geometry of Constraint Space," IIASA Research Report RR-76-3, May 1976.

3. Orchard-Hays, W., Advanced Linear-Programming Computing Techniques, McGraw Hill Book Company, 1968.

4. Dantzig, George B., Alex Orden, and Philip Wolfe, "Notes on Linear Programming," The RAND Corporation (RM series), April 1954, and many RM reports of succeeding years. These papers

constitute many of the original documents on the development of linear programming theory, computational methods, and application. They may be hard to obtain.

5. Dantzig, George B., Alex Orden, and Philip Wolfe, _Linear Programming and Extensions_, Princeton University Press, 1963. Perhaps the best single source of references.

6. Graves, Robert L., and Philip Wolfe (eds), _Recent Advances in Mathematical Programming_, McGraw-Hill Book Company, 1963.

7. Markowitz, H.M. "The Elimination Form of the Inverse and Its Application to Linear Programming," _Management Science_, vol. 3, pp. 255-269, April 1957.

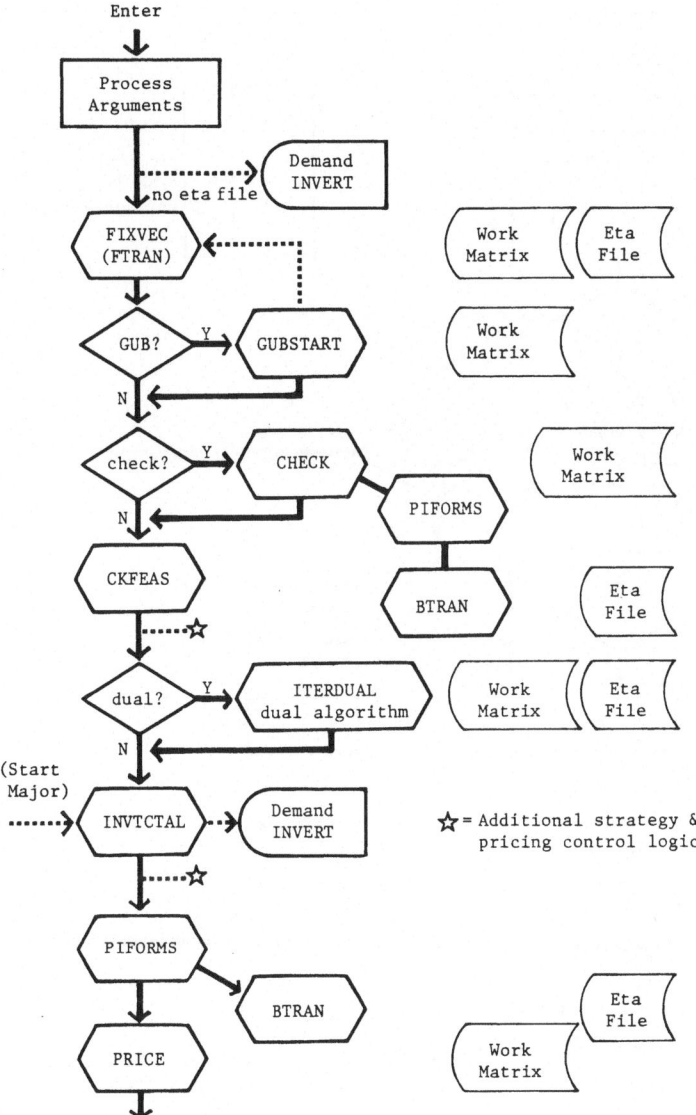

Figure 1:   ITERATE START UP

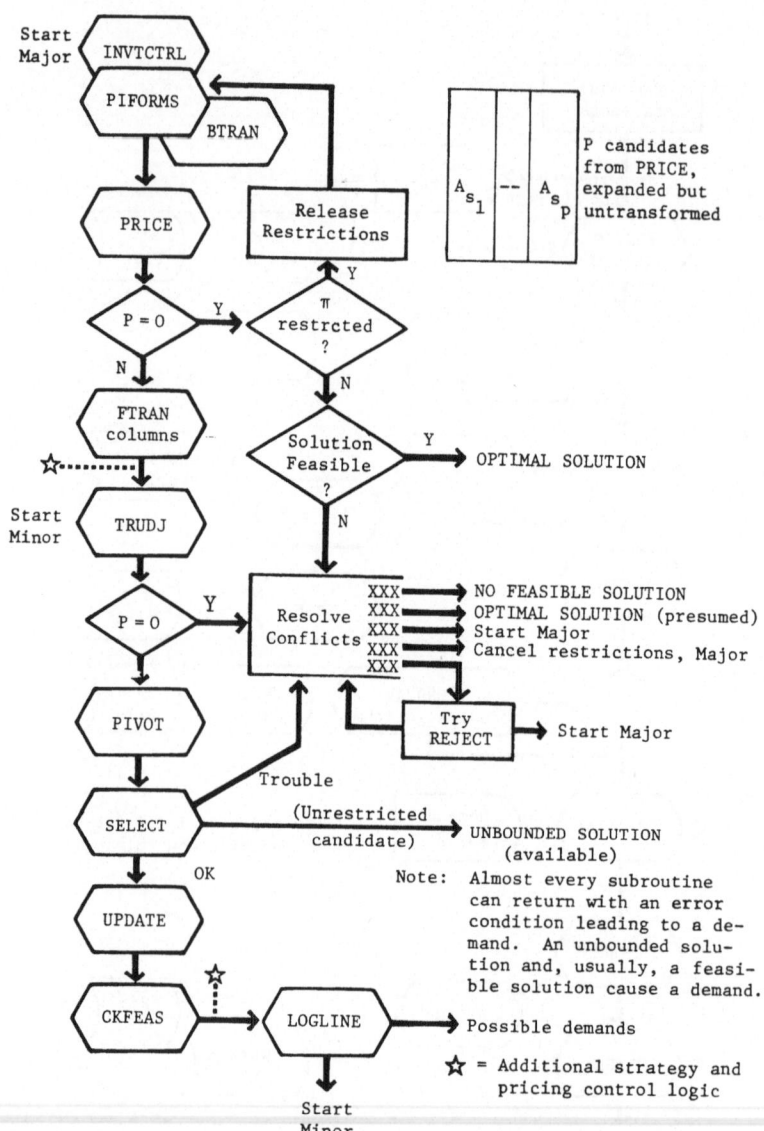

Figure 2:   SIMPLEX ITERATIONS

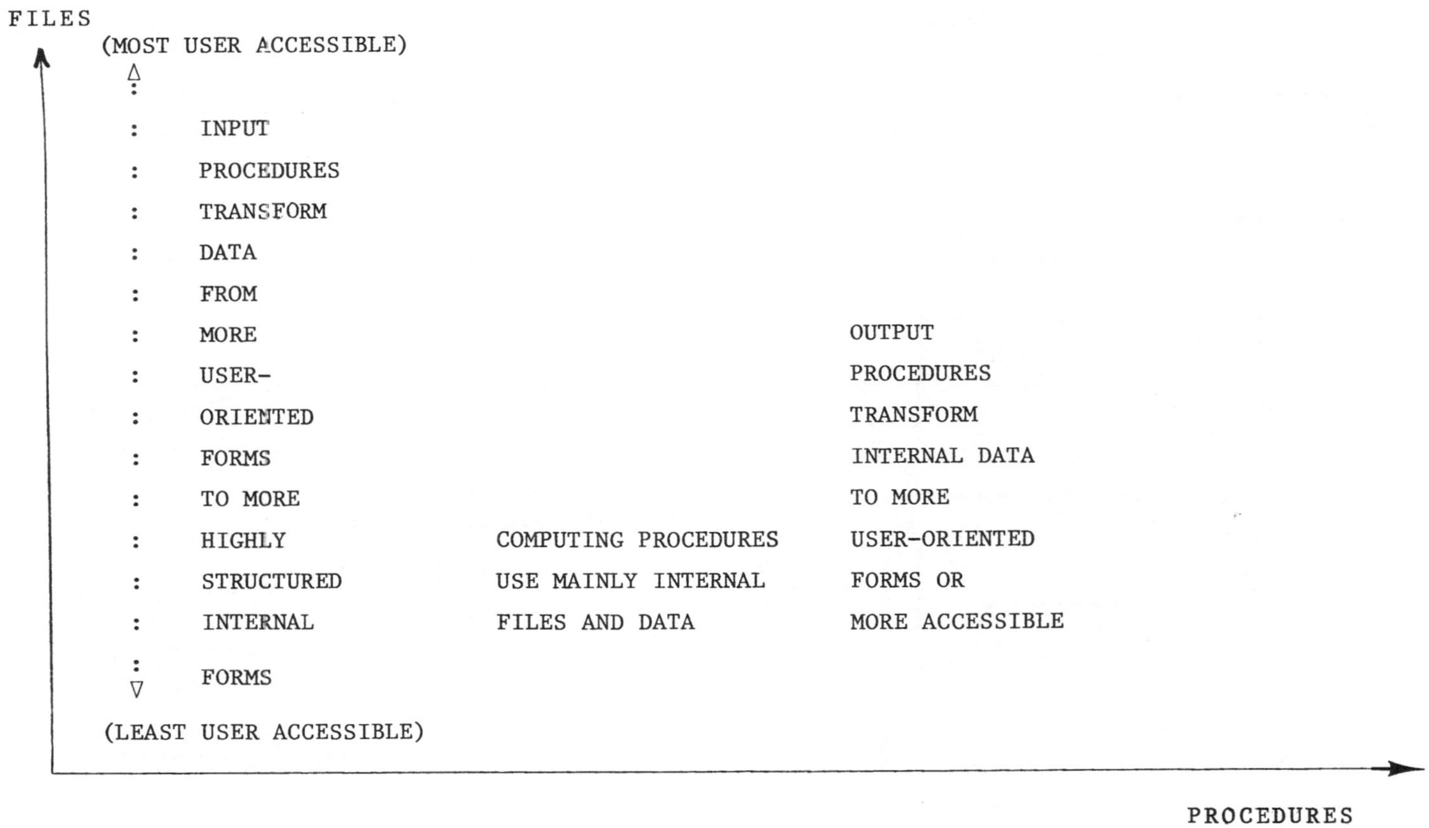

FILES

(MOST USER ACCESSIBLE)

INPUT
PROCEDURES
TRANSFORM
DATA
FROM
MORE
USER-
ORIENTED
FORMS
TO MORE
HIGHLY
STRUCTURED
INTERNAL
FORMS

(LEAST USER ACCESSIBLE)

COMPUTING PROCEDURES
USE MAINLY INTERNAL
FILES AND DATA

OUTPUT
PROCEDURES
TRANSFORM
INTERNAL DATA
TO MORE
USER-ORIENTED
FORMS OR
MORE ACCESSIBLE

PROCEDURES

Figure 3

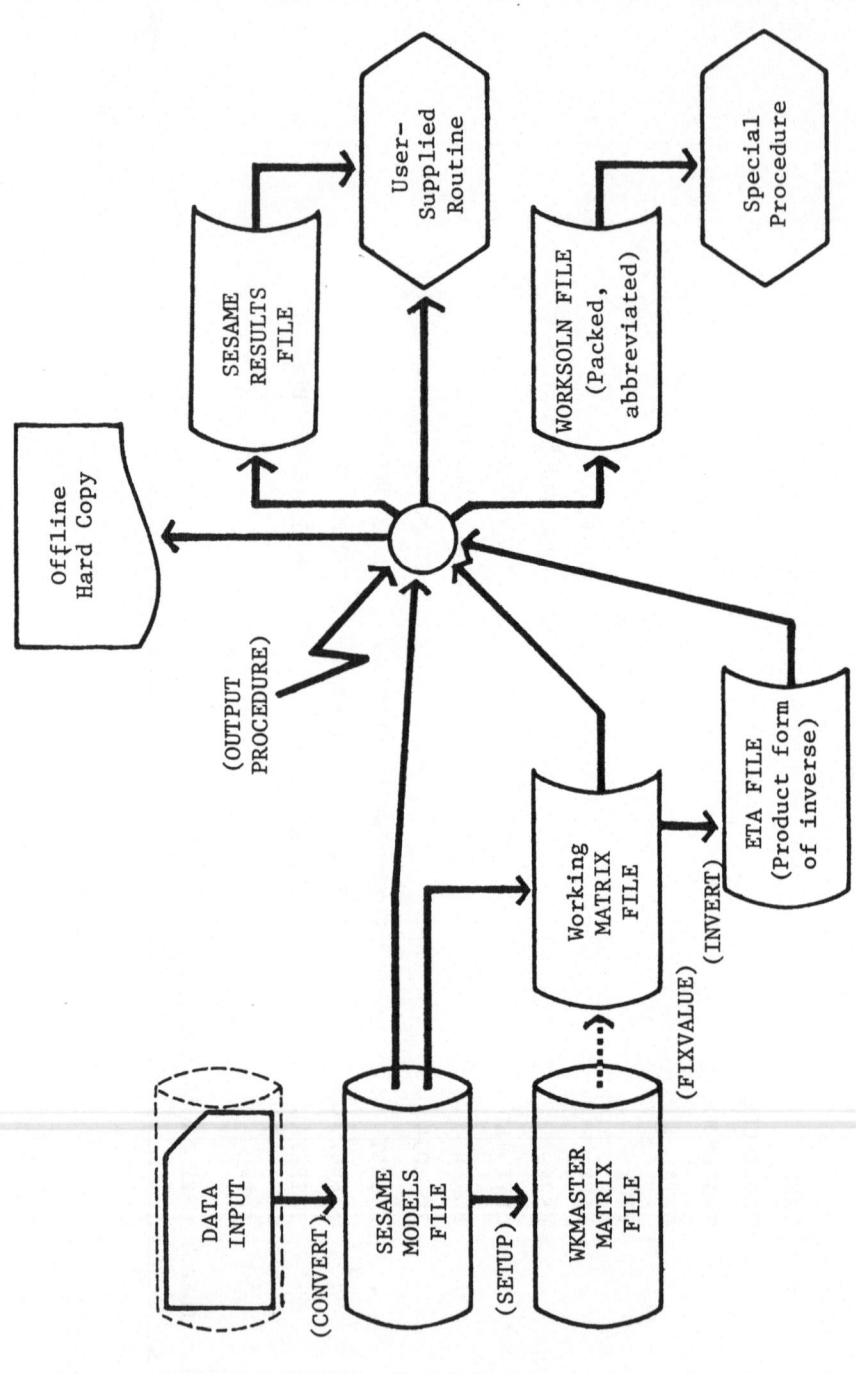

Figure 4: TRANSFORMATION OF DATA TO DIFFERENT FILE LEVELS

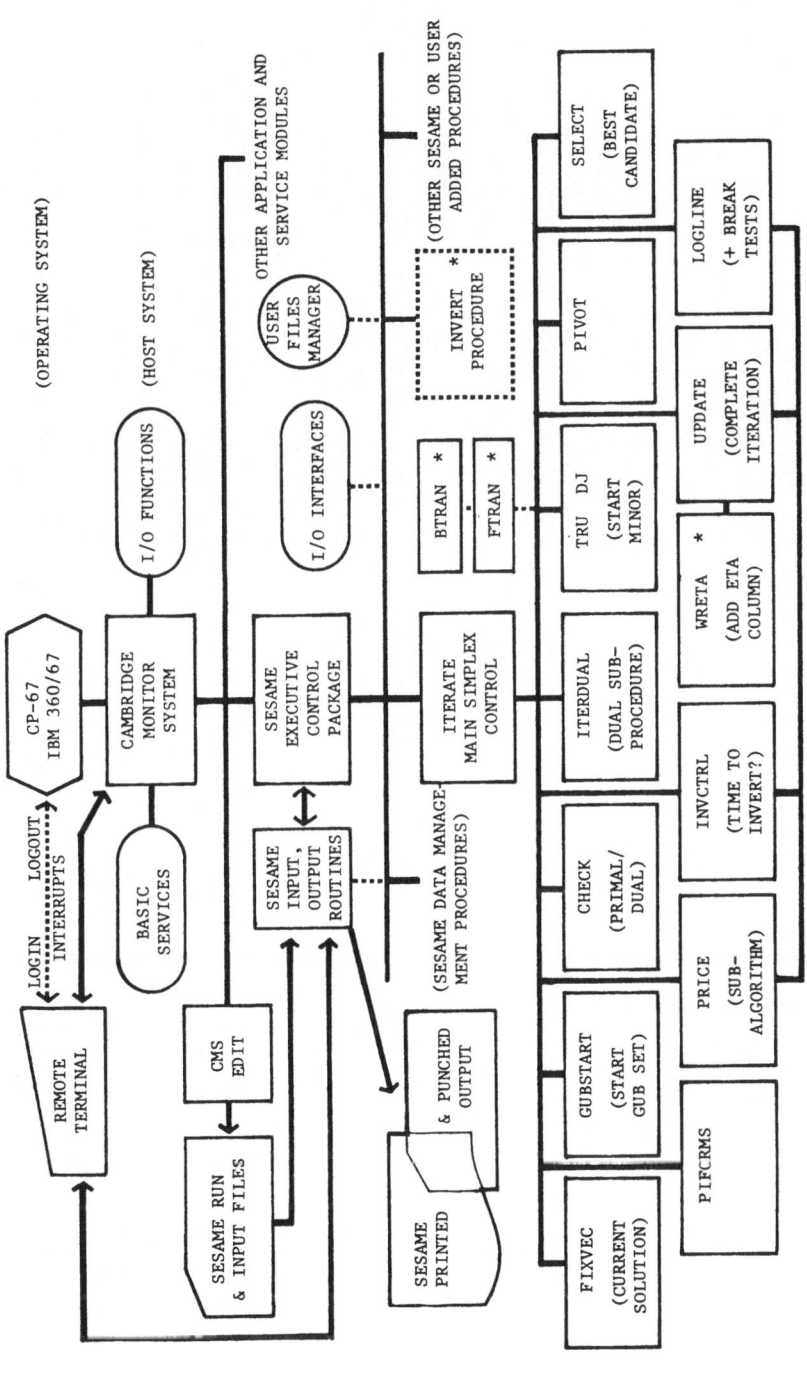

Figure 5: SOFTWARE SYSTEM STRUCTURE VIEWED AS A LINE AND STAFF ORGANIZATION

* Product form of inverse.

Procedure	Keyboard	Display	Level 1 Files	MODELS	RESULTS	TABLES	USERMPAS	MAPSFILE	Master Matrix	Work Matrix	Eta File	CR and Core	Reports
				Level 2				Level 3					
MPFILES	(R)	W											
FREECORE		W											
PATCH	R	W											
CONVERT			R	W									W
CARDOUT			W	R									W
BROWSE	R	W		R/W	R								
DATAMAT	R	W	R/W	R/W	R	R/W		R				R/W	W
VALUES	R	W	R	R								W	W
MAPIN		R		R					W			W	
MAPOUT		W		R					R			R	
LISTMAP		W					R	R					
MOVEMAPS	(R)	W					W/R	R/W					
COMPREST				(Reform tree file structure)									
PURGE	R	W		(Purge and reform tree file)									
SETUP	(R)	W		R				R	W	W	(init) W/R		
SETUPRNT		W									R		
MATDUMP				R				R	R	R			W
FIXVALUE									R	W	(init) W/R		
INVERT										R	W	R/W	W
ITERATE		W								R	R/W	R/W	W
SAVE								W			R		
RESTORE								R			W		
RIMPARA		W								R	R/W	R/W	W
STRPARA		W								R	R/W	R/W	W
MAPGEN	(R)	W		R				W		R	R	R/W	
BOOL	(R)	W						R+W					
STATUS		W										R	W
REGNDUMP												R	W
VARY	R	W	R	R						R	R	R/W	W
SOLUTION	(R)			R	W			R		R	R	R/W	W
TABLEAU	(R)			R	W			R		R	R	R/W	W

R = read, (R) indicates that command really includes input
W = write; under Display indicates a main output, not mere interactive dialogue.
  Display and Reports more flexible than shown.

Figure 6: DATA FLOW AMONG PROCEDURES

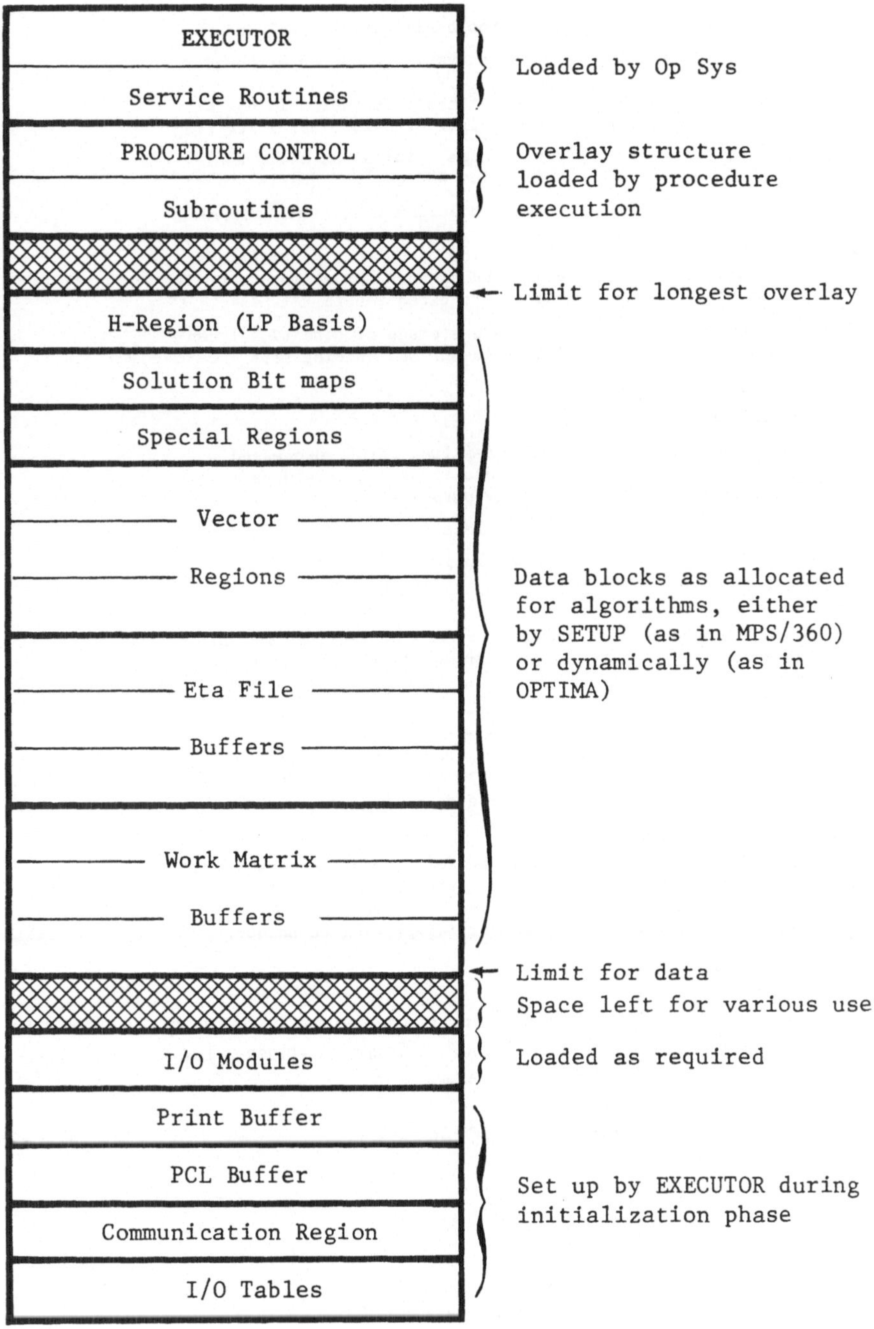

Figure 7: MPS CORE PARTITION

Name	Size	Usage
BMAP	(m+fill)+n+pad bits	Indicates basic variable/columns
KMAP	Same length as BMAP	Indicates variables at upper bound
BASIS	(m+1) all words (4-byte)	J-nos. of basic variables in basis order; first byte is feasibility flag
LIMITS	(m+1) double words	Finite upper limits for basic variables plus GUB chains. (Basis order)
BETA	(m+1) double words	Current solution vector. (Basis order)
BSCGUB	G 24-byte items where G = min(m, no. GUB sets)	Information on GUB-set members in basis and anchors for chains in LIMIT. Represents extension to expanded basis
PACVEC1 PACVEC2 PACVEC3	Three areas each long enough to hold longest packed column from work matrix (except RHS columns)	Transient storage of conditional candidate in Gub and pricing sets
ALPHA1 ALPHA2	(m+4) double words plus 2-ds trailer for GUB	Candidates from PRICE, processed throughout iteration. Used variously for many purposes.

—————————— End of deterministic allocation ——————————

Area below allocated by pseudo-optimization with
attempt to honor requested number of alpha regions.

ALPHA3 . . . ALPHA7	Maximum number of alpha regions varies among systems; SESAME ' max = 7	One or more may be required for some of the parametric algorithms.
Eta-file buffers	Length is determined as part of optimization and the number; min = 2	Complex buffering scheme for eta-file but usually file is all in-core most times except on very large models.
Work matrix buffers	Length is determined as part of optimization, also number that depends in part on model size; may all fit in one buffer	Complex buffering scheme for work matrix but often file is in-core or need be fed only over many iterations due to partial-pricing technique.

Note: Scratch file buffers may also use same buffer space for temporary use, e.g., in INVERT.   Some systems also use alpha regions as temporary buffers.

Figure 8:   ALLOCATION OF DATA STORAGE

A:(rownm, colnm)	Element(s) of the structural part of the LP model.
B:(rownm, rhsnm)	Element(s) of the LP RHS(s) as stored in the model.
C:(colnm, case) C:colnm	Composite cost coefficient(s) from LP results. If second form used, case is from prior SET CASE.
D:(colnm, case) D:colnm	Reduce cost element(s) from LP results.
E:name	Local real variable, type D.
F:subrout(art$_1$,...)	Reference to single-valued function subprogram with result assumed type D. "subrout" must have been declared with LOAD. Arguments any valid references.
G:tabnm(stub, head)	Reference to table with type D body elements. "stub" and "head" can take a variety of forms including names, indices, auto-indexing and name-matching.
H:tabnm(stub, head)	Reference to table whose rows contain text strings. "head" is stylized denoting row layouts.
I:name	Local integer variable, type H.
J:mapname	An (entire) bit map in MAPSFILE.
K:(ROW, rownm) K:(COL, colnm)	Existence and inclusion in map previously loaded of an LP model row or column. Result is -1, 0 or +1.
L:arrayname	FORTRAN-style array declared by ALLOC and used as argument to F: reference or CALL.
L:arrayname(i,j)	Reference to element of array, numerical i,j only.
M:tabnm(stub, head)	Reference to table with symbolic body elements.
N:name	Local symbolic variable.
O:letter	One of the 26 pre-defined 0-1 (on-off) switches.
P:(rownm, case) P:rownm	Dual structural variable(s) for LP results. (pi row)
Q:name	Local logic variable (T, F).
R:(gubnm, case) R:gubnm	GUB set value, i.e., implicit RHS value used, from LP results. (Not available from LP model.)
S:($name, case) S:$name	CR value when TABLEAU case recorded. (Limited set)
T:(LP-stub,LP-head,case) T:(LP-stub, LP-head)	Tableau value(s) from LP results. (Bit maps may not be used for selection, but masks allowed.)
U:(rownm, case) U:rownm	Value of LGL variable(s) (slacks) from LP results.
V:(rownm, case) V:rownm	Row value(s) from LP results.
W:(rownm, indic, case) W:(rownm, indic)	Lower limit (indic=LL), upper limit (UL), or status (ST) of row from LP results.
X:(colnm, case X:colnm	Value of STR variable(s) (X-variables) from LP results.
Y:	Same as W: but for STR variable.
Z:	Same as S: but for SOLUTION case.

Figure 9: DATAMAT PREFIXES

<u>Head and stub references</u>: A zero for a stub referent implies the head; a zero for a head referent implies the stub; both may not be zero.

<u>Auto-indexing</u>: The form !n for n=1...q implies automatic indexing over all rows or columns of a table or array. If the same form is used twice, the shorter limit governs. Small n is nested within larger. One arithmetic operator may be used with each expression involving !n but if this results in zero, it is considered out of range and not a head or stub referent.

> G:TAB(!1, !2) = 0.0

The table is zeroed.

> G:TAB(!1,!1) = 1.0

The diagonal is set to ones. The table need not be square.

> G:TAB(1,!1) = !1 + 10

The first row is set to 11, 12, ...

> G:TAB(!1, !1-1) = .5

The subdiagonal is set to values of .5.

> M:TRANS(!2, !1) = M:SYMB(!1, !2)

As much as possible of the transpose of the upper left corner of M:SYMB is copied to the upper left corner of M:TRANS.

> L:WORK(!1, !2) = G:TAB(!1, !2)

As much as possible of the upper left corner of the table is copied to the upper left corner of the array.

<u>Name-matching</u>: The form "n for n=1,...,9 implies name matching between a pair of lists, either heads or stubs in any combination. The two lists need not be the same length or in the same order. Smaller n is nested within larger and, for equal n, auto-indexing within name-matching.

> G:WORK("1, "2) = G:TAB("1, "2) * E:SCALE

Elements from G:TAB which have stub,head identifiers that also occur in G:WORK are multiplied by E:SCALE and become elements of G:WORK with those identifiers. Unmatched positions are not changed.

<u>General</u>

> M:HEAD(!1, TAB) = TAB & G:TAB(0, !1)

The column of M:HEAD named TAB takes on values equal to the head names of G:TAB prefixed with TAB, or as many as possible.

> G:N:NAME(!1, N:COL) = G:WORK(!1, N:COL)

The G-table whose name is in N:NAME is expected to have a column whose name is in N:COL. If it does not, the net effect is a no-operation. If it does and table G:WORK has a column of the same name, the values in this column (or as many as possible) are copied to the table on the left. If G:WORK has no such column, the column on the left takes on zero values.

Figure 10: TABLE AND ARRAY REFERENCING

General (‾)indicates optional

(‾CALC‾)   result = numerical-valued expression

(‾MANIP‾)   result = symbolic-valued expression

(‾LOGIC‾)   result = logical-valued expression

DIMEN   I:name = table stub or head length or element symbolic reference

TIME   N:name   (Time of day in form hh:mm:ss)

CVTR   Arithmetic result = symbolic expression (looking like number)

Table Construction and Maintenance

TABLE   Direct definition of all parts with set of lines

STUB   Generate or extend stub-only table with symbolic expression

FORM   Create empty table from combinations of other table stubs and heads or by stylized generation

READTAB   Read tables, rows, or body updates from card-image file with created table of names of tables referenced and action codes

REFORM   Create empty table from enfiled LP model row and/or column identifiers with option for variable types in first column

ENFILE   Enfile tables selectively or en masse with list option

RECALL   Recall tables selectively or en masse with list option

ERASE   Erase one table from file

Display and Reports

NOTE   Print comment on- and/or off-line, single or double space

DISPLAY   (LOG class)

REPORT   (REPORT class) Display one or several local variables, one or several classes of variables, one or several tables, one or all set of table-types, or one or more components of model under construction. Formats are pre-defined and fixed

FORMAT   FORTRAN-like format for use by PRINT, PUNCH or (stylized)AUTOFORM

PACE   Start new page off line

HEADING   Define one to 9 levels of headings for off-line reports

FOOTING   Define a footnote for use with AUTOFORM

PRINT   FORMAT-formatted line with arbitrary lists, including auto-
PUNCH   indexing and dummy indexing in FORTRAN style

AUTOFORM   FORMAT-controlled output of table body with optional H-table stubs and (multi-line) column heads, wide page extension and with option for "picture" format

Calculations over Sets

FETCH   Loads a general map from SESAME MAPSFILE for K: prefix use

DOT   Takes inner products of two vectors from MODELS and RESULTS files with restriction of range of summation specified with either a mask or general map

Figure 11:   DATAMAT VERBS EXCEPT MATRIX GENERATION

Summation convention; When referencing MODELS or RESULT elements in an arithmetic expression, summation over a set specified as in DOT is recognized

Special Controls

LOAD   LOAD assembled/compiled routines for CALL or F:references

ALLOC   Allocate space for 2-dimensional FORTRAN-style arrays REAL*4 or REAL*8. Reference by indexing only

CALL   Call loaded routine with FORTRAN linkage convention

DEMAND   Set demand to be honored by SESAME after exit

EXIT   Unconditional exit from DATAMAT back to SESAME

Execution Controls in Macros and DATARUN Files (plus RUN)

NAME   Heads a program deck in macro or DATARUN file

LOOP   Auto-indexing or name matching loop based on conditional expression

CONTINUE Terminates range of nearest preceding LOOP verb

SKIP   Skip forward, backward, to beginning of deck or to a label[1]

TALLY   Conditional form of SKIP based on a count-down of an I:variable

IF   Conditional form of SKIP based on a logical expression being true

IFNOT   Same as IF but for expression false

GOTO   Unconditional transfer of control to a lable, executed in file reading routine without further analysis or parsing

QUIT   In macro, interpreted as "return to main program." In DATARUN file interpreted as "return to console" with option to continue in file. From terminal, same as EXIT. Requires a command typed at the terminal.

?Y/N   Requires a "y" or "n" response from terminal. (Yes or No)

ENDATA   Terminates program deck in macro or DATARUN file. Interpreted like QUIT for macro, as unconditional exit in DATARUN file.

RUN   Initiates execution of a program deck in a DATARUN file, from the terminal or from another such deck. In the latter case, the first deck and its file is terminated with no return option. RUN may not be used in a macro.

Multi-Purpose

SET   Set file names, model names, print controls, activate virtual punch, specify case name for RESULTS file, and control automatic flip-flop of O:switches in IF statements. Also defines macro library for which purpose it must be first after LOAD, if any.

DELETE   Delete in-core tables and arrays. Delete any row, column, RHS, range set or bound set for model under construction.

MACROS   A macro is invoked by using its name as a verb. If it take substitutable arguments, these are specified on the same line and may often be made to appear as a user-defined command.

---

1. A label has the form //symbol where "symbol" is limited to 6 characters Transfering to a label means to start execution at the line following. A dynamic symbol table for labels is maintained automatically in DATARUN deck execution. A different scene is used for macros.

Figure 11 (continued)

A model is generated in a working data base (WDB) and then enfiled. (ENFILE)

NEWMODEL

Initiates a new, null model in the WDB. Either NEWMODEL, SUBMODEL or REVISE must be issued before any other matrix generation verb, but only one.

REVISE [DUMMY]

Copies a model from a file to the WDB for revision. If DUMMY is specified, the model is not copied but a table for INDIRECT names is created. This is used for creating new indirect vector in core.

SUBMODEL

A variant of REVISE for generating a decomposition submodel. No algorithm is presently available for utilizing such submodels.

ROW   row-name-exp[<type>][, col-name-exp[<type>] = value-exp [,...]]

One or more rows may be defined, including their types. For each row, one or more elements may be defined including the definition of any new column and, possibly, a special type. Several expressions after the first comma may appear. A zero value does not cause a definition.

COL   col-name-exp [<type>][, row-name-exp[<type>] = value-exp [,...]]
      The action is just the transpose of ROW.
RHS   rhs-name-exp [, row-name-exp[<type>] = value-exp [,...]]

The action is the same as COL but for right-hand-sides which have no type.

Note: The model component verbs may appear in any order. Rows, columns, etc. are defined in order of first occurrence in any context.

INDIRECT $\begin{Bmatrix} GET \\ PUT \end{Bmatrix} \begin{Bmatrix} G:tabname \\ G:N:name \end{Bmatrix}$

Retrieves or defines the name of indirects in the WDB in the form of a G-table. Used for model construction, revision, and for changing values in core. The in-core vector is referenced as $INDVECT, a convention

---

GUB   gub-set-name <type>
PRSET   pricing-set-name
MARKER Marker-name

Define special column set markers. Order is intrinsically important.

INSERT $\begin{Bmatrix} ROW \\ COL \\ RHS \end{Bmatrix} : \begin{Bmatrix} identifier \\ 'FIRST' \end{Bmatrix}$
ENDINS

Permit controlled order of insertions when this is necessary

RANGE   (Same as RHS but for range sets and no row-type permitted.)

BOUND   bound-name, col/gub-name = value(s)

One or more bound sets may be defined. Has involved syntax rules.

COMBINE (Uses special vector-linear-form expressions for rows, cols, rhs-s.)

MERGE   model-name-reference

Merges an entire model from a file into model in WDB. Recommended for creating large models in parts. All components literally merged.

Use   DELETE for entire rows, columns, rhs-s, etc.

Figure 12: DATAMAT MATRIX GENERATION VERBS

SQRT(arg)	Square root
SIN(arg)	Sine of arg in radians
COS(arg)	Cosine of arg in radians
ATAN(arg)	Radian value of Arctan(arg)
LOG(arg)	Natural logarithm
EXP(arg)	e^{arg}
LOGIO/arg	Common logarithm
EXP10	10^{arg}

Examples

E:BETA = EXP(I:T * LOG(1.0 / (1.0 + I:DISCOUNT/ 100.0)))

    Execution: (1) I:DISCOUNT/100.0 is computed as real since one factor is.
                    (2) The reciprocal of 1.0 plus the above is an argument to LOG.
                    (3) The value of the log is multiplied by I:T as real since
                           the log is a real factor. This is the argument to EXP.
                    (4) The real value of the exponential is stored in E:BETA,
                           i.e., it becomes the current value of E:BETA.

I:MAG = LOG10(E:GNP) + .5

    Execution: (1) The log to base 10 of E:GNP is computed as real.
                    (2) One-half is added to the above for rounding.
                    (3) The rounded result is truncated to an integer and becomes
                         the current value of I:MAG.

```
LOOP G:COORD(!1,0) <NE>
     G:COORD(!1,MAG)=SQRT(G:COORD(!1,X)*G:COORD(!1,X)+G:COORD(!1,Y)*G:COORD(!1,Y))
     G:COORD(!1,AMP)=1.5707963
     IF G:COORD(!1,X) <EQ> 0.0,1
     G:COORD(!1,AMP)=ATAN(G:COORD(!1,Y)/G:COORD(!1,X))
CONTINUE
```

    Execution: The LOOP statement has a dummy condition to force looping over
                    all rows of the table G:COORD. This table has (at least) four
                    columns named X, Y, MAG, and AMP. The X,Y coordinates are al-
                    ready in the tables and the magnitude and amplitude of all
                    points so defined are to be computed. The magnitude is com-
                    puted as the square root of the sum of the squares. The ampli-
                    tude is first set to $\pi/2$ in case X=0. (It is implied that all
                    Y=0.) If X≠0, the amplitude is computed.

Figure 13:   USE OF REAL FUNCTIONS

For illustration, assume the following values exist:

    N:ONE = A1Zbbbbb   N:TWO = 2BC9bbb   (b = blank character)

<u>Concetenation</u>: Append 2nd operand to last non-blank of 1st operant.

    N:ONE & N:TWO   gives   A1Z2BC9b

FILL: Blank characters in 1st operand are replaced by corresponding
       positions from 2nd operand.

    FILL(N:ONE, N:TWO)   gives   A1Z9bbb

<u>Mask</u>: For zero or blank positions in 2nd operand, characters in first
       operand are replaced with blank. Result is automatically packed
       to left and blank filled on right unless inhibited by LEAVE.

    MASK(N:ONE, '0*')   gives   1bbbbbbb   ('0*' - 0*bbbbbb)

Shift: The first operand is left circularly shifted the number of posi-
        tions specified by the second operand which is an integer.

    SHIFT(N:TWO, 3)   gives   92BCbbbb

Leave: Inhibits automatic justification of its argument. Applies only
        to first level of nested arguments.

    LEAVE(MASK(N:ONE, '0*')) gives b1bbbbbb

    LEAVE(SHIFT(N:TWO, 3)) gives 9bbbb2BC

<u>Bump</u>: The last nonblank character of the first operand is incremented by
       the second operand which is an integer. This is done in mixed mode
       numeric and alphabetic with carry left, but skipping any characters
       except digits and letters. Suppose

        N:STUFF   has the value A9Z..9.b

      BUMP(N:STUFF, 2) gives B0A..1.b

          as follows: . on right is skipped
                      9+2 = 1 with carry left
                      .. are skipped
                      Z+1 = A with carry left
                      9+1 = 0 with carry left
                      A+1 = B

Combined example: Suppose N:EX has value MAN bbbbb and N:AMP value DATAbbbb

    FILL(SHIFT(LEAVE(MASK(N:EX & N:AMP, '**0****')) 3), TTTTTTT)

gives successively:

          MANDATAb   Concatenation
          MAbDATAb   Mask and Leave
          DATAMAbb   Shift 3 with auto-justification
          DATAMAT   Fill

Selection example:

    LOOP MASK(G:TAB(0, !1), '00X') <EQ> C

The loop is executed only for head symbols which have C in 3rd position.

Figure 14: SYMBOLIC FUNCTIONS

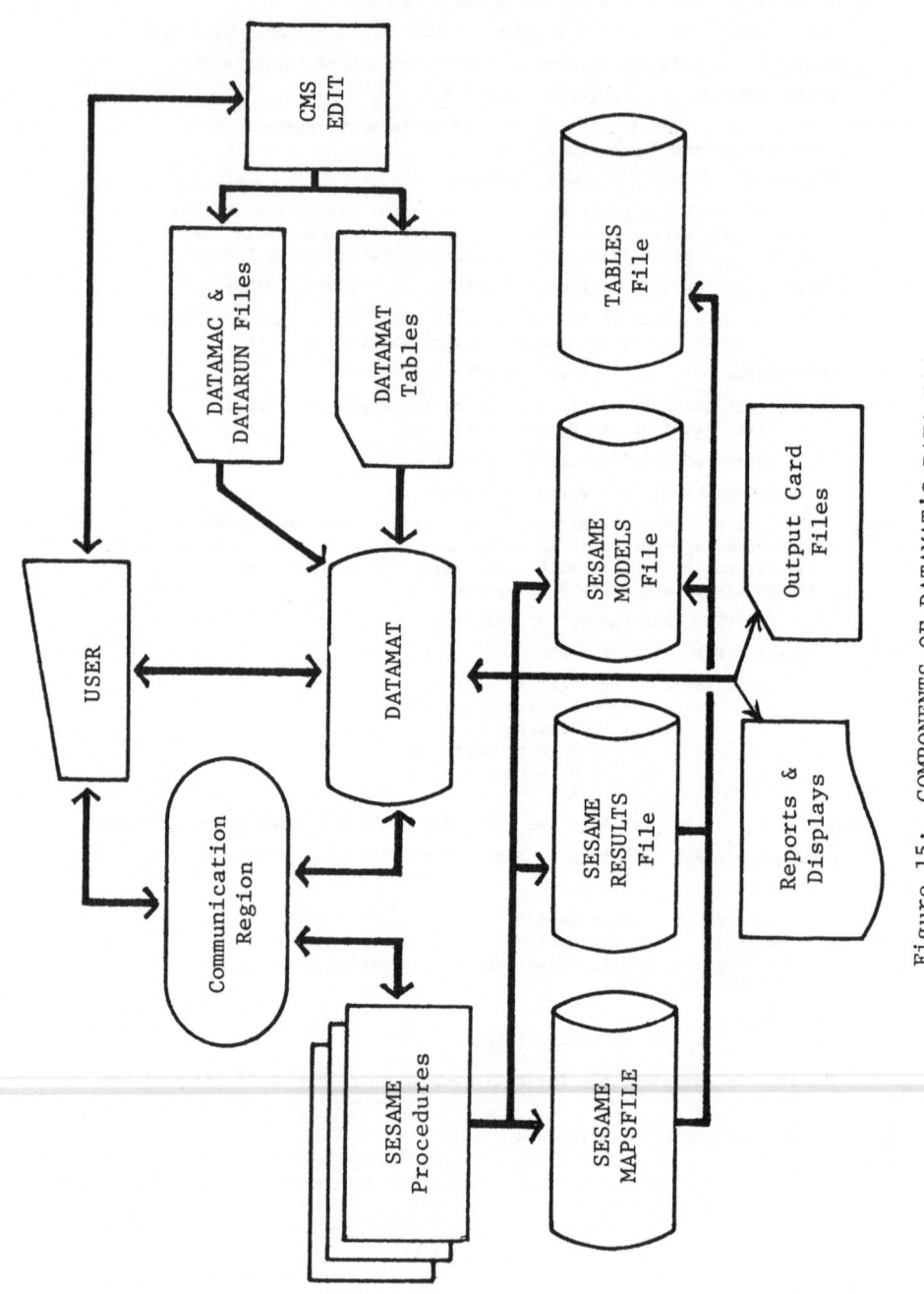

Figure 15: COMPONENTS OF DATAMAT'S DATA BASE

ELEMENTS OF NUMERICAL LINEAR ALGEBRA

T.J. Dekker

Department of Mathematics, University of Amsterdam,
Roetersstraat 15, Amsterdam

ABSTRACT. Elementary vector and matrix operations, Gaussian
elimination and triangular decomposition, orthogonal triangularisation, singular value decomposition, error analysis, implementations
in numerical program libraries.

SUMMARY

1. Elementary vector and matrix operations

We consider real vectors, i.e., elements of a real finite-
dimensional Euclidian vector space and real matrices representing
linear transformations from one vector space into another.

Some important elementary vector and matrix operations, used
in solving numerical linear algebraic problems, are the following:

(a) scalar product and multiplication, i.e., vector times vector
     and matrix times vector or matrix; these operations are used in
     triangular decomposition (i.e., factoring a matrix into the
     product of a lower and an upper triangular matrix), in the cal-
     culation of residuals and in various other algorithms;

(b) elementary elimination, i.e., adding a scalar multiple of a
     vector (or row or column of a matrix) into another one; this
     operation is used in Gaussian elimination and in many variants
     of the simplex algorithm; and

(c) plane rotation, elementary reflection and projection (elemen-
     tary reflection is multiplication by an elementary Householder

matrix); these operations are used in <u>orthogonal triangulari-</u>
<u>sation</u> (i.e., factoring a matrix into the product of an ortho-
gonal and an upper triangular matrix) and in various other
algorithms involving orthogonal matrices.

The factorizations mentioned have the purpose to reduce linear
algebraic problems to simpler ones. [See the various textbooks
mentioned in the Bibliography below.]

2. Gaussian elimination and triangular decomposition

A system of linear algebraic equations can be solved by means
of Gaussian elimination or by the method, mathematically but not
numerically equivalent, of triangular decomposition. Interchanges
of rows and/or columns (pivoting) are usually needed to maintain
numerical stability, and for sparse matrices also to preserve
sparseness as much as possible. [See for treatments on numerical
stability, e.g., Wilkinson (1963 & 1965) and Stewart (1973) and on
sparse problems Young (1971), Gustavson, Liniger & Willoughby (1970)
and variuos publications in Willoughby (1968), Rose & Willoughby
(1972) and Bunch & Rose (1976).]

Elimination as well as triangular decomposition are also used
in the simplex algorithm for solving linear programming problems.
Here interchanges are needed not only for the purposes mentioned
above, but also to obtain the next step towards an optimal solution.
In practice, it may be difficult to meet the three requirements
mentioned. [See Reid (1971) and various papers in Bunch & Rose
(1976), in particular Saunders (1976) for the triangular decomposition method due to Bartels and Golub.]

3. Orthogonal triangularisation

Orthogonal triangularisation is used for solving linear least
squares problems and (as a special case) linear systems of equations.
For the latter problem, orthogonal triangularisation is about a
factor or two slower than triangular decomposition or Gaussian
elimination, but in some situations slightly more stable.

Orthogonal triangularisation can be achieved in two main ways:
modified Gram-Schmidt method (which is a numerically stable variant
of the corresponding classical method) and Householder triangularisation (which uses elementary reflections).

In orthogonal triangularisation, one sometimes uses interchanges
to increase numerical stability. Here the interchanges are much
less important, however, than in Gaussian elimination or triangular

decomposition. [See Lawson & Hanson (1974), Polak (1971), Stewart (1973) and the papers by Å. Björck and by P.E. Gill & W. Murray in Bunch & Rose (1976).]

4.   Single value decomposition

A linear least squares problem is called degenerate if its matrix does not have full rank.

Orthogonal triangularisation leads to a satisfactory solution of a linear least squares problem only when it is not degenerate. Otherwise, one should use singular value decomposition, i.e., factoring a matrix into the product of an orthogonal matrix, a non-negative diagonal matrix and another orthogonal matrix. The diagonal elements of the middle factor are called the singular values of the matrix. The number of singular values not equal to zero is equal to the rank of the matrix.

The singular value decomposition has several applications. It is important not only for calculating the numerical rank of a matrix and for solving degenerate linear least squares problems, but also for many practical applications in statistics.

The singular value decomposition is in some sense related to the eigensystem, of a matrix, i.e., its system of eigenvalues and eigenvectors.

In fact, the singular value decomposition and the eigensystem of a matrix are identical when the matrix is symmetric positive (semi-) definite, and they contain essentially the same numerical information when the matrix is normal, i.e., commutes with its transpose.

For a non-normal matrix (and especially a non-diagonalisable one) however, the singular value decomposition gives quite other information about the matrix than its eigensystem. [See Lawson & Hanson (1974) and Stewart (1973).]

5.   Error analysis

Error analysis involves analysis of the linear algebraic problems considered as well as analysis of the numerical algorithms used to solve these problems. A problem is called well-conditioned if its solution is not very sensitive to perturbations of the data. A numerical algorithm is called stable if the errors due to the numerical calculations are not larger than the errors due to perturbations of the data.

An error analysis can be _a priori_ or _a posteriori_. In the latter case, one calculates a solution of a certain problem and a corresponding residual and uses this residual to calculate or estimate an error bound.

An important technique for various numerical algorithms is the _backward_ analysis; in this technique one shows that the computed solution is the exact solution of a slightly perturbed problem. [See Wilkinson (1963 & 1965) and Stewart (1973).]

6. Implementations in numerical program libraries

A good algorithm must be stable and efficient. A good implementation of an algorithm in a (sub-)program must, moreover, be _reliable_ and _robust_. Reliable means that every failure is reported; robust means that the implemented algorithm works for a wide class of problems including difficult ones and yields results which, within the limitations of the machine, are (almost) optimal.

In the last decade several good implementations of good algorithms have been produced and included in numerical program libraries. At this moment the largest libraries available on a wide range of machines are IMSL and NAG. [See for these and other libraries or packages the bibliography on this subject below.]

BIBLIOGRAPHY

Textbooks

1. C.G. Broyden, _Basic Matrices_, MacMillan Press, 1975.

2. G.E. Forsythe and C.B. Moler, _Computer Solution of Linear Algebraic Systems_, Prentice-Hall, 1967.

3. L. Fox, _Introduction to Numerical Linear Algebra_, Clarendon-Press, 1964.

4. B. Noble, _Applied Linear Algebra_, Prentice-Hall, 1969.

5. G.W. Stewart, _Introduction to Matrix Computations_, Academic Press, 1973.

6. J.H. Wilkinson, _Rounding Errors in Algebraic Processes_, Her Majesty's Stationary Office/Prentice-Hall, 1963.

7. J.H. Wilkinson, _The Algebraic Eigenvalue Problem_, Clarendon-Press, 1965.

Books on specific problems

1. C.L. Lawson & R.J. Hanson, Solving Least Squares Problems, Prentice-Hall, 1974.

2. E. Polak, Computational Methods in Optimization, Academic Press, 1971.

3. J.K. Reid, Large Sparse Sets of Linear Equations, Academic Press, 1971.

4. D.M. Young, Iterative Solution of Large Linear Systems, Academic Press, 1971.

Proceedings and papers on sparse matrices

1. J.R. Bunch and D.J. Rose (ed.), Sparse Matrix Computations, Academic Press, 1976.

2. F.G. Gustavson, W. Liniger and R. Willoughby, Symbolic Generation of an Optimal Crout Algorithm for Sparse Systems of Linear Equations, J. ACM 17, p. 87-109, 1970.

3. D.J. Rose and R.A. Willoughby, Sparse Matrices and Their Applications, Plenum Press, New York, 1972.

4. M.A. Saunders, A Fast Stable Implementation of the Simplex Method Using Bartels-Golub Updating, p. 213-226. In: Bunch and Rose, 1976.

5. R.A. Willoughby, ed., Sparse Matrix Proceedings, IBM Yorktown Heights, 1968.

Program libraries and packages

1. T.J. Dekker and W. Hoffmann, ALGOL 60 Procedures for Numerical Algebra, Parts 1 and 2, Mathematical Centre Tracts 22 and 23, Amsterdam, 1968.

2. International Mathematical and Statistical Libraries, Inc., FORTRAN subroutines library.

3. Numerical Algorithms Group Ltd., Oxford, England, FORTRAN, ALGOL 60 and ALGOL 68 subprograms libraries.

4. NUMAL: Numerical ALGOL 60 library, Mathematical Centre, Amsterdam.

5. NATS: National Activity to Test Software, EISPACK, Package of Matrix Eigensystem Routines in FORTRAN.

6. B.T. Smith et. al., <u>Matrix Eigensystem Routines - EISPACK Guide</u>, Lecture notes in Computer Science, Springer-Verlag, 1974.

7. J.H. Wilkinson and C. Reinsch, ed., <u>Handbook for Automatic Computation, Vol. II Linear Algebra</u>, Springer-Verlag, 1971.

A TUTORIAL ON MATRICIAL PACKING

HARVEY J. GREENBERG

Energy Information Administration
Washington, D.C. 20461

ABSTRACT. This tutorial describes advanced data structures for
representing matrices, as implemented in many (large-scale)
mathematical programming systems. It functionally separates
the "endogenous matrix file" from the "exogenous matrix vile."
The exploitation of sparsity and super-sparsity is the primary
foundation.

This tutorial describes fundamental data structures to
represent a large matrix. The technology has been developed
from linear programming systems, but it can be applied directly
to any "matricial program." A matricial program is one which
can be represented by a matrix (or more formally a tensor). An
example of a class of nonlinear matricial programs is the multi-
nomial forms embodied in geometric programming. Further, the
data structures we shall describe may be extended in several ways
to represent more general nonlinear programs.

When we say a matrix is large, we mean it has at least 1,500
rows and 10,000 columns. Clearly, we would not want to use a
simple array structure and reserve 15,000,000 storage locations.
Even small-to-medium size matrices are of the order 800x5,000,
so we need something more sophisticated than an array representation.

Fundamental to the development of matricial packing is understanding what a matrix is. To a mathematician a matrix is a
linear transformation from one vector space into another; to an
engineer it is a rectangular array of numbers. The view we shall
take in our computer science orientation is that a matrix is a

"file", that is a collection of records with a prescribed structure.

Before we consider the types of matrix files relevant to the design of a mathematical programming system, let us note that real models produce matrices where most of the matrix elements are zero. This is an important observation because we can avoid storing zeroes by designing the records to identify only nonzeroes. Arithmetic operations, such as addition or multiplication, have predictable results for the zeroes, and they may be avoided, thus resulting in a savings of time as well as space. Retrieval operations, such as determining a matrix element value for given row and column specification, can begin with zero as a default and search for a nonzero, terminating with the appropriate conclusion.

When a matrix has a high percentage of zeroes, it is called "sparse," and when it has few zeroes, it is called "dense." More precisely, we have the following

DEFINITION: The sparsity of an m by n matrix is the ratio of the number of zero elements to the product, m*n. The density is 1 - sparsity.

Small models, say with 300-800 rows and 500-1200 columns, tend to have a density of approximately .5 - 2%; medium models, say with 800-1500 rows and 1200-7000 columns tend to have a density of approximately .05 - .3%; very large models, say more than 2500 rows and more than 30,000 columns tend to have less than .01% density. It is generally true that the larger the model the lower the density, which is one important reason we can represent them for effective processing.

To gain some insight as to why this is true, consider the standard transportation model with s sources and d destinations. The matrix size is (s+d+1) rows and s*d columns (if every link is present) and every column has exactly two ones in it for the supply-demand constraints plus a cost of flow in the objective row. Therefore the density is less than 3/(s+d+1), which decreases with increases in the problem dimensions.

More generally, a modeller cannot define activities with more than a few row elements; in practice, he would tend to use more activities rather than fewer complicated ones. This results in the rule-of-thumb: a column will typically have 5 nonzeroes, regardless of the number of rows. This seems to be true with a small variance. Thus, if we assume each column count is less than some constant, c, independent of row size (where c is about 7), then

$$\text{density} \leqq \frac{c*n}{n*m} = c/m.$$

Thus, as the number of rows gets large, the density decreases.

2. ENDOGENOUS MATRIX FILE

2.1 Basic Structures

Let us now consider the types of matrix files which are relevant to the design of a mathematical programming system. The one we shall consider first is the endogenous matrix file. This is to be constructed for use during iterations with the primal simplex method, and it represents a single problem.

Under the rules of the primal simplex method the only access to the endogenous matrix file is for a given column; in many designs one simply proceeds column by column in a sequential fashion to find one which corresponds to an activity that shows promise of improving the objective function. Thus, let us suppose that the basic type of access and operation to be performed is characterized by:

(1) access by column, and

(2) compute inner product of a column with another vector, stored as a linear list.

The access by column suggests that each record represents the activity's column, including any relevant values such as scale, translation or bound values. Therefore, we define columnar form to mean that record j corresponds to activity j. All of the schemes we shall consider for the endogenous matrix file will be of columnar form. There is an obvious symmetry in developing a row form representation.

Storage as an array results in a linear list with the location (or address) given by the following linear equation:

$$\text{LOC}(A_{ij}) = \text{LOC}(A_{00}) + cnj + ci$$

where

> n = number of columns + extra information (e.g., scale, bounds).
> c = number of addressible units to store a value.

The units are number of addressible entities, (e.g., bytes or words), using high precision (e.g., word on CDC 6000's, double word on IBM 370's or UNIVAC 1108).

Since we know most models are sparse, let us consider more compact data structures, resulting in nonlinear lists with variable record sizes, depending upon the density.

GENERAL COLUMNAR FORM:

The j-th record corresponds to the j-th activity and may include a "header" to provide record separation plus other information about the activity.

Figure 1:   Schematic of Columnar Form

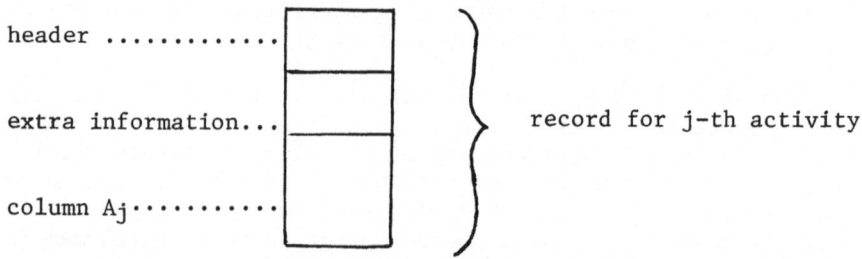

header ....

extra information...   } record for j-th activity

column A_j...........

We shall consider the header and the extra information later. Our concern now is with the representation of the column other than the array form.

Let us begin with an elementary scheme,

BASIC SEQUENTIAL COLUMNAR FORM (BSC):

Each data item for the column in the j-th record corresponds to a nonzero element and appears as the couple: (VALUE, ROW INDEX).

In order to illustrate BSC let us assume, temporarily, that no extra information is needed, and the header simply contains the number of nonzeroes in the column.   Then, consider the following matrix:

$$
A= \begin{array}{c}
 \\
0 \\
1 \\
2 \\
3 \\
4
\end{array}
\begin{array}{cccc}
1 & 2 & 3 & 4 \\
\left[\begin{array}{cccc}
4.0 & 3.0 & 1.0 & 0 \\
1.0 & -1.0 & 0 & 1.0 \\
0 & 2.0 & 0 & 0 \\
-1.0 & 1.0 & 0 & 0 \\
0 & 0 & 2.0 & 1.0
\end{array}\right]
\end{array}
$$

The endougenous matrix file for this matrix will have 4 records, as illustrated in Figure 2 below:

Figure 2: Schematic of Example BSC

3	...header for column 1
4.0, 0 1.0, 1 -1.0,3	
4	...header for column 2
3.0,0 -1.0,1 2.0,2 1.0,3	
2	...header for column 3
1.0,0 2.0,4	
2	...header for column 4
1.0,1 1.0,4	

Let us now consider how to perform an inner production using BSC. Let $X(1), \ldots, X(m)$ be an array (i.e., linear list representation of a vector). At the risk of seeming trivial, notice that

$$
(X, A_j) = \sum_{i=1}^{m} A_{ij} * X(i) = \sum_{i:A_{ij} \neq 0} A_{ij} * X(i),
$$

so only nonzeroes are needed in computing the inner product. Further, the order of summation is of no (theoretical) consequence, so the row indices stored in BSC format need not be in sort order.

ALGORITHM BSCPROD: Given an array, $X(1)$,...,$X(m)$, and a column in BSC format with the k-th data item of the form (v_k, i_k), where $1 < = i_k < = m$, this algorithm computes the inner product, (X, A_j), and puts the result into PROD.

step 1 (initialize): set PROD=0, set k=1 and perfrom step 2 until end-of-record is reached.

step 2 (add term): retrieve (v_k, i_k) and set PROD $\leftarrow$ PROD + $v_k*X(i_k)$; advance k.

Of course, since we may compute the inner product for more than one column in the endogenous matrix file, an exogenous pointer is maintained to locate the column's header; algorithm BSCPROD simply shows the elementary scheme for one column. It should be noted that because we inherently avoid the multiplication and addition (step 2) for the zero elements, the BSC form takes less time than the array form to compute to an inner product. Now let us consider storage requirements.

For an array the storage is m n locations for the matrix elements plus whatever is needed for the extra information. In BSC we incur the extra storage for the headers and the row indices. We have, for BSC,

$$STORAGE = n \ (h+x) + (v+i) \ Z,$$

where

$n=$ number of columns
$h=$ size of header
$x=$ size of extra information
$v=$ size of nonzero value
$i=$ size of index value
$Z=$ number of nonzeroes

Then, the ratio of BSC storage to the array storage is,

$$R = (h+x)/(m+x) \ + \ (v+i) \ DENSITY/(1+x/m).$$

The first term is relatively small, especially for large row size; the second term becomes small when the density is low. For definiteness we may take the word (say on CDC 6000's) as a basic

storage unit in the array.   Then consider h=1, x=0 and v+i= 1.25.
This yields a storage ratio,

$$R = 1/m + 1.25*DENSITY.$$

For large m the BSC form takes less space when DENSITY < .80.
Since we typically have DENSITY << .50 (often less than .05), the
BSC form generally takes <u>much</u> less space than an array representation of a matrix.   Further, by sacrificing some precision we can
take v+i=1, in which case only the headers contribute extra
storage, and this is negligible even for high density.

Now let us consider another scheme based upon the observation
that most models have a prevalance of plus or minus ones.   If we
could distinguish them, then we could save time by avoiding multiplication during the computation of an inner product; further, if
the data structure distinguishes them, then we do not have to store
their values.   This leads to the

PARTITIONED   SEQUENTIAL   COLUMNAR   FORM   (PSC)

> The data items for the column in the j-th record
> is partitioned into 3 sections with the following
> structure:
>
> section 1:   row index list associated with i: $A_{ij}=1$
>
> section 2:   row index list associated with i: $A_{ij}=-1$
>
> section 3:   BSC form for i:$A_{ij} \neq 0,1,-1$.

Using our former example let the header contain the length of
each of the three sections.   Then, we have a structure illustrated in Figure 3.

ALGORITHM PSCPROD: Given an array, X(1), ...,X(m), and a column
in PSC, this algorithm computes the inner product,
(X,A_j) and puts the result into PROD.

step 1 (initialize):   set PROD =0.

step 2 (+1 section):   for each row index, i, in the
+1 section, set PROD ← PROD + X(i).

step 3 (-1 section):   for each row index, i, in the
-1 section, set PROD ← PROD - X (i).

step 4 (BSC section): for each data item, (v,i), in the
BSC section, set PROD ← PROD + v*X(i).

Figure 3: Schematic of Example PSC.

1,1,1	...header for column 1
1	...+1 section
3	...-1 section
4.0,0	...BSC section

1,1,2	...header for column 2
3	...+1 section
1	...-1 section
3.0,0	...BSC section
2.0,2	

1,0,1	...header for column 3
0	...+1 section
2.0,4	...BSC section

2,0,0	...header for column 4
1	...+1 section
4	

Notice that we save the multiplication for the ones in the "ones sections" (steps 2 and 3), but there is extra "overhead" in performing the loops, compared to algorithm BSCPROD. An exact comparison would depend on the particular machine. It should also be noted that the ± 1's may be combined in one section by placing the sign on the row index. The tradeoff is in the loop overhead in algorithm PSCPROD. If there is only one section for ones, then the sign would be tested for each row index in order to use

$$PROD \leftarrow PROD + X(i)$$

or

$$PROD \leftarrow PROD - X(-i)$$

in the accumulation step over the ones section. If the number of ones is "small," the combined section is better because only one loop is used. Conversely, if there is a "large" number of ones, the extra loop is better to avoid a comparison at each step. The threshold is machine dependant. (For IBM 370's it is about 4 to 5, making the combined section typically preferrable.)

Now consider the storage requirements for PSC. We have

$$\text{STORAGE} = n(H+x) + Zi + gv,$$

where

n = number of columns
H = header size
x = size for extra information
Z = number of nonzeroes
i = size of index
g = number of general nonzeroes ($\neq 0, 1, -1$)
v = size of value

Compared to BSC we save $(Z-g)$ $v-$ $(H-h)n$, that is the number of ones (+ or -) times the size of general values, plus a possible difference in header space. Typically, ones are very prevalent and account for a high percentage of the density. Further, the difference in header space is relatively negligible in large models. Thus, PSC storage requirements are much less, as a rule.

Now let us consider an alteration in the BSC format based upon the observation that many nonzero values appear many times throughout the matrix, even if we do not count the ones (which could be represented with PSC form). For reasons that become clear only when studying many models and how they are generated, the number of distinct constants is much less the number of non-zeroes. Perhaps one type of model where this is evident is one involving time periods, where the same submatrix is replicated because those sets of relations exist in every time period. Another explanation is that the "raw data" is relatively small compared to the matrix which gets generated from this raw data; thus, it is "likely" that the same number will appear in many places. Of course, highly structured models, such as ones with a large embedded network are inherently supersparse with an abundance of ± 1.

Whatever the reason, it is generally the case that many nonzero values are replicated. If we assume that it takes less space to store an index (some pointer) than a nonzero value (in high precision), then we may construct an "inverted file" structure for the endogenous matrix file. This is the same technique used in compiler design, where we setup a literal pool, that is a table of constants. Then, instead of (v, i) containing the value and row index as in BSC, we let v be an index to identify the location in the literal pool whose contents is the nonzero value. This leads to the following scheme.

INVERTED SEQUENTIAL COLUMNAR FORM (ISC):

> The column in the j-th record has one data item per non-
> zero in the form: (VALUE INDEX, ROW INDEX), where the
> value index locates the nonzero value in a LITERAL POOL.

Of course, we may combine PSC with ISC by using ISC form in
section 3 (instead of BSC). However, let us illustrate ISC with
our example and not use PSC form.

Figure 4: Schematic of Example ISC.

		LITERAL POOL		
3	...header for column 1			
1,0				
2,1			index	value
3,3			1	4.0
4	...header for column 2		2	1.0
4,0			3	-1.0
3,1			4	3.0
5,2			5	2.0
2,3				
2	...header for column 3			
2,0				
5,4				
2	...header for column 4			
2,1				
2,4				

We shall consider an inner product algorithm for the ISC format,
and extension to combine with PSC should be straightforward.

ALGORITHM ISCPROD: Given an array, $X(1),\ldots,X(m)$, and a column
in ISC, this algorithm computes the inner product,
(X,A_j), and puts the results into PROD.

> step 1 (initialize): set PROD = 0 and perform step 2
> until an end-of-record is reached.

> step 2 (add term): retrieve (v,i) data item, and set
> V=VALUE(v) (from the literal pool of values), set
> PROD $\leftarrow$ PROD + V*X(i).

We see that there is an extra retrieval in step 2 compared with
algorithm BSCPROD, so algorithm ISCPROD will generally be slower.
However, let us consider the storage requirements.

We have
$$STORAGE = n \ (h+x) + 2 \ Z \ i + v \ V,$$
where

n = number of columns
h = header size
x = size for extra information
Z = number of nonzeroes
i = size of index
v = size of value
V = number of distinct nonzeroes

The difference between ISC and BSC is $Z \ i + v \ (V-Z)$. Dividing this by $Z \ v$ we consider $i/v + V/Z \ -1$. Therefore, if the ratio of distinct nonzeroes to the total number of nonzeroes (V/Z) is sufficiently small, then ISC takes less space (including the storage for the literal pool) than BSC. For definiteness consider $i/v = 1/4$; then we may conclude ISC uses less space if $V/Z < 3/4$. It is generally true that $V/Z < 1/2$, so ISC typically takes <u>much</u> less space than BSC.

If we accept the claim that ISC form uses much less space than BSC, and we combine it with the space-saving PSC form, then we may be able to avoid costly I/O by keeping the entire endogenous matrix file in core. This may more than compensate for the time lost in step 2 of algorithm ISCPROD.

Now let us consider how to establish the literal pool. When a value is received as input to be added to the endogenous matrix file, we must search the literal pool to see if it is there. If so, then we want the index number to insert into the associated data item; if not, then we want to add it as a new entry to the literal pool and insert it into the associated data item. A technique for doing this efficiently is known as "hashing."

Hashing is the process of computing an address (or index) from an input key (the nonzero value in our case). This process is carried out with the use of a "hash function" which is the associated mapping from the set of input keys to the set of addressees (or indices). We shall not take up the entire subject of hashing here, but we shall describe one such process suitable for our needs.

Let h be a function which has domain equal to the representation of a floating point value, which is our input. Its range shall be the integers from 1 to L, where L is to be prescribed. One example is to let $L=2^k$, so a string of k bits is a binary representation of $h(v)$. Now partition the input, v, into fields, each of length k. Treating these fields as a separate binary string we can use arithmetic or boolean operations to form $h(v)$. For definiteness, consider k=8 (e.g., byte on IBM 370's), and let v be represented by 64 bits (double word on IBM 370's). Then, there are 8 fields. We can take the exclusive-OR operation among the 8 fields to obtain h(v). Here is a list of hash values for this particular function with the representation found on IBM 370's:

Table 1: Hash Values for Setting Up Literal Pool

Value	Hecadecimal Representation				Hash Value
1.0	4110	0000	0000	0000	81
- 1.0	C110	0000	0000	0000	209
10.0	41A0	0000	0000	0000	225
-10.0	C1A0	0000	0000	0000	97
2.0	4120	0000	0000	0000	97
0.5	4080	0000	0000	0000	192
0.333	C055	5326	17C1	BDA5	46
8.0	4180	0000	0000	0000	193
17.0	4211	0000	0000	0000	83
0.99	40FD	70A3	D70A	3D70	254
- 2.0	C120	0000	0000	0000	225

To illustrate, consider h(1.0). Expanding the hexidecimal representation into binary form we have 01000001 00010000 0...0, so that the exclusive-OR among the eight fields (viz., bytes) yields the 8-bit string, 01010001. This is the binary representation of 81.

Given a hash function, such as the one just described, let the hash value be a list number, pointing to a linear list called HEADS. If h(v)=i, then we look at HEADS(i). If it is zero, then this means the value, v, has not appeared before, and we create a list by adding v to the literal pool and setting HEADS(i) to point to it (as the first member of this list). If HEADS(i) is not zero, then it points to the literal pool, and we begin a search through a linked list starting at this first member. If v is found, our task is complete upon noting the associated value index; otherwise, v is added to the literal pool and the associated list is updated with this new insertion. This procedure is given by the following algorithm (to be applied to one entering value.

ALGORITHM ENTERV: Given the input value, v, and the associated hash value, h(v), the value index is obtained and put into INDEX. In the event no space remains and v must be inserted, OVERFLOW is reached. The following information is included:

HEADS...linear list of list heads whose length is the range of the hash function, h;

POOL....literal pool of constants between location 1 and MAX;

LINK....parallel list to POOL containing links for (multiple) value lists;

LAST....pointer to last member of POOL.

TOLERANCE...Monnegative value.

Initially (before first entry) all of the above information (except TOLERANCE) is zero.

step 1   (Start with list head): set INDEX=HEADS(h(v)).

step 2   (Is list empty?): if INDEX=0, go to step 4; else, if / POOL(INDEX)-v / $\leq$ TOLERANCE, STOP; else, set j=LINK(INDEX).

step 3   (Does the list end here?): if j=0, go to step 4; else set INDEX=j, and go to step 2.

step 4   (Add entry.): if LAST=MAX, exit OVERFLOW; else, advance LAST $\leftarrow$ LAST+1, set LINK(LAST)=INDEX, HEADS (h(v))=LAST, POOL(LAST)=v and INDEX=LAST. EXIT.

If we apply algorithm ENTERV to each of the values listed in our example, then we obtain the following literal pool:

Table 2: Literal Pool for Example

HEADS			LITERAL POOL		
LOC	VALUE	LOC	VALUE	LINK
46	7	1	1.0	0
81	1	2	- 1.0	0
83	9	3	10.0	0
97	5	4	-10.0	0
192	6	5	2.0	4
193	8	6	0.5	0
209	2	7	0.3333	0
225	11	8	17.0	0
254	10	10	0.99	0

Notice in this example that both -10.0 and 2.0 hash to the same value (i.e., 97). This is known as a "collision," and these values are in the same list. For this example there are no other collisions, so the other lists have at most one entry. If we suppose that the hash function distributes uniformly over its range, then we will have R lists, where R is the range of h. In our particular choice of hash function, there are 256 lists. Thus, if, for example, we have 25,600 distinct nonzero entries, each list will have about 100 entries. The average search will be equivalent to a linear search through a linked list of 50 elements. If we are to use direct hashing (i.e., without a HEADS list), then one list would have 25,600 entries (at the end), so average search would appear to be equivalent to search through a list with 12,800 elements. However, the situation is worse. If the range of h has exactly 25,600 locations, then many collisions will occur (i.e., 2 distinct inputs hashing to the same address). This necessitates searching the range of h to find an unused location. To avoid a high frequency of collisions, it is desirable to allocate more than the anticipated number of distinct inputs for the range of h. The unused locations would also have to be interrogated, and the average search would be 1/2 the range. More importantly, since this secondary table method produces a contiguous list of constants, there is no wasted space after the creation process terminates. Compression cannot be applied to the resulting literal pool from direct hashing without revising the pointers already set in the endogenous matrix file.

It is to be emphasized that HEADS and LINK are no longer needed once the literal pool is constructed, so they may be returned to the "storage manager" for other usage. Further, the literal pool can be relocated to gain compactness since the stored value index is only relative to the base, which can be reset.

Summarizing, we have considered three basic elementary data structures for the endogenous matrix file, namely Basic Sequential Columnar Form (BSC), Partitioned Sequential Columnar Form (PSC), and Inverted Sequential Columnar Form (ISC). The "sequential" refers to the fact that the records are stored sequentially, and the "columnar form" means that the matrix is stored by columns (since that is to be the method of access using the primal simplex method) with the j-th record corresponding to the activity j.

2.2 GROUPING ACTIVITIES

We shall now consider a more advanced data structure designed to avoid explicit representation of certain rows by grouping activities and using their contiguity to implicitly represent certain kins of constraints. Let suppose that we can expect some rows to be of the following form:

$$(0\ldots\ldots0\ 1\ 1\ 1\ \ldots\ 1\ -1\ \ldots\ -1\ 0\ \ldots\ 0)\ X\ \begin{matrix}\leq\\=\\\geq\end{matrix}\ g.$$

That is, we have a group of activities, placed in sequence, so that their coefficients in a particular row form a set of +1's followed by a set of -1's. The constraint is that this difference must relate to the "group value," g, with one of the three prescribed relations ($\leq$, = or $\geq$). With scaling we can always generate one such row, but what is more important many models have a prevalance of such rows in their natural form. For example, all supply rows of a transportation problem may be put into this form, thus grouping all activities with the same source; similarly, all destination rows may be represented by grouping all activities with same destination. In these cases the set of -1's is empty, and the group value is the supply or demand values, respectively. Another type of constraint fitting this form is "balance equations," where g=0. Hence, consider the following

MARKED GROUP COLUMNAR FORM (MGC):

The General Columnar Form is used with a marker used to identify groups. The structure of a marker is similar to a header with a tag bit allocated to distinguish between a marker and header.

The marker includes information to identify the group value and the numbers of +1 members and -1 members which follows the marker.

One example of a marker is illustrated in Figure 5.

Figure 5:   Schematic of Group Marker

$\begin{matrix}-\\+\end{matrix}$	t	n1	n2	g

bit 1 = tag ('-' if marker; '+' if header)
t = type of group (e.g., form of inequality)
n1= number of +1's
n2= number of -1's
 g= group value

Let us illustrate MGC, using the above marker, with a transportation problem having 2 sources and 3 destinations. We have

$$\begin{bmatrix} 1 & 1 & 1 & & & \\ & & & 1 & 1 & 1 \\ 1 & \cdot & & 1 & & \\ & 1 & & & 1 & \\ & & 1 & & & 1 \end{bmatrix} \quad \begin{array}{l} < = s1 \\ < = s2 \\ > = d1 \\ > = d2 \\ > = d3 \end{array}$$

$\left.\begin{array}{l} < = s1 \\ < = s2 \end{array}\right\}$ supplies

$\left.\begin{array}{l} > = d1 \\ > = d2 \\ > = d3 \end{array}\right\}$ demands

Let $t = 1$ represent the group type (which is the same for each of the three groups). Note that $n1 = 2$ and $n2 = 0$ in each group, so MGC, with PSC for the records, produces the structure illustrated in Figure 6.

Figure 6: Schematic of Exampe MG

-,1,2,0,d1	... marker for group 1 (flow into d1)
+,1,0,0 1	...header for column 1
+,1,0,0 2	...header for column 4
-,1,2,0,d2	... marker for group 2 (flow into d2)
+,1,0,0 1	...header for column 2
+,1,0,0 2	...header for column 5
-,1,2,0,d3	... marker for group 3 (flow into d3)
+,1,0,0 1	...header for column 3
+,1,0,0 2	...header for column 6

When the groups do not overlap, such as the above example, then the structure is less complicated and certain alogrithmic advantages may be deduced. This is known as "Generalized Upper Bounding." (However, even if the disjointness is violated, it is important to note the concept of using markers to represent certain row structures implicitly.) If a marker takes the same space as three indices, then we need the groups to have more than three members to take less space than PSC without groups. Some marking schemes take less than three indices. For example, we can distinguish the case g=0 with one bit, thus reducing to two indices. Similarly, we can distinguish the case where n2=0.

When employing a special algorithm such as Generalized Upper Bounding or Variable Upper Bounding, where disjointness of groups is assumed, the inner product algorithm need not change. The dual price associated with an equality special row is never computed since it does not effect pricing and candidate selection. (After terminating, the dual price of a special row is computed using the (modified) reduced cost of the activity.)

3. EXOGENOUS MATRIX FILES

Now let us consider the exogenous matrix file. This is designed primarily for storage and retrieval of information when the analyst is creating the problem (or revising one previously created). Therefore, we are not interested in a data structure designed for efficiency of arithmetic operations. Further, we shall be interested in access by element, by row or by column. In fact, we may be interested in access by submatrix. However, since we know that once the problem is generated, we shall convert to establish an endogenous matrix file, we may want certain information to be activity-directed. Putting the details of that issue aside for the moment, let us point out an important feature to be included.

To facilitate report writing, as well as making data base management tasks transparent, it is desirable to identify rows and columns by name, rather than merely by index number. For example, an activity corresponding to flow of goods from Dallas to New York in October may be named 'DAL.NY.OCT.' Since there may be other flows out of Dallas, one may wish to retrieve all flow out of Dallas in October by the mask, 'DAL.*.OCT' to represent a restriction on total flow out of Dallas in October.

Thus, let us take, as the basic retrieval operation, the tabulated information (i.e., array form of submatrix) from an input key of the form, (ROW MASK, COLUMN MASK). By using no asterisks (*) we are retrieving a single element. If the row mask has all asterisks, then we are retrieving the submatrix whose column names match the column mask. For the basic storage operation let us simply take the key to be (ROW NAME, COLUMN NAME). This syntax is simpler to deal with, so we shall consider it first.

A basic structure consists of a list of row names and

another list of column names, each with associated information. One way to represent this is a linear list with 3 data items per record:

ROW NAME, COLUMN NAME, VALUE.

(VALUE, here and elsewhere, can be the actual value, or it can be a pointer to a literal pool.) The difficulty with this structure is that when a new entry is declared, the entire list must be interrogated to see if it is there. This would be all right if the list remains small; however, for large problems there may be on the order of 50,000 entries, so linear search would not be very fast.

The search process can be accelerated if a sort order is maintained (say on ROW NAME first, then on COLUMN NAME). However, insertion of a new entry then becomes costly.

We shall describe a binary search tree representation which has been successful in practice. More sophisticated structures are not described here in the interest of space. Our definitions follow Knuth [6].

A binary tree is defined recursively as follows. An empty set is a binary tree. A binary tree of n nodes, symbolized by T_n, is the triple (T_L, ROOT, T_R), where L+R=n-1. We call T_L the "left subtree" and T_R the "right subtree." Associated with each node is a key whose set of values is totally ordered. A binary search tree is a binary tree whose nodes correspond to key values with the following property:

if node p is in the left subtree of node q,
then KEY (p) < KEY(q);

if node p is in the right subtree of node q,
the KEY (p) > KEY(q).

BASIC BINARY TREE REPRESENTATION

Each node cosists of 4 fields as follows: (KEY, INFO, LLINK, RLINK), where 'KEY' is the information to be kept in order, 'INFO" is other information associated with node, 'LINK' is the left link, pointing to the root of the left subtree, 'RLINK' is the right link, pointing to the root of the right subtree.

It is convenient to let '0' be a terminal marker, so if the left subtree of a node is empty, we set LLINK(node)=0. However, notice that the number of terminal markers in each binary tree is

precisely one more than the number of nodes. This follows from
the fact that each node, except the root, has precisely one node
pointing to it, called the "father" node, and no node points to
the root. By using a single bit (viz., the sign bit) to tag the
link field as terminal, the remaining space in the link field may
be released to provide threads back to fathers that aid in traversal. We shall return to this point shortly. First, let us consider basic algorithms needed to utilize a binary search tree.

ALGORITHM FINDKEY: Given an input key, K, and a nonempty binary
    search tree located by ROOT, the nodes are interrogated
    until the key is matched or it is discovered to be
    absent. If the key is matched, then its location is
    put into L and control transfers to SUCCESSFUL. If the
    key is not matched, then its father node location is
    put into L, and control transfers to UNSUCCESSFUL.

    step 1 (Begin with root.):   set L=ROOT.

    step 2 (Test key.): if K > KEY(L), go to step 3;
           else, if KEY(L) > K, go to step 5; else, exit
           SUCCESSFUL.

    step 3 (Move right.): set L1=RLINK(L).

    step 4 (Test for termination.): if L1 <=0, exit
           UNSUCCESSFUL; else, set L=L1 and go to step 2.

    step 5 (Move left.): set L1=LLINK(L) and go to
           step 4.

It should be noted that in algorithm FINDKEY we are using
the location number, rather than node number, as an index. These
can be made equal by adjusting L to account for translation and
scale (i.e., number of addressible units per record associated
with a node if record size is constant; this only requires the
INFO field to be a constant size).

Before dealing the storage and retrieval operations with the
exogenous matrix file, which uses binary search trees as its
representation, let us consider the general use of algorithm
FINDKEY. Let us suppose we wish to store a new input consisting
of (K,I), where K=KEY, and I=INFO field. If we exit SUCCESSFUL,
then this may signal an error (e.g., duplicate name which is
not allowed), or it may be the case that we wish to revise the
information by overwriting with I onto INFO field. If we exit
UNSUCCESSFUL, then this may be a new input (e.g., new column or
row declaration), and algorithm FINDKEY identifies the father node
from which we can complete the insertion (see algorithm NEWKEY

below). Now suppose we wish to retrieve information, given K=KEY, and put this information into I. We apply algorithm FINDKEY. If the exit is SUCCESSFUL, then L locates the node, and we can extract INFO for completion of the retrieval. If the exit is UNSUCCESSFUL, then this may mean an error (e.g., input key misspelled), or we may have just wanted to check if this key is present.

ALGORITHM NEWKEY: Given (K,I) as an input key-information couple, and a binary search tree located by ROOT, (K,I) is inserted into its proper order unless it is already present, in which case control transfers to DUPLICATE (with L pointing to node). In the event no room remains to complete the insertion, control transfers to OVERFLOW.

step 1   (Setup control and interrogate tree.): Execute algorithm FINDKEY. If exit is SUCCESSFUL, go to step 2. If exit is UNSUCCESSFUL, go to step 3.

step 2   (Key found.): exit DUPLICATE.

step 3   (Location of father node found.): Fetch space from AVAIL list; if none, exit OVERFLOW; else, place location into LNEW.

step 4   (Insert.): Set LLINK(LNEW)=RLINK(LNEW)=0 and INFO(LNEW)=I. If K>KEY(L), SET RLINK(L)=LNEW; else, set LLINK(L)=LNEW.

step 5   (Set pointer.): Set L=LNEW and EXIT.

Let us now describe a binary tree representation of the exogenous matrix file. We define two such trees, one for rows and one for columns. Let ROOTR and ROOTC designate their roots, respectively. In each case the key is the name and the order relation is the lexicographical ordering by character representation (e.g. if names are letters, ordering is alphabetical). The INFO field for the row tree contains the followng:

(1)   row index number (based on order of entrance)

(2)   row type (L,G,E or N)

(3)   right-hand-side value

For the column tree the INFO field contains the following:

(1) bounds

(2) pointer to (linked) list of nonzeroes.

To illustrate what we have described thus far, consider the following exogenous matrix file:

Table 3: Example Exogenous Matrix File Using Binary Tree Structures

	LOC	KEY	INFO	LLINK	RRLINK
ROOTR	1	S1	1,L,10	3	9
ROOTC	2	S1D1	11,100	0	6
	3	D1	2,G,10	0	4
	4	OBJ	3,N,0	5	0
	5	D2	4,G10	0	7
	6	S1D2	12,103	0	8
	7	D3	5,G,10	0	0
	8	S1D3	13,106	0	10
	9	S2	6,L,15	0	0
	10	S2D1	21,109	0	11
	11	S2D2	22,112	0	12
	12	S2D3	23,115	0	5

LOC	INFO
100	1,1.0,101
101	2,1.0,102
102	3,50.0,0
103	1,1.0,104
104	4,1.0,105
105	3,60.0,0
106	1,1.0,107
107	5,1.0,108
108	3,70.0,0
109	6,1.0,110
110	2,1.0,111
111	3,80.0,0
112	2,1.0,113
113	4,1.0,114
114	3,90.0,0
115	2,1.0,117
116	5,1.0,117
117	3,90.0,0

This represents the following transportation matrix:

	S1D1	S1D2	S1D3	S2D1	S2D2	S2D3	
OBJ	50	60	70	80	90	90	
S1	1	1	1				$\leq$ 10
S2				1	1	1	$\leq$ 15
D1	1			1			$\geq$ 5
D2		1			1		$\geq$ 10
D3			1			1	$\geq$ 10
bounds:	11	12	13	21	22	23	

To see how this structure works, suppose we want to interrogate the right-hand-side of row S2. Using algorithm FINDKEY, we start at ROOTR, which is location 1. Since S2>S1, we move to the right-i.e., using RLINK, we go to location 9. Now the name matches, and we can retrieve RHS(S2)=15 from the third item in INFO. Now suppose we want the nonzero list of activity S1D3. Starting at ROOTC, we discover S1D3>S1D1, so we move to the right-i.e., using RLINK, we go to location 6. Again, we discover S1D3>S1D2, so we move to location 8, where we match the column name. The second item in INFO is the pointer to the nonzero list, and its value is 106. Thus, we go to location 106, where we have a nonzero in row 1 (named S1) whose value is 1.0. The third item is the link to the location of the next nonzero for column S1D3, that is 107. This tells us row 5 (named D3) has a nonzero whose value is 1.0. The pointer is 108, so a third nonzero is in row 3 whose value is 70. Since the pointer value is 0, there are no more nonzeroes in this column.

Now let us consider the storage operation when the input is of the form, (ROW NAME, ROW INFO, COLUMN NAME, COLUMN INFO). Our task here is to update the two trees and the memory pool of non-zeroes when we receive an input in this form. If a nonzero already exists in the position identified by (ROW NAME, COLUMN NAME), or if the row has been previously declared, but with different charac-teristics (e.g., right-hand-side), then we must decide whether this is to be declared an error or whether a revision is intended. We shall adopt the latter.

ALGORITHM HEREIS: Given (ROW NAME, TYPE, RHS, COLUMN NAME, BOUND, NONZERO VALUE),
The exogenous matrix file is updated by the implied addition or revision. If no room remains and an addition is required, control transfers to OVERFLOW.

step 1   (Find row number.): Execute algorithm NEWKEY with ROOT=ROOTR and (K,I)= (ROW NAME,* TYPE, RHS). If exit is DUPLICATE, go to step 3; else, continue.

step 2   (New row.): Set M ← M+1 and INFO (L, 1)=M, where L was returned by NEWKEY.

step 3   (Update row information.): Set i=INFO(L, 1), INFO(L, 2)= TYPE and INFO(L, 3)=RHS.

step 4   (Find column.): Execute algorithm NEWKEY with ROOT=ROOTC and (K,I)= (COLUMN NAME, BOUND,*). If exit is DUPLICATE, go to step 5; else go to step 6.

step 5   (Look for revision): Set h=INFO(L,2) and interrogate nonzero list (whose head is located by h). If i is present, change the nonzero value to NONZERO VALUE and EXIT.

step 6   (Add new nonzero.): add NONZERO VALUE to nonzero list (whose head is located by h), set INFO(L,2)=HEAD LOCATION and EXIT.

The use of '*' is merely to indicate anything can be put there since its value is not part of the input, and only the system knows what its value is. For example, the row index number (step 1) and the column pointer (step 4) are internal to the data structure design. It should also be noted that the addition of a row or a new nonzero may result in OVERFLOW, already considered by algorithm NEWKEY.

To illustrate how algorithm HEREIS may be employed for matrix generation consider the transportation problem with M sources and N destinations. Let us name the i-th source row as Si and the j-th destination row as Dj; let the activity corresponding to flow from source i to destination j be named SiDj. For example, for M=2 and N=3 we would have the diagram which appears on the following page.

	S 1 D 1	S 1 D 2	S 1 D 3	S 2 D 1	S 2 D 2	S 2 D 3	
OBJ	x	x	x	x	x	x	
S1	1	1	1				<=x
S2				1	1	1	<=x
D1	1			1			>=x
D2		1			1		>=x
D3			1			1	>=x
BOUNDS	x	x	x	x	x	x	

(where 'x' denotes an arbitrary nonzero, and 'OBJ' is the name of the objective row).

Consider a FORTRAN-like language that uses algorithm HEREIS as a subroutine to generate a matrix, given the dimensions (M, N) and the objective values in the array, COST (which is two-dimensional with COST (i, j) corresponding to the objective value of activity SiDj). Further, let SUPPLY and DEMAND be two 1-arrays to provide right-hand-sides for rows (Si) and (Dj), respectively.

PROGRAM TRANSGEN: This program generates the matrix for the transportation problem.

```
DIMENSION COST (10, 20), SUPPLY (10), DEMAND (20), BOUNDS
1(10, 20)

CALL INPUT (COST, BOUNDS, SUPPLY, DEMAND, M, N)

S='SO'

DO 10 I=1, M

S=INCR(S)

D='DO'

DO 10 J=1, N

D=INCR(D)

IF (BOUNDS(I,J).LE.O)GO TO 10

A=S&D

B=BOUNDS(I,J)
```

```
        CALL HEREIS (S, 'L', SUPPLY(I), A,B, 1)

        CALL HEREIS (D, 'G', DEMAND(J), A,B, 1)

        CALL HEREIS ('OBJ', 'N', 0, A, B, COST(I,J))

10      CONTINUE

        STOP

        END
```

Before we look at the effects of this primitive program, note the function 'INCR' is intended to increment the name with the rules that INCR('S1')='S2', etc. The definition of the assignment 'A=S&D' is the cacatenation, which we have added to the syntax.

Now consider the two trees generated. The row names appear in the order S1, D1, OBJ, D2, ..., Dn, S2, ..., Sm. This produces the following search tree:

Figure 7: Example Row Tree

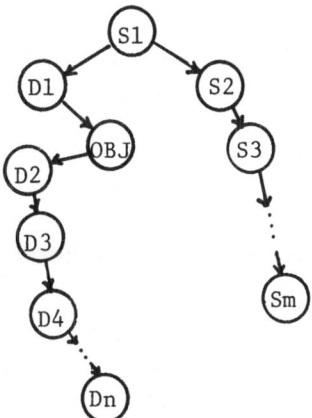

The column names are entered in sort order (i.e., lexicographically increasing) to yield the following:

134

Figure 8:   Example Column Tree

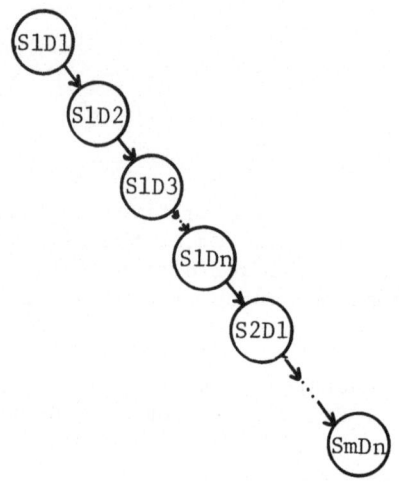

This situation is rather unfavorable if we were to retrieve on a
one-at-a-time basis because the tree depth is so great.

If the DO loops are reversed in program TRANSGEN, then the
order of declaration becomes:

    rows: D1, S1, OBJ, S2, ..., Sm, D2, ..., Dn
    columns: S1D1, S2D1, ..., SmD1, S1D2, S2D2, ...

This changes the shapes of the row and column trees and hence
changes the access time. The general question of optimal trees
has received some attention, but the issue here is much more
specialized and is an avenue for further research.

Now let us consider basic retrieval operations in some detail.
The INFO field of a node in the row or column tree may contain
solution information (which is inserted upon command once the
optimization process is executed). In that case retrieval is used
for report writing or for initiating the optimization process using a solution obtained previously. For rows we may include the
associated row activity level and the dual price; for columns we
may include activity level and the reduced cost. It is generally
recommended that solution information be kept in a separate file,
which we can call the SOLUTION FILE, rather than included in the

exogenous matrix file. This point is not crucial to the analysis of retrieval since the structure of the solution file would essentially be the same, although the INFO field would contain different information.

If a particular row is named, algorithm FINDKEY can be used to retrieve the associated information in the row tree; the same is true for retrieval in the column tree. Similarly, if an element is to be retrieved from the couple, (ROW NAME, COLUMN NAME), then we can first use ROW NAME to retrieve the row index number; then, we can interrogate the nonzero list for the column associated with COLUMN NAME. In both portions of the retrieval, algorithm FINDKEY can be used directly. However, it is common to specify a mask rather than just one name and retrieve the submatrix (maybe just a subset of rows or a subset of columns) for any names that match. It is less efficient to retrieve one-at-a-time ignoring the fact that we have a mask and starting at the root each time, than to consider mask retrieval directly.

Let us simplify the problem by considering only a column mask as input with the output being the associated columns, say as an array. For example, consider our transportation problem just described and suppose we assign 'S1.*' as the column mask. Then, we shall retrieve the following submatrix:

	S1D1	S1D2	...	S1Dn
S1	1	1	...	1
OBJ	COST(1,1)	COST(1,2)	...	COST(1,n)
D1	1			
D2		1		
.			.	
.				.
.				.
Dn				1

We shall <u>thread</u> the tree with the LLINK and RLINK values at terminal markers, and we shall use the sign bit to tag the distinction between an ordinary left or right link from a (upwards) thread to a sort neighbor as follows:

LLINK(node) =—sort predecessor if no left subtree.

RLINK(node) =—sort successor if no right subtree.

For example, our row tree would be threaded as follows (dotted arrows for threads):

Figure 9:   Example of Threaded Binary Search Tree

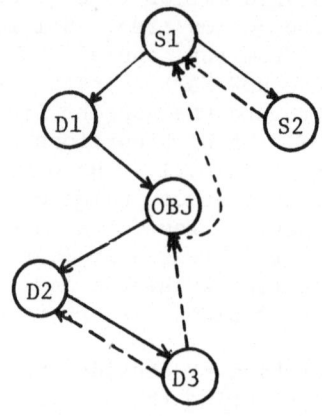

REPRESENTATION:

LOC	KEY	LLINK	RLINK
1	S1	2	6
2	D1	0	3
3	OBJ	4	-1
4	D2	-2	5
5	D3	-4	-3
6	S2	-1	0

Note that two terminal markers are retained (viz., D1 and S2), one for the first member and one for the last member of the sort order. We can apply algorithm FINDKEY to locate the node with the smallest key value matching the mask. Then we use the threads to traverse the tree in sort order, until the node with the largest key value is visited, by applying

ALGORITHM NEXT: Given the node at location, L, the location of
                 the node with the key in sort succession is put into
                 LNEXT.

                 step 1 (Test RLINK.): Set LNEXT=RLINK(L). If LNEXT <
                         0, set LNEXT ← -LNEXT and STOP. If LNEXT=0,
                         exit NONE.

step 2 (Search to left.): if LLINK(LNEXT > 0, set
LNEXT=LLINK (LNEXT) and repeat step 2; else,
STOP.

Applying algorithm NEXT at the node with key=D3 (so L=5), we
first set LNEXT=-3. Since this is negative, node 3 is determined
as the successor (with key=OBJ). If we apply it to node 1, we
enter step 2 with LNEXT=6. The first entrance into step 2 results
in termination with LNEXT remaining equal to 6 (so S2 follows S1
in the sourt order).

The efficiency of algorithm NEXT depends upon how many times
step 2 must be performed, so let us analyze this frequency.

What is the expected number of times step 2 must be performed if L is a "random" node in the tree? Knuth [6] shows that this
average is 1. A sketch of that proof is as follows. First, note
there are n+1 threads (or terminal links) in a tree with n nodes.
Therefore, the probability that step 2 is not executed at all is
(n+1)/2n, which is slightly more than 1/2. If step 2 is entered,
the chances of only one execution is (n-2)/2(n-1), slightly less
than 1/2. In general, the expected value is approximately

$$E_n \doteq 1/2 \quad (0)+ 1/4 \quad (1)+ 1/8 \quad (2)+ \ldots = \sum_{i=0}^{n-1} i \ (1/2)^{i+1}$$

$$\doteq 1 - (n+1) \quad (1/2)^n \approx 1.$$

We have considered the important storage and retrieval
operations associated with our exogenous matrix file using a binary
search tree as the basic data structure. We now wish to consider
additional operations associated with model revision.

Additions of rows or columns is in the mainstream of the
previous descriptions, and in-place revisions (such as changing a
bound value) can be handled with simple overwrite using algorithm
HEREIS. What remains is a method to perform deletions.

We shall begin by ignoring threads and consider the tree in
Figure 10 which appears on the following page. The keys appear
inside the node, and the sort order is indicated near each node.
We shall take the sort order number to be the location number
during this analysis.

The easiest deletion is when the node has empty left and
right subtrees, as in the case of node 6 (with key = M). Such
nodes are called leaves, and they may be deleted merely by breaking the link from the father node.

Figure 10: Example Binary Search Tree

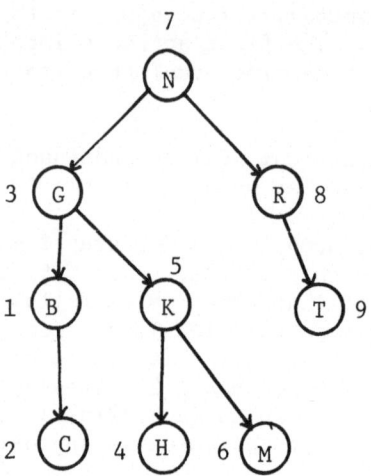

The next easiest case is when the node has one nonempty subtree, as for example node 1 (with key = B). In this case we
adjust the link of the father node to point to its son, i.e., have
node 3(G) point to node 2(C) instead of node 1(B), which then becomes deleted.

Now consider deleting node 5(K), which has two sons, 4(H) and
6(M). Every node in this subtree, with root at node 5, belongs in
the left subtree of node 3 (the father node of the one we wish to
delete). Therefore, sort order is maintained, except for the
position of K, if we exchange the contents (KEY and INFO) of node
5 with one of its subtree roots. The right subtree root, node 6,
may be chosen to produce:

Figure 11: Subtree for Deletion Operation

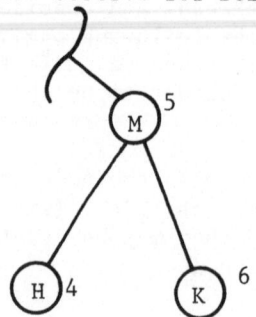

Now the node to be deleted is number 6. Since it is a leaf, we can complete the deletion.

The basic idea is to exchange the node to be deleted with one of its sons until it becomes a leaf or has only one son. In those cases deletion is trivially completed. Let us state the algorithm and then look at deleting node 3(G) in the tree illustrated in Figure 11.

ALGORITHM DELETE: Given a binary search tree and a node at location L with its father node at F such that LLINK(F)= L, this algorithm deletes the node at L while maintaining the conditions of a binary search tree.

  step 1   (Test for leaf.): If node L is a leaf, set
           LLINK(F) = LLINK(L) and STOP; else, set L1 =
           LLINK(L) and L2 = RLINK(L).

  step 2   (Test for empty subtree.): If L1 = 0, set
           LLINK(F) = L2 and STOP; else if L2= 0, set
           LLINK(F) = L1 and STOP; else, go to step 3.

  step 3   (Exchange.): Set T = KEY(L), KEY(L) = KEY(L1),
           KEY(L1) = T, INFO(L) = INFO(L1), F = L, L = L1
           and go to step 1.

Let us apply algorithm DELETE to our binary search tree pictured above for L = 3(G) and F = 7(N). Since node 3 is not a leaf, we enter step 2 with L1 = 1 and L2 = 5. Both subtrees are nonempty, so we proceed to step 3 where we exchange nodes 1 and 3. This procedure leads to the following:

Figure 12:   Example of Deleting a Node with
             Algorithm
             DELETE

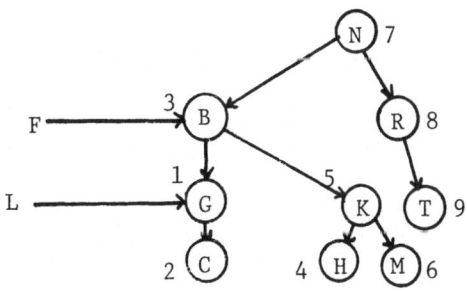

Note that F and L were reset to 3 and 1, respectively. We next go back to Step 1. Node 1 is not a leaf, so we set L1=0 and L2=2. We enter step 2 to find only one subtree. This results in setting LLINK(3)=2, thereby deleting (logically) node 1. We then have

Figure 13: A Next Step in Applying Algorithm DELETE.

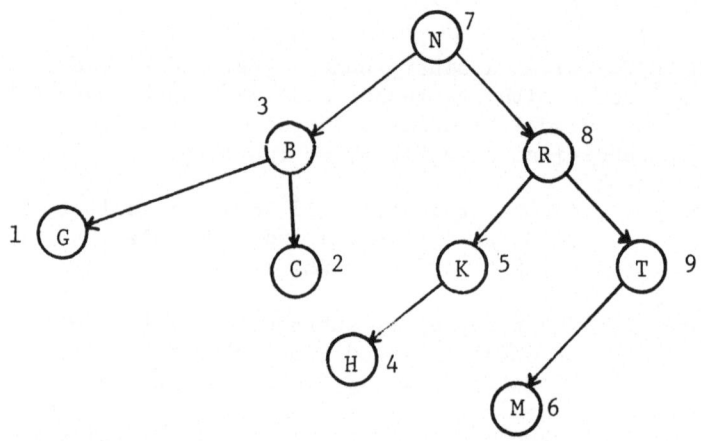

If the node to be deleted is the right son of its father (i.e., RLINK(F)=L), then a similar algorithm applies, except we exchange to the right.

In conclusion, it is to be emphasized that the binary search tree is not the only (or best) candidate for representing the exogenous matrix file. It is a useful starting point. Alternatives are beyond the scope of this tutorial.

ACKNOWLEDGEMENT

Much of the material in this tutorial is based upon unpublished works of James E. Kalan (University of Texas) and Dennis C. Rarick (Management Science Systems). I am grateful for having learned from each of them.

Bibliographic Notes

Sparsity schemes were introduced to LP codes by
William Orchard-Hays (see references 4 and 9). The processing of
sparse matrices has received a great deal of attention by others
as well (see references 2, 11 and 12). Comparative discussions
on different structures, in particular bit map versus pointer
list for placement of nonzeroes, has appeared in references 3, 7,
8, 9 and 10. The notion of the partitioning scheme (PSC), and
the inverted file structure (ISC) is due to Kalan [5]. For broad
coverage of hashing (as in ISC) and for searching (as in the
operations on the exogenous matrix file) see references 2, 6 and
10. Advanced features, in particular complexity analysis, may
be found in references 1 and 6.

REFERENCES

1) A. V. Aho, J. E. Hopcroft and J. D. Ullman (1974), The Design and Analysis of Computer Algorithms, Addison-Wesley, Reading, MA.

2) G. G. Dodd (1969) "Elements of Data Management Systems," ACM Comp. Surv., 1, 117-133.

3) H. J. Greenberg and J.E. Kalan (1976), "Representations of Networks," NCC Proceedings, N.Y., 939-943.

4) H. A. Judd (1956), "The Storage Allocation of the LP Code, " RAND Rept. P-907, Santa Monica, California.

5) J. E. Kalan (1971), "Aspects of Large-Scale, In-Core Linear Programming," Proc. ACM., 304-313.

6) D. Knuth (1968), The Art of Computer Programming, Volumes 1 and 3, Addison-Wesley, Reading, MA.

7) D. Lefkovitz (1975), "The Large Data Base File Structure Dilemma," J. of Chem. Inf. & C.S., 15, 14-19.

8) D. T. MacVeigh (1975), Effect of Data Representation on Efficiency of Sparse Matrix Operations, Masters Thesis, University of North Carolina, Chapel Hill, N.C.

9) W. Orchard-Hays (1968), Advanced Linear Programming Computing Techniques, McGraw-Hill, New York, N.Y.

10) U. W. Pooch and A. Nieder (1973), "A Survey of Indexing Techniques for Sparse Matrices," ACM Comp. Surv., 5, 109-133.

11) J. K. Reid (1971), Large Sets of Linear Equations, Academic Press, New York, N.Y.

12) R. A. Willoughby (1969 and 1972), Sparse Matrix Proceedings, IBM, Yorktown Heights, N.Y.

PIVOT SELECTION TACTICS

HARVEY J. GREENBERG

Energy Information Administration
Washington, D.C.   20461

INTRODUCTION

The simplex method iterates by ascertaining whether the current basis can be improved by an exchange between two columns. This raises many tactical variations aimed at reducing overall computing cost to reach a conclusion. In order to understand some of these options and their relative merits we shall first proceed along the rationale introduced by Dantzig in his original form of the simplex method which inherently defines a pivot selection rule. Moreover, we shall temporarily impose the following conditions:

(1)   the current basis is feasible,

(2)   feasibility shall be maintained,

(3)   only a nonbasic activity can be a candidate for the incoming vector.

Let us consider what happens if we keep all nonbasic activities at their current bound, but we allow the j-th activity level to vary by the amount of change, t. In order to maintain the equations we require

$$B\ Z(t) + t\ A_j = b',$$

where B is the current basis, $Z(.)$ is the vector of associated basic activity levels, A_j is the column associated with the j-th activity, and b' is the right-hand-side translated to account for nonbasic activities at nonzero bound. Multiplying by B^{-1} we observe the more tractible form given by

$$Z(t) = BETA - t\ (B^{-1}\ A_j),$$

where $BETA = B^{-1}b'$ (the current activity levels of the basic variables).

The objective function, $z(t)$, is one of the basics, say the 0-th. Letting c_0 be the associated unit vector we can extract the 0-th equation by

$$z(t) = (e_0, BETA) - t\ (e_0 B^{-1}, A_j).$$

We note that the only dependence on j is the column, A_j, residing in the (endogenous) matrix file. We would first compute $e_0 B^{-1}$ and store it as an array which we call PI; then, the effect of changing the j-th activity level on the objective value is given by the equation

$$z(t) = OBJ - t\ (PI, A_j),$$

where $OBJ = (e_0, BETA)$ (the current objective value). The change in objective function value is therefore given by the product,

$$\Delta z(t) = t\ D_j,$$

where $D_j = (PI, A_j)$ (the <u>reduced cost</u>).

Recapitulating what we have so far, we form a <u>pricing vector</u>, PI, by transforming the objective vector relative to the current basis; namely, forming $PI = e_0 B^{-1}$. Upon considering activity j we form the inner product between the pricing vector and the associated column in the matrix file. This inner product is the reduced cost and measures the rate of change in the objective value.

Under condition 2 we know that the actual activity level of the j-th vector will be restricted, so its change (t) can be of only one sign. Namely, if the j-th activity is at lower bound, then we require t> = 0, and if it is at upper bound, then we require t< = 0. Therefore, without actually knowing what value t could be without violating feasibility for the basic variables, we can reject an activity if its reduced cost is not of the same sign required by t (in order to have no increase in the objective we seek to minimize). Dantzig's rule in the early version of the simplex method finds the nonbasic activity whose reduced cost is of appropriate sign and is largest in magnitude. The rationale is that choosing the activity with the largest rate of improvement "should" produce the best improvement. Subsequent experimentation has led to discoveries which we shall consider shortly. For now we consider Dantzig's initial candidate selection rule, namely choosing the activity whose reduced cost is largest (in magnitude) among those of appropriate sign (to improve the objective function). This results in half the pivot selection rule since this defines only the incoming activity. Before considering the other half, let us state this portion as a pricing algorithm.

ALGORITHM MAXDJ: Given PI this algorithm finds the activity having largest absolute reduced cost of nonoptimal sign. If this is positive, the internal id is stored into J.

step 1 (initialize): set DJ=0 and J=1.

step 2 (compute reduced cost): if activity is basic, go to step 5; else, set $d=(PI,A_j)$.

step 3 (truncate): if activity j is at upper bound, set $d \leftarrow -d$.

step 4 (test): if d<=DJ, go to step 5; else, set $DJ \leftarrow d$ and $J \leftarrow id(j)$.

step 5 (next): increment $j \leftarrow j+1$; if j<=n, go to step 2; else, STOP.

If we exit this algorithm with DJ=0, then this means the current basis is optimal, and we are ready to terminate the optimization process. On the other hand, if an incoming vector is found, then we begin the third phase, namely, row selection.

Returning to our equations of the form,

$$Z(t) = BETA - t\ (B^{-1}A_j),$$

we can determine the greatest magnitude of t that maintains feasibility. First we form

$$ALPHA = B^{-1}A_j,$$

which transforms the vector, A_j, into coordinates relative to our current basis. We may then consider the i-th basic variable with the equation

$$Z_i(t) = BETA_i - t\ ALPHA_i.$$

If t is to be non-negative (determined by the sign of the j-th reduced cost), then Z_i decreases if $ALPHA_i > 0$ and increases if $ALPHA_i < 0$. This means that if $|t|$ were permitted to become large enough, a bound imposed on the i-th basic variable may become violated. The threshold is found by solving

$$\text{BOUND} = \text{BETA}_i - t \, \text{ALPHA}_i \; .$$

Table I below lists all possibilities for the incoming (non-basic) status (at lower bound, so change is to be nonnegative, or at upper bound, so change is to be nonpositive). If the i-th basic variable is "free" (i.e., both bounds are infinite), then it cannot block the incoming variable (i.e., imposes no limit on the change). However, if at least one of the bounds is finite, then for $|t|$ large enough the i-th basic variable would be driven to an infeasible activity level. The thresholds are the entries in Table I.

For example, if both bounds are finite and $\text{ALPHA}_i > 0$, then increasing values of t from zero (so $t > 0$) would drive the value of $Z_i(t)$ to the lower bound, a_i, when t reaches the value $(\text{BETA}_i - a_i)/\text{ALPHA}_i$. Similarly, if t decreases from zero (so $t < 0$), then $Z_i(t)$ increases for $\text{ALPHA}_i > 0$ and reaches its upper bound when $t = (\text{BETA}_i - u_i)/\text{ALPHA}_i$.

TABLE I. Thresholds imposed by the i-th basic variable on the change in activity level of the incoming variable

INCOMING BASIC	SLOPE	AT LOWER BOUND ($t \geq 0$)	AT UPPER BOUND ($t \leq 0$)
FREE ($a_i = -\infty, u_i = \infty$)		∞	$-\infty$
LOWER BOUND ONLY ($a_i > -\infty, u_i = \infty$)	$\text{ALPHA}_i > 0$	$(\text{BETA}_i - a_i)/\text{ALPHA}_i$	$-\infty$
	$\text{ALPHA}_i < 0$	∞	$(\text{BETA}_i - u_i)/\text{ALPHA}_i$
UPPER BOUND ONLY ($a_i = -\infty \; u_i < \infty$)	$\text{ALPHA} > 0$	∞	$(\text{BETA}_i - u_i)/\text{ALPHA}_i$
	$\text{ALPHA} < 0$	$(\text{BETA}_i - u_i)/\text{ALPHA}_i$	$-\infty$
BOTH BOUNDS ($a_i > -\infty, u_i < \infty$)	$\text{ALPHA}_i > 0$	$(\text{BETA}_i - a_i)/\text{ALPHA}_i$	$(\text{BETA}_i - u_i)/\text{ALPHA}_i$
	$\text{ALPHA}_i < 0$	$(\text{BETA}_i - u_i)/\text{ALPHA}_i$	$(\text{BETA}_i - a_i)/\text{ALPHA}_i$

Further, an incoming variable may block itself and merely switch from one bound to its other one. In this case there is no pivot exchange, and the basis remains current. Of course, the change in the nonbasic status is recorded, and BETA is updated to account for the changes in activity levels. Note that in this case the same PI vector is used for the next iteration.

If we agree to break ties arbitrarily, then Table I can be used to construct an algorithm that makes the row choice for an incoming vector. Namely, if the variable blocks itself, then no pivot exchange takes place and we update as we just described above. If no basic variable is blocking (i.e. all thresholds are infinite), and if the variable does not block itself, then we have reached a conclusion, namely the objective is unbounded. (To see this, note that we may proceed to drive the incoming variable to infinity while maintaining feasibility and improving the objective function at a rate equal to the reduced cost.) In the remaining case a basic variable is blocking, and this defines the <u>pivot row</u>, or equivalently the vector to leave the basis in exchange with the incoming vector.

However, instead of testing which case we are to look up for each nonzero $ALPHA_i$, we may proceed to define a limiting value, THETA, for the change, which is initially equal to the bound difference, u_j-a_j (or the negative, as appropriate). This may be infinite since the bounds need not be finite. Then, we may test our limit for each nonzero $ALPHA_i$ to see if the i-th basic variable would exceed any of its bounds, keeping a machine representation of infinity to avoid special tests. Thus, THETA may become reduced (in magnitude), and it will reach its least (absolute) value at a <u>blocking</u> basic variable, if any exists. The following algorithm proceeds along these lines.

ALGORITHM CHUZR: Given BETA, ALPHA and THETA= $(u_j-a_j)sign(D_j)$, the basic variables are scanned for possible blockage. If the i-th basic variable is blocking, then p is set to i; otherwise, if there are no blocking variables, p is set to 0.

> step 1 (initialize): set p=0 and perform step 2 for i: $ALPHA_i \neq 0$.

> step 2 (test threshold): compute z=$BETA_i$-THETA*$ALPHA_i$.

>> (a) If z < a_i, set THETA←($BETA_i-a_i$)/$ALPHA_i$, p←i, and z←$BETA_i$-THETA*$ALPHA_i$; else, continue to (b).

>> (b) If z>u_i, set THETA←($BETA_i-u_i$)/$ALPHA_i$, p←i.

After termination of algorithm CHUZR we test THETA against infinity; if equal, then we conclude unboundedness; otherwise, we test p. If p=0, then the variable blocks itself, and we perform the simple update of switching to its other bound, with no change of basis; otherwise, the value of p identifies the basic variable to depart, or more directly identifies the pivot row choice by which the exchange can be made.

We now wish to consider some of the variations in the pivot selection rule just described. There are three phases to pivot selection (not counting the actual update which follows); namely, we have

(1) form a dual price vector, PI;

(2) price activities to obtain one or more candidates or else ascertain the current basis is optimal;

(3) choose the pivot row and one of the incoming candidates or else ascertain the problem is unbounded or else indicate a simple change of nonbasic bound status.

PHASE I

Let us begin with forming the dual price vector, PI. Under the stated conditions it was a simple matter of setting the COST vector to e_0 and then transforming to $PI=COST*B^{-1}$. If the objective is a composite of rows, say the sum of rows 0 and 1 in the matrix file, then we would simply set $COST=e_0 + e_1$ and obtain PI in the same manner. In general, we can obtain any linear combination of rows of B^{-1} by setting COST to the coordinates and then transforming by the equation $PI=COST*B^{-1}$. Our concern in forming the dual price, at least for the present, is exclusively with the formation of COST. The tricky case is when the current basis is not feasible, so the objective function is chosen to drive towards feasibility using the basic mechanism of linear programming, and the simplex method in particular.

If a basic variable is feasible (i.e., its activity level is within its bounds), then we do not want it to contribute to the objective function, at least not for the approach we shall consider here. If a basic variable violates its lower bound (i.e., $BETA_i < a_i$), then we wish to drive it up (i.e., increase its activity level); if it violates its upper bound (i.e, $BETA_i > u_i$), then we wish to drive it down (i.e., decrease its activity level). We may not be able to simultaneously drive all violations towards feasibility, so we consider what we can do to ensure that the sum of the infeasibility tends to diminish. That is, we want the pricing algorithm, once it has PI, to select only those candidates which show a rate of decrease for the sum of infeasibility. Our only question, therefore, is what COST vector accomplishes this?

The true sum of infeasibility, as a function of the variables, is not linear (and is zero over feasible points), but we can use linear programming if we consider local behavior only. That is, we want COST to reflect a direction towards decreasing the sum of infeasibility. This can be accomplished by setting COST as follows:

$$
COST_i = \begin{cases} 1 & \text{if } BETA_i > u_i \\ -1 & \text{if } BETA_i < a_i \\ 0 & \text{otherwise.} \end{cases}
$$

To see this let us develop an expression for the sum of infeasibility as a function of the driving parameter, t. Assuming t is of appropriate sign and sufficiently small in magnitude, the only feasibility violations will be in the basic variables. Consider the i-th basic variable, $Z_i(t)$, which satisfies the basic equation,

$$
Z_i(t) = BETA_i - t \, ALPHA_i.
$$

Then, the contribution to the sum of infeasibility by the i-th basic variable is as follows:

$$
f_i(t) = \begin{cases} a_i - Z_i(t) & \text{if } Z_i(t) < a_i \\ Z_i(t) - u_i & \text{if } Z_i(t) > u_i \\ 0 & \text{else.} \end{cases}
$$

We shall find it useful to introduce the following notation:

$$
(X)^+ = \begin{cases} X & \text{if } X > 0 \\ 0 & \text{else.} \end{cases}
$$

Then, we may write

$$
f_i(t) = (a_i - Z_i(t))^+ + (Z_i(t) - u_i)^+.
$$

If $BETA_i < a_i$, then

$$
f_i(t) = a_i - BETA_i + t \, ALPHA_i \quad \text{for } |t| \text{ sufficiently small,}
$$

so $-ALPHA_i$ is the rate of decrease of infeasibility of the i-th basic variable. If $BETA_i > u_i$, then

$$f_i(t) = BETA_i - t\ ALPHA_i - u_i \text{ for } |t| \text{ sufficiently small,}$$

so $ALPHA_i$ is the rate of decrease of infeasibility of the i-th basic variable. Temporarily ignoring degeneracy (where $BETA_i$ equals one of the bounds, a_i or u_i), the only remaining case is when $a_i < BETA_i < u_i$. In this case,

$$f_i(t) = 0 \text{ for } |t| \text{ sufficiently small,}$$

so the rate of change is zero.

Thus, we want COST to be chosen such that

$$RATE = (COST*B^{-1}, A_i) = \sum_{i \in I^-} ALPHA_i + \sum_{i \in I^+} ALPHA_i,$$

where

$$I^- \equiv \{i: COST_i = -1\} \quad \text{and} \quad I^+ = \{i: COST_i = 1\} .$$

In summary, by setting COST to the vector above, placing +1, -1 or 0 in coordinates which correspond to activity levels which currently violate the upper bound, lower bound or neither (i.e., feasible), respectively, we obtain a PI vector which lets us compute the rate of change in the sum of infeasibility for an activity by computing the usual inner prosuct, (PI, A_j). In the absence of degeneracy, this value is precisely the desired rate; more generally, it is an optimistic estimate, not accounting for the new infeasibilities that would be introduced even for marginal change.

Using a row selection rule which does not permit new infeasibilities, we may obtain zero gain in the degenerate case (depending upon the sign of the associated ALPHA-vector coordinate). Let us defer this point until later, but we may immediately note some variations in our choice of COST-vector. For example, we could select the index, say q, corresponding the most violated bound-- i.e., largest $f_i(0)$ value. Then, upon setting $COST = e_q$, we are tending to minimize the maximum infeasibility, and $(COST, ALPHA) = ALPHA_q$ yields the rate of change. Since degeneracy would not contribute to the rate of this change, our measure is exact unless there is a tie (i.e., q not unique); however, we still may obtain zero gain if the row selection rule does not permit new infeasibilities.

Algorithm FORMSUM (below) forms the PI vector in accordance with what we have described. While we have indicated that phase I (infeasibility) has many variations, we have not mentioned the types of PI-vectors that can be useful during phase II; only the prescribed objective COST has been considered, yielding the usual reduced cost for pricing. We shall correct this oversight when analyzing pricing tactics.

ALGORITHM FORMSUM: Given the feasibility status, the row id of the (phase II) objective, say row 0, and given the BETA vector, the PI vector is formed to be used during pricing.

      step 1 (initialize): if the basis is feasible, set COST=0, $COST_0$=1 and go to step 3; else, perform step 2 for each i.

      step 2 (form phase I objective): set $COST_i$=0. if $BETA_i$< a_i, set $COST_i$ = -1; else, if $BETA_i$> u_i, set $COST_i$ = 1.

      step 3 (transform COST): compute the solution to the linear system, PI*B = COST.

Now we consider pivot row selection and algorithm CHUZR in particular.

For definiteness, and to avoid tedious notation, let us temporarily suppose all variables are simple nonnegative (so a_j=0 and u_j = ∞ for all j). We know phase I cannot result in a conclusion of unboundedness since the sum of infeasibility is bounded by zero. Therefore, a basic variable must be blocking, say the p-th, so that

$$THETA = BETA_p/ALPHA_p,$$

where $ALPHA_p$> 0. (Note the associated entry in Table I.)

If $BETA_p$ >0 (i.e., if the p-th basic variable is currently feasible), then the interpretation of "blocking" is accurate under our condition of disallowing new infeasibilities. However, if $BETA_p$< 0, this means the p-th basic variable is currently infeasible and is driven up to zero from its negative activity level. This disagrees with the meaning of "blocking," and we feel motivated to let the variable pass through zero, yielding no blockage on the incoming variable (although the rate reflected by D_j is no longer accurate, so care must be taken if this is the only remaining infeasibility). Unfortunately, algorithm CHUZR would look at the threshold,

$$z = BETA_p - THETA*ALPHA_p$$

and test if z<0. Since THETA >=0, $BETA_p$ <0 and $ALPHA_p$ >0, we would conclude z<0 and modify THETA to the (negative) value, $BETA_p/ALPHA_p$. This results in an incorrect value of THETA!

The problem is that if the basic variable is currently in-feasible, we should permit it to pass through its threshold value into feasible range; that is, do not declare it blocking. Further, if an infeasible activity is tending further away from its feasible range, we should let it do so and not declare it blocking (which means a reversal in the direction of the incoming variable); we are assured that other variables are moving towards feasibility at a combined rate large enough to offset this unfavorable move-ment (since D_j > 0). For the present, we retain the rule which does not permit new infeasibilities and traps a variable once it enters its feasible range. This means that while we permit a basic variable to increase above its lower bound (become feasible from below), we do not allow it to violate its upper bound. The rationale is that it is "good" to keep the number of infeasibili-ties low.

ALGORITHM CHRUZI: This algorithm extends algorithm CHUZR to account for phase I blockage.

    step 1 (initialize): If the system is in phase II, execute algorithm CHUZR and STOP; else, set p= 0 and perform step 2 for i: $ALPHA_i$ $\neq$0.

    step 2 (test threshold): compute z= $BETA_i$ - THETA* $ALPHA_i$.

        (a) If z<a_i and $BETA_i$> =a_i, set THETA=($BETA_i$- a_i)/$ALPHAi$, z = $BETA_i$ - THETA*$ALPHA_i$, p=i; else continue to (b).

        (b) If z >u_i and $BETA_i$ <=u_i, set THETA=($BETA_i$- u_i)/$ALPHAi$ and p = i.

Note that step 1 transfers to algorithm CHUZR if we are in phase II. This is to avoid the extra tests in step 2 for each nonzero $ALPHA_i$. Further, note that no blockage occurs when z<a_i and $BETA_i$< a_i since this means either we are driving the i-th basic vari-able towards its feasible range and permit it to pass through a_i, or we are driving it further away and could do nothing about it here.

To see when algorithm CHUZRI necessarily yields a strict de-crease, let us examine the actual sum of infeasibility. For con-venience let us again temporarily suppose that all variables are simply nonnegative, except the row variable associated with the objective which we shall designate as the 0-th basic variable (i.e., a_j = 0 and u_j = ∞ for all j >0, and a_0= -u_0 = -∞). Recall we defined the function,

$$(X)^+ \equiv \begin{cases} X & \text{if } X > 0 \\ 0 & \text{else.} \end{cases}$$

Then, the sum of infeasibility is given by

$$S(t) \equiv \sum_{i=i}^{m} (t \text{ ALPHA}_i - \text{BETA}_i)^+ .$$

In particular, the current sum of infeasibility is

$$S(0) = \sum_{i=i}^{m} (-\text{BETA}_i)^+ .$$

Consider a small change, $t = \varepsilon > 0$, and partition the indices according to the following:

$$I^- = i:\{\text{BETA}_i < 0\}, \quad I^0 = \{i: \text{BETA}_i = 0\} \quad \text{and} \quad I^+ = \{i: \text{BETA}_i > 0\}.$$

Then, for ε sufficiently small we have

$$S(\varepsilon) = \sum_{i \in I^-} (\varepsilon \text{ ALPHA}_i - \text{BETA}_i) + \sum_{i \in I^0} \varepsilon (\text{ALPHA}_i)^+$$

$$= \varepsilon \{ \sum_{i \in I^-} \text{ALPHA}_i + \sum_{i \in I^0} (\text{ALPHA}_i)^+ \} + S(0),$$

where we note

$$S(0) = \sum_{i \in I^-} (-\text{BETA}_i).$$

Recall how COST was formed in algorithm FORMSUM. The resulting reduced cost satisfies

$$D_j \equiv (\text{COST } B^{-1}, A_j) = (\text{COST, } B^{-1}A_j) = (\text{COST, ALPHA}).$$

In scalar notation we have

$$D_j = \sum_{i \in I^-} \text{ALPHA}_i .$$

In other words, the reduced cost, used to indicate rate of change in the sum of infeasibility, is the sum of coordinates of the ALPHA-vector associated with infeasible basic variables (i.e., with $i:$ $\text{BETA}_i < 0$).

Substituting this into our equation for $S(\varepsilon)$ we obtain

$$S(\varepsilon)-S(0) = - \varepsilon(D_j - \sum_{i \in I^0}(ALPHA_i)^+).$$

We selected j because its reduced cost is positive (i.e., $D_j>0$). Therefore, the only way to have

$$S(\varepsilon)>=S(0) \text{ for } \underline{all} \ \varepsilon \text{ sufficiently small}$$

is to have

$$\sum_{i \in I^0}(ALPHA_i)^+ \geq D_j.$$

In this case the gain will be zero, and the incoming variable is blocked by a degenerate basic variable. In the absence of degeneracy, I^0 is empty, so

$$S(\varepsilon)<S(0) \text{ for all } \varepsilon \text{ sufficiently small.}$$

This results in positive gain, meaning that the (global) sum of infeasibility strictly decreases.

Thus, as in phase II we have a simple proof of positive gain and hence of convergence if we assume no degeneracy.

Now let us consider another row selection scheme to be used during phase I aimed at further reducing the sum of infeasibility. Let us continue to maintain all variables simply nonnegative (except the objective row activity). Let us also maintain that the incoming variable must have a feasible activity level (so $t \geq 0$). However, let us relax the condition that all feasible basic variables must remain feasible. Instead, we shall solve the one-variable, non-linear optimization problem,

$$\text{minimize } S(t): t \geq 0.$$

We do not yet know if a solution exists with the property that one of the basic variables will be driven to zero (its only bound), thereby retaining the basic simplex method which relies on such a pivot exchange. Therefore, let us impose this as a condition, at least until we are ready to prove the imposition unnecessary.

Then, there are a finite number of vaules for t, and the best one (i.e., yielding minimal sum of infeasibility) is THETA. Namely, we consider the thresholds defined by

$$T_i = \begin{cases} BETA_i/ALPHA_i & \text{if } i\epsilon I \\ \infty & \text{else,} \end{cases}$$

where $\quad I \equiv \{i>0: ALPHA_i \neq 0 \text{ and } BETA_i/ALPHA_i \geq 0\}.$

Then, $\quad S(T_k) = \sum_{i=1}^{m} (T_k ALPHA_i - BETA_i)^+$ for $k\epsilon I$,

and we choose the index $p \epsilon I$ to

minimize $\{S(T_k): k\epsilon I\}.$

(Note that I cannot be empty if $D_j > 0$.)

A brute force method to perform the minimization is to explicitly compute $S(T_k)$ for every k in I and select the minimal one to be p (breaking ties arbitrarily for now). We shall consider a better scheme which requires only two passes through the ALPHA vector and avoids computation of the sum of infeasibility.

To help focus our ideas let us consider the following example:

row index	transformed vector	basic activity level	threshold	sum of infeasibility
i	$ALPHA_i$	$BETA_i$	T_i	$S(T_i)$
1	2	-10	∞	∞
2	3	9	3	16
3	-4	-8	2	14
4	-2	-2	1	16
-	-	-	0	20 current

Figure 1 shows the (global) sum of infeasibility, $S(t)$, as a function of the driving variable, t. Let us review the construction of this curve.

Throughout, the first basic variable is moving further away from its feasible range (by the equation $Z_1(t)=-10-2t$) at a rate of 2 (per unit of t). Variable two is currently feasible and will not contribute to the sum of infeasibility until t >3. Variables three and four are both moving towards feasibility at a combined initial rate of -6. Thus, the reduced cost is 4 (minus the sum of ALPHA vector coordinates associated with infeasible activities (i.e., with i: $BETA_i<0$)). This is the initial rate of decrease (-slope) shown in the sum of infeasibility curve.

At t=1 the status of the fourth basic variable changes since it then becomes feasible. Only variables one and three continue to be infeasible, and the rate of change increases to -2. The sum of infeasibility continues to decrease, but at the increased rate, -2, until t=2. Now the third variable becomes feasible. At this point the sum of infeasibility starts to increase at a rate of 2, corresponding here to the movement in variable one. At t=3 variable two becomes zero and is about to contribute to the sum of infeasibility at a rate of 3. Thus, the rate of change of the sum of infeasibility increases to 5 and remains constant for t>3 (since there are no additional changes in status).

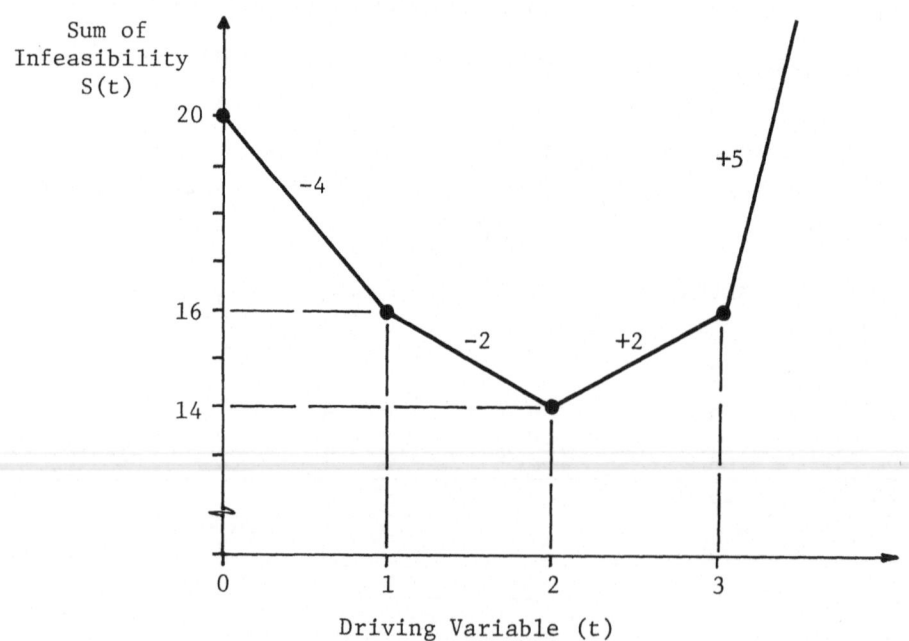

Figure 3.1: SUM OF INFEASIBILITY CURVE FOR EXAMPLE-- SLOPES INDICATED ABOVE EACH LINEAR PORTION

We notice that $S(t)$ is piece-wise linear, having a constant rate between threshold values. At each threshold value, the rate increases (in general may remain constant, but cannot decrease). After the final threshold value, $S(t)$ is linearly increasing at constant rate.

Figure 2 illustrates another possibility, where the rate of change is 0 between two threshold values. This can even occur initially, corresponding to the case of zero gain. Figure 3 illustrates the case when the sum of infeasibility can be driven to zero, which happens once (at most) during phase I.

Taking Figure 1 as the "typical" case (but not ignoring the other cases), we accept the fact that $S(t)$ has the indicated properties. Roughly, the reason for the nondecreasing rates of change is that the function, $S(t)$, changes linearly until a basic variable changes its status. If it goes from infeasible to feasible, the rate begins to include the new movement away from feasibility. Thus, in either case the rate worsens (i.e., increases). Further, these status changes happen only at threshold values.

We now consider a two-pass scheme. Begin by computing thresholds, maintaining sort order on the threshold values. In the second pass start with

$$\text{RATE} = -D_j < 0,$$

and adjust RATE by ALPHA_{p_K} when considering the k-th (sorted) threshold value corresponding to variable p_K. As long as RATE<0 we continue; the first time RATE >=0, we stop with the previous basic row index as our optimal choice of p (with T_p= THETA). Notice this works properly in the cases illustrated by Figure 2 and Figure 3. Also note that THETA is globally minimal, so the imposition which requires $t=T_i$ for some i in I is unnecessary.

This is described by the following

ALGORITHM CHUZRGLOBAL: Given D_j, ALPHA and BETA in phase I, a pivot row (p) is selected to minimize the sum of infeasibility.

step 1 (initiate): perform step 2 for i: $\text{ALPHA}_i \neq 0$, then set RATE=$-D_j$, k=1 and go to step 3.

step 2 (compute threshold): set T= ∞.

i) if $\text{BETA}_i < a_i$ and $\text{ALPHA}_i < 0$, set T = $(\text{BETA}_i - a_i)/\text{ALPHA}_i$; else, if $\text{BETA}_i > u_i$

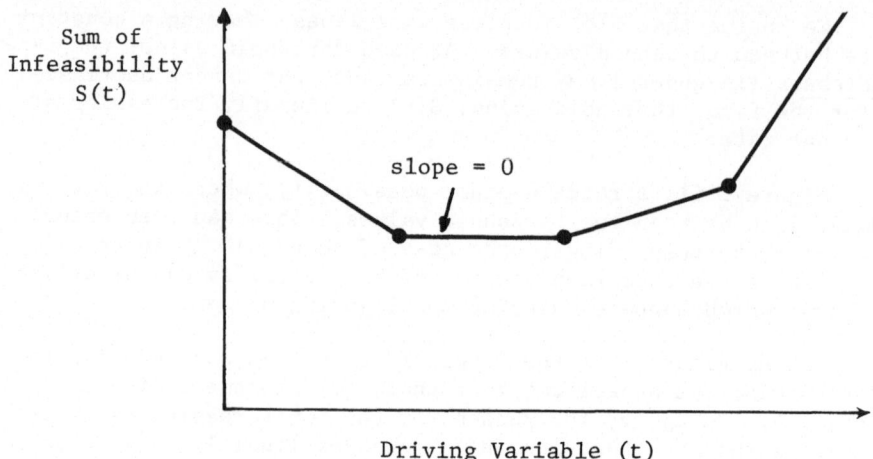

Figure 3.2:   ILLUSTRATION OF ALTERNATIVE GLOBAL MINIMA,
              WHERE THE RATE IS ZERO BETWEEN TWO THRESHOLDS

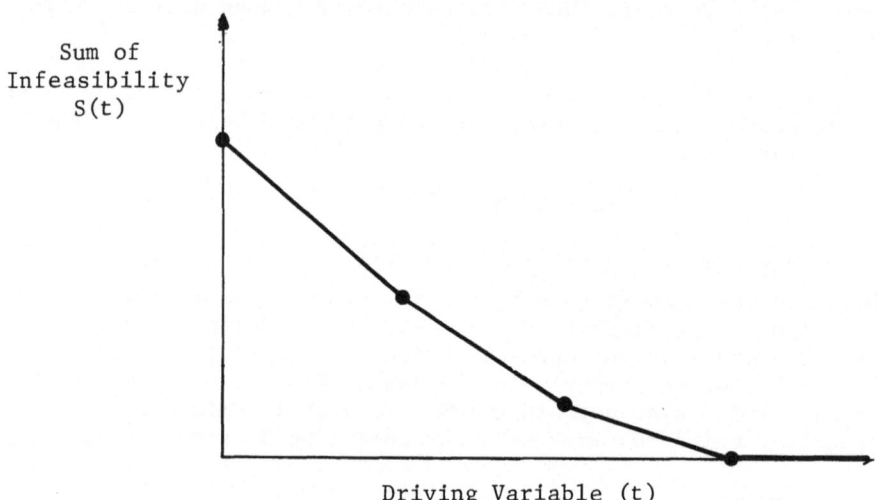

Figure 3.3:   ILLUSTRATION OF SUM OF INFEASIBILITY REACHING ZERO

and $ALPHA_i > 0$, set $T = (BETA_i - u_i)/ALPHA_i$;
else, if $ALPHA_i < 0$ and $a_i > -\infty$, set
$T = (BETA_i - a_i)/ALPHA_i$; else if $ALPHA_i > 0$ and $u_i < \infty$, set $T = (BETA_i - u_i)/ALPHA_i$.

ii) enter (T, i) into list sorted by T.

step 3 (traverse list to find best pivot row): set RATE $\leftarrow$ RATE-$ALPHA_{i_k}$. if RATE $\geq$ 0, STOP; else, set $p = i_k$,

increment k and repeat step 3.

Let us apply algorithm CHUZRGLOBAL to our example. Steps 1 and 2 result in the following:

k	T(k)	ID(k)
1	1	4
2	2	3
3	3	2
4	∞	1

At step 3 we begin with RATE=-4 ($-D_j$). For k=1 we have i_1=ID(1)=4, so RATE$\leftarrow$RATE-$ALPHA_4$=-4-(-2). Since RATE <0, set $p = i_1$=4. The next member (k=2) has i_2=ID(2)=3, so RATE$\leftarrow$RATE-$ALPHA_3$=-2-(-4)=2. Since RATE > 0, we STOP with p=4 our pivot row selection.

PRICING

Now we turn our attention to pricing tactics. Recall that algorithm MAXDJ interrogates every nonbasic activity and selects the one activity whose absolute reduced cost is largest. Three of the implied rules imbedded in that description is that "every" activity is interrogated, only "one" activity is selected, and the criteria used in the selection is the "reduced cost". We shall consider variations in all of these rules, but one condition that so far seems needed is the conclusion we can make if all reduced costs show rates of degradation in the objective. Despite the fact that this state is reached only once, it seems necessary to include a computation of reduced cost to detect optimality; we also want these reduced costs available when we reach optimality because they provide sensitivity information for the user. Before we consider broader issues of tactical variations in the three rules noted, let us observe one of the simple improvements.

If a variable is fixed (i.e., its bounds are finite and equal), then it must block (i.e., the change must be zero). Therefore, regardless of how large its reduced cost may be, the actual change

in objective value (i.e., the _gain_) is zero. Further, if we would
enter it into the basis anyway, it would block the next entry whose
ALPHA coordinate is not zero. This means there is no point in
considering it as a candidate, at least under the usual row
selection such as the CHUZR algorithm. One modification is to skip
nonbasic fixed variables during pricing; we essentially regard them
as "out of the problem" once they become nonbasic.

We begin to see that the activity resulting in largest gain
might be a better choice, and this depends both on the reduced
cost (rate of objective change) and the resulting activity level,
THETA. Unfortunately, the actual value of THETA is not known
until the basic variables are interrogated, as in the CHUZR
algorithm. This means that to compute the gain for each activity
(having reduced cost of appropriate sign to show promise of improvement) we must expend more computational effort. In particular, we
would "need" the ALPHA vector associated with a candidate to compute
its associated THETA; the gain is the (absolute) product, GAIN=
THETA*D_j. We have at one extreme expending great computational
effort to obtain an activity with greatest gain versus an inexpensive cost (viz., compute inner product) which does not describe
the net benefit, only the rate. Is there a compromise?

This question assumes that activities with large gains are
preferred over activities with small gains (possibly no gain).
There is no theoretical justification for this, and one can construct examples where the MAXDJ pricing algorithm leads to fewest
number of steps overall. However, practice indicates that a "best
gain criterion" is effective in keeping the total number of iterations nearest to minimal. Therefore, we consider the rationale
that if we can predict the gain through an inexpensive pricing
mechanism (not with certainity, but with some indication of "good-
ness" in the prediction), then we can expect to do better than by
selecting the activity with largest reduced cost.

Before we consider pricing variations, we must consider the
issue of identifying an optimal basis (which happens only once).
Until something better is invented, we shall always compute the
usual PI vector, as in FORMSUM, and interrogate the reduced cost
of an activity under consideration. We shall reject the activity
if its reduced cost is not of appropriate sign to show promise of
gain. Therefore, we retain the property that if we scan the entire
matrix and find no candidates, then the current basis must be optimal.

There are several observations to be made before we consider
what criteria looks useful beyond the size of the reduced cost
(which was the sole criterion in algorithm MAXDJ). First, we can
construct another PI vector, call it PI2, at the same time we compute the ususal PI (in the same loop of the program, thus avoiding
associated extra overhead computational costs). Let us say that

PI2=V*B^{-1}, where V is a vector to be described. The inner-product, (PI2, A$_j$) then produces a linear combination of the coordinates of the ALPHA vector associated with A$_j$ (i.e., ALPHA=B^{-1}A$_j$). To see this we note

$$(PI2,A_j) = (V B^{-1},A_j) = (V,B^{-1}A_j) = (V,ALPHA).$$

The usual PI-vector simply yields the sum of ALPHA coordinates associated with the objective described by COST. Here we have a general linear combination described by V.

Let us consider an immediate benefit from this observation, namely how we can deal with degeneracy in a practical manner. Define

$$V_i = \begin{cases} +1 & \text{if } BETA_i = a_i \\ -1 & \text{if } BETA_i = u_i \\ 0 & \text{else.} \end{cases}$$

Then let PID = V*B^{-1}. This provides the following measure of degeneracy:

$$DSUM \equiv (PID,A_j) = \sum_{i \in I^+} ALPHA_i - \sum_{i \in I^-} ALPHA_i,$$

where $I^- \equiv \{i: BETA_i = a_i\}$ and $I^+ \equiv \{i: BETA_i = u_i\}$.

If DSUM >0, then we may conclude that ALPHA$_i$>0 for some i in I$^+$ or ALPHA$_i$<0 for some i in I$^-$; in either case this implies zero gain under a row selection rule that prevents the incoming variable from becoming infeasible. Unfortunately, DSUM < =0 is inconclusive, but at least we can reject some of the offensive activities from candidacy (namely when DSUM >0).

The fact that there appears to be motivation for computing multiple PI vectors to aid during pricing may suggest that extra regions of storage should be reserved for such arrays. Let us suppose this is the case, so we have room for several arrays, each of size m (= number of rows). The row selection rule may use some of these to avoid waste and improve the pivot selection. Namely, the pricing rule may select _several_ candidates on the basis of some criteria (say largest reduced cost for which DSUM < =0). For definiteness suppose the pricing rule is allowed to select up to

K candidates, each showing a promise of gain. Then, we can compute the ALPHA vectors for each of the k (< =K) candidates and compute associated gains. The final pivot selection may be based upon a best gain criterion from the list of candidates.

Thus, if we use a region reserved for PI vectors during pricing, this region becomes available during row selection and may be gainfully employed during this final phase of pivot selection. Overall, this appears to be a good compromise between computing the gain for every activity versus computing the gain for only the one activity selected to enter the basis. This is called multiple pricing, and the regions reserved for PI vectors and ALPHA vectors are called ALPHA regions (although they may just as well be called "PI regions" except for the order of discovery).

In addition to multiple pricing there are two other related tactical variations which are simple, so let us consider them before returning to variations in the criteria.

First, instead of scanning the entire matrix file (which may require I/0) to select the best K candidates, we may look at only a portion. Beginning with the activity we left off with at the last scan, we look for candidates. One tactic is to keep scanning until K are found (or the entire matrix is scanned in case there aren't K candidates). If K=1, this is equivalent to accepting the first activity showing promise of gain. Experience indicates that there are better schemes which are compromises between taking the first K and scanning the entire matrix for the best K.

One of these schemes is to replace the new candidate with the worst one saved in the candidate list if it is better. Then, we may count the number of replacements and halt the scan when this number gets "large." Alternatively, we could compute the ratio of number of replacements to number of activities interrogated. This may serve as a probability indicator for hope of improvement, so when it becomes "small," we halt the scan.

The process of scanning only a portion of the matrix file is called partial pricing and is subject to many variations; we have mentioned at least two. Usually, the stopping rule depends upon the multiple pricing scheme used, particularly on the value of K.

Second, another pricing tactic is called sectional pricing. The activities are partitioned into sections, usually stored contiguously in the matrix file with markers or pointers, and the multiple and partial pricing schemes are applied to each section. Another partial pricing mechanism is used to determine how many sections are interrogated during this "major pricing iteration".

Let us collect the tactics into a prototype pricing algorithm model.

ALGORITHM MODEL PRICE: A list of candidates is obtained, each showing promise of gain. If none exists, this is indicated (to deduce optimality).

(1) price activity j by specificed criteria and REJECT or ACCEPT; in the latter case skip to step (3);

(2) apply the multiple pricing mechanism (resulting in rejection or insertion into the candidate list);

(3) test stopping rule described by the partial pricing mechanism, and either STOP or go to step (4);

(4) determine next activity by sectional pricing rule and go to step (1).

An algorithm conforming to the PRICE model is performed every major iteration. At an optimal solution, the entire matrix file is scanned, and the resulting candidate list is empty. Otherwise, a nonempty list of candidates is created, and minor iterations (if K >1) are performed using row selection and restricted pricing schemes which are applied only to the activities in the candidate list.

One way to perform the minor iterations is to view the candidate list plus the basic variables as a subproblem and find a solution for it. This process is called total suboptimization. Alternatively, one can dismiss a basic variable once it leaves the basis and terminate when none of the candidates could be entered with positive gain. This process is called partial suboptimization.

We now want to return to choice of criteria used in step (1) of the PRICE algorithm model. So far we have considered two criteria: (1) reduced cost (D_j), and (2) reduced cost with DSUM<=0 (to avoid zero gain). It is important to recall that both D_j and DSUM are computed by an inner product once the two associated PI vectors are computed (at a major iteration). This is regarded as inexpensive (versus computing ALPHA for each candidate, which is regarded as expensive). Whether or not the computation of multiple PI vectors is really "inexpensive" depends upon the other tactics used.

Now let us consider other criteria. First, another observation to be made is the dependence of the reduced cost and of THETA on the scales used to describe the problem represented by the numbers in the matrix file. Let us consider, for example, what happens if we scale activity j so that $A_j' = s_j A_j$, where $s_j > 0$. (The bounds also get scaled, where we similarly denote $a_j' = s_j a_j$ and $u_j' = s_j u_j$.)   If we leave the basic variables unscaled and consider only the nonbasic activity, j, then we know PI is the same, and the reduced cost changes by the equation,

$$D_j' = (PI, A_j') = (PI, s_j A_j') = s_j (PI, A_j') = s_j D_j.$$

Thus, the reduced cost changes proportionally to the same scale factor.

This means at least two things. First, the analyst that formulated the problem used a scale (even if it be without awareness), so there may be no good reason for a larger reduced cost, relative to another reduced cost (of another activity), to indicate any real preference of such an activity. Second, this raises the issue of constructing scales (on-the-fly) that provides a more meaningful comparison between two activities on the basis of their reduced cost values.

By similar analysis the incoming activity level (THETA), using a row selection rule such as in algorithm CHUZRI, is affected as follows:

$$THETA' = BETA_p/ALPHA_p' = BETA_p/(s_j ALPHA_p) = THETA/s_j.$$

We have assumed the p-th basic variable is blocking, and we noted

$$ALPHA' = B^{-1}A_j' = s_j B^{-1}A_j = s_j ALPHA.$$

Thus, the value of THETA is inversely proportional to the column scale which implies the gain is unaffected by scale.

In attempting to predict gain, or at least obtain a measure, say DGAIN, with the property that a relative order between two activities on the basis of their DGAIN yields a better then even chance that their gains are similarly ordered, we would want DGAIN to be independant of column scales for the two competing activities.

Keeping with the idea of using a linear combination of ALPHA vector coordinates, let DSUMGAIN be one which is not zero and consider

$$DGAIN = D_j/|DSUMGAIN|.$$

By the same argument used in deriving the equation, $D_j' = s_j D_j$, we note

$$\text{DSUMGAIN'} = (V, \text{ALPHA'}) = s_j \; (V, \text{ALPHA}) = s_j \; \text{DSUMGAIN}.$$

Therefore, DGAIN is independent of the nonbasic column scale.

Now let us consider how V may be chosen to induce $\text{PIGAIN} = V*B^{-1}$ which in turn lets us compute the associated DSUMGAIN using the inner product, (PIGAIN, A_j). Let us once more temporarily assume that all variables (except the 0-th, corresponding to the objective row activity) are simply nonnegative with no explicit upper bound. Let us also suppose we are in phase II with no degeneracy (so BETA>0). Then, define

$$V_i = 1/\text{BETA}_i, \text{ for } i>0 \text{ and } V_0 = 0.$$

This produces

$$\text{DSUMGAIN} = \sum_{i=1}^{m} \text{ALPHA}_i/\text{BETA}_i.$$

It is not difficulat to prove that DSUMGAIN, and hence DGAIN, is independent of row scales (other than the objective row which we can take as +1 since this will not affect comparison between two activities). Of course, we could let $V_i=1$, but obtaining row scale independence, just as in the true gain, is quite desirable; further, each term is a potential threshold, and thus holds some relation to 1/THETA. However, let us explore further than just the independence of row scale and a superficial relation to THETA.

Let $\text{THETA} = \text{BETA}_p/\text{ALPHA}_p$ (with p the associated pivot row selection as in algorithm CHUZR), and define

$$\text{DSUM} = \sum_{i \neq p} \text{ALPHA}_i/\text{BETA}_i = \text{DSUMGAIN} - 1/\text{THETA}.$$

Then, we have

$$\text{DGAIN} = \frac{D_j}{\left| \text{DSUM} + 1/\text{THETA} \right|}.$$

Since THETA >0, we have

$$\text{DGAIN} = \frac{\text{THETA}*D_j}{\left| 1 + \text{THETA}*\text{DSUM} \right|} = \frac{\text{GAIN}}{\left| 1 + \text{THETA}*\text{DSUM} \right|}.$$

Let us analyze the relative attractiveness of activity j when its DGAIN value is larger than another activity's, say the k-th, so that $\text{DGAIN}_j > \text{DGAIN}_k$. We know that either

or
$$GAIN_j > GAIN_k$$

$$|1 + THETA_j * DSUM_j| < |1 + THETA_k * DSUM_k|.$$

In the first case we have the desired result, namely that we selected the activity of greater gain. Now consider the second case.

Suppose both terms are positive inside the absolute value signs, so that we have

$$0 < 1 + THETA_j * DSUM_j < 1 + THETA_k * DSUM_k.$$

Let us continue to simplify the analysis by considering only nonnegative variables and phase II status (so BETA >0). Then one possible implication is that the j-th activity has a greater amount of scaled (by $1/BETA_i$ to yield row scale-free) ALPHA vector coordinates. Roughly, this would suggest that the net sum of new BETA coordinates would be greater if activity j were entered into the basis compared to entering activity k. This is desirable since the net increase of basic activity levels suggests greater gains on subsequent pivots.

Unfortunately it is also possible that $0 < THETA_j < THETA_k$ (consistent with $GAIN_j < GAIN_k$ and $DSUMGAIN_j > DSUMGAIN_k$). Therefore, this measure cannot guarantee that the selection leads to the best possible, whether "best" be in terms of immediate gain or in terms of leading to fewest number of iterations.

Nevertheless, the possibilities favoring activity j (over activity k) do seem to outweigh the opposite conclusion. The real question is, "To what degree is this relative measure able to make good selections?" Presently, only empirical evidence is available, and it suggests that this method of measurement is much better than using only the reduced cost.

Now let us turn our attention to other ways of "dynamically scaling" the reduced cost in an effort to select activities that show greater promise of gain.

Another way to obtain a measure which is independent of column scale is to divide the reduced cost by the norm of the ALPHA-vector since

$$\| ALPHA' \| = s_j \| ALPHA \|$$

This actually has a deeper meaning which we now describe. From the basic equations we note that the change in position of the basic variables (i.e., change in activity levels) is given by

$$\Delta Z(t) \equiv A(t) - Z(0) = -t \ \mathrm{ALPHA}.$$

Therefore, the distance travelled by the basic variables is

$$D(t) = |t| \ \ || \ \mathrm{ALPHA} \ ||.$$

In particular, in order to change the incoming variable by one unit (to obtain a gain of $|D_j|$), the basic variables must move $||\mathrm{ALPHA}||$ units.

The rate of change in objective value per unit of distance is defined to be the GRADIENT and satisfies the following:

$$\mathrm{GRADIENT} = \frac{dZ_0}{dD} = \frac{dZ_0}{dt} \div \frac{dD}{dt} \ ,$$

so we have

$$\mathrm{GRADIENT} = D_j / \ ||\mathrm{ALPHA}||.$$

Let us now see how we might compute $||\mathrm{ALPHA}||$ efficiently. Initially, if we start with B=I (all row activities basic), then ALPHA=A_j for each j. Therefore, at the time the matrix file is created we can compute (once and for all) $||A_j||$ for each j. Now it is a matter of determining how to update $||\mathrm{ALPHA}||$ when the basis changes by pivot exchange, (p,q); that is, A_q enters the basis in exchange for the p-th basic variable (i.e., pivoting on row p).

For j=q, the update is simple because ALPHA=e_p; thus, $||\mathrm{ALPHA}||$ = 1 for the entering activity (as well as for every basic variable). Thus, we are concerned with the nonbasic variables, including the one which just became nonbasic.

Let the new ALPHA vector of the j-th activity be denoted ALPHA', and let α be the ALPHA vector A_q before the pivot exchange. Recall that pivot equations are

$$\mathrm{ALPHA'}_i = \mathrm{ALPHA}_i - \alpha_i \ \mathrm{THETA} \ \text{for} \ i \neq p,$$

where $\quad \mathrm{THETA} \equiv \mathrm{ALPHA'}_p = \mathrm{ALPHA}_p / \alpha_p.$

It is convenient to write this in the following vector form:

$$\mathrm{ALPHA'} = \mathrm{ALPHA} - \alpha \ \mathrm{THETA} + e_p \ \mathrm{THETA}$$

(where recall that 'e_p' denotes the p-th unit vector).

Then,

$$||\text{ALPHA}'||^2 = (\text{ALPHA}', \text{ALPHA}')$$

$$= ||\text{ALPHA}||^2 + (1+||\alpha||^2)\ \text{THETA}^2 + 2\ \text{THETA}$$

$$(-(\alpha, \text{ALPHA}) + \text{ALPHAp} - \alpha_p\ \text{THETA}).$$

From the definition of THETA we note that $\text{ALPHA}_p = \alpha_p\ \text{THETA}$, so

$$||\text{ALPHA}'||^2 = \text{THETA}\ ||\text{ALPHA}||^2 + \text{THETA}^2(1+||\alpha||^2) - 2\ \text{THETA}\ \alpha, \text{ALPHA}).$$

Define NORM_j to be $||\text{ALPHA}||^2$, which is the quantity we are to maintain, so that the above equation becomes

$$\text{NORM}'_j = \text{THETA}*\text{NORM}_j + \text{THETA}^2(1+ \text{NORM}_q) - 2\ \text{THETA}\ (\alpha, \text{ALPHA}).$$

The quantity, NORM_j, is the saved value we wish to update, and NORM_q is the saved value of the new entrant into the basis. Hence, these two quantities are immediately available. The value of THETA is the p-th coordinate of the new ALPHA vector associated with activity j; this can be obtained by using another PI vector, namely $\text{PIP} = e_p B^{-1}$ (for the new basis). Then, as before we have $(\text{PIP}, A_j) = \text{ALPHA}_p' = \text{THETA}$.

The last term to consider is the inner product, (α, ALPHA), where α was computed when A_q entered the basis and could be saved. One approach which has been taken is to suppose that either $\text{ALPHA}_p=0$, in which case THETA = 0, or that α is orthogonal to ALPHA. If either of these conditions hold, the last term is zero. If we agree to ignore this last term anyway, then we have the following approximation:

$$T_j' \approx \text{THETA}*T_j + \text{THETA}^2\ (1+T_q),$$

and we use it as an equation to update T_j.

The accuracy of this approximation may be measured by computing the square norm, $||\text{ALPHA}||^2$, for a selected activity, namely q. Then, upon comparing with the approximation, Tq, we could decide whether to re-initialize all approximations.

To see if gross inaccuracies immediately appear let us consider the value associated with the p-th basic variable that has just left the basis. The new ALPHA vector for Z_p is

$$\text{ALPHA}' = e_p - \alpha\text{THETA} + \text{THETA}\ e_p,$$

where $\quad \text{THETA} = 1/\alpha_p$

since its old ALPHA vector was e_p.

Then,

$$\| \text{ALPHA}' \|^2 = 1 + \text{THETA}^2 (1+\| \alpha \|^2) - 2 \text{ THETA } (\alpha, e_p).$$

Observe that

$$\text{THETA } (\alpha, ep) = \text{THETA}*\alpha_p = 1$$

This means the approximation overestimates the norm initially. Since ALPHA is known, we could use the exact relation rather than approximate. Thus, making this a special case we set

$$T'_{i_p} = \{\text{THETA } (1 + \| \alpha \|^2) - 1\},$$

where $\| \alpha \|$ is computed (as well as THETA) from the ALPHA vector of the incoming activity.

Each time a variable enters the basis its T-value is reset to one since we know ALPHA = e_p. When a variable leaves the basis, its T-value is reset to its (theoretically) precise value, not using an approximation. However, the T-values of other non-basic variables are updated by an approximation.

Now let us consider an alternative to dropping the inner product term, (α, ALPHA). From the pivot equations we have

$$(\alpha, \text{ALPHA}) = (\alpha, \text{ALPHA}') + \text{THETA}*\alpha_p - 2 (\alpha, \text{ALPHA}').$$

Now the only quantity not saved is (α, ALPHA'). However, since this is an inner product with the new (computed) ALPHA vector, we can obtain it by using PIALPHA = $\alpha*B^{-1}$ (with the new basis) followed by the usual inner product,

$$\text{DALPHA} = (\text{PIALPHA}, A_j) = (\alpha, \text{ALPHA}').$$

In summary, we start with $T_j = \| A_j \|^2$ for each j (corresponding to B=I). At a major pricing iteration we form two extra PI-vectors, namely PIP (to get THETA) and PIALPHA (to get (α, ALPHA')). When we perform a (p,q)-pivot exchange, we save α, and we update the i_p-th norm by

$$T'_{i_p} = \text{THETA } (1+\| \alpha \|^2)/\alpha_p^2 - 1.$$

Next we update the other nonbasic activities (which can be done in conjunction with pricing if partial pricing is not used) by the (exact) equation,

$$T'_j = T_j^2 + T^2 + \text{THETA}*T_q^2*(T-2) - 2\text{THETA}*\alpha_p - 2 \text{ DALPHA}$$

where

DALPHA = (PIALPHA,A$_j$).

Actually, setting T'$_q$=1 is not necessary since the norms of ALPHA-vectors in the basis are always one, and we used that fact directly. (Nowhere do we use T$_i$ for the i-th basic variable, and upon leaving the basis, the associated norm is computed, rather than updated.)

Recapitulating the entire pricing mechanism, we begin with several PI vectors, which have been previously computed; one PI vector is used to obtain the usual reduced cost (in either phase I or II); one is used to help predict zero gain the presence of degeneracy; one is used to provide a scale-free measure of gain; and two more may be computed to measure gradient. Upon considering an activity, it is immediately rejected if its reduced cost is not of appropriate sign. Otherwise, the 0-gain predictor (in the presence of degeneracy) is computed; the activity is rejected if one candidate has already been selected and this one shows zero gain. (Note that we may have to accept a candidate even if we know there will be zero gain because we cannot rule out the possibility of future gains; only when all reduced costs have appropriate signs (i.e., showing rate of degradation only) can we conclude optimality.)

If a candidate is selected for further consideration, then it is compared with other candidates selected earlier during this major pricing iteration. This results in rejection or insertion into the candidate list (replacing the worst of the former candidates if the list was full). This phase of screening is known as "multiple pricing," and the auxiliary PI vectors are used in making the comparison.

Counting the number of replacements, or some other measure of "hope," a stopping rule is designed to avoid scanning the entire matrix file each major iteration. This tactic is known as "partial pricing." Finally, instead of always scanning the matrix file activity-by-activity in a sequential fashion, we may scan several "sections" independently. The sections represent a partitioning of the activities into logical groups, and each group usually consists of activities stored sequentially (though this is not necessary). Rules for partitioning and interrogating the activities determine a "sectional pricing" tactic.

Before concluding our description of pricing let us examine sectional pricing tactics more closely. The nature of the matrix generator is such that there is an inherent grouping of related activities. The reason problems become large is generally due to a multiplicative effect in forming activities. For example, an activity may represent flow of goods from a "source" to a "destination". This activity is the product of two <u>attributes</u>, namely source and destination. Mnemonically, an activity may be named by the format

     s&d.

For example, if a source is located in Dallas and a destination is located in New York, then flow may be named

     DAL&NY.

Many models have more than two attributes (eg., adding time periods), but two shall suffice for our consideration.

In mathematical notation we often see

     "let x_{ij} = flow from source i to destination j."

This is another representation of the same entity. A matrix generator may involve a 2-level loop resulting in a matrix file which appears in the following schemetic:

$$i=1 \left\{ \quad j=1,\ldots,J \right.$$

$$\vdots \qquad \vdots$$

$$i=I \left\{ \quad j=1,\ldots,J \right.$$

A partitioning scheme may be to partition the activities into sections, so the i-th section contains activities corresponding to $(x_{ij}: j=1,\ldots,J)$--flow out of the i-th source. The pricing mechanism would then be treating each source independently; if algorithm MAXDJ is applied to each section, then a new destination is found for the i-th source such that upon re-routing flow, a net reduction in cost (or increase in profit) is obtained.

Structurally, I-pointers may be kept to access the (i,1)-th activity (the first in each section). Alternatively, the (i,J)-th activity record could point back to the (i,1)-th activity record, thus permitting traversal of the i-th section. Then, I-pointers can be reserved to point to a particular activity in each section; these would be changing, depending upon information gained at the previous major pricing iteration when this section was interrogated. For example, when a section is completely priced, the "best" activity is selected and the pointer is updated to point to this activity. During subsequent iterations, this activity may leave the basis and hence become a candidate. Using the pointer this activity is priced first (in the section), and if it is found to be "good", then it is selected with no further pricing within that section. Alternatively, the pointer may point to the second best activity in a section when it was priced. If this distinguished activity prices unfavorably (i.e., has nonpositive truncated reduced cost), then the entire section can be priced (and the pointer updated). Still another variation is to employ partial pricing in a section but start at the pointer value.

The following algorithm incorporates the many tactics described. It excludes the gradient measure because partial pricing is used.

ALGORITHM PRICE: Given

criteria....... (i) PI, PID, $PIGAIN$

multiple pricing (ii) K, $FIRST$, $C(1),\ldots C(K), J(1),\ldots, J(K)$

partial pricing (iii) $MAXR$

sectional pricing (iv) N, $SECTION(1),\ldots SECTION(N)$,

this algorithm produces a list of candidates in the J-array, sorted by order of preference (in the parallel C-array).

step 1 (initialize): Set $k=0$, $s=FIRST$, $r=0$ and $J(h)=C(h)=0$ for $h=1, \ldots, k$.

step 2 (new section):
(a) Set $j=SECTION(s)$, $JBEST=j$ and compute $d=(PI, A_j)$.
(b) If $X_j = u_j$, set $d \leftarrow -d$.
(c) If $d \leq 0$, go to step 3; else, compute $d1=(PID, A_j)$.
(d) Set $JBEST = j$ and $DGAIN = 0$. If $d1 > 0$, go to step 3; else, set $DGAIN = d$ and go to step 4.

step 3   (price section): (starting with j) interrogate
         section number s and find j* such that DGAIN*
         is maximal. If DGAIN* >0, set DGAIN=DGAIN* and
         JBEST= j*. Go to step 4.

step 4   (compare with worst candidate): If $C(K) \geq$ DGAIN,
         go to step 5; else set $C(K)$ = DGAIN, $J(K)$ = JBEST
         and $r \leftarrow r + 1$. Sort parallel arrays C and J on
         descending values of $C(.)$.

step 5   (test for stopping): If r = MAXR, set FIRST = s
         and STOP; else, set $s \leftarrow (s+1)$ mod (N+1). If s =
         FIRST, STOP; else, go to step 2.

In algorithm PRICE we enter sections at the activity indenti-
fied by SECTION(s) (which may be a location pointer rather than the
activity's index number), and we first compute its truncated reduced
cost. If it is not of appropriate sign, we enter step 3 to price
the entire section. Otherwise, we compute the degeneracy measure
to test for zero gain. Except when the candidate list is empty,
the activity would be immediately rejected if we know it will have
zero gain. In case we enter it into the list, despite zero gain
(to avoid false indication of optimality), the merit rating used
is zero, so it will be replaced as soon as we find an activity
with indication of positive gain. If step 3 is entered, then
every activity in section s is interrogated, and the best DGAIN
is found. Thus, step 4 is entered either with the best DGAIN from
the section or with the distinguished activity from the section,
and the associated reduced cost shows the rate of improvement.

Step 4 compares the representative of section s with the
candidates taken from other sections. By maintaining a sort (there
are variations) we know that $C(K)$ is the worst value (and may be
0 if less than K candidates have been found so far). If a replacement is made, then the counter, r, is incremented; otherwise, the
only significant test in step 5 is whether we have made a complete
matrix pass.

Step 5 uses a simple partial pricing tactic in limiting the
number of replacements.

CONCLUSION

In conclusion, we have considered pivot selection tactics
for phases I and II. The departure from early phase I methodology
presented is the global minimization of the sum of infeasibility
and allowance of new infeasibilities. This method was tried in
the early developments but not entered into a commercial code
until Rarick's rediscovery and implementation into WHIZARD.

Phase II tactics here focused on pricing, particularly on the criteria for candidate selection. The use of auxiliary PI vectors to estimate gain was invented by Kalan. The dynamic scaling approach, using the GRADIENT, was invented by Harris; the exact update was discovered by Greenberg and Kalan (and independently by Goldfarb). Partial, multiple and sectional pricing appeared in the early developments by Orchard-Hays.

AN INTERACTIVE QUERY SYSTEM FOR MPS SOLUTION INFORMATION

R.P. O'Neill

Department of Energy and Louisiana State University

ACKNOWLEDGEMENTS. Many of the ideas of the conception and design phases of this system were generated in discussions with Harvey Greenberg who originally perceived its need. Charles Everett and Reginald Sanders were very helpful in the system's final development.

ABSTRACT. This paper describes the design, development and use of an interactive query system for the MPS solution. A packed data structure is presented which reduces the storage requirement of the file by an order of magnitude allowing larger files to be resident in core. The language syntax is described and examples are presented.

INTRODUCTION

Large scale mathematical programming models present data handling problems that have long been realized by those working directly in this area. These problems are sometimes of such a subtle nature that they are not realized or dismissed as trivial by those working indirectly in this area (i.e., theory of large-scale mathematical programs). For example, listings of the solution file and the matrix are often well over 10,000 lines forcing a very tedious and awkward process for examining information on an ad hoc basis. These problems can be resolved by the introduction of interactive software that allows the user to request specific information via commands and have the selected information listed at a user terminal or other chosen media.

At the Department of Energy (DOE), the Project Independence Evaluation System (PIES) solution output uses approximately 12,000 lines of printed output and occupies approximately 180 tracks of disk (3330) space in filed output form. There is often a need to print selective portions of the solution with little lead time. In order to satisfy this need a system of query programs, called PERUSE, has been written that provide the analyst with a tour through an MPS solution file, pausing only to list information of interest to the analyst while avoiding information gluts and manual paging through stacks of output.

In the following sections an overview of the software, the data structure for the packed solution file, the syntax of the interactive commands, and a sample session in TSO are presented. Finally, the current use of the system at DOE along with some future plans for interactive software are discussed.

2. SOFTWARE OVERVIEW

There are two FORTRAN programs that form the heart of the query system: READPACK and SCAN3. READPACK is a load module created from a FORTRAN program that reads the filed solution output and packs the file into data structure approximately one-tenth the original file size (the data structure for the packed file is given in Section 3). SCAN3 is a load module created from a FORTRAN program that accepts query commands as input, parses the commands and searches the core resident packed solution file to answer the query. Supporting software to execute these programs is available under TSO and SUPERWYLBUR.

In SUPERWYLBUR (a text editor/batch submission system) one or both of the programs can be executed by calling a macro that queries the user and modifies requesite JCL prior to initiating a batch run. In TSO CLISTs are used to interactively request and respond to requests for information from the user.

3. DATA STRUCTURE OF THE PACKED FILE

In order to answer queries without long terminal delays it is necessary to have the solution file core resident. As presently constituted the solution file contains redundant information. For example, if a row status is EQ (i.e., an equality row), the activity level, lower bound and upper bound have the same value and consequently, only one needs to be stored. Moreover, the information stored for every row and column contains some redundant information. This section describes the data structure that was created which reduces the storage required for the solution file to one-tenth its size allowing for core resident storage.

The overall data structure is contained in a FORTRAN common block. The first word gives the length of the file in words; the second word is a pointer to the first column; the remaining space is reserved for records containing the solution file information.

One variable length record is created for each row and column information grouping in the solution. Each record starts on a full word boundary and has the following format:

field:	1	2	3	4
	Length of the records in words	Status bit map	name	values ((one per word)
length in bytes:	2	2	8	0 to 20

The first field in the record is a halfword integer containing the length of the record in words indicating the beginning of the next record.

The second field is a status bit map which is accessed in FOR-TRAN as a halfword integer. If an integer is viewed as a sum of powers of 2, multiplied by variables with values of zero or one, then each integer has a unique representation in terms of these 0-1 variables. Therefore, each set of on-off bit settings has a unique integer associated with it and vice versa. Each bit will be referenced by the power of 2 it represents.

bit	Value	Meaning
0	1	status is lower limit
1	0	status is basic
2	1	status is equality (or fix)
3	1	status is upper limit
4	1	status is feasible
5	0	activity level is 0.0
6	0	cost (or slack) is 0.0
7	0	lower level is 0.0
8	1	no lower bound
9	0	no upper bound
10	0	and bit 9 = 1, upper limit is zero
11	0	reduce cost (or dual activity level) is zero
12-15		not used

The third field is an eight-byte name field extracted from the solution file.

The fourth field is a variable length field of from one to five words. Each entry is a single precision floating point number. The meaning of each entry is determined by the status bit map as follows:

if the activity level is not zero, it is stored in the first available location;

if the cost or slack value is not sero, it is stored in the next available location;

if a lower limit exists, and it is not zero, and the status is not lower limit or equality, then the lower limit is stored in the next available location;

if an upper limit exists, and it is not zero, and the status is not upper limit or equality, then the upper limit is stored in the next available location;

if the reduced cost (or dual activity) is not zero, then it is stored in the next available location.

There is no possible instance of solution information that would require all five numeric values associated with a row or column to be stored. Moreover, it is possible that no values need be stored. The experience with the PIES and other solution output files is that an average of 1.5 to 2.0 values are stored.

4. SYNTAX FOR PERUSE COMMANDS

PERUSE commands are subdivided into fields. The fields are blank delimited and must appear in proper order. Currently, there are six different field types: the command, qualifier, mask, conditional print, and average field. The command field is required for each command. The commands are divided into three categories: information, control, and comment. The information commands are DISPLAY, ADD, and AVERAGE. The control commands are VERIFY, NO-VERIFY, PROMPT, NOPROMPT, HEADING, and END. A comment is recognized by an * in column one causing the parser to ignore the input line. In the syntax descriptions that follow the underlined portions are the shortest acceptable abbreviations for the element.

Information Command Syntax

DISPLAY $\begin{Bmatrix} ALL \\ COLUMNS \\ ROWS \end{Bmatrix}$ mask   [conditional phrase]   [print options]

DISPLAY INFEASIBILITIES   [print options]

ADD $\begin{Bmatrix} \text{ALL} \\ \text{COLUMNS} \\ \text{ROWS} \\ \text{INFEASIBILITIES} \end{Bmatrix}$ mask [conditional phrase] [print options]

AVERAGE $\begin{Bmatrix} \text{A} \\ \text{R} \\ \text{C} \end{Bmatrix}$ mask   [conditional phrase] [average]

    The DISPLAY command displays from the solution file information governed by the remaining fields. The ADD computes sums for values found in the solution file. The values in the sum are controlled by the remaining fields. The AVERAGE command computes averages and weighted averages associated with information in the solution file.

    For the information commands, the command field is followed by the qualifier field which contains one of the following options:

    All meaning search both row and column names
    ROWS meaning search only row names
    COLUMNS meaning search only column names
    INFEASIBILITIES meaning search for the infeasibilities.

    Following the qualifier is the mask field which is mandatory except when the qualifier field contains INFEASIBILITIES. The mask is any 1 to 8 character string consisting of alphanumeric characters or asterisks. If the string is less than 8 characters the parser left justifies the string and fills to 8 characters with asterisks. The search is satisfied by matching a row or column name with the mask. A match occurs when the non-arbitrary characters of the mask are the same as the variable name. Any character is considered a match for an asterisk.

    The conditional field is always optional, allowing the user to discriminate further in the choice of information and must have one of the following two forms:
FOR arg1 repol arg2
    arg1 and arg2 must be one of the following:

      X, for activity level;
      C or S, for the cost or slack value;
      L, for the lower limit;
      U, for the upper limit;
      D, for the dual activity or reduced cost; or
      any valid floating point number

    relop must be one of the following:

      GE, GT, LT, NE or EG.

(the meaning is the same as in FORTRAN. Note that periods do not preceed and succeed the relational operator).

or

$$\underline{F}OR\ \underline{S}TATUS\ =\ \begin{Bmatrix} BS \\ LL \\ UL \\ EQ \end{Bmatrix}$$

where

> BS indicates a basic variable;
> LL indicates a variable at its lower limit;
> UL indicates a variable at its upper limit;
> EQ indicates a variable at a fixed value.

If no conditional field is present, all names satisfying the mask are taken.

The print field allows the user flexibility in printing certain types of information. Any combination of the activity level, cost or slack, lower limit, upper limit, and reduced cost or dual activity fields can be requested.

The print option appears as:

$$[X]\ \begin{bmatrix} C \\ S \end{bmatrix}\ [L]\ [U]\ [D].$$

The symbols may appear in any order and have the same denotation as in the conditional. If the symbol appears, the corresponding field will be printed. When it appears, the print field is always the last and if omitted, the default is the complete list. The symbols may be separated by commas. If a variable contains no lower limit, $-.7273E76$ (smallest floating-point number) will be printed and if there is no upper limit, $-.7273E76$ (largest floating-point number will be printed).

The average field is used only with the AVERAGE command. It describes the arguments for the weighted average and appears as follows:

> $\underline{A}VE$ arg1 $\underline{B}Y$ arg2
>
> arg1 and arg2 must be one of the following:
>
> X, C, S, L, U, D (as in the conditional phase) or N (the number of variables satisfying both the mask and the conditions).

When the field appears, the average of arg1 weighted by arg2 is calculated. If omitted, the average of the activity levels (X) will be calculated.

Control Commands

VERIFY   - copy the input command to the output file;
NOVERIFY - do not VERIFY (default)
PROMPT   - print the prompt INPUT A COMMAND (default);
NOPROMPT - do not PROMPT;
H   - in column 1 causes the information in columes 2
             through 72 to be printed on the output file;
END   - causes termination of the session.

VERIFY, NOVERIFY, PROMPT, and NOPROMPT cause switches to be set, and the control is in effect until changed.

When a syntax error is found, the system provides diagnostic information. Two examples are presented below. In the first example the qualifier field is incorrectly specified, and in the second example, the rational operator is not valid. (User suppled commands are in lower case and the system's prompts and responses are in upper case.)

```
        INPUT A COMMAND
    dis xol ad*dfin

    ****** SYNTAX ERROR IN THE COMMAND ******

    INCORRECT SPECIFICATION IN QUALIFIER FIELD
    USE A, I, R OR C.
    THE ERROR OCCURRED BETWEEN COLUMNS 6 AND 6
            1         2         3         4         5         6
    123456789012345678901234567890123456789012345678901234567890


    DISP XOL AD*DFIN
      TRY AGAIN

      INPUT A COMAND
    disp r lmbcj**r for x tg L

    ****** SYNTAX ERROR IN THE COMMAND ******
    RELATIONAL OPERATOR INCORRECTLY SPECIFIED IN THE FOR (COND.)
    PHRASE THE ERROR OCCURRED BETWEEN COLUMNS 17 AND 23
            1         2         3         4         5         6
    123456789012345678901234567890123456789012345678901234567890
    DISP R LMBCJ**R FOR X TG L
      TRY AGAIN

      INPUT A COMMAND
```

5. DISCUSSION AND EXAMPLES

The PERUSE system has been operational at the DOE since the spring of 1977 and has proved very useful. The process of debugging a run with analytical (formulation or data) errors, as opposed to one with mechanical (software or hardware) errors, is often a long and tedious process. The solution file alone is over two hundred pages which creates difficulties in tracing problems. With PERUSE, needed information can be requested by a simple command or a series of commands. Additionally, the run output is now two hundred pages thinner, killing fewer trees. Some examples of the system's use are presented below.

For our first example, we shall illustrate how the system can be used to determine if a model change has been correctly implemented or if a policy has achieved its goal. For example, suppose that a proposed policy is intended to create economic incentives for electric utilities to switch from natural gas to some other fuel. To determine the impact of this policy, the total quantity of natural gas used by utilities can be obtained with the following command:

```
          INPUT A COMMAND
        add col ungg*u* for x gt 0. x

     THE      3 ACTIVITIES WITH MASK UNGG*U**
          HAVE THE FOLLOWING SUM(S):
                  ACT LEVEL
               184.62
```

The information from the previous command can be expanded by asking for individual activities to be displayed with the following command:

```
     INPUT A COMMAND
     disp col ungg*u* for x gt 0.
     NAME STATUS   ACT LEVL    COST   LIMIT  ULIMIT       RED COST
     UNGG9U41 BS    4.4303    .38000   .0    .72370E+76    .0
     UNGG7U71 BS    1.4623    .40000   .0    .72370E+76    .0
     UNGG2U91 BS   178.72     .83000   .0    .72370E+76    .0

       3 ACTIVITIES WITH MASK UNGG*U** SATISFY THE CONDITION
         THE SUM OF THEIR ACT. LEVELS IS 184.62
```

The above response gives the analyst the utility regions that are receiving gas and the supply regions from which the gas is purchased.

The command structure allows the analyst to respond expedittously to requests for summary information not produced by a static

report writer. For example, the amount of hi-sulfur/low-btu coal
that is available at a production cost of less that $26 per ton
can be obtained summing the upper bounds on the appropriate activities as follows:

```
INPUT A COMMAND
add col pci**** for c lt 26.   u

THE   68 ACTIVITIES WITH MASK PCI*****
   HAVE THE FOLLOWING SUM(S):
            ULIMIT
          381.32
```

The average delivered price of gasoline used in the transportation
sector of the economy can be obtained by taking the average of dual
variables of the rows that collect gasoline from the transportation
activities weighted by their activity levels (i.e., demands) as
follows:

```
INPUT A COMMAND
ave rows dd*gstr ave d by x

THE WEIGHTED AVERAGE FOR THE   10 ACTIVITIES SATISFYING THE
   CONDITION AND MASK DD*GSTR* IS -28.417
```

Dropping the sign, the average delivered price of gasoline is
$28.42 per barrel.

The system has been used to create quick-and-dirty reports that
can be designed and implemented in an hour or less. Its output has
been used to drive a graphics package to display primary fuel supply
curves. Moreover, analysts who are mainly interested in specific
subsets of the output and often are not directly involved in the
effort, can obtain at remote stations, the information they need
without direct assistance.

The success of PERUSE has demonstrated the need and usefulness
of interactive software in this area. Consequently, two new systems are under development. One will be a system to execute interactive queries on a packed matrix. This system will allow the
analyst to trace paths through the matrix on a graph where the nodes
are the columns (or rows). An edge is defined between two nodes
when each column (row) has a nonzero coefficient in the same row
(column). The other system will allow analysts to alter the starting point for the algorithmic process in the inter-active fashion
in order to reduce CPU time.

MODELING AND SOLVING NETWORK PROBLEMS

F. Glover* and D. Klingman**

*College of Business, University of Colorado, Boulder
**Center for Cybernetic Studies, University of Texas,
Austin

Design and Implementation of Optimization Software

OVERVIEW. The growth of the computer industry has had a profound
influence on many areas, perhaps affecting none more dramatically
than the area of management science. A virtual explosion of new
knowledge about ways to solve optimization problems in industry
and government has occurred since World War II, much of it intimately dependent on the capability provided management scientists
by the computer to record and manipulate extremely large amounts
of data. Without this capability, many of the tools of management
science would be mere theoretical niceties.

The advent of the computer has given rise to the development
of computer-based planning models. The techniques for building,
solving, refining, and analyzing such models have undergone a
steady evolutionary development as computer hardware has changed.
This evolution has recently spawned the embryo of two new and important technologies, network computer implementation technology
and NETFORM (network formulation) technology.

The first technology has emerged from recent research on new
solution algorithms and implementation techniques for solving network problems [2, 3, 5, 11, 13, 14, 17, 18, 28]. The fruits of
this research have dramatically reduced the cost of solving linear
and mixed integer network type problems. This cost reduction, significantly, has been entirely above and beyond any reductions af-
forded by changes in computer hardware or compilers. For example,
the cost of solving network problems with 2400 equations and
500,000 arcs on an IBM 360/65 has been reduced from a conservative

estimate of $10,000 in 1968 to $300 in 1976 by these advances. In addition, these advances have stimulated the development of new modeling techniques for handling a multitude of problems that arise in applications of scheduling, routing, resource allocation, production, inventory management, facilities location, distribution planning, and other areas.

These new modeling techniques [12, 15, 16, 18] are mathematically and symbolically linked to network and augmented network structures and are called NETFORM (network formulation) technology. A major attribute of the NETFORM technology is that it allows users to conceptualize formulations of their problems graphically. The pictorial aspect of this technology has proven to be extremely valuable in both communicating and refining problem interrelationships without the use of mathematics and computer jargon. Thus it protects the non-technical person against technical legerdemain and exaggerated claims of model "realism." Another powerful attribute of this technology is that it often yields a model that can be solved as a sequence of linear network problems.

One purpose of this paper is to briefly describe each of these technologies and to demonstrate the power of these technologies when used in concert to model and solve real world applications. We argue on the basis of practical experience that these advances overcome many of the conceptual design and computational difficulties of previous optimizing procedures and provide the type of technologies required of truly useful planning tools. Our experience with these tools has led us to the conclusion that the weakest link in developing effective computer-based planning models is no longer in the computer and management science tools themselves, but rather in the way these new tools are used. The ultimate test and worth of these tools, however, depends on their use by practitioners. Thus the more important purpose of this paper is to convey a sense of what is now possible and offer some insights that will make it easier for others to improve and use these developments.

In subsequent sections we present examples of how algebraic models can be viewed graphically, describe several real-world applications that have profited by the use of NETFORM techniques, compare and contrast the implementational network computer codes with commercial linear programming codes, and briefly discuss how network techniques may be integrated into linear programming codes to produce the next generation of linear programming systems.

PART I: MODELS AND MODELING TECHNIQUES

PURE NETWORK MODELS

Pure network problems actually embody a group of distinct model

types. This group includes shortest path, assignment, transportation, and transshipment problems. Any of these network problems
can be characterized by a coefficient matrix which has at most one
+1 and one -1 entry in each column. For the sake of brevity we
will focus attention on the most general of these model types.

Transshipment Problem

The most general pure network structure that appears in numerous applications--either directly, or as a subproblem--is the transshipment model. An illustration of this model for a cash flow problem is depicted in Figure 1.

The arrows shown in Figure 1 are called arcs and circles are
called nodes. In this cash flow network, the nodes may be thought
of as corresponding to subsidiaries in different locations. The
supplies and demands--which are shown in the directional triangles
leading into a node for a supply and out of a node for a demand--
may be thought of as representing excess or deficit cash positions.
Thus, nodes A, B, and C have excess funds, nodes D and E have no
funds, and nodes F and G have deficit funds. The arcs indicate the
ways to transfer cash from one subsidiary to another. For instance,

Figure 1

Capacitated Transshipment Cash Flow Problems

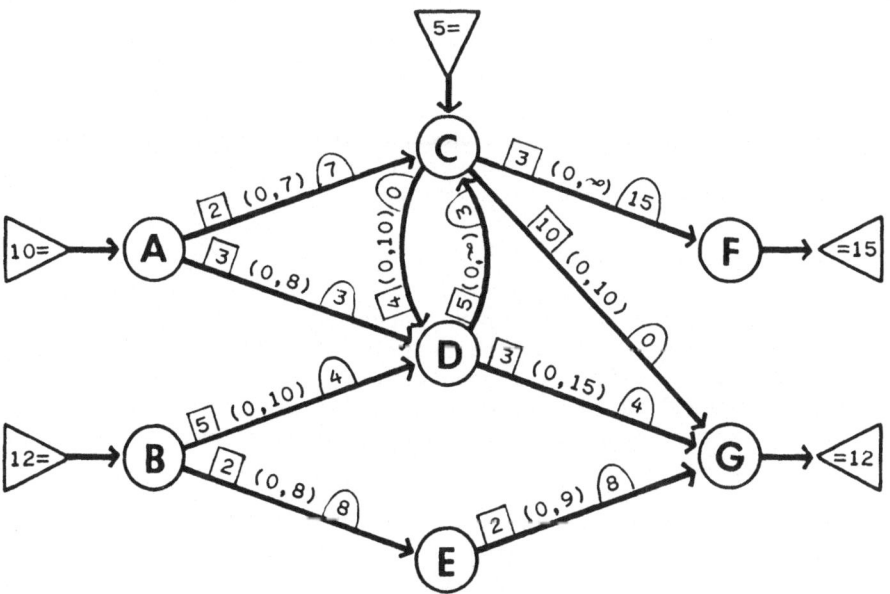

the arc from node A to node C indicates that it is possible to
transfer funds from subsidiary A to subsidiary C. The absence of
an arc between a pair of subsidiaries indicates that it is not possible to transfer funds directly between them (thought it may be
possible to transfer funds indirectly by means of a sequence of
arcs). Each arc has a lower bound, upper bound, and cost. The
lower and upper bounds appear within the parentheses and the cost
within the rectangle on an arc. For example, Figure 1 indicates
that the arc from node A to node C has a lower bound of 0, an upper bound of 7, and a cost of 2.

The objective in the transshipment problem is to determine how
much to ship along each arc within the limits stipulated by the
bounds in order to satisfy all supplies and demands and to minimize total cost. By satisfying supplies and demands we mean the
total flow into the node minus the total flow out must equal its
demand, and the total flow out of the node minus the total flow in
must equal its supply. For all other nodes the flow into the node
must equal the flow out. The numbers in the semi-circles on the
arcs in Figure 1 illustrate a solution which satisfies these node
equations and the bound requirements.

It is quite important to understand how a transshipment problem may be stated mathematically in order to appreciate the connections between graphical and algebraic structures.

To state a network problem algebraically, define a variable
for each arc. For example let X_{ij} denote the flow on the arc from
node i to node j and c_{ij} denote the unit cost on this arc. Henceforth, an arc will be denoted as an ordered pair (i,j) where the
first component specifies the from node and the other component
specifies the to node.

Next create the objective function for the problem as an expression involving the costs and variables. For the problem in
Figure 1, the objective function would be:

$$2X_{AC}+3X_{AD}+5X_{BD}+2X_{BE}+4X_{CD}+3X_{CF}+10X_{CG}+5X_{DC}+3X_{DG}+2X_{EG}.$$

Upon identifying the objective function, create a constraint
for each node which expresses the restriction on flow into and out
of the node. To do this, it is convenient to view a supply as an
inflow and a demand as an outflow. Then the requirement at each
node can be expressed as Total Inflow = Total Outflow, or in particular, Total Inflow - Total Outflow = 0. Upon transposing any
constant term of this equation to the right hand side, supplies
being denoted as negative quantities and demands as positive
quantities. To see this, consider constructing the "Total
Inflow - Total Outflow = 0" equation for node C in

Figure 1. The total flow into node C consists of the 5 units of supply and $(X_{AC}+X_{DC})$. The total flow out of node C is $X_{CF}+X_{CG}$ $+X_{CD}$. Thus we have $5+X_{AC}+X_{DC}-(X_{CF}+X_{CG}+X_{CD})=0$, or after transposing the constant term, $X_{AC}+X_{DC}-X_{CF}-X_{CG}-X_{CG}-X_{CD}= -5$. Thus, the supply of 5 becomes expressed as a negative quantity because of its move- ment to the right hand side of the equality sign. On the other hand, a demand, which is included in the outflow that is subtracted in the "Inflow-Outflow" equation appears as a positive quantity when moved to the right hand side. This also discloses, incidentally, that a supply may be viewed as a negative demand, and vice versa.

The entire algebraic statement of the capacitated transship- ment problem shown in Figure 1 is as follows:

Minimize:

$$2X_{AC}+3X_{AD}+5X_{BD}+2X_{BE}+4X_{CD}+3X_{CF}+10X_{CG}+5X_{DC}+3X_{DG}+2X_{EG}$$

Subject to:

$$
\begin{aligned}
-X_{AC} -X_{AD} && = -10 \\
-X_{BD} -X_{BE} && = -12 \\
X_{AC} \quad -X_{CF} -X_{CG} +X_{DC} && = -5 \\
X_{AD} +X_{BD} \quad -X_{DC} -X_{DG} && = 0 \\
X_{BE} \quad -X_{EG} && = 0 \\
X_{CF} && = 15 \\
X_{CG} \quad +X_{DG} +X_{EG} && = 12
\end{aligned}
$$

$0 \leqq X_{AC} \leqq 7$; $0 \leqq X_{AD} \leqq 8$; $0 \leqq X_{BD} \leqq 10$; $0 \leqq X_{BE} \leqq 8$; $0 \leqq X_{CD} \leqq 10$;

$0 \leqq X_{CD}$; $0 \leqq X_{CF}$; $0 \leqq X_{CG} \leqq 10$; $0 \leqq X_{DC} \leqq 15$; $0 \leqq X_{EG} \leqq 9$.

It is important to observe that each X_{ij} appears in exactly two node equations, i.e., the equation for node i and the equation for node j. Since X_{ij} contributes to the outflow of the node i equa- tion and to the inflow of the node j equation, it appears with a coefficient in -1 in the former and with a coefficient of +1 in the latter. Thus, each column of the coefficient matrix has one -1 and one +1 entry. If the restrictions at the nodes are stated as in- equalities rather than equations (i.e., Total Inflow - Total In- flow = +0 or Total Outflow $\leqq$ 0), then slack or surplus variables are added to convert these constraints to equations and it is admis- sible for columns to contain a single non-zero entry. Inequality restrictions at nodes generally arise by stipulating that supplies or demands must be "at least" or at most" a certain amount.

Note that, by means of these observations, it is possible to
represent any LP problem whose coefficient matrix has at most one
+1 and one -1 entry per column as a transshipment problem simply
by reversing the above steps. That is, to construct a graph that
corresponds to such a problem, create a node for each constraint
and an arc for each variable, affixing supplies, demands and bounds
in the manner indicated.

APPLICATIONS OF PURE NETWORK PROBLEMS

Pure network problems provide models for numerous mathematical
optimization problems and major components of many additional problems. For example, inventory maintenance [9,29,31] typically exhibit an underlying network structure. A cousin of the inventory
maintenance problem is the so-called PERT/CPM problem, which seeks
the best way to sequence a complex set of interdependent activities.
The PERT/CPM framework, which constitutes one of the simplest network model forms, has been used in a variety of practical applications (including construction of the Polaris submarine) and has been
reported to save enormous dollar costs and greatly speed the completion of complex projects.

Problems involving the effective management of resources often
exhibit network structures and are becoming increasingly important
in government and industry. Direct network formulations of water
resource management problems, for example, are finding use in a
number of states. In these, canals, river reaches, and pipelines
take the role of arcs, while reservoirs and pumping stations take
the role of nodes. Planning over time frequently looms as a major
consideration in these applications.

The Texas Water Development Board and the government of Poland,
for example, use a succession of simulations of alternative "supply
configurations," and solve the resulting network for each simulation run. (The step of finding the optimum solution to each network problem is used to determine the best response to meet demands for water use, given a particular supply configuration.)
Roughly five hundred such runs are made each month. The feasibility
and cost-effectiveness of such runs of course owes heavily to the
efficiency of solving the underlying networks.

The problem of determining flows and heads in a general pipeline system (such as in municipal water systems) with reservoirs,
pumps, gate and check valves, given fixed inputs and withdrawals
has been recently shown in [25] to be equivalent to a convex transshipment problem under the assumption of convex head losses. Such
problems are easily solved as ordinary transshipment problems by

using a piecewise linear approximation of the convex function. Since the convexity requirements are usually satisfied for real pipe networks, this is an example of another class of real-world problems which now can be handled by network procedures with far greater effectiveness than by the procedures applied to these problems in the past.

Another important instance of the use of network models occurs in manpower promotion and assignment problems. AT&T has developed such models in order to guarantee acceptable hiring and promotion policies in accordance with HEW rules and regulations.

A number of cash-management problems have also recently been modeled as transshipment problems. These models include sources of funds in addition to cash (such as maturing accounts and notes receivable, sales of securities, borrowing, etc.) and use of funds other than a single "investment." The generalized network model to be discussed subsequently makes it possible to further incorporate discount, interest, and other financial considerations directly into the model.

Many nonlinear problems involve network subproblems. One of the most basic and prevalent forms of nonlinear problems is the fixed-charge network problem, whose major offshoots include the extremely important genre known as "location" problems. The nonlinear element of a fixed-charge network is the fixed-charge arc which has the following special property; whenever the arc is "used" (i.e., permitted to transmit flow), a charge is incurred that is independent of the amount of flow across the arc. Fixed-charge networks have been used to model problems of plant and warehouse location, equipment purchasing and leasing, personnel hiring and offshore oil drilling platform location, among others.

To provide a fuller appreciation of the ingredients of such models, we will not discuss in detail an example from an important practical application.

Production Planning and Distribution Application

A major U.S. car manufacturer has developed and implemented a transshipment model for production planning and distribution decisions. This model is noteworthy for demonstrating the value of networks in interactive decision-making. Figure 2 illustrates this application.

The problem, simplified, is to determine the number of cars of each of the three models (m:1, m:2, and m:3) to produce at the Atlanta and Los Angeles plants (represented by the "Atl." and "L.A." nodes), and then to determine how many each of these car models to ship from each plant to the distribution centers in Pittsburgh and Chicago (represented by the "Pitt." and "Chi." nodes.) The objective is to identify a production-distribution plan that minimizes total cost.

Figure 2

Production Planning and Distribution

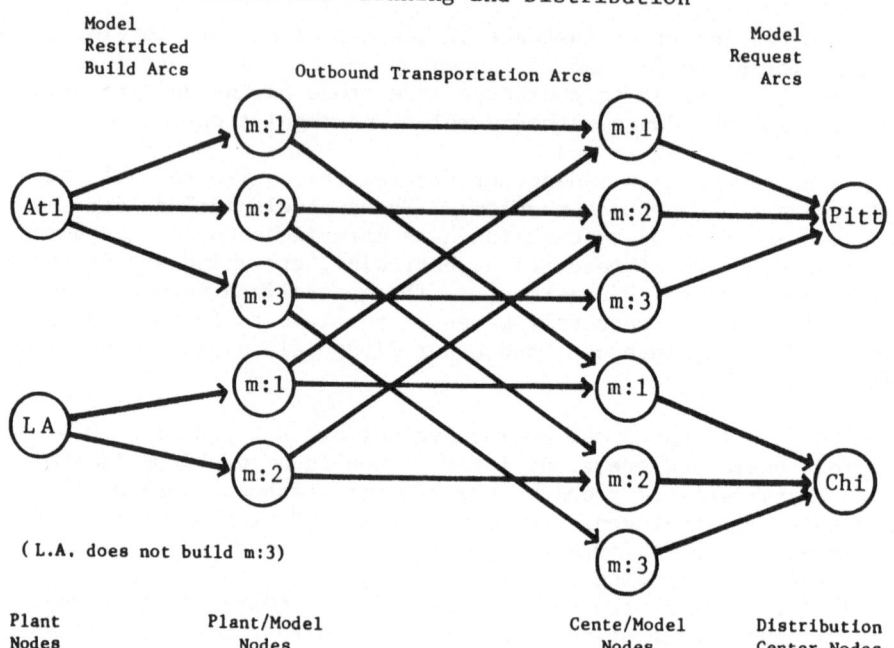

Model
Restricted
Build Arcs

Outbound Transportation Arcs

Model
Request
Arcs

(L.A. does not build m:3)

| Plant
Nodes | Plant/Model
Nodes | Cente/Model
Nodes | Distribution
Center Nodes |

Bounded supplies are associated with the Atl. and L.A. nodes, indicating the least and most that can be produced at these plants. In addition, upper and lower bounds are placed on the various arcs emanating from these two nodes to control the minimum and maximum number of each particular car model that can be produced at these plants. Similar bounds (capacity restrictions) can also be placed on other arcs. For instance, if there is a limit on the number of m:1 cars that can be shipped from Atlanta to Pittsburgh, then this appears as an upper bound restriction on the "top-center" arc in the network. Finally, the number of each particular model required at Pittsburgh and Chicago is handled by placing bounds on the "far right" arcs. For example, if exactly 4,000 m:3-type cars are required in Chicago, then 4,000 becomes both the lower and upper bound on the m:3-Chi. arc.

An interesting feature of this model is not only that it coordinates the production and distribution decision, but that it handles a multi-commodity problem in a "single-commodity" framework. That is, the three models m:1, m:2, and m:3 are distinct commodities being shipped through the network, but their identities never get mixed or confused, as could be possible in some network models. This illustrates the importance of getting the "right" network formulation.

The typical size of this problem for a particualr division (e.g., Pontiac, Ford, Dodge, etc.) is 1,200 nodes and 4,000 arcs. The company initially used a version of the SHARE out-of-kilter code [26] to solve these problems. The solution time ranged from 10 to 20 minutes on an IBM 370/145 and required 150K bytes of computer memory. Using the transshipment code of [1,14] the problem was solved in less than 20 seconds on the company's IBM 370/145, using only 80K bytes of computer memory, thus making it possible to solve such problems in an on-line computer mode. In fact, due to the nature of the decision-making environment of this application, the company has developed an on-line real time production planning and distribution system which is linked to a graphics display terminal and an English language input processor. This system is currently being used at several administrative levels within in the corporation hierarchy for planning purposes.

Today, by using the interactive on-line network system and utilizing visual displays, plant executives are able to discuss their goals and assumptions in a very short time. Answers to questions of the form "What if we do this?" are quickly obtained and evaluated. In fact, the executives typically are able to evaluate 150-200 production plans each quarter with the aid of the network system.

GENERALIZED NETWORK

The generalized network (GN) problem represents a class of LP problems that heretofore has received only a small portion of the attention it deserved. Recently, however, with the identification of many new generalized network applications and with the emergence of computer codes able to solve these problems efficiently, generalized networks are coming to be appreciated as rivaling or even surpassing pure networks in their practical significance. Generalized networks include pure networks as a special case in which the non-zero entries in a column, is actually the broadest classification of linear network-related problems. Practical settings in which such GN problems arise include resource allocation, production, distribution, scheduling, capital budgeting, as well as other problem types which will be elaborated on subsequently.

As previously noted, the most effective procedures for modeling and communicating pure network problems are based on viewing these problems as directed graphs. A generalized network problem can also be represented as a directed graph using the following conventions. Whenever the problem has a bounded optimal solution, the coefficient matrix can be transformed so that at least one entry in any column with two non-zero entries is -1. In this way, a directed arc is created that leads from the node associated with the -1 to the node associated with the other non-zero entry. (If both entries are -1, the arc may be directed either way.) A single non-zero entry in a column is represented by an arc that touches only one node (which is both its starting and ending point).

There is an important distinction between arcs in pure network problems and arcs in GN problems. An arc of a generalized network has a multiplier associated with it. This multiplier is the non-zero coefficient associated with the node at the head of the arc (i.e., the terminal node of the directed arc). In pure networks, this multiplier is always +1.

We will illustrate these ideas for the following GN problem.

Minimize: $1X_{12}+5X_{13}+3X_{23}+1X_{24}-4X_{32}-9X_{34}$

Subject to:
$$-1X_{12}-1X_{13} = -5$$
$$2X_{12} \quad -1X_{23}-1X_{24}+1/3X_{32} = 0$$
$$1/2X_{13}+1X_{23} \quad -1X_{32}-1X_{34} = 0$$
$$-15X_{24} \quad +3X_{34} = 10$$

$$0 \leq X_{12} \leq 3, \quad 0 \leq X_{13} \leq 4, \quad 0 \leq X_{23} \leq 6$$
$$0 \leq X_{24} \leq 5, \quad 0 \leq X_{32} \leq 3, \quad 0 \leq X_{34} \leq 7$$

The network associated with this problem is shown in Figure 3. As with pure network problems, each row of the coefficient matrix is associated with a node and each column with an arc. That is, a node corresponds to a problem equation and an arc corresponds to a problem variable. Consequently, each arc has a cost, lower bound, and uppper bound. Costs are shown in Figure 3 within the squares and bounds are shown within parentheses. Arc multipliers are shown with triangles.

Flow across an arc in a generalized network problem is acted upon by the nonzero multiplier so that the amount starting out on an arc will not necessarily be the amount arriving at the opposite end. Specifically, the flow entering the arc is multiplied by the value of the multiplier to produce the quantity of flow leaving the arc. For example, if 2 units start on an arc from node 1 to node 2 in Figure 3, the multiplier of 2 will cause 4 units to arrive at node 2. Likewise, 10 units starting on the arc from node 2 and node 4 will result in 2 units arriving at node 4 since the multiplier in this case is 1/5. It is important to keep in mind that the arc's cost, lower bound, and upper bound refer only to the units of flow entering the arc.

Figure 3

Generalized Network

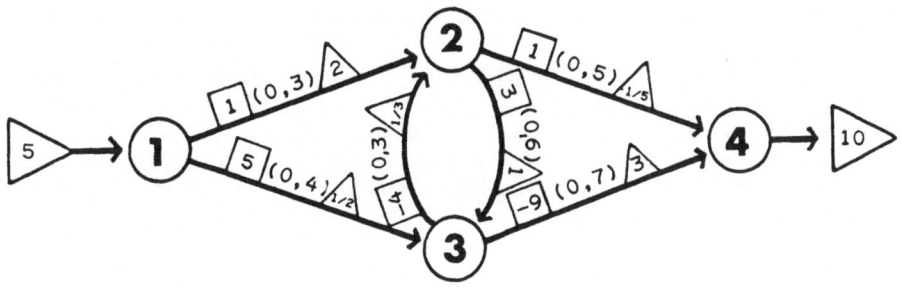

APPLICATIONS OF GENERALIZED NETWORKS

As already indicated, generalized networks can successfully model many problems that have no pure network equivalent. This is made possible by the use of arc multipliers, which may be interpreted in two ways. First, multipliers can be viewed as modifying the amount of flow of some particular item. By means of flow modification, generalized networks can model such situations as evaporation, seepage, deterioration, breeding, interest rates, sewage treatment, purification processes with varying efficiencies, machine efficiency, and structural strength design. However, it is also possible to interpret the multiplication process as transforming one type of item to another. This interpretation provides a way to model such processes as manufacturing, production, fuel to energy conversions, blending, crew scheduling, manpower to job requirements, and currency exchanges. The following applications lend insight into the possible use of generalized networks. (See [6,12, 15,16]).

A complete water distribution system with losses has been modeled by Bhaumik [4] as a generalized network problem. This model is primarily concerned with movement of water through canals to various reservoirs. However, the model must also consider the retention of water over several time periods. The multipliers in this case represent the loss effect due to both evaporation and seepage.

Turner and Gilliam [10] have proposed a file reduction model which has the form of a generalized transportation model with a single extra constraint. This model is designed to facilitate the reduction of extremely large microdata files to smaller, statistically representative files. The objective, in this case, is to minimize the amount of information lost in the reduction process. The arcs represent paths from the original records to the reduced records. A non-zero flow on an arc implies that the originating record is to be represented by the terminal record. The multipliers on the arcs are used to insure that the reduced file is truly representative of all of the original records.

Kim [23] has utilized generalized networks to represent copper refining processes. The electrolytic refining procedure, in this case, is modeled by a large d-c electrical network. The arcs are current paths and the multipliers representing the appropriate resistances. In this way, Kim analyzes the effect of short circuits in the refining process.

Charnes and Cooper [6] identify applications of generalized networks for both plastic-limit analysis and warehouse funds-flow models. In plastic-limit analysis, the network is generated by forming the equations for horizontal and vertical equilibrium and by employing a coupling technique. The warehouse funds-flow model is actually a multi-time period model. The arcs are used to represent sales, production, and the inventory holding of both products and cash. The multipliers are introduced to facilitate the conversions between cash and products.

A cash management problem has been modeled as a generalized network by Crum [7]. This model for the multi-national firm incorporates transfer pricing, receivables and payables, collections, dividend payments, interest payments, royalties, and management fees. The arcs represent possible cash flow patterns and the multipliers represent costs, savings, liquidity changes, and exchange rates. Other applications include machine loading problems [6,8, 30], blending problems [6,30], the caterer problem [8,30], and scheduling problems such as production and distribution problems, crew scheduling, aircraft scheduling, and manpower training [6,8, 30].

INTEGER GENERALIZED NETWORKS

The foregoing uses the arc multipliers represent just a part of their full range of application. An especially significant realm of application, only recently discovered, is based on the fact that flows on particular arcs must occur in integer (whole number) amounts. Introducing the integer requirement into the GN problem enables it to model an unexpected diversity of applications, including problems such as shceduling variable length television commercials into time slots, assigning jobs to computers in computer networks, scheduling payments on accounts where contractual agreements specify "lump sum" payments, and designing communication networks with capacity constraints.

These, and many other applications that make use of integer requirements in GN problems, are founded on the new modeling principla we call NETFORM (network formulation) principles. The power of NETFORM techniques is illustrated by the fact that they enable any 0-1 LP problem to be modeled as an integer GN problem [16,18]. These techniques can also accommodate mixed integer 0-1 LP problems where the continuous part of the problem is a transportation, transshipment or generalized network problem itself. An illustration in [30] shows how contemporary financial capital allocation models can be modeled as integer GN problems. Important real world applications with such a "mixed" structure also include a variety of plant location models, energy models, and physical distribution models.

The NETFORM representation is able to rigorously express all of the elements of these problems that would ordinarily require expression in an abstract algebraic form, as by customary mathematical programming formulation techniques. Consequently, it effectively replaces the obscure and unilluminating algebraic representation by an equivalent, but much easier to understand, pictorial representation. But the advantages of the NETFORM approach do not end here, for we have found that its underlying network-related structures can be exploited by special solution methods that are substantially more efficient than the methods previously developed for the algebraic representations.

Figure 4 illustrates a useful modeling device commonly employed

Figure 4

Generalized Network with Interger Flow Restrictions

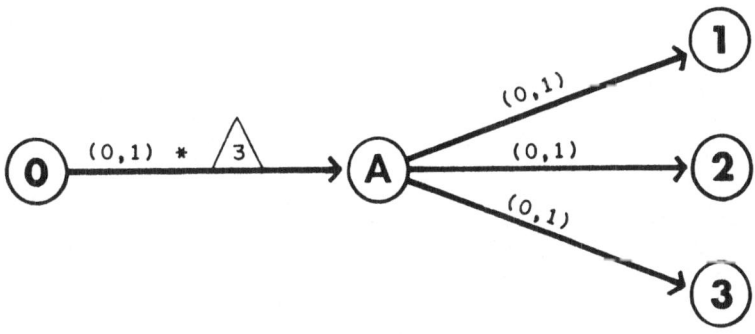

in the NETFORM approach. The bounds, costs, and multipliers are depicted by the same conventions employed before. In addition, the asterisk on the arc from node 0 to Node A indicates that its flow must be an integer. Since the bounds on the arc constrain the flow to lie between 0 and 1, and the integer requirement rules out all "fractional" values, the only acceptable flow values are excatly 0 and 1. If the flow is 0, then $3 \cdot 0 = 0$ and no flow gets transmitted to node A. But if the flow is 1, then 3 units are transmitted to node A. Further, because of the upper bounds of 1 on each of the three arcs leaving node A, the only possible way to distribute the 3 units flowing into node A is to send exactly one unit to each of the nodes 1, 2, and 3. Thus by giving all arcs bounds of 0 and 1, and introducing a generalized arc, the following effect has been achieved: when the flow on the arc from node 0 to node A is 0, the flow on each of the three arcs out of node A is 0; when the flow on the arc from node 0 to A is 1, the flow on each of the three arcs out of node A is 1.

The extension of this device to handle an even more useful set of conditions is illustrated in Figure 5. This figure is the same as before except that multipliers have not been added to the three arcs leaving node A. For concreteness, we may suppose this diagram represents an investment decision: to invest in project A (if the flow on the arc from 0 to A is 1) or not to invest in project A (if the flow on the arc from 0 to A is 0). Then the nodes 1, 2, and 3

Figure 5

An Equipment Investment

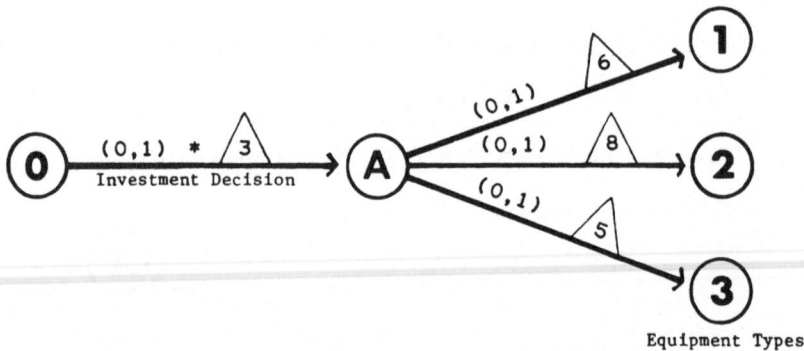

identify different components of this investment project. In this example, the investment project is set in an equipment purchase context, and nodes 1, 2, and 3 represent different equipment types. In other contexts, these nodes might represent different types of aircraft in a fleet, different parcels of land in a real estate venture, different types of stock in a portfolio, etc.

The multipliers on the arcs into nodes 1, 2, and 3 represent the quantities of each component of project A (each type of equipment) that would be acquired if in fact the decision is made to invest in that project. By the conventions and flow relationships previously described, the diagram of Figure 5 transforms the investment into its components in precisely the manner desired; i.e., in particular a flow of 1 on the arc from node 0 to node A (representing the decision to invest) translates into six units of Equipment 3 at node 3. The combination of arc multipliers and the 0-1 integer gives rise to what generally is called an integer network or a 0-1 generalized network. The kinds of uses to which this NET-FORM modeling tool can be put are demonstrated more fully by the following real-world applications.

Air Force Course Scheduling

Undergraduate Flight Training (UFT) graduates are required upon graduation to take advanced flight training and survival training courses enroute to their first operational assignment. Advanced flight training is offered only in formal schools usually by the Major Air Command, the principal aircraft user. UFT graduates must also take from one to four survival training courses which are only offered at certain times, have enrollment limits, and may have prerequisites. The identification of schedules is further complicated by attandance requirements at Combat Crew Training courses, various modes of transportation, the number of dead days in the pipeline, the opportunity for the UFT graduates to take leave as desired, etc.

To solve this UFT graduate scheduling problem, the Air Force developed a computer program (called the UFT Pipeline Scheduling Model) which generates from one to five feasible least cost schedules for each graduate. Using these schedules and course enrollment limits, the personnel manager in the Training Pipeline Management Division manually assigns each graduate to one of his feasible schedules. Clearly, this is a difficult and time-consuming task to do by hand; further, the total cost of these manual assignments may be far from optimal.

In search of a better way, the Air Force formulated this problem as an integer programming problem. We have reformulated this integer programming problem as the 0-1 GN problem shown in Figure 6.

In this diagram, the node M_i represents the ith man and has a supply of exactly 1. Each man node is connected by arcs to its set of man/schedule nodes. Each connecting man/schedule arc has a multiplier a_{ij} equal of the number of classes in the schedule and a cost c_{ij} equal to the cost of assigning man i to his j^{th} schedule. The asterisk again indicates that flow must be integer-valued. The arcs enamating from a man/schedule node in Figure 6 lead to the individual

200

Figure 6

UFT NETFORM FORMULATION

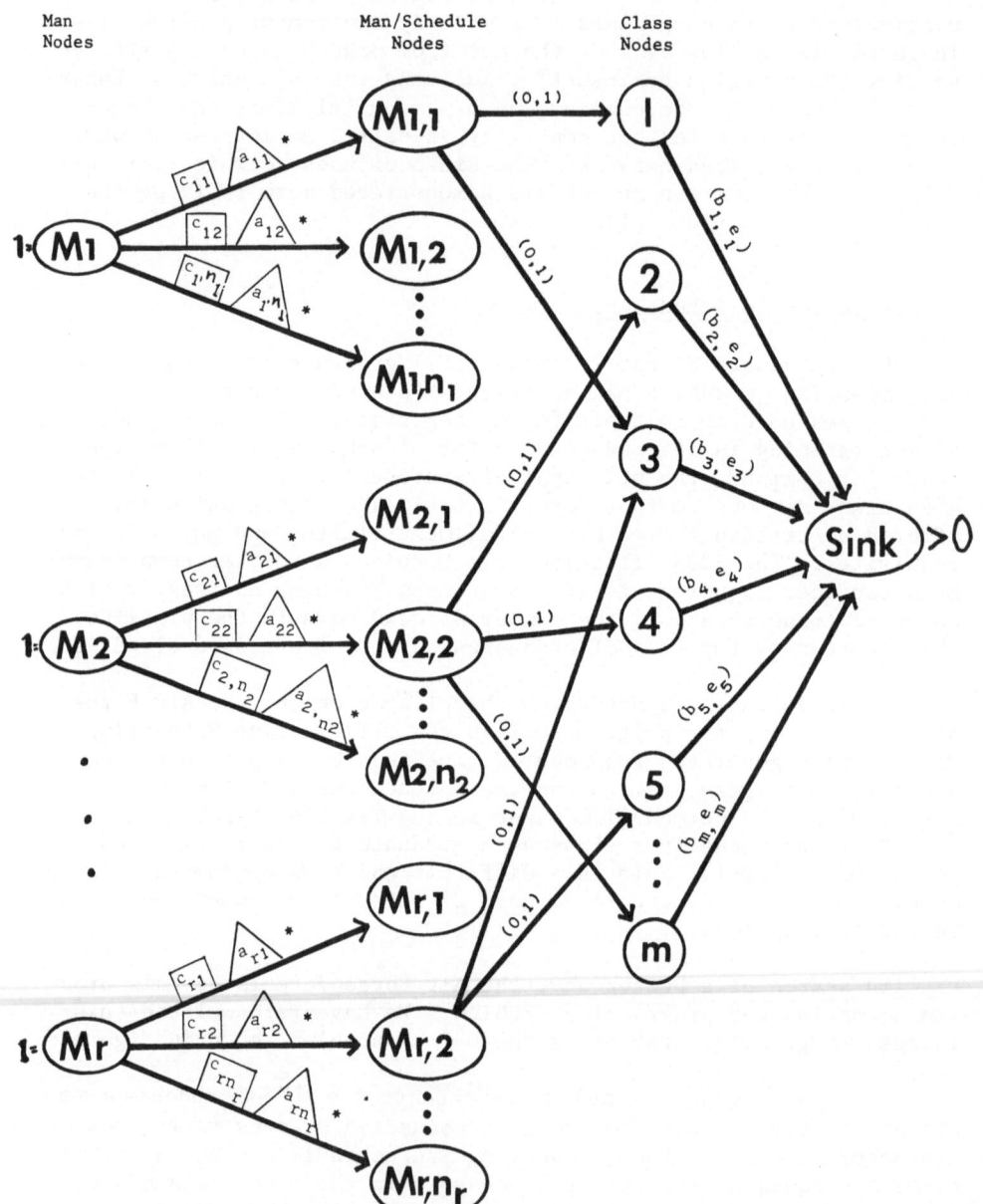

classes making up the schedule. Each of these arcs has an upper bound of one. Thus, if a particular schedule is "selected," then every class in the schedule is also automatically selected. The objective is to pick a schedule for each man that will minimize the value of the assignments on the overall program, subject to the upper and lower attendance limits for each class, expressed as bounds on the arcs from class nodes to the sink nodes of Figure 6. All arc costs, except for those attached to the man/schedule arcs, are thus equal to 0.

Typically the UFT problem involves 120 men, 200 classes, and 460 schedules, giving rise to a 0-1 formulation with 520 constraints and 460 0-1 variables. The 0-1 GN formulation involves 460 0-1 variables, 2,200 continuous variables and 780 nodes. This represents a fair increase in size as an LP problem, but provides a relatively small GN problem. The 0-1 GN problem of this application was solved using a specialized branch and bound procedure with GN subproblems. The optimal solution was often found and verified after only 30 seconds and in some cases only required a total solution time of 10 seconds on a CDC 6600. This is exceptionally fast for a 460 x 520 zero-one LP problem.

Refueling Nuclear Reactors

Another problem whose solution has been improved by the use of the NETFORM concept is a mixed integer programming problem for determining the minimum cost refueling schedule for nuclear reactors. This problem was initially modeled by Kazmersky [22] as a mixed integer programming problem with no apparent connection to networks. However, after working closely with Dr. Kazmersky, we discovered a way to express the problem by a NETFORM representation that was not only equivalent to the original formulation but that also succeeded in reducing the size of the problem. The transformation of the original problem to a 0-1 GN problem will not be shown because the mathematics is somewhat intricate and the original formulation by itself consumes more than twenty pages of [22]. However, making use of the 0-1 GN formulation, we were able to develop a branch and bound solution procedure which solved GN subproblems. Using this computer system, four versions of this problem were solved using data supplied by the TVA. The first three versions, while requiring half an hour to two hours to solve on an IBM 370/168 using MPSX, were easily solved in 10 to 20 minutes using the 0-1 formulation and the specialized solution approach. The fourth version was by far the most difficult, involving 173 constraints, 126 zero-one variables, and 511 continuous variables. The original mixed integer formulation was run for eight hours on an IBM 370/168 using MPSX and then taken off the machine to avoid further computer run costs. At the end of this time the best (minimum cost) solution obtained had an objective function value of $136,173,440. With a time limit of

30 minutes imposed on the 0-1 GN solution effort, a solution was obtained that had an objective function value of $125,174,727, which constitutes more than a $10,000,000 improvement. Consequently, this application shows that the use of the NETFORM approach can provide improved solutions for problems too complex to be solved optimally (within practical time limits) by standard approaches.

GENERALIZED ASSIGNMENT MODEL

A cousin to the inter generalized network problem, which is in fact a special case, is the so-called generalized assignment model. The nodes of this model (as in classical assignment and transportation models) are divided into two sets. The nodes of the first set are called origin nodes and only have arcs leaving them while the nodes of the second set are called destination nodes and only have arcs entering them. See Figure 7. Each origin node has a supply of exactly one and each destination node, subscripted by the index i, has a demand of at least (or at most) d_i. Additionally, <u>each</u> arc has a cost, a multiplier, and an integer (0-1) restriction. For example, c_{11}, r_{11}, and the asterisk on the arc between origin node 1 and destination node 1 of Figure 7 indicate the cost, multiplier, and integer requirement on the arc.

Figure 7

Generalized Assignment Problem

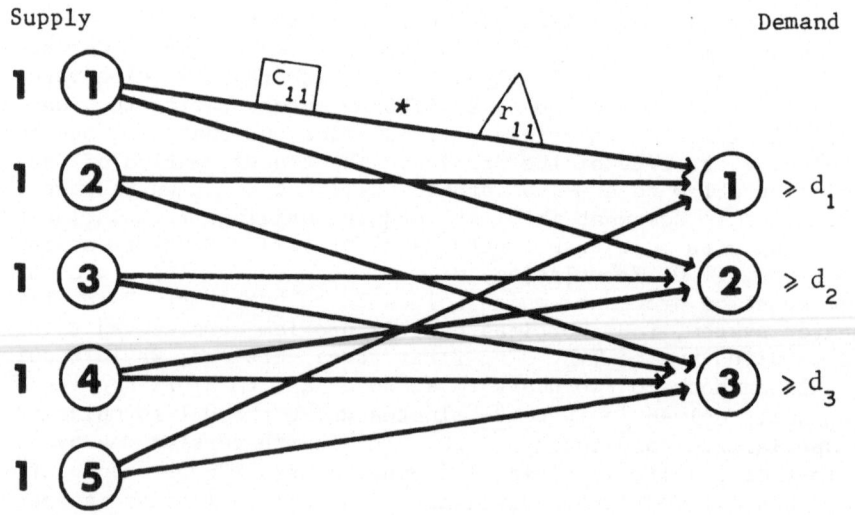

The name "generalized assignment model" is due to an instance of the model in which it is desired to assign personnel (at the origin nodes) to jobs (at the destination nodes). Each job has a

demand that requires at least a certain number of "standard man-
hours" (i.e., man-hours of an individual at a standard skill level)
to be devoted to that job during a specified interval (weekly,
monthly, etc). The multiplier r_{ij} on an arc represents the number
of standard man-hours a given person can contribute to a given job
during the interval. Note that an individual will have different
multiplier values on different arcs as the result of possessing a
skill that exceeds or falls below the standard. An adiitional requirement is that each person can only be assigned to one job (integer requirement). In contrast to the classical assignment problem [6,8,30], however, a job may have several persons assigned to
it in order to satisfy its demand.

In another application, the origin nodes are visualized as
checking accounts and the destination nodes as days of the month.
The demands are "at most" requirements ($\leq d_j$) and represent daily
auditing capacity. Each account must be assigned to a day of the
month and the multipliers represent the auditing effort required
for the account.

A further application of this model involves the assignment of
ships to shipyards for overhaul. The origin nodes in Figure 7 can
represent the ships and the destination nodes shipyards. Like the
last application, the demands are "at most" requirements and represent shipyard capacity in days. The multiplier represents the number of days required for the overhaul at the shipyard. The "cost
coefficients" could be a weighted combination of attributes such as
transportation costs, overhaul costs, desirability of assigning the
ship to this yeard, etc. The objective would then be to minimize
total "cost."

A major real world application of this problem that demonstrates
the nature and practical value of its model structure more fully will
now be described.

Optimal Lot-Sizing and Machine Loading for Multiple Products

The generalized assignment model described in this section is
currently being used by a major manufacturing firm for large-scale
task allocation. The problem involves the determination of lot-
sizes for each of n products and the assignment of production to
m machines in such a way that combined set-up, production, and
holding cost per unit time is minimized. The principal characteristics of the problem are:

1. The planning horizon is a single period, t weeks in length.

2. The products are designed to meet different needs and can-
    not be substituted for one another. Production of each

product is a single-stage process.

3. Lot-sizes are selected from a predetermined finite set of ℓ possible lot-sizes.

4. All lots of any single product must be produced on the same machine.

5. The machines work in parallel. They are similar in function, but they may differ in their rate and cost of operation. Some machines may be capable of producing several (or all) of the products while others may be more specialized.

6. The production capacities of all machines over the planning horizon are known constants. Each machine can produce only one product at a time.

7. Demand for each product is assumed to occur continuously at a known constant rate.

These characteristics give rise to the following mathematical model.

A binary valued decision variable x_{ijk} is introduced which is defined to be 1 if project j is produced on machine i in the kth possible lot-size and 0 otherwise. The combined set-up, production, and holding cost (per unit time) incurred when product j is produced on machine i in the kth possible lot-size is denoted by c_{ijk}. Similarly, r_{ijk} denoted the capacity required on machine i to produce product j in the kth possible lot-size. Finally, b_i denotes the aggregate production capacity of machine i over the t week planning horizon.

The problem is to determine values for the variables that Minimize:

$$\sum_{i=1}^{m} \sum_{j=1}^{n} \sum_{k=1}^{\ell} c_{ijk} x_{ijk} \tag{1}$$

Subject to:

$$\sum_{i=1}^{m} \sum_{k=1}^{\ell} x_{ijk} = 1 \text{ for } j = 1,\dots,n \tag{2}$$

$$\sum_{j=1}^{n} \sum_{k=1}^{\ell} r_{ijk} x_{ijk} \overset{\leq}{=} b_i \text{ for } i = 1,\dots,m$$

$$x_{ijk} = 0 \text{ or } 1 \text{ for } i = 1,\ldots,m;$$

$$j = 1,\ldots,n; \ k = 1,\ldots,\ell. \tag{3}$$

Constraints (1) and (3) together insure that one and only one machine and lot-size combination is selected for each product. Constraint (2) insures that each machine is assigned production tasks commensurate with its capacity.

It is clear from the formulation above that the model is designed only to load the machines and that it does not schedule the work on each machine. In fact, the lot-sizes selected by the model may generate scheduling conflicts on any given machine. Although such potential conflicts are important in theory, they have not caused any difficulty in practice. Moreover, managers primarily use the model for capacity planning and prefer to retain the option of scheduling on the basis of what is "hot." Thereby, they retain the prerogative of determining the precise sequence and timing for implementing the candidate assignment over the horizon, in accordance with the objectives of this application. This provides flexibility to make adjustments to special conditions and changed demands, while simultaneously aiding planning functions (such as evaluating the possible use of overtime shifts in periods when the candidate assignments tax weekly production capacities.). For this type of flexibility and responsiveness to the needs of management, and to further support the analyses based on alternative assumptions of demands and capacities, it is especially important to be able to solve the model quickly for different (or recently updated) sets of data. Thus, the success of the application depends in large measure on the ability to solve the problem efficiently.

The firm in which this application arises initially tried to solve the problem using the efficient 0-1 code RIP 30-C developed by Geoffrion at UCLA. This proved to be unsuccessful for two reasons: (1) the large array requirements of RIP 30-C made it impossible to accommodate large problems; and (2) the method required excessive computation times even to solve problems with no more than 50 variables.

Consequently, it was apparent that an alternative solution approach was needed. The first step of our effort to identify such an approach was to characterize the network related structure of the problem, which in this case turns out to be a generalized assignment structure, as already intimated.

Although this is not immediately apparent from the algebraic statement, if equations (1) and (2) are written out (replacing (1) by its negative), the coefficient matrix has only two non-zero entries per column, which are -1 and r_{ijk}. Thus this problem can be represented graphically in the usual fashion by letting a node represent each equation and an arc each variable. Figure 8 illustrates the resulting graph. The two sets of nodes for this problem consist of a product node set and a machine node set. The arcs joining the nodes in these sets correspond to the variables x_{ijk}; the cost and multiplier of each of these arcs correspond to the cost and resource consumption of the associated variable.

This graphical representation as a generalized assignment problem led immediately to identifying an appropriate solution method. In particular, extremely effective techniques for solving such problems have been developed by Ross and Soland [27] and imbeded in a computer code called BIG-A.

A comparison of the BIG-A code with the RIP 30-C code for this problem shows that the BIG-A code is from 300 to 1000 times faster. In addition, the BIG-A code readily handles problems of up to 4000 variables within available computer memory. Thus, the firm now

Figure 8

NETFORM Representation

Product Nodes   Machine Nodes

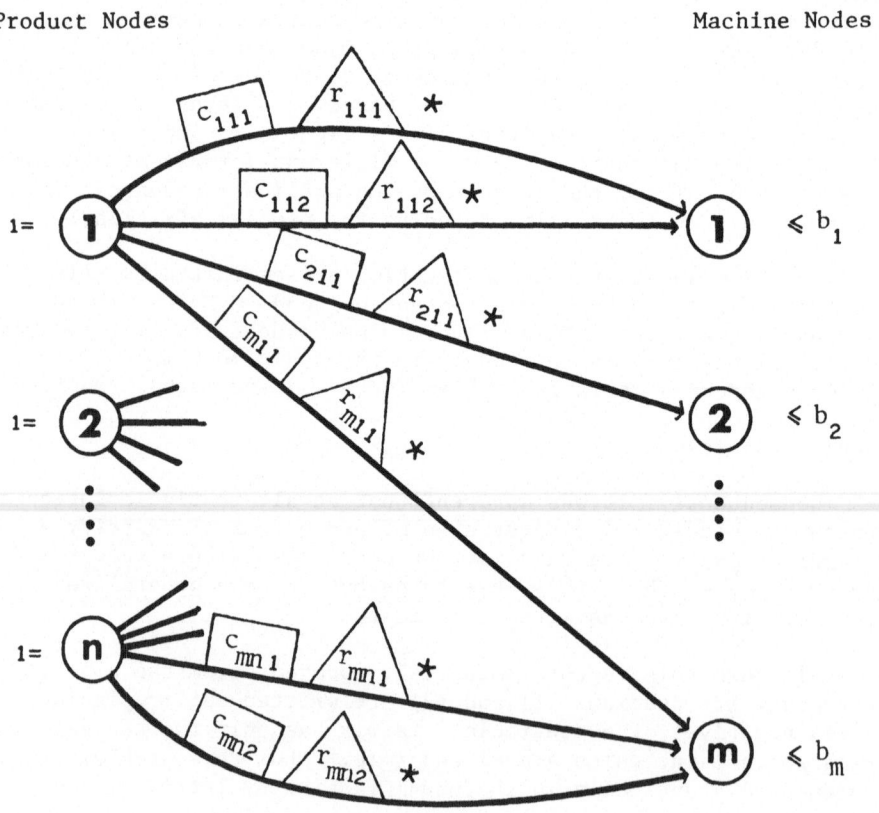

uses the graphical formulation coupled with the BIG-A code to solve
the problem. This approach has made it possible to solve problems
with 106 machines, 182 products, 4 lot-size options per machine/
product combination and 3772 zero-one variables in .64 seconds on
a CDC 6600.

PART II: ALGORITHMS AND IMPLEMENTATIONS

Part II of the paper is divided into three sections. The first
section presents a computational comparison of current network codes
with the state-of-the-art LP code, APEX-III. Section two briefly
compares and contrasts the implementation logic of network codes and
LP codes. The final section discusses how these implementation procedures can be merged to provide a new generation of LP codes.

The discussion in each of these sections is devoted to sketch-
ing the concepts and innovations that represent the highlights of
the field. A minutely detailed coverage of these topics would fill
a book. Thus the intent of each section is to provide the reader
with an executive summary rather than a microscopically focused account of these topics.

COMPARISON RESULTS

Part I presented a diverse spectrum of practical applications
and some impressive computational statistics for solving these problems by means of recent advances in network-related modeling and
solution technology. In this section we take a closer look at the
form of these advances in the realm of solution methods, and provide fuller insight into their practical significance by presenting
the results of empirical tests of the new methods against a leading
example of the state-of-the-art in solution systems that does not
incorporate the network technology. In particular, we report computational comparisons of the new network codes against APEX-III on
a wide array of network problems of varying structures.

These results are not biased by variations in computer hardware: all problems were solved on the same machine. Further, an
attempt was made to execute the codes when the computer had the
same type of job load. Even with these safeguards, minor differences
between two solution times should be statistically ignored and the
focus should be on order of magnitude differences. For this reason, the times reported are for large problems so that timing variations become less significant.

Table I contains solutions times on 15 network problems using
APEX-III on a CYBER-74. The first set of problems consists of assignment problems and the reported network solution times were

TABLE I

(times are in billing units)

PROBLEM TYPE	no. of equations	no. of variables	APEX III		Network Code	
			solution times	cost	solution times	cost
Assignment	400	1500	231.85	$ 41.73	1.16	$ .21
	400	2250	336.37	60.55	1.34	.24
Transportation	200	1300	105.68	19.02	.94	.17
	200	1500	124.53	22.42	1.07	.19
	200	2000	164.94	29.69	1.21	.22
Transshipment	400	1306	174.83	31.47	1.51	.27
	1000	2900	833.63	150.05	5.28	.95
Generalized networks	250	4000	453.02	81.54	16.65	3.00
	250	4000	742.61	133.67	14.74	2.65
	500	5000	1044.34*	187.98	22.55	4.06
	1000	6000	1633.64*	294.06	50.22	9.04
Singularly constrained generalized networks	200	2000	205.87	37.06	16.10	2.90
	200	1000	130.18	23.43	11.38	2.05
	500	4000	943.25	169.79	32.72	5.89
	1000	6000	1875.55*	$337.60	83.13	$14.96

*Not optimal after 10,000 iterations.

obtained using the AP-AB code of [3]. The solution times indicate that the AP-AB code is roughly 200 times faster than APEX-III on assignment problems.

The network code times reported on the transportation and transshipment problems were obtained using the ARC-II code of [2]. Again the network solution times are substantially superior (on the order of 130 times faster than APEX-III). The fourth set of solu-times are for generalized network problems. The network code times refer to the NETG code [12].

The relative superiority of network code times to APEX-III is smaller for generalized networks than for pure networks. The code NETG is on the order of 50 times faster than APEX-III on generalized networks; nevertheless, this superiority is dramatic, especially in terms of computer costs for solving such problems.

The final set of test results are for LP problems composed on a GN problem augmented by an arbirtrary linear constraint. This problem-type is called the singularly constrained generalized net-work problem. The network code times refer to NETSG [20] code and are approximately 25 times faster than APEX-III. The results even for this class of constrained generalized networks are more than an order of magnitude faster than available with the advanced LP sys-tem.

In addition to improving solution speed, the network proces-sing techniques have the noteworthy advantage of requiring less computer memory to solve a problem. This allows larger problems to be solved without resorting to external storage devices, which can incur significant cost increases due to lengthened computer run times. Further, the reduced memory requirements enable many com-puter-based decision systems that would otherwise be excluded from this option to be used in an interactive real-time processing en-vironment.

Yet another important advantage of the network codes is their portability. All of these codes are written in standard FORTRAN IV. Several beneficial consequences result. For example, this portability feature allows easy transfer of the network component of a computer-based decision system to a new computer. It also greatly facilitates imbedding the code as a subroutine within a larger system.

A final computational advantage, which will be discussed in the next section, is reduced round-off error. Taken together, the im-pressive array of advantages of the network solution codes makes it clear why their use in industry and government applications is rap-idly increasing.

IMPLEMENTATION APPROACHES

As pointed out in the preceding sections, linear network problems are special types of LP problems and can thus be solved using
any standard LP solution technique. Improvements in LP inversions
and reinversion processes, data compactification, and pivot strategies have provided dramatic increases in the efficiency of primal
simplex LP computer codes in recent years. In many cases, special
structures such as GUB constraints (which are embodied within network problems) are detected by current LP codes. This information
is then used to reduce storage requirements and to simplify operations. Despite these improvements, we saw in the preceding section
that the special purpose primal simplex network solution systems
dwarf the LP systems in their efficiency. In this section we examine some of the reasons for this, and undertake to trace their
more significant implications.

Undoubtedly, the primary reason for the superiority of network
codes over LP codes is the fact that the latter, with the exception
of the GUB feature, are based primarily on algebraic or arithmetic
processing. That is, these codes maintain and update a basis inverse by manipulating numbers. Further, the representation of a
variable to enter the basis is computed by matrix multiplication.

By contrast, the most efficient methods for solving network
problems are based on replacing arithmetic operations with "logical" operations. More precisely, these solution procedures are
based on viewing the problem in a graphical context (just as in
the case of network modeling ideas discussed previously). In particular, the network codes AP-AB, ARC-II, NETG, and NETSG (for assignment, transshipment, generalized, and singularly constrained
generalized networks, respectively) all store the coefficient matrix and basis matrix as graphs using computer list structures.

The use of such computer list structures reduces the amount
of work needed to perform the algorithmic steps and the amount of
computer memory required to store essential data. For example,
network codes normally store only the cost coefficient, the upper
bound, and the "to" node for each column of the coefficient matrix.
(In the case of a GN problem, the multiplier is also stored.) In
this way, problem data can often be resident in central memory even
for large-scale problems.

In particular, the most popular way of storing a network is to
use a linked list structure. In this method, all of the arcs that
begin at the same node are stored "together" under the name of their
"from" node and each is represented (distinguished from the others)
by recording only its "to" node, cost, and upper bound. A pointer
is then kept for each node which indicates the block of computer
memory locations for the arcs beginning at this node. The set of

arcs emanating from node u is called the <u>forward star</u> of node u
[11]. If the nodes are numbered sequentially from 1 to the number
of nodes, and the arcs are stored consecutively in memory such that
the arcs in the forward star of node i appear immediately after the
arcs in the forward of node i-1, then this method, called the for-
ward star form requires only $|N| + 2|A|$ units of memory for pure
uncapacitated problems, $|N| + 3|A|$ for pure capacitated problems,
and $|N| + 4|N|$ for capacitated generalized network problems where
$|N|$ denotes the number of nodes and $|A|$ the number of arcs. Figure
9 illustrates the storage of a pure network in forward star form.
As before, the number in the square attached to an arc of the network diagram is the cost. Note that the supplies and demands of
the nodes are not stores in central computer memory since a starting basis is selected whose flows satisfy node conservation and
the updated flows after each iteration also satisfy node conservation.

Figure 9

Forward Star Form

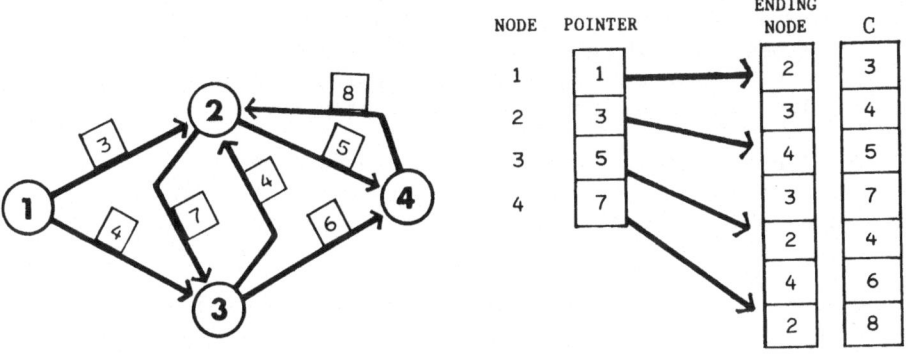

Network basis matrices, like network coefficient matrices, have
a graph structure. Moreover, the graph structure of a basis matrix
is very special, consisting either of disjoint trees or of trees
coupled with one additional arc (called quasi-trees [12]). The
basis of a pure network consists of a single tree and the basis of
a GN problem consists of one or more trees and quasi-trees. These
trees and quasi-trees can be stores and updated with remarkable efficiency by special linked list and labeling procedures that have
been developed in the past few years [2,3,13,17,28].

A common way of representing a tree in a computer is to think
of the root node r as the highest in the rooted tree with all nodes
hanging below it. If nodes i and j are endpoints of a common arc
in the rooted tree such that node i is closest to the root, then i
is called the predecessor of node j and node j is called an immediate successor of node i. The tree is then represented by keeping

a pointer list which contains for each node w ≠ r, its predecessor. This upward pointer is called the predecessor of node w and is denoted by p(w). For convenience, we will assume that the predecessor of the root, p(r), is zero.

Figure 10 illustrates a tree rooted at node 1, the predecessor of the nodes and other functions to be described subsequently. The predecessor of a node is identified in the p array. For example, the predecessor of node 16 is node 5.

It is important to note that the direction of the arcs in Figure 10 correspond to the orientation induced by the predecessor ordering and do <u>not</u> necessarily correspond to the direction of the basic arcs in the network. Thus, it is necessary to keep track of each basic arc's true direction. In performing the various tree traversals required by the simplex algorithm, we say that arc (i,j) is traversed in the forward direction if it is traversed from node i to node j (i.e., in accordance with its network direction) and is traversed in the reverse direction otherwise.

Most primal simplex codes keep another list indexed by the node numbers and associated with tree T. This list contains for each node v a label d(v), whose value is the current dual variable value of this node. Henceforth, d(v) will be called the node potential of node v. The root r has a node potential of zero.

In Figure 10 the number in the square on each arc indicates the cost of the arc. The entries in the d array identify dual variable values which satisfy complementary slackness for the basis variables. That is, for each basic arc (i,j), $-d(i) + d(j) = c_{ij}$.

Figure 10 illustrates additional tree information expressed as node functions, which <u>can be used</u> in the computer implementation procedures.

The first of these functions, the thread function [2,17], is denoted by t(x). This function is a downward pointer through the tree. As illustrated in Figure 10 by the small dashed line, function t may be thought of as a connecting link (thread) which passes through each node exactly once in a top to bottom, left to right sequence, starting from the root node. For example, in Figure 10, $t(1) = 2$, $t(2) = 4$, $t(4) = 5$, $t(5) = 16$, $t(16) = 8$, etc.

Letting n denote the number of nodes in the tree, the function t satisfies the following inductive characteristics:

a) The set $\{r, t(r), t^2(r), \ldots, t^{n-1}(r)\}$ is precisely the set of nodes of the rooted tree, whereby convention $t^2(r) = t(t(r))$, $t^3 = t(t^2(r))$, etc. The nodes $r, t(r), \ldots, t^{k-1}(r)$ will be called the antecedents of node $t^k(r)$.

Figure 10

Tree Labeling Techniques

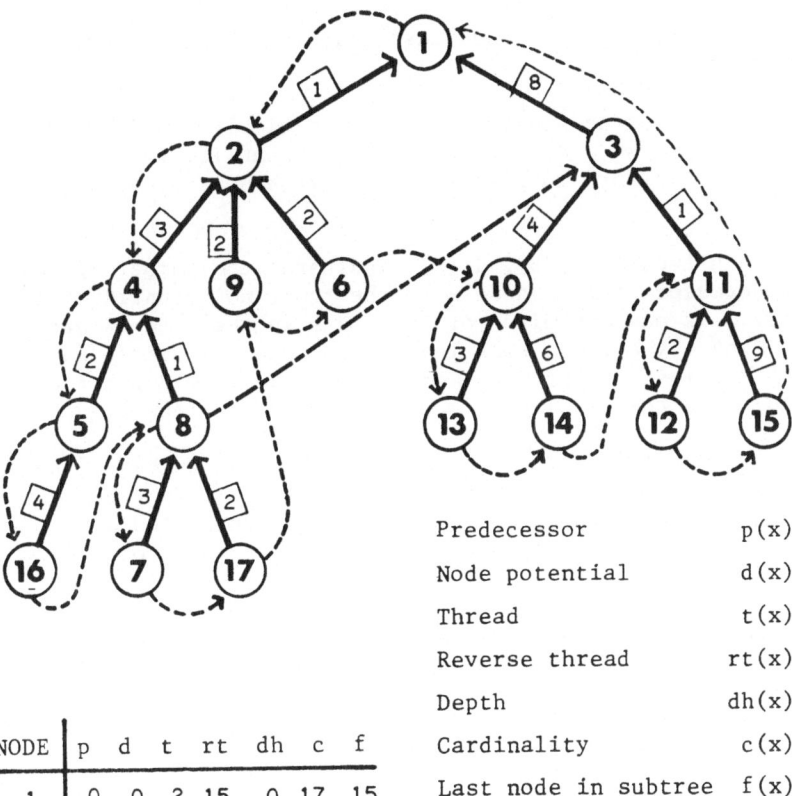

Predecessor	p(x)
Node potential	d(x)
Thread	t(x)
Reverse thread	rt(x)
Depth	dh(x)
Cardinality	c(x)
Last node in subtree	f(x)

NODE	p	d	t	rt	dh	c	f
1	0	0	2	15	0	17	15
2	1	1	4	1	1	9	6
3	1	8	10	6	1	7	15
4	2	4	5	2	2	6	17
5	4	6	16	4	3	2	16
6	2	3	3	9	2	1	6
7	8	8	17	8	4	1	7
8	4	5	7	16	3	3	17
9	2	3	6	17	2	1	9
10	3	12	13	3	2	3	14
11	3	9	12	14	2	3	15
12	11	11	15	11	3	1	12
13	10	15	14	10	3	1	13
14	10	18	11	13	3	1	14
15	11	18	1	12	3	1	15
16	5	10	8	5	4	1	16
17	8	7	9	7	4	1	17

b) For each node i other than node $t^{n-1}(r)$, t(i) is one of the nodes such that p(t(i)) = (i), if such nodes exist. Otherwise, let x denote the first node in the predecessor path of i to the root that has an immediate successor y and y is not an antecedent of node i. In this case, t(i) = y.

c) $t^n(r)$ = r; that is, the "last node" of the tree threads back to the root node.

The reverse thread function, rt(x), is simply a pointer that points in the reverse order of the thread. That is, if t(x) = y, then rt(y) = x. Figure 10 also lists the reverse thread function values.

The depth function [28], dh(x), indicates the number of nodes in the predecessor path of node x to the root, not counting the root node itself. If one conceives of the nodes in the tree as arranged in levels--where the root is at level zero, and all nodes "one node away from" the root are at level one, etc.--then the depth function simply indicates the level of a node in the tree. (See Figure 10.)

The cardinality function, c(x), specifies the number of nodes contained in the subtree associated with node x in the tree. By the nodes in the subtree associated with node x, we mean the set of all nodes w such that the predecessor path from w to the root contains x. (See Figure 10.)

The last node in a subtree function, f(x), specifies the last node in the subtree of x that is encountered when traversing the nodes of this subtree "in thread order." More precisely, f(x) = y where y is the unique node in the subtree of x such that t(y) is not also a node in the subtree of x. (See Figure 10.)

Note that both the domain and the range of each of the above discrete functions consist of the set of nodes and thus are independent of the number of arcs. Since |N| is the maximum number of nodes that could be in the tree, a one dimensional array of size |N|, called a node length array, is allocated to each function during computer implementation. The procedures for updating the values of the functions when the tree is reconfigured is discussed in [2,13,17,28]. Current network codes use only a subset of these functions. For example, the code [1] that we developed for the U.S. Treasury to solve problems with 50,000 nodes and 62 million arcs on a UNIVAC 1108 uses only the predecessor, node potential, and thread functions because of central memory limitations. The most efficient code, ARC II [3], whose times are reported in the previous section, uses the predecessor, thread, last node, node potential, and cardinality functions. The previously fastest code PNET-I [14] uses the predecessor, thread, node potential, and depth functions. The selection of which functions to use in developing a code largely depends on the developers trade-off utility between c.p.u. times and central memory.

The original problem data (compactly stored) and the basis matrix (sorted via linked lists) are the only data elements kept by network codes. No basis inverse is stored. In LP systems, inverses generally require considerable amounts of storage and involve numerous (error-producing) arithmetic operations. In network systems, the specialized labeling rules (that are designed to exploit the linked list storage structures) operate on the basis graph in a manner that obviates the use of a basis inverse.

Fundamental Steps of Special Problem Primal Simplex Codes

The fundamental pivot, or basis exchange, step of the simplex method will now be briefly reviewed in the graphical setting. Assume that a primal feasible starting basis (possibly containing artificial arcs) has been determined and is represented as a rooted tree. To evaluate the nonbasic arcs to determine whether any of them "price out" profitably, and therefore are candidates to enter the basis, it is necessary to determine node potentials (values for the dual variables) $d(i)$ which satisfy complementary slackness; i.e., which yield $-d(i) + d(j) = c_{ij}$ for each basic arc. Because of redundancy in the defining equation of pure network problems, one node potential may be specified arbitrarily. The root node is customarily selected for this purpose and assigned a potential of zero, whereupon the potentials of the other nodes are immediately determined in a cascading fashion by moving down the tree using the thread function and identifying the value for each node from its predecessor using the equation $-d(i) + d(j) = c_{ij}$. This highly efficient labeling procedure for traversing the tree to initialize and update these node potential values is fully described in [1,3 17].

A feasible basic solution is optimal if the updated cost coefficient $\pi_{ij} = (-d(i) + d(j) - c_{ij})$ is nonpositive for all the nonbasic arcs with flow equal to its lower bound (without loss of generality we will assume that all lower bounds are 0 henceforth) and nonnegative for all nonbasic arcs with flow equal to U_{ij}. If the solution is not optimal, then a nonbasic arc which violates the nonnegativity or nonpositivity requirement for π_{ij} is selected to enter the basis. If the flow on the selected arc is zero (U_{ij}), then the simplex method attempts to increase (decrease) this flow. The arc to leave the basis is determined by: (1) finding the unique path in the basis tree, called the basis equivalent path, which connects the two nodes of the entering arc, and (2) isolating a blocking arc in this path whose flow goes to zero or its upper bound ahead of (or at least as soon as) any others as a result of increasing or decreasing the flow on the entering arc.

An increase (decrease) in the flow of the incoming arc causes a corresponding increase (decrease) in the flow of all basis equivalent path arcs traversed in the forward direction and a corresponding decrease (increase) of all basis equivalent path arcs traversed in the reverse direction. Thus, if a forward direction arc already has a 0 flow or a reverse direction arc already has a U_{ij} flow, then such an arc qualifies as a blocking arc and the incoming arc cannot be assigned a non-zero flow change. By using the predecessor and cardinality function in combination, one can quickly and efficiently simultaneously find the basis equivalent path and a blocking arc. To illustrate, suppose arc (8,3) in Figure 10 is the entering arc. Its basis equivalent path can be found by first examining the cardinality function of the nodes associated with the entering arc; namely, $c(8) = 3$ and $c(3) = 7$. Since $c(8) < c(3)$, find the predecessor of node 8. Compare $c(3)$ with $p(c(8)) = c(4) = 6$ and simultaneously determine the maximum flow change possible on the basis link between nodes 8 and 4. Continue this process of traversing the predecessor path of the current node with the smaller cardinality value until the "two" current nodes have the same cardinality value. If these "two" nodes are the same node, stop. The basis equivalent path has been traversed and a blocking arc found. Otherwise, continue from either of the two current nodes until the stopping criterion is satisfied.

It is important to note that the above procedure can be substantially improved computationally by augmenting the stopping criterion to stop when a zero flow change arc is encountered. Since computational testing has shown that 90 percent of the pivots made in solving network problems are degenerate, this augmented rule substantially improves solution times [1,2,12].

Once the entering and leaving arcs are known, the basis exchange is completed simply by updating the flow values on the basis equivalent path, determining new node potentials for the new basis tree, and updating the other functions used to represent the tree. Only a subset of the node potentials change during a pivot and these can be updated rather than being determined from scratch. (In a capacitated problem, the entering and leaving arcs can be the same arc. In this case, the updating is very simple.)

To update the node potentials, assume that the nonbasis arc (p,q) is to enter into the basis and the basic arc (r,s) is to leave the basis. If arc (r,s) is deleted from the basis (before adding arc (p·q)), two subtrees, K and $\overline{K}$, are formed, each containing one of the two nodes of the incoming arc (p,q). Let K denote the subtree which does not contain the root node of the full basis. The node potentials for the new basis may be obtained [13] by updating only those potentials of the nodes in K or $\overline{K}$, as follows. If p is in K, add $\delta = -d(p) + d(q) - c_{pq}$ to the potentials of each node in K. Otherwise, q is in K and $-\delta$ is used in the above operations.

(Note that $\delta \stackrel{>}{=} 0$ if arc (p.q) is nonbasic with zero flow and $\delta \stackrel{<}{=} 0$ if arc (p,q) is nonbacis with U_{pq} flow.)

The above procedure can be efficiently performed uy using the thread function to simultaneously locate K and update the node potentials. Further, since the node potentials in either subtre K or $\overline{K}$ can be updated, the above procedure can be substantially enhanced [2] by using the cardinality to select the smaller tree and updating its node potentials.

The procedures for updating the functions to represent the tree directly depend on which of the functions are being used. [2] describes these procedures when the predecessor, thread, cardinality, and last node functions are used. [17] describes these procedures when the predecessor and thread are used. The discussion in [17] can be easily modified when the depth function is used in conjunction with the predecessor and thread functions.

If the latter two combinations are used, the updating procedures basically involve rerooting subtree K at its associated node of the entering arc and attaching this rerooted subtree to $\overline{K}$ via the entering arc. As shown in [2], when the predecessor, thread, cardinality, and last node functions are used, either subtree can be efficiently rerooted and attached to the other subtree. This has several important computational advantages when integrating the operations of finding the basis equivalent path, the leaving variable, updating the node potentials, and updating the functions used to represent the tree.

Network Basis Traversal and Relations to Inverse Updating

The network labeling and list procedures provide a means for traversing (and modifying) relevant portions of the basis tree. The basis tree is given a "top-to-bottom" orientation by the predecessor and thread functions. Accordingly, there are two major types of traversal required to execute the basis exchange steps, called "upward traversal" and "downward traversal."

The first, upward traversal, is associated with operations normally requiring pre-multiplication by the inverse, such as determining the representation of a variable to enter the basis. This operation is performed by traversing the unique paths from selected nodes up to their "junction" point. Simultaneously, the equivalent triangular system of basis equations is solved, in effect, by back substitution. This approach has two advantages. First, original problem data are used to compute the representation; thus, roundoff error is minimized. Second, operations involving elements of the basis representation with weights of zero, or the execution of checks to identify such elements, are eliminated since the upward traversal of the basis graph isolated the elements that receive non-zero weights.

Downward traversal is analogous to post-multiplication by the inverse. This operation is used to calculate updated dual variable values (node potentials) associated with the problem nodes. At each iteration, new dual values must be computed for the nodes in a particular subtree associated with the arc leaving the basis. (The set of nodes whose potentials must be updated for GN problems has a slightly more complex characterization.) These nodes can all be encountered, and their new node potentials determined, by downward traversal using the thread function. For a pure network, it is only necessary to add a constant to the potential of each node in the subtree. In the case of a GN problem, each new value is computed by a simple operation which is equivalent to solving an equation in just one variable. An additional computational advantage of this procedure is that only the dual variables whose values change are examined at each iteration. Thus this operation again strictly eliminates checking or performing arithmetic operations on zero elements.

Integrated Operations

In the better network codes, the updating of the dual variables is integrated with the updating of the basis graph. The complete basis exchange step involves finding the representation of the arc to enter the basis, determining the arc to leave the basis, updating the node potentials, and restructuring (and partly re-orienting) the basis graph by removing the arc leaving the basis and inserting the arc entering the basis. This last step, which is equivalent to updating the basis inverse, is accomplished simply by changing a few pointers in the list structures: no arithmetic operations are involved and, consequently, no round-off error introduced. The integration of this basis update with the dual update, by which both processes are carried out simultaneously, is made possible by the specialized labeling procedures [2].

These advantageous features of network systems have motivated researchers to develop extensions for solving LP problems with embedded networks. The NETSG code is an instance of one such extension. The next section briefly describes the fundamental ideas underlying such extensions and indicates their potential value.

EXPLOITING EMBEDDED NETWORK STRUCTURE

The procedures for exploiting embedded network structure are based on partitioning the coefficient matrix of an LP problem into network and non-network components. Such a partitioning scheme arranges the rows so that each column has at most two non-zero entries in the first m rows out of a total of m + q rows. By reference to this partitioning, a basis compactification procedure is employed that induces an identical row partitioning on the basis matrix B so that B can be expressed in the form

$$
B = \begin{bmatrix} G_m & E_q \\ A_m & A_q \end{bmatrix}
$$

The submatrix G_m is an m x m basis for the underlying network (or networks) composing the first m row of the LP problem. The basis inverse B^{-1} may be stated relative to this same partition as:

$$
B^{-1} = \begin{bmatrix} (G_m^{-1} + G_m^{-1} E_q Q^{-1} A_m G_m^{-1}) & (-G_m^{-1} E_q Q^{-1}) \\ -Q^{-1} A_m G{-1} & Q^{-1} \end{bmatrix}
$$

where $Q = A_q - A_m G_m^{-1} E_q$.

The motivation for this partitioning is to factor out the matrix G_m. By its connection with the network, G_m may be stored as a graph and any operations involving G_m^{-1} may be performed by the special labeling and basis traversal techniques discussed in the preceding section. This means that G_m^{-1} need not be explicitly generated and the full basis inverse B^{-1} can be determined simply by referring to the partitioned components of the basis B and the q x q matrix Q^{-1}. Thus, Q^{-1} may be viewed as the working basis inverse for such problems. Since the row (and column) dimension of Q^{-1} is equal to the number of non-network constraints of the LP problem, the algorithmic steps of the simplex method can be executed much more efficiently and with considerably less demand on computer memory by merging the network updating of G_m^{-1} with the standard of updating of Q^{-1}. The benefits previously discussed for dealing with network basis updating thereby carry over to the partitioned LP problem with only the residual portion of the basis associated with Q^{-1} being subject to the slower customary process with its greater attendant susceptibility to round-off error and numerical inaccuracy. In addition, since the ordering of the rows to achieve the partition need be done only once (and often will automatically be accomplished by the initial formulation), the augmentation of commercial LP systems with such a "special order network" (SON) features would constitute a noteworthy and beneficial enhancement.

The development of the SON feature will in our opinion produce the next major computational advance in large-scale linear programming. In fact, it should have a more profound effect than the development of generalized upper bound (GUB). This belief is based on the following:

1) GUB is a specialization of these procedures. This can be seen simply by observing that the GUB constraints can be scaled and summed to form another constraint which, when appended to the GUB constraints, yields a network.

2) SON extends GUB in several important ways. For example, it eliminates the non-overlapping variable requirement of GUB in an efficient manner. Other attempts to accomplish this by "generalized GUB" procedures do not share the computational power of network techniques.

3) Computational experience with the SON feature in prototype applications involving both a simple form of the problem, solved completely by SON, and a fully general form of the problem solved partly by SON, already demonstrate that substantial computational savings are possible. In particular, the NETSG code, previously reported to be 25 times faster than APEX-III (and with substantially better memory requirements), is a direct application of SON to the situation of a single arbitrary linear constraint, where the network portion is a generalized network with arbitrary multipliers.

At the opposite end of the spectrum, we have implemented a "first pass" execution of the SON feature for a major automobile manufacturer engaged in solving more general LP problems with large imbedded network components. The firm was solving LP problems of this application on an IBM 370/145 using MPSX, incurring computer run times in excess of 30 minutes per problem. We superimposed a network system on the MPSX system in a manner designed to operate on the network portion of the problem to produce an advanced starting basis for MPSX. This "first pass" application by itself reduced the total solution time from over 30 minutes to 10 minutes.

SON and Integer Programming

There is another important application of the SON feature that extends beyond its use in solving LP problems. This application has to do with solving pure and mixed integer programming (IP) problems. Current research has shown that the best solution approach is to use formulations which keep the number of integer variables as small as possible and which yield strong LP relaxations, rather than minimizing the number of constraints. Fortunately, the IP problem manipulation schemes for obtaining stronger LP relaxations often induce network structure. This result is largely unrecognized presently by many IP practitioners and even by researchers.

To illustrate this statement, consider the constraint

$$x_1 + x_2 + x_3 - 3x_4 = 0$$

where x_1, x_2, x_3, x_4 are 0-1 variables. It is well known that re-placing this constraint by the constraints:

$$s_1 + x_1 = x_4$$

$$s_2 + x_2 = x_4$$

$$s_3 + x_3 = x_4$$

yields a stronger LP relaxation. Note however that by performing elementary row operations this latter set of constraints is equivalent to:

$$0 = x_1 - x_2 \qquad\qquad +s_1 - s_2$$

$$0 = \qquad x_2 - x_3 \qquad\qquad +s_2 - s_3$$

$$0 = \qquad\qquad x_3 \qquad\qquad\qquad s_3 - x_4$$

Subtracting these constraints produces $0 = -x_1 - s_1 + x_4$. Appending this equation to the others yields a network.

By combining the IP problem manipulation approach with the SON feature the working basis inverse of the LP problem would be reduced by the number of constraints that would otherwise be added to accommodate relationships of the form indicated. Thus the addition of the SON feature to commercial LP systems would substantially overcome the problem expansion concern of many practitioners when using stronger IP/LP formulations.

The above example is only one of many important uses of the SON feature in integer programming. Almost every practical IP application - fixed charge, location allocation, project selection, capacity expansion, and set-up scheduling problems have substantial network substructures.

In sum, it seems clear that the SON feature would constitute an important computational advance for large-scale LP and IP. Presently however, no LP or IP system has this feature. The full extent of the advantages to be derived from the SON feature needs to be established by extensive testing in diverse applications. The potential of the approach, in our opinion, strongly merits such a thorough implementation and analysis.

REFERENCES

1. Analysis, Research, and Computation, Inc., "Development and Computational Testing on a Capacitated Primal Simplex Trans-shipment Code," ARC Technical Research Report, P.O. Box 4067 Austin, Texas 78765.

2. R. Barr, F. Glover, and D. Klingman, "Enhancements of Spanning Tree Labeling Procedures for Network Optimization," Research Report CCS 262, Center for Cybernetic Studies, University of Texas at Austin, 1976.

3. R. Barr, F. Glover, and D. Klingman, "The Alternating Basis Algorithm for Assignment Problems," Research Report CCS 263. Center for Cybernetic Studies, University of Texas at Austin, 1977.

4. G. Bhaumik, Optimum Operating Policies of a Water Distribution System with Losses, Unpublished Dissertation, University of Texas at Austin, August, 1973.

5. G. Bradley, G. Brown, and G. Graves, "Design and Implementation of Large Scale Primal Transshipment Algorithms," Technical Report NPS55BZBW76091, Naval Postgraduate School, Monterey, California, 1976.

6. A. Charnes and W. Cooper, Management Models and Industrial Applications of Linear Programming, Vols. I and II, Wiley, New York, 1961.

7. R. Crum "Cash Management in the Multinational Firm: A Constrained Generalized Network Approach," Working Paper, The University of Florida, Gainesville, Florida, 1976.

8. G. Dantzig, Linear Programming and Extensions, Princeton University Press, Princeton, New Jersey, 1963.

9. J. Evans, "A Single Commodity Network Model for a Class of Multicommodity Dynamic Planning Problems," Working Paper, University of Cincinnati, 1975.

10. G. Gillam and J. Turner, "A Profile Analysis Network Model to Reduce the Size of Microdata Files," Working Paper, Office of Tax Analysis, Office of the Secretary of the Treasury, Washington, D.C., 1974.

11. J. Gilsinn and C. Witzgall, "A Performance Comparison of Labeling Algorithms for Calculating Shortest Path Trees," NBS Technical Note 772, U.S. Department of Commerce, 1973.

12. F. Glover, J. Hultz, D. Klingman, and J. Stutz, "A New Computer-Based Planning Tool," Research Report CCS 258, Center for Cybernetic Studies, University of Texas at Austin, 1976.

13. F. Glover, D. Karney, and D. Klingman, "The Augmented Predecessor Index Method for Locating Stepping Stone Paths and Assigning Dual Prices in Distribution Problems," _Transportation Science_, 6, 2 (1972), 171-179.

14. F. Glover, D. Karney, and D. Klingman, "Implementation and Computational Study on Start Procedures and Basis Change Criteria for a Primal Network Code," _Networks_, 4, 3 (1974), 191-212.

15. F. Glover, D. Klingman, "Network Application in Industry and Government," _Research Report CCS 247_, Center for Cybernetic Sudies, University of Texas at Austin, 1975.

16. F. Glover, D. Klingman, and C. McMillan, "The NETFORM Concept," Research Report CCS 281, Center for Cybernetic Studies, University of Texas at Austin, 1977.

17. F. Glover, D. Klingman, and J. Stutz, "The Augmented Threaded Index Method for Network Optimization," INFOR, 12, 3 (1974), 293-298.

18. F. Glover and J. Mulvey, "Equivalence of the 0-1 Integer Programming Problem to Discrete Generalized and Pure Networks," MSRS 75-19, University of Colorado, Boulder, Colorado, 1975.

19. R. Helgason, J. Kennington, and H. Lall, "Primal Simplex Network Codes: State-of-the-Art Implementation Technology." _Technical Report IEOR 76014_, Department of Industrial Engineering and Operations Research, Southern Methodist University, Dallas, Texas, 1976.

20. J. Hultz and D. Klingman, "Solving Singularly Constrained Generalized Network Problems," _Research Report CCS 256_, Center for Cybernetic Studies, University of Texas at Austin, 1976.

21. J. Hultz and D. Klingman, "Solving Constrained Generalized Network Problems," _Research Report 257_, Center for Cybernetic Studies, University of Texas at Austin, 1976.

22. P. Kazemersky, "A Computer Code for Refueling and Energy Scheduling Containing an Evaluator of Nuclear Decisions for Operation," Unpublished Dissertation, Ohio State University, 1974.

23. Y. Kim, "An Optimal Computational Approach to the Analysis of a Generalized Network of Copper Refining Process," Presented at the Joint ORSA/TIMS/AIIE Conference, Atlantic City, New Jersey, 1972.

24. D. Klingman and R. Russell, "On Solving Constrained Transportation Problems," Operations Research, 23, 1 (1975), 91-107.

25. M. Collins, L. Cooper, and J. Kennington, "Solving the Pipe Network Analysis Problem Using Optimization Techniques," Technical Report IEOR 76008, Southern Methodist University, 1976.

224

26. "Out-of-Kilter Network Routine," SHARE Distribution 3536, SHARE Distribution Agency, Hawthorne, New York, 1967.

27. T. Ross and R. Soland, "A Branch-and-Bound Algorithm for the Generalized Assignment Problem," _Mathematical Programming_, 9 (1975), 91-103.

28. V. Srinivasan and G. Thompson, "Accelerated Algorithms for Labeling and Relabeling of Trees with Applications for Distribution Problems," JACM, 19, 4 (1972), 712-726.

29. H. Taha, _Operations Research_, The Macmillan Company, New York, 1971.

30. L. Tavis, R. Crum, and D. Klingman, "Implementation of Large-Scale Financial Planning Models: Solution Efficient Transformations," _Research Report CCS 267_, Center for Cybernetic Studies, University of Texas at Austin, 1976.

31. H. Wagner, _Principles of Operations Research_, Prentice-Hall, Englewood Cliffs, New Jersey, 1969.

INTEGER PROGRAMMING CODES

E.L. Johnson and S. Powell*

IBM, Thomas J. Watson Research Center (Johnson)
London School of Economics (Powell)

1. INTRODUCTION

In this brief survey of codes, we try to focus on the differences between commercial codes and other codes in use. In particular, we speculate as to why more sophisticated methods have not been incorporated into commercial codes and which methods seem likely to be implemented.

One overall remark which should be made at the outset is that commercial codes seem to be directed at large linear programs with few integer variables while most codes developed for experimentation are for pure integer problems with relatively small linear programming formulations. Sometimes the methodology employed for pure problems is simply not adaptable to the mixed problem. In any case, testing and extending a method in the environment of a large linear programming system may not be easy.

2. COMMERCIAL CODES

In July 1977 Land and Powell [17] found 11 maintained commercially available codes for solving mixed integer linear programming problems. Table 1 gives the name of the code, the name of the organization responsible, the computers for which the code is written, the approximate date of the first release and the code's status.

---

*This research has been supposed by the U.K. Science Research Council.

TABLE 1

The Commercial Codes

Code	Organization	Computer	Date	Under Development
Apex III	Control Data	Cyber 70 series, models 72,73,74, and 76; Cyber 170 6000 series 76000 series	1975	Yes
FMPS	Sperry-Univac	1100 series	1976	Yes
Haverley-MIP	Haverley Systems	IBM 360 and 370 series; Univac 90/30	1970	No
LP400	ICL	System 4-70 and 4-50	1970	No
MIP	IBM	360 and 370 series	1969	No
MIP/370	IBM	370 series	1974	Yes
MPS	Honeywell	Series 60 (level 66)	1973	Yes
Ophelie	SIA	CDC 6600	1972	No
Sciconic	Scicon	Univac 1100 series	1976	Yes
Tempo	Burroughs	B7000 series B6000 series	1975	No
XDLA	ICL	1900 series	1970	No

All the codes are MIP codes; that is, they can all handle problems in which some of the variables are continuous, and some (or all) are restricted to take integer values. A binary variable is restricted to take values zero or one and an integer variable is restricted to integer values between specified lower and upper bounds. All the codes can handle binary variables. Integer variables can be handled by all the codes except FMPS and Haverley-MIP. Apex III allows bivalent variables which must take either the value zero or an upper bound, which need not be one. A semi-continuous variable is restricted to take the value zero or any value greater than or equal to one. These variables are only available in Sciconic.

Beale and Tomlin [2] in 1970 introduced the concept of special ordered sets. There are two types, SOS1 and SOS2. A SOS1 is a set of variables such that at most one of the variables may take a non-zero value, and a SOS2 is a set of variables such that at most two adjacent variables may take non-zero values. A SOS1 is useful when a selection of one from a set of alternatives has to be made. A SOS2 is useful when there is a non-linear function (or functions) in the model, either in the objective function or among the constraints, and where separable programming techniques may yield local rather than global optima to the linear approximation. Sets in some form are present in 8 of the 11 codes.

Branching does not take place on the individual variables (except in FMPS) in the set. Branching in a set involves excluding (that is setting to zero) alternatively the variables on one side or the other of the branch point. Beale and Tomlin defined a con-straint in the model as a 'reference' row associated with a set that is used to determine the branch point of the set. In the codes where a reference row need not be supplied, the branching is done by assigning weights in some other way. Commonly the weights are the sequence numbers 1,...,p.

Probably as the result of introducing sets with the minimal change to the data input, all the codes, except Tempo, require that a set variable is a member of only one set, that is the sets do not overlap. Tempo is not restricted this way, as the sets are not specified by the user but by an analysis of the model by the code.

Table 2 summarizes the variants of special ordered sets that are available in each code.

2.1 Branch and Bound

All eleven codes solve mixed integer or pure integer program-ming problems by a branch and bound algorithm. All the codes start

TABLE 2

Special Ordered Sets

	Set variables must add to one?	Variables in set must be consecutive?	May have a reference row?	Must have a reference row?	Sets must be disjoint?	SOS2
Apex III	No	Yes	No	No	Yes	Yes
FMPS	Yes	No	No	No	Yes	No
Haverley-MIP	no special set facility					
LP400	Yes	Yes	Yes	No	Yes	No
MIP	no special set facility					
MIP/370	Yes	Yes	Yes	No	Yes	No
MPS	Yes	Yes	No	No	Yes	No
Ophelie	no special set facility					
Sciconic	No	Yes	Yes	Yes	Yes	Yes
Tempo	Yes	No	No	No	No	No
XDLA	Yes	Yes	Yes	No	Yes	Yes

by relaxing the integrality conditions and solving the resultant continuous linear programming problem. The branch and bound algorithm can be represented as a tree search and the initial continuous solution constitutes the first node in the tree of solution. Having created the first node, a simple form of branch and bound is as follows.

1. Select a node from the tree that does not satisfy the integer conditions. If there are none the algorithm is complete and the best integer solution found (if any) is the optimum.

2. Choose as the branching variable a variable which does not satisfy the integer conditions.

3. Branch to create (usually) two subproblems. Together the two subproblems exclude the current value of the branching variable but do not exclude any feasible integer solution. These two subproblems constitute two new nodes of the tree.

4. Solve neither, one or both of the subproblems. A node is said to be fathomed if the solution of the subproblem is a better integer solution, or is infeasible or has a value of the objective function worse than a known integer solution. A fathomed node is removed from the list of nodes. Return to step 1.

There are many variants on this simple branch and bound algorithm (see Geoffrion and Marsten [9]). Also within an algorithm there are many choices to be made: possibly the two most important are the choice of branching variable and the choice of node for further development.

2.2 Choice of branching variable

There is a wide variety of rules used for the choice of variable to branch upon and most of the codes offer the user a choice. Table 3 summarizes the choice available to each code. The same rules are used to select a set for branching; details of these are given in Land and Powell [17].

It is widely accepted that branching upon variables in the order of their importance can accelerate the progress of the algorithm. All the codes, except LP400, enable the user to define a priority list. The variable selected as the branching variable is that variable not satisfying the integer conditions with the highesr priority.

Penalties, which are described by Tomlin [22], are used by five codes, Apex III, LP400, MPS, Tempo and XDLA, to select the branching variable. Penalties provide guaranteed bounds on the function from branching in each direction on a variable. However, they are costly to compute and only provide information on the function value very close to the current solution.

TABLE 3

Choice of Variable to Branch Upon

	Priorities	Penalties	Pseudo-costs	Integer infeasibility	Pseudo-shadow costs
Apex III	✓	✓		✓	
FMPS	✓				
Haverley- MIP	✓			✓	
LP400		✓			
MIP	✓		✓		
MIP/370	✓		✓	✓	
MPS	✓	✓	✓	✓	
Ophelie	✓			✓	
Sciconic	✓				✓
Tempo	✓	✓	✓		
XDLA	✓	✓		✓	

Pseudo-costs, which are described by Benichou, Gauthier, Girodet, Hentges, Ribière and Vincent [4] are used by four codes, MIP, MIP/370, MPS and Tempo. Pseudo-costs are an estimate of the total effect of branching upwards or downwards on a variable. The disadvantage of pseudo-costs is that they do not provide a guaranteed bound on the function. The up and down pseudo-costs of the jth variable, PCU_j and PCL_j, are computed as

$$PCU = \frac{\Delta^+ x_o}{1-f_j} \quad \text{and} \quad PCL_j = \frac{\Delta^- x_o}{f_j}$$

where, on branching on the jth variable, $\Delta^+ x_o$ and $\Delta^- x_o$ are the absolute change in the functional value on the up and down branches, and f_j is the fractional part of the value of x_j before branching.

There are many integer infeasibility options for selecting the branching variable. All of them involve considering the fractional part of the value of a variable with a non-integral value. The details of these options are given in Land and Powell [17].

Pseudo-shadow costs, which are used only in Sciconic, have been described by Beale and Forrest [1]. At the input stage the user may specify up and down pseudo-shadow prices, p_i^+ and p_i^- for each constraint, i, and q_j^+ and q_j^-, up and down pseudo-costs for each integer variable. The pseudo-shadow costs and pseudo-costs must be strictly positive and in the absence of any user specification these values are taken as .0005 except for p_i^+ and p_i^- of the objective function, p_i^- on a less-than-or-equal-to constraint and p_i^+ on a greater-than-or-equal-to constraint whose values are zero. The estimated degradation in the objective function, or the estimated cost of satisfaction, in forcing an integer variable, x_j, to the integer above its current value is

$$D_j^+ = \{q_j^+ + \sum_i \max(p_i^+ a_{ij}, -p_i^- a_{ij}, \pi_i a_{ij})\} (1-f_j)$$

and in forcing x_j to the integer below is

$$D_j^- = \{q_j^- - \sum_i \min(p_i^+ a_{ij}, -p_i^- a_{ij}, \pi_i a_{ij})\} f_j$$

where π_i is the current dual value of the ith constraint, a_{ij} is the coefficient in the matrix of constraints, f_j is the fractional part of the value of x_j and the summation is over all rows including the objective function. The default rule in selecting the branching variable, x_k, is

$$\theta_k = \max_j \theta_j, \text{ where } \theta_j = \min(D_j^+, D_j^-).$$

2.3 Choice of node

An option in all of the codes except FMPS, on branching, is to solve either one or both of the newly created subproblems and then select one for further development. FMPS, on branching, solves both subproblems and then selects the node for further development from all nodes in the tree. On reaching a fathomed node, LP400, Ophelie and XDLA select the node that was last created as the one for further development, that is they follow the LIFO strategy. All the other codes, on reaching the fathomed node, select the node for further development from all the nodes of the tree. The node is chosen on the basis of a criterion. Table 4 indicates which criteria are used by each code.

The value of a node is a bound on the value of an integer solution that may be derived from a node. In the codes using

TABLE 4

Choice of Node Criteria

	Value of node	Best projection	Pseudo-cost est.	Sum of integer infeas.	Norm est.	Pseudo-shadow costs	Percent. error
Apex III	✓	✓					
FMPS	✓	✓		✓			
Haverley-MIP	✓						
LP400			LIFO strategy				
MIP	✓		✓				
MIP/370	✓		✓				
MPS	✓	✓	✓	✓			
Ophelie			LIFO strategy				
Sciconic						✓	✓
Tempo					✓		
XDLA			LIFO strategy				

penalties the value of a node is the functional value of the sub-problem $\pm$ the minimum penalty. The $\pm$ means + when minimizing and - when maximizing. In other codes the value of a node is the functional value of the subproblem.

The best projection estimate is an estimate of the value of an integer solution that may be derived from a node. The estimate is the degradation in the value of the objective function that is expected to be necessary to drive the sum of integer infeasibilities to zero. That is

$$BP_k = x_o^k + \left(\frac{|x_I - x_o^o|}{s_o} \right) * s_k$$

where BP_k is the BP value at node k, x^o and x^k are the functional value of the initial continuous problem and the problem at node k, x_I the value of an integer solution, s_o and s_k is the sum of integer infeasibilities at the continuous optimum and at node k. The integer infeasibility of an integer variable x_j is

$$\min(f_j, 1-f_j)$$

where f_j is the fractional part of the value of x_j.

The pseudo-cost estimate is functional value of the node plus (when minimizing) the sum of the degradations in the value of the objective function that will result from driving each variable to an integer value. That is

$$PCE_k = x_o^k + \sum_j \min (PCL_j f_j, PCU_j (1 - f_j))$$

where PCE_k is the pseudo-cost estimate at node k, PCL_j and PCU_j are the lower and upper pseudo-costs of variable j, and x_o^k and f_j are as defined above.

The sum of integer infeasibilities at node k, SIF_k, is

$$SIF_k = \sum_j \min (f_j, 1 - f_j).$$

The norm estimate at node k, NE_k, is

$$NE_k = \frac{depth^2}{|PCE_k - x_o^o|}$$

where 'depth' is the depth of node k within the tree, PCE_k is the pseudo-cost estimate at node k and x^o_o is the functional value of the initial continuous problem.

The pseudo-shadow cost estimate at node k, $PSCE_k$, is an estimate of the cost of satisfying all the integer infeasibilities. It is the functional value of node k, x^k_o, plus (when minimizing) the sum of the estimate of the cost of satisfying each integer infeasibility. That is

$$PSCE_k = x^k_o + \sum_j \min (D^+_j, D^-_j)$$

where D^+_j and D^-_j are defined in section 2.2.

The percentage error criterion is a measure of the error of an estimate; it was defined by Forrest, Hirst and Tomlin [6]. At node k the percentage error, PE_k is

$$PE_k = \frac{x_I - PSCE_k}{x^k_o - x_I} * 100$$

where $PSCE_k$ is the pseudo-shadow cost at node k, x_I is the value of a known integer solution and x^k_o the functional value at node k.

3. CUTTING PLANE CODES

The codes are all applicable only to the pure integer case and almost all are based on Gomory's work or some extension of it. The Land and Powell code [16] is easily available and documented. Trauth and Woolsey [23] have done a computational study of a number of codes.

Other ideas which have been discussed but are not in the available codes include: primal cutting plane methods, enumeration cuts, intersection cuts, cuts from corner polyhedra and subadditive functions, cuts from outer polars, and facets of polyhedra for special problems such as the travelling salesman and node packing problem.

Experience with cutting plane codes seems to be mixed. Martin [18] has reported being able to solve large crew-scheduling problems with his cutting plane code. The original hope for cutting plane codes was that since they convert an integer program into a linear program and since the simplex method works well in solving linear programs, cutting plane methods should have the same success in solving integer programs. However, the reality seems to be that degeneracy and high dimensional polyhedra are not well understood. We do not understand why the simplex method, which can iterate through every vertex in contrived examples, works as well as it does for the vast majority of practical problems. Some problems are easily solved with cutting plane codes while other similar problems seem to run forever.

There are two readily apparent problems in implementing cutting plane methods in present linear programming systems. The first is that in using cutting planes in connection with most simplex codes the rows for cuts must be set up at the outset and carried along as inactive rows for the entire run. Adding and deleting rows in a linear program is not so easy (except in the Land and Powell programs which are specifically designed to do just that). The second and more serious problem is that all large linear programming codes are tailored for sparse matrices. The usual cutting plane methods generate dense matrices, and if a code is expected to handle such matrices efficiently, the design of the code would have to be altered.

One way to get around the problem of adding rows is to solve the dual of the problem so that columns are added. However, the number of rows is then the number of variables, excluding slacks, which may be large. In pure integer problems the number of variables one can handle is not so large, but if cutting planes were ever to be used in mixed problems, the number of variables there would seem to preclude solving the dual problem.

Finally, it is hard to rule out cutting planes in the long run. For special problems, principally the travelling salesman problem, Miliotis [19], Hong and Padberg [14], recent success seems promising. However, it is unlikely that any commercial code will implement cutting planes in the near future.

4. ENUMERATION CODES

We make the distinction between branch-and-bound and enumeration in how the free (not yet fixed) integer variables are treated. In branch-and-bound, they are allowed to take on fractional values as given by the solution of a linear program. In enumeration, they are kept at some choice of integer values.

For the pure integer problem, linear programs need not be solved. Truncation can be on the basis of feasibility, objective value, or logical information on the variables. Even for the pure integer problem, however, it seems better to occasionally solve some linear programs, Garfinkel and Nemhouser [7]. When we allow branch-and-bound to do some enumeration at nodes and enumeration to solve linear programs at the nodes, the distinction between the two becomes somewhat fuzzy.

Use of logical or Boolean constraints in enumeration seems to be helpful, Spielberg [21]. Hammer and Nguyen [13] and Spielberg [20] use information such as $x_i \vee x_j$ so that if x_j is fixed at 0 then x_i can be set to 1 immediately. These logical constraints are kept outside the linear program and are used to fix several variables at once, where possible.

Use of cutting planes to strenghten the linear programs solved appears to be helpful, Guignard [12], in some problems. Adjoining cutting planes to the linear program in branch-and-bound does not always help because branching tends to drive the cuts out of the basis. There may well be hybrid methods developed, but more work needs to be done to ensure that the combined methods are not using the same restrictions, e.g., integality of the basic variables.

5. GROUP METHODS, LAGRANGIAN RELAXATION, AND BENDERS DECOMPOSITION

The main computational work with group methods has been that of Gorry, Northup and Shapiro [11]. Their results seem encouraging for the pure integer problem. They solve the group problem for all right-hand sides, which requires, at worst, order D^2 work where D is the determinant of the optimum basis. Then they use the group solution to get good bounds in an enumeration over the non-basic variables. This method has the advantage that the work required in the group part of the problem can be determined in advance once the linear program is solved. If the determinant D is too large, they advocate a weakening of the linear program to try to get a smaller determinant. See [5] for other work using group methods.

Geoffrion [8] has done considerable work with Lagrangian and Benders methods. These methods seem to be well suited to some problems, even to some mixed integer problems. However, Benders' decomposition [3] for solving the general mixed integer problems seems to be unsuccessful. There was a commercial code using that method, and it has been changed to a branch-and-bound method.

6. SPECIAL PROBLEMS

We first discuss network formulations. The work of Glover and Klingman [10] seems to show that problems having a network structure can be solved in much smaller times using the speed of network flow codes to solve those special classes of linear programs.

Development of network capabilities is independent of any integer programming considerations, but once such a capability exists, it would be possible to extend these network formulations to pure integer problems. A remaining question is how broad a class of problems can be successfully treated by these methods.

Although any pure 0-1 problem can be converted to this form [10a], performance will depend on how much underlying network structure is present.

Among special problems for which much work has been done, we would mention the following: travelling salesman, matchings, matroids, set packing and covering, knapsack, plant location, and fixed charge problems. There are codes written especially for these problems. Plant location is perhaps the most likely one to have a commercial code written for it. Enumeration methods [21] have been employed with some success here.

7. POSSIBLE IMPROVEMENTS IN COMMERCIAL CODES

In this section, we would like to speculate on likely changes in commercial codes and to give some reasons that other methods will not be implemented.

First, most of the special problems seem too narrow for the development of commercial codes to solve only one of them. There may well be proprietary codes already written for some, but commercial codes depend on a large general market. The most likely candidates might be network formulations and plant location.

For general pure integer problems, it is very hard to say what a commercial code would look like if something other than branch-and-bound were implemented. The branch-and-bound commercial codes presently in existence may solve pure problems reasonably well. There are some techniques which would probably speed them up on pure problems. At least one of them, MIP/370, specifies different options for pure problems. When we return to likely candidates for implementation, we will mention three possible improvements which apply both to mixed and pure problems.

It is unlikely that any commercial code would employ cutting planes alone at this time. However, it is hard to rule out future developments in cutting plane theory, and, in any case, cutting planes may be part of hybrid algorithms for the pure problem.

Enumeration codes with effective heuristics frequently find good solutions in a short time but need some bounds or other methods to guide the search and to be sure that there are not much better solutions still to be found.

The group approach and Lagrangian methods are other possibilities for pure problems; the latter could also be applied to mixed problems.

Three small, but promising, techinques which could very well be incorporated into current commercial codes are: (1) preprocessing; (2) logical constraints; and (3) enumeration at nodes of the branch-and-bound tree.

Preprocessing could be used to tighten up the linear program and to find logical constraints. At present, reduce techniques can be applied to integer programs, but these do not use the integer restrictions. Exactly what could be done is hard to say, but it seems like a promising area.

Logical constraints can be kept outside of the linear program and used in various ways. Special ordered sets of type 1 applied to a set of 0-1 variables is an example already implemented in almost all commercial codes. Other possibilities are open and, because of the success of special sets, seem like good candidates for future development.

Another possibility, which applies mainly to the pure problem, is enumeration at nodes of a branch-and-bound tree. A simple version of this enumeration is simply to round the fractional answer and try it. The difficulty in the mixed case is that a linear program in the continuous variables must be solved for each trial integer solution.

REFERENCES

[1] E.M.L. Beale and J.J.H. Forrest, "Global optimization using special ordered sets," Mathematical Programming 10, pp. 52-69.

[2] E.M.L. Beale and J.A. Tomlin, "Special facilities in a general mathematical programming system for nonconvex problems using ordered sets of variables," in: Proceedings of the Fifth International Conference on O.R., J. Lawrence, Tavistock Publications, London 1970, pp. 447-454.

[3] J.F. Benders, "Partitioning procedures for solving mixed-variable programming problems," Numerisehe Mathematik 4, pp. 238-252.

[4] M. Beuichou, J.M. Gauthier, P. Girodet, G. Hentges, G. Ribière, and O. Vincent, "Experiments in mixed-integer linear programming," Mathematical Programming 1, pp. 76-94.

[5] H.P. Crowder and E.L. Johnson, "Use of cyclic group methods in branch and bound," in: Mathematical Programming, T.C. Hu and S. Robinson (eds.), Academic Press, New York, 1973, pp. 213-226.

[6]   J.J.H. Forrest, J.P.H. Hirst and J.A. Tomlin, "Practical solution of large mixed integer programming problems with UMPIRE," Management Science 20, No. 5, pp. 736-773.

[7]   R.S. Garfinkel and G.L. Nemhouser, Integer Programming, John Wiley and Sons, 1972.

[8]   A.M. Geoffrion, "Lagrangian relaxation and its uses in integer programming," Mathematical Programming Study 2, pp. 82-114.

[9]   A.M. Geoffrion and R.E. Marsten, "Integer programming algorithms: a framework and state-of-the-art survey," Management Science 18, pp. 465-491.

[10]   F. Glover and D. Klingman, "Modelling and solving network problems," in these proceedings.

[10a] F. Glover and J. Mulvey, "Equivalence of 0-1 programs to discrete generalized and pure networks," MSRS-19, University of Colorado, Boulder, Colorado.

[11]   G.A. Gorry, W.D. Northup and J.F. Shapiro, "Computational experience with a group theoretic integer programming algorithm," in Mathematical Programming 4, pp. 171-192.

[12]   M. Guignard, "Inequalities valides de Gomory-Johnson," Journees de Combinatiore AFCET, 1971.

[13]   Hammer and Nguyen "POSS - a partial order in the solution space of bivalent programs," Centre Rech. Method 163, University of Montreal, 1972.

[14]   S. Hong and M.W. Padberg, "A computational study for the traveling salesman problem," to be published in the Proceedings of DO77, North-Holland.

[15]   E.L. Johnson and K. Spielberg, "Inequalities in branch and bound programming," in: Optimization Methods for Resource Allocation, R. Cottle and J. Krarup (eds.), English University Press Ltd., 1974.

[16]   A. Land and S. Powell, Fortran Codes for Mathematical Programming: Linear, Quadratic and Discrete, John Wiley and Sons, 1973.

[17]   A. Land and S. Powell, "Computer codes for problems of integer programming" to be published in the Proceedings of DO77.

[18]   G. Martin, "An accelerated euclidean algorithm for integer linear programming," pp. 311-318, in: Recent Advances in Mathematical Programming 10, R.L. Graves and P. Wolfe (eds.), McGraw-Hill, 1963.

[19]   P. Miliotis, "Integer programming approaches to the travelling salesman program," Mathematical Programming 10, pp. 367-378.

[20] K. Spielberg, "Minimal preferred variable reduction for zero-one programming," Report 320-3013, IBM, Phil. Scientific Center, 1972.

[21] K. Spielberg, "Enumerative methods in integer programming," to be published in the Proceedings of D077.

[22] J.A. Tomlin, "Branch and bound methods for integer and non-convex programming," in: Integer and Non-linear Programming, J. Abadie (ed.), North Holland 1970.

[23] C.A. Trauth and R.E. Woolsey, "Integer linear programming, 'A study in computational efficiency," Management Science 15, pp. 481-493.

SOME CONSIDERATIONS IN USING BRANCH-AND-BOUND CODES

E.L. Johnson

IBM T.J. Watson Research Center
P.O. Box 218
Yorktown Heights, NY 10598

We discuss here considerations in using codes based on solving linear programs in order to obtain bounds and to help choose branching variables. The remarks are not meant to apply to strictly enumerative codes where linear programs are not solved.

Unlike much of mathematical programming, integer programming problems are frequently so difficult and so unpredictable that improving a code or finding a faster code may not make much difference; the problems may require hours in any case. There are marginal improvements possible, of course, and, for some problem classes, effective heuristics may cause striking reductions in time needed to find reasonable good solutions. Some of these heuristics are available as options in some codes, and we include discussions of some of them here. However, even with faster codes and more heuristics, there remains a large body of virtually unsolvable problems due to the exponential explosion in running times.

Some users of mathematical programming codes have had the experience of spending several months formulating an integer program and collecting data for it and then encountering running times sufficiently long to force termination of the project without obtaining answers.

We do not claim here to eliminate this class of intractable problems, but we will give three considerations which may be helpful and which are, in our opinion, the types of considerations a user should consider in setting up his problem for branch-and-bound codes.

1   STRONGER LINEAR PROGRAMMING RELAXATIONS

To illustrate this point, we use an example [6] where a user had encountered very long running times and was contemplating abandoning his efforts. The problem was one of assigning production facilities to supply demand points via warehouses. This problem differed from the usual transhipment problem in that there were several product classes and all had to be supplied to a given demand point from one warehouse.

For each product class ℓ, the problem was to minimize a linear objective function, representing the costs of production and shipping, subject to:

$$S_{ij}^{\ell} \geq 0, \; T_{ij}^{\ell} \geq 0; \tag{I.1}$$

$$\sum_{j} S_{ij}^{\ell} \leq a_{i}^{\ell}; \tag{I.2}$$

$$\sum_{i} S_{ij}^{\ell} = \sum_{k} T_{jk}^{\ell}; \tag{I.3}$$

$$\sum_{j} T_{jk}^{\ell} = d_{k}^{\ell}; \tag{I.4}$$

where the variables are:

S_{ij}^{ℓ} the amount shipped from plant i to warehouse j of product class ℓ;

T_{jk}^{ℓ} the amount shipped from warehouse j to demand point k of product class ℓ;

and the coefficients are:

a_{i}^{ℓ} the production capacity of plant i for product class ℓ;

d_{k}^{ℓ} the demand at k for product class ℓ.

In order to incorporate the single warehouse restriction a variable

$$X_{jk} = \begin{cases} 1 \text{ if warehouse j supplies demand point k;} \\ 0 \text{ otherwise;} \end{cases}$$

was introduced along with the constraint

$$\sum_{\ell} T_{jk}^{\ell} = (\sum_{\ell} d_k^{\ell})X_{jk}. \tag{I.5}$$

The formulation here has been simplified somewhat, but still captures the essence of the difficulty. For a problem with about 30 plants, 30 warehouses, 4 product classes, and 600 demand points, there were about 2,000 0-1 variables and 20 hours of running on an IBM 370/158 did not yield even the first integer answer.

In looking at the problem we see that the X_{jk} will, in the linear programming relaxation, take on the fraction of total demand supplied to demand point k from warehouse j when the transhipment problems are solved separately for each product class. In this example, they tend to be fractional because almost no plant makes all four product classes. The warehouses are located at a plant, so the transhipment problems tend to use the nearest plant which makes the given product class.

The problem was reformulated with (I.5) replaced by

$$T_{jk}^{\ell} = d_k^{\ell} X_{jk}. \tag{I.6}$$

This formulation allowed the variables T_{jk}^{ℓ} to be eliminated from the problem with (I.4) replaced by

$$\sum_{j} X_{jk} = 1. \tag{I.7}$$

However, the fact that the linear program became smaller is not very important. The dramatic improvement obtained by using (I.6) over (I.5) came because when the linear program was solved only 4 0-1 variables were at fractional values (out of 2,000) and after one more minute of CPU time an optimum integer answer was found and proven optimum.

The linear program with (I.6) requires that the same fraction of every product class come from every warehouse to demand point. This linear programming relaxation, while still a relaxation of the real problem, does make the stringent requirement that if a plant makes only one product class and wants to ship some of it to a nearby demand point, then it must bring in the same fraction of the demand for other product classes and ship them along with the one product class it produces.

Geoffrion and Graves used this stronger form of the linear program in a more complex setting [5] and have emphasized making a strong linear programming relaxation. This same type of considera-

tion arose in the plant location problem [2,4,7]. The general subject has been written about by Williams [8].

In this case, the stronger form of the linear program was
immediately seen to be better by the interpretation of the 0-1
variables in the linear relaxation of the integer program. We
suggest as a general guide to successfully modeling integer programming problems that one should ask what the 0-1 variables will do in
the linear programming solution and what their interpretation is in
that solution. If many are likely to be fractional, if the objective value is likely to be far from an integer objective, and if
the 0-1 variables themselves carry no special restrictions, then
branch-and-bound codes are likely to be dismal failures because
they will degenerate to enumeration without bounds.

More concretely, a stronger linear program has a smaller
feasible region. In principle, we would like to have the linear
program be the convex hull of feasible points of the integer program. However, the constraints of that linear program are generally impossible to know and could be very numerous. Only in a few
special cases, such as matchings or matroids, are they known. The
convex hull of feasible integer points does give us an ideal linear
program which we would like ours to be close to. One consideration
of much less importance is the number of constraints in the linear
program. There is a much better chance to solve large linear programs than to go through an exponentially large branch-and-bound
tree without effective bounds.

2   WEAKER INTEGER RESTRICTIONS

Another example should help illustrate this next point. The
problem arose in retail store marketing and was worked on by myself,
Richard Chen of retail marketing, and Harlan Crowder [3]. It involved installation of new checkout equipment for a chain of retail
stores. The stores are divided into classes $\ell = 1,...L$. For each
class ℓ, there is an installation cost $C_{\ell t}$ for installing the
equipment in time period t and there is a return of $B_{\ell rt}$ in time
period t for an installation in class ℓ at time r, $1 \leq r < t$. An
initial amount of capital K is made available for installation, and
returns from previous installations can be used to pay for other
installations. There are M_ℓ total stores of class ℓ. Our initial
integer programming formulation was:

$$x_{\ell t} \geq 0 \text{ and integer, } \ell = 1,...,L, \ t = 1,..., T;$$

$$- \sum_{\ell=1}^{L} C_{\ell 1} x_{\ell 1} - P_1 = -K;$$

$$- \sum_{\ell=1}^{L} \sum_{r=1}^{t-1} B_{\ell rt} x_{\ell r} - \sum_{\ell=1}^{L} C_{\ell t} x_{\ell t} + P_{t-1} - P_t = 0, \quad t = 2,\ldots,T;$$

$$\sum_{t=1}^{T} x_{\ell t} \leq M_\ell, \quad \ell = 1,\ldots,L;$$

maximize P_T.

Here, P_t is the carryover of dollars from period t to period $t+1$, and the objective is to maximize the final cash position P_T.

This formulation requires every installation to begin and be completed in the same time period. After some consideration, motivated by use of S2 sets [1], we realized that an installation need not be finished in the same time period but must be completed in the next time period. An integer programming formulation of this requirement is obtained from the previous one by dropping the requirement $x_{\ell t}$ integer and adjoining the restrictions:

$$d_{\ell t} \geq 0 \text{ and integer, } \ell = 1,\ldots,L, \quad t = 1,\ldots,T;$$

$$\sum_{k=1}^{t} x_{\ell k} - d_{\ell t} \leq 0, \quad \ell = 1,\ldots,L; \quad t = 1,\ldots,T-1;$$

$$\sum_{k=1}^{t+1} x_{\ell k} - d_{\ell t} \geq 0; \quad \ell = 1,\ldots,L; \quad t = 1,\ldots,T-2;$$

$$\sum_{k=1}^{T} x_{\ell k} - d_{\ell,T-1} = 0.$$

These restrictions require that there be an integer between each successive S_t given by

$$S_t = \sum_{k=1}^{t} x_{\ell t}.$$

That is, if S_t has a fractional part, then S_{t+1} must be at least as large as the next integer. In other words, the activity level $x_{\ell t+1}$ must be at least as large as 1-(fractional part of S_t). Thus, the installation represented by that fractional part of S_t is begun in time period t and completed in time period $t+1$.

The reason that any fractional $x_{\ell t}$ cannot be viewed in this way is that the linear programming model starts giving the fraction of the returns from an installation as soon as it is made. For example, if 1/3 of an installation is made in time period 5 and the other 2/3 in time period 9, the linear program gives 1/3 of the return $B_{\ell t}$ in each of time periods 6,7,8, and 9. If the other 2/3 is done in period 6, as allowed here, then the returns are $(1/3)B_{\ell 56}$ in period G and $(1/3)B_{\ell 5t} + (2/3)B_{\ell 6t}$ for $t \geq 7$. This linear interpolation of returns and costs was considered acceptable in our problem so long as the interpolation was over adjacent time periods.

The second form of integer restriction is a strict relaxation of the earlier formulation. In practice, the order of improvement in running times, even with a larger linear program, was of the order of five.

3   MAINTAIN INTEGER FEASIBILITY AND FIND EARLY INTEGER SOLUTIONS

The same example can be used to illustrate a third point about solving problems with branch-and-bound codes.

When first solving our integer program, many minutes were required before an integer answer was found. In looking at the output, it became clear that the problem was that integer decisions on installation were being made far out in the time horizon based on returns from the linear program in the earlier time period. However, when the variables in earlier time periods were forced to be integer, there was no feasible answer. In other words, we over-installed in later time periods based on too-optimistic estimates of returns, i.e., based on the linear rather than the integer returns.

We reordered the variables, and branched on the variables in that order, so that $x_{\ell s}$ came before x_{mt} for any $s < t$ and all ℓ and m. Then, any feasible linear program contained a feasible integer answer, one of which could be obtained by moving out the time horizon investing as much as possible.

Using branch-and-bound codes, it is very important to find good integer solutions as early as possible. This goal will not be achieved if the linear program at a node being followed contains no integer answer. It may require several branches before this integer infeasibility is discovered.

In this case, it was possible to assure that linear programming feasibility implied integer feasibility. The reductions in running times were of the order of five when this good branching order was introduced. Finally, we were able to solve problems with L = 3,

$T = 36$, $M_1 = 8$, $M_2 = 10$, $M_3 = 12$, and $K = \$200,000$ in about 5 minutes using MPSX-MIP/370 on a 370/168.

4   SUMMARY

We can summarize these three points by saying that the linear program should be as close as possible to the integer program. In the first case, the linear program was made tighter; in the second, the integer problem was relaxed while still giving usable answers; and in the third case we try to avoid feasible linear programs which contain no integer feasible point. These considerations cannot always be used for a particular problem, but they are the type of considerations one should make in analyzing mixed integer formulations to be solved with branch-and-bound codes.

REFERENCES

1.   E.M.L. Beale and J.A. Tomlin, "Special facilities in a general mathematical programming system for non-convex problems using ordered sets of variables," Proc. Fifth Int. Conf. of Operational Res., J. Lawrence (ed.), Venice, Tavestock Pub., London, 1969, pp. 8.21-8.28.

2.   O. Bilde and J. Krarup, "Bestemmelse af Optimal beliggenhed af produktionssteder," Res. Report IMSOR, Techn. Univ. of Denmark, 1967.

3.   R. Chen, H.P. Crowder, and E.L. Johnson, "An integer programming formulation of the installation scheduling problem," IBM RC 6196, IBM Research, Yorktown Heights, NY 10598, 1976.

4.   P.S. David and T.L. Ray, "A branch-and-bound algorithm for the capacitated facilities location problem," Naval Res. Log. Quart. 16(1969), 331-344.

5.   A.M. Geoffrion and G.W. Graves, "Multicommodity distribution system design by Bender's decomposition," Management Science, 20(1974), 822-844.

6.   E.L. Johnson, T.G. Mairs, G.W. Wakefield and K. Spielberg, "On a production allocation and distribution problem," 1977.

7.   K. Spielberg, "Algorithms for the simple plant-location problem with some side conditions," Operations Research 17(1969), 85-111.

8.   H.P. Williams, "Experiments in the formulation of integer programming problems," Math. Programming Study 2: Approaches to Integer Programming, M.L. Balinski (ed.), 1974, 180 197.

QUADRATIC PROGRAMMING

E.M.L. Beale[§] and Regina Benveniste[†]

Imperial College of Science & Technology[§,†]
University of London, and
Manpower Services Commission[†]

ABSTRACT. Following a general introduction to the theory of quadratic programming, the paper describes computational aspects of a new algorithm for convex quadratic programming. The algorithm is presented in detail in Benveniste (1976). An essential feature is that the only information needed about the objective function is the gradient direction at successive trial solutions (and the value of the objective function at the final solution). The constraints are handled as in the Reduced Gradient Method. The method is essentially a generalization of the method of Conjugate Gradients. But pure Conjugate Gradients, although finite, require a complete restart whenever the set of active constraints changes. If storage space is available, the algorithm stores additional directions in a way that avoids the need for a complete restart.

The method is conceived as being particularly appropriate for problems with a large number of variables but where gradients can be computed without requiring a large amount of data storage. This is true in particular when the Hessian is sparse. But the experimental computer program seems to be quite fast on small dense problems.

I. INTRODUCTION

Quadratic programming is the name given to the problem of minimizing a quadratic function of variables subject to linear equality and inequality constraints. Many finite algorithms have been developed for solving a convex quadratic programming problem, and many of these also find a local optimum to a nonconvex problem. Several methods for finding a global optimum to a nonconvex problem using either branch and bound or cutting planes have also been proposed, but their computational status is less certain.

This paper considers three classes of method. Section 2 is concerned with methods based on a direct analysis of the Kuhn-Tucker conditions. The fact that these conditions reduce to linear equations in the primal and dual variables is in a sense the fundamental reason why finite methods are possible for these problems. These methods work with a square matrix of dimension $m + n$, where m is the number of constraints and n the number of variables. Section 3 considers methods based on representing the objective function as a sum of squares of linear functions, or as a difference of such sums of squares if it is not convex. Section 4 considers methods related to Reduced Gradient Method due to Wolfe (1963). In particular it outlines the program for a new method due to Benveniste (1976). Section 5 analyzes some computational results with this program.

2. METHODS BASED ON THE KUHN-TUCKER CONDITIONS

We may write a general quadratic programming problem in the form:

Minimize $\quad f(x_1, \ldots, x_n) \equiv \sum_j c_j x_j + (1/2) \sum_j \sum_k h_{jk} x_j x_k,$

subject to the constraints $\quad \sum_j a_{ij} x_j \quad = b_i \, (i = 1, \ldots, m)$

$$0 \leq x_j \leq U_j.$$

If π_i denotes the dual variable, or Lagrange Multiplier, on the <u>ith</u> constraint, the problem is to minimize

$$L = -\sum_i b_i \pi_i + \sum_j (c_j + \sum_i \pi_i a_{ij}) x_j + (1/2) \sum_j \sum_k h_{jk} x_j x_k.$$

Hence, if $u_j = \partial L / \partial x_j$, we see that

$$u_j = c_j + \sum_i \pi_i a_{ij} + \sum_k h_{jk} x_k.$$

So the problem reduces to finding values of the variables x_j, u_j and π_i satisfying the $m + n$ linear equations

$$\sum_k a_{ik} x_k = b_i \, (i = 1, \ldots, m)$$

$$u_j - \sum_i \pi_i a_{ij} - \sum_k h_{jk} x_k = c_j \quad (j = 1, \ldots, n).$$

subject to the further conditions that

$$0 \leqq x_j \leqq U_j \quad (j = 1, \ldots, n)$$

$$u_j \leqq 0 \text{ when } x_j = U_j, \quad u_j \geqq 0 \text{ when } x_j = 0$$

and $u_j = 0$ when $0 < x_j < U_j$.

These further conditions can be achieved by using the simplex method to solve the equations with restrictions on the choice of variable to enter the basis. Wolfe (1959) produced such a method, which has been further developed by Dantzig (1963), Lemke (1968) and many others.

Current thinking about such methods is based on the notion of complementarity. If A_i denotes the artificial variable associated with the ith constraint, then the primal variable A_i and the dual variable π_i form a complementary pair. And similarly the primal variable x_j and the dual variable u_j form a complementary pair. A complementary basis is one containing exactly one member of each complementary pair. The corresponding complementary basic solution must be a local optimum unless a basic primal variable lies outside its bounds, or unless a basic dual variable u_j lies outside the bounds associated with the trial value of the complementary primal variable x_j (i.e., if $u_j < 0$ when x_j is nonbasic at its lower bound or if $u_j > 0$ when x_j is nonbasic at its upper bound).

If the initial complementary basic solution is not optimum, then we make a sequence of simplex iterations until we reach another complementary basic solution.

Given an infeasible complementary basic solution, we choose a basic primal variable that exceeds its upper bound and decrease the complementary dual variable, or else we choose a basic primal variable that falls short of its lower bound and increase the complementary dual variable. We use the standard rules for choosing a pivotal column, that is to say we prevent any basic primal or dual variable that is within its bounds from violating them. If the variable complementary to the outgoing basic variable is nonbasic, then we bring it into the basis (in the appropriate direction) at the next iteration. Otherwise we have a new complementary basic solution to analyze. Note that if a dual variable becomes nonbasic, and the complementary primal variable then flips between its lower and upper bounds, the dual variable must then be made basic again with the opposite sign to the one it had before.

This approach requires only a modest change to a simplex linear programming code, and it can therefore take advantage of sparseness in the matrices $\underset{\sim}{A}$ and $\underset{\sim}{H}$.

Fletcher (1971) and Keller (1973) present variants of this approach that are somewhat further from the mechanics of the simplex method, but which find local optima to arbitrary nonconvex quadratic programming problems. Fletcher's algorithm takes special care over numerical accuracy. But, as noted in the introduction, it is cumbersome to have to work with a square matrix of dimension $m+n$, particularly if the quadratic terms are essentially a perturbation of an otherwise linear programming problem. So other approaches are also worth considering.

3. METHODS BASED ON SUMS OF SQUARES

Any convex quadratic function can be expressed as a sum of squares of linear functions. And this is a compact way to express it if the rank r of the Hessian matrix H is much smaller than n, since the objective function can then be written in the form

$$\sum_{j=1}^{n} c_j x_j + (1/2) \sum_{\ell=1}^{r} z_\ell^2 ,$$

where
$$z_\ell = \sum_{j=1}^{n} d_{\ell j} x_j .$$

One way to exploit this structure is to use convex separable programming. This can find an arbitrarily close approximation to the solution without any branching or bounding. In principle this is an infinite algorithm, and must be regarded as inelegant. But the approach is more attractive if the objective function is not convex. The objective function can then be written in the form

$$\sum_{j=1}^{n} c_j x_j + (1/2) \sum_{\ell=1}^{r} s_\ell z_\ell^2 ,$$

where each s_ℓ is ± 1. We can therefore find a global optimum using S2 sets, as described for example by Beale (1978). If there are several terms with negative s_ℓ this can still be a painful process, and the pain can perhaps be mitigated by further analysis. If there are equality constraints, they can be used to eliminate variables from the objective function. This is worthwhile if it reduces the value of r, particularly if it reduces the number of terms with $s_\ell = -1$. And alternative ways of forming the objective function may yield worthwhile reductions in the possible ranges of values of those z_ℓ for which $s_\ell = -1$.

4. METHODS BASED ON REDUCED GRADIENTS

Beale (1955) presented a method that concentrates on the constraint matrix, using information about the Hessian only to provide data for selecting search directions. It can be regarded as a variant of the Reduced Gradient Method due to Wolfe (1963), with free nonbasic variables introduced to make search directions conjugate. But the algorithm still uses explicit data on the Hessian, and is somewhat inefficient when new constraints are encountered. Both these disadvantages are overcome in a new method due to Benveniste (1976).

In this method, the reduced gradient of the objective function at successive trial solutions is calculated as a function of the gradient of the objective function. This is the only information used about the objective function. The method of conjugate gradients could then be used to develop a finite algorithm using these gradients. But this would require a complete restart when the reduced problem changes.

It is a feature of this algorithm that no such restart is necessary provided storage is available to store some directions along which optimization was successful. When the reduced problem changes, linear transformations of the stored directions are formed which span a subspace of the space in which we optimize the new reduced problem. Since optimization in that subspace has already been completed we have to generate fewer search directions. This facility generally reduces the total computation time.

We now consider the organization of the Computer Program for this method. We use standard terminology, but we subdivide the nonbasic variables at any iteration in to two sets:

Restricted, which remain at their upper or lower bounds, at least for this iteration, and

Independent, over which optimization takes place.

The Program contains 8 main steps as follows:

1) The main program originally calls routine RDDATA which reads the input. This consists of specifications of the number of variables, number of constraints, the linear coefficients of the objective functions, the nonzero elements of half the symmetric Hessian matrix H, the nonzero elements of the A matrix, the right hand side coefficients b, and the inequality signs of the constraints (0 specified for equality, 1 for less than or equal sign, and -1 for greater than or equal sign). Upper bounds for variables may be specified. Lower bounds equal to zero are assumed for all variables.

The nonzero elements of the Hessian and the A matrix are defined and stored compactly one column after the other. Record
is kept of the index of the first element of each column.
Storing the elements by column was preferred to facilitate
faster retrieval when vector products are formed with the columns of the A matrix.

The same routine adjusts the coefficients of the A matrix and
vector b so that they correspond to less than or equal constraints, and introduces the slack variables. Some error
detection is also performed. The input cards are printed as
they are read.

2) After a successful termination of RDDATA the main program calls
routines FIRSTB that finds a first basis, the unit matrix, and
CHKFEA and CORECT which detect and correct any infeasibilities
in a manner common to several L.P. and Q.P. algorithms.

We also need to define an initial set of independent variables.

3) The program now calls routine NEWIVS to select variables to be
added to the independent set, and thus define a new reduced
problem. These variables are chosen among those which have
values equal to either lower or upper bounds. (All other
variables are basic or already independent.) For the selection
of the new independent variables two strategies have been
tested:

a) All variables with favourable reduced gradients are
included in the independent set.

b) The variable with the most favourable reduced gradient
is included in the independent set.

Overall, the second strategy seems to require less computing
time.

If a new independent set is defined we have a new reduced
problem to solve. If no new variable was added to the independent set we have reached a local optimum to the quadratic
programming problem so we go to 8.

4) Routine GENQI is called to generate a new search direction in
the space of the independent variables. The new direction is
a function of the reduced gradient at the present trial point,
the last search direction, the rate of change of the reduced
gradient along that direction, as well as similar statistics
related to conjugate directions spanning the subspace in which
we have already optimized.

5) Routine CALCMU is called to calculate the distance to the new optimal point along the new search direction. This distance is adjusted if the upper or lower bound of any variable would otherwise be violated, and the variable then becomes restricted to that bound. The new trial point is thus located.

If no variable is to be restricted to its bound we go to 7.

6) Otherwise we have a new reduced problem. If the variable to be restricted is independent, routine RESTRI is called to update the relevant tables about the change of status of the variable. If a basic variable is to become restricted, routine RESTRB perform the corresponding updating of tables and the change of basis that will make one of the independent variables basic in the place of the basic variable that becomes restricted. This is done by an ordinary simplex iteration. An explicit inverse is used, but a triangular factorization of the basis could be used instead.

In both cases routine LINCOM is called to calculate the new reduced gradient and make the linear transformations of any stored conjugate directions so that they are relevant to the new reduced problem.

7) Routine CHKOPT checks whether we have reached the optimal solution to the present reduced problem. It also stores information about the last search direction if optimization along it was not interrupted and storage is provided.

8) Routine EXIT is called to print the output. This includes all information specified by the input cards and the details about the optimal solution. These are the optimal value, the final reduced gradient for all variables and slacks, their status, as well as the inverse. If the problem is found infeasible or unbounded an appropriate message is printed.

Presently a table recording the total time spent and its distribution in the various routines is produced.

5.   COMPUTATIONAL PERFORMANCE

The algorithm has been tested on 30 problems of varying size and density of Hessian. The number of variables ranged from 4 to 40. The number of constraints ranged from 1 to 5, and the density of the Hessian from 2.5 percent to 100 percent.

The total time used for each problem was compared with the time taken by a version of Beale's algorithm by Land and Powell (1973) for problems with less than 20 variables. For all such problems the new algorithm performed better. The improvement ranged from 8 percent to 50 percent with an overall average of 29 percent.

Although the highest improvement is noted for problems with a large number of variables, or problems with a sparse Hessian, there is no indication that the performance for the small or dense problems is much below average.

A study was made of the variation of the total time used as a function of the allocation of storage for storing search directions. The storage allocation D_{MAX} ranged from provision for 0 to 20 directions. It was found that extra storage allocation reduced the total time as long as extra directions were actually stored and if fewer search directions were generated. The value of D_{MAX} for which the minimum time occurred varied from problem to problem. Overall the total time for all problems occurred for D_{MAX} = 12 and did not change much for greater values of D_{MAX}, probably because only two problems stored more directions.

The table below summarizes the distribution of time in the various routines and the effect of changing D_{MAX} from 0 to 20.

We can see that the increase of D_{MAX} reduces the total time by 4 percent corresponding to an 11 percent reduction of the total computation time (excluding the input and output time). The reduction is mainly due to limiting the number of calls of routine CALCMU. The effect is partially cancelled by the increase of time per call for most routines and especially for RESTRB and GENQI. The latter used up more time regardless of the fact that it was called 36 percent less frequently.

It is conceivable that for some problems the algorithm may store so many directions as to increase the time per call of the routines enough to cancel any saving of time due to the reduction in the frequency of calling them.

REFERENCES

1. E.M.L. Beale, On Minimizing a Convex Function Subject to Linear Inequalities, in: J. Roy. Statist. Soc. (B) 17 pp. 173-184, 1955.
2. E.M.L. Beale, Nonlinear Programming Using a General Mathematical Programming System, Proceedings from the 1977 NATO Summer School, 1978.
3. R. Benveniste, A Quadratic Programming Algorithm Using Conjugate Search Directions, Submitted for publication, 1976.
4. G.B. Dantzig, Linear Programming and Extensions, Princeton University Press, 1963.
5. R. Fletcher, A General Quadratic Programming Algorithm, in: J. Inst. Maths. Applics. 7, pp. 76-91, 1971.

INFORMATION RECORDED FOR 30 P.Q. PROBLEMS

	TIME in msecs			Number of calls			Time per call		
	$D_{MAX}=0$ (1)	$D_{MAX}=20$ (2)	difference (3)	$D_{MAX}=0$ (4)	$D_{MAX}=20$ (5)	difference (6)	$D_{MAX}=0$ (7)	$D_{MAX}=20$ (8)	difference (9)
1. Subroutine FIRSTB	7	10	3	30	30	0	.23	.33	.10
2. Subroutine CHKFEA	13	4	-9	49	49	0	.27	.08	-.19
3. Subroutine CORECT	52	50	-2	30	30	0	1.73	1.67	-.06
4. Subroutine GENQI	64	108	44	272	175	-97	.24	.62	.38
5. Subroutine CALCMU	5140	4140	-1000	270	175	-95	19.04	23.66	4.62
6. Subroutine RESTRB	18	163	145	27	27	0	.67	6.03	5.36
7. Subroutine RESTRI	0	1	1	17	17	0	0	.06	.06
8. Subroutine LINCOM	1206	1245	39	44	44	0	27.41	28.30	.89
9. Subroutine CHKCPT	140	122	-18	260	165	-95	.54	.74	.20
10. Subroutine NEWIVS	151	217	66	261	261	0	.58	.83	.25
11. Subtotal for computation	6791	6060	-731						
12. INPUT	6287	6212	-75	30	30	0	209.57	207.06	-2.51
13. OUTPUT	5014	5093	79	30	30	0	167.13	169.77	2.64
14. TOTAL	18902	17365	-727						

258

6. E.L. Keller, The General Quadratic Optimization Problem, in: Mathematical Programming 5, pp. 311-337, 1973.
7. A.H. Land and S. Powell, Fortran Codes for Mathematical Programming, John Wiley, 1973.
8. C.E. Lemke, On Complementary Pivot Theory, in: Mathematics of the Decision Sciences, Part I, Ed. by G.B. Dantzig and A.F. Veinott, American Mathematical Society, Providence, R.I., pp. 95-114, 1968.
9. P. Wolfe, The Simplex Method for Quadratic Programming, in: Econometrica 27, pp. 382-398, 1959.
10. P. Wolfe, Methods of Nonlinear Programming, in: Recent Advances in Mathematical Programming, Ed. by R.L. Graves and P. Wolfe, McGraw Hill, New York, pp. 67-86, 1963.

NONLINEAR PROGRAMMING USING A GENERAL MATHEMATICAL PROGRAMMING SYSTEM

E.M.L. Beale

Scientific Control Systems Ltd., and
Scicon Computer Services Ltd.

ABSTRACT. This paper describes two approaches to the solution of nonlinear programming problems using a general mathematical programming system. Conjugate Gradient Approximation Programming is a development of the Method of Approximation Programming due to Griffith and Stewart (1961), which now incorporates many of the concepts of the Generalized Reduced Gradient Method due to Abadie and Carpentier (1969). Special Ordered Sets and Linked Ordered Sets are developments of Separable Programming due to Miller (1963), using ideas from Beale and Tomlin (1970), Beale and Forrest (1976) and Beale and Forrest (1977). This approach finds global optima, using Branch and Bound methods where necessary, to programming problems where the objective function and all constraints are defined as sums of products of functions of single arguments.

Scicon Computer Services Ltd. have implemented both approaches, and the algorithmic and operational aspects of the resulting software are described. Both approaches arise from a single canonical form for a nonlinear programming problem, viewing it as a linear programming problem in some linear variables where the coefficients of the variables and the right hand sides may be functions of the nonlinear variables. But the approaches are nevertheless addressed to fundamentally different types of problems. The use of Approximation Programming is appropriate where it is only convenient to define the local behaviour of the objective function and constraints in the neighbourhood of any trial solution. The formulae defining this local behaviour may be extremely complex, and this causes no particular difficulty, but there can be no guarantee of reaching a global optimum to a nonconvex problem. The use of Special Ordered Sets is appropriate when it is convenient to represent the global behaviour of the objective and constraint functions by explicit

formulae. Global optima can then be found, and integer variables
can be included in the model if required. Of course on large nonconvex problems it may not be feasible to complete the search and
therefore one may not achieve a guaranteed global optimum.

1.   INTRODUCTION

If we say that a problem is nonlinear, we have not really said
anything about what it is. So numerical methods for nonlinear programming form a large and untidy subject. They include methods for
essentially unconstrained optimization problems with a few inequality
constraints added to exclude physically foolish solutions. They
also include methods for essentially linear programming problems
with a few nonlinear constraints, or a few decision variables that
introduce product terms when they interact with other decision variables. This paper is about methods that use the linear programming
facilities of a general mathematical programming system. When applied to large sparse problems these methods take advantage of the
steady improvements that have been made over the past 20 years in
implementations of the simplex method. And, unlike more specialist
software, they benefit automatically from future developments as
soon as they are implemented in the mathematical programming system
being used. If progress over the next 5 years is as rapid as it
has been over the past 5 years then this will be very important.
The methods, and the software, can and have been applied to problems
that are neither large nor sparse, although they have no special
advantages for such problems.

One distinction between different types of optimization software is whether the problem is defined locally or globally. Local
definition means that the user supplies a routine to compute the
values, and perhaps the derivatives, of the objective and constraint
functions for any given set of trial values of the decision variables. The standard optimization software then interacts with this
routine as often as necessary. This is the way that standard hill-
climbing software works. On the other hand global definition means
that the user supplies a complete specification of the problem, and
the standard optimization software continues without interruption
until the problem is solved. This is the way that standard linear
programming software works. When discussing algorithms, we cannot
distinguish clearly between these approaches, since the routines
to calculate the objective and constraint functions for a particular class of problems can be incorporated within the optimization
software, leaving only the data defining a particular problem to be
defined globally. But at the level of software this distinction is
valid and important. Both approaches have merit, and both have been
used in conjunction with general mathematical programming since
about 1960. This paper discusses recent developments of which I
have first-hand experience: in other words developments by Scicon

Computer Services Ltd.

Software using local definition has been based on the Method of Approximation Programming, due to Griffith and Stewart (1961). It is the more flexible approach, since the user has only to provide local linear approximations to the objective function and the constraints. In many applications these approximations need a substantial amount of computing, but this does not affect the rest of the system. On the other hand, this approach cannot guarantee to find global optimum solutions to problems with several local optima.

Software using global definition has been based on Separable Programming. Methods for applying this approach to nonconvex problems were published by Miller (1963). In its original form, this approach found local optima to problems defined by piecewise linear approximations to all nonlinear functions. Various methods have been used to refine these approximations automatically within the mathematical programming system, and also to find global optima using branch and bound methods.

Section
problem of defining a canonical form for a general nonlinear programming problem. Then Sections 3 and 4 discuss algorithmic and operational aspects of software using local definition of the problem. Sections 5 and 6 discuss algorithmic and operational aspects of software using global definition of the problem. Finally the Appendix presents a detailed point concerning line searches using cubic approximations that is apparently unpublished and may be of some general interest.

2.   A CANONICAL FORM FOR A NONLINEAR PROGRAMMING PROBLEM

In many, perhaps most, computer applications, input and output requires at least as much attention from the analyst and programmer as the calculations taking place between. As a preliminary to input, it seems appropriate to consider what is a suitable canonical form for the mathematical description of a nonlinear programming problem. Theorists may write:

Minimize

$$f(\underset{\sim}{x}),$$

subject to

$$g_i(\underset{\sim}{x}) \leq b_i \qquad (i = 1 \ldots m).$$

But this provides no way of indicating that the problem may be largely linear. Griffith and Stewart (1961) therefore introduced

the concepts of <u>linear variables</u> and <u>nonlinear variables</u>. Denoting
the linear variables by x_j $(j = 1...n)$ and the nonlinear variables
by y_r $(r = 1,...k)$, they defined the problem as

Minimize

$$G = \sum_{j=1}^{n} a_{ij} x_j + g_1(y_1,...y_k),$$

subject to

$$\sum_{j=1}^{n} a_{ij} x_j + g_1(y_1,...y_k) = b_i \quad (i = 2,...m)$$

$$0 \leq x_j \qquad\qquad\qquad (j = 1,...n)$$

$$L_r \leq y_r \leq U_r \qquad\qquad (r = 1,...k).$$

Beale (1974) suggests that the concept of a linear variable should
be generalized by allowing any set of decision variables to be regarded as linear if the problem reduces to a linear programming
problem whenever the remaining, nonlinear, variables are all given
fixed values. This extends the Griffith and Stewart formulation by
allowing the coefficients of the linear variables to be functions
of the nonlinear variables. The problem can then be written as
follows:

Maximize x_o subject to the constraints

$$x_o + \sum_{j=1}^{n} a_{oj} x_j \qquad\qquad = b_o$$

$$\sum_{j=1}^{n} a_{ij} x_j \qquad\qquad = b_i \quad (i = 1,...m)$$

$$0 \leq x_j \qquad\qquad \leq B_j \quad (j = 1,...n)$$

$$L_r \leq y_r \qquad\qquad \leq U_r \quad (r = 1,...k),$$

where the coefficients a_{ij} and b_i may be either constants or functions of the k nonlinear variables $y_1...y_k$.

This reformulation sometimes greatly reduces the number of
variables that have to be classified as nonlinear; although there
are real problems in which the only linear variables are the slacks

that have been introduced to turn all the constraints into equations, except for simple upper and lower bounds on individual variables.

With this more general approach we need to distinguish the set N of linear variables with some nonconstant coefficients and the set C of linear variables with constant coefficients. The variables in N must all have finite upper and lower bounds, although the variables in C need not.

3. ALGORITHMIC ASPECTS OF METHODS USING LOCAL DEFINITION

The next two sections discuss Scicon's approach to Approximation Programming, which is called Conjugate Gradient Approximation Programming. Its theory is described in Beale (1974), and a substantially revised version of the algorithm is given by Batchelor and Beale (1976). These revisions have taken place over the past few years as a result of client problems becoming more difficult and needing a more powerful algorithm. Following a general description of the current algorithm, this Section comments on those changes from the original algorithm that may be relevant in other contexts.

The method uses a general mathematical programming system to solve a sequence of linear programming subproblems, or steps, based on local linear approximations to the objective function and the constraints calculated at the current trial solution. For theoretical purposes it is helpful to think of the method as a variant of the Reduced Gradient Method, introduced by Wolfe (1963) and generalized to nonlinear constraints by Abadie and Carpentier (1969). As indicated in Section 2, we express all constraints as equations, except for lower and upper bounds on individual variables. Given any feasible trial solution, we can therefore use the constraints to solve for some variables in terms of the others, and we can then divide the variables into three categories:

Basic, or dependent, variables.
Nonbasic variables at their absolute lower or upper bounds.
Other nonbasic variables.

Assuming that the nonbasic variables at their absolute lower or upper bounds cannot usefully be changed, the problem of finding a better trial solution is then essentially a problem of unconstrained optimization in the other nonbasic variables.

We call these other nonbasic variables the Independent Variables. Some research workers prefer the term Superbasic Variables. We choose an appropriate set of independent variables by making an Exploratory Step in which each nonlinear variable y_r is restricted to lie within some standard tolerance t_r of our current best estimate for its value. A variable is then treated as independent if it is nonbasic in our optimum solution to the exploratory step and has a value that differs by more than its standard tolerance from both its absolute lower and upper bounds. Note that a linear variable can never become independent because it is not restricted by tolerances and can therefore never be nonbasic except at its absolute lower or upper bound.

Following each exploratory step, we reduce all the standard tolerances by a common factor. We then solve a set of further steps in which the independent variables are given fixed values, or zero tolerances, but the other nonlinear variables are allowed to vary by their standard tolerances about their trial values and the linear variables are allowed to vary between their absolute lower and upper bounds. These steps can be regarded as function evaluations in the space of the independent variables. But we also obtain all first derivatives for a negligible amount of extra work, since these are the negatives of the reduced costs d_r of the independent variables y_r. (To do this we need to prevent the Mathematical Programming System from suppressing the independent variables from the Work File on the grounds that their lower bounds equal their upper bounds.)

The unconstrained optimization process in the space of the independent variables than involves carrying out a sequence of line searches. In prin 'ple we could use any sensible unconstrained optimization procedure, but in practice we use a variant of the method of conjugate gradients in order to be able to handle a possibly very large number of independent variables. To start the line search we have trial values for all variables, and we make local linear approximations to the objective function and all constraints. When we solve the resulting linear programming subproblem, we generally obtain new values for the basic variables, but this causes no difficulty as long as they are within standard tolerances of their trial values. We can therefore think of this as taking one step of Newton's method for solving the nonlinear constraints for the basic variables, so in this respect the method is similar to that of Robinson (1972). The tolerances ensure the stability of the method, although if they become relevant the corresponding objective function value and reduced costs may be inaccurate. /

We also use the same local linear approximations to indicate the rates of change of the values of the basic variables with respect to distance along the line of search in the space of the independent variables. The calculation of these directional derivatives is not a standard facility in mathematical programming systems, but it is straightforward and is available in SCICONIC. So the next set of trial values for the basic variables takes account both of the errors in the previous set and the consequences of changing the values of the independent variables. Linear constraints are treated exactly, provided that all variables remain within their bounds. And even for nonlinear constraints there is no need to iterate between steps in the tangent plane to the constraints and steps returning to the feasible region.

It is perhaps worth noting that the differences in the reduced costs at different points on the line search include the effects of the differences in the linear approximations to any nonlinear constraints. So the conjugate gradient algorithm is in effect acquiring and using information about the Hessian of the Lagrangian function, and not merely of the objective function itself.

The set N_I of independent variables remains unchanged throughout each major iteration, except that a variable y_r is dropped from N_I if its optimum value found in a line search lies within t_r of either L_r or U_r. This may mean that variables remain or become dependent when they should really be independent. Each step will then usually change such variables by their standard tolerances from their trial values, and this tends to create an oscillation in the value of the LP objective function calculated in successive steps. This may in turn mean that an interpolation during a line search will fail to improve on the two bracketing solutions. We have a standard response to any trouble of this kind: we make a new Exploratory Step, choose a new set of independent variables and (at the following step) reduce the standard tolerances. The existence of this general recovery procedure means that we do not have to find specific solutions to unexpected problems during line searches. We refer to the steps between successive Exploratory Steps as a Major Iteration.

The precise rules are that the Major Iteration continues until either

(a) we have a trial solution in which no independent variable has a nonzero reduced cost;

(b) the optimum value in a line search has been bracketed between a feasible and an infeasible LP subproblem, and no independent variable y_r differs by more than t_r in the two bracketing subproblems;

(c) an interpolation between two feasible or two infeasible LP subproblems in a line search has failed to find a significantly better value of the objective function, and no independent variable y_r differs by more than t_r in the two bracketing subproblems, or

(d)   an interpolation between two feasible or two infeasible LP
      subproblems in a line search has failed to find a significantly
      better value of the objective function, and we cannot find a
      suitable point on the line at which to look for a better value.

In Cases (a) or (d), the LP problem just solved is treated
as the Exploratory Step for the next major iteration. Any
independent variable y_r not within t_r of either L_r or U_r will
remain independent for the next major iteration.

In Cases (b) and (c), another interpolation is made as the
Exploratory Step for the next major iteration. The tolerances
on all nonlinear variables are set to their standard values;
so a variable that was independent throughout the previous
major iteration and never approached its lower or upper bound
can now become dependent.

Interpolation in line searches is based on fitting cubic
approximations to the values of the objective function and the basic
variables, using the values and first derivatives at the end points
of the interval in which interpolation is taking place. The detailed formulae are developed in the Appendix, since the conventional formulae given by Fletcher and Powell (1963) are not always
appropriate.

It does not seem worthwhile repeating the precise rules for
carrying out line searches, or for choosing between gradient and
conjugate gradient search directions. These are described by
Batchelor and Beale (1976). The other major change from the original version of the method that seems to be of major importance
is the method of scaling the variables when calculating gradients.

Scaling is a significant factor in any optimization method
that uses gradients, since the problem is then trivial if the objective function has approximately hyperspherical contours, and the
extent to which this is so can be significantly affected by scaling.
To the extent that the contours are approximately hyperellipsoids,
they can be transformed into hyperspheres by a general linear
transportation of variables, but not necessarily by a simple re-
scaling of individual variables. It is therefore tempting for a
mathematician to conclude that scaling of individual variables is
an unimportant topic. But this overlooks two factors:

(a)   The initial scalings of different variables may be completely
      arbitrary, particularly if the variables have different physi-
      cal dimensions.

(b)   Hessian matrices are often sparse, and this introduces a de-
      gree of independence between variables, or at least between
      sets of variables. The extreme case where all off-diagonal

elements of the Hessian vanish is of course the one where scaling of individual variables gives the best possible linear transformation.

We therefore investigate scaling of individual variables in more detail. The gradient direction in the space of the independent variables y_r has direction ratios $-d_r$, but if we define new variables, say $z_r = y_r/s_r$, where the s_r are scale factors, then the gradient direction in the space of the z_r has direction ratios $-s_r d_r$, and this corresponds to the direction in the space of the y_r with direction ratios $-s_r^2 d_r$. So we can choose scale factors to give these quantities arbitrary magnitudes, although we cannot change their signs. All this is well known. But it is not so clear what to do about it. When there are many decision variables, bad scaling can cause a few variables to have reduced costs that are of a constant sign and nearly constant magnitude over many steps. And this is particularly galling if we then stop the process on the grounds that the trial solution is not changing much.

Our solution to this problem is to use "statistical scaling." That is to say, we consider each variable independently and observe the variation in the values of d_r from step to step. We treat these as random variables, and compute exponentially weighted moving averages d_{Mr} and d_{Vr} of their means and variances. We then choose the scale factors s_r so that the variances of the scaled gradients $-s_r d_r$ are all set to unity. In other words we put $s_r^2 = 1/d_{Vr}$.

We are quite pleased with the results of this, but one consequence is worth further attention. If a particular reduced cost d_r becomes very large at one step, this will make d_{Vr} very large and s_r^2 correspondingly small. If at later steps this d_r takes more normal values, the direction ratio $-s_r^2 d_r$ will remain very small and the variable y_r will remain almost constant. This is not a serious problem for us, because the values of d_{Mr} and d_{Vr} are re-initialized after each Exploratory Step. But the point needs to be borne in mind by anyone thinking of adapting this approach to other algorithms.

We have used the algorithm on some toy problems with no constraints other than (in one case) a simple lower bound on one variable. We chose those studied by Sargent and Sebastian (1972). This has helped us to understand the properties of the algorithm, and the results may be of some interest:

The algorithm took

- 77 iterations to solve Rosenbrock's problem;

- 77 iterations to solve Rosenbrock's problem with a lower bound of zero on x_2;

94 iterations to solve the Helical Valley problem;

119 iterations to solve Powell's Quartic; and

257 iterations to solve Wood's problem.

We believe that these are reasonably satisfactory figures for a method that is really addressed to a quite different type of problem.

Serious use of the current version of the system has been confined to a sequence of oil production porblems for the Kuwait Oil Company. The latest problem solved has 2,336 constraints, 408 nonlinear variables and 3,984 linear variables. This was run for 54 steps and the resulting solution was accepted as adequate for practical purposes.

4. OPERATIONAL ASPECTS OF METHODS USING LOCAL DEFINITION

Our scheme for operating Conjugate Gradient Approximation programming is not as smooth as it could be.
convinced that we could do very much about it, because tne major task in a large problem is to produce a Matrix Generator to create a data tape for a linear programming subproblem given any set of trial values of the variables and tolerances on the nonlinear variables. The whole system consists of 6 programs.

1. Input, which reads the data, checks and prints them, and transfers them to backing store for later use.

2. A Mathematical Control Program, which decides whether or not to stop, and if not selects trial values and tolerances.

3. A Matrix Generator, producing the data-tape for the next LP subproblem.

4. The LP system (SCICONIC) that solves the LP subproblem and produces directional derivatives if needed.

5. A Short Report Writer, which reads the LP solution, makes a short report, and stores the values of the variables, the reduced costs and the directional derivatives for transmission to the Control Program. A Basic Variable is recorded as having a Reduced Cost that represents the number 1 when interpreted as an integer, which is a very small number indeed when interpreted as a floating point number.

6. A Long Report Writer, which produces a detailed report on the final solution to the problem.

A Control Stream is provided to instruct the Operating System for the Computer to run Program 1, and then to loop through Programs 2, 3, 4 and 5 as often as necessary, and finally to run Program 6. In fact this Control Stream is generated by a FORTRAN program.

Programs 1, 3, 5 and 6 are written in FORTRAN and are specific to any application of the system. Program 2 is also written in FORTRAN. It is in principle a general purpose program, but there is one problem-specific part of the operation that we have included here. This concerns the fact that the Control Program assumes that the optimum values of the nonlinear variables are stored in a single one-dimensional array followed by all the linear variables with non-constant coefficients. And similarly for the reduced costs and directional derivatives. Equally the program produces new trial values and tolerances in the same way. But the other programs store these data in separate arrays, with one array for each type of variable and often with more than one subscript. So we must pack the data into linear arrays at the start of the Control Program and reverse the process at the end of the Control Program. And we have found it most convenient to include both operations within the Control Program.

It would be logical to generate the constant coefficients in the matrix once for all, and to regenerate only the variable coefficients at each step. But we have not incorporated this facility. We do arrange for the data to be read directly into a Problem File for SCICONIC, so there is no conversion of data to BCD at the end of Program 3 to be read and converted back at the start of Program 4. But this is a standard option with matrix generators for SCICONIC, and not specific to nonlinear programming.

One thing that we can perhaps take credit for is that the Row and Column names in the LP subproblems are fully under the user's control, being created in the Matrix Generator. The standard output from SCICONIC is not usually printed after each iteration, but it can be produced for the final solution and for any intermediate solution of interest. This is often important, in particular for special analyses dependent on the Shadow Prices or the Reduced Costs that are not covered by the standard report writer program.

5. ALGORITHMIC ASPECTS OF METHODS USING GLOBAL DEFINITION

The next two sections discuss Scicon's approach to the task of solving nonlinear programming problems by feeding a complete specification of the problem into a general mathematical programming system. Following the original work on Separable Programming by Miller (1963), we do this by representing the problem as a formally linear programming problem with additional restrictions on the values of some of the variables. Following the introduction of Special Ordered Sets by Beale and Tomlin (1970), we switched our interest from methods for finding local optima to methods for finding global optima to similarly posed problems by Branch and Bound. This approach incidentally allows problems to contain integer variables as well as nonlinear functions.

Both of the papers cited above are concerned with problems in which all nonlinearities are expressed as sums (or differences) of piecewise linear functions of single arguments. Beale and Forrest (1976) relaxed the requirement that the functions be piecewise linear. Their methods are also applicable to functions that are defined analytically under mild restrictions that are discussed in more detail below.

In principle, this covers a very wide range of problems, but in practice the representation of products of variables may be clumsy, whether this is done by using logarithms, or by differences of two squares. Beale and Forrest (1977) have therefore introduced the concept of Linked Ordered Sets, which can be used to find global optimum solutions by branch and bound to problems with nonlinear functions expressed as sums of products of nonlinear functions of single arguments. This is related to the canonical form for nonlinear programming suggested in Section 2 above, since if we take fixed values for all the nonlinear variables we can obviously find conditional global optimum values for all the linear variables without any further branching.

The algorithmic task is therefore to find a simply computed guaranteed upper bound on the value of the objective function when the nonlinear variables are allowed to vary within finite ranges. It turns out that if each of the coefficients a_{ij} and b_i is a function of a single nonlinear variable, then we need only carry out branching operations on the permitted ranges of values of these variables. More general functions require the introduction of intermediate variables, but we never need to branch on the values of any of the linear variables as defined in Section 2.

Let us now see how this works in more detail.

Suppose that the nonlinear function $f(z)$ occurs in either the objective function or a constraint of an otherwise linear programming problem, and suppose in the first instance that the argument z can take only a finite number of possible values, say Z_k for $k = 0,1,...K$. Then we can introduce a set of nonnegative variables λ_k for $k = 0,1,...K$ and write

$$\sum_k \lambda_k = 1$$

$$\sum_k Z_k \lambda_k - z = 0.$$

These rows are called the Convexity and Reference Rows respectively for the set. The nonlinear function $f(z)$ is then represented by the linear function

$$\sum_k f(Z_k) \lambda_k$$

if we impose the further restriction that not more than one of the λ_k may be nonzero. And if we solve the linear programming problem without this further restriction we obtain an upper bound on how good the solution can be.

Furthermore, in order to sharpen this bound we can carry out branch and bound operations on the set of λ-variables that are allowed to take nonzero values. Specifically, if λ_{k_1} is any member of the set, we note that in any valid solution

either $\qquad \lambda_0 = \ldots = \lambda_{k_1} = 0$

or $\qquad \lambda_{k_1+1} = \ldots = \lambda_K = 0.$

By making this dichotomy we can replace our original linear programming problem by two new linear programming subproblems that include all valid solutions to the original problem while excluding the solution to the previous linear programming approximation. We can therefore solve the problem by a Branch and Bound process.

In the above formulation, the set of λ-variables is known as a Special Ordered Set of Type One, or S1 set, since only one member may ultimately be nonzero. But we may relax the formulation and allow two adjacent members of the set to be nonzero. This is then known as a Special Ordered Set of Type Two, or S2 set. It amounts to permitting linear interpolation to $f(z)$ between adjacent given values of the argument Z_k. The modification to the branching rule is simply that

either $\qquad \lambda_0 = \ldots = \lambda_{k_1-1} = 0$

or $\qquad \lambda_{k_1+1} = \ldots = \lambda_K = 0.$

This is the formulation originally introduced by Miller (1963). He achieved the necessary conditions on the λ_k by preventing a variable from entering the basis if any nonadjacent member of the set was currently in the basis. This approach provides a local optimum solution without any branching or bounding.

By introducing several such nonlinear functions, in general with different arguments, we can build up sums and differences of nonlinear functions of single arguments. But in practice we often need to consider products of variables, so let us see how these can be accommodated.

Suppose that we wish to represent $x_j f_j(z)$ for $j = 1,...J$, where the x_j and other variables of the problem, or possibly linear functions of such other variables. We suppose again that z must take one of the values Z_k for $k = 0,...K$, and that $X_{MINj} \leq x_j \leq X_{MAXj}$.

We now introduce $2J$ sets of nonnegative variables λ_{jvk} for $j = 1,...J$, $v = 1$ or 2, $k = 0,...K$, and write

$$\sum_k \lambda_{j1k} \quad + \quad \sum_k \lambda_{j2k} \quad = 1.$$

This is the Convexity Row.

$$\sum_k Z_k \lambda_{j1k} \quad + \quad \sum_k Z_k \lambda_{j2k} - z \quad = 0.$$

This is the Reference Row.

$$\sum_k X_{MINj} \lambda_{j1k} \quad + \quad \sum_k X_{MAXj} \lambda_{j2k} - x_j \quad = 0.$$

Then if $z = Z_{k_1}$ we can represent the nonlinear functions $x_j f_j(z)$ by the linear functions

$$\sum_k X_{MINj} f_j(Z_k) \lambda_{j1k} \quad + \quad \sum_k X_{MAXj} f_j(Z_k) \lambda_{j2k} \, ,$$

if we impose the further restriction that $\lambda_{jvk} = 0$ whenever $k \neq k_1$. This restriction must hold for all j and v. We therefore treat the sets of variables λ_{jvk} as Linked S1 Sets, and carry out Branch and Bound operations on the first and last values of k for which these variables may take nonzero values for all j and v simultaneously.

Beale and Forrest (1976) show how Special Ordered Sets can be used when z is a truly continuous variable. Provision must then be made for introducing new variables λ_k while solving linear programming subproblems. The procedure used is essentially a special case of the Decomposition Principle introduced by Dantzig and Wolfe (1960). There remains the global optimization problem of choosing a value of z for which the corresponding λ_k is within ε of the most negative reduced cost. Beale and Forrest (1976) define a finite algorithm for this using ideas similar to those used by Brent (1973). They require that each f(z) can be written in the form

$$f(z) = \sum_i \Pi_i f_i(z)$$

where

(a)   each $f_i(z)$ is twice differentiable,

(b) $f_i(z)$, $f_i'(z)$ and $f_i''(z)$ can be calculated for any z, and

(c)   the range of possible values of z can be divided a priori into a finite number of intervals such that $f_i''(z)$ is monotonic within each interval.

Further algorithmic details are given in the cited papers and in Beale (1977).

6.   OPERATIONAL ASPECTS OF METHODS USING GLOBAL DEFINITION

The MPS formats developed by IBM for input and output of linear or integer programming problems have become a de facto industry standard, to the benefit of all parties. But it is not obvious how these should be extended to cover the non-standard facilities discussed in the previous section. It is perhaps too much to expect general agreement on input formats for nonlinear programming problems, since the expression of the problem will inevitably be influenced by the algorithmic approach used. Nevertheless, a statement of Scicon's current practice may be of interest. Both the design and implementation of this are largely the work of my colleague J.J.H. Forrest.

The users of Special Ordered Sets, and of Linked Ordered Sets, have to analyze their problems mathematically to express them in a formally linear manner. The linear part of the model is then represented in standard MPS formats, except that there is always a pseudo-objective-function row with the reserved name 'MARKER'. (This name must appear in the Rows Section.)

Special Ordered Sets of variables not containing analytical functions are separated from other variables in a way that is very similar to that used by IBM for Separable Programming. They start with a Header Card as follows

Cols 2-3	S1 (for S1 sets), or S2 (for S2 sets)
Cols 5-12	Any Unique Name
Cols 15-22	'MARKER'
Cols 25-32	'SETORG'
Cols 40-47	The Name of the Reference Row (used in Branch and Bound operations)
Cols 50-62	A number representing the maximum possible value of the sum of all the variables in the set. This is normally 1.0, but some nonstandard uses of Special Ordered Sets allow larger values. This number is used only in the calculation of bounds.

They end with a card as follows:

Cols 5-12	Any Unique Name
Cols 15-22	'MARKER'
Cols 25-32	'SETEND'.

As things stand, sets containing analytical functions cannot contain any other variables. And any function must be of a specified type, each of which contains three numerical parameters. The types that exist at the time of writing are as follows:

Type 1	$Az^2 + Bz + C$	
Type P	$Az^B + C$	(where $z \geq 0$)
Type E	$Az^{Bx} + C$	
Type L	$A\ln Bz + C$	(where $Bz > 0$)
Type N	$A(z+C)^B$, where B is a small integer, either positive or negative. Where B is negative, the user must ensure that $-C$ is not within the range of possible values of z.	

A single row may contain more than one function. So for example a low-order polynomial can be defined by a function of Type 1, plus one or more functions of Type N with different parameters.

The input formats for Analytical Functions are as follows:

There is a header card, which is the same as that for an ordinary Special Ordered Set except that the Cols 2 and 3 contain the letters FN.

This is followed by data cards for one "pseudo-vector" that defines all the members of the set. It has a name like that of any other vector, but the fields normally reserved for numerical values only contain numbers when the entry in that row is a constant for all members of the set.

There must be an entry in the row 'MARKER' with the pseudo-value 'FUNCTN'. And the entries in the rows where the coefficients are not constant come in sets of three, defining the values of the parameters A, B and C for the function in question. The first Character of the field defining the pseudo-value then contains the character ', the second character contains the code for the function type, the third character contains the code for the parameter (i.e., A, B or C) and the remaining 9 characters give the numerical value of the parameter.

The end card is the same as that for any other Special Ordered Set.

The range of possible values of the argument z is defined in the BOUNDS section. The default value of the lower bound is zero, but an upper bound must be specified, by a card punched as follows:

Cols 2-3   UP

Cols 5-12   The Bound Set Name

Cols 15-22   The Name given to the Pseudo-Vector

Cols 25-36   The Upper Bound on the argument.

Any links between Ordered Sets are defined in the Run Stream together with information about priorities and strategies to be used for the global optimization process. There must be one card per set, punched as follows:

Cols 2-3   Indicator for the type of set, as follows

          L1   A single set of variables defined
                explicitly

          L2   A member of a pair of sets of variables defined explicitly and sharing
                a convexity row

          N1   A single set of variables defined as
                an analytic function

          N2   A member of pair of sets of variables
defined as an analytic function and
sharing a convexity row

Cols 5-12   The Name of the Set (i.e., the vector name on
the header card for the set)

Cols 15-   LINK for the first of the Linked Ordered Sets

                      LINKEND for the last of the Linked Ordered
Sets with a single common argument

                      Blank otherwise.

Pairs of sets with a common convexity row must appear together
in this list. Single sets of variables only occur in some non-
standard applications of Linked Ordered Sets not considered in this
paper.

One modification to the standard MPS output formats is necessary in order to make the information on analytic functions intelli-
gible. All members of a set defined by analytic functions have the
pseudo-vector name used to define the set. So they are distinguished
on the COLUMNS section of the output by giving the Reference Row
Entry in the space normally reserved for the Input Cost.

REFERENCES

1.   J. Abadie and J. Carpenter, Generalization of the Wolfe Reduced
        Gradient Method to the Case of Nonlinear Constraints, in:
        Optimization, ed. by R. Fletcher, Academic Press, London and
        New York, 1969, pp. 37-47.
2.   A.S.J. Batchelor and E.M.L. Beale, A Revised Method of
        Conjugate Gradient Approximation Programming, Paper presented
        to the Ninth International Symposium on Mathematical Program-
        ming at Budapest, 1976.
3.   E.M.L. Beale, A Conjugate Gradient-Method of Approximation
        Programming, in: Optimization Methods for Resource Allocation,
        ed. by R.W. Cottle and J. Krarup, English Universities Press,
        1974, pp. 261-277.
4.   E.M.L. Beale, Branch and Bound Methods for Integer Programming,
        Paper presented at the Conference D077 in Vancouver,
        Canada, August 1977.
5.   E.M.L. Beale and J.A. Tomlin, Special Facilities in a General
        Mathematical Programming System for Non-Convex Problems Using
        Ordered Sets of Variables, in: Proceedings of the Fifth
        International Conference on Operational Research, ed. by
        J. Lawrence, Tavistock Publications, London, 1970, pp. 447-
        454.

6. E.M.L. Beale and J.J.H. Forrest, Global Optimization Using Special Ordered Sets, Mathematical Programming 10, 1977, pp. 52-69.
7. E.M.L. Beale and J.J.H. Forrest, Global Optimization as an Extension of Integer Programming, to appear, 1977.
8. R.P. Brent, Algorithms for Minimization without Derivatives, Prentice Hall Inc., Englewood Cliffs, New Jersey, 1973.
9. G.B. Dantzig and P. Wolfe, Decomposition Principle for Linear Programming, Operations Research 8, 1960, pp. 101-111.
10. R. Fletcher and M.J.D. Powell, A Rapidly Convergent Descent Method for Minimization, in: Computer Journal 6, 1963, pp. 163-168.
11. R.E. Griffith and R.A. Stewart, A Nonlinear Programming Technique for the Optimization of Continuous Processing Systems, in: Management Science 7, 1961, pp. 379-392.
12. C.E. Miller, The Simplex Method for Local Separable Programming, in: Recent Advances in Mathematical Programming, ed. by R.L. Graves and P. Wolfe, McGraw Hill, New York, 1963, pp. 89-100.
13. S.M. Robinson, A Quadratically Convergent Algorithm for General Nonlinear Programming Problems, in Mathematical Programming 3, 1972, pp. 145-156.
14. R.W.H. Sargent and D.J. Sebastian, Numerical Experience with Algorithms for Unconstrained Minimization, in: Numerical Methods for Nonlinear Optimization, ed. by F. Lootsma, Academic Press, London and New York, 1972, pp. 45-68.
15. P. Wolfe, Methods of Nonlinear Programming, in: Recent Advances in Mathematical Programming, ed. by R.L. Graves.

APPENDIX

Cubic Interpolation to Maximize a Function of One Variable

Suppose that we were given the values f_o and f_h of a differentiable function $f(x)$ for $x = x_o$ and $x = x_o + h$ respectively, and the corresponding first derivatives f_o' and f_h'.

If $f_o' > 0$, and either $f_h < f_o$ or $f_h' < 0$, then the function has a local maximum at some point $x = x_o + \theta h$, where $0 < \theta < 1$, and we can approximate θ by maximizing a cubic approximation to $f(x)$ fitted to the known data.

If the cubic approximation to $f(x_o + \theta h)$ is denoted by $a_0 + a_1\theta + a_2\theta^2 + a_3\theta^3$, then

$$f_o = a_0$$

$$f_h = a_0 + a_1 + a_2 + a_3$$

$$hf_o' \quad = \quad a_1$$

$$hf_h' \quad = \quad a_1 + 2a_2 + 3a_3.$$

To solve these equations for a_0, a_1, a_2 and a_3 it turns out to be convenient to write

$$t_1 = f_o' - 3(f_h - f_o)/h + f_h' .$$

Then, since $a_0 = f_o$ and $a_1 = hf_o'$, it follows that

$$a_2 + a_3 = f_h - f_o - hf_o' = h(-(1/3)t_1 - (2/3)f'0 + (1/3)f_h')$$

and

$$2a_2 + 3a_3 = hf_h' - hf_o' = h(- f_o' + f_h').$$

So

$$a_2 = - h(t_1 + f_o')$$

and

$$a_3 = h(2/3)t_1 + (1/3)f_o' + (1/3)f_h').$$

But the values of θ for which $f(x_0 + \theta h)$ is stationary are the roots of the quadratic equation

$$a_1 + 2a_2\theta + 3a_3\theta^2 = 0,$$

i.e.,

$$\theta = \{-a_2 \pm \sqrt{a_2^2 - 3a_1a_3}\} /3a_3.$$

To establish the appropriate sign, note that if $a_3 < 0$, we want the larger root, while if $a_3 > 0$ we want the smaller root. So in both cases the negative sign is appropriate and we write

$$\theta = -\{a_2 + \sqrt{a_2^2 - 3a_1a_3}\} /3a_3.$$

This is a good formula if $a_2 \geq 0$, but otherwise it can produce serious rounding-off errors. We therefore derive an alternative formula by multiplying top and bottom by

$$a_2 - \sqrt{a_2^2 - 3a_1a_3}$$

and see that

$$\theta = - \frac{a_2^2 - (a_2^2 - 3a_1a_3)}{3a_3(a_2 - \sqrt{a_2^2 - 3a_1a_3})} = - \frac{a_1}{a_2 - \sqrt{a_2^2 - 3a_1a_3}}$$

This is a good formula if $a_2 < 0$.

If we now substitute for a_1, a_2 and a_3 we find that

$$a_2^2 - 3a_1a_3 + h^2(t_1^2 - f_0'f_h'),$$

so we compute

$$t_2 = t_1 + f_0',$$

and if $t_2 > 0$ we write

$$\theta = -\frac{a_1}{a_2 - \sqrt{a_2^2 - 3a_1a_3}} = \frac{f_0'}{t_2 + \sqrt{t_1^2 - f_0'f_h'}}.$$

while if $t_2 \leq 0$ we write

$$\theta = -\frac{a_2 + \sqrt{a_2^2 - 3a_1a_3}}{3a_3} = \frac{t_2 - \sqrt{t^2 - f_0'f_h'}}{t_1 + t_2 + f_h'}.$$

The first of these formulae is equivalent to that quoted by Fletcher and Powell (1963), and is usually appropriate. But if f_0' is very small, as it can be, this is ill conditioned and the second formula should be used.

THE DESIGN AND IMPLEMENTATION OF SOFTWARE FOR UNCONSTRAINED
OPTIMIZATION

Philip E. Gill and Walter Murray

INTRODUCTION

This paper is concerned with the design of software for the
unconstrained minimization problem

P1 $\qquad$ minimize $F(x)$,
$$ x $$

where $F(x)$ is a twice-continuously differentiable function of n
variables $x = (x_1, x_2, \ldots, x_n)^T$.

The solution of this problem by a single all-powerful method
is not possible. Methods are therefore designed to solve particular
categories of problems, each category being defined by the properties
of the function $F(x)$ and the order of the derivatives which can be
defined by the user.

The mathematical software available to solve these problems is
generally in one of two forms. The first form is a self-contained
program which is available for solving a single problem category;
such programs are generally written by those undertaking research in
optimization in order to test the features of a new method. The
second form consists of part of a collection of routines known as a
program library which are conceived and written within a unified
framework to be available to a general community of users. It is

primarily this second type of software which will be discussed in this paper and as a consequence we seek theoretical methods which, while catering for the different problem categories, nevertheless involve the same basic operations of the optimization process. In this way a set of basic modules can be shared by methods for solving various categories of problems. It is not our intention here to give a detailed derivation of the theory of all methods available. We are more concerned with those aspects of optimization theory which impinge upon software design. For further details of the basic theory, the reader should refer to the references cited in the text. If there is a particular algorithm which in our view most effectively solves a certain category of problem, we shall concentrate on that method. However, if a promising method is relatively new, its merits vis à vis its competitors will be discussed so that readers unacquainted with the technique may form their own conclusions.

We shall define the gradient vector $g(x)$ as the vector whose ith element is $\frac{\partial F(x)}{\partial x_i}$ and the Hessian matrix $G(x)$ as the symmetric matrix whose (i,j)th element is $\frac{\partial^2 F(x)}{\partial x_i \partial x_j}$. All the algorithms discussed in this paper generate a sequence of estimates $\{x^{(k)}\}$ of the optimal point x*. Many do so by generating a search direction $p^{(k)}$ and a step length $\alpha^{(k)}$ such that $x^{(k+1)} = x^{(k)} + \alpha^{(k)} p^{(k)}$; those which have the additional property that $F(x^{(k)} + \alpha^{(k)} p^{(k)})$ $< F(x^{(k)})$ are known as descent methods. In order to simplify some of the formulae we shall denote $F(x^{(k)})$, $g(x^{(k)})$ and $G(x^{(k)})$ by $F^{(k)}$, $g^{(k)}$ and $G^{(k)}$.

1.1 The structure of a program library

A good program library should have a routine for each of the following categories

Properties of F(x)	Type and order of derivatives available
F(x) Univariate	F(x) only
F(x) sum of squares	F(x) and g(x)

Properties of F(x)	Type and order of derivatives available
G(x) large and sparse	F(x), g(x) available but expensive to compute
G(x) cannot be stored	F(x), g(x) and G(x)
	F(x), g(x) and some G(x).

In this paper we shall give a description of a technique for each of these categories. However, there are other equally important aspects of optimization software design which are not concerned with the actual minimization of the function. Before the minimization can commence the user must provide routines which evaluate the function F(x) and, optionally, its higher derivatives. We have found that it is worthwhile providing 'service' routines which check these user-provided routines for programming errors or mistakes in the differentiation. This can be done by means of finite differences. If first derivatives are being checked, finite differences of the function values are used; if second derivatives are being checked, the gradient vector may be differenced. In both cases the difference is made along just two independent vectors which are chosen so as not to give any special values of the function or gradient. Similarly, a service routine can be used to set values of any parameters which the inexperienced user may find difficult to provide. For example, to solve an unconstrained problem with a quasi-Newton method based upon finite-difference approximations to gradients, a finite-difference interval must be provided for each variable. A service routine can be provided which determines a sensible set of finite-difference intervals. For more details see Gill, Murray, Picken and Wright (1977).

2. UNIVARIATE MINIMIZATION AND STEP-LENGTH ALGORITHMS

2.1 Univariate minimization methods

The univariate minimization problem is to find the point α^* at which the function $f(\alpha)$ attains its minimum value over the interval $[a,b]$. Problems of this type occur in their own right, but more often they are a subproblem within a general descent method for multidimensional minimization. In the latter case we require $\overset{*}{\alpha}$, the solution of

UP1   minimize $f(\alpha) = F(x^{(k)} + \alpha p^{(k)})$, $\alpha \in [0,\infty)$.

Many descent methods require only a crude solution of UP1 and we shall consider this problem directly in Section 2.2. However, it is important to note that the most effective techniques for computing a step length which is not a univariate minimizer utilize many of the results of this section.

We shall assume that initially we have an interval [a,b] in which the $\overset{*}{\alpha}$ is known to lie. The interval [a,b] is known as the interval of uncertainty and the points a and b are said to bracket the minimum value of $\overset{*}{\alpha}$. The basic strategy of univariate minimization methods is progressively to reduce the size of this interval. The usefulness of any estimate $\bar{\alpha}$ of the minimum obtained by these methods depends mainly on our knowing that it lies within a very small interval of uncertainty.

Any method for solving UP1 belongs to one of three categories.

(a) Function comparison methods. These techniques reduce the interval of uncertainty by evaluating the function at points within [a,b] and comparing their magnitude. Typical of methods in this class are Fibonacci search, Golden-section search (see Kiefer, 1953 and Johnson, 1955) and successive approximation (Berman, 1966). The advantage of methods of function comparison is that they are guaranteed to be convergent for the class of unimodal functions, and in most cases an a priori upper bound on the number of function evaluations can be given. The major disadvantage of this type of method is that the rate of convergence is at best linear. This is because the quantity by which the value of the function varies over the interval of uncertainty is ignored.

(b) Successive function interpolation. The main feature of this class of methods is that the function $f(\alpha)$ is approximated by a simple function $\hat{f}(\alpha)$ which agrees exactly with $f(\alpha)$ in either

function value of function value and derivatives at a certain number
of points. Naturally $\hat{f}(\alpha)$ must be a function whose minimum is
easily determined and so it is normally chosen to be a quadratic or
cubic polynomial. However, there are many ways in which $\hat{f}(\alpha)$ can
be chosen to reflect the behaviour of $f(\alpha)$ more closely. For
example, if $f(\alpha)$ is a sum of squares of the form

$$f(\alpha) = F(x^{(k)} + \alpha p^{(k)}) = \sum_{j=1}^{m} \phi_j (x^{(k)} + \alpha p^{(k)})^2,$$

where $\phi_j (x^{(k)} + \alpha p^{(k)})$ is a non-linear function, a low-order polynomial $\hat{\phi}_j (\alpha)$ can be fitted to each function ϕ_j. Similarly, if
$F(x)$ is a barrier function derived from a constrained minimi-
zation problem, it has a singularity. In this case an interpolating function can be constructed which has a similar singularity but with a minimum which is easily found (see Murray and
Wright, 1976).

If $\hat{f}(\alpha)$ is a quadratic polynomial, the new approximation to $\overset{*}{\alpha}$
is the stationary point of a quadratic polynomial agreeing with
$f(\alpha)$ in the function value at three known points. If $\hat{f}(\alpha)$ is a
cubic, the new approximation to $\overset{*}{\alpha}$ is the stationary point of a
cubic whose function value and first derivative are identical to
those of $f(\alpha)$ at two known points.

Provided the old values of the function bracket the minimum
and exact arithmetic is used, the stationary points of the interpolating cubics and quadratics will also lie in the interval and
consequently the interval of uncertainty must be reduced.

If, as in the case of function-comparison methods, we insist
that the point discarded is such that the new set of points still
brackets the minimum, a high function value may be retained for
some while and the convergence can be significantly impeded. A
natural alternative is to discard the point corresponding to the
highest function value since this point is likely to be the least
useful in any subsequent interpolations. It can be shown that
under mild conditions on $f(\alpha)$, if such an algorithm converges, it

does so at a superlinear rate (see Brent 1973). Unfortunately, the interval defined by the new set of points need no longer bracket the minimum and under these circumstances the interpolation formula cannot be relied upon to yield a function value which is lower than any of those used in the interpolation formula.

(c) Safeguarded successive-interpolation schemes. This class of methods is designed to overcome the disadvantages of function comparison and polynomial interpolation schemes when used alone by combining the two methods into a single hybrid algorithm. Methods in this class have the guaranteed convergence properties of the function-comparison methods together with the superlinear asymptotic rate of convergence of successive polynomial interpolation schemes. The basic strategy is to use polynomial approximation provided that the predicted step lies within some interval; otherwise a step of a function-comparison method is used. Two points bracketing the minimum are always kept but the best (i.e., the lowest) values of the function obtained up to that time are used to compute the approximating polynomial.

During the earlier stages of the interpolation, that is, before the superlinear convergence sets in, the best points can tend to be bunched together at one end of the interval of uncertainty. Figure 2.1 depicts this situation in the case where $\hat{f}(\alpha)$ is a quadratic polynomial: a and b are the current upper and lower bounds on the minimum, x is the best point obtained so far, w is the previous value of x and v is the worst of the three points. This situation can arise when, owing to an overestimation of the initial step length, the function value at b is large. The subsequent point x obtained by interpolation will be close to the first point. The intervals d_1 and d_2 can often be of different orders of magnitude with $|d_2| \gg |d_1|$.

Conversely when certain types of penalty and barrier functions are being minimized, the function values on one side of the minimum rise more rapidly than values on the opposite side, often giving a configuration of points with $|d_1| \gg |d_2|$.

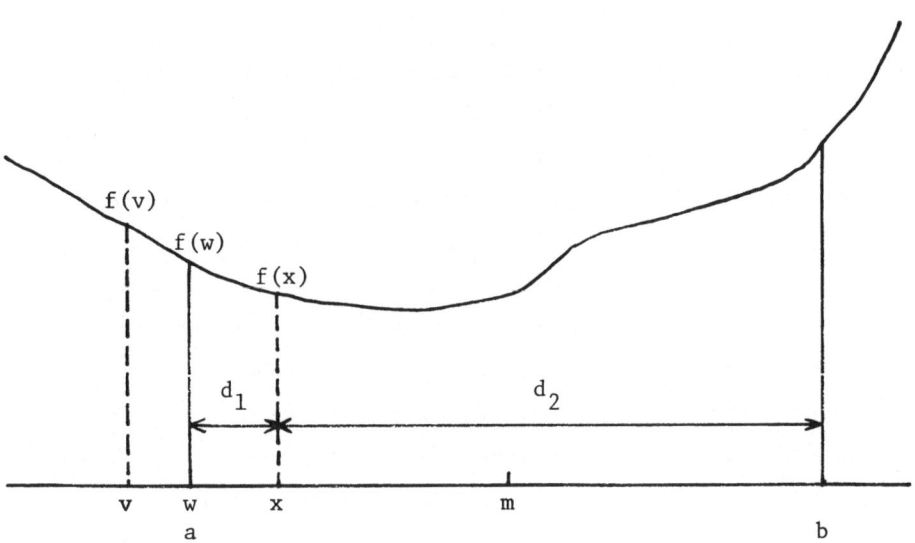

Fig. 2.1.

In either of the situations just described, repeated use of a
step obtained by function comparison is common. Unfortunately, a
large number of such steps is necessary to reduce the length of the
large interval significantly. What is required is a scheme which
will give, when necessary, a point which is biased towards x, the
best point available at that stage.

To avoid taking a large number of function comparison steps
when d_1 and d_2 are of widely differing size we suggest that an
artificial bound m be constructed <u>within</u> the interval of uncertainty
when the points are in an extrapolation configuration (see Figure
2.1). This bound should be computed so that the interval $|m - x|$
is obtained with an exponent which is the average of the exponents
of the two intervals $|d_1|$ and $|d_2|$. If the predicted point lies be-
yond m, the predicted point is set equal to the bound. The reader
is referred to Gill and Murray (1974a) for further details.

<u>Starting the safeguarded successive interpolation scheme.</u>
Before a safeguarded interpolation scheme can commence, enough
interpolating points must be known to define the new approximation.

The way in which these points are obtained depends upon the nature of $f(\alpha)$.

$\underline{f(\alpha)\ \text{a general univariate function.}}$ If $\hat{f}(\alpha)$ is a quadratic polynomial and $[a,b]$ is the initial interval of uncertainty, three points within $[a,b]$ are required. The "optimal" placing of three points in an interval so that the final interval of uncertainty is minimized, regardless of the behaviour of the function, is $x_1 = a + (b-a)/3$, $x_2 = a + 2(b-a)/3$ and, if $f_1 < f_2$, $x_3 = x_1 + \varepsilon$ or, if $f_1 > f_2$, $x_3 = x_2 + \varepsilon$ where ε is a small positive scalar. This gives a final interval of uncertainty of length $\varepsilon + (b-a)/3$. This optimal placing is not satisfactory since an unfortunate choice of ε can lead to significant cancellation error during the first step of the interpolation process. Furthermore, we have a situation of the type discussed in the last section, where one interval is significantly larger than the other. A placing of points which gives no problem during the subsequent interpolation, yet leads to only a marginal increase in the resulting interval of uncertainty is $x_1 = a + 2(b-a)/5$, $x_2 = a + 3(b-a)/5$ and, if $f_1 < f_2$, $x_3 = a + (b-a)/5$, or if $f_1 > f_2$, $x_3 = a + 4(b-a)/5$. This gives an interval of uncertainty of length $2(b-a)/5$.

If cubic interpolation is used, the optimal process of bisection can be used without difficulty.

$\underline{f(\alpha)\ \text{derived from a general descent method.}}$ In this case the initial points can be obtained from information relating to a specific descent method. For example, the unit step is usually a good prediction of the minimum along the direction of search, or a step can be computed by using the gradient and function value at $\alpha = 0$. The more difficult problem is to obtain a set of points which bracket the minimum. An efficient method is to use successive interpolation to predict the position of a minimum. Since the process is one of extrapolation, safeguards are needed in the form of a bound upon the step taken. A natural choice of bound is the point which would be obtained by a simple extrapolation in multiples of a fixed scalar.

2.2 Step-length algorithms

Many descent methods have been proposed for which it is claimed that solution of a linear search subproblem is unnecessary (see for example Davidon 1975, Fletcher 1970). In most cases this claim is intended to advertise the fact that certain properties of the method will hold without our necessarily calculating the exact point $\overset{*}{\alpha}$ which solves the minimization problem UP1. We believe that the quest for an algorithm in which a <u>single</u> evaluation of F(x) is made per iteration is ill-advised and certain to be fruitless. As soon as more than one evaluation of F(x) is made, the way in which those values are computed becomes important.

The earliest attempts to specify values of α other than $\overset{*}{\alpha}$ involved finding any value of α satisfying a criterion which ensured the convergence of the underlying descent method for general multidimensional problems. It is possible to prove the convergence of a general descent method with the aid of any one of the following conditions:

c1. $\alpha^{(k)}$ is the smallest solution of UP1;

c2. $\alpha^{(k)}$ is the smallest root of

$$[g(x^{(k)} + \alpha p^{(k)}) - \eta g^{(k)}]^T p^{(k)} = 0 \qquad \eta \varepsilon [0,1) \quad (2.1)$$

c3. $\alpha^{(k)}$ satisfies the inequalities

$$0 < - \mu_1 \alpha^{(k)} g^{(k)T} p^{(k)} \leqq F^{(k)} - F^{(k+1)} \leqq - \mu_2 \alpha^{(k)} g^{(k)T} p^{(k)},$$

where μ_1 and μ_2 are arbitrary scalars satisfying $0 < \mu_1 \leqq \mu_2 < 1$.

Of the three conditions, c3 is the only one suitable for defining values of $\alpha^{(k)}$ for general functions. (The computation of an $\alpha^{(k)}$ which satisfies c1 or c2 would be very inefficient in practice since the only way to guarantee that $\alpha^{(k)}$ is the smallest minimum of UP1 or the smallest root of (2.1) is to compute <u>every</u> minimum or <u>every</u> root.) Several algorithms have been suggested based on the condition c3 (Goldstein and Price 1967, Fletcher 1970). They all involve choosing $\alpha^{(k)}$ as 1, w, w^2, w^3,...($0 < w < 1$) until c3 is satisfied for some values of μ_1 and μ_2. The fundamental disadvantage of this type of technique is that any iterative scheme based upon taking arbitrary multiples of a fixed scalar can give a slow rate of congergence of $F(x^{(k)} + w^j p^{(k)})$ to the required value. Another disadvantage is that such algorithms are not flexible enough for general application. The majority of descent methods are such that fewer function evaluations are required to find the minimum of $F(x)$ if an "inexact" univariate minimization is performed. However, the decrease in the number of function evaluations is accompanied by an increase in the number of iterations. A consequence of this is that if the housekeeping time per iteration is relatively greater than the time required to compute the value of the function, an exact linear search can be advantageous. Algorithms for multivariate minimization utilizing a crude step length should be used only if the cost of a function evaluation is significantly less than the work to perform a single iteration. If this is not the case there is no simple way in which values of μ_1 and μ_2 can be chosen so that the accuracy of the univariate minimization is increased.

A rapidly convergent algorithm for which the accuracy can be varied to suit the problem is based upon the following condition on $\alpha^{(k)}$:

c4.　$\alpha^{(k)}$ is defined such that $\alpha^{(k)} = w^{\bar{j}}\bar{\alpha}$, where

$$\left| g(x^{(k)} + \overline{\alpha p}^{(k)T} p^{(k)} \right| \leq - \eta g^{(k)T} p^{(k)}, \quad \eta \in [0,1), \quad (2.2a)$$

and　　　$$F^{(k)} - F^{(k+1)} \leq - \mu a^{(k)} g^{(k)T} p^{(k)}, \quad 0 < \mu < 1/2. \quad (2.2b).$$

The important property of this condition is that if μ is chosen as a small value then, unless $f(\alpha)$ is a pathologically ill-behaved function, any value $\bar{\alpha}$ satisfying (2.2a) automatically satisfies (2.2b). In this case condition c4 is equivalent to specifying that $\alpha^{(k)}$ should satisfy the relationship

$$\left| g(x^{(k)} + \alpha^{(k)} p^{(k)})^T p^{(k)} \right| \leq - \eta g^{(k)T} p^{(k)}, \quad \eta \in [0,1).$$

The scalar $\bar{\alpha}$ is computed as the first number of a sequence of estimates to α^* generated by safeguarded successive interpolation which
satisfies (2.2a). The value of η is specified by the user and can
be used to give a step length which is well-suited to the problem
being solved. If η is chosen as 0.9 the algorithm will generally
give a "crude" value of $\alpha^{(k)}$ as the initial point of the repeated
interpolation algorithm, provided it satisfies (2.2b). If η is
chosen as zero, $\alpha^{(k)}$ is identical to the solution of UP1.

2.3 Software design

In this section we shall touch upon the aspects of software
design for a computer routine for computing a step length. Our aim
is to describe a routine which has the property that its major components can be used by as many other optimization routines as possible, yet remains efficient when used in any particular application.

Two alternative step-length algorithms should be available.
For the most common type of problem where $g(x)$ can be obtained
with approximately the same amount of work as $F(x)$, the safeguarded
cubic interpolation algorithm is appropriate. If $g(x)$ is relatively
expensive to compute, however, it is preferable to use quadratic interpolation with (2.2a) of condition c4 replaced by

$$\left| \frac{F(x)^{(k)} + \sigma p^{(k)}) - F(x^{(k)} + \bar{\alpha} p^{(k)})}{\sigma - \bar{\alpha}} \right| \leqq - \eta g^{(k)T} p^{(k)},$$

where σ is any estimate of α^* such that $\sigma < \alpha$.

All computer software must allow for the fact that the finite-
precision arithmetic of the machine being used will lead to round-
off error in the calculation of the objective function and the quantities involved in the definition of $\alpha^{(k)}$. Round-off error may
cause a theoretically unimodal function to become non-unimodal
within intervals comparable to the machine precision. For this
reason it is sensible to evaluate the function only at points which
are further apart than a certain value δ which is related to the

machine precision (see Brent, 1973; Gill and Murray 1974a). This
scheme also helps to reduce cancellation error during an interpolation. A further safeguard against unnecessary round-off error is
to treat one of the points defining the current interval of uncertainty as the origin and to scale the other defining points in relation to it.

Another desirable feature is the facility for enforcing an
upper bound λ upon the step length taken (that is, the final $\alpha^{(k)}$
must satisfy $\|\alpha^{(k)}p^{(k)}\| \leqq \lambda$). This bound can be used in several
ways: to prevent overflow in the user-supplied function routine;
to increase efficiency by ensuring that F(x) is evaluated only at
sensible values of x; to prevent the step-length algorithm from
returning an inordinately large step because no smaller step would
satisfy the convergence criterion; to guarantee that the new point
$x^{(k)} + \alpha^{(k)}p^{(k)}$ remains feasible when the step-length routine is
being used for constrained minimization.

The technique for ensuring that $\alpha^{(k)}$ is bounded above is not
straightforward. The simple expedient of evaluating F(x) at the
boundary and using the interval $[0,\lambda]$ as an initial interval of
uncertainty can be very inefficient if $\overset{*}{\alpha} <<< \lambda$ or the derivative
of $f(\alpha)$ is negative at λ. For further details the reader is referred to Gill and Murray (1974a).

In the design of optimization software in FORTRAN, an important
consideration is that of the control structure of the step-length
routine. If the routine is to be used by other multi-variate minimization routines, the computation of F(x) may involve the evaluation of many auxiliary quantities such as constraint values and
their derivatives, estimates of Lagrange multipliers, and penalty
parameters. The computation of these auxiliary quantities requires
the use of workspace and user-supplied subroutines. The amount of
workspace and the number of auxiliary subroutines will vary with the
application. If a completely general step-length subroutine is to
be constructed in FORTRAN the parameter list of the subroutine which
computes the value of F(x) must include all possible work arrays and

subroutine names which are likely to be used to define F(x). This
leads to a complicated and cumbersome algorithm which must be continually updated as further applications are found. A way of avoiding this problem is to separate the step-length subroutine into two
modules. The first module contains the majority of the code and
computes a single trial step using safeguarded interpolation. The
second module sets up the initial conditions for the safeguarded
interpolation to commence and repeatedly computes the problem functions at the trial points specified by the first module. The code
for the first module is problem-independent and forms the basic
routine for computing the step length. For each application a
different "outer" module is available which sets up the initial
conditions for the interpolation, calls the "inner" module and computes the problem function and all its auxiliary quantities. This
control structure is called reverse communication and was suggested
by Lawson and Krogh (see Krogh 1969).

3. SECOND-DERIVATIVE METHODS

The most effective numerical techniques for optimization are
modelled upon Newton's method. In this method the sequence of
directions can be regarded as solutions of a sequence of unconstrained quadratic problems of the form

$$\underset{p}{\text{minimize}} \left\{ Q(p) = 1/2 p^T G^{(k)} p + g^{(k)T} p + F^{(k)} \right\} . \tag{3.1}$$

If $G^{(k)}$ is positive definite, the level surfaces of the quadratic
function $Q(p) = Q(x - x^{(k)})$ are ellipsoids whose principal axes are
the eigenvectors of $G^{(k)}$ with lengths proportional to the recipro-
cals of the eigenvalues of $G^{(k)}$. The ellipsoid defined by
$Q(x - x^{(k)}) = F(x^{(k)})$ is tangent to the level surface of F(x) at $x^{(k)}$,
and its centre lies at the point $x^{(k)} + p^{(k)}$.

The solution of each quadratic subproblem is defined by the
equations

$$G^{(k)}p^{(k)} = - g^{(k)}. \tag{3.2}$$

If $G^{(k)}$ is always positive definite then Newton's method is usually very effective. Difficulties arise because for general functions it is only in the neighbourhood of the minimum $\overset{*}{x}$ that we can be sure that $G^{(k)}$ is positive definite. It is easy to verify from (3.2) that if $x^{(k)}$ is a saddle point then Newton's method fails to generate a new point since $p^{(k)}$ is the zero vector. The only way to generate a lower value of $F(x)$ in such circumstances is to determine a direction of so-called <u>negative curvature</u> which satisfies $p^{(k)T}$ $\cdot G^{(k)}p^{(k)} < 0$. Methods which improve upon Newton's method have mainly been concerned with catering for indefinite matrices $G^{(k)}$ and the computation of a direction of negative curvature when required.

Gill and Murray (1974b) have suggested obtaining $p^{(k)}$ by using a modified matrix $\overline{G}^{(k)} = G^{(k)} + E^{(k)}$, where $E^{(k)} = \text{diag}(E_1, E_2, \ldots, E_n)$ is such that if $G^{(k)}$ is sufficiently positive definite then $\overline{G}^{(k)} = G^{(k)}$. The matrix $E^{(k)}$ is formed during the computation of the factorization $\overline{G}^{(k)} = L^{(k)}D^{(k)}L^{(k)T}$ where $L^{(k)}$ is a unit lower-triangular matrix and $D^{(k)} = \text{diag}(d_1, d_2, \ldots, d_n)$. If we solve the triangular systems

$$L^{(k)}v = - g^{(k)}, \quad L^{(k)T}\overline{p} = D^{(k)-1}v, \tag{3.3}$$

then $\overline{p}$ is a descent direction. Alternatively if $\|E^{(k)}\| > 0$ and we solve

$$L^{(k)T}\hat{p} = \sigma e_s, \tag{3.4}$$

where e_s is the sth column of the identity matrix, $d_s - E_s \leq d_j - E_j$ for all j, and σ is chosen such that $\hat{p}^T g^{(k)} \leq 0$, then $\hat{p}$ is a direction of negative curvature. (Note that $\overline{p}$ also may be a direction of negative curvature, but unlike $\hat{p}$, it is not guaranteed to be so.)

Gill and Murray set $p^{(k)}$ equal to $\overline{p}$ except in the neighbourhood of a saddle point, where $\hat{p}$ is used. It can be shown that for this algorithm the sequence $\{x^{(k)}\}$ converges to $\overset{*}{x}$. The capability of computing local minima rather than just stationary points is a fundamental advantage of second derivative methods.

If we define

$$p^{(k)} = \frac{\bar{p}}{1 = \phi \, \|\bar{p}\|_2} + \frac{\sigma \phi \hat{p}}{\|\hat{p}\|_2} \, , \tag{3.5}$$

where $\phi = \sum\limits_{j=1}^{n} E_j$, then it is not necessary to switch from p to $\hat{p}$ in the neighborhood of a stationary point.

Almost any stable factorization of $G^{(k)}$ can be used to construct a satisfactory Newton-type method similar to the Gill-Murray algorithm. For example, Graham (1976) has proposed using the Dax and Kaniel (1974) factorization

$$G^{(k)} = P^{(k)-1} L^{(k)} D^{(k)} L^{(k)T} P^{(k)-T},$$

where $L^{(k)}$ and $D^{(k)}$ have the same structure as in the Gill-Murray algorithm and $P^{(k)}$ is a trivially invertible matrix. In this case a descent direction $\bar{p}$ can be defined as a solution of the equations

$$P^{(k)-1} L^{(k)} \bar{D}^{(k)} L^{(k)T} P^{(k)-T} \bar{p} = - g^{(k)},$$

where $\bar{d}_j$ is the larger of $|d_j|$ and a small positive constant related to the computer word length. Similarly a direction of negative curvature is given by $\hat{p}$ where

$$L^{(k)T} P^{(k)-T} \hat{p} = \sigma e_s$$

with σ chosen as before and the index s chosen so that $d_s \leq d_j$ for all j.

Similar algorithms can be constructed based on factorizations of the form $M^{(k)} D^{(k)} M^{(k)T}$ where $M^{(k)}$ is an easily-invertible matrix. Fletcher and Freeman (1975) have proposed an algorithm utilizing the triangular factorization of Bunch and Partlett (1971). In this case $D^{(k)}$ is a block diagonal matrix whose blocks are at most 2×2. Fletcher and Freeman argue that if $G^{(k)}$ is indefinite then one should always use a direction of negative curvature. Such a strategy could be applied to all Newton-type methods; however, there is no computational evidence to suggest that such an approach is advantageous. Moreover, methods using only negative curvature to modify Newton's method cannot be proved convergent to local minima.

We have tested extensively a wide variety of Newton-type methods and although most perform well, none has performed consistently better than the Gill-Murray algorithm. Since this is the simplest stable algorithm and it can be extended readily to sparse problems and constrained problems, it is the method we recommend.

4. FIRST-DERIVATIVE METHODS

4.1 Finite-difference techniques

The task of analytically differentiating a function $F(x)$ twice with respect to each of the n variables and then coding these second derivatives within a subroutine can be a formidable one, even for moderate values of n. In such circumstances it is usually better to use a method which requires only first derivatives.

An algorithm requiring only first derivatives can be constructed by using one of the modified-Newton methods discussed in the last section but with the Hessian matrix approximated by finite differences of the gradient vector. The approximation is given by $1/2(Y + Y^T)$ where Y is a matrix whose jth column is given by

$$y_j = (g(x^{(k)} + h_j e_j) - g^{(k)})/h_j,$$

with e_j the jth column of the identity matrix and h_j the finite-difference interval.

Finite-difference algorithms work very well in practice; they are robust and behave in a similar way to the modified-Newton algorithms which they are intended to emulate. However, for moderate to large values of n, the $n + 1$ gradient evaluations required every iteration can be prohibitively expensive unless the matrix $G^{(k)}$ is sparse (see Gill and Murray, 1974c). Quasi-Newton methods were devised to overcome this problem. They are based upon the formation of an approximation to the Hessian matrix using differences of the gradient vector along successive directions of search obtained during the minimization process rather than along the coordinate directions.

4.2   Quasi-Newton methods

At each point $x^{(k)}$ a matrix $B^{(k)}$ is known which approximates $G^{(k)}$ in some sense and a step $s^{(k)}$ is taken such that $x^{(k+1)} = x^{(k)} + s^{(k)}$. At $x^{(k+1)}$ a matrix $B^{(k+1)}$ is computed which differs from $B^{(k)}$ by a matrix of low rank (usually one or two).   In most algorithms $s^{(k)}$ is computed by defining

$$s^{(k)} = \alpha^{(k)} p^{(p)}, \tag{4.1a}$$

where

$$B^{(k)} p^{(k)} = - g^{(k)}. \tag{4.1b}$$

This is directly analagous to the definition of $p^{(k)}$ when second derivatives are available.

In order to avoid the problem of inverting the matrix $B^{(k)}$ when computing $p^{(k)}$, early numerical implementations recurred the inverse-Hessian approximation $H^{(k)}$.   In any practical computation, however, it is advantageous to recur a matrix facorization of $B^{(k)}$ itself and use it to solve the equations for $p^{(k)}$.   (We shall consider this point in more detail when we discuss the numerical implementation of Quasi-Newton methods in Section 4.6.)   From a theoretical point of view it is of no consequence whether methods use $H^{(k)}$ or $B^{(k)}$. Needless to say, since we prefer implementations based on recurring the factorization of an approximate Hessian, we shall concentrate our discussion on the recurrence of $B^{(k)}$.

We mentioned earlier that $n + 1$ gradient evaluations are required to compute a close approximation to the Hessian matrix at $x^{(k)}$.   If a single gradient evaluation is made every iteration, only a part of the information about G can be determined at any one time and there are an infinite number of ways in which this information can be combined with $B^{(k)}$ to give $B^{(k+1)}$.   The most effective method of utilizing the gradient evaluation is to impose upon $B^{(k+1)}$ a finite-difference condition involving the step taken, $s^{(k)} = x^{(k+1)} - x^{(k)}$, and the gradient difference, $y^{(k)} = g^{(k+1)} - g^{(k)}$, namely, the so-called <u>quasi-Newton condition</u>

$$B^{(k+1)} s^{(k)} = y^{(k)}. \tag{4.2}$$

Note that if $F(x)$ is a quadratic function with Hessian matrix G then $Gs^{(k)} = y^{(k)}$.

The imposition of the quasi-Newton condition still does not imply that the elements of $B^{(k+1)}$ will look anything like the elements of $G(x^{(k+1)})$. For example, the modification formula

$$B^{(k+1)} = B^{(k)} + \frac{1}{w^T s^{(k)}} (y^{(k)} - B^{(k)} s^{(k)}) w^T$$

satisfies (4.2), yet w may be any n-vector, provided that it is not orthogonal to $s^{(k)}$. If we are to expect rapid convergence of the sequence $\{B^{(k)}\}$ to G it is necessary to impose further conditions upon each matrix $B^{(k)}$. An obvious first step is to allow only symmetric approximate matrices. We can go further and require $B^{(k)}$ to be positive definite. This has some theoretical justification because $G(x)$ must be positive definite in the neighbourhood of a strong local minimum. If $B^{(k)}$ is positive definite and $p^{(k)}$ is computed from (4.1b) then a positive value of $\alpha^{(k)}$ exists such that the value of $F(x)$ is lower than at $x^{(k)}$. This implies that if an iterative scheme is used to compute $\alpha^{(k)}$, we are more likely to know an accurate first approximation to $\alpha^{(k)}$, (see Section 2). The maintenance of positive-definiteness also makes it easier to guarantee the numerical stability of the low-rank updating process and allows the use of the LDL^T factorization to solve Equation (4.1b).

A common set of additional conditions placed upon the matrix $B^{(k+1)}$ are the following:

$$B^{(k+1)} s^{(j)} = y^{(j)}, \tag{4.3}$$

for some set of $s^{(j)}$, $f \leq k$. If (4.3) applies for n vectors $s^{(j)}$

and they are linearly independent then the scheme has finite termination for a quadratic function since

$$B^{(k+1)} s^{(j)} = y^{(j)}$$
$$= Gs^{(j)},$$

and if S is the matrix whose columns comprise the vectors $s^{(j)}$,

$$B^{(k+1)} S = GS,$$

giving $B^{(k+1)} = G$ since S is invertible. (Note that it is essential that the directions $s^{(j)}$ are linearly independent if this proof of of finite termination is to apply.)

4.3 The one-parameter class of modification formulae

If we require the correction to $B^{(k)}$ to be symmetric and of rank one only then the quasi-Newton condition (4.2) uniquely defines $B^{(k+1)}$ to be

$$B^{(k+1)} = B^{(k)} + \frac{q^{(k)} q^{(k)T}}{q^{(k)T} s^{(k)}} \, ,$$

where $q^{(k)} = y^{(k)} - B^{(k)} s^{(k)}$. This correction is usually referred to as the symmetric rank one (SR1) update. If we require the additional property that $B^{(k+1)}$ is positive definite if $B^{(k)}$ is positive definite, we must define a suitable rank-two correction.

Consider the formula

$$B^{(k+1)} = B^{(k)} + \frac{y^{(k)} y^{(k)T}}{y^{(k)T} s^{(k)}} - \frac{B^{(k)} s^{(k)} (B^{(k)} s^{(k)})^T}{s^{(k)T} B^{(k)} s^{(k)}} \, . \qquad (4.4)$$

Provided $y^{(k)T} s^{(k)}$ is non-zero this formula satisfies (4.2) for all values of k. If a value of $\alpha^{(k)}$ is chosen which satisfies condition c4 of Section 2.2, then $g^{(k+1)T} p^{(k)} - g^{(k)T} p^{(k)}$ is non-zero and consequently $y^{(k)T} s^{(k)} = \alpha^{(k)} (g^{(k+1)T} p^{(k)} - g^{(k)T} p^{(k)})$ does not vanish and (4.4) is well defined. The modification (4.4) is known as the BFGS formula owing to its simultaneous discovery

by Broyden (1970), Fletcher (1970), Goldfarb (1970), and Shanno
(1970).

The BFGS formula may be generalized, yet still be made to
satisfy (4.2) by adding a term $W^{(k)}$ such that $W^{(k)} s^{(k)} = 0$. This
leads us to consider a general one-parameter class of formulae of
the form

$$
B_\phi^{(k+1)} = B_\phi^{(k)} + \frac{y^{(k)} y^{(k)T}}{b} - \frac{B_\phi^{(k)} s^{(k)} s^{(k)T} B_\phi^{(k)}}{a}
$$

$$
+ \phi^{(k)} a \left[\frac{y^{(k)}}{b} - \frac{B_\phi^{(k)} s^{(k)}}{a} \right] \left[\frac{y^{(k)}}{b} - \frac{B_\phi^{(k)} s^{(k)}}{a} \right]^T , \qquad (4.5)
$$

where $a = s^{(k)T} B_\phi^{(k)} s^{(k)}$, $b = y^{(k)T} s^{(k)}$ and $\phi^{(k)}$ is a scalar function
of $y^{(k)}$ and $B^{(k)} s^{(k)}$. The SR1 update corresponds to $\phi^{(k)} = b/(b-a)$
and is an update for which (4.5) is not always defined.

(If we had preferred to work with $H^{(k)} = B^{(k)-1}$ rather than
$B^{(k)}$ itself, we should have obtained the formula

$$
H_\psi^{(k+1)} = H_\psi^{(k)} + \frac{s^{(k)} s^{(k)T}}{b} - \frac{H_\psi^{(k)} y^{(k)} y^{(k)T} H_\psi^{(k)}}{a}
$$

$$
+ \psi^{(k)} a \left[\frac{s^{(k)}}{b} - \frac{H_\psi^{(k)} y^{(k)}}{a} \right] \left[\frac{s^{(k)}}{b} - \frac{H_\psi^{(k)} y^{(k)}}{a} \right]^T
$$

where $c = y^{(k)T} H_\psi^{(k)} y^{(k)}$, $b = y^{(k)T} s^{(k)}$ and $\psi^{(k)}$ is a scalar function of $H_\psi^{(k)} y^{(k)}$ and $s^{(k)}$. The formula defined by $\psi^{(k)} = 0$ is
known as the DFP update (see Fletcher and Powell, 1965) and it
corresponds to the member of the one-parameter family defined by
$\phi^{(k)} = 1$. The DFP and BFGS updates are examples of 'dual' or 'complementary' updates, and for any formula satisfying the condition
(4.2) there automatically exists another satisfying $s^{(k)} = H^{(k+1)} y^{(k)}$
under the transformation $s^{(k)} \to y^{(k)}$, $y^{(k)} \to s^{(k)}$, $B^{(k)} \to H^{(k)}$,
$B^{(k+1)} \to H^{(k+1)}$ applied to 4.5).

In general, if $F(x)$ is a quadratic function and $\alpha^{(k)}$ is an arbitrary step length, the approximate Hessian $B_\phi^{(k+1)}$ does not satisfy

(4.3) However, the following result indicates that, for a quadratic function, if the step length solves UP1 of Section 2.1 then (4.3) does hold. Moreover, the $s^{(j)}$ are linearly independent and consequently the algorithm has finite termination.

Result 4.1 (finite termination for the one-parameter family). Let $B_\phi^{(0)}$, $B_\phi^{(1)}$, ..., $B_\phi^{(n)}$ be a well-defined sequence of matrices obtained using (4.5) with $s^{(k)} = x^{(k+1)} - x^{(k)} = \alpha^{(k)} p^{(k)}$, where $B_\phi^{(k)} p^{(k)} = - g^{(k)}$ and $\alpha^{(k)}$ defined as the solution of UP1. If $F(x)$ is a quadratic function with a positive-definite Hessian matrix G then the sequence of directions $\{s^{(j)}\}$ and corresponding gradient differences $\{y^{(j)}\}$ satisfy

$$B^{(k+1)} s^{(j)} = y^{(j)}, \quad 0 \le j \le k \le n-1,$$

$$s^{(j)T} Gs^{(i)} = 0, \quad 0 \le i \le n-1, \quad 0 \le j \le n-1, \quad i \ne j. \quad (4.6)$$

The set of directions which satisfy (4.6) are linearly independent and are known as conjugate directions.

The conditions under which $B_\phi^{(k+1)}$ is positive definite can be found by rearranging (4.5) to be of the form

$$B_\phi^{(k+1)} = B_\phi^{(k)} U^{(k)},$$

where

$$U^{(k)} = I + \frac{B_\phi^{(k)-1} y^{(k)} y^{(k)T}}{b} - \frac{s^{(k)} s^{(k)T} B_\phi^{(k)}}{a}$$

$$+ \phi^{(k)} a \left[\frac{B_\phi^{(k)-1} y^{(k)}}{b} - \frac{s^{(k)}}{a} \right] \left[\frac{B_\phi^{(k)-1} y^{(k)}}{b} - \frac{s^{(k)}}{a} \right]^T,$$

$$= B_\phi^{(k)-1} B_\phi^{(k+1)}.$$

Taking determinants of both sides gives

$$\det(B_\phi^{(k+1)}) = \det(B_\phi^{(k)}) \det(U^{(k)}).$$

The determinant of a matrix is equal to the product of its eigenvalue and consequently if $B_\phi^{(k)}$ is positive definite, $B_\phi^{(k+1)}$ will be positive definite if the product of the eigenvalues of $U^{(k)}$ is positive. If $n \geq 3$ the matrix $U^{(k)}$ has $n-2$ unit eigenvalues; the two remaining eigenvalues and their corresponding eigenvectors are given by the following result (Davidon, 1975).

Result 4.2 (eigenvalues and eigenvectors of $B_\phi^{(k)-1}B_\phi^{(k+1)}$).
The eigenvectors of $U^{(k)}$ corresponding to the non-unit eigenvalues are $v_1 = B_\phi^{(k)-1}y^{(k)} - \lambda_2 s^{(k)}$ and $v_2 = B_\phi^{(k)-1}y^{(k)} - \lambda_1 s^{(k)}$ where λ_1 and λ_2 are the eigenvalues of $U^{(k)}$ corresponding to v_1 and v_2 respectively. The eigenvalues λ_1 and λ_2 satisfy the equations

$$\lambda_1 + \lambda_2 = \frac{1}{b}[\phi^{(k)}(ac - b^2)/b + b + c],$$

$$\lambda_1\lambda_2 = \frac{1}{ab}[b^2 + \phi^{(k)}(ac - b^2)],$$

where $c = y^{(k)T}B_\phi^{(k)-1}y^{(k)}$.

If $B_\phi^{(k)}$ is positive definite then $a > 0$ and if $\alpha^{(k)}$ satisfies Condition c4 of Section 2.2 then $b > 0$. Consequently Result 4.2 implies that $B_\phi^{(k+1)}$ will be positive definite if

$$\phi^{(k)} > - b^2/(ac - b^2). \tag{4.7}$$

Application of the Schwartz inequality gives $ac - b^2 > 0$ and so the one-parameter family is positive definite over an infinite interval with lower end point equal to $- b^2/(ac - b^2)$.

Before examining other values of $\phi^{(k)}$ we recall the following surprising result which was proved by Dixon (1972) for the sequence $\{H_\psi^{(k)}\}$.

Result 4.3 (quasi-Newton methods generate identical points).
Let $F(x)$ be any twice continuously-differentiable function. Let $\{x_1^{(k)}\}$ be a sequence of points generated by the modification rule (4.5) with $\phi^{(k)} = \phi_1^{(k)}$. Let $\{x_2^{(k)}\}$ be another sequence generated with $\phi^{(k)} = \phi_2^{(k)}$ but with the same starting point and initial Hessian approximation. Let $p_1^{(k)}$, $p_2^{(k)}$, $\alpha_1^{(k)}$, $\alpha_2^{(k)}$, $B_1^{(k)}$ and $B_2^{(k)}$

denote the corresponding values of $p^{(k)}$, $\alpha^{(k)}$ and $B_\phi^{(k)}$ respectively. If each of the sequences $\{B_1^{(k)}\}$ and $\{B_2^{(k)}\}$ is well-defined with $\alpha_1^{(k)}$ and $\alpha_2^{(k)}$ the minima of $F(x^{(k)} + \alpha p_1^{(k)})$ and $F(x^{(k)} + \alpha p_2^{(k)})$ which are nearest to the point $\alpha = 0$, then

$$B_1^{(k)} = B_2^{(k)} + \left[\frac{\phi_2^{(k-1)}}{p_2^{(k-1)T} g^{(k-1)}} - \frac{\phi_1^{(k-1)}}{p_1^{(k-1)T} g^{(k-1)}} \right] g^{(k)} g^{(k)T}, \qquad (4.8)$$

$$\alpha_1^{(k)} p_1^{(k)} = \alpha_2^{(k)} p_2^{(k)}. \qquad (4.9)$$

Equation (4.9) implies that all the members of the one-parameter family obtain the same sequence $\{x^{(k)}\}$ when exact univariate searches are used. The Equation (4.8) implies that all the approximate Hessian matrices generated by the one-parameter family differ by a matrix of rank-one. Thus if a $B_\phi^{(k+1)}$ cannot be guaranteed to be positive definite since $\phi^{(k)}$ does not satisfy (4.7), $B_\phi^{(k+1)}$ differs from a positive-definite matrix by a rank-one matrix only.

It might appear that Result 4.3 removes any further interest in investigating other values of $\phi^{(k)}$. However, numerical experience shows that a significant decrease in the amount of computational effort can often be achieved by accepting values of $\alpha^{(k)}$ which do not necessarily minimize $F(x)$ along $p^{(k)}$ (see Section 2.2). In this event, Result 4.3 is not necessarily relevant and we still seek a formula which in some sense gives better results than others.

Before considering other values of ϕ we shall discuss a remark-able phenomenon which occurs if we monitor the number of function evaluations required to minimize a general nonlinear function using exact linear searches with the BFGS and DFP modification rules. As predicted by Result 4.4 the number of iterations is identical for both methods. However, far fewer function evaluations are required by the BFGS update. The methods are identical apart from the dif-ference in values of ϕ, and the difference in the numerical behaviour is due only to the choice of the initial step length in the poly-nomial interpolation algorithm.

One possible explanation of this phenomenon is based on the following result.

<u>Result 4.4.</u> Let two sequences $\left\{B_1^{(k)}\right\}$ and $\left\{B_2^{(k)}\right\}$ be computed for which Result 4.3 applies. If $B_1^{(k)}$ and $B_2^{(k)}$ are positive definite and $\phi_1^{(k)} \geq \phi_2^{(k)}$ then $\alpha_1^{(k)} \geq \alpha_2^{(k)}$ for all k.

If we take $\phi_1^{(k)} = 1$ (the DFP formula) and $\phi_2^{(k)} = 0$ (the BFGS formula) then $\alpha_{DFP}^{(k)} \geq \alpha_{BFGS}^{(k)}$ for all k. If an initial step of unity is taken at the kth iteration, we should expect DFP to require fewer function evaluations than BFGS if $\alpha_{DFP}^{(k)} \leq 1$ and more if $\alpha_{BFGS}^{(k)} > 1$. Since there is no reason to suppose otherwise we should expect both algorithms to use approximately the same number of function evaluations. However, the situation changes if the choice of the first step α_e along the direction of search is given by

$$\min \left\{1, \; -2(F^{(k)} - F_e/g^{(k)T}p^{(k)}\right\} \tag{4.10}$$

where F_e is some estimate of the solution with $F_e < F^{(k)}$. Suppose that $\alpha_{BFGS}^{(k)} = 1$ and the initial step taken by the BFGS algorithm is also unity. It follows from (4.10) and Result 4.4 that $\alpha_{DFP}^{(k)} \geq 1$ and the initial step taken by the DFP algorithm is unity then $\alpha_{BFGS}^{(k)} < 1$. If, in contrast, $\alpha_{DFP}^{(k)} = 1$ and the initial step taken by the DFP algorithm is unity, then $\alpha_{DFP}^{(k)} \leq 1$. In this case however, it is possible that the initial step taken by the BFGS algorithm is also less than unity. We have observed that $\alpha_{BFGS}^{(k)}$ is often closer to unity than $\alpha_{DFP}^{(k)}$ in practical problems. The tendency of the DFP algorithm to under-predict the position of the minimum along a particular direction of search may be a partial explanation of why the BFGS algorithm is superior for general minimization.

<u>The convex class of modification formulae.</u> A property of quasi-Newton methods which is just as remarkable as that indicated by Result 4.3 is that they work so effectively when an exact linear search is <u>not</u> performed. The fact that this behaviour has no theoretical basis has caused concern for some years. Fletcher (1970)

noted that the better quasi-Newton modification formulae have the property that, when F(x) is quadratic, the eigenvalues of the matrix $R^{(k)} = G^{1/2}(B^{(k)})^{-1}G^{1/2}$ tend monotonically to unity as k increases, regardless of the step $\alpha^{(k)}$ taken. He showed that this property holds for all members of the so-called convex class of formulae for which $\phi^{(k)} \in [0, 1]$. Note that we still have the problem of choosing a particular value of ϕ.

Optimally-conditioned updating formulae. The directions of search obtained by using a quasi-Newton method can be regarded as solutions of a sequence of quadratic problems analogous to (3.1) but with $G^{(k)}$ replaced by $B^{(k)}$. The magnitude of the eigenvalues of $B^{(k)}$ determines the geometry of the ellipsoidal level surfaces of each quadratic function. The shape of these ellipsoids varies with the particular choice of modification rule; the more elongated the ellipsoids become, the closer the direction of search becomes to a vector which is orthogonal to the direction of steepest descent. Numerically this implies that it is more difficult to locate a value of $\alpha^{(k)}$ which sufficiently decreases the function. A good measure of how the geometry of the quadratic functions varies with the eigenstructure of $B^{(k)}$ is the condition number $\kappa(B^{(k)})$ of $B^{(k)}$. (The condition number $\kappa(X)$ of a general matrix X is defined as the square root of the ratio of its largest and smallest singular values. If X is symmetric this ratio is equal to the ratio of its largest and smallest eigenvalues.) The more elongated are the level surfaces of the quadratic approximation, the greater is the condition number of $B^{(k)}$.

Infinitely many members of the one-parameter family safisfy the quasi-Newton condition (4.2) and give a positive-definite update to $B^{(k)}$. A possible choice of $\phi^{(k)}$ is that which gives a positive-definite correction and minimizes the condition number of $B_\phi^{(k+1)}$. It is not possible to define analytically the value of $\phi^{(k)}$ which exactly minimizes $\kappa(B_\phi^{(k+1)})$ but we can define a value which minimizes a bound on $\kappa(B_\phi^{(k+1)})$.

Result 4.5 (bound on the condition number of $B_\phi^{(k+1)}$. If $B_\phi^{(k)}$ is positive definite and $U^{(k)}$ is defined as $B_\phi^{(k)-1}B_\phi^{(k+1)}$ then

$$\kappa(B_\phi^{(k+1)}) \leq \kappa(B_\phi^{(k)})\kappa(U^{(k)}).$$

Result 4.6 (the condition number of $U^{(k)}$). The condition number of $U^{(k)}$ is equal to the ratio of its largest and smallest eigenvalues.

The non-unit eigenvalues of $U^{(k)}$ can be found by solving a quadratic equation whose sum and product of roots is given by Result 4.2. These roots are then

$$\frac{b+c}{2b} + \frac{\phi(ac-b^2)}{2b^2} \pm \left[\left\{ \frac{c-b}{2b} + \frac{\phi(ac-b^2)}{2b^2} \right\}^2 + \frac{(ac-b^2)}{ab}\cdot\left\{1 + \phi\left(\frac{a-b}{a}\right)\right\} \right]^{1/2} \quad (4.11)$$

and the optimal ϕ is given by the solution of

$$\min \frac{\max\{\lambda_1, 1\}}{\min\{\lambda_2, 1\}} \text{ subject to } \lambda_2 > 0 \quad (4.12)$$

where $\lambda_1 \geq \lambda_2$.

Result 4.7 (optimally-conditioned formula). The solution of (4.12) is given by

$$\phi_{OC} = \begin{cases} \dfrac{b(c-b)}{ac-b^2}, & b \leq 2ac/(a+c), \\[2ex] \dfrac{b}{b-a}, & b > 2ac/(a+c). \end{cases}$$

Note that when $b > 2ac/(a+c)$ the optimally conditioned (OC) update is equal to the symmetric rank-one (SR1) update. When b is less than a and c, the OC update is in the convex class and the SR1 update is not positive definite; when b is equal to a the OC and BFGS updates are the same and the SR1 update is not defined; when b is equal to c the OC and DFP updates are the same and the SR1 update is singular; when b is between a and c but less than their harmonic mean $2ac/(a+c)$, the OC update has rank two and is not in the convex class; and when $b \gtreqless 2ac/(a+c)$, the OC and SR1 updates are identical.

Schnabel (1976) has suggested imposing on the problem (4.12) an additional constraint which restricts the ϕ to lie in the convex class. He has shown that this additional constraint does not significantly increase the condition number of $B_\phi^{(k+1)}$. This strategy can be used to resolve the dilemma of finding which value of ϕ to choose for the convex class of formulae.

4.4 Quasi-Newton methods which do not require exact linear minimizations to give finite termination

The SR1 update has the property that it is not necessary to use exact linear searches in order to ensure finite termination for quadratic functions. Moreover, provided the vectors $s^{(j)}$ are linearly independent, the algorithm has finite termination regardless of how the sequence $\{s^{(j)}\}$ is computed. This is in contrast to other members of the one-parameter family which require $s^{(k)}$ to be computed from (4.1a) and (4.1b). The finite-termination property derives from the following result.

Result 4.8. If $F(x)$ is a quadratic function and $s^{(j)}$ is any vector which satisfies $B^{(k)} s^{(j)} = y^{(j)}$, then the matrix $B^{(k+1)}$ defined by the SR1 update satisfies

$$B^{(k+1)} s^{(j)} = y^{(j)}.$$

This result implies that, for a quadratic function, once a step $s^{(j)}$ satisfies the quasi-Newton condition, it satisfies it for all $k \geqq j$. Thus conditions (4.3) apply and the algorithm has finite termination, provided the vectors $\{s^{(j)}\}$ are linearly independent.

Unfortunately the SR1 update has a number of unpleasant properties. Even for positive-definite quadratic functions the formula may not be well-defined. Furthermore the value of $\phi^{(k)}$ corresponding to the SR1 update does not necessarily satisfy (4.7) and $B^{(k+1)}$ may be indefinite.

Notwithstanding these difficulties, many methods have been proposed which are based upon the SR1 update (see Davidon 1959, 1968; Broyden 1967; Murtagh and Sargent 1968, 1969; Powell, 1970; Cullum and Brayton 1976). This popularity is due not only to the theoretical desirability of finite termination without exact linear searches: despite the need to alter the modification to maintain the positive definiteness and boundedness of the approximate Hessian, the SR1 update is very competitive with other algorithms.

Recently, Davidon (1975) has suggested a method which gives finite termination without exact linear searches, yet avoids the possibility of the approximate Hessian's becoming unbounded. Let $u^{(k)}$ be any vector orthogonal to previous steps, that is

$$u^{(k)T}s^{(j)} = 0, \quad j = 0,1,\ldots,k-1.$$

If we define $q^{(k)} = y^{(k)} - B^{(k)}s^{(k)}$, then the formula

$$B^{(k+1)} = B^{(k)}+\gamma_1 q^{(k)}q^{(k)T}+\gamma_2(q^{(k)}u^{(k)T}+u^{(k)}q^{(k)T})+\gamma_3 u^{(k)}u^{(k)T}, \quad (4.13)$$

satisfies the conditions (4.3 for any previous step which satisfies $B^{(k)}s^{(j)} = y^{(j)}$ because $q^{(k)T}s^{(j)} = 0$ and $u^{(k)T}s^{(j)} = 0$. Provided $q^{(k)T}s^{(j)}$ and $u^{(k)T}s^{(j)}$ do not vanish simultaneously, the scalars γ_1, γ_2 and γ_3 can be chosen so that the quasi-Newton condition (4.2) is satisfied. If $s^{(k)}$ is orthogonal to both $q^{(k)}$ and $u^{(k)}$ the value of $u^{(k)}$ must be altered: we shall see later in this section that the choice $u^{(k)} = y^{(k)}$ is often sensible.

The vector $u^{(k)}$ can be recurred from iteration to iteration, $u^{(k+1)}$ being that vector lying in the subspace spanned by $q^{(k)}$ and $u^{(k)}$ which is orthogonal to $s^{(k)}$. For example, $u^{(k+1)}$ can be computed as

$$u^{(k+1)} = (u^{(k)T}s^{(k)})q^{(k)} - (q^{(k)T}s^{(k)})u^{(k)}.$$

For practical computation we require particular values of γ_1, γ_2 and γ_3 which give a positive-definite update and we need to be able to define a sensible value of $u^{(k)}$ when $s^{(k)}$ is orthogonal to both $q^{(k)}$ and $s^{(k)}$. However, rather than repeat the analyses of previous sections for the general class of updates defined by (4.13), we quote the following result of Davidon (1975) which shows that we can rearrange them to be of a form such that many of the standard results pertaining to the one-parameter family (4.5) apply.

Result 4.9. Let $\bar{s}^{(k)} = P^T s^{(k)}$ and $\bar{y}^{(k)} = Py^{(k)}$ where P is the matrix

$$P = \frac{q^{(k)} q^{(k)T} B_\phi^{(k)-1}}{q^{(k)T} B_\phi^{(k)-1} q^{(k)}} + \frac{z^{(k)} z^{(k)T} B_\phi^{(k)-1}}{z^{(k)T} B_\phi^{(k)-1} z^{(k)}},$$

with $z^{(k)} = q^{(k)} - \left(\dfrac{u^{(k)T} B_\phi^{(k)-1} q^{(k)}}{u^{(k)T} B_\phi^{(k)-1} u^{(k)}} \right) u^{(k)}$. The one-parameter

class of formulae

$$B_\phi^{(k+1)} = B_\phi^{(k)} + \frac{\bar{y}^{(k)} \bar{y}^{(k)T}}{\bar{b}} - \frac{B_\phi^{(k)} \bar{s}^{(k)} \bar{s}^{(k)T} B_\phi^{(k)}}{\bar{a}}$$

$$+ \phi^{(k)} \bar{a} \left[\frac{\bar{y}^{(k)}}{\bar{b}} - \frac{B_\phi^{(k)} \bar{s}^{(k)}}{\bar{a}} \right] \left[\frac{\bar{y}^{(k)}}{\bar{b}} - \frac{B_\phi^{(k)} \bar{s}^{(k)}}{\bar{a}} \right]^T , \quad (4.14)$$

with $\bar{a} = \bar{s}^{(k)T} B_\phi^{(k)} \bar{s}^{(k)}$, $\bar{b} = \bar{y}^{(k)T} \bar{s}^{(k)}$ and $\phi^{(k)}$ a scalar function of $\bar{y}^{(k)}$ and $B_\phi^{(k)} \bar{s}^{(k)}$, satisfies the quasi-Newton condition $B_\phi^{(k+1)} s^{(k)} = y^{(k)}$ and is equivalent to the family (4.13).

Result 4.2 implies that $B_\phi^{(k+1)}$ will be positive definite if

$$\bar{b} > 0 \text{ and } \phi^{(k)} > - \bar{b}^2 / (\bar{a}\bar{c} - \bar{b}^2)$$

where $\bar{c} = \bar{y}^{(k)} B^{(k)-1} \bar{y}^{(k)}$. However, in this case, unlike the other where $B_\phi^{(k+1)}$ is defined in terms of $s^{(k)}$ and $y^{(k)}$ directly, we cannot guarantee that $\bar{b} > 0$ and consequently $B_\phi^{(k+1)}$ may be indefinite.

This problem can be avoided by choosing $y^{(k)}$ as the value for $u^{(k)}$ when $\bar{b} < 0$. It is easily verified that in this case $\bar{s}^{(k)} = P^T s^{(k)} = s^{(k)}$ and $\bar{y}^{(k)} = Py^{(k)} = y^{(k)}$ and the update reverts to its equivalent form in the one-parameter family (4.5), for which $b > 0$.

The class of updates defined by (4.14) is known as the <u>projected one-parameter family</u> since P is a matrix which projects vectors on to the space spanned by $y^{(k)} - B^{(k)} s^{(k)}$ and $u^{(k)}$.

4.5 Other updating formulae and generalizations

More general classes of updating formulae can be defined which require the specification of more than one parameter. Oren and Luenberger (1974) suggest the two-parameter family

$$B^{(k+1)} = \eta B^{(k)} + \frac{y^{(k)} y^{(k)T}}{b} - \frac{\eta B^{(k)} s^{(k)} s^{(k)T} B^{(k)}}{a}$$

$$+ \eta \phi^{(k)} a \left[\frac{y^{(k)}}{b} - \frac{B^{(k)} s^{(k)}}{a} \right] \left[\frac{y^{(k)}}{b} - \frac{B^{(k)} s^{(k)}}{a} \right]^T, \qquad (4.15)$$

where $\eta = \beta \left(\frac{b}{a} \right) + (1 - \beta) \frac{c}{b}$ with a, b and c defined as in the family 4.5. Formula (4.15) is equivalent to scaling the approximate Hessian matrix by the factor η before updating and is known as the self-scaling formula. If β, $\phi \in [0, 1)$ the updates in this family are such that if $F(x)$ is a quadratic function with minimum value $F(\overset{*}{x})$ and (4.15) is applied with exact linear searches then the sequence of condition numbers of the matrices

$$R^{(k)} = G^{1/2} \left[B^{(k)} \right]^{-1} G^{1/2}$$

is monotonically decreasing. The motivation for looking at this quantity is that the bound on the rate of convergence is of the form

$$F(x^{(k+1)}) - F(\overset{*}{x}) \leq \left[\frac{\kappa(R^{(k)}) - 1}{\kappa(R^{(k)}) + 1} \right]^2 (F(x^{(k)}) - F(\overset{*}{x})). \qquad (4.16)$$

It is not clear whether these properties are relevant to practical
problems since they are valid only when exact linear searches are
made and F(x) is quadratic. Moreover, (4.16) is only a <u>bound</u> on
the convergence rate and it tells us little about the convergence
rate which is actually achieved in practice. A fundamental disadvantage of the self-scaling formulae is that for a quadratic function, $B^{(n+1)}$ is not equal to G (see Brodlie, 1977 for a more detailed discussion of these points).

There is still the task of choosing particular values of β and
ϕ. Oren and Spedicato (1976) and Spedicato (1975) have shown that
$\eta = \left(\frac{c}{a}\right)^{1/2}$ and $\phi = 1/(1 + (ca/b^2)^{1/2})$ are the values which minimize
the ratio of the largest to smallest eigenvalues of $B^{(k)-1}B^{(k+1)}$
subject to the requirement that ϕ, $\beta \in [0, 1]$.

Brodlie (1977) has considered the case $\beta = 1$ in some detail
and he prefers this value for two reasons. Firstly it is not
necessary to compute the quantity $c = y^{(k)}B^{(k)-1}y^{(k)}$; secondly,
the formula obtained by $\beta = 1$ has the property that

$$s^{(k)T}B^{(k+1)}s^{(k)} = y^{(k)T}s^{(k)}$$

and

$$s^{(k)T}(\eta B^{(k)})s^{(k)} = \frac{s^{(k)T}(s^{(k)T}y^{(k)})B^{(k)}s^{(k)}}{s^{(k)T}B^{(k)}s^{(k)}}$$

$$= s^{(k)T}y^{(k)}.$$

Thus for a quadratic function the curvature along $s^{(k)}$ is correct
before and after updating.

Generalizations. The results of this section and Sections
4.3 and 4.4 indicate that an updating formula can be constructed
by utilizing any combination of the properties of the one-parameter
family, self scaling and finite termination without exact linear
searches. For example, we may use the BFGS formula as originally
defined, or a self-scaling BFGS formula, or a BFGS formula for
which finite termination is assured for quadratic functions without

the need for exact univariate minimizations. However, there is
still the question of which update should be used for general
application. We shall address this problem further in the next
section.

4.6 Quasi-Newton methods: software design

By far the most important decision affecting software design
is whether to recur the approximate inverse Hessian matrix $H^{(k)}$,
or an LDL^T factorization of the approximate Hessian, $B^{(k)}$. Although
it is immaterial which form is used in theoretical analysis, we
believe that the recurrence of the LDL^T factorization has significant advantages when the algorithms are implemented on a computer.

If the matrix $B^{(k+1)}$ is known to be positive definite from
theoretical considerations its factors can be computed in such a
way that $B^{(k+1)}$ is positive definite regardless of any rounding
errors made. This is a very important property since, if $B^{(k+1)}$
is near-singular, only a small perturbation may be required to make
the modified matrix indefinite or singular. If round-off error
causes $H^{(k+1)}$ to become indefinite this might be noticed only in
subsequent iterations when $p^{(k)}$ fails to be a descent direction.
The remedy generally applied in this situation is to reset $H^{(k)}$ to
the identity matrix. This is a drastic strategy, since any useful
information in $H^{(k)}$ is discarded along with the bad.

The LDL^T factorization provides an estimate of the condition
number of $B^{(k)}$. It can be shown that $\kappa(B^{(k)}) \geq d_{mx}/d_{mn}$, where d_{mx}
and d_{mn} are the largest and smallest diagonal elements of $D^{(k)}$.
Moreover, we have observed in practice that this lower bound is
generally a realistic estimate of the condition number. When the
minimization has been completed, the estimated condition number can
be used to give an indication of whether or not the algorithm has
converged successfully.

On the rare occasions when the matrix $B^{(k)}$ is so ill conditioned that the computed value of $p^{(k)}$ is likely to have no correct

figures, the LDL^T factorization is easily modified so that its condition number does not exceed a fixed upper bound (see Gill, Murray and Pitfield, 1972). Any quasi-Newton algorithm with this modification and a step-length algorithm based on one of the conditions c1 - c4 will give a sequence $\{x^{(k)}\}$ which is convergent to a stationary point of a twice-continuously differentiable function $F(x)$.

The amount of work required for a single iteration of a quasi-Newton method based upon recurring the LDL^T factorization is approximately the same as that for an algorithm based upon recurring $H^{(k)}$. The modification of the triangular factors after a rank-two updating is more expensive than updating the inverse but in most cases, this extra expense is balanced by savings elsewhere. For example, if the BFGS formula is employed and $s^{(k)}$ is defined as in (4.1) we have

$$B^{(k+1)} = B^{(k)} + \frac{y^{(k)}y^{(k)T}}{y^{(k)T}s^{(k)}} + \frac{g^{(k)}g^{(k)T}}{g^{(k)T}p^{(k)}}$$

and it is not necessary to compute any additional matrix-vector products to define $B^{(k+1)}$. Similarly, forming $\eta B^{(k)}$ for any of the self-scaling formulae requires just n multiplications since $\eta B^{(k)} = L^{(k)}(\eta D^{(k)})L^{(k)T}$, yet the formation of $\eta H^{(k)}$ requires $n^2 + 0(n)$ multiplications.

Modifying the LDL^T factors. Before the factors can be modified, the rank two correction must be in the form

$$B^{(k+1)} = B^{(k)} + \beta_1 ww^T + \beta_2 zz^T, \tag{4.17}$$

where w and z are vector combinations of $y^{(k)}$ and $B^{(k)}s^{(k)}$, and β_1 and β_2 are scalars. There are an infinite number of ways in which a general rank-two correction can be expressed in this form. For example, consider the formula

$$B^{(k+1)} = B^{(k)} + \frac{(\lambda_1-1)u_1 u_1^T}{u_1^T B^{(k)-1} u_1} + \frac{(\lambda_2-1)u_2 u_2^T}{u_2^T B^{(k)-1} u_2}, \tag{4.18}$$

where $u_1^T B^{(k)-1} u_2 = 0$. It can be verified that the vectors $B^{(k)-1} u_1$ and $B^{(k)-1} u_2$ are the eigenvectors of $B^{(k)-1} B^{(k+1)}$ with λ_1 and λ_2 their corresponding eigenvalues. If the update is a member of the one-parameter family (4.5), Result 4.2 implies that $u_1 = y^{(k)} - \lambda_1 B^{(k)} s^{(k)}$ and $u_2 = y^{(k)} - \lambda_2 B^{(k)} s^{(k)}$ where λ_1 and λ_2 are defined by (4.11). In this case we have

$$u_1^T B^{(k)-1} u_1 = a\lambda_2^2 - 2b\lambda_2 + c$$

and

$$u_2^T B^{(k)-1} u_2 = a\lambda_1^2 - 2b\lambda_2 + c$$

Formula (4.17) is still not ideal for our purpose since considerable unnecessary cancellation may occur if $\|\beta_1 ww^T + \beta_2 zz^T\|_2$ is very small compared to $\|\beta_1 ww^T\|_2$. This situation occurs if we add a very large correction and immediately remove it, and it can be remedied if we rearrange (4.17) to be

$$B^{(k+1)} = B^{(k)} + \sigma_1 uu^T + \sigma_2 vv^T$$

where $\|u\|_2 = \|v\|_2 = 1$ and $u^T v = 0$. The relationship

$$\beta_1 ww^T + \beta_2 zz^T = \sigma_1 uu^T + \sigma_2 vv^T$$

is an explicit statement of the spectral decomposition of the matrix $A \equiv \beta_1 ww^T + \beta_2 zz^T$, that is, σ_1 and σ_2 are the eigenvalues of A with u and v their corresponding eigenvectors. This deomposition can be effected with the aid of the following result. (This result utilizes the properties of <u>Householder matrices</u>, which can be chosen to reduce a given vector to a multiple of a column of the identity matrix; see Wilkinson, 1965, pp. 152-160.)

<u>Result 4.10</u> (Spectral decomposition of $\beta_1 ww^T + \beta_2 zz^T$). Let P_1 be a Householder matrix chosen such that $P_1 w = \|w\|_2 e_1$. If $\bar{z}$ denotes the vector $P_1 z$, τ the scalar

$$\left(\sum_{j=2}^{n} \bar{z}_j^2\right)^{1/2} ,$$

then σ_1 and σ_2 are the eigenvalues of the 2×2 matrix

$$\begin{bmatrix} \beta_1 \|w\|_2^2 + \beta_2 \bar{z}_1^2 & \beta_2 \tau \bar{z}_1 \\[2ex] \beta_2 \tau \bar{z}_1 & \beta_2 \tau^2 \end{bmatrix} .$$

If t_1 and t_2 are the eigenvectors corresponding to σ_1 and σ_2 and P_2 is the Householder matrix which is chosen such that

$$P_2 \bar{z} = (\bar{z}_1, \tau, 0, \ldots, 0)^T ,$$

then

$$u = P_1^T P_2^T \begin{bmatrix} t_1 \\ 0 \end{bmatrix} \quad \text{and} \quad v = P_1^T P_2^T \begin{bmatrix} t_2 \\ 0 \end{bmatrix} . \; \blacksquare$$

As a final safeguard against the possibility of overflow within the updating procedures, the modification should be scaled so that

$$B^{(k+1)} = B^{(k)} \pm uu^T \pm vv^T ,$$

after which the factors of $B^{(k)}$ can be updated using the following two results (see Gill, Murray and Saunders, 1975).

Result 4.11 (Positive rank-one correction). The recurrence relations for forming the factors $\overline{LDL}^T = LDL^T + uu^T$ are as follows.

(i) Define $t_0 = 1$, $u^{(1)} = u$;

(ii) for $j = 1, 2, \ldots, n$ compute

$$P_j = u_j^{(j)}, \quad t_j = t_{j-1} + p_j^2 / d_j$$

$$\bar{d}_j = d_j t_j / t_{j-1}, \quad \beta_j = P_j / (d_j t_j)$$

if $\bar{d}_j / d_j > 4$ then set

$$\bar{1}_{rj} = (t_{j-1}/t_j)1_{rj} + \beta_j u_r^{(j)}$$

$$u_r^{(j+1)} = u_r^{(j)} - p_j 1_{rj}$$

$$r = j+1,\ldots,n;$$

otherwise set

$$u_r^{(j+1)} = u_r^{(j)} - p_j 1_{rj}$$

$$\bar{1}_{rj} = 1_{rj} + \beta_j u_r^{(j+1)}$$

$$r = j+1,\ldots,n.$$

When a negative correction $\overline{LDL}^T - vv^T$ is made, care must be taken lest round-off errors perturb the factors to be those of an indefinite matrix.

Result 4.12 (Negative rank-one correction). The recurrence relations for forming the factors $\overline{LDL}^T = LDL^T - vv^T$ are as follows:

(1) Solve the equations $Lp = v$ and define $t_{n+1} = 1 - p^T D^{-1} p$; if $t_{n+1} \overset{\le}{=} \varepsilon$ set $t_{n+1} = \varepsilon$, where $\varepsilon(\varepsilon > 0)$ is the relative machine precision;

(ii) for $j = n, n-1,\ldots,1$ set

$$t_j = t_{j+1} + p_j^2/d_j, \quad \bar{d}_j = d_j t_{j+1}/t_j,$$

$$\beta_j = - p_j/(d_j t_{j+1}), \quad u_j^{(j)} = p_j,$$

$$\bar{1}_{rj} = 1_{rj} + \beta_j u_r^{(j+1)}$$

$$u_r^{(j)} = u_r^{(j+1)} + p_j 1_{rj}$$

$$r = j+1,\ldots,n.$$

If the modified matrix is theoretically guaranteed to be positive definite then the exact value of t_{n+1} must be positive. The effect of replacing the computed value of t_{n+1} by ε when it is negative is commensurate with error made in computing $\bar{B} = B - vv^T$. It can be easily verified that $\bar{d}_j, j = 1,2,\ldots,n$ is guaranteed to be positive, irrespective of any rounding errors made during the computation.

Choice of updating formula. The work required to apply the modification to the approximate Hessian matrix varies with each formula chosen. If (4.1) is used to compute the direction of search, the SR1 update is the least expensive, requiring no additional matrix-vector products. In contrast the OC update in the projected one-parameter family requires the additional computation of the vectors $B^{(k)-1}y^{(k)}$ and $B^{(k)-1}u^{(k)}$. Our experience is that, of all the numbers of the straightforward one-parameter family, the BFGS and OC updates give the best overall performance. It is more difficult to choose between these two formulas: on some problems the BFGS requires significantly fewer function evaluations, but on others the situation is reversed. Currently we use the BFGS update because it requires less work per iteration (the OC update requires an additional term $B^{(k)-1}y^{(k)}$). Our experience with the class of projected methods of (4.14) is that there is not yet enough numerical evidence to warrant the additional computation or complication involved.

4.7 Conjugate-direction algorithms

When n is so large that it is impossible to store the approximate Hessian matrix in the machine, one of the class of so-called conjugate-direction methods that does not require the storage of any matrices must be used.

Methods for the positive definite function $F(x) = 1/2x^T Gx + c^T x$. In Result 4.1 we defined a set of conjugate directions, which satisfy

$$p^{(i)T}Gp^{(j)} = 0, \quad 0 \leq i \leq n-1, \quad 0 \leq j \leq n-1, \quad i \neq j.$$

If P is the matrix whose columns comprise these directions then

$$P^T GP = D,$$

where D is a diagonal matrix. If we transform the variables of the quadratic function such that $x = Pz$ then

$$F(z) = 1/2z^T Dz + c^T Pz$$

is a separable function in z which can be minimized in n steps by performing an exact linear search along each of the vectors $p^{(k)}$ in turn.

The set of mutually-conjugate directions can be obtained by defining $p^{(o)}$ as the steepest-descent direction and computing each subsequent direction $p^{(k)}$ as a linear combination of $g^{(k)}$ and the previous k search directions,

$$p^{(k)} = - g^{(k)} + \sum_{j=0}^{k-1} \gamma_j p^{(j)}. \tag{4.19}$$

This equation implies that $p^{(k)}$ is a linear combination of $g^{(0)}$, $g^{(1)}, \ldots, g^{(k)}$, in which case the following result applies.

Result 4.13 (see Fletcher, 1972). If an exact linear search is made at each iteration and each $p^{(k)}$ is a linear combination of $g^{(o)}, \ldots, g^{(k)}$ then $g^{(j)T} g^{(k)} = 0$, for all $j < k \leqq n$. ∎

This result and the conjugacy conditions:

$$p^{(k)T} G p^{(j)} = 0, \quad 0 \lesseqgtr j < k \tag{4.20}$$

can be used to compute the γ_j in (4.19) as

$$\gamma_{k-1} = y^{(k-1)T} g^{(k)} / y^{(k-1)T} p^{(k-1)}, \quad \gamma_j = 0, \ j = 0,1,\ldots,k-2,$$

where $y^{(k-1)} = g^{(k)} - g^{(k-1)}$. This gives the recurrence relations for the so-called conjugate-gradient algorithm

$$p^{(o)} = - g^{(o)}, \quad p^{(k)} = - g^{(k)} + \beta^{(k)} p^{(k-1)}, \tag{4.21a}$$

where $\quad \beta^{(k)} = y^{(k-1)T} g^{(k)} / y^{(k-1)T} p^{(k-1)}. \tag{4.21b}$

The orthogonality of the gradient vectors can be used to give the following equivalent definitions of $\beta^{(k)}$.

$$\beta^{(k)} = y^{(k-1)T} g^{(k)} / \| g^{(k-1)} \|_2^2, \quad \text{(Polak and Ribière, 1969), } \tag{4.22}$$

$$\beta^{(k)} = \| g^{(k)} \|_2^2 / \| g^{(k-1)} \|_2^2, \quad \text{(Fletcher and Reeves, 1964).} \tag{4.23}$$

It is useful if the conjugate directions can be generated without the need for an exact linear search. Two related techniques suggested by Dixon (1975) and Nazareth (1975) are based upon finding values of γ_j for the linear combination

$$p^{(k)} = -y^{(k-1)} + \sum_{j=0}^{k-1} \gamma_j p^{(j)}. \tag{4.24}$$

Pre-multiplying (4.24) successively by $y^{(k-1)T}$ and $y^{(k-2)T}$ and using the conjugacy conditions (4.20) we obtain

$$\gamma_{k-1} = y^{(k-1)T} y^{(k-1)} / y^{(k-1)T} p^{(k-1)},$$

$$\gamma_{k-2} = y^{(k-2)T} y^{(k-1)} / y^{(k-2)T} p^{(k-2)},$$

$$\gamma_j = 0, \quad j = 0, 1, \ldots, k-3.$$

This gives the algorithm

$$p^{(0)} = -g^{(0)}, \quad p^{(1)} = -y^{(0)} + \|y^{(0)}\|_2^2 / y^{(0)T} p^{(0)} p^{(0)},$$

$$p^{(k)} = -y^{(k-1)} + \beta^{(k)} p^{(k-1)} + \gamma^{(k)} p^{(k-1)}, k = 2, \ldots, n-1$$

$$\beta^{(k)} = \|y^{(k-1)}\|_2^2 / y^{(k-1)T} p^{(k-1)}$$

$$\gamma^{(k)} = y^{(k-2)T} y^{(k-1)} / y^{(k-2)T} p^{(k-2)}.$$

$$\tag{4.25}$$

This scheme does not automatically produce the minimum $\overset{*}{x}$ because we are not computing $\alpha^{(k)}$ by means of exact linear searches. However, using the following result we can obtain the solution by recurring one more vector.

Result 4.14. If $\{p^{(k)}\}$ is a set of conjugate directions and $s^{(k)} = \alpha^{(k)} p^{(k)}$ then

$$G^{-1} = \sum_{i=0}^{n-1} s^{(i)} s^{(i)T} / s^{(i)T} y^{(i)}.$$

The minimum of the quadratic is given by

$$\overset{*}{x} = x^{(0)} - G^{-1}g^{(0)}$$

$$= x^{(0)} - \sum_{i=0}^{n-1} s^{(i)}s^{(i)T}g^{(0)}/s^{(i)T}y^{(i)}.$$

The vector on the right-hand side of this expression can be accumulated in a single n-vector as the solution proceeds. We can avoid the necessity of storing $g^{(0)}$ by using the relation

$$g^{(k)} = g^{(0)} + \sum_{i=0}^{k-1} y^{(i)}$$

and the conjugacy condition $y^{(i)T}s^{(k)} = 0$ to show that $s^{(k)T}g^{(0)} = s^{(k)T}g^{(k)}$.

Thus the solution $\overset{*}{x}$ is given by $\overline{x}^{(n)}$ where

$$\overline{x}^{(0)} = x^{(0)}, \quad \overline{x}^{(k+1)} = \overline{x}^{(k)} - \rho^{(k)}s^{(k)}$$

where $\quad \rho^{(k)} = s^{(k)T}g^{(k)}/s^{(k)T}y^{(k)}$.

A problem with the recurrence relations (4.25) is that $p^{(k)}$ cannot be guaranteed to be a descent direction (i.e., we cannot guarantee $p^{(k)T}g^{(k)} < 0$) unless an exact linear search is made. In practice this implies that unless either $p^{(k)}$ is changed in sign when $g^{(k)T}p^{(k)} > 0$ or a sufficiently accurate linear search is made, the iteration breaks down.

Conjugate-direction methods for general nonlinear functions. Conjugate-direction methods can be applied to general nonlinear functions in several ways. Two possibilities are to repeat the n iterations described earlier in a cyclic fashion, resetting $p^{(k)}$ to the steepest-descent direction every n iterations; or to continue to use the recurrence relations for $p^{(k)}$ indefinitely. The following result proved by Powell (1976) gives useful insight into which method is more efficient.

Result 4.15. If F(x) is a quadratic function and $p^{(0)}$ is an arbitrary vector such that $p^{(0)T}g^{(0)} < 0$ then either termination is

obtained within (n+1) iterations or convergence to the solution
occurs at a linear rate (the latter being the more likely even-
tuality).

Clearly, if the sequence of estimates of the solution moves
into a region where the function is quadratic, in general we can
expect only linear convergence unless resetting takes place, so
that $p^{(o)} = -g$.

Other possibilities for the nonlinear case are to reset more
or less often than every n iterations, or to use resetting directions other than $-g^{(k)}$ (see Beale 1972, Powell 1975).

It is important to note that when F(x) is not quadratic,
Formula (4.23) is no longer identical to (4.22) and (4.21) since
the gradient vectors are no longer orthogonal. Further (4.22) and
(4.21b) have the advantage of being such that the angle between
$p^{(k)}$ and the steepest-descent direction is always less than $\pi/2$
(Powell, 1976). This property can be used to prove that the
sequence $\{x^{(k)}\}$ converges to a stationary point of F(x) under very
mild conditions on the problem. There is little to choose between
(4.22) and (4.21b) but we prefer (4.21b) since it guarantees that
$y^{(k-1)T} p^{(k)} = 0$ even when F(x) is non-quadratic.

There is still not conclusive evidence concerning the relative
merits of (4.21a) and (4.25). However, if the user can afford to
store the extra three n-vectors $y^{(k-2)}$, $p^{(k-2)}$ and $\bar{x}^{(k)}$ then the
recurrence relations (4.25) appear to give the more robust algorithm, provided a fairly accurate linear search is made every
iteration.

In comparison with quasi-Newton methods, the performance of
practical implementations of conjugate-direction methods is dis-
appointing. The methods require significantly more function evaluations and are less robust. To some extent this behaviour is due
to the fact that, on a quadratic function, round-off errors cause
the directions to lose their conjugacy rapidly, but the increase in
the number of function evaluations is incurred mainly in the finding
of the step length. A good choice of step length is far more

crucial for conjugate-direction algorithms than for quasi-Newton algorithms. In general the direction of search rarely approximates the Newton direction and consequently the unit step is a poor initial approximation of $\alpha^{(k)}$ for the safeguarded interpolation algorithm. Moreover, it is a feature of conjugate-direction algorithms that the performance does not improve as the linear search tolerance is decreased. This situation applies when the theoretical properties of the algorithm do not depend upon the use of an exact linear search.

Despite these drawbacks the conjugate-direction algorithm has an important place in any numerical software library since there are many practical problems for which alternative methods require prohibitively large amounts of storage space.

5. METHODS WHICH DO NOT REQUIRE DERIVATIVES

If $F(x)$ is a general twice-continuously differentiable function, yet its derivatives are too difficult or expensive to evaluate, the best minimization methods available are based on using quasi-Newton or conjugate-gradient methods with finite-difference approximations to the gradient vector.

Consider the forward-difference formula

$$\bar{g}_j^{(k)} = \frac{1}{h_j} (F(x^{(k)} + h_j e_j) - F^{(k)}),$$

where h_j is the finite-difference interval and e_j is the jth column of the identity matrix. The vector $\bar{g}_j^{(k)}$ is subject to two types of error. The first is the truncation error,

$$E_t = \bar{g}_j^{(k)} - g_j^{(k)},$$

and the second is the cancellation error

$$E_c = \bar{g}_j^{(k)} - fl(\bar{g}_j^{(k)}),$$

where $fl(\bar{g}_j^{(k)})$ denotes the value of $\bar{g}_j^{(k)}$ obtained by using floating-point arithmetic.

Result 5.1. If $\bar{g}_j^{(k)}$ is computed in floating-point arithmetic on a computer with relative machine precision ε, then crude estimates of E_t and E_c are given by

$$|E_t| \sim \frac{h_j^2}{2} |G_{jj}^{(k)}|,$$

and

$$|E_c| \sim 3\varepsilon \left[2|F^{(k)}|/h_j + 1 \right]. \tag{5.1}$$

The main consideration in the implementation of finite-difference techniques is the choice of h_j; if h_j is too large the truncation error will be unacceptable, if h_j is too small the elements of $\bar{g}^{(k)}$ will be swamped by cancellation error. One solution of this problem is to choose h_j so that it approximately balances estimates of $|E_c|$ and $|E_t|$. However, we must emphasize that if a quasi-Newton method is used, the diagonal elements of the approximate Hessian matrix should not be used to estimate the truncation error since low-rank modification methods do not in general give good element-by-element approximations to the Hessian matrix. This fact is illustrated by Result 4.3 which states that even if the gradient vector is known exactly, the approximate Hessian matrices of the one-parameter family differ by a matrix of rank-one.

If the problem is well-scaled, the square root of the relative machine precision is a good value of h_j which approximately balances the cancellation error and truncation error. Alternatively, if the problem is not well-scaled, h_j can be chosen by a 'service' routine (see Section 1.1) which balances an estimate of the truncation error (obtained by approximating E_{jj} by finite differences) with the estimate of the cancellation error (5.1).

Whatever the value of h_j chosen, it should be held constant for as long as possible. This is because many useful properties of the quasi-Newton method or conjugate-gradient method will be abrogated if h_j varies from iteration to iteration (see Gill and Murray, 1972).

As the gradient becomes smaller (either during the final stages of the minimization or even at points remote from the solution), the relative truncation error causes a significant deterioration in the direction of search so that the elements of the vector $s^{(k)}$ become artifically small. When this happens the gradient vector must be reestimated with the central-difference formula

$$\frac{1}{h_j} \left[F(x^{(k)} + he_j) - F(x^{(k)} - he_j) \right], \tag{5.2}$$

and the search direction recomputed. The central-difference formula gives smaller truncation error, but requires an additional n function evaluation.

The cancellation error also increases as the solution is approached until eventually no correct figures remain in the finite-difference estimate. The total loss of figures must be postponed as long as possible. This can be done by using (5.2) when $|E_c|/|\bar{g}_j^{(k)}|$ becomes large.

6. METHODS FOR THE NON-LINEAR LEAST-SQUARES PROBLEM

In a large number of practical problems the function $F(x)$ is a sum of squares of non-linear functions

$$F(x) = \sum_{i=1}^{m} \left[f_i(x) \right]^2.$$

In this case the gradient vector and Hessian matrix are given by $2J(x)^T f(x)$ and $2(J(x)^T J(x) + Q(x))$ where $J(x)$ is the $m \times n$ Jacobian matrix of $f(x)$ whose ith row is

$$\nabla f_i(x) = (\partial f_i/\partial x_1, \partial f_i/\partial x_2, \ldots, \partial f_i/\partial x_n)^T,$$

$$Q(x) = \sum_{i=1}^{m} f_i(x) G_i(x)$$

and $G_i(x)$ is the Hessian matrix of $f_i(x)$.

The Newton equations $G^{(k)} p^{(k)} = -g^{(k)}$ have the special form

$$(J^{(k)T} J^{(k)} + Q^{(k)}) p_N^{(k)} = J^{(k)T} f^{(k)},$$

where $p_N^{(k)}$ denotes the Newton direction of search. If $\|f\|_2$ tends to zero as $x^{(k)}$ approaches the solution $\overset{*}{x}$, the second derivative term $Q(x)$ also tends to zero and $P_N^{(k)}$ can be approximated by the solution of the normal equations

$$J^{(k)T} J^{(k)} p_{GN}^{(k)} = -J^{(k)T} f^{(k)}. \tag{6.1}$$

This choice of direction gives the <u>Gauss-Newton method</u>, $P_{GN}^{(k)}$ being the solution of the linear least-square problem,

$$\underset{p}{\text{minimize}} \ \|p_N^{(k)} - p_{GN}^{(k)}\| \ / \ \|p_N^{(k)}\| \ = 0(\varepsilon).$$

<u>Result 6.1.</u> If $J^{(k)}$ is of full column rank and $\|Q^{(k)}\| = \varepsilon$

then $\| \ _N^{(k)} - \ _{GN}^{(k)}\| \ / \ \| \ _N^{(k)}\| \ = 0(\varepsilon).$

If $J^{(k)}$ is of full column rank, $\alpha^{(k)}$ is chosen to satisfy any one of the conditions C1 – C4 and $F(\overset{*}{x}) = 0$, then the Gauss-Newton method will ultimately converge at the same rate as Newton's method, despite the fact that only first derivatives are required.

A popular alternative method suggested by Levenberg (1944) and Marquardt (1963) is to compute $x^{(k+1)}$ as $x^{(k)} + p_M^{(k)}$, where $p_M^{(k)}$ is the solution of

$$(J^{(k)T} J^{(k)} + \lambda^{(k)} I) p_M^{(k)} = -J^{(k)T} f^{(k)},$$

with $\lambda^{(k)}$ a non-negative scalar. Trial values of λ are used to give $F(x^{(k+1)}) < F^{(k)}$.

The Gauss-Newton and Levenberg-Marquardt algorithms are not intended to solve the class of so-called "large-residual problems" for which ε does not tend to zero at the solution. Dennis (1973) has suggested that such problems are best tackled by including a quasi-Newton approximation $M^{(k)}$ of the second derivative term $Q(x)$; the matrix $M^{(k+1)}$ being chosen to satisfy the condition

$$(2J^{(k+1)T}J^{(k+1)} + M^{(k+1)})s^{(k)} = y^{(k)} \qquad (6.2)$$

analagous to (4.2), where $s^{(k)} = x^{(k+1)} - x^{(k)}$ and $y^{(k)}$
$= 2(J^{(k+1)}f^{(k+1)} - J^{(k)T}f^{(k)})$.

Any one of the updating formulae mentioned in Section 4 may
be used, but it should be noted that the property of n-step termination does not apply in this case since we are not directly approximating the quadratic term of the Taylor expansion of the sum of
squares. For this reason (6.2) is the only meaningful condition
which can be applied to $M^{(k+1)}$ and this is insufficient to ensure
that $J^{(k+1)T}J^{(k+1)} + M^{(k+1)}$ is a good element-by-element estimate
of $J^{(k+1)T}J^{(k+1)} + Q(x^{(k+1)})$.

Our experience with the Gauss-Newton method is that if it converges, it converges very rapidly. Betts (1976) utilizes this
phenomenon by using a Gauss-Newton method until no further progress
can be made, at which point a switch is made to a technique based
upon a quasi-Newton approximation to $Q(x)$. The matrix $M^{(k)}$ is updated at every iteration regardless of whether or not a quasi-
Newton step is taken (Bett's algorithm incorporates the SR1 update).

All the algorithms considered so far assume that the Jacobian
matrix does not become near-singular at any point $x^{(k)}$. Unfortunately least-squares problems are such that J is often by-nature ill-
conditioned because $F(x)$ is often derived from a parameter-estimation
problem where the underlying mathematical model is not well defined.
The following result was proved by Gill and Murray (1976a).

Result 6.2. If $J^{(k)}$ is singular then the vectors $p_M^{(k)}$ and
$p_{GN}^{(k)}$ lie wholly in the range of the matrix $J^{(k)T}J^{(k)}$. Since it
is unlikely that $p_N^{(k)}$ satisfies the same property, $p_M^{(k)}$ and $p_{GN}^{(k)}$
differ from $p_N^{(k)}$ by a vector whose norm is independent of ε.

Moreover, it can be shown that Result 6.2 applies for the
quasi-Newton direction if $M^{(o)}$ is chosen as the zero or identity
matrix (as is invariably the case in practical implementations).

Gill and Murray (1976b) have proposed an algorithm which can

be viewed as a modification of the Gauss-Newton method to allow
convergence for large-residual and rank-deficient problems.

Consider the singular-value decomposition of the matrix $J^{(k)}$

$$J^{(k)} = U \begin{bmatrix} S \\ 0 \end{bmatrix} V^T,$$

where $S = \text{diag}(\sigma_1, \sigma_2, \ldots, \sigma_n)$ is the matrix of singular values
with $\sigma_{i+1} \leq \sigma_i (1 \leq i \leq n-1)$, U an $m \times m$ orthonormal matrix and V
an $n \times n$ orthonormal matrix. The rank of $J^{(k)}$ is given by the index
$r_J (1 \leq r_J \leq n)$ such that $\sigma_j = 0$ for $j > r_J$. If we define $S_1 =$
$\text{diag}(\sigma_1, \sigma_2, \ldots, \sigma_{r_J})$ with V_1 the columns of V corresponding to
S_1 then it can be shown that

$$P_{GN}^{(k)} = -V_1 S_1^{-1} f_1,$$

where f_1 is the vector of first r_J components of $U^T f^{(k)}$. The theoretical basis of the Gill-Murray method is that, if necessary, the
Gauss-Newton direction can be corrected by adding the vector

$$h = -V_2 (V_2^T Q^{(k)} V_2)^{-1} V_2^T Q^{(k)} P_{GN}^{(k)}.$$

Result 6.3   (Gill and Murray, 1976b).   If we define

$$P_{GM}^{(k)} = P_{GN}^{(k)} + h \text{ and } \|Q^{(k)}\| = \varepsilon, \text{ then}$$

$$\|P_{GM}^{(k)} - P_N^{(k)}\| / \|P_N^{(k)}\| = O(\varepsilon).$$

In order to extend the algorithm to cater for large-residual
problems we define the grade of $J^{(k)}$ to be an index r such that
$1 \leq r \leq r_J$ and we define the matrices $S_1 = \text{diag}(\sigma_1, \sigma_2, \ldots, \sigma_r)$,
$S_2 = \text{diag}(\sigma_{r+1} \ldots, \sigma_{r_J})$ with V_1, V_2, f_1 and f_2 the corresponding
columns of V and elements of $U^T f^{(k)}$ respectively. The vector

$$P_1^{(k)} = V_1 S_1^{-1} f_1 \qquad (6.3a)$$

can be interpreted as the Gauss-Newton direction in the subspace V_1 and the vector

$$h = -V_2(S_2^2 + V_2^T Q^{(k)} V_2)^{-1}(S_2 f_2 + V_2^T Q^{(k)} p_1^{(k)}) \qquad (6.3b)$$

its correction.

The grade of the matrix used depends upon the progress of the minimization. If the Gauss-Newton direction is satisfactory then $r = r_J$ and the step is not corrected; otherwise r is chosen such that the function is reduced satisfactorily every iteration. Note that if we allow $S_1 = 0$ and $S_2 = S$ in our set of allowable partitions (that is, if we define the zero grade of $J^{(k)}$) then the algorithm is equivalent to Newton's method.

There are three practical algorithms based upon (6.3) which can be implemented - one using a quasi-Newton approximation to $Q(x)$, one using finite differences of $J^{(k)}$ along the columns of V_2 and one using $Q^{(k)}$ explicitly. In all of them the modified LDL^T factorization must be used to solve (6.3b). This ensures that the algorithm is convergent for problems with indefinite Hessian matrices.

The quasi-Newton algorithm uses the BFGS updating formula

$$M^{(k+1)} = M^{(k)} + \frac{y^{(k)} y^{(k)T}}{y^{(k)T} s^{(k)}} - \frac{W^{(k)} s^{(k)} s^{(k)T} W^{(k)}}{s^{(k)T} W^{(k)} s^{(k)}},$$

where $W^{(k)} = J^{(k+1)T} J^{(k+1)} + M^{(k)}$. The advantage of using this form of the BFGS update is that if $J^{(k+1)T} J^{(k+1)} + M^{(k)}$ is positive definite, then $J^{(k+1)T} J^{(k+1)} + M^{(k+1)}$ is also. Because it is the elements of $M^{(k)}$ which are updated (as opposed to the LDL^T factors) any modification need not be in the symmetrical form $M^{(k+1)} = M^{(k)} \pm vv^T \pm uu^T$. Gay (1976) has shown that the type of modification which minimizes the cancellation error in this case is given by

$$M^{(k+1)} = M^{(k)} + uv^T + vu^T,$$

where $u = y^{(k)} + \left[\dfrac{y^{(k)T}s_s^{(k)}}{s^{(k)T}w^{(k)}s_s^{(k)}} \right]^{1/2} w^{(k)}s_s^{(k)}$ and

$$v = \frac{1}{2y^{(k)T}s_s^{(k)}} \left[y^{(k)} - \left[\frac{y^{(k)T}s_s^{(k)}}{s^{(k)T}w^{(k)}s_s^{(k)}} \right]^{1/2} w^{(k)}s_s^{(k)} \right].$$

7. CONCLUSIONS

In order to solve all unconstrained minimization problems efficiently it is necessary for a wide variety of algorithms to be available. The similarity of each of these algorithms may be exploited by means of a software library in which a basic set of program modules is shared by all the various algorithms. We believe that a good program library should contain the following algorithms: (the algorithms are designated as in the NPL FORTRAN library with the reference section given in parenthesis).

(i) MNA, a modified-Newton algorithm using first and second derivatives (§3);

(ii) MNAF, a modified-Newton algorithm using finite-difference approximations to the second derivatives (§3 and §4.1);

(iii) QNMDER, a quasi-Newton algorithm using first derivatives (§4.2);

(iv) QNMDIF, a quasi-Newton algorithm using function values only (§4.2 and §5);

(v) CNGRDR, a conjugate-direction algorithm using first derivatives (§4);

(vi) CNGRDF, a conjugate-direction algorithm using function values only (§4 and §5);

(vii) UNIGRD, a univariate minimization algorithm using first derivatives (§2.1);

(viii) UNIFUN, a univariate minimization algorithm using function values only (§2.1).

Available for use (as appropriate) with the above subroutines are the following auxiliary subroutines.

(ix) LNSRCH, a step-length algorithm using cubic interpolation with first derivatives (§2.2);

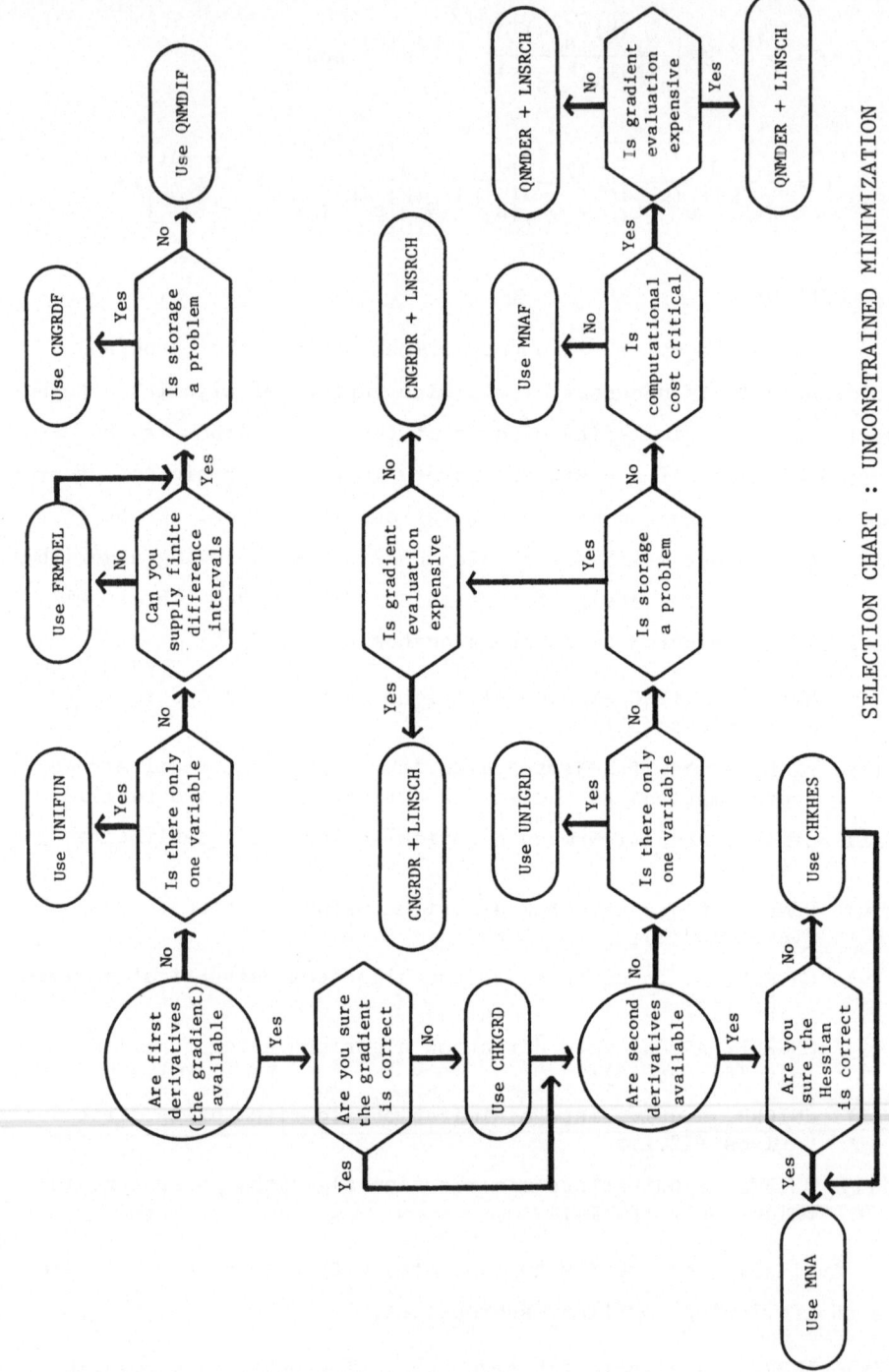

SELECTION CHART : UNCONSTRAINED MINIMIZATION

(x)   LINSCH, a step-length algorithm using quadratic interpolation with function values only (§2.2).

(xi) CHKHES, a subroutine to check the user-supplied second
derivatives (§1.1);

(xii) CHKGRD, an algorithm to check the user-supplied first derivatives (§1.1);

(xiii) FRMDEL, an algorithm to compute a sensible set of finite-
difference intervals for QNMDIF and CNGRDF (§1.1).

It is important that the user should choose the subroutine
most appropriate to his specific problem.   The selection chart given
on the previous page enables the user to make these choices readily.

REFERENCES

1.   E.M.L. Beale, A derivation of conjugate gradients, in:
Numerical methods for nonlinear optimization, ed. by F.A.
Lootsma, Academic Press, London and New York, 1972, 39-43.
2.   G. Berman, Minimization by successive approximation, SIAM
J. Numer. Anal., 1966, 3, 123-133.
3.   J.T. Betts, Solving the nonlinear least squares problem:
application of a general method, J. Optimization Theory Appl.
1976, 18, 469-484.
4.   R.P. Brent, Algorithms for minimization without derivatives,
Prentice-Hall, New Jersey, 1973.
5.   K.W. Brodlie, An assessment of two approaches to variable
metric methods, to be published, 1977.
6.   C.G. Broyden, Quasi-Newton methods and their application to
function minimization, Math. Comput., 1967, 21, 368-381.
7.   C.G. Broyden, The convergence of a class of double-rank
minimization algorithms, J. Inst. Maths. Applics., 1970, 6,
76-90.
8.   J.R. Bunch and B.N. Partlett, Direct methods for solving
symmetric indefinite systems of linear equations, SIAM J.
Numer. Anal., 1971, 8, 639-655.
9.   J. Cullum and R.K. Brayton, Some remarks on the symmetric rank
one update, IBM Research Centre Report RC 6157, Yorktown
Heights, New York, 1976.
10. W.C. Davidon, Variable metric method for minimization, Argonne
National Laboratory Report ANL-5990 (Rev.), 1959.
11 . W.C. Davidon, Variance algorithm for minimization, Comput. J.,
1968, 10, 406-410.
12. W.C. Davidon, Optimally conditioned optimization algorithms
without line searches, Math. Program., 1975, 9, 1-30.
13. A. Dax and S. Kaniel, Pivoting techniques for symmetric
decomposition, Institute of Mathematics, The Hebrew University
of Jerusalem, Jerusalem, Israel, 1974.

332

14. J.E. Dennis, Some computational techniques for the nonlinear least squares problem, Numerical solution of systems of non-linear algebraic equations, ed. by Byrne and Hall, Academic Press, London and New York, 1973.

15. L.C.W. Dixon, Quasi-Newton algorithms generate identical points, Math. Program., 1972, 2, 383-387.

16. L.C.W. Dixon, Conjugate gradient algorithms: quadratic termination without linear searches, J. Inst. Maths Applics1, 1975, 15, 9-18.

17. R. Fletcher, A new approach to variable metric algorithms, Comput. J., 1970, 13, 317-322.

18. R. Fletcher, Conjugate direction methods, Numerical methods for unconstrained optimization, ed. by W. Murray, Academic Press, London and New York, 1972, 73-86.

19. R. Fletcher and T.L. Freeman, A modified Newton method for minimization, Dundee University Numerical Analysis Report No. 7, 1975.

20. R. Fletcher and M.J.D. Powell, A rapidly convergent descent method for minimization, Comput. J., 1963, 6, 163-168.

21. R. Fletcher and C.M. Reeves, Function minimization by conjugate gradients, Comput. J., 1964, 7, 149-154.

22. D. Gay, Representing symmetric rank 2 updates, NBER Working Paper Series, Working Paper No. 124, 1976.

23. P.E. Gill, G.H. Golub, W. Murray, and M.A. Saunders, Methods for modifying matrix factorizations, Math. Comput., 1974, 28, 505-535.

24. P.E. Gill and W. Murray, Quasi-Newton methods for unconstrained optimization, J. Inst. Maths Applics., 1972, 9, 91-108.

25. P.E. Gill and W. Murray, Safeguarded steplength algorithms for optimization using descent methods, NPL NAC Report No. 37, 1974a.

26. P.E. Gill and W. Murray, Newton-type methods for unconstrained and linearly-constrained optimization, Math. Program., 1974b, 7, 311-350.

27. P.E. Gill and W. Murray, Methods for large-scale linearly-constrained problems, Numerical methods for constrained optimization, ed. by P.E. Gill and W. Murray, Academic Press, London, 1974c, 93-147.

28. P.E. Gill and W. Murray, Nonlinear least squares and nonlinearly constrained optimization; Numerical Analysis, Lecture Notes in Mathematics No. 506, ed. by G.A. Watson, Berlin-Heidelberg-New York, Springer Verlag, 1976a, 134-147.

29. P.E. Gill and W. Murray, Algorithms for the solution of the non-linear least-squares problem, NPL NAC Report No. 71, 1976b.

30. P.E. Gill, W. Murray, S.M. Picken, and M.H. Wright, The design and structure of a Fortran library for optimization, Stanford University Systems Optimization Laboratory Technical Report SOL 77-7, 1977.

31. P.E. Gill, W. Murray, S.M. Picken, M.H. Wright and H.M. Barber, Subroutine FRMDEL, NPL Algorithms Library Report No. E4/06/Fortran/11/75, 1975.

32. P.E. Gill, W. Murray, and R.A. Pitfield, The implementation of two revised quasi-Newton algorithms for unconstrained optimization, NPL NAC Report No. 11, 1972.

33. P.E. Gill, W. Murray, and M.A. Saunders, Methods for computing and modifying the LDV factors of a matrix, Math. Comput., 1975, 29, 1051-1077.

34. D. Goldfarb, A family of variable metric updates derived by variational means, Math. Comput., 1970, 24, 23-26.

35. A. Goldstein and J. Price, An effective algorithm for minimization, Numer. Math, 1967, 10, 184-189.

36. S.R. Graham, A matrix factorization and its application to unconstrained minimization, Project thesis for BSc (Hons) in Mathematics for Business, Middlesex Polytechnic, Enfield, Middlesex, 1976.

37. S.M. Johnson, Best exploration for a maximum isFibonaccian, RAND Corporation Report RM-1590, 1955.

38. J. Kiefer, Sequential minimax search for a maximum, Proc. Am. Math. Soc., 1953, 4, 503-506.

39. F.T. Krogh, VODQ/SVDQ/DVDQ - Variable order integrators for the numerical solution of ordinary differential equations, Section 314 subroutine write-up, Jet Propulsion Laboratory, Pasadena, California, 1969.

40. K. Levenberg, A method for the solution of certain problems in least squares, Q. Appl. Math., 1944, 2, 164-168.

41. D. Marquardt, An algorithm for least squares estimation for non-linear parameters, SIAM J. Appl. Math., 1963, 11, 431-441.

42. W. Murray and M. Wright, Efficient linear search algorithms for the logarithmic barrier function, Systems Optimization Laboratory Technical Report SOL 76-18, Stanford University, California, 1976.

43. B.A. Murtagh, and R.W.H. Sargent, A constrained minimization method with quadratic convergence, Optimization, ed. by R. Fletcher, Academic Press, London and New York, 1969, 215-246.

44. B.A. Murtagh and R.W.H. Sargent, Computational experience with quadratically convergent minimization methods, Comput. J., 1970, 13, 185-194.

45. L. Nazareth, A conjugate direction algorithm without line searches, Applied Mathematics Division, Argonne National Laboratory, Argonne, Illinois, 1975.

46. S.S. Oren, On the selection of parameters in self-scaling variable metric algorithms, Math. Program., 1974, 7, 351-367.

47. S.S. Oren, Self-scaling variable metric (SSVM) algorithms II: Implementation and Experiments, Management Science, 1974, 20, 863-874.

48. S.S. Oren and D.G. Luenberger, Self-scaling variable metric (SSVM) algorithms I: Criteria and sufficient conditions for scaling a class of algorithms, Management Science, 1974, 20, 845-862.

49. S.S. Oren and E. Spedicato, Optimal conditioning of self-scaling variable metric algorithms, Math. Program., 1976, 10, 70-90.

334

50. E. Polak and G. Ribiere, Note sur la convergence de methodes des directions conjugees, Rev. Fr. Inform. Rech. Operation 16-R1, 1969, 35-43.

51. M.J.D. Powell, Rank one method for unconstrained optimization, Nonlinear and integer programming, ed. by J. Abadie, Amsterdam, North-Holland, 1970, 139-156.

52. M.J.D. Powell, Some global convergence properties of a variable metric algorithm for minimization without exact line searches, AERE Report CSS 15, 1975.

53. M.J.D. Powell, Restart procedures for the conjugate gradient method, AERE Report CSS 24, 1975.

54. M.J.D. Powell, Some convergence properties of the conjugate gradient method, Math. Program., 1976, 11, 42-49.

55. R.B. Schnabel, Optimal conditioning in the convex class of rank two updates, AERE Report CSS 36, 1976.

56. D.F. Shanno, Conditioning of quasi-Newton methods for function minimization, Math. Comput., 1970, 24, 647-656.

57. E. Spedicato, On condition numbers of matrices in rank-two minimization algorithms, Towards global optimization, ed. by L.C.W. Dixon and G.P. Szego, North-Holland, Amsterdam, 1975, 196-210.

58. E. Spedicato, A variable metric method for function minimization derived from invariancy to nonlinear scaling, J. Optimization Theory Appl., 1976, 20, 315-329.

59. J.H. Wilkinson, The Algebraic Eigenvalue Problem, Oxford University Press, London, 1965.

THE GRG METHOD FOR NONLINEAR PROGRAMMING

J. Abadie

Electricité de France and University Paris-Dauphine
Paris, France

1. INTRODUCTION

The main concepts of the GRG method (an abbreviation for the "Generalized Reduced Gradient" method) go back to the years 1964-1965 [1] (readers interested in a more detailed presentation in the English language are referred to [2]). After some preliminary numerical experiments showed that the method might indeed not be devoid of some good qualities, a first general code was written, and much to our surprise, was ranked first in the Colville study [3] of 1968, comparing some 30 methods using 8 nonlinear test-problems. A new code was written in 1969 [4,5], with increased robustness, accuracy, and speed. This code contained the Fletcher-Reeves conjugate gradient method [6] instead of a less efficient acceleration procedure. Computation time was divided, on the average, by a factor of 3. This code was again ranked first in a new, privately circulated Colville study [7], which was summarized in a paper that appeared in the Proceedings of the Princeton Symposium on Mathematical Programming [8]. The new code, however, did not contain any antidegeneracy procedure, and was not easy to use: for instance, the user had to write himself the problem in standard form, including slack and artificial variables. A partial revision was then made in 1971 [9]. Both codes were used at a number of places, with some success, but also some failures -- the great majority of them due to the fact that the user must have some knowledge of both the GRG method and numerical analysis to give correct values to the various parameters and tolerances. Each of the other few failures, of course, lead to modifications which increased the size and complexity of the program. My own experience with graduate students in Business or Engineering, who were interested in the method only to a certain extent, but were much more

keen on solving some specific problem, drove me to the conclusion
that the code should be rendered as easy to use as possible, even
at the sacrifice of some computer time. The corresponding revised
version is called GRGA [10]. At the present moment, work is in
progress to include variable metric methods [11], with the same
stringent conditions on easiness in use, robustness and accuracy.

There have been other implementations of the GRG method. Let
met quote, among others: Heltne and Liittschwager [12,13];
Gabriele and Ragsdell [14]; Lasdon, Waren, Ratner and Jain [15,16]
(see also Arvind Jain's Thesis, Stanford University [17], and [18]);
Lasdon and Waren GRG2 [19].

All the inplementations so far quoted are intended to solve
small to moderate nonlinear programming problems (up to, say, $m = 50$
constraints and 100 variables, not including the bounds on the
variables among the constraints), because no provision, or almost
none, is made for sparseness, and because the methcd involves inverting, or factorizing, an $m \times m$ nonsingular matrix. Though the
size quoted above may be increased up to, say, 100 constraints and
300 variables, large problems need other implementations to be
solved.

The GRG method has the nice property that any progress in
large sparse matrices, or in solving large sparse <u>linear</u> equations,
or any progress in the simplex method for <u>linear</u> programming, can
be implemented into a GRG code with a reasonable amount of work.
This has been done for the first time, to my knowledge, by Peschon
and Peterson [20], who used our 1969 GRG card deck, suitably transformed as far as our inversion subroutine and a few others are
concerned, to solve the so-called "Optimum Power Flow Problem,"
sometimes also called "Economic Dispatch Problem" (this problem
is described below). Their modifications, however, are very
specific, and can solve only this special problem. Time reported
to solve a typical case with 500 nonlinear equality constraints
(plus bounds, plus some other side inequality constraints) and
1000 variables is one minute on a CDC 6400.

In his thesis, Arne Drud [21] designed a code which can solve
fairly large dynamic econometric models (or optimal control models)
using the GRG method as explained in the original paper [2], and
the Lasdon-Waren LSGRG code [19] is aimed at solving nonlinear
programming problems which are sparse and mostly linear ("sparse"
here means that the Jacobian matrix of all problem functions is
sparse, and "mostly linear" means that most elements of the
Jacobian are constant). I will describe below my own views on some
problems, which include both the Optimum Power Flow and the optimal
control problems [22,23,24].

In addition, many of the concepts of the GRG method have been
implemented in codes which use as well different approaches; see

for instance, for large problems, the successful Conjugate Gradient Approximation Programming of Beale [25]. The GRG approach was used by Kowalik [26] in solving, for the Bonneville Power Administration, a long range planning problem of hydroelectric electricity production for the West Coast of the United States, with some 3000 constraints and 6000 variables. Due to the tree structure of rivers and basins, the basic variables were numbered in such a way that the basis matrix was constant and upper triangular. Upper and lower bounds on the basic variables were taken care of via penalty terms added to the objective function.

To terminate this introduction, it is worth noticing that some variant of the GRG method reduces, in the case where all the constraints are linear, to the Wolfe reduced gradient method [27, 28], and some other variant, in the case of linear programming, to the Dantzig simplex method.

Let me state here, as an example of a large system easy to describe, the Optimal Flow Problem. We are given an electrical transmission system, described by the AC power flow equations

$$P_i - C_i = \sum_j G_{ij} V_i V_j \cos(\theta_i - \theta_j - \alpha_{ij})$$

and a second equation of the same type, with sine instead of cosine, and other values of the constants G_{ij}, α_{ij}. The variables are: P_i, the power produced at node i; V_i, the voltage magnitude at node i; θ_i, the phase angle at node i (there is also another variable, Q_i, corresponding to P_i in the second equation). The variables are further restricted by lower and upper bounds on V_i, P_i, Q_i, and on the difference $\theta_i - \theta_j$ (lower bound opposite to upper bound). C_i is the known power consumption at node i. At consumption nodes, $P_i = Q_i = 0$; at production nodes, $C_i = 0$. The index i relates to node, and the summation is over all adjacent nodes. Two hundred to 500 nodes are usual figures. The objective function to be minimized is the sum of the power production costs.

2.   OUTLINE OF THE GRG METHOD

Consider a mathematical programming problem in the following standard form:

Maximize $\varphi(X)$

subject to: $f(X) = 0$, $a \leq X \leq b$,

where X stands for $(X_1, \ldots, X_n)^T$, and similarly for a,b, and where $f(X)$ is the column vector whose components are $f_1(X), \ldots, f_m(X)$. We assume that all functions are real-valued continuously differentiable, and even twice continuously differentiable wherever necessary.

A point X is said to be feasible if $|f_i(X)| \leq \varepsilon_0$, for $i = 1$, ...,m, where ε_0 is some preassigned small constant (in fact, a vector of ε_i would be more appropriate).

Notice that any mathematical program can be put into the standard form, by introduction of non-negative slack variables, if there are inequalities (other than bounds on the variables) among the constraints, and by allowing some of the bounds to be $+\infty$ or $-\infty$ if necessary. The standard form is adopted here for ease in notations and discussion.

Assume that we know some feasible point X^o. We make the following nondegeneracy assumption. The vector X can be split into two components: an m-dimensional component y (the basic part), and x, a component of dimension $n - m$ (the nonbasic part), such that the following two properties hold:

(H1) y^o is strictly between bounds; and

(H2) the square $m \times m$ matrix $\partial f / \partial y$, computed at X^o, is nonsingular.

By the implicit function theorem, there exists, in some neighborhood V of x^o, a unique continuous function (mapping), say y(x), such that f(x,y(x)) is identically zero in V. In addition, y(x) has a continuous derivative dy/dx, which can be computed by the chain rule:

$\partial f / \partial x + (\partial f / \partial y)(dy/dx) = 0$,

or, more conveniently,

$dy/dx = - (\partial f / \partial y)^{-1}(\partial f / \partial x)$.

In what follows, we call A the jacobian of f(X) <u>computed at</u> X^o. Similarly, we set:

$B = \partial f / \partial y$, $N = \partial f / \partial x$ (computed at X^o).

Substituting y(x) into the objective function $\varphi(x,y)$, we obtain the <u>reduced function</u>

$\phi(x) = \varphi(x,y(x))$,

the gradient of which at x^o is, by the chain rule again:

$g = \partial \varphi / \partial x + (\partial \varphi / \partial y)(dy/dx)$

(all derivatives computed at X^o). Setting

$c = \partial \varphi / \partial x$, $d = \partial \varphi / \partial y$ (computed at X^o), we have the following formula for the <u>reduced gradient</u> g:

$$g = c - d\,B^{-1}\,N.$$

Let us define the <u>projected reduced gradient</u> p (in the space of g) by its components:

$$p_j = 0 \quad \text{if} \quad x_j^{\,o} = a_j \quad \text{and } g_j < 0;$$

$$p_j = 0 \quad \text{if} \quad x_j^{\,o} = b_j \quad \text{and } g_j > 0;$$

$$p_j = g_j \quad \text{otherwise.}$$

It is convenient to set

$$u = d\,B^{-1},$$

hence

$$d - uB = 0, \quad c - uN = g.$$

It is a simple matter to verify that the Kuhn–Tucker condition for the problem in standard form reduces to p = 0, and that u is the row-vector of multipliers corresponding to the equations $f(X) = 0$. We assume from now on that $p \neq 0$.

The following relations

$$x_j = a_j \quad \text{if} \quad x_j^{\,o} = a_j \quad \text{and} \quad g_j < 0,$$

$$x_j = b_j \quad \text{if} \quad x_j^{\,o} = b_j \quad \text{and} \quad g_j > 0,$$

define what we call the <u>face</u> (at x^o), denoted by F. The row-vector p (the projected reduced gradient) is also named the projection of g onto F.

Let h be any non-zero column-vector in F such that ph > 0: the vector h is an ascent direction for the reduced function $\phi(x)$.

There is a striking analogy with what is usually done in linear programming, where y(x) can be computed in close form. This is generally not the case if the constraints $f(X) = 0$ are non-linear. Even if close form is available actual substitution may very well be undesirable. Here is an example.

Suppose the problem is

$$\text{minimize } x_1^2 + x_2^2$$

$$\text{subject to } x_1^2 + b^2(x_2 - c)^2 \leq d^2,$$

where b,c,d, for a moment, are positive numbers without any relationship with the previous b,c,d. Assuming bc > d, the solution
of this convex problem is $x_1 = 0$, $x_2 = c - d/b$. The standard form
is

$$\text{minimize } x_1^2 + x_2^2$$

$$\text{subject to } x_1^2 + b^2(x_2 - c)^2 + x_3 - d^2 = 0, \quad x_3 \geq 0.$$

Taking x_1 as the basic variable, it is an easy matter to express
x_1 as a function of the nonbasic variables x_2, x_3. Substitution
into the objective function gives the reduced function

$$x_2^2 - b^2(x_2 - c)^2 - x_3 + d^2, \quad x_3 \geq 0,$$

the infimum of which is $-\infty$ ($x_3 \to +\infty$). Of course what is lacked
here is the domain of definition of the function $x_1(x_2, x_3)$ in
close form. We must then add the inequality

$$b^2(x_2 - c)^2 + x_3 \leq d^2,$$

and, consequently, the problem is not simplified. We leave to the
reader the pursuance of this example, which illustrates that the
main point in this section is not so much to simplify the problem
than to compute the reduced gradient g, the projected reduced
gradient p, and to check for the Kuhn-Tucker condition p = 0 by
means of tractable computations. If p ≠ 0, an improved feasible
point is computed by the GRG method.

The GRG method consists of the following steps:

Step 0. Assume some feasible X^o is known.

Step 1 is conveniently divided into substeps.

  1.1 Compute the jacobian A and the gradient of the
      objective function;

  1.2 Determine a splitting of X into (x,y), and corres-
      pondingly of A into (N,B), such that y^o is
      strictly between bounds and B is nonsingular;
      invert B.

  1.3 Compute the lagrange multipliers u and the reduced
      gradient g.

  1.4 Determine the face F and the projection p of g
      onto F.

  1.5 If p is zero (or almost zero in some sense), then
      terminate; otherwise:

Step 2. Choose some ascent direction h in F.

Step 3.   Choose a first stepsize θ_1.

Step 4.   Maximize, with respect to θ, the function

$$\psi(\theta) = \mathcal{P}(x^o + \theta h, y(x^o + \theta h)) = \phi(x^o + \theta h)$$

with more or less accuracy (the linear search).
For each value of θ under consideration, this step
requires solving the following system of m equations:

$$f(x^o + \theta h, y) = 0$$

where y is the m-dimensional vector of unknowns;
let us call SOLVEQ the corresponding subroutine.

Step 5.   Assuming Step 4 succeeds, an improved feasible
point is obtained, which replaces X^o. Return to
Step 1.

3.   SUMMARY OF IMPLEMENTATION

Before giving some details on the implementation of our GRG
code, let me point out that it was designed to include the Fletcher-
Reeves conjugate gradient method with restart every $1 + \dim(F)$ iterations, where $\dim(F)$ is the dimension of the face F. This group
of iterations is called a cycle. All the iterates of a given
cycle belong to the same face. A cycle may be terminated for a
variety of reasons, before reaching the normal restart after $1 +$
$\dim(F)$ iterations. At each restart, a new face is computed, and
the new ascent direction is the projected reduced gradient $h = p^T$.

In order to use the Fletcher-Reeves conjugate gradient procedure, the basis indices to be chosen in Step 1.2 at any iteration
within a cycle should be the same. Hence, provided no basic variable has reached a bound from one iteration to the next, the set
of column indices of B should remain unaltered. However, the
basis B can tend to be singular. Consequently, some test should
be applied to see if the basis is not too badly conditioned, and,
in case some unpleasantness appears, provision should be made to
recompute a new better basis. This lead to consider two inversion
subroutines: INV1 to invert a matrix B with known columns, and
another one, INV2, to choose a basis B from among the columns j of
A which are candidates (those columns which correspond to variables
strictly between bounds). INV1 operates as in the revised simplex
method. INV2 chooses first to introduce in the basis all the
logical variables (slacks and artificials) which are candidates,
because this will not affect the conditioning of the matrix B,
and will facilitate the computation of its inverse. At each step
of INV2, a new row of A is considered and updated, and the largest
element (in absolute value) is taken as the next pivot, provided
it is far enough from zero. If there is an updated row in which
no pivot can be found, INV2 is called a failure and, subsequently,

the current point X^o is called degenerate. Note that INV1 calls
INV2 if no suitable pivot can be found.

Of course, this inversion may be replaced by some factorization, such as the product form of the inverse (used in our first
GRG code), or, better, a LU factorization, followed by the
Bartels-Golub procedure [29] for changing basis, as implemented
in the MINOS code of Murtagh and Saunders for linear constraints
[30]. The LU factorization requires only $m^3/3$ computations (1 computation is 1 addition plus 1 multiplication), against m^3 computations for the explicit inverse of B, not to speak of increased
stability. One may also begin with a LU factorization at the
beginning of the iteration, followed by an elementary matrix
factor for each change of basis, like in some implementation of
the simplex method. This will not be memory consuming in GRG,
because a new LU has to be computed anyway at the beginning of
each iteration (we are thinking to non-linear constraints, leaving
aside the case of linear constraints); in addition, there are not
so many basis changes at each iteration.

In Step 2, at any start of a Fletcher-Reeves cycle, the
ascent direction is $h = p^T$; within a cycle, the conjugate gradient
direction is computed by using the formula recommended by Fletcher
and Reeves:

$$h = g^T + (|g|^2/|\bar{g}|^2)\bar{h},$$

where $|g|$, $|\bar{g}|$ are euclidean norms, and $\bar{g}$, $\bar{h}$ refer to the previous
g, h. Other formulae have been proposed, and some have been tried
within our implementation; they did not show any significant difference in the average.

Step 3 is crucial: if the first stepsize θ_1 is too small or
too large, the number of calls to SOLVEQ in Step 4 may be very
large. In addition, if θ_1 is too large, the iterative method contained in SOLVEQ might either diverge or converge too slowly. I
found the following considerations of some use.

First, limit θ_1 by requiring $x^o + \theta h$ to be between bounds.
Let t' be the corresponding positive upper limit.

Second, compute the tangent vector (h^T, k^T) at X^o, i.e., the
vector k such that $Nh + Bk = 0$, or, explicitly,

$$k = - B^{-1}(Nh),$$

and further limit θ so that $y^o + \theta k$ be between bounds. Let t'' be
the corresponding upper limit.

Third, assume that $\phi(x)$ is well approximated by a quadratic

$$g(x - x^o) - (1/2)(x - x^o)^T Q(x - x^o),$$

where Q is some symmetric positive definite matrix. The optimal choice for θ in the search direction h is

$$\theta = (gh)/(h^T Q h).$$

Let us call λ and μ the smallest and largest eigenvalues of Q, and $|h|$ the euclidean norm of h. From

$$0 < \lambda |h|^2 \leqq h^T Q h \leqq \mu |h|^2,$$

we have

$$gh/\mu |h|^2 \leqq \theta \leqq gh/\lambda |h|^2.$$

Suppose on the other hand that $\bar{\theta}$ was the optimal value of θ found, in the previous iteration, by the linear search (Step 4), and designating again by $\bar{g}$, $\bar{h}$ the values of g, h at this previous iteration, we have

$$\lambda \leqq \overline{gh/\theta} |\bar{h}|^2 \leqq \mu.$$

Let us set EST$(-1) = \overline{gh/\theta} |\bar{h}|^2$. From a few previous iterations, we have an estimate λ_2 of λ (by excess value) by taking the minimum of EST(-1), EST(-2),..., and similarly an estimate μ_2 of μ by taking the maximum of the same quantities EST(-1), EST(-2),... Having those estimates inherited from past history, we are left, in the current iteration, with the interval

$$0 < t_1 = gh/\mu_2 |h|^2 \leqq \theta \leqq gh/\lambda_2 |h|^2 = t'''$$

The upper limit t''' is taken into account in our code. Let t be the smallest of the three limits t', t'', t'''. To further limit t, we make a very rough maximization of $(x^o + \theta h, y^o + \theta k)$ in the interval $(0,t)$; this involves a very few calls to the objective function φ and none to the constraints or derivatives. This procedure might seem complicated, and may easily be replaced by some simpler one. Let me state that taking t as the smallest of t', t'', t_1 lead to less satisfactory results on the Colville test problems.

Step 4 heavily depends on the efficiency of the subroutine SOLVEQ, and on the efficiency of the successive choices of θ in the linear search. Let us take the two points in succession.

In our GRG code, SOLVEQ always uses a pseudo-Newton method to solve, with respect to y, the system

$$f(x^o + \theta h, y) = 0.$$

The iterates being y^1, y^2,..., the formula is

$$y^{k+1} = y^k - B^{-1}f(x^o + \theta h, y^k).$$

Newton's method corresponds to computing B at the current point (appearing in the parenthesis of the preceding formula), while our B is the one which has been computed at X^o in Step 1.2, and whose inverse B^{-1} is currently in the machine memories. The method is ascertained to converge if the starting point y^1 is close enough to the solution. In [24] we took $y^1 = y^o$ with some success. Our general code, however, always take $y^1 = y^o + \theta k$ (on the tangent, see above details on Step 3). Consequently, the pseudo-Newton method converges if θ is small enough. The following precautions are taken.

If the number of Newton iterations overpasses a preassigned number NEVL = 20 (controllable by the user), then SOLVEQ is declared a failure (see below for some possible exceptions).

Set ERR equal to the maximum error on the constraint equations at the current Newton iteration. If ERR $> 10^{12}\varepsilon_o$, or if the current ERR is more than 10 times the preceding one, failure is again declared (this number 10 can be changed to 2, or even to 1, but better not at the first Newton iteration).

We know that the convergence of this pseudo-Newton iteration is asymptotically linear. At iteration number 6, provided no basis change has occured in iterations 1 to 5, an estimate is made, from iterations 2 to 5, of the rate of convergence; this estimate is used to see if there is a chance to have ERR $\leq \varepsilon_o$ within the next 12 iterations, otherwise failure is declared (this number 12 is automatically adjusted if the user wants, say, NEVL = 10 instead of 20).

When iteration number NEVL is reached, the code extrapolates again, as above, to see if there is a chance to succeed in 9 more iterations, otherwise Newton's method is termed a failure, and the 20 iterations are lost.

A change of basis is needed if some basic variables go out of their respective bounds during the Newton iterations. This will be discussed later (subroutine COB).

Let us now describe the one dimensional optimization (the linear search in Step 4).

Let θ_1 be the first stepsize, as obtained from Step 3. If Newton is a failure, then θ_1 is replaced by $\theta_1/10$, and Newton is repeated. As soon as Newton is a success, the linear search continues as below.

For shortening, set $DIR = (h^T, k^T)$, so that $X + \theta DIR$ stands for $x + \theta h$, $y + \theta k$.

Let θ_1 be the first value for which Newton is a success, and let X^1 be the corresponding feasible point. Since the scalar product gh, which is a known positive number, clearly is the derivative of $\psi(\theta)$ for $\theta = 0$, we are able to make a quadratic fit, which gives a value $\theta*$. If $\theta*$ is equal to θ_1 within 10 percent, we set $\theta* = \theta_1$, and $\theta*$ is termed optimal. If $\theta* < 0$ or $\theta* \geq 2\theta_1$, the next trial value is $2\theta_1$, so the next starting point for Newton's method is $X^1 + \theta_1 DIR$. If $0 \leq \theta* \leq \theta_1/10$, θ_1 is replaced by $\theta_1/10$, and, after replacement, the next starting point for Newton's method is $X^O + \theta_1 DIR$, and the process above is repeated. In all other cases, the value of the objective function at $\theta*$ is computed (calling again SOLVEQ), and the linear search terminates with the best feasible point so far achieved. We are left with the case where $X^1 + \theta_1 DIR$ is the starting point for Newton's method: if the latter fails, the linear search terminates at X^1; if, on the contrary, Newton is a success and the value of the objective function is the best so far achieved, let X^2 be the point obtained. The next starting point for Newton's method is $X^2 + \theta_2 DIR$, where θ_2 is equal to $3\theta_1$, $2\theta_1$ or $1.5\theta_1$, depending on the number of iterations needed in the previous call to SOLVEQ. If Newton is a failure, the linear search terminates at X^2; if it is a success and the point X^3 thus obtained gives the objective function a better value than X^2, the next starting point for Newton's method is $X^3 + \theta_3 DIR$, where θ_3 again is equal to $3\theta_2$, $2\theta_2$ or $1.5\theta_2$. This process is repeated until Newton is a failure (end of linear search with the last point for which Newton was a success), or until Newton is a success and the value of the objective function at the corresponding feasible point is worst; we have now three consecutive values of θ, say a, b, c, with b better (in terms of the objective function) than a and c, to form a quadratic fit, which gives a value $\theta*$. If $\theta*$ is equal to b within 10 percent, then we set $\theta* = b$, $\theta*$ is declared optimal, and the linear search terminates; otherwise, the objective function is computed at $\theta*$, and the best of b and $\theta*$ is termed optimal.

I have no claim this is a good method. First, no control of the optimization accuracy is introduced; second, there may be too many Newton's iterations. I was guided by the feeling that, if the search does not terminate with a successful quadratic fit, the final convergence of the Fletcher-Reeves method may be very slow. Indeed, in case $\theta*$ is not termed optimal, the next iteration begins with a gradient direction (find a new face F and set $h = p^T$) and restarts a new Fletcher-Reeves cycle.

In the increasing values process, θ may very well overpass the value t' above which some nonbasic variables may go outside of their bounds. Each of those variables is then reset to its nearest bound before the new SOLVEQ is called. If θ overpasses t", the same strategy is applied to the basic variables, and usually results in SOLVEQ calling COB (change of basis). If θ becomes greater than t' or t", the Fletcher-Reeves cycle terminates anyway, though this is not compelling, as is shown by Beale and Benveniste [31], at the cost of additional storage, in the case of quadratic programming; it is an open question to know whether the latter method can be extended to more general cases.

During the course of Newton iterations in SOLVEQ, it may happen that iterates number 1 to k are within bounds, but iterate number k + 1 violates (at least) one of the bounds. A linear interpolation is then made to find, on the line segment joining the last two iterates, the point which is the closest to the last one, and still is feasible. In Figure 1, where the crosses mark the successive iterates starting from X^1 on the tangent at X^0, this happens for iterates number 2 and 3. The linear interpolation gives point c. Let us say that the linear interpolation sets some basic variable y_r at some of its bounds, while the other basic variables are strictly between bounds (the special case where more than one variable is simultaneously at some of their bounds after the linear interpolation is left aside; it simply requires more than one change of basis). The COB (change of basis) subroutine is then called. The variable y_r leaves the basis, and is replaced by some other nonbasic variable x_s which enters the basis. At the end of the COB subroutine, we have the inverse of the new B, formed from the old B by replacing the column corresponding to y_r by the column of N corresponding to x_s. In Figure 1, if x_2 is chosen to enter the basis, the Newton iterations will continue, and converge (hopefully) to point a. There may be many such changes of basis (the reader may see what happens if x_1 enters the basis). Lasdon, Fox, and Ratner [18] (see also Lasdon and Waren, [19], this Proceedings) recommend continuing the Newton iterations, without changing B, until convergence occurs or Newton fails. On Figure 1, this procedure will lead from point number 3 to point ℓ. They then consider θ as a new variable, $y_r(\theta) = 0$ as a new equation, and return to point b (the corresponding iterates are not marked on Figure 1). I am not in favour of this strategy, not so much because it might result in more Newton iterations, but rather because bounds sometimes serve to delimit the region where a function is defined, for instance $x \geq 0$ for $x^{2.5}$, or $x \geq 10^{-8}$ for log x. Gabriele and Ragsdell [14] suggested to converge from c to b on Figure 1. I propose to use the following formulae (not yet implemented in our GRG code), where β is the inverse of B, and β_r is the row r of B (corresponding to the basic variable y_r which just hit a bound). Setting

$$x^i = \theta_i h, \ x^{i+1} = \theta_{i+1} h, \ \Delta X = x^{i+1} - x^i, \ \Delta\theta = \theta_{i+1} - \theta_i,$$

we must have

347

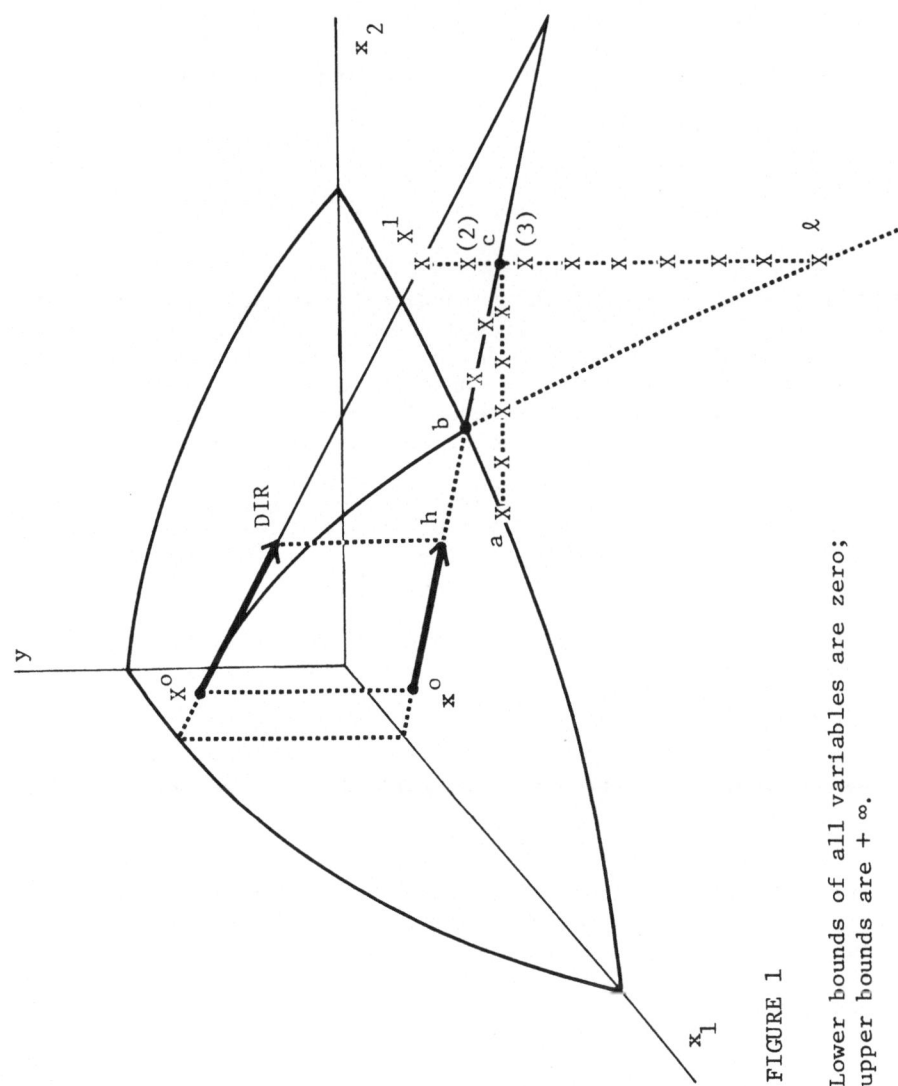

FIGURE 1

Lower bounds of all variables are zero;
upper bounds are + ∞.

$$\Delta x = h\Delta\theta.$$

Hence Newton's method consists in solving

$$f(X^i) + B\Delta y + Nh\Delta\theta = 0$$

$$\Delta y_r = 0.$$

Letting β denote the inverse of B, the final formulae are:

$$\Delta\theta = (1/k_r)\beta_r f(X^i)$$

$$\Delta y = k\Delta\theta - \beta f(X^i)$$

$$\Delta y_r = 0,$$

where k is, as in the preceding sections, the basic component of the tangent direction DIR, already computed (see details of Step 3), and where k_r is the component of index r. The last equation is, mathematically speaking, a consequence of the preceding two. For the machine, however, this equation permits to avoid y_r^{i+1} leaving its bound, due to rounding errors.

It seems to me that, in order that convergence from c to b takes place, one should have $\Delta\theta < 0$; in all cases then where k_r and $\beta_r f(X^i)$ are not of opposite signs, X^1 should be moved to a point much closer to X^o on the tangent.

The change of basis (COB) is done in the following way: suppose a basic variable y_r must leave the basis, and let β_r be the row r of the inverse of B. The row-vector $w = \beta_r N$ is computed, at least for the candidate columns (corresponding to nonbasic variables not at some bound). We must balance between two advantages in choosing a variable x_s to replace y_r. The corresponding pivot in w should be large in absolute value, for increasing numerical stability, and x_s should be far from its bounds. Whatever be the choice between these two objectives, a pivot is chosen, and a pivoting operation is done, as in the simplex method. Other rules must be applied in case of degeneracy (nonbasic variables at some bound are candidates), or in case no pivot is found (failure is declared; if COB is called from Newton, the latter is also called a failure; measures are then taken in the subroutine which called Newton).

Let us turn to the stopping criterion I use in GRGA. If the problem is convex, that is, the objective function $\varphi(X)$ to be maximized is concave and the constraints are $f_i(X) \leqq 0$, where the left-hand side consists of convex functions, then, at least near the optimum where the row-vector u of multipliers is non-negative, the lagrangian, considered as a function of X, with fixed u, is concave. Thus we have

$$\mathscr{P}(X) - uf(X) \leqq \mathscr{P}(X^0) - uf(X^0) + [\mathscr{P}'(X^0) - uf'(X^0)](X - X^0),$$

where the primes (') indicate derivatives (i.e., gradients). Assuming that the non-zero slack variables are in the basis, this gives

$$\mathscr{P}(X) \leqq \mathscr{P}(X^0) + g(x - x^0).$$

The right hand side is certainly increased by

$$g(x - x^0) = \Sigma g_i(x_i - x_i^0) \leqq \Sigma' g_i(b_i - x_i^0) + \Sigma'' g_i(a_i - x_i^0),$$

where now the (') indicates summation over the indices i such that $g_i > 0$, and (") summation over negative g_i. Finally, the following expression

$$DELTAFI = \Sigma' p_i(b_i - x_i^0) + \Sigma'' p_i(a_i - x_i^0)$$

is an upper bound on the error on the maximum value of $\mathscr{P}(X)$ when it is approximated by $\mathscr{P}(X^0)$. Our main stopping criterion is then

$$DELTAFI \leqq EPS1* |\mathscr{P}(X^0)|$$

(with a small modification if $\mathscr{P}(X^0)$ is near zero). There are also other stopping criteria; they almost never enter into action.

The Newton tolerance ε_0, named EPSILO, is quite crucial. If taken too large, the GRG method does not work; if too small, it does not have any meaning. Let us look into the latter. Suppose we have one linear constraint written, for a moment, as $f(X) = aX - 1000$. The machine will check if $|aX - 1000| \leqq$ EPSILO. Suppose the job is run in single precision arithmetics and the user sets EPSILO $= 10^{-12}$, on a machine with 8 decimal places: it is clear the test is meaningless. The user is not always aware of this point. In the present example, the program itself can take the following decision: compute f(o), and give EPSILO a value

$$EPSILO = |f(o)| \times 10^{-n},$$

where n depends on the machine precision. In GRGA, all functions f(X) are computed for a number of points, and the program will derive a reasonable value of EPSILO. In fact, the latter is a first value, which purposely is much too large for good precision. At the same time, EPS1 is 1000 times the final EPS1. Once the problem is declared solved with the first EPS1 and the first EPSILO (there are a number of other tests as well, which permits stopping before completion), then EPS1 is divided by 10, EPSILO is

divided by 1000, a call is made to Newton's method; if the latter
is successful, the new EPSILO becomes active, otherwise the old is
kept. This is repeated three times in the solution run.

We did not say until now how to deal with degeneracy. More
precisely, we assume now that the m rows of the jacobian A are
independent, but that INV2 was not able to determine a square
m x m non-singular submatrix B of A whose columns correspond to
variables strictly within bounds. The best to do in this case
seems to consider the GRG method as a realization of a tangent
direction method [32], [23], where an improving tangent direction
Y may be found by solving the following system

$$gY > 0$$

$$AY = 0$$

$$Y_i \geq 0 \text{ if } X_i^o = a_i$$

$$Y_i \leq 0 \text{ if } X_i^o = b_i.$$

This can easily be done by the simplex method (with antidegeneracy
procedure, preferably) to maximize gY under the constraints listed
above, and stopping at an extreme ray. A by-product of this calculation will be the inverse of the basis B. In the actual implementation of GRG, it has been chosen instead not to worry about degeneracy of the kind just described, as long as it is possible to make
a positive move in the direction DIR, i.e., as long as t" (see
above, detailed discussion on Step 3) is not zero. If t" = 0, the
code will continue as in the simplex method of linear programming.
Take the largest (in absolute value) element of the projected
reduced gradient p, say p_s, and try moving the corresponding nonbasic variable x_s in the direction given by the sign of p_s, so the
ascent direction p is a unit vector (with a + 1 or a - 1). This
usually results in a succession of basis changes at the same point
X^o, until some positive t" is found. This works in practice,
though without any theoretical ground; it would probably be better
to change this procedure to the former one described above.

4.   THE GRGA CODE FROM THE USER'S POINT OF VIEW

Though the GRGA code is not a production code, it is easy to
use. The problem should first be set in the following standard
form:

Maximize $\varphi(X)$

subject to

$$f_i(X) \leqq 0, \quad i = 1, \ldots, NIN$$

$$f_i(X) = 0, \quad i = NIN + 1, \ldots, NIN + NEQ$$

$$a_j \leqq X_j \leqq b_j, \quad j = 1, \ldots, NV$$

(inequalities numbered first, with $\leqq$ only, and then equations; objective function to be maximized; all variables with specified lower and upper bounds). These specifications are not very troublesome for small problems. If need be, it would be easy to have more flexibility.

The user will then be asked the following to describe his problem:

1. In a subroutine LECTUR, he will state, in his own preferred format, the number of variables, NV (excluding slacks and artificials; the program will take care of that); the number of inequalities and equations, NIN and NEQ; he will indicate (by 0 or 1) if his objective function is general or linear, and will do the same for the constraints (an indicator equal to 1 if they are all linear, to 0 in the contrary). He may set both indicators to zero, at a possible cost of increased computing time. (In case of a linear programming problem, both indicators are set to 1; the program will behave more or less like the simplex method). The user will then give values to all the non-zero bounds, and all the non-zero upper bounds. He may also give, in the same way, a starting point, though this is optional. He may also, optionally, set his own values to such parameters as EPSILO, though it is not recommended, at least for a first run. He will also state the values of all the non-zero constant derivatives of the objective function or the constraint functions, so they will no more be computed again.

2. In a subroutine PHIX, he will state what the objective function $\varphi(X)$ is.

3. In a subroutine CPHI, he will do the same for the constraint functions.

4. In a subroutine GRADFI he will give the formulae for the non-constant components of gradient of the objective function; if he resents the idea of having to write FORTRAN statements for the derivatives, he may use what he prefers; he may, for instance, have a single statement in GRADFI, which is CALL GRADEL: the code with then compute all derivatives, using central differences.

5. He will do the same, in a subroutine JACOB, for the jacobian of the constraints. Again, the code contains a subroutine JACDEL which the user can call, as the single statement in JACOB.

Having thus described his problem, it remains to make a call:

CALL MAXIMA (0,0).

If verification of the derivatives is needed, the first 0 is replaced by a 3; if higher accuracy than the usual one (which has always proved to be sufficient) is needed, the second zero is replaced by a larger integer. If the verification of derivatives is asked for, and errors are detected, the run is stopped with a specific message which points to the errors.

In this way, the average user is expected to be able to use the code after a half-hour learning. Intentionally, the code will stop if the number of variables exceeds 100, or the number of constraints (excluding bounds) exceeds 50, and will issue a message. It also stops at a preassigned value on the number of iterations (the user can choose any number he wants).

5. SOME APPLICATIONS OF THE GRG METHOD

One should always distinguish between the GRG method, and a GRG code, which contains the machine implementation of some variant of the GRG method (possibly many variants). In addition, the GRG method can be implemented for special problems. I have already quoted Kowalik's work [26]. In [22] is developed a GRG method for solving discrete optimal control problems with bounds on the state variables as well as on control variables; the equations take the form

$$x^{t+1} = f(x^t, u^t, t), \quad t = 0, \ldots, T-1;$$

vector x^t between bounds, $t = 0, \ldots, T$;

vector u^t between bounds, $t = 0, \ldots, T-1$.

The main idea is to use as often as possible the explicit form of the evolution equation. Only if some state variable is at some bound, say x_i^{t+1}, then the code will look for a variable u_i^t (the same value of t) to replace it in the basis, if at all possible. Later on, Mehra and Davis used this simple idea [33]. This concept was exploited also in [24], where the solutions of many problems are given, two being typical. The first one, the Jacobson and Lele problem [34] is to

minimize $x_0(1)$,

subject to $x_0' = x_1^2 + x_2^2 + 0.005u^2$;

$x_1' = x_2$;

$$x_2' = -x_2 + u;$$

$$x_1(o) = 0;$$

$$x_2(o) = -1;$$

$$x_2(t) \leq 8(t-5)^2 - 0.5.$$

Primes (') denote time derivatives. The time interval $(0,1)$ was divided into 100 equal steps, and the ordinary 4th-order Runge-Kutta method was used in [24]. The difficulty of course is due to the last inequality, without which the problem can be chiefly reduced to an unconstrained problem in 100 variables $u(1), \ldots, u(100)$. Figure 2 shows the x_2-trajectory. The second problem which will be mentioned here is the Kendrick and Taylor model of Korea [35], [36], which has 6 state variables, 9 control variables, 8 intermediate variables, and 30 one-year periods. The model is too long to be described here. Complete formulation with data can be found in [35] and [24].

As another instance of the same general principle, let us return to a general GRG code. Assuming that it is possible to call any particular constraint function separately, we may save computation time by the following procedure [22] -- put all slack variables which are not at some bound in the basis, use Newton's method to solve for the other basic variables, using only tight constraints. At each Newton iteration, use the iterate so obtained to compute the values of the basic slacks, and check for bounds. This check can be made only periodically, or even only once for all after convergence of Newton's iteration (Lasdon et al.). Newton's method, applied to the whole system of equations, including slacks, give different iterates, as far as the values of the basic slacks are concerned.

Readers are referred to [23] for problems which, in a natural way, are attached to a graph: the electrical distribution network in case of the Optimal Power Flow Problem, a chain in the case of the ordinary optimal control problem.

In the Optimal Flow Problem (see end of Section 1), there are thousands of constraints of the type

$$\theta_i - \theta_j \leq \pm b_{ij},$$

where θ_i, θ_j are variables, and b_{ij} are non-zero bounds. According to what has just been said, we momentarily disregard all constraints which are not tight. Let us construct an undirected graph in the following way: (i,j) is an arc if and only if one of the two constraints $\theta_i - \theta_j \leq b_{ij}$, $\theta_i - \theta_j \leq -b_{ij}$ is tight. Suppose this graph has a cycle, say $(1,2,3,4,5,1)$. Then there

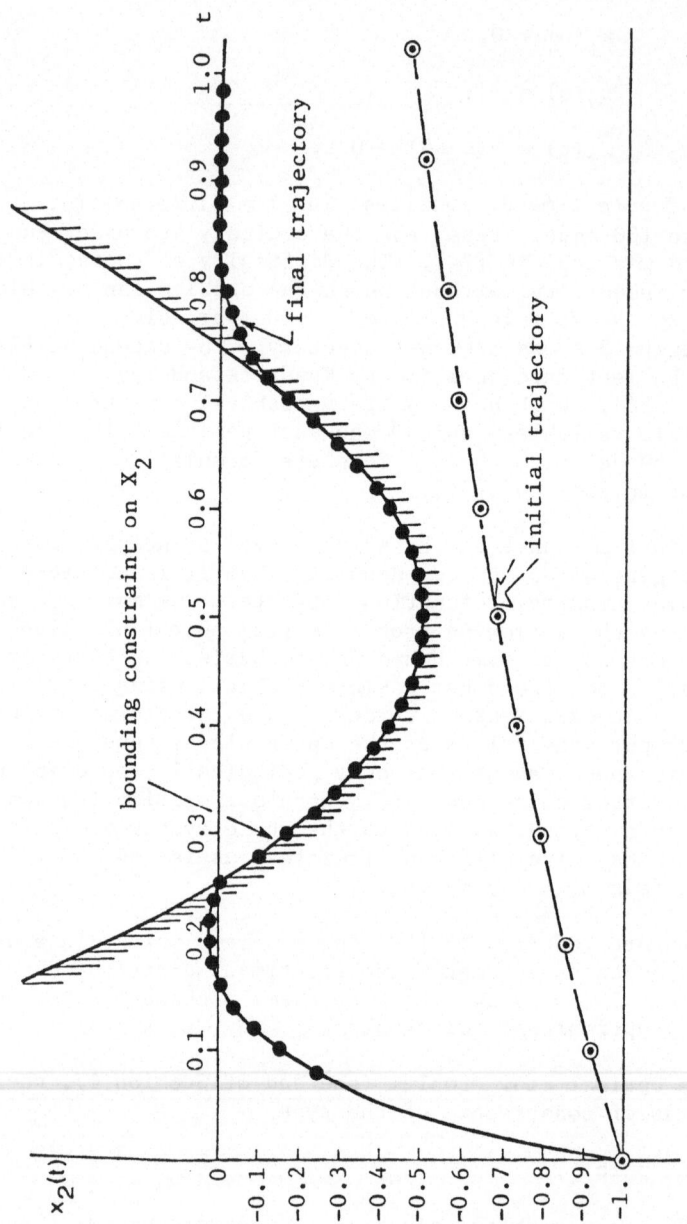

Jacobson and Lele Problem: Trajectory of x_2, initial trajectory corresponds to $u(t)=-0.21$

FIGURE 2

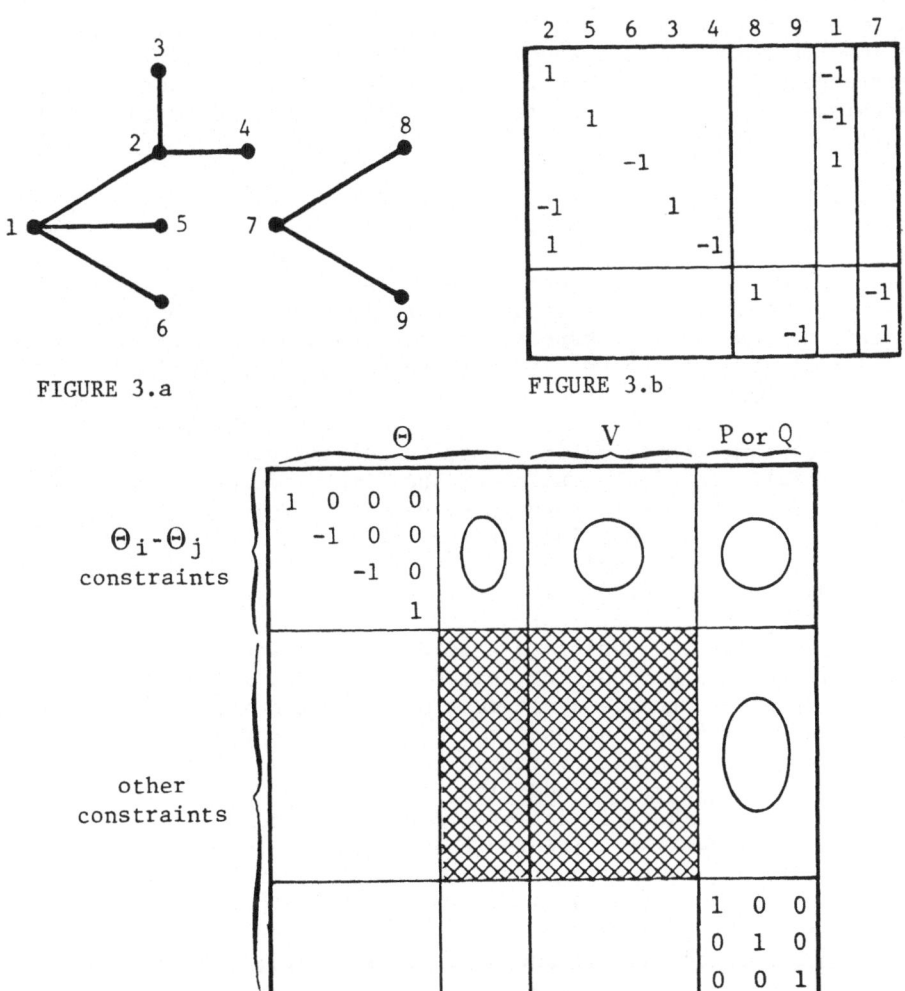

FIGURE 3.a   FIGURE 3.b

FIGURE 3.c

should be a combination, with coefficients +1 or -1, of b_{12}, b_{23}, b_{34}, b_{45}, b_{51}, which gives zero. Excluding such special cases, there is no cycle. The graph, then, is composed of a certain number of disconnected trees. Let two such trees be shown in Figure 3.a. Correspondingly, we have a lower triangular square matrix L, plus, for each tree, one column of +1, -1 and zeros (Figure 3.b). We may now add or subtract, if need be, successive columns of L to these special bordering columns, making them zero. This corresponds to substitute (Figure 3.b) $x_2 = x_1 + b_{21}$,

$x_5 = x_1 + b_{51}$, and so on. Each addition or subtraction of a column is carried out through the whole basis matrix (i.e., the corresponding substitution is made through the whole set of constraints). This gives the matrix of Figure 3.c. Only the hatched part has to be inverted.

6.   GRG WITH VARIABLE METRIC METHOD

There is now sufficient evidence to be sure that, for small to moderately large unconstrained optimization problems, variable metric methods are far superior to the conjugate gradient. The reader is referred to Dennis and Moré for a recent unified survey [37]. Convergence is speeded up for a variety of reasons, among which is the fact that, after a few iterations, the steplength $\theta = 1$ has some justification, and, consequently, we shall be largely relieved of the choice of the first steplength θ_1. See Dixon [38], [39] for a thorough discussion. This should result in a fewer number of iterations in the linear search. Preliminary experiments [11] in implementing the Fletcher strategy [40] in our GRG code show good promise.

When using the conjugate gradient method and some nonbasic variable reaches a bound, or leaves a bound, or if there is some change of basis, then a cycle must be restarted again (see, though, Beale and Benveniste, already quoted, for an approach to this question). When using a variable metric method, restart is not (or less) necessary. In addition, if some nonbasic variable leaves a bound, there is at least something which can be done -- augment the inverse hessian (or the hessian) with a unit row and a unit column (the 1 being at the diagonal intersection). This gives a positive definite matrix, which should not be so bad to consider as the inverse hessian of the augmented problem. Murtagh and Saunders have another approach [30], but their procedures, besides embodying a discernible level of ad hoc strategy, would be too costly to implement in a GRG code for nonlinear constraints.

If on the contrary a nonbasic variable hits a bound, then a row and a column has to be removed from the hessian, which is easy. Suppose the variable metric method under consideration deals with the inverse hessian

$$\begin{pmatrix} H_1 & a \\ a^T & b \end{pmatrix}$$

where the last row and column correspond to the variable to be removed. It is a simple matter to verify that the new inverse hessian should be

$$H_1 - ab^{-1}a^T,$$

a very simple update formula.

The case where there is a change of basis is more complicated. Let us set

$$L(X) = \varphi(X) - uf(X),$$

where u is as defined by the GRG method, at X^o. The primes (') and (") denoting gradients and square matrices of second partial derivatives, we have

$$\phi'(x^1) = (c,d)\begin{pmatrix} I \\ -B^{-1}N \end{pmatrix}$$

that is, setting for simplicity

$$P = B^{-1}N,$$

$$\phi'(x^o) = \varphi'(X^o)\begin{pmatrix} I \\ -P \end{pmatrix}.$$

Similarly, for each function $f_i(X)$:

$$f'_i(X^o)\begin{pmatrix} I \\ -P \end{pmatrix} = 0.$$

Differentiating a second time with respect to x at x^o, we obtain:

$$\phi''(x^o) = \begin{pmatrix} I \\ -P \end{pmatrix}^T \varphi''(X^o)\begin{pmatrix} I \\ -P \end{pmatrix} + \varphi'(X^o)\frac{\partial}{\partial x}\begin{pmatrix} I \\ -P \end{pmatrix}$$

$$0 = \begin{pmatrix} I \\ -P \end{pmatrix}^T f''_i(X^o)\begin{pmatrix} I \\ -P \end{pmatrix} + f'_i(X^o)\frac{\partial}{\partial x}\begin{pmatrix} I \\ -P \end{pmatrix}.$$

Multiplying by $-u_1,\ldots,-u_m$ and adding, we get

$$\phi''(x^o) = \begin{pmatrix} I \\ -P \end{pmatrix}^T L''(X^o)\begin{pmatrix} I \\ -P \end{pmatrix} + L'(X^o)\begin{pmatrix} 0 \\ -\frac{\partial P}{\partial x} \end{pmatrix}.$$

Note that $L'(X^o) = (\partial L/\partial x, \partial L/\partial y)$, computed at X^o, and that $\partial L/\partial y = 0$ at X^o. It then follows

$$\phi''(x^o) = \begin{pmatrix} I \\ -B^{-1}N \end{pmatrix}^T (\varphi''(X^o) - uf''(X^o))\begin{pmatrix} I \\ -B^{-1}N \end{pmatrix}$$

where $uf''(X^o)$ means the sum of the square matrices $u_i f''_i(X^o)$. Near the optimum, u will not change very much, so we consider it as a constant, even when we change basis (this may not be true far from the optimum). The rows of the matrix $B^{-1}N$ are indexed

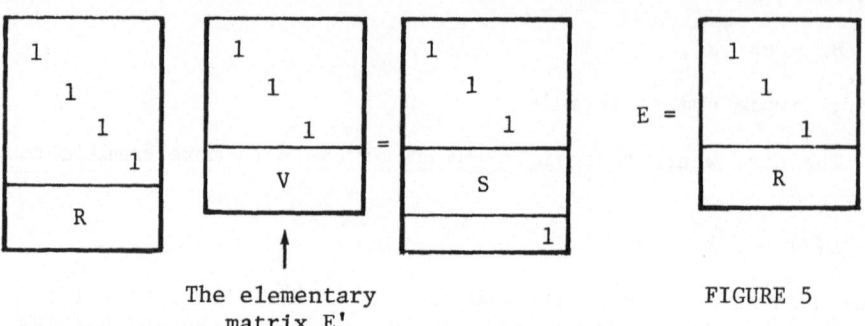

The elementary
matrix E'

FIGURE 4

FIGURE 5

as the columns of B, i.e., the row indices of P are the basis
indices. Suppose row R of -P (index r) is to leave the basis,
to be replaced by some row S (index s). This can be done, using
a row-elementary matrix E' as a right multiplier (see Figure 4).
The matrix multiplication shows that, in fact, V = S, from which
follows that the inverse E of E' is as exhibited in Figure 5.

Finally, the new inverse hessian $\tilde{H}$ is related to the previous
inverse hessian H by the formula

$$\tilde{H} = EHE^T,$$

where the row R of E is $-\beta_r N$, already computed when seeking a
pivot in row r (see details of COB), while the other rows of E
are unit rows.

This updating formula should be used with great care if the
point under consideration is not close to the optimum, because
the lagrange multipliers u depends on the basis, and $\varphi''(x^0)$
$- uf''(x^0)$ consequently changes with the basis (a notable
exception is the case of linear constraints).

7. FINAL REMARK AND CONCLUSION

Let us call degree of freedom of an optimization problem,
assumed to have a unique solution, the number of variables which
are not at some bounds (in the standard form, slacks included)
minus the number of equations. If the degree of freedom is zero,
the optimal solution is, so to speak, at a vertex (as is usually
the case in linear programming). For this kind of problem, I am
not sure that conjugate gradients or variable metric methods make
any difference. Even an ordinary pure straight gradient might be
sufficiently quick. At the other extreme are problems with hundreds or thousands of degrees of freedom. In my opinion, this is
where the GRG method helps. Imagine a problem currently solved
in the utility industry, the Optimal Power Flow Problem quoted at

the beginning of this paper. This problem usually has 500 non-linear equations, 1000 variables, plus side constraints. If treated by a penalty method, or an augmented lagrangian method, the underlying unconstrained optimization has a degree of freedom of 1000. Using GRG, it cannot be more than 1000 minus 500, i.e., 500, and this has to be diminished by the number of variables at some bound, and by the number of tight side inequality constraints, leaving a small degree of freedom, and, at peak hours, a very small one.

The GRG concept has been useful in solving problems of small to very large size, the latter for special problems with special coding. Some general code already exists for a large class of economic models, and some general codes for large sparse nonlinear problems are being developed. They will certainly prove useful for problems with a small to moderately large degree of freedom.

REFERENCES

1. J. Abadie and J. Carpentier, "Generalisation de la méthode du gradient réduit de Wolfe au cas de contraintes non-linéaires," Note HR6678, Electricité de France, Paris, Octobre 1965.

2. J. Abadie and J. Carpentier, "Generalization of the Wolfe Reduced Gradient Method to the Case of Nonlinear Constraints," in: Optimization, R. Fletcher (ed.), Academic Press, London and New York, pp. 37-47, 1969.

3. A.R. Colville, "A Comparitive Study of Nonlinear Programming Codes," IBM New York Scientific Center Report 320-2949, 1968.

4. J. Abadie and J. Guigou, "Gradient réduit généralisé, Note HI069, Electricité de France, Paris, April 1969.

5. J. Guigou, "Présentation et utilisation du code GRG," Note HI102, Electricité de France, Paris, June 1969.

6. R. Fletcher and C.M. Reeves, "Function Minimization by Conjugate Gradients," Computer J. 7, 149-154, 1964.

7. A.R. Colville, "Non-linear Programming Study Results as of June 1970," private circulation.

8. A.R. Colville, "A Comparative Study on Nonlinear Programming Codes," in: Proceedings of the Prineceton Symposium on Mathematical Programming, H.W. Kuhn (ed.), Princeton University Press, Princeton, N.J., 1970.

9. J. Guigou, "Présentation et utilisation du code GREG," Note HI582, Electricité de France, Paris, May 1971.

10. J. Abadie, "Méthode du Gradient Réduit Géneralisé: le code GRGA," Note HI1756, Electricité de France, Paris, February 1975.

11. Amr. H., Haggag, "Etudes d'algorithmes d'optimisation non linéaires: une variante de GRGA" Thèse de Docteur-Ingènieur, CNRS No. TD493, G-12-76, Université Pierre et Marie Curie, Paris, 1976.

12. D.R. Heltne and Liittschwager, "Users' Guide for GRG73," The University of Iowa, Iowa City, September 1973.

13. D.R. Heltne, "Technical Appendices to GRG 73," The University of Iowa, Iowa City, September 1973.

14. G.A. Gabrielle and K.M. Ragsdell, "The Generalized Reduced Gradient Method: A Reliable Tool for Optimal Design," ASME Publication 75-DET-103, June 1975.

15. L.S. Lasdon, A.D. Waren, M.W. Ratner, A. Jain, "GRG System Documentation," Technical Memorandum CIS-75-01, Computer and Information Science Department, Cleveland State University, Cleveland, Ohio, November 1975.

16. L.S. Lasdon, A.D. Waren, M.W. Ratner, A. Jain, "GRG User's Guide," Technical Memorandum CIS-75-02, Computer and Information Science Department, Cleveland State Univeristy, Cleveland, Ohio, November 1975.

17. A. Jain, "The Solution of Nonlinear Programs using the Generalized Reduced Gradient Method," Technical Report SOL 76-6, Systems Optimization Laboratory, Department of Operations Research, Stanford University, March 1976.

18. L.S. Lasdon, R.L. Fox, and M.W. Ratner, "Nonlinear Optimization Using the Generalized Reduced Gradient Method," Revue Française d'Automatique, Informatique et Recherche Operationnelle, RAIRO, No. V3, November 1974, 73-103.

19. L.S. Lasdon and A.D. Waren, "Generalized Reduced Gradient Software for Linearly and Nonlinearly Constrained Problems," this Proceedings, 1977.

20. J. Peschon and N.M. Peterson, "Optimization and Simulation Computations in Advanced Energy Control Centers for Electric Power Utilities," in: Proceedings - XX International Meeting, The Institute of Management Sciences, E. Shlifer, Y.E. Orgler, and R. Joffe (eds.), Jerusalem Academic Press, 1973, Vol. I, pp. 138-143.

21. A. Drud, "Methods for Control of Complex Dynamic Systems," IMSOR Publication NR. 27, The Institute of Mathematical Statistics and Operations Research, The Technical University of Denmark, Lyngby, Denmark, 1976.

22. J. Abadie, "Application of the GRG Algorithm to Optimal Control Problems," Ch. 8 in: Integer and Nonlinear Programming, J. Abadie (ed.), North-Holland Publishing Company, Amsterdam, 1970.

23. J. Abadie, "Optimization Problems with Coupled Blocks," Economic Computation and Economic Cybernetrics Studies and Research, Bucharest, 1970, No. 4, pp. 5-26.

24. J. Abadie and M. Bichara, "Résolution de certains problemes de commande optimale," RAIRO, No. V2, May 1973, pp. 77-105.

25. E.M.L. Beale, "Nonlinear Programming Using a General Mathematical Programming System," this Proceedings, 1977.

26. C.R. Gagnon, R.H. Hicks, S.L.S. Jacoby, J.S. Kowalik, "A Nonlinear Programming Approach to a Very Large Hydroelectric System Optimization," Math Programming, 6, 1974, pp. 28-41.

27. P. Wolfe, "Methods of Nonlinear Programming," in: Recent Advances in Mathematical Programming, Graves and Wolfe (eds.), McGraw-Hill, New York, 1963, pp. 67-86.

28. P. Wolfe, "Methods for Nonlinear Constraints," in: Nonlinear Programming, J. Abadie (ed.), North-Holland Publishing Company, Amsterdam, 1967, pp. 97-131.

29. R.H. Bartels and G.H. Golub, "The Simplex Method of Linear Programming Using LU Decomposition," Comm. ACM, 12, 1969, pp. 266-268.

30. B. Murtagh and M. Saunders, "Nonlinear Programming for Large Sparse Systems," Technical Report SOL 76-15, Systems Optimization Laboratory, Department of Operations Research, Stanford University, August 1976.

31. E.M.L. Beale and R. Benveniste, "Quadratic Programming," this Proceedings, 1977.

32. J. Abadie, "Solution des questions de dégénérescence dans la méthode GRG," Note HI 143, Electricité de France, Paris, September 1969.

33. R.K. Mehra and R.E. Davis, "A Generalized Gradient Method for Optimal Control Problems with Inequality Constraints and Singular Arcs," 1971 Joint Automatic Control Conference, St. Louis, Missouri, August 11-13, 1971.

34. D.H. Jacobson and M.M. Lele, "A Transformation Technique for Optimal Control Problems with a State Variable Inequality Constraint," IEEE Transactions AC-14, Vol. 5, 1969, 457-464.

35. D. Kendrick and L. Taylor, "A Dynamic Nonlinear Planning Model for Korea," in: Practical Approaches to Development Planning, I. Adelman (ed.), The Johns Hopkins Press, Baltimore, Maryland, 1969.

36. D. Kendrick and L. Taylor, "Numerical Solutions of Nonlinear Planning Models," Econometrica, 38, 1970, pp. 453-467.

37. D.E. Dennis and J.J. Moré, "Quasi-Newton Methods, Motivation and Theory," SIAM Review 19, No. 1, 1977, pp. 46-89.

362

38. L.C.W. Dixon, "The Choice of Steplength, a Crucial Factor in the Performance of Variable Metric Algorithms," in: <u>Numerical Methods for Nonlinear Optimization</u>, F.A. Lootsma (ed.), Academic Press, London, 1972.

39. L.C.W. Dixon, "Nonlinear Optimization: A Survey of the State of the Art," in: <u>Software for Numerical Mathematics</u>, D. Evans (ed.), Academic Press, London, 1974.

40. R. Fletcher, "A New Approach to Variable Metric Algorithms," <u>The Computer Journal</u> 13, No. 3, 1970, pp. 317-322.

GENERALIZED REDUCED GRADIENT SOFTWARE FOR LINEARLY AND NONLINEARLY
CONSTRAINED PROBLEMS

L.S. Lasdon and A.D. Waren

Operations Research Department, Case Western Reserve
University, Cleveland, Ohio

Department of Computer and Information Science,
Cleveland State University, Cleveland, Ohio   44115

1.   INTRODUCTION

Generalized Reduced Gradient (GRG) algorithms for nonlinearly
constrained problems were first developed by Abadie [1]-[2] who
also designed the first GRG software. Recently a number of other
versions of GRG have been developed and implemented, [16]-[17].

This paper discusses three such versions and describes their
FORTRAN software implementations. These are GRG2, developed by
Lasdon, Waren et. al., for general nonlinear problems; MINOS,
developed by Murtagh and Saunders, for large sparse linearly con-
strained problems [3]; and LSGRG, developed by Lasdon, Jain and
Saunders, for large sparse, nonlinearly constrained problems.

Section two of this paper briefly describes GRG algorithms,
primarily from the point of view of the three implementations
mentioned above. In section three a summary of desirable features
for general NLP software is presented. The last three sections are
each devoted to one of the above GRG codes. They provide more
detailed information on software implementation and present some
computational results.

2.   BRIEF DESCRIPTION OF GRG ALGORITHMS

GRG algorithms are designed to solve problems of the following general form:

Problem P1

$$\text{Minimize } f(x)$$

subject to

$$g(x) = b$$

$$lb \leq h(x) \leq ub$$

$$1 \leq x \leq u$$

where x is a vector of n variables, f is the objective function, g is a vector of m equality constraint functions, h is a vector of p inequality constraint functions and 1,u,lb,ub are vectors of lower and upper bounds.

By introducing appropriate slack variables, the inequality constraints can be converted to equalities. In addition, since a central feature of GRG algorithms is their approach to handling equalities, the remainder of this section will deal with the following specific problem:

$$\text{minimize } f(x) \tag{1}$$

subject to $\qquad\qquad\qquad g(x) = 0 \tag{2}$

$$1 \leq x \leq u \tag{3}$$

There are many possible GRG algorithms. Their underlying concepts are described in reference [4]. This section briefly describes the version currently implemented in GRG2 and LSGRG and, to some extent, MINOS.

GRG algorithms use the m equality constraints (2) to solve for m of the variables, called the basic variables as in L.P., in terms of the remaining n-m nonbasic variables. Denoting the basic and nonbasic variables as x_b and x_{nb} respectively, the constraint equations become

$$g(x_b, x_{nb}) = 0.$$

The Jacobian matrix of g may be similarly partitioned as

$$\frac{\partial g}{\partial x} = \left(\frac{\partial g}{\partial x_b} , \frac{\partial g}{\partial x_{nb}} \right) = (B, B_{nb}) \tag{4}$$

where, for simplicity, the variables are assumed renumbered so the basics are the first m components of x.

Let $\bar{x}$ be the current feasible point (i.e., satisfies constraints (2) and (3)). Then the specific variables to be chosen as the basic variables must be selected so that B, evaluated at $\bar{x}$, is nonsingular. In this case the constraints (2) can be solved (at least conceptually) for x_b in terms of x_{nb} to yield the basics as a function of the nonbasics, $x_b(x_{nb})$. This representation is valid for all x_{nb} sufficiently near $\bar{x}_{nb}$. The objective function is then reduced to a function of x_{nb} only,

$$f(x_b(x_{nb}), x_{nb}) = F(x_{nb}) \tag{5}$$

and the original problem (1) - (3) (at least in the neighborhood of $\bar{x}$) is transformed to a simpler <u>reduced problem</u>

$$\text{minimize } F(x_{nb})$$

subject to the bounds on x_{nb}. The function F is called the <u>reduced objective</u> and its gradient ∇F the <u>reduced gradient</u>.

GRG algorithms solve the original problem (1) - (3) by solving (perhaps only partially) a seqence of reduced problems, which are usually solved by a gradient method. At a given iteration, with nonbasic variables x_{nb} and basic variables $\bar{x}_b$, the reduced gradient is computed as follows:

(a) Solve $\quad B^t \Pi = \partial f / \partial x_b \tag{6}$

for the simplex multiplier vector Π;

(b) Compute the reduced gradient

$$\frac{\partial F}{\partial x_{nb}} = \frac{\partial f}{\partial x_{nb}} - \Pi^t B_{nb} \tag{6a}$$

Note that all partial derivatives are evaluated at the current point $\bar{x}$

Following Saunders [3] the nonbasic variables are further partitioned into s superbasic variables, x_s, which are strictly between their bounds and n-m-s remaining nonbasic variables, x_n, which are at one of their bounds. In the codes discussed here, the reduced gradient with respect to the nonbasic variables, $\partial F / \partial x_n$, is used only to determine if one of these variables should be released from a bound to join the superbasic set. This decision can be made at each iteration, as in GRG2, or after an optimization over the current superbasics, x_s, is completed, as in MINOS and LSCRC. In either case, the reduced gradient with respect to the current superbasics, $\partial F / \partial x_s$, is used to form a search direction, d. Both conjugate gradient and variable metric methods have been used to determine $\bar{d}$. Then a one dimensional search is initiated, whose goal is to solve the problem

$$\underset{\alpha \geq 0}{\text{minimize }} F(\bar{x}_{nb} + \alpha d)$$

In the above $\bar{d}$ has been extended to include zero components for the non-basics at bounds. This minimization is done only approximately, and is accomplished by choosing a sequence of positive values $\{\alpha_1, \alpha_2, \ldots,\}$ for α. For each value α_i, $F(\bar{x}_{nb} + \alpha_i \bar{d})$ must be evaluated. By (5), this is equal to

$$f(x_b(\bar{x}_{nb} + \alpha_i \bar{d}), \bar{x}_{nb} + \alpha_i \bar{d})$$

so the basic variables $x_b(\bar{x}_{nb} + \alpha_i \bar{d})$ must be determined. These satisfy the system of equations

$$g(x_b, \bar{x}_{nb} + \alpha_i \bar{d}) = 0$$

where $\bar{x}_{nb}$, α_i, and $\bar{d}$ are known and x_b is to be found. If x_b appears non-linearly in any constraint then this system must be solved by an iterative procedure. Usually, a variant of Newton's method is used.

In the case of nonlinear constraints, the one dimensional search can terminate in three different ways. First, Newton's method may not converge. If this occurs on the first step, α_1 is reduced and we try again. Otherwise, the search is terminated. Second, if the Newton method converges, some basic variables may be in violation of their bounds. Then the codes discussed here determine a new α value such that at least one such variable is at its bound and all others are within their bounds. If, at this new point, the objective is less than at all previous points, the one dimensional search is terminated. A new set of basic variables is determined and solution of a new reduced problem begins. Finally, the search may continue until an objective value is found which is larger than the previous value. Then a quadratic is fit to the three α_i values bracketing the minimum. F is evaluated at the minimum of this quadratic, and the search terminates with the lowest F value found. The reduced problem remains the same.

An important feature of this algorithm is its attempt to re-turn to the constraint surface at each step in the one dimensional search. This differs from earlier strategies suggested by Abadie [1] and by Luenberger [5], which involve linear searches on the tangent plane to the constraint surface prior to returning to that surface. We have not experimented with such strategies, choosing to return to the surface each time because it was simpler and we felt it would lead to a more reliable algorithm. Computational experience presented later shows that, if properly implemented, this strategy can be developed into an algorithm that is both reliable and efficient.

3. DESIRABLE FEATURES OF NLP SOFTWARE

This section lists what we believe to be desirable features of NLP software. The problem to be solved is in the form of P1 (see first page of section 2), and the features were compiled with all-FORTRAN software in mind, although many are desirable independent of the programming language used. Later sections discuss the various GRG codes in terms of these features.

3.1 Input Features

(a) Ability to assign names to variables and constraints. This helps interpretation of solution output and can highlight critical variables or constraints.

(b) Ability to specify the type for each problem function and variable, independently of their order. Function types are: objective, equality, lower bounded, upper bounded, both upper and lower bounded and function to be ignored. Variable types are: free, fixed, and bounded as above. If bound values for each constraint can also be specified independently then constraints can be deleted, added, or modified, and the objective can be changed all without affecting the subroutine(s) used to compute function values. Given similar flexibility for variables, many variations of a given problem may be run with little effort, a mode of use which dominates in practice.

(c) Only one mandatory user provided subroutine which computes the values of the problem functions. If derivatives are needed then the system should provide an option to compute them automatically using numerical differencing or to use a user provided subroutine. The coding of subroutines for first partial derivatives can be time consuming and error prone. Second derivatives are worse, often almost impossible. Of course, if a well coded subroutine for evaluating analytic derivatives is available, much computing time can be saved since advantage can be taken of terms common to the various functions and their derivatives. Clearly any constant partial derivative terms need be computed only once. Wolfe [6] indicates that such methods usually reduce the time required to compute all partial derivatives from n times t_f (this is needed for forward differencing, where t_f is the time to evaluate the functions) to k times t_f, with $1 \leqq k \leqq 3$. We have seen examples where k has been significantly less than 1.

368

(d) A run time revise capability, allowing modification of some problem data after the given problem has been solved, but leaving all the rest unchanged. Such a facility permits a sequence of different problems to be solved in one run.

(e) Error checking and direct echo back of all input data.

(f) An input deck divided into sections, each section with a header card and an END card and with most sections optional. This also helps in checking input data.

(g) Default values for all controllable program tolerances and parameters, as well as for all problem data for which these seem reasonable. This minimizes input from the occasional user and yet retains, for the sophisticated user, a high degree of control enabling "tuning" for the specific application.

3.2 Output Features

(a) Tabular formats for output of initial data and final solution information. MPS output formats are a good example. This allows easy inspection of output for large problem.

(b) Multiple print levels, to facilitate both production and debugging runs.

(c) Dump and restart capabilities, to facilitate long runs, and recovery from error conditions.

(d) Availability of a periodic detailed print for every kth iteration.

(e) Ability to change print levels after a specified number of iterations.

(f) Availability of an option for checking any user provided analytic derivative computations.

3.3 Ease of Use Features

(a) Well documented at both the user and system level.

(b) Easy to use as part of a larger system.

(c) Minimal storage requirements.

(d) Dynamic storage allocation - code contains at most a few arrays that must be dimensioned by the user, depending on problem size. All working and data arrays are stored in these. This permits solution of small problems using only the storage needed, while placing no limit on the size of the problem that can be accommodated except for the amount of core available.

(e) Machine independent – requires no or minimal modification to run on machines of various vendors.

3.4 Problem Solving Capabilities

(a) Ability to solve unconstrained problems efficiently, with or without bounds on the variables.

(b) Finite termination for quadratic programs, and enhanced efficiency for the linear constraint case.

(c) Capable of handling nonlinear equality constraints efficiently.

(d) Able to start from feasible or infeasible starting points, and to generate a sequence of improved feasible points once feasible

(e) Deals with bounds on the variables separately, i.e., without counting them as g_i constraints.

(f) Capable of handling large sparse problems efficiently by exploiting sparsity.

(g) Fast and robust.

4. DESCRIPTION OF GRG2

4.1 Overview

GRG2 is a revision of an earlier version [4], over 50 copies of which have been distributed. The current version incorporates all of the input and output features listed in section 3. In terms of problem solving capabilities, only feature (f) is absent (but LSGRG has this feature).

This code is composed of a main program and a number of subroutines, written in FORTRAN IV. A diagram of the major subroutine structure is shown below in Figure 1.

The function of Main is to dimension the 1-dimensional array, z, in which all working and data arrays are stored, and to call GRG. The functions of the remaining subroutines are listed in Table 1.

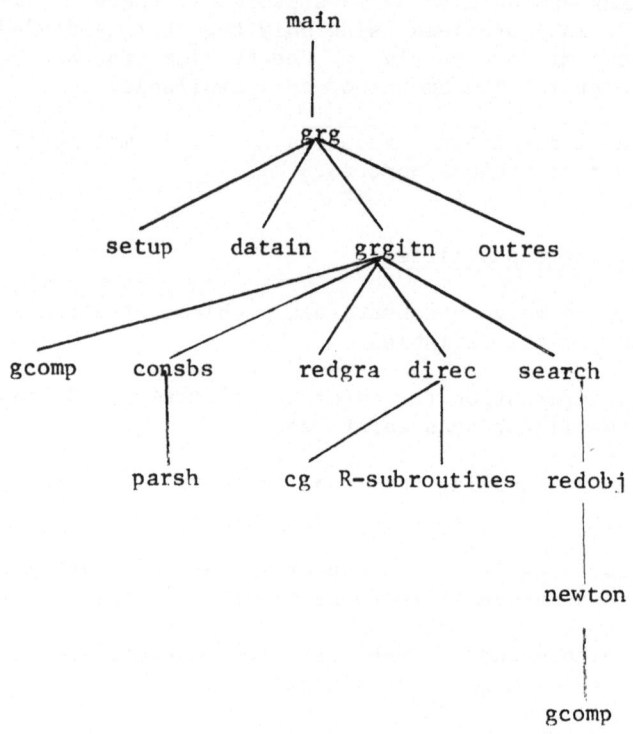

Figure 1: SUBROUTINE STRUCTURE OF GRG2

1.	SETUP	Computes addresses of all data and working arrays within the z array, using problem dimensions read in prior to call.
2.	DATAIN	Reads input data.
3.	OUTRES	Prints solution results.
4.	GRGITN	Controls main iterative loop. Computes initial basis inverse and calls DIREC to compute search direction. Calls one dimensional search subroutine SEARCH. Tests for optimality.
5.	CONSBS	Computes Basis Inverse, BINV.
6.	PARSH	Given current X and G vectors, computes array GRAD, whose (i,j) element is the

partial derivative of g_i with respect to x_j. May be user supplied. If not, there is a system subroutine PARSH which computes GRAD by forward difference approximation.

7.	REDGRA	Given BINV and GRAD, computes Lagrange multiplier vector π, and reduced gradient of either phase I or phase II objectives, GRADF.
8.	DIREC	Computes search direction.
9.	R-SUBROUTINES	These update an upper triangular matrix R, where $R^T R$ is an approximation to the Hessian matrix $\partial^2 F/\partial x_s^2$.
10.	CG	Computes search direction d using one of several conjugate gradient methods.
11.	SEARCH	Performs one dimensional search.
12.	REDOBJ	Computes values of basic variables for given values of nonbasics by calling NEWTON. Takes action if NEWTON does not converge. Checks for constraint violations. If any are violated, finds feasible point where some initially violated constraint is binding and others satisfied.
13.	NEWTON	Uses Newton's Method to compute values of basic variables for given value of nonbasics. If convergence not achieved, sets flag and returns.
14.	GCOMP	User supplied subroutine. Given current X vector, computes vector of m function values G, one of which is the objective, the others constraints.

Table 1: FUNCTIONS OF MAJOR GRG2 SUBROUTINES

The following sections describe the most important of these subroutines.

4.2 Subroutine GRGITN

GRGITN starts by calling GCOMP to evaluate the initial constraint and objective values. If any constraints are violated, a phase I procedure is entered in which the objective is the sum of absolute values of constraint violations. Then the basis inverse B^{-1}, and the reduced gradient, ∇F, are computed.

The current x is considered optimal if either of two tests is met. The first test checks if the Kuhn-Tucker optimality conditions are satisfied to within EPSTOP, a small positive number which can be controlled by the user, with default value 10^{-4}. The second optimality test checks if the fractional change in the objective is less than EPSTOP for NSTOP consecutive iterations. NSTOP has a default value of 3.

If x is not optimal, a search direction, d, is generated, and the tangent vector, v, corresponding to d is computed, using the formula

$$v = B^{-1}B_{nb}d.$$

The vector v contains the directional derivatives of the basic variables in the direction d. After computing v, a CHUZR subroutine is called, an implementation of Paula Harris' CHUZR, which computes the largest step that can be taken in the direction d before any basic variable violates a bound, assuming that all variables change linearly with derivatives v. If this step is judged to be too small, the current basis is termed degenerate. Subroutine CHUZQ then selects a superbasic variable which can replace one of the basic variables which is threatening to violate a bound. A pivot operation is performed to accomplish this change of basis, and control is transferred to REDGRA to recompute the reduced gradient. Note that the variables are unchanged in such a degenerate iteration. Both subroutines CHUZR and CHUZQ were obtained through the courtesy of Michael Saunders, and are minor modifications of corresponding subroutines in MINOS.

If the basis is not degenerate then, after computing the search direction d, the one dimensional search subroutine is called. If the search finds an improved point, a new iteration is started. If the search fails, a sequence of actions is attempted. These are: (1) set $d = -\partial F/\partial x_{nb}$, (2) release from its bound some nonbasic variable whose reduced gradient component indicates it wants to leave. If both fail, the program stops with appropriate error messages.

GRG2 is designed to solve small to medium size, dense, highly nonlinear problems. Hence, all elements of the basis matrix may change as x changes. For this reason, the basis is reinverted after each line search, rather than updated, and the inversion routine, CONSBS, has a free choice of which variables to use as basic variables. Further, if the number of currently binding constraints is nb, the basis inverse formed is only of dimension nb. This corresponds to a suggestion of Abadie's in [2], where slack variables of inactive constraints are excluded from the basic set.

In the remainder of this section, the basic variables are renamed y and the nonbasics x. This simplifies the notation considerably.

4.3 Subroutine DIREC

DIREC computes the search direction d. If the number of superbasic variables is less than a user supplied value (default value n), d is computed using a variable metric algorithm [7]. Otherwise, a conjugate gradient method is used.

The variable metric algorithm in GRG2 updates an approximation to the Hessian $\partial^2 F/\partial x^2$ rather than its inverse. Further, again following Murtaugh and Saunders [3], this approximate Hessian is maintained in facorized form, i.e., as $R^T R$, where R is an upper triangular matrix. The updating formula used is the complementary DFP formula:

$$\bar{R}^T\bar{R} = R^T R + \frac{1}{ah^T d} hh^T + \frac{1}{g^T d} gg^T$$

In the above, R and $\bar{R}$ are the previous and updated matrices respectively, h is the change in $\partial F/\partial x$ in the last one dimensional search, α is the step size determined by the search, and g is $\partial F/\partial x$ at the start of the search.

To insure stability, all modifications to R are implemented using elementary orthogonal matrices (plane rotations). The 2 subroutines used, obtained through the courtesy of Michael Saunders, are:

$$\text{R1ADD:} \quad \bar{R}^T\bar{R} = R^T R + zz^T$$

$$\text{R1SUB:} \quad \bar{R}^T\bar{R} = R^T R - zz^T.$$

These use forward and backward sweeps of plant rotations respectively, as described in [8].

The alternative of using a conjugate gradient (CG) method was added to deal with problems with many superbasic variables, where the dimension of the (dense) matrix R may require excessive storage. CG methods require storage of at most a few vectors of dimension equal to the number of superbasics. Five variants have been included in a subroutine CG (again implemented by Saunders).

These include formulas due to Fletcher and Reeves [9], Polak and
Ribiere [10], Perry [11], and two derived as 1-step versions of
the DFP and complementary DFP variable metric formulas.

Subroutine DIREC must deal with the possibility that a superbasic variable may have hit a bound during the previous linesearch.
If so, and a CG method is being used, the CG method is restarted
(d is set to $-\partial F/\partial x$). If the variable metric method is being
used, R can be modified by deleting the appropriate column, and
transforming the resulting matrix back to upper triangular form
(see [3] for details). If a new superbasic variable is added by
releasing a nonbasic variable from its bound, a unit vector column
is added to R. The logic for releasing a nonbasic variable from
its bound is as prescribed by Goldfarb, in [12].

If the set of basic variables and/or binding constraints, as
determined by CONSBS, is not the same as at the previous iteration,
DIREC resets R to the identity matrix. By contrast, MINOS is able
to update R in this situation, since its constraints are linear
and the basis changes by replacing a single basic column by a
superbasic one.

Note that both the CG and the variable metric methods minimize
quadratic functions in as many line searches as there are variables.
Hence, assuming only a finite number of basis changes, GRG2 is finite
for quadratic programs (as are the other 2 GRG codes discussed here).

4.4 Subroutine SEARCH

This subroutine finds an approximation to a first local minimum
for the problem

$$\text{minimize } F(\bar{x} + \alpha\bar{d})$$
$$\alpha$$

where d is always a direction of descent. It searches for three
α values, A, B and C which satisfy

$$0 \leq A < B < C$$

$$F(\bar{x} + A\bar{d}) \geq F(\bar{x} + B\bar{d}) \leq F(\bar{x} + C\bar{d})$$

Then the interval [A,C] contains a local minimum of $F(\bar{x} + \alpha\bar{d})$. A
quadratic in α is passed through A, B, and C, with its minimum at D.
The best point, B or D, is taken as an estimate of the optimal α
and a return is made. The initial step size is determined in a
similar way to that described in [4]. SEARCH then operates in two
phases, halving the initial step size (if necessary) until an improved point is found, or doubling the step size until the minimum
is bracketed. In each phase the nonbasic variables are changed,
and subroutine REDOBJ is called to compute the reduced objective F.

The search is terminated if REDOBJ produces an improved point at which either a basic variable or a previously loose constraint is at a bound.

SEARCH must also deal with the possibility that the Newton algorithm may fail to converge. If so, and an improved point has already been found, the search is terminated; otherwise the step size is halved. The search is also terminated, at an improved point, if more than 6 Newton iterations were required to evaluate that point. Experience has shown that the next NEWTON call usually will not converge.

The strategy of terminating the search if an improved point has already been found and Newton did not converge or took too many iterations was not adopted initially. Earlier versions of the code attempted to push on with the line search by recomputing B^{-1} at the last feasible point found and cutting the step taken to 1/3 its previous value. The current strategy has been found to be much superior. Now B^{-1} is computed only once, at the beginning of each one dimensional search, where it is needed any way to comput ∇F. In a set of six test problems, the current strategy required about half the function and gradient evaluations of the older one (see [4] for details), and also significantly reduced the number of times B^{-1} is evaluated. This strategy plus a rather conservative choice of initial step size, plays a large part in making an algorithm which returns to the constraint surface each time efficient.

Recently, much interest has been expressed in "step size" algorithms [13] - [14] to replace the line search. These attempt to obtain only a "sufficient" decrease in the objective, rather than to find its minimum. We have opted for a "sloppy" attempt to find the minimum because of its "inside-out" nature, i.e., a small initial step is taken, then increased if necessary. This approach is more likely to remain within the radius of convergence of Newton's method, viz., that range of α values for which Newton will converge, with B^{-1} evaluated only at $\alpha = 0$. This radius imposes an upper bound on α of unknown value. Most step-size strategies choose large α values first (e.g., $\alpha = 1$ in [15]), then reduce them if necessary, and hence are more likely to exceed this bound. The fact that the number of Newton iterations required to evaluate $F(x + \alpha d)$ increases as α increases also works against "outside-in" strategies. These same comments also apply to algorithms which do a one dimensional search on the tangent plane to the constraints prior to returning to the constraint surface, as in [16] - [17], and [5].

4.5 Subroutine REDOBJ

This subroutine evaluates the reduced objective function $F(x + \alpha d)$ for given x, α, and d. It does so by attempting to solve the system of nb (possibly nonlinear) equations

$$g_i(y, \bar{x} + \alpha\bar{d}) = 0 \qquad i \in IBC \tag{7}$$

for the nb basic variables y, where IBC is the index set of binding constraints. As in [1] and [2], this is accomplished in subroutine NEWTON, using the pseudo-Newton algorithm

$$y_i^{k+1} = y_i^k - B^{-1}(\bar{X}) g_B(y_i^k, x_i) \qquad k = 0,1,2,\ldots \tag{8}$$

where

$$x_i = \bar{x} + \alpha_i \bar{d}, \qquad\qquad \alpha_0 = 0$$

$$y_i = y(x_i)$$

$$X_i = (y_i, x_i), \quad X_0 \equiv \bar{X}$$

and g_B is the vector of binding constraints. Note that y_i^k is the kth estimate of y_i. The algorithm is called pseudo-Newton because B^{-1} is evaluated once at the initial point of the search, $\bar{X}$, instead of being reevaluated at each step of the algorithm, as in the standard Newton Method.

An initial estimate of the basic variables, y_i^0 is computed either by linear or quadratic extrapolation. As in [1], the linear extrapolation uses the tangent vector

$$v = -B^{-1} \left(\frac{\partial g}{\partial x} \right) \bar{d} \tag{9}$$

In our code, v is computed at $\bar{X}$. It is used to find initial values, y_1 by the formula

$$y_1^0 = y_0 + \alpha_1 v \tag{9a}$$

Using these initial values, Newton finds the feasible point X_1. Then, at X_1, v is not recomputed. The old v is used, but emanating now from X_1, to yield the next set of initial values as

$$y_2^0 = y_1 + (\alpha_2 - \alpha_1)v$$

Using these, Newton finds a new point X_2. This procedure is repeated until the one dimensional search is over.

Quadratic extrapolation may also be used to obtain initial estimates of the basic variables, at the user option. Initially, linear extrapolation is used. After the first feasible point, X_1, is found, quadratic functions are fit to the value and slope at $\alpha = 0$, and the value at α_1 of each basic variable. These are used to predict their values at $\alpha = a_2$. Subsequent quadratics are fit to the values of the basic variables at α_i, a_{i-1}, α_{i-2} ($i \overset{\geq}{=} 2$).

Newton is considered to have converged if the condition

$$\text{NORMG} = \max_{i \in \text{IBC}} |g_i(X_t)| < \varepsilon$$

is met within ITLIM iterations. Currently $\varepsilon = 10^{-4}$ and ITLIM = 10. If NORMG has not decreased from its previous value (or the above condition is not met in 10 iterations) Newton has not converged.

Once Newton has converged, possible constraint violations must be checked. There are several reasons why the current step α may be too large;

1) A strictly satisfied constraint may have violated an upper or lower bound.

2) A constraint in IABOVE, the set of constraints initially violating their upper bounds, may violate a lower bound.

3) A constraint in IBELOW may violate an upper bound.

4) A basic variable may violate a lower or upper bound.

If any of these cases hold, α is reduced to a value α^* where no constraints are violated and at least one new constraint is equal to a bound. To determine this constraint, an estimate is made of α^*, using linear interpolation between the current and previous values of the violated constraints.

The next step determines whether case 4 or one of cases 1-3 is to be dealt with, according to which has the smallest linear estimate of $*$. Assuming case 1-3 as an example, we then wish to solve the system

$$g_i(y(\alpha), \bar{x} + \alpha\bar{d}) = 0. \qquad i \in \text{IBC}$$

$$g_L(y(\alpha), \bar{x} + \alpha\bar{d}) = 0.$$

(10)

where α is a new variable and $g_L = 0$ a new equation. This system is solved by the same Pseudo-Newton method used to solve for the basic variables. The Jacobian for this system is

$$J = \left[\begin{array}{c|c} B & c \\ \hline d & w \end{array} \right]$$

where

$$d = \partial g_L / \partial y$$

$$w = (_\partial g_L /_\partial x)^T d$$

and c is an nb component column vector whose elements are $(\partial g_i / \partial x)^T d$. Newton iterations with J as coefficient matrix are easily carried out, since B^{-1} is known.

The basis change procedure here, based on solving (10) and then calling CONSBS, differs from that of Abadie in [1] and [2]. In Abadie's procedure the basic variables y_i^k in (8) are checked for each k. If any violate their bounds, one is selected to leave the basis, an entering variable is chosen, and a pivot operation updates B^{-1}. The Newton iteration (8) then continues. This could lead to "false" basis changes, since violation of a bound during the iterative process does not imply violation when the process converges. Newton's method need not converge componentwise monotonically. Failure to converge could also lead to a false basis change. In addition, if the (Abadie) basis change is accomplished, the new point may have an objective value larger than $F(\overline{x})$, which makes proof of convergence unlikely. Our procedure avoids both these objections, perhaps at the expense of slightly more computation. We feel that the (presumed) increase in reliability makes the extra work worthwhile.

4.6 Subroutine CONSB

This subroutine selects a set of basic variables and computes the basis inverse, B^{-1}. A call to PARSH computes the gradients of the objective and all constraints at the current point. The gradients of the binding constraints are stored in the same array where the pivoting to compute B^{-1} is done. This entire tableau is transformed by each pivot.

Pivot elements in this tableau are determined as follows. After each pivot, for each unpivoted column, the element of largest absolute value in its unpivoted rows is determined, and the maximum of all these elements, MAXELT, is computed. The pivot column is then chosen as that unpivoted column whose associated variable is farthest from its nearest bound, subject to the constraint that its largest element is greater than or equal to r*MAXELT, $0 < r < 1$. The current value for r is 0.1. The pivot is then made in the largest unpivoted element of this column.

Computational Results

At the time this paper is written (May, 1977), computational testing of GRG2 is not yet complete. Preliminary results indicate that it is from slightly to moderately faster than its predecessor, GRG, (described in [4]), and more robust. Computational results of this latter code on the 24 problems specified in appendix A of [18]* are shown in table 2. All problems were solved on an IBM 370/145 at Cleveland State University.

In this table, the Newton Average is the total number of iterations of the quasi-Newton method (see section 4.5) divided by the number of times solution of a nonlinear system was attempted, i.e, the number of calls to subroutine NEWTON. The Colville standard time is obtained by dividing the execution times by 77.83, the time in seconds required to run the Colville standard timing program (see [18]) on the 370/145. These numbers provide some means (admittedly imperfect) for other investigators, using different computers, to compare results.

GRG solved all problems (number 21 needed scaling) in the sense that at least a local minimum was found. In all but two of the problems (6 and 14) the final objective values attained by GRG starting with the initial points specified in [18] either matched the solutions specified in [18], to at least one part in one thousand, or were better than the solutions given it.

In problem number 6, using the starting point specified in [18], GRG reached a point with function value -1865.98 compared to -1910.361 given in [18]. However, the constraints were satisfied within 1 part in 10^{12} using GRG but only with 1 part in 20 for the solutions given in [18]. Using a different starting point (x = 0) GRG does reach an objective value of -1910.22 with constraints satisfied to 1 part in 10^{10}.

Problem number 13 "contained a myriad of local optima of many different values." Depending on the starting point used, GRG generated several different solutions. Using the initial feasible starting point in [18], GRG reaches a minimum of 261,350 compared to 250,800 in [18]. From the nonfeasible starting point GRG attains a minimum of 260,508. Starting from $x_i = 0$, $i \neq 4$, $x_4 = 2000$ GRG reaches a value 251,786.

---

*We thank Professor David Himmelblau for providing us with a card deck for these problems.

Problem Number	N,M,NEQ	Best function value reported	Best function value with GRG	Function and gradient evaluations
1	2,2,1	1.393	1.393	25,4
2	2,0,0	0.0	6.0×10^{-14}	177,25
3	2,3,0	58.903	58.903	169,17
4	10,3,3	-47.761	-47.720	77,17
4a	10,3,3	-47.761	-47.755	158,16
5	3,2,2	961.715	961.715	39,7
6	45,16,16	-1910.361	-1865.98	229,50
7	3,7,0	-1162.04	-1162.03	130,17
8	4,0,0	0.0	1.0×10^{-7}	255,43
9	4,1,0	0.0075	0.0075	89,19
10	5,10,0	-32.349	-32.349	63,9
11	5,3,0	-30,665.5	-30,665.5	16,6
11A	5,3,0	-30,665.5	-30,665.5	44,5
12	5,21,0	-1.905	-1.9051	48,6
13	5,3,0	-5,280,254	-5,280,338	19,6
14	6,4,0	255,303.5	261,350.5	118,19
14A	6,4,0	266,754.0	260,507.8	102,14
15	6,4,4	8,927.59	8,927.57	172,17
16	9,13,0	-0.8660	-0.86604	244,18
17	10,0,0	-45.778	-45.778	32,5
18	15,5,0	32.386	32.349	564,42
18A	15,5,0	32.386	32.348	399,31
19	16,8,8	-244.90	-244.90	162,37
20	24,20,14	0.05700	0.05566	200,31
21	3,0,0	0.0	0.0	6,2
22,22A	6,4,0	0.0156	0.0156	8,7
22B,22C	6,4,0	4.070	3.1358	58,9
23	100,12,0	-1,732.	-1,733.3	239,41
24	2,2,0	1.0	1.0	26,4

Table 2: RESULTS OF SOLVING HIMMELBLAU PROBLEMS

Problem Number	Equivalent Function Evaluations	One Dimensional Searches	Newton Average	Execution Time (sec)	Colville Standard Time
1	33	3	0.54	0.10	0.0013
2	227	25	0	0.44	0.0057
3	203	16	3.94	1.04	0.013
4	247	16	0	3.81	0.049
4A	318	15	2.0	3.98	0.051
5	60	6	0.5	0.24	0.0031
6	2,479	49	0	227.26	2.920
7	151	16	0.82	2.75	0.035
8	427	43	0	1.32	0.017
9	165	18	0	18.26	0.235
10	108	9	0	1.53	0.020
11	46	5	1.0	0.21	0.0027
11A	69	4	1.92	0.27	0.0035
12	78	5	1.71	1.01	0.013
13	49	5	0.33	0.16	0.0021
14	232	18	0.38	2.93	0.038
14A	186	13	0.53	2.24	0.029
15	274	16	1.75	2.41	0.031
16	406	17	2.28	4.39	0.056
17	82	5	0	1.72	0.022
18	1,194	41	2.96	18.65	0.240
18A	864	30	2.04	13.51	0.174
19	754	36	0	38.55	0.495
20	744	29	1.00	10.85	0.139
21	12	1	0	1.90	0.025
22,22A	50	6	0	0.28	0.0036
22B,22C	112	8	1.39	0.56	0.0072
23	4,339	40	0.03	570.37	7.328
24	34	3	1.17	0.08	0.0010

Table 2   (Continued)

These results were attained using the default values for all parameters in GRG, finite difference approximations for derivatives, quadratic extrapolation for basic variables, and double precision floating point computations. We also examined the effects of changing EPSTOP parameter (see section 4.2) from 10^{-4} to 10^{-3}. This reduced run time for the Himmelbalu problems; only slightly for most problems, up to 25% for some. Two problems, however, stopped significantly short of optimality. This suggests a strategy in which a loose stopping tolerance is net, the tolerance is decreased, and the procedure repeated until no significant change in objective or X values is detected. This option has recently been implemented but not yet tested.

5. MINOS

5.1 Description

MINOS is a GRG code capable of solving large, sparse nonlinear programs with linear constraints. Designed by B. Murtagh and M. Saunders, it is described in reference [3]. This section summarizes its features, using the GRG framework developed in earlier sections.

A major simplification in GRG occurs when all the constraints are linear. Then the linear extrapolation in (9a) using the tangent vector v is exact, so no iterative procedure is needed to find the basic variables for given values of the superbasics. Hence MINOS computes a vector.

$$p = (v,d)^T$$

where v is the tangent vector in (9) and d is a search direction for the superbasic variables. The basic and superbasic variables are varied according to

$$x_b = \bar{x}_b + \alpha v$$

$$x_s = \bar{x}_s + \alpha d$$

so the linesearch problem is to minimize

$$f(\bar{x}_b + \alpha v, \bar{x}_s + \alpha d, \bar{x}_n).$$

A second major simplification is that the elements of the Jacobian matrix $\partial g/\partial x$ in (4) are constants, so B is unchanged unless the set of basic variables changes. Hence B can be updated at each basis change rather than reinverted as in GRG2. In addition, the reduced gradient $\partial F/\partial x_s$ can be recomputed easily at intermediate points in the linesearch. This requires recomputing only the partial derivatives $\partial f/\partial x_b$ and $\partial f/\partial x_s$ solving

$$B^T \Pi = \partial f/\partial x_b$$

for Π and then reevaluating $\partial F/\partial x_s$ using (6a). The linesearch used is a FORTRAN translation of Gill and Murray's Algol 60 procedure _delinsearch_, which uses successive cubic interpolation with safeguards as described in [33].

In order to deal effectively with large, sparse problems, MINOS incorporates many of the efficient sparse matrix routines found in modern linear programming codes. These include

1. Fast input of the constraint data in standard MPS format* using hash tables (in particular, the method of Brent [19]) for storing row-names and distinct matrix coefficients.

2. Compact in-core storage of the constraint matrix A using an elementary version of Kalan's super-sparseness techniques [20].

3. Upper and lower bounds on all variables.

4. A version of Hellerman and Rarick's "bump and spike" algorithm P^4 [21] for determing a sparse LU factorization of the basis matrix B.**

5. Imbedding of non-spike columns of L with A.

6. Stable updating of the LU factors of B by the method of Bartels and Golub [22], [23] as implemented by Saunders [24].

7. An improved "CHUZR" procedure# for phase 1 of the simplex method, following ideas due to Rarick [25] and Conn [26].

In order to deal with large problems, it is desirable not to price (i.e., compute the reduced gradient components of) all variables at each iteration. MINOS achieves this by minimizing over the existing set of superbasics until a convergence criterion is

---

*This is the CONVERT data format described in user's manuals for the IBM systems MPS/360, MPSX and MPSX/370.

**The block-triangular structure of B is currently being found using subroutines MC13 and MC16 from the Harwell Subroutine Library (Duff [27], Duff and Reid [28]). Hellerman and Rarick's P^3 is then applied to each block.

#Implemented by J.A. Tomlin.

met. Then the nonbasics are priced and the one with the most promising reduced gradient component enters the superbasic set. The
convergence tests used when minimizing over the superbasics are [3].

$$T_1: \quad \| \Delta x_s \| \; \leq \; (\epsilon_x + \epsilon^{1/2}) \; (1 + \| x_s \|)$$

$$T_2: \quad \| \Delta F \| \; \leq \; (\epsilon_f + \epsilon) \; (1 + |f|)$$

$$T_3: \quad \| \partial F / \partial x_s \| \; \leq \; \text{TOLRG}$$

$$T_4: \quad \| \partial F / \partial x_s \| \; \leq \; \epsilon_g \; \| \Pi \|$$

where

Δx_s = change in x_s in the last iteration

ΔF = change in objective in the last iteration

ϵ_x, ϵ_f, TOLRG, ϵ_g = positive scalars

ϵ = machine precision.

The convergence criterion used is: if (T_1 and T_2 and T_3) or T_4
then price the nonbasic variables. The inclusion of T_1 and T_2
insures that the current superbasics are retained as long as sufficient progress is being made, while T_4 guarantees that a "good"
step which moves x_s to a point very close to a minimum of F is
recognized immediately. The quantity $\| \Pi \|$ is included to make the
test independent of the scaling of the objective function.

The tolerances ϵ_x, ϵ_f, TOLRG, and ϵ_g are fixed at "loose"
values initially and are then reset to "tight" values when it
appears that no other nonbasics want to enter the superbasic set.
In addition, TOLRG is varied dynamically, equated to some fraction
N_g times the norm of $\partial F / \partial x_s$ at the start of the superbasic minimization. A typical value of N_g is 0.2. Murtagh and Saunders report
in [3] that, using this convergence strategy, each subspace minimization (except perhaps the final ones) requires about 5 linesearches.

To compute search directions for the superbasic variables,
MINOS uses either a factorized implementation of a variable metric
method (if the number of superbasics is less than a user-specified
limit) or a conjugate gradient method. It is easy to prove that,
if NL is the number of variables appearing nonlinearly in the objective, then there is an optimal solution with at most NL superbasics.
Hence, in problems with, say, 50 nonlinear variables, one would
expect that no set of superbasics encountered would contain many
more than 50 variables. This permits the use of a variable metric

method (with its dense matrix R) even in problems with thousands of variables, as long as only a small fraction appear nonlinearly.

Some features of the variable metric method used are described in section 4.3. In addition, if the constraints are linear, the basis need change only when a basic variable hits a bound during a linesearch, and then by only 1 column. As shown in [3], this permits the Hessian factor R to be updated to compensate for the change, rather than resetting it as in GRG2. There is also an alternative updating for R when a new superbasic variable is added. Details of both of these are given in [3].

5.2 Computational Results

MINOS has undergone extensive testing. It has solved several difficult linear programs of staircase structure (the PILOT energy model, [30]) with about 800 rows. Several problems with nonlinear objectives have also been solved. Tables 3 and 4 summarize the results. In these tables, standard time ratio is the time required to solve the problem divided by the time to execute Colville's standard timing program [18]. This time was 83.07 sec. for unoptimized B6700 FORTRAN and 3.92 seconds on the 370/168 using an IBM FORTRAN IV (H extended) compiler with full optimization. Computations on the B6700 were done in single precision ($\varepsilon \approx 10^{-11}$) and on the 370/168 in double precision ($\varepsilon \approx 10^{-15}$). In this latter case ε_g was 10^{-6}.

Problems 5a – 5c are quadratic programs. Problem 9 is a 16 time period energy model of Mannes [31], whose objective is of the form

$$\sum_{i=3}^{16} a_i / x_i y_i^2 + \text{linear terms}$$

Problem 10 is a further development of 9 (see [32]) with a term

$$\sum_{i=1}^{16} z_i^2 \quad \text{added to the objective.}$$

6. LSGRG

LSGRG is designed to solve large, sparse nonlinear programs with both a nonlinear objective and nonlinear constraints. It is an extension of MINOS, using some of the features of GRG2 (see Section 4) to accommodate nonlinear constraints. Most of its subroutines are those of MINOS, some of which have been somewhat

Problem Number	Rows	Columns	Nonzero Elements	Nonlinear Variables	Iterations*	Evaluations of f(x), g(x)	Final no. of Superbasics	Time (secs.)	Standard Time Ratio
1	10	5	47	5	8	9	1	0.63	0.008
2	8	16	80	16	15	16	3	1.50	0.018
4	12	100	147	100	133	296	18	48.30	0.58
5a	10	24	240	24	8	8	14	1.65	0.019
5b	17	52	884	52	13	13	35	6.21	0.075
5c	19	78	1,482	78	21	21	59	13.47	0.16
6	74	83	529	15	80	40	3	37.03	0.45
7	95	200	504	24	103	72	0	42.43	0.51
8	324	425	1,404	91	348	215	0	538.3	6.48

*Includes Phase 1 iterations

Table 3: SOLUTION OF PROBLEMS 1-2, 4-8 ON BURROUGHS B6700

Problem Number	Rows	Columns	Nonzero Elements	Nonlinear Variables	Iterations	Evaluations of $f(\tilde{x})$, $f(\hat{x})$	Final No. of Superbasics	Time (secs.)	Standard Time Ratio
3	16	45	99	45	103	452	24	2.9	0.74
4	12	100	147	100	139	355	18	2.6	0.66
9a	356	1,134	4,180	0	539	0	0	33.3	8.5
9b	314	631	2,122	28	2,027	4,536	21	119.5	30.5
9c	314	631	2,122	28	1,397	2,862	21	83.6	21.3
10a	320	679	2,519	44	948	1,768	27	56.6	14.4
10b	320	679	2,519	44	236	570	29	17.5	4.5
10c	320	679	2,519	44	350	902	26	26.9	6.9

* 9a = RS8, linearized
  9b = RS8, cold start
  9c = RS8, cold start, scaled
  10a = ETA, BOUNDS = Q2NONE, cold start
  10b = ETA, BOUNDS = Q2NOFB, restart from 10a
  10c = ETA, BOUNDS = Q2BOTH, restart from 10b

Table 4: SOLUTION OF PROBLEMS 3-4, 9-10 ON IBM 370/168

modified. The major new subroutines are quite similar to subroutines SEARCH, REDOBJ, and NEWTON, discussed in Section 4. Much of the work in developing LSGRG has been done by Michael Saunders* and Arvind Jain.**

6.1 Input Features

With current technology, a nonlinear program is large if it has more than 100 variables and/or constraints. Such problems will often arise from models which were originally linear, and which have incorporated nonlinearities for greater accuracy or to deal with new problem features. This leads to NLP's which are sparse (i.e., the Jacobian matrix of all problem functions is sparse) and mostly linear (i.e., most elements of the Jacobian are constant). LSGRG attempts to exploit these aspects of problem structure in all phases of its processing. In the input phase, this implies that LSGRG formats should be compatible with existing MPS formats because (a) MPS format is a recognized standard for LP and separable nonlinear programs, (b) all commercial matrix generators generate files in MPS format and (c) many models to be solved by LSGRG are likely to be extensions of existing linear models. The current version of LSGRG extends MPS format to accommodate linear Jacobian elements by denoting the occurrence of each such element in the MPS deck by a special character. Our choice for this character is the number 999999.9, because the matrix generator language MAGEN can place only numeric characters in the numeric fields of the COLUMNS section. The input routines of MINOS were modified to create a position in storage for a nonlinear Jacobian element whenever the special character is encountered. These positions must be filled with the current value each time the nonlinear variables are changed.

The problem being solved is assumed to have the form:

$$\text{minimize} \quad x_o$$

$$\text{subject to} \quad g_i(y) + \sum_j d_{ij} y_j + \sum_j a_{ij} x_j = b_i \quad i=1,\ldots,m$$

with upper and lower bounds on all variables. The y's are those variables which appear nonlinearly in at least one function, the x's are the linear variables, and the g's are the nonlinear functions. The g's are computed by a user-supplied subroutine GCOMP which must compute the value of any specified g, (in GRG2, GCOMP computes all g's, foregoing the savings involved in computing only

---

*Applied Mathematics Division, D.S.I.R., Wellington, New Zealand.

**Energy Center, S.R.I., Menlo Park, California.

those that are needed in favor of simplicity in preparing GCOMP).
Partial derivatives of the g's may be computed by a system forward
difference routine (derivative level 0), the gradient of the objective may be computed analytically by a user supplied subroutine
while others are done by differences (derivative level 1), or all
first derivatives may be computed analytically (derivative level 2).

6.2 Algorithmic Features

We discuss here only those aspects of LSGRG which differ from
those in MINOS or GRG2. The most significant of these is the basis
updating. For large problems, reinversion after each linesearch
(as in GRG2) is too time-consuming, but if the basis contains
several nonlinear columns, all of these may change. LSGRG simply
regards each nonlinear column which has changed as having its
previous value replaced by the new one, and applies Saunders'
implementation of the Bartels-Golub LU update [24] to each such
column. This update is ideal since it is very stable, yet the
rate of growth of the L and U files is quite small. In problems
solved thus far (see Section 6.4) up to 400 updates are made before
the basis is refactorized.

The need for updating each basic nonlinear column underscores
the need to keep the number of such columns as small as possible.
There is an optimal solution and a corresponding optimal basis which
is completely linear (simply fix the nonlinear variable at their
optimal values and solve the resulting LP), but this basis is
unknown a priori, it may be degenerate or poorly conditioned, and
the algorithm may simply be forced to use nonlinear columns as
basic at some intermediate point. To keep the number of nonlinear
basic columns small, nonlinear columns are allowed to enter the
basis only if all potential pivot elements for entering alternative
columns fail certain tolerance tests. In case of a cold start where
CRASH computes an initial basis from scratch, the user may request
an all logical basis (Crash level 0), an all linear basis (Crash
level 1) or an arbitrary basis (Crash level 2).

If the constraints are nonlinear, a linesearch which requires
derivatives is impractical since recomputing ∇F requires refactoriz-
ing B. Hence LSGRG uses a version of subroutine SEARCH (see Section
4.4) rather than the linesearch of MINOS. Versions of subroutines
REDOBJ and NEWTON (see section 4.5), modified to use B in factorized
form, are used to solve for the basic variables given values of the
others.

LSGRG inherits all the startup, restart and basis preservation capabilities of MINOS. The reader should refer to the MINOS User's Guide for a detailed description of these capabilities. Very briefly, LSGRG possesses the equivalent of the following MPSX procedures with enhancements for nonlinear problems.

CRASH	Constructs initial basis
PUNCH INSERT	Communicate bases between LSGRG and external files in a form allowing changes to be made easily
SAVE RESTORE	Communicates bases in a highly compact, but not easily alterable format

6.3 Summary of the Algorithm

Given:

a)   a partition of x into basic (x_1), superbasic (x_2) and nonbasic (x_3) variables,

b)   (for simplicity) a feasible point $\bar{x} = (\bar{x}_1, \bar{x}_2, \bar{x}_2)$,

c)   a factorization of B_1, $B_1 = LU$,

d)   a triangular matrix R such that $R^T R$ approximates $\partial^2 F / \partial x_2^2$.

1.   If there are no superbasic variables, go to step 3.

2.   Compute the reduced gradient

$$\partial F / \partial x_2 = \partial f / \partial x_2 - \pi^T B_2$$

where $B_1^T \pi = \partial f / \partial x_1$.

3.   If superbasic convergence criterion is met (see section 5.1), price a partition of the columns in B_3.

a)   If all are optimal, reduce superbasic convergence tolerances and go to step 1.

b)   If tolerances are already set to "tight" levels, stop.

c)   Otherwise, choose a nonbasic to become superbasic.

4. If the basis is linear and there is only one linear superbasic variable, enter it into the basis and return to 1.

5. Adjust $\partial F/\partial x_2$ and R for the new superbasic.

6. Solve $(R^T R)\, d = -\partial F/\partial x_2$ for d, where $R^T R$ is an approximation to $\partial^2 F/\partial x_2^2$.

7. Compute the tangent vector v using

$$B_1 v = -B_2 d.$$

8. Solve the problem; min $F(\bar{x}_2 + \alpha d,\ \bar{x}_3)$ subject to the condition that x_1 and x_2 remain feasible. At each point of this search, if any constraints are nonlinear, use v to get initial estimates for x_1.

   Thus, when $\alpha = \bar{\alpha}$, set $x_2 = \bar{x}_2 + \bar{\alpha} d$

   $$x_1 = \bar{x}_1 + \bar{\alpha} v.$$

   Use a pseudo-Newton method to solve

   $$g(x_1,\ \bar{x}_2 + \bar{\alpha} d,\ \bar{x}_3) = 0$$

   for x_1. Then use these x values to compute the objective.

9. Update R. There are 3 cases:

   a) A variable in B_2 hit a bound.

   b) A variable in B_1 hit a bound.

   c) No variable hit a bound (See section 4.3 for details.)

10. If 9b, replace the leaving basic variable by a suitable variable from B_2. Update RB_2 and the factors of B, to reflect this replacement.

11. Return to step 1.

6.4 Computational Results

LSGRG has solved a set of test problems of the form

$$\text{maximize} \sum_{t=5}^{5N} \beta t \ \ln C_t$$

subject to

$$K_t - K_{t-5} - 5I_{t-5} = 0$$

$$\alpha\lambda_t^{1-b} \cdot K_t^b - C_t - I_t = 0 \qquad (t=0,5,10,\ldots,5N)$$

$$K_0 = \overline{K}_0; \ I_0 = \overline{I}_0 \qquad \text{(given)}$$

$$C_t \geq 0, \ I_t \geq 0, \ K_t \geq 0 \qquad \text{(all t)}$$

In these problems K_t represents the capital stock at the end of period t, I_t the investment in period t, and C_t the consumption. There are N periods each of length 5 years. The quantity λ_t represents the amount of labor employed and is assumed to be of the form $(1+r)^t$. The parameters α, β, r, N and b are all specified. Problems have also been solved with the alternative (linear) objective

$$\sum_{t=5}^{5N} \beta^t \cdot C_t .$$

Our thanks to Alan Manne for proposing and helping in the specification of these test problems.

These problems have 3N variables (2N nonlinear), 2N constraints, N nonlinear functions, and N distinct nonlinear Jacobian elements. The degree of nonlinearity is largely controlled by b -- if b = 1 the constraints are linear. Problems were solved with N = 10, 20, 30, 40, and b = 0.25, 0.50, 0.75, using all analytic derivatives and a cold start (CRASH level 0). Figure 3 shows a graph of CPU time versus N.

Computation time increases most rapidly for the most nonlinear problems (b = 0.25). Details of the run with N = 40 and b = 0.25 are shown in table 5. Note that the average number of Newton Iterations per Newton Call is only slightly greater than 1, so it was quite easy to solve for the values of the basic variables. This problem has 120 variables and 80 constraints, so the number of iterations and computation time does not seem excessive. All problems were solved on an IBM 370/168 at the Stanford Linear Accelerator Center under the VS/2 Operating System using a FORTRAN H Compiler (OPT=2).

7. SUMMARY AND CONCLUSIONS

This paper has discussed GRG implementations for small to medium size NLP's, large sparse NLP's with linear constraints,

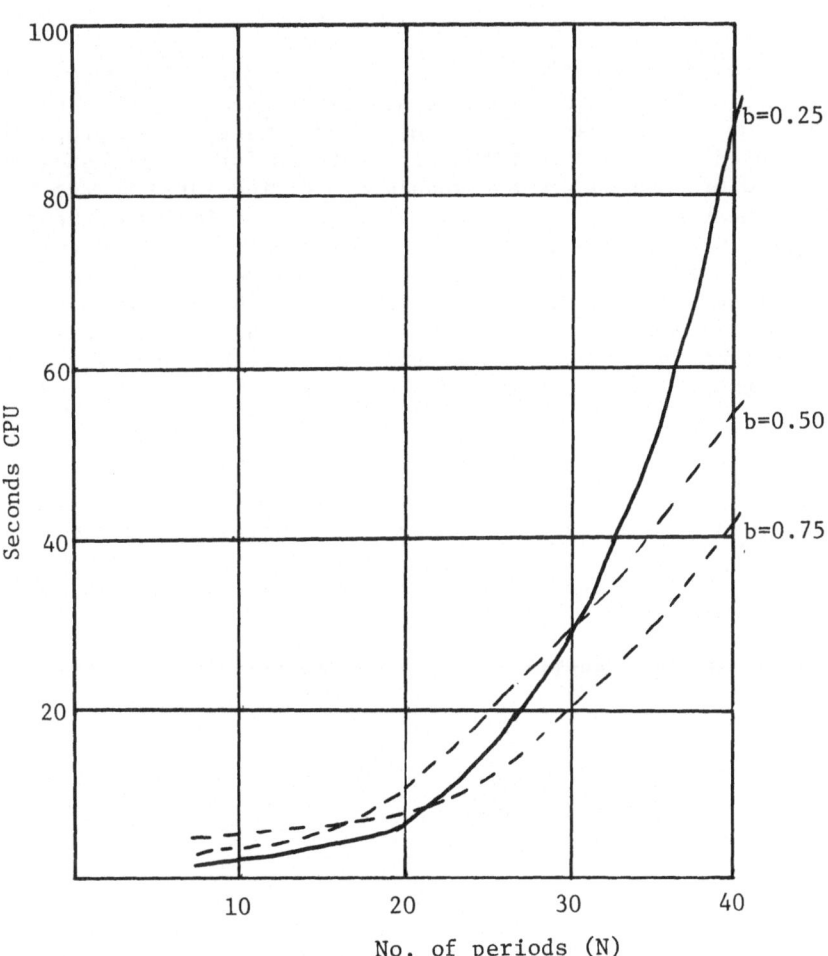

Figure 3:   SOLUTION OF LSGRG TEST PROBLEMS

Iterations:	561	Inversions:	72
Objective Function Evaluations	3,048	Objective Gradient Evaluations	667
Constraint Function Evaluations	169	Constraint Gradient Evaluations	19,253
Newton Calls	3,239	Newton Iterations	2,785

Table 5: STATISTICS FOR LARGEST RPOBLEM

and large sparse NLP's with nonlinear constraints. Research on the use of GRG for the first class of problems has been under way for from 5 to 8 years, and results indicate that, if properly implemented, GRG is one of the best methods for solving such problems. We know of no other codes capable of solving large sparse NLP's. For linear constraints, MINOS is a robust, efficient, thoroughly tested system which will not be easy to surpass. For nonlinear constraints, the concepts of LSGRG need more testing, but preliminary results are encouraging. More research is needed in all 3 cases. In addition, we need implementations of other algorithms capable of dealing with large problems, so that comparisons with the methods discussed here can be made.

REFERENCES

1. J. Abadie and J. Carpentier, "Generalization of the Wolfe Reduced Gradient Method to the Case of Nonlinear Constraints," in Optimization, R. Fletcher (ed.), Academic Press, 1969, 37-47.

2. J. Abadie, "Application of the GRG Algorithm to Optimal Control Problems," in Nonlinear and Integer Programming, J. Abadie (ed.) North Holland Publishing Co., 1972, 191-211.

3. B. Murtagh and M. Saunders, "Nonlinear Programming for Large Sparse Systems," Tech. rept. SOL 76-15, Dept of Operations Research, Stanford University, Aug. 1976.

4. L.S. Lasdon, A.D. Waren, A. Jain, M. Ratner, "Design and Testing of a GRG Code for Nonlinear Optimization", in ACM Transactions on Mathematical Software, Vol. 4, No. 1, March 1978, pp. 34-50.

5. D. Gabay and D. Luenberger, "Efficiently Converging Minimization Methods Based on the Reduced Gradient," Internal report, Department of Engineering-Economic Systems, Stanford University.

6. P. Wolfe, "Checking the Calculation of Gradients," report RC 6007, Mathematical Sciences Dept., IBM Thomas J. Watson Research Center, Yorktown, Hts., New York 10598, May 1976.

7. R. Fletcher, "A New Approach to Variable Metric Algorithms," Computer Journal 13, 1970, 317-322.

8. P.E. Gill, G.H. Golub, W. Murray and M.A. Saunders, "Methods for modifying matrix factorizations," Math. Comp. 28, 1974, 505-535.

9. R. Fletcher and C.M. Reeves, "Function Minimization by Conjugate Gradients," British Computer J. 7, 1964, 149-154.

10. E. Polak, Computational Methods in Optimization: A Unified Approach (Academic Press), 1971.

11. A. Perry, "An Improved conjugate gradient algorithm," Technical note , Department of Decision Sciences, Graduate School of Management, Northwestern University, Evanston, Illinois, March 1976.

12. D. Goldfarb, "Extension of Davidons Variable Metric Method to Maximization Under Linear Inequality and Equality Constraints," SIAM J. Appl. Math. 17, No. 4, July 1969.

13. A. Buckley, "An Alternate Implementation of Goldfarb's Minimization Algorithm," Report No. T.P. 544, AERE, Harwell, England.

14. R. Fletcher and C.M. Reeves, "Function Minimization by Conjugate Gradients," British Computer J. 7, 1964, 149-154.

15. J.S. Newell and D.M. Himmelblau, "A New Method for Nonlinearly Constrained Optimization," AICHE J. 21, No. 3, May 1975, 479-486.

16. D.R. Heltne and J.M. Liitschwager, "Users Guide for GRG 73" and "Technical Appendices to GRG 73," College of Engineering, University of Iowa, Sept. 1973.

17. C. Cohen, "Generalized Reduced Gradient Technique for Nonlinear Programming--User Writeup," Vogelback Computing Center, Northeastern University, Feb. 1974.

18. D.M. Himmelblau, Applied Nonlinear Programming, McGraw-Hill Book Co., 1972.

19. R.P. Brent, "Reducing the retrieval time of scatter storage techniques," Comm. ACM 16, 1973, 105-109.

20. J.E. Kalan, "Aspects of large-scale in-core linear programming," Proceedings of ACM Conference, Chicago, 1971, 304-313.

21. E. Hellerman and D.C. Rarick, "The partitioned preassigned pivot procedure," in: D.J. Rose and R.A. Willoughby, eds., Sparse matrices and their applications (Plenum Press, New York), 1972, 67-76.

22. R.H. Bartels, "A stabilization of the simplex method," Num. Math. 16, 1971, 414-434.

23. R.H. Bartels and G.H. Golub, "The simplex method of linear programming using LU decomposition," Comm. ACM 12, 1969, 266-268.

24. M.A. Saunders, "A fast, stable implementation of the simplex method using Bartels-Golub updating," in: J.R. Bunch and D.J. Rose, eds., Sparse Matrix Computations (Academic Press, New York and London), 1976, 213-226.

25. D.C. Rarick, An improved pivot row selection procedure, implemented in the mathematical programming system MPS III, Management Science Systems, Rockville, Maryland.

26. A.R. Conn, "Linear programming via a non-differentiable penalty function," SIAM J. Numer. Anal. (to appear).

27. I.S. Duff, "On algorithms for obtaining a maximum transversal," to appear (1976).

28. I.S. Duff and J.K. Reid, "An implementation of Tarjan's algorithm for the block triangularization of a matrix," AERE Report C.S.S. 29, Harwell, England, 1976.

29. E. Hellerman and D.C. Rarick, "Reinversion with the preassigned pivot procedure," Math. Prog. 1, 1971, 195-216.

30. S. Parikh, "Analyzing U.S. Energy Options Using the Pilot Energy Model," Technical report SOL 76-27, Operations Research Dept., Stanford University, Oct., 1976.

31. A.S. Manne, "Waiting for the Breeder," The review of economic studies symposium, 1974, 47-65.

32. A.S. Manne, "ETA: a model for Energy Technology Assessment," Working paper, John Fitzgerald Kennedy School of Government, Harvard University, Cambridge, Mass., 1975.

33. P.E. Gill and W. Murray, "Safeguarded steplength algorithms for optimization using descent methods," Report NAC 37, National Physical Laboratory, Teddington, England, 1974.

THE ALGOL 60 PROCEDURE minifun FOR SOLVING NON-LINEAR OPTIMIZATION
PROBLEMS

F.A. Lootsma

Department of Mathematics, University of Technology
Delft, Netherlands

ABSTRACT. This paper presents an ALGOL 60 procedure which has been
written to solve unconstrained and constrained optimization problems,
as well as systems of non-linear (in)equalities. The first part
gives a description of the algorithms which have been incorporated
in minifun. Basically, it is a procedure for unconstrained optimization; constrained problems and systems of (in)equalities are
solved via a penalty function. The second part gives an explanation
of the parameter list, and some additional hints and suggestions for
a proper utilization of minifun. Finally, the third part presents
a listing of minifun and a number of programming details.

NOTE. The present paper is a modified version of the author's
report 4761, published under the same name in Philips Research
Laboratories, Eindhoven, Netherlands, 1972. It is a pleasure to
acknowledge the management of the laboratory for their kind permis-
sion to distribute the original report and to publish this paper.

PART I: BASIC ALGORITHMS

1.   INTRODUCTION

The procedure minifun is an ALGOL 60 procedure designed for
solving the following problems.

a)   Unconstrained minimization. The problem to be solved reads

$$\text{minimize } g_1(x), \tag{1}$$

where x denotes an element in the n-dimensional vector space, and
g_1 the objective function.

b) Constrained minimization. The problem to be solved is posed as

minimize $g_m(x)$ subject to

$$\left. \begin{array}{l} g_i(x) \geqq 0; \ i \in I, \\ g_i(x) = 0; \ i \in E, \end{array} \right\} \tag{2}$$

where x denotes again an element in the n-dimensional vector space. The index sets I and E corresponding to the inequality and the equality constraints are disjunct, and $I \cup E = \{1, \ldots, m-1\}$. The functions $g_1, \ldots, g_{m-1}$ are the so-called constraint functions, and g_m denotes the objective function of problem (2).

c) Non-linear (in)equalities. The problem is to find an n-vector x satisfying the system of (in)equalities

$$\left. \begin{array}{l} g_i(x) \geqq 0; \ i \in I, \\ g_i(x) = 0; \ i \in E. \end{array} \right\} \tag{3}$$

The index sets I and E corresponding to the inequality and equality constraints are disjunct, and $I \cup E = \{1, \ldots, m\}$. We shall, of course, refer to $g_1, \ldots, g_m$ as the constraint functions when we are dealing with the system (3).

To sum up, the procedure minifun has been designed to deal with m problem functions ($m \geqq 1$), and we may note in passing that minifun has also special facilities to deal with simple constraints of the form $x_j \geqq 0$ or $0 \leqq x_j \leqq 1$ for some j ($1 \leqq j \leqq n$). If the problem is one of unconstrained or constrained minimization, the objective function is taken to be the last one. The remaining functions are the constraint functions which define the feasible set of the problem under consideration. It is assumed that the problem functions $g_1, \ldots, g_m$ are real-valued functions with continuous second-order partial derivatives.

The procedure minifun (minimization of functions) is virtually a procedure for unconstrained minimization, irrespectively of whether it is concerned with problem (1), (2) or (3). The constrained problem (2) is solved by sequential unconstrained minimization of a so-called penalty function for positive, decreasing values of a controlling parameter r. In solving the system (3) a sum of squares is minimized. Thus, minifun is mainly concerned with unconstrained minimization of a compound function, which is automatically generated. In this manual the compound function will be denoted by P, and variously be referred to as penalty function or P-function; the manner in which it is composed will be explained in sec. 4 and 5.

Basically, the algorithm consists of a number of iterative processes: a constrained minimum is approximated by a sequence of unconstrained minima (see sec. 4); an unconstrained minimum by a sequence of line minima (see sec. 2); and a line minimum by minima of interpolating functions (see sec. 3). The <u>convergence criteria</u> at each of these stages are based on a prescribed relative tolerance ϵ_1 and a prescribed absolute tolerance ϵ_2. Furthermore, it is possible to stipulate that the tolerance must be obtained in the value of the objective function, in the components of a minimum solution, or in both. We shall say that two successive approximations a_k and a_{k+1} of a certain quantity differ by less than the relative tolerance ϵ_1 and the absolute tolerance ϵ_2 if

$$|a_{k+1} - a_k| < \epsilon_1 |a_{k+1}| + \epsilon_2.$$

This notation and this terminology will be used to describe the convergence criteria in the sections to follow. It has been our intention to design a procedure which calculates a solution with the a priori desired accuracy.

2. UNCONSTRAINED MINIMIZATION (GENERATION OF SEARCH DIRECTIONS)

An iteration of an unconstrained-minimization technique consists of two operations: the <u>generation</u> and the <u>exploration</u> of a search direction. The following methods for generating the search direction to the next iteration point have been incorporated in minifun.

a) <u>The conjugate-direction method of Powell</u> (1964), henceforth referred to as the P64 algorithm. This method consists of a number of major cycles of $(n+1)$ linear searches each. At the beginning of a major cycle a set of n linearly independent directions is available (the unit vectors for the first major cycle). A linear search is made along these directions, whereafter a new direction is generated and explored to replace one of the old directions. Replacement is such that the danger of obtaining nearly dependent directions is avoided as much as possible (see also Kowalik and Osborne (1968) and Sargent (1973)). The algorithm terminates as soon as the initial point and the endpoint of a major cycle differ in each component by less than the relative tolerance ϵ_1 and the absolute tolerance ϵ_2, or if the distance between these two points is smaller than 10^{-10}. Thereafter, the endpoint of the cycle will be delivered as an approximation to an unconstrained minimum of the P-function.

b) <u>The variable-metric method with the updating formula derived by Broyden</u> (1970), <u>Fletcher</u> (1970) <u>and Shanno</u> (1970). This method will henceforth be referred to as the BFS algorithm. The search direction s_k emanating from the current iteration point x_k is generated by a transformation of the gradient $\nabla P(x_k)$ of P evaluated at x_k. The transformation is linear and can be written as

$$s_k = -H_k \nabla P(x_k).$$

The matrix H_k is initially set to the unit matrix, and updated according to

$$H_{k+1} = H_k + (\sigma_k^T y_k)^{-1}(\tau_k \sigma_k \sigma_k^T - \sigma_k y_k^T H_k - H_k y_k \sigma_k^T).$$

The quantities σ_k, y_k and τ_k are defined by

$$\sigma_k = x_{k+1} - x_k,$$

$$y_k = \nabla P(x_{k+1}) - \nabla P(x_k),$$

$$\tau_k = 1 + y_k^T H_k y_k / \sigma_k^T y_k.$$

The BFS algorithm terminates as soon as two successive iteration points x_k and x_{k+1} differ in each component by less than the relative tolerance ϵ_1 and the absolute tolerance ϵ_2 during n consecutive iterations. Termination will also occur as soon as one of the following conditions is satisfied:

$$\| \nabla P(x_{k+1}) \| < 10^{-10},$$

$$\| \sigma_k \| < 10^{-10},$$

$$| \sigma_k^T y_k | < 10^{-20},$$

$$| y_k^T H_k y_k | < 10^{-20}.$$

Thereafter, the point x_{k+1} will be taken as an approximation to an unconstrained minimum of P.

c) The method of Newton with the modifications proposed by Fiacco and McCormick (1968), henceforth referred to as the NFM algorithm. Let G_k denote the Hessian matrix of P evaluated at the current iteration point x_k. The matrix G_k will be factorized (see Martin, Peters and Wilkinson (1965)), and if it is found to be positive-definite, the search direction will be solved from the system

$$G_k s_k = -\nabla P(x_k).$$

Otherwise, a modified system will be solved as proposed by Fiacco and McCormick (1968). If factorization fails, then s_k will be set to the steepest-descent direction $-\nabla P(x_k)$. The NFM algorithm terminates as soon as x_k and x_{k+1} differ in each component by less than the relative tolerance ϵ_1 and the absolute tolerance ϵ_2. Termination will also occur as soon as one of the conditions

$$\|\nabla P(x_{k+1})\| < 10^{-10},$$

$$\|x_{k+1} - x_k\| < 10^{-10},$$

is satisfied. Thereafter, the point x_{k+1} will be delivered as an approximation to an unconstrained minimum of P.

3. LINEAR SEARCHES (EXPLORATION OF SEARCH DIRECTIONS)

A method for unconstrained minimization is said to have the property of <u>quadratic termination</u> (Fletcher and Powell (1963)) if it minimizes a quadratic function with a positive-definite Hessian matrix in a <u>finite</u> number of iterations. Methods with this property, like the algorithms described in the previous section, are highly efficient in a neighbourhood of a minimum, even if the function to be minimized is not quadratic. The theoretical proof of quadratic termination relies on the assumption that the next iteration point x_{k+1} is given by $x_{k+1} = x_k + \alpha_k s_k$ where α_k is the value of α which minimizes the function

$$\varphi_k(\alpha) = P(x_k + \alpha s_k).$$

In minifun, exploration of a search direction to approximate α_k is carried out with quadratic interpolation. First, three line coordinates $a < b < c$ are determined such that

$$P(x_k + as_k) \geq P(x_k + bs_k)$$

and

$$P(x_k + cs_k) \geq P(x_k + bs_k).$$

Next, the coordinate d of the point which minimizes the interpolating quadratic is determined. The search terminates if the function values $P(x_k + bs_k)$ and $P(x_k + ds_k)$ differ by less than the relative tolerance $\delta_1 = \min(\epsilon_1, 10^{-5})$ and the absolute tolerance $\delta_2 = \min(\epsilon_2, 10^{-5})$. If the convergence test fails, one of the two extreme coordinates a and c is removed in a manner which guarantees that the remaining extremes still enclose a line minimum. Thereafter, interpolation and testing is repeated. For more details, we may refer to Powell (1964), Kowalik and Osborne (1968) and Box, Davies and Swann (1969).

A line minimum is approximated by the point with the lowest P-value obtained during the linear search.

4. CONSTRAINED MINIMIZATION VIA A PENALTY FUNCTION

In solving problem (2), minifun is concerned with the penalty function

$$P(x) = g_m(x) + rb(x) + r^{-1}[\ell(x) + e(x)] \tag{5}$$

containing the logarithmic-barrier term

$$b(x) = -\sum_{i \in I_1} \ln g_i(x) \tag{6}$$

and the quadratic-loss terms

$$\ell(x) = \sum_{i \in I_2} \{\min[0, g_i(x)]\}^2 \tag{7}$$

and

$$e(x) = \sum_{i \in E} g_i^2(x).$$

The index sets I_1 and I_2 are defined by

$$I_1 = \{i | g_i(x_o) > 0; \ i \in I\},$$
$$I_2 = \{i | g_i(x_o) \leq 0; \ i \in I\}, \tag{8}$$

where x_o denotes the (user-supplied) starting point of the computations for solving (2). The parameter r in (5) controls the convergence to a minimum solution $\bar{x}$ of problem (2). Let $x(r_k)$ be a point minimizing (5) over the set

$$R_1^o = \{x | g_i(x) > 0; \ i \in I_1\}$$

for a fixed, positive value r_k or r. Under mild conditions one has

$$\lim_{k \to \infty} g_m[x(r_k)] = g_m(\bar{x})$$

and

$$\lim_{k \to \infty} \{\ell[x(r_k)] + e[x(r_k)]\} = 0$$

provided that r_k is a monotonic, decreasing null sequence as $k \to \infty$.

This provides the framework of the algorithm. For more details we may refer the reader to Fiacco and McCormick (1968) and the present author (1970, 1972a).

If certain uniqueness conditions are satisfied at a minimum solution $\bar{x}$, and if the problem functions have continuous second derivatives, then the trajectory $x(r)$ of points minimizing P is a continuously differentiable vector function of r in a neighbourhood of $r = 0$. The kth derivative of $x(r)$ exists accordingly as the problem functions admit of $(k+1)$th derivatives ($k \geqq 1$). Under certain additional uniqueness conditions $x(r)$ can be expanded in a Taylor series about $\bar{x}$. This provides the basis for extrapolation in order to obtain a more accurate approximation of $\bar{x}$.

The controlling parameter r is <u>initially</u> given the value r_o defined by

$$r_o = \max(10^{-2}, \ 10^{-2}|v^*|), \tag{9}$$

where v^* denotes an estimate of the <u>minimum value</u> $g_m(\bar{x})$ of problem (2). By the choice of r_o according to (9) we avoid the danger of using a parameter value which is too small (the minimum value of the problem should not be approximated with an excessive accuracy).

<u>Successive values</u> r_1, r_2 ... assigned to r are generated by

$$r_k = 10^{-1/3} r_{k-1}. \tag{10}$$

Thus, the controlling parameter is successively reduced by roughly 1/2. The choice of $10^{-1/3}$ makes the output more readable: starting with $r_o = 10^{-2}$ the sequence of parameters is given by 0.01, 0.00464, 0.00232, 0.001, ...

The convergence to the constrained minimum is accelerated by polynomial extrapolation using the unconstrained penalty-function minima $x(r_o)$, $x(r_1)$,... as grid points. Polynomials up to the sixth degree are employed. Let $X(k,\ell)$ denote the approximation of the constrained minimum based on $x(r_{k-\ell}),...,x(r_k)$. Sequential unconstrained minimization will be stopped as soon as the components of $X(k,\ell)$ and $X(k-1, \ell-1)$ and/or $g_m(X(k,\ell))$ and $g_m(X(k-1, \ell-1))$ differ by less than the relative tolerance ϵ_1 and the absolute tolerance ϵ_2. Thereafter, $X(k,\ell)$ is taken as an approximation of the constrained minimum.

<u>Note</u>: Many experiments indicate that polynomial extrapolation up to the <u>sixth</u> degree is not really necessary. For a variety of problems, <u>quadratic</u> extrapolation is sufficient to obtain a stable and rapid approximation of the constrained minimum. If $X(k,2)$ and $X(k+1,2)$ denote two successive approximations, then the error (the

deviation with respect to $\bar{x}$) is reduced by 10 if formula (10) is employed to decrease the value of the controlling parameter.

Note: The penalty-function minima $x(r_o)$, $x(r_1)$,... will invariably satisfy the constraints ($i \in I_1$) which are strictly satisfied at the starting point x_o. It may clearly happen that the extrapolated approximations $\bar{X}(k,\ell)$ violate some of these constraints

5.   NON-LINEAR (IN)EQUALITIES

When minifun is used to find a solution of the system (3), it minimizes the compound function

$$P(x) = \sum_{i \in I} \{(\min[0,g_i(x)]\}^2 + \sum_{i \in E} g_i^2(x). \tag{11}$$

The search directions in the process of minimizing P are generated in accordance with the Gauss-Newton method. Let x_k be the current iteration point, and let us introduce the index set

$$V(x_k) = \{i | g_i(x_k) < 0, \quad i \in I\},$$

to indicate the inequalities which are violated at x_k. Let J_k be the matrix with rows $\nabla g_i(x_k)$, $i \in V(x_k) \cup E$. Furthermore, we take d_k to denote the vector with components $g_i(x_k)$, $i \in V(x_k) \cup E$. Then the search direction s_k is obtained by solving

$$J_k^T J_k s_k = -J_k^T d_k.$$

In fact, the matrix $J_k^T J_k$ is an approximation to the Hessian matrix of the compound function (11), so that the Gauss-Newton method for solving the system (3) is closely related to Newton's method for minimizing (11).

Once a search direction has been obtained, the linear search will be carried out with the method sketched in sec. 3.

6.   ON THE CHOICE OF METHODS

In this section we shall first indicate how the methods for unconstrained minimization have been selected from the confusing variety of methods proposed in the last few years. There are two criteria by which these methods may be classified:

a)   quadratic termination (a property which was described in sec. 3);

b)   the order of the method (the highest order of the derivatives
required to generate the search directions).

Numerically, methods with the property of quadratic termination
are highly efficient in a neighbourhood of an unconstrained minimum,
but they differ in the highest order of the derivatives required to
find the successive search directions.   There are zeroth-order
methods using function values of P only; there is a large class of
first-order methods (ranging from the method of steepest descent
to the sophisticated variable-metric or quasi-Newton methods)
operating with the first derivatives of P; and lastly, there are
the second-order methods (Newton's method with several variants)
using the first and second derivatives of P.   In most cases, higher-
order methods seem to be faster than lower-order methods.   One may
take advantage of this when higher-order derivatives can easily be
supplied.

Hence, we decided that minifun should contain a method of
order 0, order 1 and order 2; all of these should have the property
of quadratic termination.

One of the best methods for unconstrained minimization without
calculating derivatives seems to be the method of Powell (1964).
It is a method with quadratic termination, and it has accordingly
been chosen as the zeroth-order method to be incorporated in minifun.

A frequently cited first-order method is the DFP algorithm due
to Davidon (1959) and Fletcher and Powell (1963).   Although a very
powerful method, it is exceeded by the BFS algorithm independently
developed by Broyden (1970), Fletcher (1970) and Shanno (1970).

In its classical form the second-order method of Newton has a
few inconveniences if the function to be minimized is non-convex
or if its Hessian matrix is singular at some iteration points.
These disadvantages are possibly removed by the modifications of
Fiacco and McCormick (1968).   We have extensively tested this promising variant of Newton's method.

For many problems it is difficult or practically impossible
to supply the first and/or second derivatives of the problem functions.   This would impose a serious limitation on the choice of
methods for unconstrained minimization.   Therefore, minifun has
been written to generate derivatives by numerical differentiation
so that the user can easily proceed to a higher-order method.   In
this paper, the order of information is understood to be the highest
order of the derivatives supplied by the user.   With the facilities
of numerical differentiation, minifun has been designed in such a
way that a first-order method may also be employed with zeroth-
order information (no derivatives), and a second-order method with

first-order information. The first-order or second-order derivatives are then obtained by numerical differentiation of the function to be minimized or its derivatives respectively. We have
omitted the possibility of using a second-order method with information of order 0 only.

The choice of the <u>linear-search method</u> described in sec. 3
(quadratic interpolation with a strong convergence criterion) has
been motivated by the author (1972b) in a comparison with other
well-known methods (golden-section algorithm, cubic interpolation,
...).

Finally, the choice of the <u>interior-exterior penalty function</u>
(with a logarithmic-barrier term and a quadratic-loss term) rests
upon arguments brought forward by Fiacco and McCormick (1968) and
by the author (1970, 1972b).

7.   PROBLEM FORMULATION, SCALING, CONSTRAINT BALANCE

Before giving directions for use it is worthwhile to pay some
attention to the problem formulation. The user should know that
<u>badly scaled or unbalanced problems</u> will lead to numerical diffi-
culties during the computations.

Theoretically, <u>improper scaling</u> might seem to be quite harm-
less. The NFM algorithm and the BFS algorithm, for instance,
minimize any quadratic function with a positive-definite Hessian
matrix in 1 or n iterations respectively. One might therefore hope
that minimization of a non-quadratic function will not be affected
by improper scaling. In practice, however, many difficulties have
been observed during the computational process. To avoid these
difficulties one could, for instance, choose the units of the
physical, chemical or other quantities in such a way that each of
the variables in the problem varies over a range of the same order
of magnitude (preferably over the interval $(0,1)$ or $(-1,1)$).
Alternatively, the units could be chosen in such a way that the
non-zero components of the <u>expected</u> minimum are of the same order
of magnitude.

Difficulties due to unbalanced constraints can easily be
explained by giving a simple example. Let us first discuss
<u>unbalanced inequality constraints</u>. The problems

$$\left.\begin{array}{c} \text{minimize } g(x,y) \text{ subject to} \\ x \geqq 0 \\ 10000 \ y \geqq 0 \end{array}\right\} \tag{12}$$

and

minimize g(x,y) subject to
$$\left.\begin{array}{c} x \geq 0 \\ y \geq 0 \end{array}\right\} \tag{13}$$

are mathematically equivalent, but numerically they are not. They give rise to different penalty functions so that the course of the computations may also be quite different. If one starts from a point with positive coordinates, the penalty function for problem (12) is automatically taken to be

$$g(x,y) - r \ln x - r \ln(10000y),$$

which clearly differs by a constant from the penalty function associated with (13). Hence, there will virtually be no difference in the computations for solving (12) or (13), if the starting point is "strictly" feasible. But if one takes a starting point which violates both constraints, the penalty function will be given by

$$g(x,y) + r^{-1}[\min(0,x)]^2 + r^{-1}[\min(0,10000y)]^2.$$

From the form of this function it is easy to understand how the numerical difficulties arise. First, an attempt is made to find a point which satisfies the second constraint. Violation of the first constraint will make only a small contribution to the value of the penalty function: this constraint violation will be hardly noticed. The remedy is obvious, however. One has to attach appropriate weight factors to the constraints of (12) so that this problem is reduced to (13). Generally, we advise the user to supply a starting point x_o for the problem (2) such that $g_i(x_o) > 10^{-10}$; $i \in I$ (see also sec. 8 and sec. 12).

Imbalance of equality constraints can be overcome in two different ways. Weight factors can be introduced, just as in the case of inequality constraints. One frequently comes across a system of equality constraints

$$g_i(x) = \tilde{g}_i(x) - b_i = 0; \, i \in E,$$

where the constants b_i differ considerably in order of magnitude. Such a system is conveniently replaced by

$$b_i^{-1} \tilde{g}_i(x) = 1; \, i \in E.$$

It is far more profitable, however, to use the equality constraints in order to eliminate some variables by solving them in terms of the remaining ones. Then the number of variables as well as the number of constraints is reduced. The inclusion of the explicit equality constraint $x_1 + x_2 = 1$, for instance, does not

give the best problem formulation. A better formulation could be
obtained if x_2 is replaced by $1 - x_1$ throughout the problem. The
explicit constraint could then be omitted without any difficulties.

8. PATHOLOGICAL BEHAVIOUR OF PENALTY-FUNCTION ALGORITHMS

The penalty-function approach for solving inequality constrained problems via unconstrained minimization is based on a
number of assumptions which are often violated in practice. The
most important assumptions (as described by the author (1970)) are
the following ones:

a)   The constraint set is a <u>compact</u>, <u>convex</u> set, and it contains
     at least one point which satisfies the inequality constraints
     with <u>strict</u> inequality sign.

b)   The objective function is defined on the constraint set, and
     <u>convex</u>.

c)   Certain conditions are satisfied which are necessary to estab-
     lish local <u>uniqueness</u> of a minimum solution $\bar{x}$, and <u>uniqueness</u>
     of the vector $\bar{u}$ of associated Lagrangian multipliers. One of
     these conditions is the strict complementarity of the Kuhn-
     Tucker point $(\bar{x}, \bar{u})$ implying that the multipliers corresponding
     to the active constraints are <u>positive</u>.

This section presents a number of examples to show the patho-
logical behaviour of penalty-function algorithms if some of these
basic assumptions are <u>not</u> satisfied.

<u>Example 1</u>. If the constraint set is unbounded, it may happen that
the penalty function has no finite minimum for $r > 0$. Consider the
two-dimensional problem

$$\text{minimize } g(x_1, x_2) \text{ subject to}$$

$$x_1 \geqq 0 \text{ and } x_2 \geqq 0,$$

where g is equal to the <u>constant</u> value c, for any x_1 and x_2. If
the starting point of the computations is strictly feasible (i.e.,
if it has positive components), the penalty function (5) for solving
this problem reduces to the logarithmic-barrier function

$$c - r \ln x_1 - r \ln x_2.$$

It is obvious that this function has no finite minimum over the
positive orthant for positive values of r. If the starting point
violates both constraints of the problem, the penalty function (5)
reduces to the quadratic-loss function

$$c + r^{-1}\{[\min(0,x_1)]^2 + [\min(0,x_2)]^2\}.$$

Difficulties would not arise here, as the reader may verify. This example shows a behaviour of barrier functions which is likely to occur if a <u>slowly varying</u> function is minimized over an <u>unbounded</u> constraint set. The remedy is obvious, however. One could introduce the additional constraint

$$x_1 + x_2 \leqq K,$$

where K is large enough to avoid that the solution to the original problem is cut off.

Example 2. Occasionally, a penalty function has a finite minimum for sufficiently small values of r only. This may happen if the constraint set is unbounded, or if constraint violations do not increase rapidly enough. Consider the one-dimensional example

minimize x subject to exp $(x) \geqq 1$.

If the starting point of the computations is feasible, the penalty function (5) for solving the problem can be written as the logarithmic-barrier function

$$x - r \ln[\exp(x) - 1].$$

Let x(r) denote the point minimizing this function over the interior of the constraint set. By differentiating and putting the derivative equal to zero, the reader can easily verify that x(r) is defined for $0 < r < 1$ only, and given by

$$x(r) = -\ln(1 - r).$$

In a similar fashion it is possible to show that the associated quadratic-loss function

$$x + r^{-1} \{\min[0, \exp(x) - 1]\}^2$$

has a finite minimum for $0 < r < 1/2$ only. This is due to the particular property that constraint violations in this problem cannot be smaller than -1.

Example 3. Convergence to an unfeasible solution may occur if the constraint set is non-convex, or even if some of the constraint functions are non-concave. Consider the one-dimensional problem

minimize x subject to

$$x^2 \geqq 4 \text{ and } x \geqq 0.$$

If the computations start from an unfeasible solution the penalty function for solving the problem is given by

$$x + r^{-1}\{[\min(0, x^2 - 4)]^2 + [\min(0, x)]^2\}.$$

On the interval $(-2, 0)$ this function reduces to

$$x + r^{-1}\{(x^2 - 4)^2 + x^2\}.$$

By differentiating and putting the derivative equal to zero one finds that a local minimum $x(r)$ in the interval $(-2, 0)$ has to satisfy the equation

$$r + 4x^3 - 14x = 0$$

whence

$$\lim_{r \downarrow 0} x(r) = -\sqrt{3.5}.$$

For further information about the dangers of starting from unfeasible solutions we refer the reader to sec. 7 and sec. 12.

Example 4. Extrapolation towards a constrained minimum is based on the theoretical result that the trajectory $x(r)$ of penalty-function minima can be expanded in a Taylor series about $r = 0$, in terms of r (see Fiacco and McCormick (1968), and Lootsma (1970)). The result is true under certain uniqueness and complementarity conditions. Let us now consider the two-dimensional example

$$\text{minimize } x_1^2 + x_2^2 \text{ subject to}$$

$$x_1 \geq 0 \text{ and } x_2 \geq 0.$$

The logarithmic-barrier function associated with the problem can be written as

$$x_1^2 + x_2^2 - r \ln x_1 - r \ln x_2.$$

The minimizing point $(x_1(r), x_2(r))$ is clearly given by

$$x_1(r) = x_2(r) = 1/2\sqrt{2r},$$

and these components are not differentiable at $r = 0$ so that a Taylor series about $r = 0$ does not exist. The problem, however, does not satisfy the condition that the Lagrangian multipliers $\bar{u}_1$

and $\bar{u}_2$ associated with the active constraints must be positive. This example shows a behaviour which is likely to occur if some of the active constraints are redundant.

PART II: USER'S MANUAL

9.   EXPLANATION OF THE PARAMETER LIST

Communication with minifun is possible via the parameters in the parameter list only; there are no global parameters in minifun. The declaration of minifun is as follows:

    procedure minifun (x,function,xtype,gtype,lin,info,first,
    second,method,n,m,raxmin,aaxmin,estimate,stop,converged,coc,
    imax);
    value n,m,raxmin,aaxmin,estimate,stop,coc,imax;
    integer info,method,n,m,stop,coc,imax;
    real raxmin,aaxmin,estimate;
    boolean converged;
    real array x; integer array xtype, gtype;
    boolean array lin;
    procedure function,first,second;
    <body>;

When minifun is called the actual parameters, which are here denoted by the corresponding formal parameters, have the following meaning.

x   real array with elements $x[1],\ldots,x[n]$; before calling minifun the starting point of the computations (a good guess at the minimum solution) must be supplied by the user and stored in x; on return x contains the solution calculated by minifun;

function procedure with three parameters x,g,i; by a call the real parameter g is evaluated for the current value of the integer parameter i and the current values of the elements in the real array $x[1:n]$; via this procedure the user supplies the problem functions as functions of the independent variables $x[1],\ldots,x[n]$; the declaration reads

    procedure function (x,g,i);
    integer i; real g; real array x;
    <body>;

xtype   integer array with elements xtype $[1],\ldots,$xtype $[n]$; the elements of xtype must be assigned the value 1,2 or 3: if x[j] is required to be an unrestricted variable

then xtype [j] must be set to 1; if x [j] is required
to be non-negative, then xtype [j] must be set to 2;
if x[j] is required to satisfy the constraints
$0 \leq x[j] \leq 1$, then xtype [j] must be set to 3;

gtype   integer array with elements gtype [1],...,gtype [m];
the elements of gtype must be assigned the values 1,
2 or 3; if the ith problem function (supplied via the
procedure function) is required to be the objective
function, then gtype [i] must be set to 1; if the ith
problem function is required to be non-negative, then
gtype [i] must be set to 2; if the ith problem function
is required to be zero, then gtype [i] must be set to
3; thus, the objective function and the constraint
functions may be given in any order, but we advise the
user to supply first the constraint functions (if any)
and thereafter the objective function of the problem
(see also sec. 1 and sec. 12);

lin   boolean array with elements lin [1],...,lin[m];
if the ith problem function is linear, then lin[i]
must be set to true; otherwise, lin[i] must be set
to false; this array is used to facilitate differen-
tation;

info   integer expression; this parameter (the order of information) must be given the value 0, 1 or 2 to indicate that no derivatives (info = 0), first derivatives
(info = 1), or first and second derivatives (info = 2)
of the problem functions will be supplied by the user;

first   procedure with three parameters x, dg, and i; by a
call the elements of the real array dg[1:n] are evaluated
for the current value of the integer parameter i and the
current values of the elements of the real array x[1:n];
it is assumed that dg[j] is the first-order partial derivative of the ith problem function with respect to x[j];
only non-zero derivatives need be supplied; the declaration reads

```
procedure first (x,dg,i);
integer i; real array x, dg;
<body>;
```

if the user does not want to supply the first derivatives,
a dummy procedure must be declared, and the parameter
info must be set to 0;

second   procedure with three parameters x, ddg, and i; by a call
the elements of the real array ddg[1:n, 1:n] are evaluated for the current value of the integer parameter i and

the current values of the elements of the real array
x[1:n]; it is assumed that ddg[j,k] is the second-order
partial derivative of the ith problem function with
respect to x[j] and x[k]; only non-zero derivatives with
j $\leq$ k (the upper-right part of the Hessian matrix) need
be supplied; the declaration reads

        procedure second (x,ddg,i)
        integer i; real array x, ddg;
        <body>;

if the user does not want to supply the second derivatives, a dummy procedure must be declared and the parameter info must be set to 0 or 1;

method   integer expression; this parameter must be assigned the
value 0, 1 or 2; if method = 0 a zeroth-order method for
unconstrained minimization will be used (the P64 algorithm without derivatives); if method = 1 a first-order
method will be used (the BFS algorithm for minimization
problems and the Gauss-Newton algorithm for non-linear
(in)equalities, both of which require first derivatives
of the problem functions); if method = 2 a second-order
method will be employed (the NFM algorithm which requires
first and second derivatives of the problem functions);
a higher-order method is often faster than a lower-order
method; generally we advise the user to set the parameter
method to the value which has been assigned to the parameter info or even to the value info +1; if method has
been given a value greater than info, the missing derivatives will be generated by numerical differentiation;
the combination info = 0 and method = 2 is not allowed;

n   integer expression; the number of variables;
m   integer expression; the number of problem functions;

raxmin   real expression; relative tolerance of the solution to
be calculated; a value of 10^{-5} is suggested;

aaxmin   real expression; absolute tolerance of the solution to
be calculated; a value of 10^{-5} is suggested;

estimate real expression; an estimate of the value of the objective function at a minimum solution; it is only used in
constrained minimization in order to find the value r_o
of formula (9);

stop   integer expression; this parameter must be assigned the
value 0, 1 or 2 to indicate that the accuracy is required
in the minimum value of the objective function (stop = 0),

414

in the components of a minimum solution (stop = 1), or
in both (stop = 2);

converged boolean variable; this parameter is set to <u>true</u> by
minifun if one of the convergence criteria is satisfied;
otherwise, converged will be <u>false</u> on return from minifun;

coc integer expression; this parameter (the conditional output control parameter) must be given the value 0, 1 or
2; if coc = 0 then no output will be given; if coc = 1
then minifun produces short output in every iteration,
and x-output in the first and the last iteration of an
unconstrained-minimization cycle; in addition to this,
x-output appears in every iteration if coc = 2; an
explanation will be given in sec. 10;

imax integer expression; the maximum number of iterations
permitted by the user.

10. OUTPUT

The procedure minifun has been designed for use with the
Electrologica X8 computer. It calls some of the output procedures
and a time procedure available in the ALGOL 60 system.

<u>Short output</u> is a single-line summary of the current iteration
presenting the iteration number, the value of the penalty function
and the length of its gradient both evaluated at the current iteration point, the distance between the current and the preceding
iteration point, and the time elapsed since the start of the computations.

<u>X-output</u> is a print of the current iteration point (solution
vector) and the gradient of the penalty function at this point.

<u>G-output</u> is a print of the values of the problem functions
at the current iteration point, and the current approximation
(dual solution) of the Lagrangian multipliers of problem (2).

Some messages may be given during the computations. They are
self-explanatory so that they do not need to be discussed here.

The subroutines and procedures of scientific software libraries (for numerical problems such as the solution of linear
equations, the integration of differential equations, etc.) are
normally written without standard output provisions. For optimization procedures, which are frequently used to improve a guess
at an optimum solution, output provisions are indispensable. This
is a common experience in linear programming and we have accordingly

incorporated standard output facilities in minifun (see Lootsma 1975)).

11. EXAMPLE

In sec. 14 an example is shown where minifun is called to compute the distance between the set of points (x_1, x_2, x_3) such that

$$x_1^2 + x_2^2 + x_3^2 \leqq 5,$$

and the set of points (x_4, x_5, x_6) satisfying the constraints

$$(x_4 - 3)^2 + x_5^2 \leqq 1,$$

$$4 \leqq x_6 \leqq 8.$$

The problem functions are supplied via the procedure distance, and their first and second derivatives via the procedures ddistance and dddistance respectively. By setting the arrays gtype and lin the user indicates how these functions have to be processed. Thus, a constraint function is evaluated when distance is called for i such that $1 \leqq i \leqq 4$, and the objective function when i = 5. The starting point is chosen to be (1,1,1,3,0,5). Thereafter, minifun is called to solve the problem.

12. POSSIBLE TRAPS

The facilities for numerical differentiation in minifun can also be used to check the derivatives supplied by the user. Errors in the derivatives are extremely dangerous since they do not reveal themselves in the early stages of the minimization process. Several iterations, reducing the penalty function considerably, may be carried out before the process suddenly stops. To recognize the last obtained iteration point as an erratic solution is only possible if the user has a thorough knowledge of his problem, or if he tries to find a solution from different starting points. An easy and often satisfactory check, however, is obtained by comparison of the derivatives with their numerical approximations, both evaluated at the starting point of the minimization process. So, minifun checks first derivatives by comparing them with differences of function values, and second derivatives by comparing them with differences of first derivatives. The maximum relative deviation is printed. If this is more than 1% we advise the user to look for errors in the derivatives which he has given.

Any gradient method for minimizing a function is essentially using local information so that it can only produce a local minimum. Therefore, the starting point of the minimization process should be a good guess at a global solution. Furthermore, one should try to solve a given problem from different starting points. If the same solution is produced in all these runs it may indeed be a global minimum.

If the problem is one of constrained minimization, and if the starting point is unfeasible, convergence to an unfeasible point may occur (see also sec. 7 and sec. 8). The procedure has probably located undesired local minima of the penalty function or, and this may even be worse, there is no solution to the constraints at all. An unconstrained-minimization method cannot distinguish between these two cases. The user should inspect the problem formulation and/or restart the computations from another point. It is worth noting that minifun can be used to generate a better starting point, if the objective function is taken to be the last of the problem functions. The parameter m must be set to the number of constraints. The objective function is then ignored, and minifun reduces the infeasibilities in an attempt to find a solution to the constraints. Thereafter, the parameter m must be set to the number of problem functions, and minifun must be called again to solve the constrained minimization problem, starting from the point which has just been generated.

If the penalty function decreases below reasonable limits, this may be an indication that a finite solution does not exist. The user should then check whether the problem formulation is correct and whether the proper constraints are imposed. Define a constraint set which is bounded!

In sec. 7 we argued that improper scaling may lead to numerical difficulties during the minimization process. It could be helpful to choose the units of the physical, chemical or other quantities of the problem in such a way that each of the variables varies over a range of the same order of magnitude (preferably over the interval (0,1) or (-1,1)). Alternatively, the units could be chosen in such a way that the non-zero components of the expected minimum are of the same order of magnitude.

13. PERFORMANCE

The performance of minifun on a few well-known test problems may be found in a paper by the present author (1972b), where several unconstrained-minimization methods and several linear-search methods are compared. For these problems, quadratic interpolation with a strong convergence criterion (QUs) was almost consistently successful in the P64, the BFS and the NFM algorithm. Hence we

removed the other linear searches from previous versions of minifun. The performance of the present version is displayed in the
rows corresponding to QUs, in the tables I-IX of the cited paper.

The significance of numerical differentiation in minifun and
a preliminary comparison with other programs for non-linear optimization have been described by the author (1975). The general
conclusions are as follows. Minifun is somewhat slower than some
FORTRAN programs based on the reduced-gradient method. Mostly,
differentiation should be used as far as possible. Thus, if the
user is not in a position to supply first derivatives, the BFS
algorithm should be used (method = 1) with numerical approximations
to the first derivatives (info = 0); if he cannot supply second
derivatives, the NFM algorithm should be employed (method = 2) with
numerical approximations to the second derivatives (info = 1).

Practical experience has shown that minifun can be used to
solve problems with up to 50 variables and 50 constraints.

PART III: PROGRAMMING DETAILS

14. STRUCTURE AND LISTING OF MINIFUN

The procedure minifun consists mainly of a number of procedures to compute the penalty function and its derivatives, and to
carry out unconstrained minimization of the penalty function.

The main program of minifun checks the values assigned to
various parameters in order to decide whether the problem to be
solved has the type (1), (2) or (3). The parameter values are
printed out (if desired), and the procedures errorgrad and error-
hess are called to compare the analytical derivatives supplied by
the user and the numerical derivatives, both evaluated at the
starting point. Thereafter, a cycle for (sequential) unconstrained
minimization is set up. Unconstrained minimization is carried out
by the procedure rcycle, and extrapolation by the procedure extra-
pol. The convergence test for constrained-minimization problems
is applied at the end of the cycle with the procedure ready.

The main program of the procedure rcycle generates the search
directions according to the methods explained in sec. 2 and 5.
The procedures penalty, gradient, and hessian are used to compute
the penalty function, and its first and second derivatives respectively. The procedure quadsearch controls the linear search and
calls the procedure move (to locate an interval embracing a line
minimum; see sec. 3) and the procedure interpol (to approximate
a line minimum by quadratic interpolation). The procedure
cholesky is used to factorize the Hessian matrix (see sec. 2) and
to solve the system (4).

The penalty function (5) is evaluated by the procedure penalty, but the index sets I_1 and I_2 defined by (8) and the index set E corresponding to the equality constraints are determined at other places. The main program of minifun incorporates all the inequality constraints in a barrier term. The main program of rcycle, at last, generates the sets I_1 and I_2; the inequality constraints violated at the starting point are transferred to the loss term (7); the remaining inequality constraints constitute the barrier term (6). The procedure transfer is called by penalty to avoid the generation of very large numbers during the calculation of the logarithmic-barrier term.

If an objective function has not been supplied by the user, the penalty function (11) will be generated. The main program of minifun takes care of this.

Output during unconstrained minimization will be given by the procedure output1. A detailed account of the number of function, gradient, and Hessian-matrix evaluations will be supplied via the procedure output2. Finally, the results of extrapolation will be printed via the procedure output3.

The listing on the pages to follow shows a program where minifun is called to solve the example of sec. 11.

15. SYSTEM PROCEDURES CALLED BY MINIFUN

The following procedures, which are called by minifun, do not need to be declared in an ALGOL 60 program for the Electrologica X8 computer in Philips Research Laboratories.

procedure absfixt (n,m,x); value n,m,x;
integer n,m; real x; comment when this procedure is called the absolute value of x will be printed in fixed-point representation: one space, n decimal digits (leading zeroes being replaced by spaces), decimal point, m decimal digits, one space (if m = 0 the decimal point is not printed); <body> ;

procedure carriage (n); value n; integer n; comment causes the printer to advance the paper n lines and to take the print position at the beginning of the line; <body> ;

procedure flot (n,m,x); value n,m,x; integer n,m; real x; comment when this procedure is called the value of x will be printed in floating-point representation: sign, decimal point, n decimal digits, the symbol 10, sign, m decimal digits (leading zeroes being replaced by spaces), one space; <body> ;

```
begin comment  example where minifun is called to compute the
distance between the set of points (x[1],x[2],x[3]) such that
            x[1]↑2 + x[2]↑2 + x[3]↑2 < 5,
and the set of points (x[4],x[5],x[6]) satisfying the constraints
            (x[4] − 3)↑2 + x[5]↑2 ≤ 1,
            4 < x[6] < 8.
— the starting point of the search is chosen to be (1,1,1,3,0,5);


procedure  minifun(x, function, xtype, gtype, lin, info, first, second,
method, n, m, raxmin, aaxmin, estimate, stop, converged, coc, imax);
value  n, m, raxmin, aaxmin, estimate, stop, coc, imax;
integer  info, method, n, m, stop, coc, imax;
real  raxmin, aaxmin, estimate;
boolean  converged;
real array  x; integer array  xtype, gtype;
boolean array  lin;
procedure  function, first, second;
begin real  initr, factor, fmin, dfmin, starttime;
    integer  i, j, k, ieff, cycle, maxcycle, order,
    np, ng, nh, nsearch, nrp, mpn;
    boolean  bounded, objective, constraints, nlp, heading,
    nonneg, incorrect;
    real array  xrmin, xmin, dxmin[1:n], gmin, urmin, umin[1:m],
    xtable[1:n, 0:6], utable[1:m, 0:6], rtable[0:6];
    boolean array  logp[1:m+2×n];


    procedure rcycle(r, xr, ur, raxr, aaxr); value r;
    real r, raxr, aaxr; real array  xr, ur;
    comment  unconstrained minimization to compute an r-minimum
    xr[1:n] and the associated dual multipliers ur[1:m] with relative
    and absolute accuracy raxr and aaxr respectively;
    begin integer  itercnt, counter, reset, rule, pvalues, pointer, maxm;
        boolean  def, fail;
        real  prxr, dprxr, dprp0, sugstep, descent, gradl, distance, maxdp,
        ln10, racc, aacc;
        real array  grad, dir, sigma, yvec, dp0[1:n], h[1:n, 1:n],
        gxr[1:m], dgxrdx[1:m, 1:n], step[0:n];


        real procedure penalty(p, t, q, gt, reject, pvalues);
        integer reject, pvalues; real  t; real array  p, q, gt;
        comment computes the problem functions gt[1:m] and the penalty
        function at the point p[1:n] + t × q[1:n] — reject indicates
        whether this point is feasible or not: it is the index of the
        first encountered, violated constraint;
        begin integer  i, j; real  product, barrier, loss, pen;
            real array  xt[1:n];
            pvalues := pvalues + 1;
            penalty := pen := loss := 0; reject := 0;
            barrier := 0; product := 1;
            for j := 1 step 1 until n do xt[j] := p[j] + t × q[j];
```

```
if  nonneg or  bounded then
for  j := 1 step 1 until n do
begin real  xtj,ytj; integer  xtypej;
  xtypej := xtype[j];
  if  xtypej = 2 or  xtypej = 3 then
  begin  xtj := xt[j];
    if  logp[m+j] then
    begin if  xtj > ᵣ–10 then
      begin  product := product x xtj;
        transfer(product,barrier)
      end else
      begin  reject := m+j; nrp := nrp+1; goto  fin end
    end  of logarithmic transformation else
    if  xtj < 0 then  loss := loss + xtj↑2
  end  of handling nonnegative variable;
  if  xtypej = 3 then
  begin  ytj := 1 – xtj;
    if  logp[mpn+j] then
    begin if  ytj > ᵣ–10 then
      begin  product := product x ytj;
        transfer(product,barrier)
      end else
      begin  reject := mpn+j; nrp := nrp+1; goto  fin end
    end  of logarithmic transformation else
    if  ytj < 0 then  loss := loss + ytj↑2
  end  of handling upper bound
end  of j loop;
for  i := 1 step 1 until m do
begin real  gti; integer  gtypei;
  function(xt,gt[i],i);
  gti := gt[i]; gtypei := gtype[i];
  if  gtypei = 1 then  pen := pen + gti else
  begin if  gtypei = 2 then
    begin if  logp[i] then
      begin if  gti > ᵣ–10 then
        begin  product := product x gti;
          transfer(product,barrier)
        end else
        begin reject := i; nrp := nrp + 1; goto fin end
      end of logarithmic transformation
      else if  gti < 0 then  loss := loss + gti↑2
    end of handling inequality constraints
    else if  gtypei = 3 then  loss := loss + gti↑2
  end of transforming constraints
end of i loop for generating barrier and loss term;
penalty := pen + loss/r –
r x (barrier + (if  product=1 then  0 else  ln(product)));
np := np + 1;
fin:
end  of penalty;
```

```
procedure  transfer(p, sumln);  real   p, sumln;
begin if  p < ₁₀–40 then
   begin  p := p × ₁₀+40;  sumln := sumln – 40 × ln10 end ;
   if  p > ₁₀+40 then
   begin  p := p × ₁₀–40;  sumln := sumln + 40 × ln10 end
end  of transfer;


procedure  gradient(xt, gt, dgtdx, dptdx);
real array   xt, gt, dgtdx, dptdx;
comment  computes gradients dgtdx[1:m,1:n] of problem
functions and gradient dptdx[1:n] of penalty function
at the point xt[1:n] — the array gt[1:m] must contain the
values of the problem functions at this point;
begin real   r1 ; integer  1, j;  boolean  add1 ;
   real array   dxt, dg[1:n];
ng := ng + 1 ;
for  j := 1 step  1 until  n do
begin  dptdx[j] := 0;
   dxt[j] := ₁₀–3 × abs(xt[j]) + ₁₀–6;
end  of initiating;
for  1 := 1 step  1 until  m do
for  j := 1 step  1 until  n do  dgtdx[1, j] := 0;
for  1 := 1 step  1 until  m do
begin real   gt1;  integer   gtype1;
   gt1 := gt[1]; gtype1 := gtype[1];
   add1 := true ;
   if  gtype1 = 1 then  r1 := 1 else
   if  gtype1 = 2 then
   begin if  logp[1] then  r1 := –r/gt1 else
      if  gt1 < 0 then  r1 := 2 × gt1/r else
      add1 := false
   end  of handling inequality constraints else
   if  gtype1 = 3 then  r1 := 2 × gt1/r;
   if  add1 then
   begin comment  find first derivatives of g1 ;
      for  j := 1 step  1 until  n do  dg[j] := 0;
      if  info ≥ 1 then  first(xt, dg, 1) else
      begin comment  numerical differentiation;
         for  j := 1 step  1 until  n do
         begin real   xtj, gdelta;
         xtj := xt[j]; xt[j] := xtj + dxt[j];
         function(xt, gdelta, 1);
         if  lin[1] then  dg[j] := (gdelta – gt[1])/dxt[j]
         else
         begin  dg[j] := gdelta; xt[j] := xtj – dxt[j];
            function(xt, gdelta, 1);
            dg[j] := (dg[j] – gdelta)/(2 × dxt[j])
         end  of generating j–th element;
         xt[j] := xtj;
```

```
          end  of j loop;
        end  of computing first derivatives;
        for  j := 1 step 1 until  n do
        begin dptdx[j] := dptdx[j] + r1 × dg[j];
          dgtdx[i,j] := dg[j]
        end  of adding constraint gradients
      end  of test for satisfied constraints in loss term
    end  of i loop;
    if  nonneg or  bounded then
    for  j := 1 step 1 until  n do
    begin real  xtj,ytj,dptdxj; integer  xtypej;
      xtypej := xtype[j]; dptdxj := dptdx[j];
      if  xtypej = 2 or  xtypej = 3 then
      begin xtj := xt[j];
        if  logp[m+j] then
        dptdxj := dptdxj − r/xtj else
        if  xtj < 0 then
        dptdxj := dptdxj + 2 × xtj/r
      end  of handling nonnegative variable;
      if  xtypej = 3 then
      begin ytj := 1 − xtj;
        if  logp[mpn+j] then
        dptdxj := dptdxj + r/ytj else
        if  ytj < 0 then
        dptdxj := dptdxj − 2 × ytj/r
      end  of handling upper bound;
      dptdx[j] := dptdxj
    end  of j loop;
  end  of gradient;


  procedure  hessian(xt,gt,dgtdx,hxt);
  real array  xt,gt,dgtdx,hxt;
  comment  computes the hessian matrix hxt[1:n,1:n] of the
  penalty function at the point xt[1:n] — the arrays gt[1:m]
  and dgtdx[1:m,1:n] must contain the values and the first
  derivatives of the problem functions at this point;
  begin real  r11,r2; integer  i,j,k;
    boolean  add11,add2;
    real array  dxt,dgtdxi,dgdeltadx[1:n],ddg[1:n,1:n];
    nh := nh + 1;
    for  j := 1 step 1 until  n do
    for  k := j step 1 until  n do  hxt[j,k] := 0;
    for  j := 1 step 1 until  n do
    dxt[j] := 10−3 × abs(xt[j]) + 10−6;
    for  i := 1 step 1 until  m do
    begin real  gti; integer  gtypei;
      gti := gt[i]; gtypei := gtype[i];
      add11 := true ; add2 := (not  lin[i]) and  method = 2;
      for  j := 1 step 1 until  n do
      dgtdxi[j] := dgtdx[i,j];
```

```
if  gtypei = 1 then
begin add11 := false ; r2 := 1 end else
if  gtypei = 2 then
begin if  logp[i] then
    begin r11 := r/gti↑2; r2 := -r/gti end else
    begin if  gti < 0 then
       begin r11 := 2/r; r2 := 2 × gti/r end else
       add11 := add2 := false
    end  of handling satisfied constraints in loss term
end  of handling inequality constraints else
if  gtypei = 3 then
begin r11 := 2/r; r2 := 2 × gti/r end ;
if  add11 then
for  j := 1 step 1 until  n do
begin real  factor;
   factor := r11 × dgtdxi[j];
   for  k := j step 1 until  n do
   hxt[j,k] := hxt[j,k] + factor × dgtdxi[k]
end  of adding product of constraint gradients;
if  add2 then
begin comment  find second derivatives of gi;
   for  j := 1 step 1 until  n do
   for  k := j step 1 until  n do  ddg[j,k] := 0;
   if  info = 2 then  second(xt,ddg,1) else
   begin comment  numerical differentiation; real  xtj;
      for  j := 1 step 1 until  n do
      begin  xtj := xt[j]; xt[j] := xtj + dxt[j];
         for  k := j step 1 until  n do
         dgdeltadx[k] := 0;
         first(xt,dgdeltadx,1);
         for  k := j step 1 until  n do
         ddg[j,k] := (dgdeltadx[k] - dgtdxi[k])/dxt[j];
         xt[j] := xtj;
      end  of j loop
   end  of computing second derivatives;
   for  j := 1 step 1 until  n do
   for  k := j step 1 until  n do
   hxt[j,k] := hxt[j,k] + r2 × ddg[j,k]
   end  of adding hessian of constraints
end  of i loop;
if  nonneg or  bounded then
for  j := 1 step 1 until  n do
begin real  xtj,ytj,hxtjj; integer  xtypej;
   hxtjj := hxt[j,j]; xtypej := xtype[j];
   if  xtypej = 2 or  xtypej = 3 then
   begin  xtj := xt[j];
      if  logp[m+j] then
      hxtjj := hxtjj + r/xtj↑2 else
      if  xtj < 0 then
      hxtjj := hxtjj + 2/r
```

```
      end  of handling nonnegative variable;
      if  xtypej = 3 then
      begin ytj := 1 - xtj;
         if  logp[mpn+j] then
         hxtjj := hxtjj + r/ytj↑2 else
         if  ytj < 0 then
         hxtjj := hxtjj + 2/r
      end  of handling upper bound;
      hxt[j,j] := hxtjj
   end  of j loop;
end  of hessian;


procedure  quadsearch(point, prpoint, gpoint, s, sugstep,
racc, aacc, directed);
value  racc, aacc;  real  prpoint, sugstep, racc, aacc;
boolean  directed;
real array  point, gpoint, s;
comment  linear search along direction s[1:n] from point[1:n]
— sugstep is the initial step size in the search direction
— directed indicates whether a search in both senses
(positive and negative) is necessary or not;
begin integer  i, j, sense;
   real  a, b, c, pra, prb, prc;
   real array  ga, gb, gc[1:m];
   pvalues := 0;
   a := b := c := 0; pra := prb := prc := prpoint;
   for  i := 1 step 1 until  m do
   ga[i] := gb[i] := gc[i] := gpoint[i];
   if  sugstep ne  0 and  sum(j, 1, n, abs(s[j])) ne  0 then
   begin  sense := sign(sugstep);
      move(point, s, a, b, c, pra, prb, prc, ga, gb, gc, sugstep,
      sense, pvalues);
      if  directed then
      begin  sugstep := sugstep/2; sense := 2 × sense end else
      begin  sugstep := - sugstep; sense := - sense end ;
      if  a = b or  b = c then
      move(point, s, a, b, c, pra, prb, prc, ga, gb, gc, sugstep,
      sense, pvalues);
      interpol(point, s, a, b, c, pra, prb, prc, ga, gb, gc,
      pvalues, racc, aacc);
   end  of search;
   shift1(b, b, prpoint, prb, gpoint, gb);
   for  j := 1 step 1 until  n do
   point[j] := point[j] + b × s[j];
   sugstep := b
end  of quadsearch;


procedure  shift1(y, z, pry, prz, gy, gz);
real  y, z, pry, prz;  real array  gy, gz;
begin integer  i; y := z; pry := prz;
```

```
    for i := 1 step 1 until m do  gy[i] := gz[i]
end of shift1 ;

procedure  move(point, s, a, b, c, pra, prb, prc, ga, gb, gc, sugstep,
sense, pvalues);
integer  sense, pvalues; real  a, b, c, pra, prb, prc, sugstep;
real array  point, s, ga, gb, gc;
comment  locates three coordinates a, b, and c along the
search direction such that pra ≥ prb and prb < prc;
begin integer  nsteps, idle; real  d, prd, multiplier;
    real array  gd[1:m]; boolean  further;
    further := true ; multiplier := 2;
    for  nsteps := 1 while  pvalues < 50 and  further do
    begin  d := b + sugstep;
      prd := penalty(point, d, s, gd, idle, pvalues);
      if  idle > 0 then
      begin  sugstep := sugstep/2; multiplier := 0.5 end else
      if  prd < prb then
      begin if  sense > 0 then  shift1(a, b, pra, prb, ga, gb) else
        shift1(c, b, prc, prb, gc, gb);
        if  sense=2 or  sense=-2 then  further := false else
        sugstep := multiplier × sugstep;
        shift1(b, d, prb, prd, gb, gd)
      end else
      begin if  sense > 0 then shift1(c, d, prc, prd, gc, gd) else
        shift1(a, d, pra, prd, ga, gd);
        if  sense=1 or  sense=-1 then  further := false else
        sugstep := sugstep/2
      end  of testing feasible trial point d
    end  of nsteps loop
end  of move;

procedure  interpol(point, s, a, b, c, pra, prb, prc, ga, gb, gc,
pvalues, racc, aacc);
integer  pvalues; real  a, b, c, pra, prb, prc, racc, aacc;
real array  point, s, ga, gb, gc;
comment  repeated quadratic interpolation to approximate
a line minimum;
begin integer  nsteps, idle; real  pa, pc, d, prd;
    real array  gd[1:m]; boolean  further;
    further := true ;
    for  nsteps := 1 while  pvalues < 50 and  further do
    begin comment  d minimizes interpolating quadratic;
      pc := (a − b) × (prc − prb);
      if  pc = 0 then  d := (b + c)/2 else
      begin  pa := (b − c) × (pra − prb);
        d := if  pa = 0 then  (a + b)/2 else
        0.5 × ((a + b) × pc + (b + c) × pa)/(pa + pc)
      end  of computing d;
      prd := penalty(point, d, s, gd, idle, pvalues);
```

```
        if idle > 0 then
        begin shift1 (d, b, prd, prb, gd, gb);
          if coc ne 0 then
          begin carriage(2);
            printtext({ line search in troubles, });
            printtext({ probably non-convex constraint set })
          end of message
        end of alarm;
        if (b ne 0 or prd le prb) and
        abs(prd - prb) < racc × abs(prd) + aacc then
        further := false ;
        if d < b then
        begin if prd le prb then
          begin shift1 (c, b, prc, prb, gc, gb);
            shift1 (b, d, prb, prd, gb, gd)
          end else shift1 (a, d, pra, prd, ga, gd)
        end else
        begin if prd le prb then
          begin shift1 (a, b, pra, prb, ga, gb);
            shift1 (b, d, prb, prd, gb, gd)
          end else shift1 (c, d, prc, prd, gc, gd)
        end of rearranging a, b, c;
      end of quadratic interpolation;
end of interpol;

procedure cholesky(a, s, b, def, fail);
real array a, s, b; boolean def, fail;
begin integer i, j, k; real xx, yy, zz;
  real array diag, y[1:n];
  for j := 1 step 1 until n do
  s[j] := y[j] := diag[j] := 0;
  def := true ; fail := false ;
  for i := 1 step 1 until n do
  for j := 1 step 1 until i do
  begin xx := a[j, i];
    if i = j then
    begin for k := j - 1 step -1 until 1 do
      begin yy := a[i, k];
        zz := a[i, k] := yy/diag[k];
        xx := xx - yy × zz
      end of k loop;
      if xx le 0 then
      begin def := false ; y[i] := 1 end ;
      if xx = 0 then
      begin fail := true ; goto solve end ;
      diag[i] := xx
    end of generating diagonal elements else
    a[i, j] := xx - inprod(k, 1, j-1, a[i, k], a[j, k])
  end of i and j loop;
solve: if fail then
```

```
begin for  j := 1 step 1 until  n do  s[j] := -b[j];
end  of setting s to -b else
begin if  def then
   begin comment  solution of ly = b;
      for  j := 1 step 1 until  n do
      y[j] := b[j] - inprod(k,1,j-1,a[j,k],y[k]);
      comment  solution of dus = y;
      for  j := n step -1 until  1 do
      s[j] := y[j]/diag[j] - inprod(k,j+1,n,a[k,j],s[k])
   end  of solving as = b else
   begin comment  solution of us = y;
      for  j := n step -1 until  1 do
      s[j] := y[j] - inprod(k,j+1,n,a[k,j],s[k]);
   end  of finding direction with negative curvature
   end  of finding direction if decomposition is successful
end  of cholesky;


procedure  output1 ;
begin integer i,j;
   if itercnt = 0 ∧ nlp then
   begin carriage(2);
      printtext({ begin of cycle }); absfixt(2,0,cycle);
      printtext({ for r equal to }); flot(3,3,r)
   end ;
   comment short output;
   if heading then
   begin carriage(2); printtext({ iteration   });
      printtext({ penalty value      gradient length });
      space(8); printtext({ distance });
      space(10); printtext({ time });
   end of printing the heading;
   nlcr; absfixt(6,0,ieff); space(6); flot(6,3,prxr); space(7);
   if  method > 1 then  flot(6,3,gradl) else  space(14);
   space(7); flot(6,3,distance);
   space(5); absfixt(4,2,time - starttime);
   if  method = 2 and not  def then
   begin space(3); if  fail then
      printtext({ h not factorized }) else
      printtext({ h indefinite })
   end  of messages;
   heading := false ;
   comment end of short output;
   if ieff = 0 ∨ converged ∨ coc = 2 then
   begin comment x-output; carriage(2);
      printtext({  variable    solution vector    });
      printtext({ gradient of penf });
      for j := 1 step 1 until n do
      begin nlcr; printtext({x }); absfixt(4,0,j); space(6);
         flot(6,3,xr[j]); space(7);
         if  method > 1 then  flot(6,3,grad[j])
```

```
      end of printing iteration point and gradient;
      heading := true
   end of x-output;
   if ieff = 0 ∨ converged then
   begin comment g-output; carriage(2);
      printtext(⊀ function    function values      ⊁);
      if nlp ∧ converged then
      printtext(⊀ dual solution ⊁);
      for i := 1 step 1 until m do
      begin nlcr; printtext(⊀gx⊁); absfixt(4,0,i); space(6);
         flot(6,3,gxr[i]); space(7);
         if nlp ∧ converged then flot(6,3,ur[i])
      end of printing function values and dual solution;
      heading := true
   end of g-output;
   if nlp ∧ converged then
   begin carriage(2);
      printtext(⊀ end of cycle ⊁); absfixt(2,0,cycle);
      printtext(⊀ for r equal to ⊁); flot(3,3,r)
   end
end of output1 for printing iteration data;

real procedure min(a,b); value a,b; real a,b;
min := if a < b then a else b;

comment start of main program of rcycle;
itercnt := counter := 0; distance := 0; converged := false ;
pvalues := 0; def := true ; fail := false ;
ln10 := ln(10);
restart: prxr := penalty(xr,0,xr,gxr,reset,pvalues);
if reset > 0 then
begin logp[reset] := false ; goto restart end ;
for j := 1 step 1 until n do
for k := 1 step 1 until n do
h[j,k] := if j = k then 1 else 0;
if method = 0 then
begin for j := 1 step 1 until n do
   step[j] := if xr[j] = 0 then 1 else xr[j]
end else
if method = 1 and objective then
begin comment compute gradient in starting point;
   gradient(xr,gxr,dgxrdx,grad);
   gradl := sqrt(inprod(j,1,n,grad[j],grad[j]));
   converged := gradl < ₁₀-10
end else
if (method = 1 and not objective) or method = 2 then
begin comment compute gradient and hessian in starting point;
   gradient(xr,gxr,dgxrdx,grad);
   gradl := sqrt(inprod(j,1,n,grad[j],grad[j]));
   converged := gradl < ₁₀-10;
```

```
    hessian(xr,gxr,dgxrdx,h)
end  of initializing;
rule := if  nlp and  stop = 0 then  1 else  stop;
racc := min(₁₀-5,abs(raxr));
aacc := min(₁₀-5,abs(aaxr));
if coc ne 0 then  output1 ;
for  itercnt := itercnt + 1 while not  converged and
ieff le  imax do
begin comment unconstrained-minimization cycle;
    if  method = 0 then
    begin comment  method of powell(1964);
        pointer := itercnt - (itercnt:(n+1)) x (n+1);
        if  pointer = 1 then
        begin dprp0 := prxr;
            for  j := 1 step  1 until  n do  dp0[j] := xr[j]
        end  of storing starting point of (n + 1) iterations;
        for  j := 1 step  1 until  n do
        dir[j] := if  pointer = 0 then
        xr[j] - dp0[j] else  h[pointer,j];
        if  pointer = 0 then
        step[pointer] := sqrt(inprod(j,1,n,dir[j],dir[j]));
        sugstep := step[pointer];
        for  j := 1 step  1 until  n do  sigma[j] := xr[j];
        dprxr := prxr; nsearch := nsearch + 1 ;
        quadsearch(xr,prxr,gxr,dir,sugstep,racc,aacc,method≥1 );
        dprxr := dprxr - prxr;
        for  j := 1 step  1 until  n do
        sigma[j] := xr[j] - sigma[j];
        distance := sqrt(inprod(j,1,n,sigma[j],sigma[j]));
        if  pointer = 1 then  maxdp := 0;
        if  pointer > 0 and  maxdp < dprxr then
        begin  maxdp := dprxr; maxm := pointer end ;
        if  sugstep ne 0 then  step[pointer] := sugstep;
        if  pointer = 0 and  dprxr ne 0 and
        sugstep x sqrt(maxdp/dprxr) ge  1 then
        begin comment  set up new directions;
            for  k := maxm step  1 until  n - 1 do
            for  j := 1 step  1 until  n do
            h[k,j] := h[k+1,j];
            for  j := 1 step  1 until  n do
            h[n,j] := dir[j];
            for  k := maxm step  1 until  n-1 do
            step[k] := step[k+1];
            step[n] := step[0]
        end  of generating new set of directions;
        if  pointer = 0 then
        begin dprp0 := dprp0 - prxr;
            for  j := 1 step  1 until  n do
            dp0[j] := xr[j] - dp0[j];
            if  inprod(j,1,n,dp0[j],dp0[j]) < ₁₀-20 then
```

```
        converged := true ;
        if  ready(prxr,dprp0,xr,dp0,raxr,aaxr,rule) then
        converged := true
    end  of testing the accuracy
end  of method of powell else
if  method = 1 and  objective then
begin comment  broyden-fletcher-shanno algorithm;
    for  i := 1 step  1 until  n do
    dir[i] := - inprod(j,1,n,h[i,j],grad[j]);
    descent := inprod(j,1,n,grad[j],dir[j]);
    sugstep := if  descent = 0 then  0 else
    -sign(descent) × min(1,1/abs(descent));
    for  j := 1 step  1 until  n do  yvec[j] := grad[j];
    for  j := 1 step  1 until  n do  sigma[j] := xr[j];
    dprxr := prxr; nsearch := nsearch + 1 ;
    quadsearch(xr,prxr,gxr,dir,sugstep,racc,aacc,method>1 );
    dprxr := dprxr - prxr;
    for  j := 1 step  1 until  n do
    sigma[j] := xr[j] - sigma[j];
    distance := sqrt(inprod(j,1,n,sigma[j],sigma[j]));
    gradient(xr,gxr,dgxrdx,grad);
    gradl := sqrt(inprod(j,1,n,grad[j],grad[j]));
    for  j := 1 step  1 until  n do
    yvec[j] := grad[j] - yvec[j];
    if  ready(prxr,dprxr,xr,sigma,raxr,aaxr,rule) then
    counter := counter + 1 else  counter := 0;
    if  counter ge  n or  gradl < ₁₀-10 or
    distance < ₁₀-10 then  converged := true else
    begin comment  update direction matrix;
        real  sigmay,yhy,tau; real array  hy[1:n];
        for  i := 1 step  1 until  n do
        hy[i] := inprod(j,1,n,h[i,j],yvec[j]);
        sigmay := inprod(j,1,n,sigma[j],yvec[j]);
        yhy := inprod(j,1,n,yvec[j],hy[j]);
        if  abs(sigmay) < ₁₀-20 ∨ abs(yhy) < ₁₀-20 then
        converged := true ;
        tau := 1 + yhy/sigmay;
        for  i := 1 step  1 until  n do
        for  k := 1 step  1 until  i do
        h[k,i] := h[i,k] := h[i,k] + (tau × sigma[i] × sigma[k]
        - sigma[i] × hy[k] - hy[i] × sigma[k])/sigmay;
    end  of updating
end  of bfs-algorithm else
if  (method = 1 and not  objective) or  method = 2 then
begin comment  method of gauss-newton or newton;
    cholesky(h,dir,grad,def,fail);
    descent := inprod(j,1,n,grad[j],dir[j]);
    sugstep := if  descent = 0 then  0 else
    -sign(descent) × min(1,1/abs(descent));
    for  j := 1 step  1 until  n do  sigma[j] := xr[j];
```

```
        dprxr := prxr; nsearch := nsearch + 1;
        quadsearch(xr,prxr,gxr,dir,sugstep,racc,aacc,method≥1);
        dprxr := dprxr - prxr;
        for j := 1 step 1 until n do
        sigma[j] := xr[j] - sigma[j];
        distance := sqrt(inprod(j,1,n,sigma[j],sigma[j]));
        gradient(xr,gxr,dgxrdx,grad);
        gradl := sqrt(inprod(j,1,n,grad[j],grad[j]));
        if gradl < n-10 or distance < n-10 or
        ready(prxr,dprxr,xr,sigma,raxr,aaxr,rule) then
        converged := true else
        hessian(xr,gxr,dgxrdx,h)
    end of gauss-newton or newton;
    ieff := ieff + 1;
    if nlp and converged then
    for i := 1 step 1 until m do
    begin if gtype[i] = 1 then ur[i] := 1 else
        begin if gtype[i] = 2 then
            begin if logp[i] then ur[i] := r/gxr[i] else
            ur[i] := if gxr[i] < 0 then -2 × gxr[i]/r else 0
            end of computing multipliers for inequalities
            else if gtype[i] = 3 then ur[i] := 2 × gxr[i]/r
        end of computing constraint multipliers
    end of generating dual solution;
    if coc ne 0 then output1
    end of unconstrained minimization;
end of rcycle for unconstrained minimization of penalty function;

procedure extrapol(t,arg,order,dim,target,result);
integer order,dim; real target; real array t,arg,result;
begin integer j,k,l; real beta;
    real array aid[0:order,0:order];
    for j := 1 step 1 until dim do
    begin comment extrapolate j-th element;
        for l := 0 step 1 until order do
        aid[0,l] := t[j,l];
        for k := 1 step 1 until order do
        for l := k step 1 until order do
        begin beta := (arg[l-k] - target)/(arg[l-k] - arg[l]);
            aid[k,l] := beta × aid[k-1,l] + (1 - beta) × aid[k-1,l-1]
        end of building aid table;
        result[j] := aid[order,order]
    end of j loop
end of extrapol;

procedure output2;
begin carriage(2);
    absfixt(5,0,np + ng × n + nh × n × (n + 1)/2);
    printtext(∤ aequivalent function evaluations ∤);
    nlcr; absfixt(5,0,np);
```

```
      printtext(⊀ evaluations of penalty function ⊁);
      if  nsearch ne  O then
      begin  nlcr; absfixt(5,0,np/nsearch);
        printtext(⊀ evaluations of pen. f. per line minimum ⊁);
      end ;
      nlcr; absfixt(5,0,ng);
      printtext(⊀ evaluations of gradient of penalty function ⊁);
      nlcr; absfixt(5,0,nh);
      printtext(⊀ evaluations of hessian matrix of penf ⊁);
      nlcr; absfixt(5,0,nrp);
      printtext(⊀ rejected points due to constraint violation ⊁)
end of output2 for printing number of function evaluations;

procedure  output3;
begin integer  i,j; carriage(2);
    printtext(⊀ extrapolation, cycle ⊁); absfixt(2,0,cycle);
    printtext(⊀ , order ⊁); absfixt(2,0,order);
    carriage(2);printtext(⊀ variable   solution vector ⊁);
    for j := 1 step 1 until n do
    begin nlcr; printtext(⊀x ⊁);
      absfixt(4,0,j); space(6); flot(6,3,xmin[j])
    end of x-output;
    carriage(2);printtext(⊀ function   function values      ⊁);
    printtext(⊀ dual solution ⊁);
    for i := 1 step 1 until m do
    begin nlcr; printtext(⊀gx⊁); absfixt(4,0,i); space(6);
      flot(6,3,gmin[i]); space(7); flot(6,3,umin[i])
    end of g-output; heading := true
end of output3 for printing extrapolated solutions;

boolean procedure  ready(f,df,x,dx,reps,aeps,stop);
real  f,df,reps,aeps; integer  stop; real array  x,dx;
begin integer  j; ready := true ;
    if  stop = 0 ∨ stop = 2 then
    begin if  abs(df) > reps × abs(f) + aeps then
      begin ready := false ; goto  exready end
    end  of testing accuracy in function value;
    if  stop = 1 ∨ stop = 2 then
    begin for  j := 1 step 1 until  n do
      if  abs(dx[j]) > reps × abs(x[j]) + aeps then
      begin ready := false ; j := n end
    end  of testing accuracy in position;
exready:
end  of ready;

real procedure  err(a,b); value a,b; real  a,b;
err := if  a = 0 then  abs(b) else  abs((a-b)/a);

procedure  errorgrad(x); real array  x;
begin integer  i,j,ierror;
```

```
real  xj,dxj,error,errorg,gdelta,dgj;
real array  dg[1:n];
errorg := 0;
for  i := 1 step 1 until m do
begin for  j := 1 step 1 until n do  dg[j] := 0;
   first(x,dg,i);
   for  j := 1 step 1 until n do
   begin  xj := x[j]; dxj := ₁₀-3 × abs(xj) + ₁₀-6;
      x[j] := xj + dxj; function(x,gdelta,i);
      dgj := gdelta;
      x[j] := xj - dxj; function(x,gdelta,i);
      dgj := (dgj - gdelta)/(2 × dxj);
      x[j] := xj;
      error := err(dg[j],dgj);
      if  errorg < error then
      begin  errorg := error; ierror := i end
   end of j loop
end of i loop;
carriage(2); printtext(⊀ max rel error ⊁);
flot(3,3,errorg); printtext(⊀ in gradient of function ⊁);
absfixt(4,0,ierror)
end of errorgrad;


procedure errorhess(x); real array x;
begin integer i,j,k,ierror;
   real  xj,dxj,error,errorh;
   real array  dgdelta,diag[1:n],ddg[1:n,1:n];
   errorh := 0;
   for  i := 1 step 1 until m do
   begin for  j := 1 step 1 until n do
      for  k := j step 1 until n do  ddg[j,k] := 0;
      second(x,ddg,i);
      for  j := 1 step 1 until n do
      begin  xj := x[j]; dxj := ₁₀-3 × abs(xj) + ₁₀-6;
         x[j] := xj + dxj;
         for  k := 1 step 1 until n do dgdelta[k] := 0;
         first(x,dgdelta,i);
         diag[j] := dgdelta[j];
         for  k := j+1 step 1 until n do
         ddg[k,j] := dgdelta[k];
         x[j] := xj - dxj;
         for  k := 1 step 1 until n do dgdelta[k] := 0;
         first(x,dgdelta,i);
         diag[j] := (diag[j] - dgdelta[j])/(2 × dxj);
         for  k := j+1 step 1 until n do
         ddg[k,j] := (ddg[k,j] - dgdelta[k])/(2 × dxj);
         x[j] := xj;
         for  k := j step 1 until n do
         begin  error := if  j = k then
            err(ddg[j,j],diag[j]) else
```

```
            err(ddg[j,k],ddg[k,j]);
            if  errorh < error then
            begin  errorh := error; ierror := 1 end
        end  of k loop
     end  of j loop
  end  of i loop;
  carriage(2); printtext(< max rel error >);
  flot(3,3,errorh); printtext(< in hessian of function >);
  absfixt(4,0,ierror)
end  of errorhess;


comment  start of main program of minifun;
starttime := time;
ieff := np := ng := nh := nsearch := nrp := 0;
heading := true ; maxcycle := 0;
objective := constraints := nlp := false ;
nonneg := bounded := false ;
mpn := m + n;
initr := 1; factor := 10^(-1/3);
for i := 1 step 1 until  mpn + n do  logp[i] := false ;
for j := 1 step 1 until n do xrmin[j] := xmin[j] := x[j];
incorrect := false ;
for j := 1 step 1 until n do
begin comment  check xtype;
   if  xtype[j] < 1 or  xtype[j] > 3 then
   incorrect := true ;
   if xtype[j] = 2 then nonneg := constraints := true ;
   if  xtype[j] = 3 then
   nonneg := constraints := bounded := true ;
   for k := 0 step 1 until 6 do xtable[j,k] := 0
end of checking types of variables;
for i := 1 step 1 until m do
begin comment  check gtype;
   if  gtype[i] < 1 or  gtype[i] > 3 then
   incorrect := true ;
   if gtype[i] = 1 then objective := true else
   if gtype[i] = 2 V gtype[i] = 3 then constraints := true ;
   for k := 0 step 1 until 6 do utable[i,k] := 0
end of checking constraint types;
if objective ∧ constraints then
begin initr := abs(estimate)/100;
   if initr < _p-2 then initr := _p-2;
   maxcycle := 20; nlp := true ;
   for i := 1 step 1 until  mpn + n do  logp[i] := true
end of initiating constrained minimization;
if coc ne 0 then
begin  carriage(2);
   printtext(< information, order >);
   absfixt(2,0,info); nlcr;
   printtext(< unc min method      >);
```

```
absfixt(2,0,method); nlcr;
printtext(∤ stopping rule      ∤);
absfixt(2,0,stop); nlcr;
printtext(∤ rel accuracy       ∤);
flot(3,3,raxmin); nlcr;
printtext(∤ abs accuracy       ∤);
flot(3,3,aaxmin); nlcr;
carriage(2);
printtext(∤  variable ∤); space(4); printtext(∤ type ∤);
for j := 1 step 1 until n do
begin nlcr; absfixt(6,0,j); space(3); absfixt(6,0,xtype[j])
end of printing types of variables;
carriage(2);
printtext(∤  function ∤); space(4);
printtext(∤ type ∤); space(4); printtext(∤ linear? ∤);
for i := 1 step 1 until m do
begin nlcr; absfixt(6,0,i); space(3); absfixt(6,0,gtype[i]);
   space(6);
   if lin[i] then printtext(∤ yes ∤) else
   printtext(∤ no ∤)
end of printing types of constraints;
end of printing input;
if coc ne 0 and info ge 1 then errorgrad(xrmin);
if coc ne 0 and info = 2 then errorhess(xrmin);
converged := false ;
if info < 0 or info > 2 or method < 0 or
method > 2 or (info = 0 and method = 2) or
stop < 0 or stop > 2 or coc < 0 or coc > 2 or
imax < 0 or incorrect then
begin carriage(2);
   printtext(∤ incorrect parameter value(s) ∤);
end of input checking else
for cycle := 0,cycle + 1 while cycle le maxcycle do
begin comment  sequential unconstrained minimization;
   real rnew;
   rnew := initr x factor↑cycle;
   rcycle(rnew, xrmin, urmin, raxmin, aaxmin);
   if cycle = 0 then
   for j := 1 step 1 until n do x[j] := xrmin[j];
   if coc ne 0 then output2;
   if not converged then maxcycle := cycle;
   if nlp and converged then
   begin order := cycle;
      if order > 6 then
      begin order := 6;
         for k := 0 step 1 until 5 do
         begin comment update solution tables;
            for j := 1 step 1 until n do
            xtable[j,k] := xtable[j,k+1];
            for i := 1 step 1 until m do
```

```
            utable[i,k] := utable[i,k+1];
            rtable[k] := rtable[k+1]
          end  of updating
      end  of setting order of extrapolation;
      if  order > 0 then
      begin  dfmin := fmin;
         for  j := 1 step 1 until  n do  dxmin[j] := xmin[j]
      end  of saving previous solution;
      for  j := 1 step 1 until  n do
      xtable[j,order] := xmin[j];
      for  i := 1 step 1 until  m do
      utable[i,order] := urmin[i];
      rtable[order] := rnew;
      extrapol(xtable,rtable,order,n,0,xmin);
      for  j := 1 step 1 until  n do  x[j] := xmin[j];
      for  i := 1 step 1 until  m do
      function(xmin,gmin[i],i);
      extrapol(utable,rtable,order,m,0,umin);
      fmin := 0; for  i := 1 step 1 until  m do
      if  gtype[i] = 1 then  fmin := fmin + gmin[i];
      if  order = 0 then  converged := false else
      begin if  coc ne 0 then  output3;
         for  j := 1 step 1 until  n do
         dxmin[j] := xmin[j] - dxmin[j];
         dfmin := fmin - dfmin;
         if  ready(fmin,dfmin,xmin,dxmin,raxmin,aaxmin,stop)
         then  maxcycle := cycle
         else  converged := false
      end  of convergence test comparing extrapolated solutions
    end  of extrapolation towards constrained minimum
   end  of sequential unconstrained minimization
 end  of minifun;


 integer  i,j,k,info,method; boolean  converged;
 real array  x[1:6]; integer  array  xtype[1:6],gtype[1:5];
 boolean array  lin[1:5];

 procedure  distance(x,g,i);integer  i; real  g;real array  x;
 if  i = 1 then  g := -x[1]↑2 - x[2]↑2 - x[3]↑2 + 5 else
 if  i=2 then  g := -(x[4] -3)↑2 - x[5]↑2 + 1 else
 if  i=3 then  g := -x[6] + 8 else
 if  i=4 then  g := x[6] - 4 else
 if  i=5 then  g := (x[1] - x[4])↑2 + (x[2] - x[5])↑2 +
 (x[3] - x[6])↑2;

 procedure  ddistance(x,dg,i); integer  i; real array  x,dg;
 if  i = 1 then
 begin for  j := 1,2,3 do  dg[j] := -2 × x[j] end else
 if  i=2 then
```

```
begin  dg[4] := -2 × (x[4] - 3); dg[5] := -2 × x[5] end else
if  i=3 then  dg[6] := -1 else
if  i=4 then  dg[6] := 1 else
if  i=5 then
begin for  j := 1,2,3 do  dg[j] := 2 × (x[j] - x[j+3]);
    for  j := 1,2,3 do  dg[j+3] := -2 × (x[j] - x[j+3]);
end  of ddistance;


procedure  dddistance(x,ddg,i); integer  i; real array  x,ddg;
if  i = 1 then
begin for  j := 1,2,3 do  ddg[j,j] := -2 end else
if  i=2 then
ddg[4,4] := ddg[5,5] := -2 else
if  i=5 then
begin for  j := 1,2,3,4,5,6 do  ddg[j,j] := 2;
    for  j := 1,2,3 do  ddg[j,j+3] := -2
end  of dddistance;


for  j := 1,2,3,4,5,6 do  xtype[j] := 1;
for  i := 1,2,3,4 do  gtype[i] := 2;
gtype[5] := 1;
for  i := 1,2,5 do  lin[i] := false ;
for  i := 3,4 do  lin[i] := true ;
for  info := 0,1,2 do
begin  method := info;
   x[1] := x[2] := x[3] := 1;
   x[4] := 3; x[5] := 0; x[6] := 5;
   minifun(x,distance,xtype,gtype,lin,info,ddistance,dddistance,
   method,6,5,ₒ-5,ₒ-5,5,1,converged,1,500);
   carriage(6)
end  of info cycle
end  of program;
```

```
real procedure inprod (i,a,b,x,y); value b; integer i,a,b; real
x,y;
begin real s; s:=0;
    for i := a step 1 until b do
    s := s + x * y;
    inprod := s
end of inprod;


procedure nlcr; comment new line carriage return; <body> ;

procedure printtext (s); string s; comment when this procedure is
called the string s will be printed without the outermost quotes;
<body> ;

procedure space (n); value n; integer n; comment causes the prin-
ter to move over n spaces on the current line; <body> ;

real procedure sum (i,a,b,x); value b; integer i,a,b; real x;
begin real s; s := 0;
    for i := a step 1 until b do
    s := s + x;
    sum := s
end of sum;


real procedure time; comment delivers the time elapsed since the
start of the job (syntax checking) in seconds with an accuracy of
0.01 sec; <body> ;
```

16. DESCRIPTION OF SOME IDENTIFIERS

This section presents a description of some identifiers that
have been declared in minifun. The identifiers are given in alpha-
betic order, with their scope (usually a procedure body) and a
description of their meaning.

identifier	scope	description
aacc	rcycle	absolute tolerance of linear search;
add1	gradient	set to true if the first derivatives of the i-th problem function must be incorporated in the gradient of the penalty function;
add11	hessian	set to true if the first derivatives of the i-th problem function must be incorporated in the Hessian matrix of the penalty function;
add2	hessian	set to true if the second derivatives of the i-th problem function must be incorporated in the Hessian matrix of the penalty function;
barrier	penalty	logarithmic-barrier term;
bounded	minifun	set to true if at least one variable is constrained to the interval [0,1];

identifier	scope	description
constraints	minifun	set to _true_ if there is at least one constraint or constrained variable;
counter	rcycle	number of consecutive iterations during which a convergence criterion is satisfied;
cycle	minifun	cycle number of unconstrained-minimization cycle;
def	rcycle	set to _true_ by cholesky if Hessian matrix of penalty function is found to be positive definite at current iteration point;
dfmin	minifun	difference of objective function at two successive approximations of constrained minimum;
dir	rcycle	search direction;
dprp0	rcycle	difference of penalty function at starting point and end point of major cycle in Powell's (1964) method;
dxmin	minifun	difference between two successive approximations of constrained minimum (obtained by extrapolation);
fail	rcycle	set to _true_ by cholesky if factorization of Hessian matrix fails at current iteration point;
fmin	minifun	objective-function value at current approximation xmin of constrained minimum;
gmin	minifun	problem function values at current approximation xmin of constrained minimum;
ieff	minifun	number of iterations since the start of the execution;
initr	minifun	initial value of controlling parameter;
itercnt	rcycle	number of iterations since the start of the current unconstrained-minimization cycle;
logp	minifun	the i-th element $(1 \leq i \leq m)$ is _true_ if the constraint $gx[i] \geq 0$ must be incorporated in the logarithmic-barrier term; the $(m+j)$-th element $(1 \leq j \leq n)$ is _true_ if the constraint $x[j] \geq 0$ must be incorporated; the $(m+n+j)$-th element $(1 \leq j \leq n)$ is _true_ if the constraint $1 - x[j] \geq 0$ must be incorporated;
loss	penalty	quadratic-loss term;
maxm	rcycle	index of direction to be replaced by new direction in Powell's (1964) method;
multiplier	move	controls extension or contraction of search interval;
nlp	minifun	set to _true_ if an objective function _and_ constraints are present;
nonneg	minifun	set to _true_ if at least one variable must be non-negative;
nrp	minifun	number of trial points rejected because of constraint violations;

identifier	scope	description
objective	minifun	set to <u>true</u> if an objective function is present;
pointer	rcycle	iteration number within a major cycle of Powell's (1964) algorithm;
pvalues	rcycle	number of penalty-function evaluations since the start of the current linear search;
racc	rcycle	relative tolerance of linear search;
rtable	minifun	table of successive r-values to be used in the extrapolation procedure;
sense	quadsearch	indicates whether the search direction (sense > 0) or the opposite direction (sense < 0) must be explored, and whether the search interval must be extended (abs(sense) = 1) or contracted (abs(sense) = 2);
sugstep	rcycle	suggested initial step in the search direction; on return from the linear search it is the coordinate of the line minimum;
xmin	minifun	current approximation (obtained by extrapolation) of constrained minimum;
xrmin	minifun	unconstrained minimum of penalty function (r-minimum);
xtable	minifun	table of penalty-function minima to be used as grid points in the extrapolation procedure;
yvec	rcycle	difference of penalty-function gradients at two successive iteration points.

17. THE ALGOL 60 SYSTEM FOR THE ELECTROLOGICA X8

In the core memory of the Electrologica X8 at the Philips Research Laboratories, Eindhoven, Netherlands, there are at least 23000 words of 27 bits available for ALGOL 60 programs and working areas (variables, arrays, etc.).

A <u>boolean</u> variable takes one word; a <u>boolean</u> <u>array</u> takes one word for 27 elements.

An <u>integer</u> variable occupies one single word. It is represented by 26 bits and a sign bit. Thus, <u>integer</u> variables are restricted to the range (-67108863, +67108863). An <u>integer</u> <u>array</u> takes one word per element.

A <u>real</u> variable occupies two words. The floating - point representation has a mantisse of 40 bits and a sign bit, and an exponent of 11 bits and a sign bit. The relative precision of the real number is approximately 12 decimals. The absolute largest number represented in this manner is approximately 10^{628}. The

absolute smallest, non-zero number is approximately 10^{-616}.
A _real_ _array_ takes two words per element.

In cases of _overflow_ the absolute largest number ($\simeq 10^{628}$)
and the correct sign (depending on the signs of the operands in an
operation where overflow occurs) will be generated. If _underflow_
has been detected the absolute smallest number ($\simeq 10^{-616}$) and the
correct sign will be generated.

Addition and _subtraction_ will only produce an exact zero if
the two operands have equal bits. The value of the relation $a = b$
will only be _true_ if a and b are found to be equal bit after bit.

Multiplication will only produce an exact zero if at least
one of the operands is exactly 0. In all other cases the absolute
result of the operation is at least 10^{-616}.

Division of a non-zero number a by 0 will produce 10^{628} or
-10^{628}, the sign being determined by the sign of a. The value of
0/0 is undetermined.

Overflow, underflow, or division by 0 will _not_ terminate the
current job. Even a warning will not be given to the user. The
square root of a negative number is set to zero. A warning will
not be given, and the current job is continued. Similarly, the
logarithm of a non-positive number is set to -10^{628} without any
warning.

If $x < -1419$, then exp (x) is set to 10^{-616}.

If $x > 1447$, then exp(x) is set to 10^{628}.

18. DESIGN OBJECTIVES

Mostly, the solution of an optimization problem seems to go
through the following two phases. First, a practical problem is
formulated in mathematical terms, and attempts are made to solve
the mathematical problem. The answers are inspected, and possibly
several alternative formulations are used to find the most
appropriate mathematical model for the problem at hand. One or
more methods for solving the problem are employed, and comparisons
in efficiency, accuracy, etc. are made. In the second phase, as
soon as a model and a method have been chosen, the mathematical
problem is solved for several values of certain parameters in the
formulation.

The procedure minifun has primarily been designed for the first
phase where the mathematical model is tested. Hence, the following
features have been incorporated in minifun.

a)   There is a variety of unconstrained-minimization techniques, accordingly as no derivatives, first derivatives, or first and second derivatives are supplied by the user; a remarkable result of the initial tests of minifun was that a variety of linear-search methods is not really necessary.

b)   There is a flexible and uniform manner to supply the problem functions, and possibly the first and the second derivatives. The objective function, the inequality and the equality constraints may be supplied in any order (although we recommend to take the objective function as the last problem function).

c)   First and second derivatives of the problem functions can be generated by numerical differentiation of the problem functions and their first derivatives respectively. Hence, the user can easily proceed to the utilization of efficient gradient methods for unconstrained minimization. Numerical differentiation is also employed to check the analytical derivatives supplyed by the user.

d)   The starting point of the computations, which has to be given by the user, may be feasible or unfeasible. For safety reasons, the constraints which are strictly satisfied in the starting point will not be violated during the unconstrained-minimization processes.

e)   There are elaborate output facilities to follow the course of the computations and to check the model formulations.

We have always considered minifun as a blueprint or a proto-type for the development of penalty-function programs, and although optimization is mainly carried out with FORTRAN programs, we preferred to continue the development of minifun in ALGOL 60 on an Electrologica X8 Computer (in Philips Research Laboratories, Eindhoven, Netherlands). There are various reasons to justify this. The ALGOL 60 language is an elegant tool to deal with variable dimensions, and it enables the programmer to make a significant step towards a modular design if goto statements and labels are avoided. Furthermore, the ALGOL 60 compiler on the Electrologica X8 checks whether array bounds are violated, and it provides run-time error messages which refer to the line in the original source listing where the error has been detected.

Some experiences with minifun have been described in earlier papers (Lootsma (1972b, 1975)), and we can now readily draw some conclusions. Firstly, minifun provides a variety of solution strategies for unconstrained minimization as higher derivatives are supplied, but if the user proceeds to the provision of higher derivatives the efficiency of minifun does not increase as much as we originally hoped. Secondly, minifun is rather short (about

900 cards) in comparison with some other programs for nonlinear optimization (2000-3000 cards) but still longer than we
expected. Finally, using the structure of penalty-function
algorithms and reducing the number of labels and goto statements
as much as possible (without being fanatic; there are 4 labels
in minifun) we hoped that minifun could be a blueprint for the
implementation of other penalty-function programs. In view of
the versions that have been derived from it, this seems to be
possible.

ACKNOWLEDGEMENT

The procedure minifun has been developed in close contact with
users and optimization specialists. Several features of minifun
are accordingly due to their comments and criticism. I am
particularly indebted to J.D. Pearson (Department of Energy,
Washington, D.C., U.S.A.; in 1968-1970 member of the Information
Systems and Automation Department, N.V. Philips, Eindhoven,
Netherlands), J.F. Benders, J. de Jong and R. Kool (University
of Technology, Eindhoven), and J. Klozenberg (Mullard Research
Laboratories, Redhill, Surrey, England) for their stimulating
ideas and suggestions.

An earlier version of minifun published by the author in 1970
has been translated into the FORTRAN subroutine MINI by B. van
Dijk and H. Kooyman van Guldener (Data Systems Division, N.V.
Philips, Apeldoorn, Netherlands). It was extensively tested by
R. Staha and D.M. Himmelblau (University of Texas, Austin, Texas,
U.S.A.) and D. Weistroffer (Free University, Berlin). Their
experiences and comments have been very useful for the design and
development of minifun. Moreover, I was particularly encouraged
by the experiences of R. Goffin (Information Systems and Automation Department, N.V. Philips, Eindhoven) during the development
of the optimization package OPTPAC for unconstrained minimization.
I am also greatly indebted to R. Kool who tested minifun in
order to adapt it for the Burroughs B6700 computer (University of
Technology, Eindhoven).

In many establishments an ALGOL 60 procedure cannot be used,
so that a FORTRAN version is indispensible. Today, there are several
FORTRAN versions of minifun. The earliest one is due to A.
Bensasson (La Radiotechnique, Suresnes, Paris) who made a great
effort to improve Powell's (1964) method in minifun, and to incorporate the direct-search method of Hooke and Jeeves (1961) in it.
Shirley A. Lill (Computer Laboratory, University of Liverpool) and
Heather Liddell (Queen Mary College, London) modified minifun into
the ALGOL 60 procedure E04HAA and the FORTRAN subroutine E04HAF
for the library of the Numerical Algorithms Group (a joint effort
of the Computer Laboratorites in several British universities).

The NAG library is now generally available, with particular copies for Control Data, IBM, and ICL computers. Finally, D. Kraft (Institut für Dynamik der Flugsysteme, DFVLR, Oberpfaffenhofen, Germany) developed a FORTRAN version of minifun with improvements in Powell's (1964) method.

There is one source of inspiration which has previously been mentioned. The development of minifun was largely carried out on the Electrologica X8 computer in Philips Research Laboratories (Eindhoven, Netherlands) with the ALGOL 60 compiler, originally designed in the Mathematical Centre (Amsterdam, Netherlands). The ALGOL 60 language and the error diagnostics of this compiler provide more powerful and elegant facilities than I have ever experienced with ALGOL 60 and FORTRAN on Control Data, IBM, and ICL computers. It is therefore a pleasure to acknowledge J. Zonneveld and F. Kruseman Aretz (Philips Research Laboratories, Eindhoven) for the excellent computing facilities available to members of the laboratory.

REFERENCES

1.   M.J. Box. A comparison of several current optimization methods and the use of transformations in constrained problems. The Comp. J. $\underline{9}$, 67-77, 1966.

2.   M.J. Box, D. Davies and W.H. Swann. Nonlinear optimization techniques. ICI Monograph no. 5, Oliver and Boyd, London, 1969.

3.   C.G. Broyden. The convergence of a class of double-rank minimization algorithms. 1. General Considerations, J.I.M.A. $\underline{6}$, 76-90. 2. The new algorithm. J.I.M.A. $\underline{6}$, 222-231, 1970.

4.   W.C. Davidon. Variable metric method for minimization. A.E.C. Research and Development Report ANL-5990, 1959.

5.   A.V. Fiacco and G.P. McCormick. Nonlinear programming, sequential unconstrained minimization techniques, Wiley, New York, 1968.

6.   R. Fletcher. Function minimization without evaluating derivatives - a review. The Comp. J. $\underline{8}$, 33-41, 1965.

7.   R. Fletcher. A new approach to variable metric algorithms. The Comp. J. $\underline{13}$, 317-322, 1970.

8.   R. Fletcher and M.J.D. Powell. A rapidly convergent descent method for minimization. The Comp. J. $\underline{6}$, 163-168, 1963.

9.   R. Hooke and T.A. Jeeves. Direct search solution of numerical and statistical problems. J.A.C.M. $\underline{8}$, 212-229, 1961.

10.   J. Kowalik and M.R. Osborne. Methods for unconstrained optimization problems. American Elsevier, New York, 1968.

11. F.A. Lootsma. Boundary properties of penalty functions for constrained minimization. Philips Res. Repts. Suppl. no. 3, N.V. Philips, Eindhoven, Netherlands, 1970.

12. F.A. Lootsma. A survey of methods for solving constrained minimization problems via unconstrained minimization, in F.A. Lootsma (ed.), Numerical Methods for Non-linear Optimization. Academic Press, London, pp. 313-348, 1972a.

13. F.A. Lootsma. Penalty-function performance of several unconstrained-minimization techniques. Philips Res. Repts. 27, 358-385, 1972b.

14. F.A. Lootsma. The Algol 60 procedure minifun for solving non-linear optimization problems. Report 4761, Philips Research Laboratories, Eindhoven, Netherlands, 1972c.

15. F.A. Lootsma. The design of a non-linear optimization program for solving technological problems. In R. Bulirsch, W. Oettli and J. Stoer (eds.), Optimization and Optimal Control. Springer, Berlin, pp. 229-243, 1975.

16. R.S. Martin, G. Peters and J.H. Wilkinson. Symmetric decomposition of a positive-definite matrix. Numer. Math. 7, 362-383, 1965.

17. J.A. Nelder and R. Mead. A simplex method for function minimization. The Comp. J. 7, 308-313, 1964.

18. M.J.D. Powell. An efficient method for finding the minimum of a function of several variables without calculating derivatives. The Comp. J. 7, 155-162, 1964.

19. M.J.D. Powell. A survey of numerical methods for unconstrained optimization. SIAM Review 12, 79-97, 1970.

20. M.J.D. Powell. Recent advances in unconstrained optimization. Math. Progr. 1, 26-57, 1971.

21. R.W.H. Sargent. Minimization without constraints, in M. Avriel, M.J. Rijckaert and D.J. Wilde (eds.), Perspectives on Optimal Engineering Design. Prentice-Hall, Englewood Cliffs, New Jersey, pp. 37-75, 1973.

22. D.F. Shanno. Conditioning of quasi-Newton methods for function minimization. Math. of Comp. 24 , 647-656, 1970.

AN ACCELERATED CONJUGATE GRADIENT ALGORITHM

J.S. Kowalik

Academic Services, Washington State University
Pullman, Washington, U.S.A.

Considered is the problem: min $f(\underset{\sim}{x})$, where f is a real-valued function defined on Euclidean n-space denoted by E^n, and $\underset{\sim}{x}$ is a vector in E^n. A technique for determining a minimizer of f, useful in large-scale applications, is the conjugate gradient algorithm based on the quadratic function model

$$q(\underset{\sim}{x}) = 1/2(\underset{\sim}{x} - \hat{\underset{\sim}{x}})^T Q(\underset{\sim}{x} - \hat{\underset{\sim}{x}}) \tag{1}$$

with Q being positive definite and $\hat{\underset{\sim}{x}}$ a constant vector.

In recent years, more general functions than (1) have been considered as a basis for conjugate gradient methods. In particular, we consider the function

$$f(\underset{\sim}{x}) = \varepsilon_1 q(\underset{\sim}{x}) + \frac{\varepsilon_2}{2} q^2(\underset{\sim}{x})$$

which is a special case of a wider class of functions defined by $f(\underset{\sim}{x}) = F(q(\underset{\sim}{x}))$. We develop an extended conjugate gradient method which minimizes $F(q(\underset{\sim}{x}))$ in at most n steps [1]. We also discuss a procedure for restarting the conjugate gradient method based upon monitoring of the inner products of certain directions [2]. This restart procedure uses a technique due to Beale [3] for starting with any downhill direction. The resulting method, incorporating all of these features, has been applied to a set of benchmark problems and has shown, in the majority of cases, a significant improvement over the classical conjugate gradient technique.

REFERENCES

[1]   W.R. Boland, E.R. Kamgnia, and J.S. Kowalik, <u>A Conjugate</u>
      <u>Gradient Optimization Method Invariant to Nonlinear Scaling</u>,
      to appear in the Journal of Optimization Theory and Applica-
      tions.

[2]   M.J.D. Powell, <u>Restart Procedures for the Conjugate Gradient</u>
      <u>Method</u>, Report C.S.S. 24, A.E.R.E., Harwell, 1975.

[3]   E.M.L. Beale, A Derivation of Conjugate Gradients. In:
      <u>Numerical Methods for Nonlinear Optimization</u>, ed. by F.A.
      Lootsma, Academic Press, New York, pp. 39-44, 1972.

GLOBAL OPTIMA WITHOUT CONVEXITY

L.C.W. Dixon

The Numerical Optimisation Centre
The Hatfield Polytechnic
Hertfordshire, England

ABSTRACT.   In this paper the experience gained on the problem of
developing algorithms for solving the global optimisation problem
is summarised.

1.   INTRODUCTION

For the past four years a number of researchers in many countries have cooperated in the investigation of the behaviour of
algorithms that attempt to find the global optimum of a nonconvex
function. The early papers arising from this study appeared in
ref [1], and a second volume [2] will shortly appear containing,
amongst other things, the results of running many different global
optimisation codes on a standard set of nonconvex test problems.

In presenting this summary I would like to thank all the contributors who cooperated in the investigation; with special mention
of Dr. Joanna Gomulka, the S.R.C. sponsored post-doctoral research
assistant who worked on the project at Hatfield for three years.
I would also like to thank the S.R.C. and Italian C.N.R. who provided funds for the original cooperative project and North Holland
Publishing Company for agreeing to the publication of the refs [1]
and [2].

2.   THE PROBLEM

Let us consider the problem

Min $F(x)$ $x \in S \subset E^n$

where

$$S = \{x : a_i \overset{\le}{=} x_i \overset{\le}{=} b_i\}. \tag{1}$$

For convenience we shall assume that the function to be minimised is thrice differentiable. If $F(x)$ is convex then there is only one local minimum point for such a function, but for general nonconvex functions there can be many local minima and the problem is to locate that local minimum point x^* with the least function value.

Proposition 1

It is impossible to construct a deterministic algorithm that can solve the general problem (1).

Given any function $F(x)$ it is possible to modify $F(x)$ in the neighbourhood N of any point x_m, by adding a sufficiently smooth spline function which will shift the global minimum to x_m and leave $F(x)$ unaltered outside N. Therefore if a deterministic search did not enter every neighbourhood of this size the global minimum could not possibly be located. However, as the neighbourhood N can be made arbitrarily small the deterministic process would be infinitely long.

For this reason the discussion of the global optimisation problem tends to separate between deterministic algorithms that can only be applied to a restricted subset of functions $F(x)$ and to probabilistic methods for which more general statements can sometimes be made.

In either case we must accept that with a numerical algorithm it will be impossible, in general, to locate the global minimum exactly in a finite number of steps. In [24] three criteria that are often used in the location of local minima were defined:

(i) CRITERION x : $x \in A_x$ where

$$A_x = \{x : \|x - x^*\| < \epsilon \, x; \, x \in S\}.$$

(ii) CRITERION g : $x \in A_g$ where

$$A_g = \{x : \|g(x) - g(x^*)\| < \epsilon \, g, \, x \in S\}.$$

(iii) CRITERION F : $x \in A_F$ where

$$A_F = \{x : F(x) - F(x^*) < \epsilon_F, \, x \in S\}.$$

In this paper we will agree to accept any point x ε A_F as a good approximation to x* and hope that if A_F contains disjoint subsets then the algorithm will locate a point in each subset. However, for convenience in discussing the behaviour of algorithms it will usually be assumed that A_F is compact.

3. SOME PROBABILISTIC RESULTS

The probabilistic approach to global optimisation relies on the following results.

Theorem 3.1

If 1 A is any subset of S with measure m and

$$\frac{m(A)}{m(S)} \geq \varepsilon > 0,$$

and if 2 p(A,N) is the probability that at least one point of a sequence of N points drawn randomly from a uniform distribution over S falls in A, then

$$\text{Lim}_{N \to \infty} p(A,N) = 1.$$

Note 3.2

If it can be shown that the probability that an iterative process must converge to A_F (by this theorem) is assymptotically 1, it does not necessarily imply that any finite run using the iterative process will lead to a good approximation to the solution.

Algorithm 3.3: The Pure Random Search Algorithm - P.R.S.

Step 1: Evaluate F(x) at N points uniformly distributed over S. This algorithm has been extensively discussed by Brooks (1958) and Andersoen (1972). If

$$\frac{m(A_F)}{m(s)} = \alpha$$

then

$$p(A_F),N) = 1 - (1 - \alpha)^N. \tag{3.5}$$

Note 3.2

For a given function α is fixed and equation (3.5) therefore gives a probability measure that must be bettered by competitive algorithms.

4. THE USE OF LOCAL OPTIMISATION ALGORITHMS

Algorithm 4.1: The Multistart Algorithm - M.S.

Step 1: select $x^{(o)}$ at random

Step 2: start a local minimisation algorithm from $x^{(o)}$ with stopping criteria ε_g.

Step 3: Test whether this is probably the global minimum and if so STOP.

Step 4: Return to Step 1.

This general algorithm is almost certainly that most used in practice at the moment. It has many varieties largely dependent on the strategy chosen at Step 3. In the simplest version, an a priori decision is made to select $x^{(o)}$ at random N_1 times. One alternative is to choose $x^{(o)}$ at randon N_2 times and then minimise F from the subset of L such points having the least function value. Anderssen (1972) stressed the importance of testing whether a point was truly the global minimum independently of the sequence of points used to estimate it and such hypothesis testing methods will be discussed in detail later.

Let us first consider the behaviour of local minimisation algorithms on nonconvex functions. We will assume that we are using a local descent algorithm that is programmed to cope with the upper and lower bounds on x_i which define S. The modifications required in descent methods for the treatment of bounds are now known. The conditions necessary for descent methods to converge to an ε_g neighbourhood of a local minima or saddlepoint are also known (see for example Dixon (1974)). Therefore we may assume we are using a routine that will converge to an ε_g neighbourhood of either a local minimum M_j or saddlepoint Z_j. Now define $S(M_j)$ and $S(Z_j)$ for any algorithm as the set of starting points $x^{(o)}$ from which the algorithm will converge to M_j or Z_j. For such an algorithm the sets $S(M_j)$ and $S(Z_j)$, all j, must cover S.

The following definitions were first given in reference [24].

Definition 4.2

The region of attraction R_j of a local minimum M_j is the convergence set $S(M_j)$ of the gradient trajectory algorithm G.T.A.

$$\dot{x} = \frac{-g(x)}{1 + \|g(x)\|} \tag{4.1}$$

projected, when necessary, along the boundaries of S. For this algorithm the convergence sets $S(M_j)$ cover S, and the sets $S(Z_j)$ form their boundaries.

Unfortunately, the G.T.A. algorithm is known to be an inefficient local minimiser and hence the number of function evaluations per local minimisation, N_L, will be quite large.

If the algorithm were used, however, and N were chosen so that $N = N_1 N_L$ then the probability of finding a point in A_F after N function evaluation would be

$$p(A_F, N_1 N_L) = 1 - (1 - \frac{m(R_{j*})}{m(S)}) N_1 \tag{4.2}$$

where R_{j*} is the region of attraction of the global minimum.

To discuss the similar relationship for the second alternative we can introduce the Chichinadze P function (1967). He defined $P(v)$ as the probability that $F(x) < v$,

i.e., if $m(V)$ is the measure of the level set $V = \{x : F(x) < v\}$

then $\quad P(v) = \frac{m(V)}{m(S)}$. $\tag{4.3}$

If N_2 random points are uniformly distributed over S and m_i of these points have $F(x) < v_i$ then m_i/N_2 is an approximation to $P(v_i)$ which should improve as $N_2 \to \infty$. If we choose to minimise from L such points, then to a first approximation

$$p(A_f, N_2 \mid LN_L) = 1 - (1 - \frac{m(V_L \cap R_{j*})}{m(V_L)}) L \tag{4.4}$$

where

$$P(V_L) = \frac{m(V_L)}{m(S)} \doteqdot \frac{L}{N_2} .$$

If we now turn to the behaviour of more efficient local minimisers, then it is shown in ref [24] that an additional condition

$$\alpha_k = \underset{\alpha>0}{\text{Min}} \{\alpha:(g(x^{(k)} - \alpha p^{(k)})^T p^{(k)} = \mu g(x^{(k)})^T p^{(k)}\} \tag{4.5}$$

for the appropriate value of μ must be included in the linesearch if any systematic treatment of the behaviour on nonconvex functions is to be possible. This implies that no local unidirectional maxima are jumped during the linear search. This would of course require the rewriting of the line search subroutine in most local algorithms currently available. With this modification we can derive relationships equivalent to (4.2) and (4.4).

Definition 4.3

Let v_c be the maximum value of v such that the level set V has a connected subset with a closed contour contained in R_j. Then Treccani (1971,75) has shown that the contour contains a saddle-point Z_k on the boundary of R_j. Now the basin B_j of M_j is defined by

$$B_j = \{x:F(x) < F(Z_k); x \in R_j\}.$$

Theorem 4.4

A safeguarded descent algorithm converges to an ε_g neighbourhood of M_j if started from any point in B_j.

This implies that as $m(B_j) < m(S(M_j))$, the relationships equivalent to (4.2) and (4.4) are

$$p(A_F, N_1 N_L) > 1 - (1 - \frac{m(B_{j*})}{m(S)})^{N_1} \tag{4.6}$$

and

$$p(A_F, N_2 + N_L L) > 1 - (1 - \frac{m(V_1 \cap B_{j*})}{m(V_L)})^L \tag{4.7}$$

respectively.

Note 4.5

The advantage that N_L is much smaller for the efficient algorithm has to overcome the opposing disadvantage that $m(B_j*) < m(R_j*)$, and for most functions it is considered likely that this will be true.

Another simple modification of the M.S. algorithm was proposed by Hartman (1972).

Algorithm 4.6: Hartman's S2 Algorithm

Step 1: $v^+ = + \infty$

Step 2: select $x^{(o)}$ at random

Step 3: if $F(x^{(o)}) > v^+$ return to 2

Step 4: perform a local minimisation from $x^{(o)}$ to M_j and set $v^+ = F(M_j)$

Step 5: return to 2.

Note 4.7

Step 3 is an example of the Anderssen hypothesis test approach. As N, the number of random points, increases so the probability of no point being found with $v < v^+$ decreases, unless v^+ is the global minimum function value [Equ 3.5 with $\alpha = m(v^+)/m(S)$].

Note 4.8

This modification will be very effective on many functions but it is easy to construct examples where it is unlikely to be successful. Assume we have 2 local minima M_1, M_2, $F(M_1) > F(M_2)$, but with $m(V = F(M_1))$ very small, then a very large number of points are likely to be required before an improved point is found.

5.   CLUSTERING

The concept of clustering was introduced into global optimisation by Becker & Lago (1970).

Algorithm 5.1

Step 1: Select N points at random from a uniform distribution over S

Step 2: Take L of these points with the lowest function values

Step 3: apply a cluster analysis to these L points grouping them into discrete clusters, and locating the boundaries of each cluster

Step 4: return to STEP 1 with S defined as the most promising cluster.

The aim of this technique is that L should be sufficiently large to include points in the $S(M_j)$, of all "good" local minima, (i.e., all local minima with $S(M_j)$ intersecting with V_L) and that the cluster analysis should separate the different components of V_L. Since this initial algorithm two other very promising clustering algorithms have appeared, due to Torn (1976) and Price (1977). Torn modified the M.S. method in a successful attempt to reduce the number of function evaluations, N_L, associated with each starting point.

<u>Algorithm 5.2: Torn's Search-clustering Approach (1976)</u>

Step 1: select N_3 start points $x^{(o)}$; $K = 0$

Step 2: perform some R steps of a local optimiser from each $x^{(k)} \rightarrow x^{(k+1)}$

Step 3: perform a cluster analysis on the resulting points $x^{(k+1)}$; test for convergence and stop if the test is satisfied

Step 4: take a sample of points from each cluster and return to step 2 for the next iteration.

Essentially the method assumes that the initial N_3 starting points will contain some points in each Basin (set $S(M_j)$) and that as the local searches proceed these points will cluster together in each basin. The cluster analysis is intended to reduce the number of searches that are completed in each basin. This effectively reduces the value of N_L and hence for the same value of N allows the number of starting points to be increased ($N_3 > N_1$) and hence the probability that at least one will be in $S(M_j^*)$.

The efficiency of the method depends on the cluster analysis technique used and the local optimisation algorithm. Torn uses a cluster analysis technique developed by Miesel & Patrick (1972) and a random direction/local probe search as his local optimiser.

Gomulka (1977) has modified this algorithm by incorporating a variable metric routine for the local optimiser and results from both approaches are presented later.

Price (1977) has developed a simple algorithm that clusters the points as the search proceeds.

Algorithm 5.3: The Controlled Random Search (C.R.S.) Routine. Price 1977

Step 1: Select N points at random from a uniform distribution over S and calculate x_w the point with the worst function value.

Step 2: Select $n+1$ points at random from the above N points, then select one of these at random as a pole point and calculate the centroid x_G of the remaining n points. Reflect the pole point about the centroid to generate the primary trial point x_p.

Step 3: If $F(x_p) < F(x_w)$ discard x_w and calculate the new worst point x_w, including x_p among the N trial points. Return to step 2.

If $F(x_p) > F(x_w)$ and this has occurred on less than 50% of the iterations, then discard x_p and return to step 2.

Step 4: Calculate as a secondary trial point x_q, the point midway between x_p and x_G.

If $F(x_q) < F(x_w)$ discard x_w and calculate the new worst point x_w, including x_q among the N trial points. Return to step 2.

If $F(x_q) > F(x_w)$ discard x_q and return to step 2.

As the algorithm proceeds all N points are contained in the level set $F(x_w)$ which steadily decreases. In practice primary probes from randomly chosen sets spanning different components of the level set can span all S and hence may locate any missing components. The number of successful primary probes eventually decreases and secondary probes will be generated. When secondary probes are drawn from one component they tend to converge on the minimum of that component.

This is a heuristic algorithm that tends to hold clusters of points round good local minima as the iteration proceeds. Whilst it is not possible to generate formulae for the probability of its success its performance tends to be very good.

6. RANDOM DIRECTIONAL SEARCHES

As duals to the random point distributions we have considered

458

in the previous sections we can consider random search directions.

Algorithm 6.1: Random Search (R.S.)

    Step 1: Select $x^{(o)}$, $k = 0$.

    Step 2: Select $S^{(k)}$ at random from a uniform spherical distribution.

    Step 3: $x^{(k+1)} = x^{(k)} + \alpha S^{(k)}$

    Step 4: $k = k+1$ and return to 2.

There are very many varieties of such algorithm, dependent on the choice of α in step 3. If

$$\alpha = ARG \ (GLOBAL \ MIN \ (F(x^{(k)} + \alpha S^{(k)}))) \tag{6.1}$$

then Gaviano (1975) has shown $\underset{k \to \infty}{Lim} \ p(x^{(k)} \ \epsilon \ A_F) = 1.$ (6.2)

However, for the very general problem we are considering at the moment a global minimisation along the line is still not a strict possibility.

In the original R.S. algorithm due to Rastrigin (1968), α was a fixed step size h, while Bremmermann (1972) fitted a quartic to five points along the line determined by a random step length h. Both set $\alpha = 0$ if no improved point is located. It is a simple matter to modify Rastrigen's algorithm so that his h is chosen randomly and Bremmermann's algorithm so that the best of the six points along the line is accepted, and then

$$\underset{k \to \infty}{Lim} \ p(x^{(k)} \ \epsilon \ A_F) = 1$$

still holds.

In practice, however, these random search techniques are most useful when more knowledge is available about the function, as then the global line search is frequently possible.

7.   GLOBAL LINE SEARCH ROUTINES

When we have a function of one variable $f(\alpha)$, there are a number of deterministic algorithms for finding the global minima of $f(\alpha)$ providing $f(\alpha)$ satisfies a variety of different conditions.

7.1 Lipschitz Bounds on the Function

One class of function on which global optimisation is possible in a deterministic sense is those possessing a Lipschitz constant L

i.e., $|f(\alpha_1) - f(\alpha_2)| < L||\alpha_1 - \alpha_2||$ all $\alpha_1, \alpha_2 \in S.$ (7.1)

The two most well known algorithms for finding the global minimum in this case are due to Evtushenko (1970) & Shubert (1972). Both assume that the value of L is known and can fail if it is under-estimated.

7.2 Bounded Second Derivatives

The problem of finding the global minimum of a one dimensional function, when

(a)   the function is twice differentiable;

(b)   f & f' can be evaluated for any α within the allowable range; and

(c)   finite upper and lower bounds on f" can be derived within any interval,

has been investigated successfully by Brent (1972) and Beale and Forrest (1976). The latter also discuss methods for estimating the finite bounds on f" .

7.3 Polynomials

When $f(\alpha)$ is a polynomial, the method of descent from a local minimum proposed by Goldstien & Price (1972) enables the global minimum to be found in a finite number of steps. The related problem of determining all the roots of polynomial functions has been intensively studied and error analysis of many of the techniques are available. Most of these methods can be adapted to locating the global minimum of a polynomial.

We may therefore conclude that there are a large number of functions for which the global line search (6.1) is a possibility. For other functions probabalistic based line searches can be used, one example of which is described below.

7.4 Zilinskas's Method

Zilinskas (1976) has devised a technique for finding the minimum of a function $f(\alpha)$, based on the assumption that it is a sampling function of a Wiener Process.

Step 1. Calculate f at M points of a uniform grid, $\alpha_i > \alpha_{i-1}$ all i.

Step 2. Calculate $s^2 = \dfrac{1}{m-1} \displaystyle\sum_{i=2}^{m} \dfrac{(f(\alpha_i) - f(\alpha_{i-1}))^2}{\alpha_1 - \alpha_{i-1}}$.

The Wiener Process with parameter s^2 is then assumed to be the global model of the objective function, i.e., in the range $\alpha_{i-1} < \alpha < \alpha_i$ the expected value of the lower bound on f is given by

$$v(\alpha) = y - 0.3989\sigma(\alpha) \exp \left\{ - \frac{(m(\alpha) - y)^2}{2\sigma^2(\alpha)} \right\}$$

$$+0.65 \exp \left\{ -0.443\left(0.75 + \frac{m(\alpha) - y}{\sigma(\alpha)} \right)^2 \right\}$$

where y is the best value of f located so far

$$m(\alpha) = \frac{f_{i-1}(\alpha_i - \alpha) + f_i(\alpha - \alpha_{i-1})}{\alpha_i - \alpha_{i-1}}$$

$$\sigma^2(\alpha) = 49.s^2 \frac{(\alpha_i - \alpha)(\alpha - \alpha_{i-1})}{\alpha_i - \alpha_{i-1}}$$

Step 3. As $v(\alpha)$ is unimodal in the range $\alpha_{i-1} < \alpha < \alpha_i$ he minimises $v(\alpha)$ in each interval by a golden section search using 20 evaluations of $v(\alpha)$.

Step 4. At the local minimum α_J of $v(\alpha)$ having the least value, he evaluates $f(\alpha)$ and includes it in the list α_i at the appropriate point.

Step 5. Recalculates s^2 every 5th iteration.

Step 6. Checks if α_J satisfies

$$f(\alpha_{J-2}) > f(\alpha_{J-1}) > f(\alpha_J)$$

$$f(\alpha_{J+2}) > f(\alpha_{J+1}) > f(\alpha_J)$$

and if not goes to step 7.

If so he performs a local minimisation of $f(\alpha)$ using parabolic interpolation, including all points in the list α_i and returns to step 3.

Step 7.   If $f(\alpha_J) < y$, the best value of f located previously, then return to step 3.

If $f(\alpha_J) \geqq y$ then perform the golden section searches on the intervals $\alpha_{J-1} < \alpha < \alpha_J$, $\alpha_J < \alpha < \alpha_{J+1}$ and return to step 4.

The method ceases when a prescribed number of function evaluations is exceeded or the probability of having located the global minimum of the Wiener Process exceeds 0.99. In his paper he reports the performance of the algorithm on some Lipschitz bounded functions for which Shuberts method is also available and obtains the global optimum in far fewer function evaluations. It must however be noted that his method assumes that one evaluation of $f(\alpha)$ will be considerably more expensive than an evaluation of $v(\alpha)$, when this is not true; the fact that the method evaluates $v(\alpha)$ approximately 20 times as often as it evaluates $f(\alpha)$ cannot be ignored. It is therefore unlikely to be seen at its best on small cheap test functions.

8.   THE BAYESIAN APPROACH

The method due to Zilinskas described above is a one dimensional example of the general approach to the global optimisation problem developed at Vilnius. The general approach is described in a series of papers including Mockus (1975), Mockus (1977) and Mockus, Tiesis & Zilinskas (1977).

They note that as an alternative to considering the proofs of ultimate convergence of local minimisation algorithms, the following question could be posed. If the number of function evaluations is fixed in advance, which method would minimise the maximum possible deviation from the solution? They note that two solutions are known to this problem; namely if the function can be drawn from the class of continuous functions then the solution is the equi-spaced grid (Sukhorev (1971)) and if the function is known to be one dimensional and unimodal, then the method of Fibonacci is optimum (Kiefer (1953)). The sparsity of solutions to this problem led them to consider the situation where there is a probability distribution over the class of functions under consideration and the decision is to minimise the expected deviation not the maximum deviation. Such methods were termed Bayesian.

To specify a Bayesian method one must first define a probability distribution over the class of functions which might be minimised. Next one has to define the class of search methods within which the optimum method is sought and finally a loss function which measures the damage that occurs when the outcome is not the global minimum.

In the latest paper [40] the method outlined in 7.4 is extended to the n dimensional problem in two ways. First it is shown that if the probability distribution is Gaussian, then the function F is being treated as a sum of 2^n Wiener Fields. In this method the local minimisation stage is undertaken by a variable metric method (incorporating upper and lower bounds on the variables).

The second approach described there solves the problem as a series of nested one dimensional searches $\underset{X_1}{\text{Min}} \ \underset{X_2}{\text{Min}}, \ldots, \underset{X_n}{\text{Min}} \ F(X_1 \ldots, X_n)$.

The conditions for the convergence of these methods to the solution of global optimisation problem are given in Mockus (1976).

It will be noted that the hypothesis that the global optimum has been found subject to a deviation ε_F can be tested in these methods using their inherent probability distribution.

9.   HYPOTHESIS TESTING

When an inherent probability distribution is not being assumed, and a local minimum X_L has been located then the hypothesis that it is the global minimum is usually tested in one of three ways.

9.1 Random Point Selection

N points are selected at random from a uniform distribution over S, and then if no point is found with $F(x) < F(x_L)$, the probability that the level set $F(x_L)$ has a measure $m(F(x_L)) \leqq \alpha m(s)$ is given by $p(\alpha, N) = 1 - (1 - \alpha)^N$.

9.2 Random Line Searches; Bocharov (1962)

N directions are selected at random from a uniform spherical distribution. Global line searches are performed along these directions from X_L and then if no point is found with $F(x) < F(x_L)$ then the probability that the level set $F(x_L)$ casts a solid angle covering α of the unit sphere is given by $p(\alpha, N) = 1 - (1 - \alpha)^N$.

In both cases if a point is found the main routine must be restarted.

9.3 Chichinadze's P Function

Define the P function, $P(v)$ as the probability that if x is drawn from a uniform distribution over S, then $F(x) < v$.

Note that if q points are drawn at random from a uniform distribution and p points satisfy $F(x) < v$, then p/q is an estimate of $P(v)$ which is asymptotically correct with mean error proportional to $1/\sqrt{q}$.

In Archetti (1975) tests are reported on an algorithm which approximated $P(v)$ by a linear combination of prechosen functions

$$P(v) = \sum_i \lambda_i \, P_i(v).$$

The range of v was then divided at the points v_j and the optimal values of λ_i determined by minimising

$$E = \sum_j w_j \, (\frac{p_j}{q} - \sum_i \lambda_i \, P_i(v_j))^2$$

where p_j is the number of points for which $F(x) < v_j$. The root v^* of $P(v) = 0$ was then determined and the local minimum x_L accepted if either

(1) $F(x_L) < v^*$

or   (2) $\left| \dfrac{F(x_L) - v^*}{F(x_L)} \right| < \varepsilon.$

In the original paper the $P_i(v)$ were chosen to be polynomial functions, but, as was pointed out by A. Curtis, $P(v)$ will have nonpolynomial behaviour near the global minimum, and as least square polynomials do not possess uniform convergence these have been replaced in Archetti & Betro (1975) by a series of spline functions $S_K(v)$. These are splines of order $2m-1$ with K equidistributed knots. At each knot $S_K(v)$ and its first $2m-2$ derivatives are continuous. The spline function then contains $2m+K$ parameters λ which may be determined by minimising

$$E = \sum_j w_j \, (p_j/q - S_K(v_j))^2.$$

Using a result of Mikhal'skii (1974); Archetti & Betro (1975) showed that $S_K(v)$ would have uniform convergence to $P(v)$ if the number of knots K is increased with the number of points N s.t.

$$\underset{N \to \infty}{\text{Lim}} \frac{K^2(N) \log N}{N} = 0.$$

To obtain a well conditioned optimisation problem the spline $S_K(v)$ is expressed in Betro & Biase (1976) as

$$S_K(v) = \sum_{j=1}^{K+2m} \lambda_j \, B_j(v)$$

where $B_j(x)$ are the fundamental B-splines based upon the 2m-th divided differences introduced by Curry & Shoenberg (1966).

Whilst the authors have successfully used this method as a complete algorithm to solve a number of practical problems Archetti & Frontini (1975, 1977), it could obviously be used in conjunction with any other method to test the hypothesis that a given local minimum is global. It could also be used as the basis of a global unidirectional search routine.

As a word of caution we note that if none of the N points sampled is in the neighbourhood of the global minimum, then the root of $S_K(v)$ may well approach $F(x_L)$ and the local minimum would then be accepted. The acceptance of a point by this approach is therefore still a probabilistic result, where the probability depends upon both N and the relative measure of some neighbourhood around the global minimum.

10.   DETERMINISTIC METHODS

Turning now from our treatment of probabilistic techniques to that of deterministic algorithms. It will become apparent that all deterministic methods make some inherent assumption about the smoothness of the function, though this is frequently not stated explicitly.

10.1   Branin's Trajectory Method

One of the best known deterministic methods is that advocated by Branin (1971,1972). In this technique the curves

$$\underline{g}(x) = k\underline{c} \tag{10.1}$$

are followed by integrating the differential equation

$$\dot{x} = -(\text{adj } G) \text{ g.} \tag{10.2}$$

The trajectories therefore terminate when

(1)   g = 0, i.e., stationary points [essential singularities]

or   (2)   adj G is singular and g is parallel to the eigenvector corresponding to the zero eigenvalue [extraneous singularities].

It is of course true that an arc of the curve (10.1) passes through each essential singularity, it is not however true that the curve need be connected. Indeed the subclass of functions for which (10.1) is connected has not yet been determined.

In integrating the equations (10.2) a numerical integration process is used, this implies an assumption that the curve is smooth in a region of the order of the step size, and also that k varies smoothly along the arc, so that no point with k=0 is missed.

As the arcs are not connected, an integration started at a given point will only locate a given subset of minima (efficient ways of continuing curves across singularities are known and employed, Gomulka (1977)). The probability of finding the global minimum in one run is therefore increased compared with the use of a local minimisation algorithm, but the cost of one integration from a point $x^{(0)}$ to its local minimum will be considerably greater than the use of an efficient local optimiser. This is especially true as the dimension of the problem increases. In 2 dimensions the heuristic extension reported by Hardy (1975) can be very effective.

10.2   The Growing Ellipses: TTS Approach

The second deterministic method discussed in detail in Dixon, Gomulka & Hersom (1976) and Corles (1975) also has an implied smoothness assumption hidden in the numerics. Given a local minimum the method first seeks an elliptical subset of the region of attraction. This must be done by investigating the directional derivatives at the points on the surface and determining if any are negative. This is a global problem in n-1 dimensions, i.e., even if n=2 it is equivalent to a global line search and needs one of the assumptions discussed in Section 7 for the global solution to be obtainable deterministically. The difficulties outlined at the end of Corles's paper have not yet been overcome.

10.3   The Falk-Solund Approach

In Falk & Solund (1969), Solund (1971) and Falk (1973) the problem of finding the global minimum of nonconvex separable programming problems and of nonconvex geometric programming problems are treated. The method of approach is to separate the objective function (and constraints) into convex and concave terms. For these two classes of problem this is always possible. The nonconvex terms are then replaced by under-estimating linearisations, leading to a convex programming problem with a unique global minimum. This minimum can be found using an appropriate local technique. As the iteration proceeds the single convex programming problem is replaced by a set of such problems each over a subset of the space S in each of which the under-estimating linearisations are improved. The investigation of this set of problems is controlled by a branch and bound routine, for which convergence proofs are available.

The difficulties in extending this method to more general problems lie in the need to divide the function into convex and concave parts. On general problems the terms in which the function is written down will not normally be divisable in this way as one term may well be convex over parts of S and nonconvex in others.

10.4 McCormick's Method

We note that if the convex envelope of $F(x)$ could be determined then the global minimum could be found in one iteration. This is in general not possible. McCormick (1976) has however noted that it is sometimes possible numerically to determine the convex (and concave) envelopes of the functions $f(z)$ that make up the function $F(x)$. If $F(x)$ contains the term $\sin(x_1^2 - 2x_2)$ then the convex and concave envelopes of $\sin(z)$ are computable in any range $a < z < b$. As there is a limited number of such functions in general use these envelopes could be precomputed and stored. In his paper he showed that once this had been done a large subset of nonconvex programming problems would be solveable by a branch and bound routine over subsets of S that used a convex programming method at each iteration. It will be noted that the structure of the function and constraints has to be available and analysed before the program could be run.

10.5 The Beale-Tomlin-Forrest Approach

Another deterministic approach that relies on preanalysis of the problem has been developed by Beale et al, Beale & Tomlin (1970), Beale & Forrest (1976,1977). This is designed to utilise their efficient linear integer programming package. Each nonlinear function $f(z)$ is replaced by a set of linear approximations joining K nodes at which $l_j(z_j) = f(z_j)$ and the particular linear approximation applied is determined by special order sets λ_j which have the property that only one or at most two consecutive values are

nonzero. The subfunction f(z) is then replaced by the linear combination $\sum_j \lambda_j l_j$ and an additional linear equality constraint introduced, connecting the values of z and x. This process
is outlined in detail in Beale & Forrest (1977) where the detailed
equations for the seven standard test functions are presented.
The method again continues by a branch and bound process but the
branching takes place over the special ordered sets. The method
is intended for large problems with few nonlinearities and therefore the set of standard test discussed here which are all small
and fully nonlinear are not typical of the class of problems it is
designed to solve.

The final version of their method incorporates an automatic
interpolation phase intended to overcome the truncation errors
introduced by the finite number of nodes K used to represent the
nonlinear functions f(z). This involves a global minimisation of
a function of one variable (the reduced cost). The method used can
find the global optimum of a function when

(a) the function is twice differentiable;

(b) the function and its derivative can be evaluated at
any point in the range; and

(c) upper and lower bounds on the second derivative are
available in any interval.

Their method is therefore a deterministic method for finding the
global minimum under these conditions provided the function can
be preanalysed and transformed into the required form.

11. NUMERICAL RESULTS

All the contributors to TGO 2 were requested to apply their
algorithms on a set of standard test functions and to perform one
standard computation to provide a standard time. In this way results on the set of standard test functions are available using a
number of the methods outlined above. The algorithms for which
these results are available and the contributors are listed below.

1. Clustering with Random Search (Törn)

2. Clustering with Random Search (Gomulka)

3. Clustering with Variable Metric (Gomulka)

4. C.R.S. (Price)

5. Bremmermann's Algorithm (Dixon)

6. Bremmermann's Algorithm (Dixon) (modified to accept any
improved point found)

7. Random Line Search/Zilinskas Search (Dixon)

8. Descent from Local Minimum/Zilinskas Search (Dixon)

9. N-Dimensional Bayesian Search (Mockus)

10. The P function Approach (DeBiase & Frontini)

11. An efficient Branin Method (Gomulka)

12. The Beale-Forrest Algorithm (Beale & Forrest).

The results are given in detail in the relevant papers and a more detailed discussion of the comparison is given in the introduction to TGO 2. We stress again that this set of test functions are all of small dimension, are all fairly cheap to compute, and all have global optima that are relatively easy to compute as the region of attraction of the global optima is a large proportion of the total set. The algorithms that assume that a function evaluation is expensive compared with the evaluation of a probability distribution will not do well in time comparisons on these functions but the function evaluation count may give a truer indication of their performance on expensive functions. The Branin approach used analytical second derivatives and this limits the type of function evaluations. The Beale & Forrest Algorithm never computes the original function and therefore the only comparison can be on computer time. The results quoted in this summary are for 101 grid points without automatic interpolation.

Before considering the overall comparisons let us consider some subsets in detail. Torn supplied Gomulka with a listing of his algorithm, the results of his own tests on these functions are given in Torn (1977) and Gomulka ran a series of tests both with his algorithm and with the random search replaced by a variable metric algorithm. She concluded that the algorithm is very robust but its performance depends on the choice of selected parameters. Torn being more experienced with the algorithm was obviously able to choose better parameter values.

Gomulka chose her values of parameters consistent with the order of accuracy she was attempting to obtain with the algorithms being investigated at the N.O.C. and the difference in values emphasizes one difficulty in attempting to draw any conclusions from tests performed in different centres.

Turning now to the line search algorithms, these were run from a standard starting point. On the SQRN family this was a long way from the global minimum and the window of attraction of the global minimum from that region was small. Bremmermann's algorithm was trapped by a local minimum on most of the functions, the modified version that accepted any improved point did slightly better, as did the more exact Zilinskas line search. Investigation of the print-out indicated that this located the region of the global minimum along the line very consistently. On SQRN 5 the

Table 1

TORN's CLUSTERING ALGORITHM: FUNCTION EVALUATIONS

	SQRN 5	SQRN 7	SQRN 10	HARTMAN 3	HARTMAN 6	G.P.	Rcos
1. Torn's Results	3679	3606	3874	2584	3447	2499	1558
2. Gomulka's Results	6654	6084	6144				
3. Gomulka's Results with Variable Metric	7085	6684	7352	6766	11125	1495	1318

Table 2

TORN's CLUSTERING ALGORITHM: TIMES

	STANDARD	SQRN 5	SQRN 7	SQRN 10	HARTMAN 3	HARTMAN 6	G.P.	Rcos
1.	0.4	4.1	5.1	5.9	3.3	6.4	1.7	1.5
2.	2.78	47.36	43.42	56.18	46.3	132.7	6.1	7.0
3.	2.78	53.24	64.8	65.5				

Table 3

LINE SEARCH METHODS: FUNCTION EVALUATIONS

		1	2	3	4	5	6	7
5.	Bremmermann	340 L*	1700 L	2500 L	505 L	L	210 L	250
6.	Mod. Bremmermann	375 L	405 L	336 L	420 L	515	300	160
7.	Zilinskas	L	12121 L	8892 L	8641			5129
		7412 L	6082	9348	(2nd starting point)			

Table 4

LINE SEARCH METHODS: TIMES

		1	2	3	4	5	6	7
5.	2.78	2.76 L	20.02 L	37.94 L	5.80 L	L	1.50 L	2.46
6.	2.78	3.10 L	3.94 L	5.04 L	4.82 L	8.54	2.14	1.50
7.	2.78	L	784 L	600 L	486	L	220	220
		390 L	388	580				

* L denotes that a local minimum was located.

Table 5

BRANIN'S METHOD

	Function Evaluations			Times		
	1	2	3	1	2	3
11.	5500	5020	4860 (2.78)	24.9	23.62	26.64

Table 6

COMPARISON OF SUCCESSFUL METHODS I

	Function Evaluations						
	1	2	3	4	5	6	7
1. Torn	3679	3606	3874	2584	3447	2499	1558
3. Gomulka	7085	6684	7352	6766	11125	1445	1318
4. C.R.S. (Price)	3800	4900	4400	2400	7600	2500	1800
9. Bayesian (Mockus)	1174	1279	1209	513	1232	362	189
10. P. Function (DeBiase & Frontini)	620	788	1160	732	807	378	579

The Beale-Forrest algorithm cannot, of course, be included in this table as it does not evaluate the function. The number of L.P. iterations for this approach were

12. Beale-Forrest	350	850	2538	553	1016	4902	15

Table 7

COMPARISON OF SUCCESSFUL METHODS II

		1	2	3	4	5	6	7	STANDARD
1.	Torn	10	13	15	8	16	4	4	0.4
3.	Gomulka	19	23	23	17	48	2	3	2.78
4.	C.R.S. (Price)	14	20	20	8	46	3	4	3.6
10.	P. Function	23	20	30	16	21	15	14	6.0
12.	Beale-Forrest	96	258	1059	117	255	1407	1.5	0.33

window of the global minimum from the local minimum at (1., 1., 1., 1.) is so small that no improved point had been located after 2000 searches along random directions. Given the correct direction the line search located the global minimum in 31 function calls. This stresses the difficulty of hypothesis testing using line searches.

The other unsuccessful approach tested, Branin's method, had been shown to fail on the Goldstein & Price function (No 6) by Hardy. His extended method still failed to locate the minimum after 25,452 function values. From a single randomly chosen starting point Gomulka's most efficient implementation located all the minima of the SQRN family in one integration (see table 5).

If we now consider the overall comparison of the methods that were successful on these 7 functions then on the basis of function evaluations we obtain table 6.

If we now turn to the comparison of weighted times, i.e.

$$\text{Weighted Time} = \frac{\text{Time for test}}{\text{Time to calculate SQRN5, 1000 times}}$$

we obtain table 7. (Unfortunately, the times for the Bayesian approach were not recorded.) I feel it only fair to immediately point out again that these functions were not typical of the type of problem for which the Beale-Forrest approach was written and that despite this it did successfully locate each global minimum.

Of the other four methods that performed well on these function it would be unfair to attempt to place them in ranking order on the basis of these tests alone.

APPENDIX 1

Test Functions for Global Optimisation

1. SHEKEL'S FAMILY (SQRIN)

$$f(x) = -\sum_{i=1}^{m} \frac{1}{(x - a_i)^T(x - a_i) + c_i}$$

$$x = (x_1, \ldots, x_n)^T$$

$$a_i = (x_{i1}, \ldots, a_{in})^T$$

$$c_i > 0$$

Region of interest: $0 \leq x_j \leq 10$

$$j = 1, \ldots, n.$$

Consider 3 cases from the table below with

Data: $n = 4$; $m = 5, 7, 10$.

i	a_i				c_i
1	4.	4.	4.	4.	.1
2	1.	1.	1.	1.	.2
3	8.	8.	8.	8.	.2
4	6.	6.	6.	6.	.4
5	3.	7.	3.	7.	.4
6	2.	9.	2.	9.	.6
7	5.	5.	3.	3.	.3
8	8.	1.	8.	1.	.7
9	6.	2.	6.	2.	.5
10	7.	3.6	7.	3.6	.5

2.   HARTMAN'S FAMILY

$$f(x) = -\sum_{i=1}^{m} c_i \exp\left(-\sum_{j=1}^{m} \alpha_{ij}(x_j - p_{ij})^2\right)$$

$$x = (x_1, \ldots, x_n)$$
$$p_i = (p_{i1}, \ldots, p_{in})$$
$$\alpha_i = (\alpha_{i1}, \ldots, \alpha_{in})$$

p_i is an approximate location of ith local minimum; α_i is proportional to eigenvalues of Hessian at ith local minimum ; $c_i > 0$ is the height (depth) of ith local minimum (assuming that the interference of different local minima is not too strong).

Data

$$0 \leq x_i \leq 1.$$

(1) $m = 4$, $n = 3$.

i	α_i			c_i	p_i		
1	3.	10.	30.	1.	.3689	.117	.2673
2	.1	10.	35.	1.2	.4699	.4387	.747
3	3.	10.	30.	3.	.1091	.8732	.5547
4	.1	10.	35.	3.2	.03815	.5743	.8828

(2) m = 4, n = 6.

i	α_i						c_i
1	10.	3.	17.	3.5	1.7	8.	1.
2	.05	10.	17.	.1	8.	14.	1.2
3	3.	3.5	1.7	10.	17.	8.	3.
4	17.	8.	.05	10.	.1	14.	3.2

i	p_i					
1	.1312	.1696	.5569	.0124	.8283	.5886
2	.2329	.4135	.8307	.3736	.1004	.9991
3	.2348	.1451	.3522	.2883	.3047	.6650
4	.4047	.8828	.8732	.5743	.1091	.0381

3. BRANIN (RCOS)

$$f(x_1, x_2) = a(x_2 - bx_1^2 + cx_1 - d)^2 + e(1 - f) \cos x_1 + e$$

$a = 1$, $b = 5.1/(4\,\pi^2)$, $c = 5/\pi$, $d = 6$, $e = 10$, $f = 1/8\pi)$

Region of interest $=$ $\begin{array}{c} -5 \leqq x_1 \leqq 10 \\ 0 \leqq x_2 \leqq 15 \end{array}$

There are three minima,
all global, in this region.

4. GOLDSTEIN & PRICE (GOLDPR)

$$f(x_1,x_2) = [1 + (x_1 + x_2 + 1)^2 (19 - 14x_1 - 3x_1^2 - 14x_2 + 6x_1x_2 + 3x_2^2)].$$

$$[30 + (2x_1 - 3x_2)^2 (18 - 32x_1 + 12x_1^2 + 48x_2 - 36x_1x_2 + 27x_2^2)].$$

Region of interest $= \boxed{-2 \leqq x_{1,2} \leqq 2}$

Four local minima. Global
minima at $(0,-1)$ with the
value $f = 3$.

REFERENCES

1. L.C.W. Dixon and G.P. Szegö, "Towards Global Optimisation,"
    North Holland, Amsterdam, 1975.

2. L.C.W. Dixon and G.P. Szegö, "Towards Global Optimisation 2,"
    North Holland, Amsterdam, 1978.

3. R.S. Anderssen, "Global Optimisation." In: Optimisation,
    R.S. Anderssen, L.S. Jennings and D.M. Ryan, eds., University
    of Queensland Press, St. Lucia, Queensland, Australia.

4. F. Archetti, "A Sampling Technique for Global Optimisation."
    In: reference 1, 1975.

5. F. Archetti and B. Betró, "Recursive Stochastic Evaluation of
    the Level Sets Measure of Optimisation Problems," University
    of Pisa Series A, Number 21, 1975.

6. F. Archetti and F. Frontini, "A Global Optimisation Method and
    its Application to Dry Cooling Tower Design," Energia Nucleare
    N.5. (1975).

7. F. Archetti and F. Frontini, "A Global Optimisation Method and
    its Application to Technological Problems." In: reference 2,
    1978

8. E.M.L. Beale and J.J.H. Forrest, "Global Optimisation Using
    Special Ordered Sets," Mathematical Programming Vol. 10 No. 1
    pp. 52-69, 1976.

9. E.M.L. Beale and J.J.H. Forrest, "Global Optimisation as an
    Extension of Integer Programming." In: reference 2, 1978.

10. E.M.L. Beale and J.A. Tomlin, "Special Facilities in a General
    Mathematical Programming System for Nonconvex Problems Using
    Special Ordered Sets." In: Proceedings of the Fifth Interna-
    tional Conference on Operations Research, J. Lawrence, ed.,
    Tavistock Publications, London, pp. 447-454, 1970.

11. R.W. Becker and G.V. Lago, "A Global Optimisation Algorithm." In: Proceedings of the Eighth Allerton Conference on Circuits and Systems Theory, October 1970.

12. B. Betro and L. DeBiase, "A Recursive Spline Technique for Uniform Approximation of Sampled Data," University of Pisa Series A No. 31, 1976.

13. N. Bocharov and A.A. Feldbaum, "An Automatic Optimiser for the Search for the Smallest of Several Minima," Automation and Remote Control Vol. 23 No. 3, 1962.

14. F.H. Branin, Jr, "Solution of Nonlinear DC Network Problems via Differential Equations," Mem. Mexico 1970 International IEEE Conference on Systems Networks and Computers, Oaxtepec, Mexico, pp. 93-101, 1971.

15. F.H. Branin, Jr. and S.K. Hoo, "A Method for Funding Multiple Extrema of a Function of N Variables." In: Numerical Methods of Nonlinear Optimisation, F. Lootsma, ed., Academic Press, London, 1972.

16. H. Bremmermann, "A Method of Unconstrained Global Optimisation," Mathematical Biosciences 9, pp. 1-15, 1970.

17. R.P. Brent, "Algorithms for Minimisation without Derivatives," Prentice Hall Press, New York, 1972.

18. S.H. Brooks, "Discussion of Random Methods for Locating Surface Maxima," Ops Res 6, pp. 244-251, 1958.

19. V.K. Chichinadze, "Random Search to Determine the Extremum of the Functions of Several Variables," Engineering Cybernetics No. 1, pp. 115-123, 1967.

20. C.R. Corles, "The Use of Regions of Attraction to Identify Global Minima." In: reference 1, 1975.

21. Curry-Schoenberg, "On Polya Frequency Functions IV: The Fundamental Spline Functions and Their Limits," J. de Analyse Math 17, 1966.

22. L. DeBiase and F. Frontini, "A Stochastic Algorithm for G.O.P.: Its Structure and Numerical Evidence." In: reference 2, 1978.

23. L.C.W. Dixon, "Numerical Optimisation: A Survey of the State of the Art." In: Software for Numerical Mathematics, D. Evans, ed., Academic Press, London, 1974.

24. L.C.W. Dixon, J. Gomulka and S.E. Hersom, "Reflections on the Global Optimisation Problem." In: Optimisation in Action, L.C.W. Dixon, ed., Academic Press, London, 1976.

25. Y.G. Etvushenko, "Numerical Methods for Finding Global Extrema," Zh. Vychisl. Mat. mat FIZ 11, 6, pp. 1390-1403, 1971.

26. E. Fagiouli, et al., "A Mixed Deterministic/Stochastic Method for G.O.P." In: reference 2, 1978.

478

27. J.E. Falk, "Global Solutions of Signomial Programs," George Washington University, T 274, June 1, 1973.

28. J.E. Falk and R.M. Solund, "An Algorithm for Separable Non-convex Programming Problems," Management Science 15, pp. 550-569, 1969.

29. M. Gaviano, "On the Convergence of Random Search Methods..." In: reference 1, 1975.

30. A.A. Goldstein and J.F. Price, "Descent from Local Minima," Maths of Computation 25, 115, 1971.

31. J. Gomulka, "A Users Experience with Toms Clustering Algorithm," and "Numerical Experience with Two Implementations of Branins Method." In: reference 2, 1978.

32. J. Hardy, "An Implemented Extention of Branin's Method." In: reference 1, 1975.

33. J.K. Hartman, "Some Experiments in Global Optimisation," Naval Postgraduate School, Monterey NPS 55HH72051A, 1972.

34. J. Kiefer, "Sequential Minimax Search for a Maximum," Proceedings Am. Math. Soc. 4, No. 3, 1953.

35. G.P. McCormick, "Computability of Global Solutions to Factorable Nonconvex Programs: Part I," Mathematical Programming Vol. 10 No. 2, pp. 147-176.

36. A.I. Mikhal'skii, "The Method of Averaged Splines in the Problem of Approximating Dependences on the Basis of Empirical Data," Autom. and Remote Control 35, 3, p. 1.

37. J. Mockus, "On Bayesian Methods of Optimisation." In: reference 1, 1975.

38. J. Mockus, "On Bayesian Methods for Seeking the Extremum," Lecture Notes in Computer Science No. 27, Springer Verlag, Berlin, pp. 400-404, 1976.

39. J. Mockus, to appear in Proceedings of I.F.I.P. Congress, Toronto, Canada, 1977.

40. J. Mockus, V. Tieses and A. Zilinskas, "The Application of Bayesian Methods for Seeking the Extremum." In: reference 2, 1978.

41. W.L. Price, "A Controlled Random Search Procedure for Global Optimisation." In: reference 2, 1977.

42. L.A. Rastrigen, "The Stochastic Method of Search," Nauka, Moscow, 1968.

43. B.O. Shubert, "A Sequential Method for Seeking the Global Minimum of a Function," S.I.A.M. J. of Numerical Analysis 9:3, pp. 379-388, 1972.

44. R.M. Solund, "An Algorithm for Separable Nonconvex Programming Problems II: Nonconvex Constraints," Management Science 17, pp. 759-773, 1971.

45. A.V. Suckorov, "On the Optimal Strategies for Seeking an Extremum," J. Vychislitelnoj Matem i Matem Phys 11, No. 4, 1971.

46. A. Tóm. "A Search Clustering Approach to the Global Optimisation Problem." In ref 2, 1977.

47. G. Treccani, "On the Critical Points of Continuous Differentiable Functions." In ref. 1, 1975.

48. A. Zilinskas, "Optimisation of One Dimensional Multimodel Functions." To appear, 1977.

COMPUTATIONAL ASPECTS OF GEOMETRIC PROGRAMMING

M.J. Rijckaert

Instituut voor Chemie-ingenieurstechniek, Katholiek
Universiteit Leuven

ABSTRACT. The paper gives a survey of computational strageties for
geometric programming (posynomial and signomial form). It evaluates the different approaches, based on results obtained in several comparative studies. Also a few general non-linear programming algorithms participated in these tests.

Geometric programming is one of the younger members of the
family of non-linear programming techniques. Developed in the
middle sixties, it has gotten from its early start special attention in engineering circles. During its first decade, some 130
papers [36] on the subject have appeared in the open literature.
Roughly speaking, 40 percent of them focused on theoretical aspects of geometric programming. Another 40 percent illustrated
the possible applicability of GP (mainly but not exclusively in the
engineering field). The remaining 20 percent were concerned with
various computational aspects of the method. About five books were
completely or for a substantial part devoted to the subject. The
present paper will subsequently deal with the following topics:

    i)   Geometric Programming Theory
    ii)   Algorithms and Software for Geometric Programming
    iii) Theoretical Differences between Various Algorithms
    iv) Sources of Information on Computational Evidence
    v)   General Conclusions of Numerical Comparisons.

1. GEOMETRIC PROGRAMMING THEORY

We will start by summarizing the most significant theoretical

properties of geometric programs. A much more detailed and profound treatment of the geometric programming theory can be found
for the posynomial case (see later for a definition) in the original textbook on geometric programming [13] and for the signomial
case in [15] or in a recent survey paper [29]. Geometric programming deals with non-linear constrained optimization problems:

$$\min g_0(t)$$

$$\text{s.t.} \quad \sigma_k g_k(t)^{\sigma_k'} \overset{<}{=} 1 \qquad k = 1, \ldots, p \tag{1}$$

$$t_j = 0 \qquad j = 1, \ldots, m$$

with

$$\sigma_k' = \pm 1 \qquad\qquad\qquad\qquad k = 1, \ldots, p$$

$$g_k(t) = \sum_{i \varepsilon J\{k\}} \sigma_i c_i \prod_{j=1}^{m} t_j^{a_{ij}} \qquad k = 0, 1, \ldots, p$$

$$a_{ij} \text{ real constant}$$

$$\sigma_i = \pm 1 \qquad\qquad\qquad\qquad i = 1, \ldots, n$$

The above functions $g_k(t)$ are called generalized polynomials or
signomials. However, they are called posynomials when all signum
functions σ_k' and σ_i are positive. The original development of geometric programming was completely restricted to posynomial programming. (Now often called prototype GP.) Of theoretical and practical importance is the fact that posynomials can be transformed
by an exponential transformation into convex functions. Monomials
is the name given to one term posynomials.

It is worthwhile to note at this stage that the above defined
signomial program can be rearranged into a so-called reversed geometric program, involving only posynomial functions but appearing
in expressions with opposite inequality signs.

The reversed program has the form:

$$\min r_0(t)$$

$$\text{s.t.} \quad r_{m'}(t) \overset{<}{=} 1 \qquad m' = 1, \ldots, M' \tag{2}$$

$$s_m''(t) \overset{>}{=} 1 \qquad m'' = 1, \ldots, M''$$

$$t \geq 0$$

(all functions being posynomials.)

To the above stated primal program corresponds a dual program which can be formulated as:

find a stationary point of the function

$$v\,(\delta,\lambda) = \sigma_0 \left\{ \prod_{i=1} \left(\frac{c_i}{\delta_i}\right)^{\sigma_i \delta_i} \prod_{k=1}^{p} \lambda_k(\delta)^{\lambda_k \sigma_k'} \right\}^{\sigma_0}$$

s.t. $$\sum_{i\in J\{0\}} \sigma_i \, \delta_i = \sigma_0$$

$$\sum_{i=1}^{n} \sigma_i \, a_{ij} \, \delta_i = 0 \qquad\qquad j = 1,\ldots,m \qquad\qquad (3)$$

$$\lambda_k \sigma_k' = \sum_{i\in J\{k\}} \sigma_i \delta_i \qquad\qquad k = 1,\ldots,p$$

$$\delta_i \geq 0 \qquad\qquad i = 1,\ldots,n$$

$$\lambda_k \geq 0 \qquad\qquad k = 1,\ldots,p$$

$$\sigma_0 = \frac{\min g_0(t)}{|\min g_0(t)|}$$

For these non-convex signomial programs only very weak duality relations exist between so-called equilibrium solutions of (1) and (3). These equilibrium solutions satisfy the KT necessary optimality conditions.

(The global minimum of the primal program will always belong to this set of points.) Equilibrium points are defined by: a feasible solution t to primal program (1) is termed a primal equilibrium solution if there is a feasible solution δ to dual program (3) such that

$$c_i \prod_{j=1}^{m} t_j^{a_{ij}} = \delta_i \, v\,(\delta,\lambda) \qquad\qquad i \in j\{0\}$$

$$c_i \prod_{j=1}^{m} t_j^{a_{ij}} = \frac{\delta_i}{\lambda_k(\delta)} \qquad i\varepsilon J\{k\} \quad k = 1,\ldots,p$$

δ is then a dual equilibrium solution. Since for corresponding equilibrium solutions, the following relation holds

$$g_o(t) = v(\delta,\lambda)$$

primal equilibrium solutions can be computed from the corresponding dual solutions.

Unfortunately, the nature of the stationary point of the dual objective function cannot be determined for a signomial program. As a consequence, the duality theory can only play a minor computational role for the class of signomial programs. However, if the primal program contains only straight posynomials (all σ_i and σ_k equal +1), much stronger duality relations exist between the constrained primal minimum and the constrained dual maximum. Indeed in this case, the primal program can be considered convex and the nature of the dual stationary point is no longer unknown. The logarithm of the dual objective function becomes concave. The dual program corresponding to a primal posynomial program is:

$$\max v(\delta,\lambda) = \{ \prod_{i=1}^{n} (\frac{c_i}{\delta_i})^{\delta_i} \prod_{k=1}^{p} \lambda_k(\delta)^{\lambda_k} \}$$

$$\sum_{i\varepsilon J\{0\}} \delta_i = 1$$

$$\sum_{i=1}^{n} a_{ij} \delta_i = 0 \qquad j = 1,\ldots,m$$

$$\lambda_k = \sum_{i\varepsilon J\{0\}} \delta_i \qquad k = 1,\ldots,p \qquad (4)$$

$$\delta_i \geq 0 \qquad i = 1,\ldots,n$$

$$\lambda_k \geq 0 \qquad k = 1,\ldots,p$$

The following notions and definitions will prove useful in explaining the underlying ideas of some computational procedures.

Degree of Difficulty. The quantity $D = n-(m+1)$ is called the degree of difficulty by which the number of dual variables exceeds the number of dual constraints.

Reduced Dual. Since the dual constraints are all equality constraints, it is possible to eliminate some variables from the dual formulation, provided the non-negativity of these variables is guaranteed. This way a dual program can be constructed, in only D variables.

Equilibrium Equations. Passy and Wilde [28] derived the set of optimality conditions for the dual linearly constrained program. Because of their linear logarithmic form, they were called equilibrium conditions. Their number equals the above defined degree of difficulty.

$$\sum_{k=0}^{p} \sum_{i \epsilon j\{k\}} \sigma_i \nu_{id} \ln \left(\frac{\delta_i}{\lambda_k}\right) = \sum_{i=1}^{n} \sigma_i \nu_{id} \ln c_i \quad d = 1,\ldots, D \qquad (5)$$

The quantities ν_{id} are the components of D linearly independent solution vectors ν_d of the homogenized (i.e., $\sigma_o = o$) counterpart of equations (3).

Loose Constraints. The whole block of dual variables with a primal constraint should be zero for a constraint inactive at optimality. This phenomenon might cause serious computational difficulties, for which the use of slack variables might constitute one possible remedy.

However, slack variables cannot be introduced in the usual straightforward way. Kockenberger [20] therefore proposed to introduce them in a penalty-function-like-manner. Based on extensive numerical investigations, Rijckaert and Martens [32] concluded that satisfactory results can be obtained in a single pass, if corresponding to each slack variable t_s introduced in the constraints $bx_s^{-\beta}$ is added to the objective function. They advised to set β at 10^{-4} and b at 1 percent of the estimated optimal value of the objective function.

Condensation. The inequality relations between the arithmetic, geometric and harmonic mean have played a dominant role, at first in the early theoretical development and later on, in the computational evolution of the technique.

Let $u_i(t)$ $i=1,\ldots,T$ be the term of a posynomial such that

$$g(t) = \sum_{1=1}^{T} u_i(t).$$

For a given set of positive numbers ε_i such that $\sum_{i=1}^{T} \varepsilon_i = 1$ the following inequality relations hold:

$$\{ \prod_{i=1}^{T} u_i(t) \}^{-1} \leqq \prod_{i=1}^{T} \{\frac{\varepsilon_i}{u_i(t)}\}^{\varepsilon_i} \leqq \sum_{i=1}^{T} \{\frac{\varepsilon_i^2}{u_i(t)}\}$$

or terms of $g(t)$

$$(g(t))^{-1} \leqq (g'(t,\varepsilon))^{-1} \leqq (g''(t,\varepsilon)) \tag{6}$$

with

$$g'(t,\varepsilon) = \prod_{i=1}^{T} (\frac{u_i(t)}{\varepsilon_i})^{\varepsilon_i}$$

$$g''(t,\varepsilon) = \sum_{i=1}^{T} (\frac{\varepsilon_i^2}{u_i(t)}).$$

The inequalities become strict equalities if $\varepsilon_i = u_i(t)$ $i = 1,\ldots,T$. The first inequality in (6) is called the geometric inequality. The first and third term of (6) form the harmonic inequality. Both can be used in constructing an approximating program. The first by replacing a posynomial by a monomial, and operation called condensation. The second by replacing a reversed posynomial constraint $g(t) >$ by a straight posynomial constraing $g''(t,\varepsilon) < 1$.

Transformed Primal Problem. Consider again the primal problem under the logarithmic transformation

$$z_j = \ln t_j \qquad\qquad j = 1,\ldots,m.$$

This transformation together with the definition

$$y_i = \sum_{j=1}^{m} a_{ij} z_j \qquad\qquad i = 1,\ldots,n$$

leads to the following transformed primal problem.

$$\text{Min} \sum_{i\in J\{o\}} c_i \, e^{y_i}$$

$$\text{s.t.} \quad \sum_{i \in J\{k\}} c_i \, e^{y_i} \leqq 1 \qquad k = 1, \ldots, p$$

$$y_i - \sum_{j=1}^{m} a_{ij} z_j = o \qquad i = 1, \ldots, n.$$

2. ALGORITHMS AND SOFTWARE FOR GEOMETRIC PROGRAMMING

2.1 Dual Solution Methods for Posynomials

Before dicsussing alternative solution strategies, it is worthwhile to point out some general features of the dual geometric program corresponding to the posynomial primal program:

The dual program is a linearly constrained program.

The degree of difficulty has kept its literal meaning for many dual approaches as a measure of the size of the problem.

The dual objective function becomes non-differentiable in any point, where a dual variable δ_i is zero.

If one dual variable δ_i becomes zero the whole block of dual variables δ associated with the same primal constraint need to be zero. Furthermore, $\delta_i = 0$ $i \in j\{k\}$ iff $\lambda_k = 0$. This means that inactive primal constraints will form an additional obstacle for the applicability of the dual program. One way of avoiding inactive primal constraints, is to introduce, whenever needed, slack variables in the primal programs.

As mentioned earlier, this cannot be done in the usual straightforward way, but need to be done in a penalty-like manner.

(At several occasions during the subsequent paragraphs reference will be made to a set of comparative studies; the details of these stu.ies will be clarified later.)

It is evident that all nonlinear programming techniques designed for linearly constrained problems, will be applicable to the posynomial dual program, provided the above mentioned limitations are taken into account. We will however, restrict ourselves to a brief description of these methods, which, have been tested on their efficiency to solve the geometric dual program. It is clear that other possible approaches might exist and that some of them could even be better than the one mentioned here; but, at least to our knowledge, they have never been experimentally examined.

1. Linear Approximation Method [41]. Based on a linearization of the dual objective function, a feasible direction for improving the value of the same objective is found and along this direction a one-dimensional search is performed.

A code, using a LP routine based on the revised simplex method with product form of the inverse and using a cubic-interpolation method for the line minization was tested in [35].

2. Gradient Projection Method [37]. This method is a combination of Rosen's gradient projection method and a variable metric method. The gradient of the objective function is projected into the linear manifold of the set of active constraints. Doing so a projection matrix is constructed based on an approximation of the inverse of the Hessian of the objective function. In updating, this approximation remains positive definite. This approach, requiring the use of primal slack variables, was tested in [11] and [35].

3. Concave Simplex Method [4]. The dual program can be solved by the well-known concave simplex method, providing primal constraints are forced active by the use of slack variables. This approach was examined in [38].

Beck and Ecker [4] modified the procedure for selecting a new direction for improving the objective function. They adapted it to the special requirements posed by the dual geometric program (i.e., if one dual variable goes to zero, the whole block should go to zero). They also emphasized the fact that inactive primal constraints may eventually prevent the calculation of all primal variables from the dual solution. They defined for this case a so-called subsidiary program to recover the primal variables. Their code was tested in [16],[35],[38].

4. Separable Programming [21]. The dual geometric program is a linearly constrained program with a non-linear objective function, which becomes separable upon logarithmization. These two features make the dual program amenable to the use of separable programming. However, one should realize that although (v) is concave, the individual component functions are not. This means for instance that the approximating problem only a local maximum can be determined and that there is often no way of knowing how close this local maximum is to the global maximum. In [35], this technique was applied using a polygonal approximation based on 5 points. The adjustment of the gird points was performed in such a way that a variable can always return to a value lying outside the optimal line segment of the previous approximation.

5. Newton-Raphson Method [7]. This method works on the reduced dual program, for which a point satisfying the Kuhn-Tucker
optimality conditions is computed using the well-known Newton-
Raphson procedure. Precautions, however, need to be taken to guarantee that the substituted variables remain positive. This is done
by imposing a step reduction on those variables, which happen to
become negative during the interative scheme. Tested in [11] and
[35].

6. Quadratic Programming [8]. The logarithmic dual objective
function is approximated by a quadratic function and this for the
reduced dual program. Easily available analytic expressions can be
used for the gradient and the Hessian. The approximating program
is solved by quadratic programming. Dual variables are artificially
bounded from below. They are zeroed when an estimate of the primal
constraint multiplier becomes very small. Discussed in [9].

7. Augumented Geometric Program [27]. McNamara has proposed
to solve the original program upon artifically reducing its degree
of difficulty to zero. The dual of such a program is then obtained
by solving a system of linear equations. Tested as in [35].

2.2 Dual Methods for Signomials

It is important to note that, as far as the number of applications is concerned, the class of signomial problems is much more
important than the class of posynomial problems. The methods mentioned here have all been tested in practice and for all of them
the following general observations are valid.

The only possiblity by working on the dual in this case, is
to identify an equilibrium solution. The nature of the corresponding primal equilibrium solution needs then to be checked
by higher-order analysis. However, this phenomenon is due to
the type of the problem and cannot be blamed on the solution
technique.

All methods solve the optimality conditions neglecting the non-
negativity requirements on the dual variables. It should, however, be noticed that obtaining a negative solution is often
excluded in practice by the logarithmic form of the equation.

All methods mentioned below can only handle inactive inequality constraints, if slack variables are added explicitly to
the primal formulation.

1. Newton-Raphson Technique [35]. A dual equilibrium point can be obtained by solving the set of equations, consisting of the linear and dual constraints and the non-linear equilibrium equations. Such solution can be obtained by a Newton-Raphson method. Eventually if the number of non-linear (logarithmic) equations exceeds the number of linear equations, a logarithmic transformation may inverse the role of linear and non-linear equations. This method was tested in [35].

2. Lagrangian Algorithm [6]. Blau proposed an algorithm solving the dual KT conditions without eliminating the dual Lagrange multipliers. For a given value of these multipliers, the dual variables δ are completely determined. Hence one can exploit the separability of the logarithmic equations. As a consequence smaller matrices need to be inverted at each iteration. (Dimension (p+m+1) instead of (2p+m+n+1) as in the previous method.) This method has been examined in [35].

3. Dual Condensation Method [34]. The condensation algorithm, described in more detail in the section on primal methods, can also be used on the dual formulation. This approach was tested in [35].

4. Marquardt Algorithm [18]. Since the optimality conditions form a square set of non-linear equations, one could consider the well-known Marquardt method for solving this set of equations. Tested in [35].

2.3 Primal Geometric Programming Techniques

In this chapter we will not a prior make a formal difference between posynomial and signomial problems. However, it is clear that if one is dealing with a signomial problem, one should remain extremely cautious about the kind of equilibrium point obtained. For the techniques, mentioned here, the degree of difficulty has lost nearly completely its meaning.

A. Approximating a signomial by a posynomial program

1. Complementary Geometric Programming [2]. Signomial programs can be formulated as:

$$\min t_o$$

$$\text{s.t.} \quad r_k(t) - s'_k(t) \leqq 1 \qquad k = 1, \ldots, K$$

with $r_k(t)$ and $s_k'(t)$, $k = 1,\ldots,K$ posynomials.

Let

$$s_k(t) = s_k'(t) + 1$$

The constraints can then be restated as:

$$r_k(t) \cdot s_k^{-1}(t) = 1 \qquad\qquad k = 1,\ldots,K$$

The denominator is subsequently "condensed" into a monomial, creating a so-called complementary program:

$$\min t_o$$

$$\text{s.t.} \quad r_k(t) \ s_k^{-1} (t,\varepsilon) \overset{\leq}{=} 1 \qquad\qquad k = 1,\ldots,K$$

$$\varepsilon_i > 0 \qquad\qquad i\varepsilon J \ k\{,\}k = 1,\ldots,K$$

$$\sum_{i\varepsilon j\{k\}} \varepsilon_i = 1 \qquad\qquad k = 1,\ldots,K$$

It is clear that in the above procedure, posynomial constraints, if present, are left unchanged. Starting from a primal feasible solution, a series of condensed programs is constructed and their solution is guaranteed to converge to an equilibrium point of the original program.

Each condensed problem can be solved by any posynomial algorithm. However, in particular, we would like to illustrate the following technique, which can be considered as an independent primal posynomial technique, but which is conceptually closely related to the above complementarity theory. Through condensation each posynomial can be transformed into a monomial, which in his turn becomes a linear expression upon logarithmization. Hence, following the ideal of Kelley's cutting plane technique a sequence of linear programs is solved [3].

Dembo has combined the complementary idea with the cutting plane technique in one code, which also provides the possibility of computing its own feasible starting point in a phase I-procedure. Due to the use of linear programs, no precautions need to be taken to safeguard against inactive constraints. The use of the cutting plane technique urges to state upper and lower bounds on each primal variable. This algorithm has been tested in [11],[35], [38].

In an alternative approach, the reduced dual of the complementary program has been solved by Fletcher and Reeves' conjugate gradient method [39]. This approach has been tested in [11],[35].

The reduced dual of the complementary program has also been solved by a Newton-Raphson method. Tested in [11],[25]. Also the quadratic programming approach was used to solve the complementary posynomial program. Discussed in [9].

2. Use of harmonic inequality [14]. As mentioned before, the harmonic inequality can be applied to transform reversed constraints into straight posynomial constraints. The following posynomial program then results:

$$\min g_0(t)$$

$$\text{s.t. } g_k(t) \leqq 1 \qquad\qquad k = 1,\ldots,K'$$

$$g_k''(t,\varepsilon) \leqq 1 \qquad\qquad k = 1,\ldots,K''$$

$$\varepsilon_i \geqq 0 \qquad \sum_{i \in J\{k\}} \varepsilon_i \qquad k = 1,\ldots,K''$$

Jefferson [19] proposed an algorithm, that maximizes the reduced dual of the above program by means of a modified Newton method. After calculating a feasible starting point, one dimensional searches are performed until the dual maximum is obtained. New weights are then computed and a new pass of the iteration is begun. Slack variables are introduced, when needed during the computations. Their implementation is, however, different from what has been told before and for details the reader is referred to [19]. The approach has been studied in [11],[25],[35].

B. Direct Primal Approach

3. Direct Primal Condensation [34]. Rijckaert and Martens have proposed to solve directly the primal KT optimality conditions, provided that all primal constraints are guaranteed to be active through the introduction of slack variables. The geometric inequality is then used to condense the optimality conditions into monomial equations, which become linear upon logarithmization. Hence, only a set of linear equations needs to be solved iteratively. This approach has been tested in [11],[35]. The code provides the possibility of a two-level approach where in the second level inactive constraints (positive slack variables) are dropped. The code works equally well for posynomial as for signomial problems.

4. Transformed Primal Program [32]. Reklaitis and Wilde proposed a primal code that works on the transformed program. It uses the differential algorithm of Wilde and Beightler, which can be seen as a generalized reduced gradient technique. (Using an active constraint strategy to accommodate inequalities.) The code has been tested on posynomial programs [38], but can, of course, be extended to handle signomial programs by the complementary principle.

3. GENERAL NON-LINEAR PROGRAMMING TECHNIQUES

It is clear that every general purpose non-linear programming technique can be used to solve the primal program. We will mention here only these possibilities, which have been tested in practice against geometric programming approaches. Their occurrence in this context is therefore not to be interpreted as proof of their excellent qualities among general non-linear programming codes. Since these codes are usually well known, we will be extremely brief in their description.

1. Penalty Function Methods. This approach has been tested in [11],[38].

2. Generalized Reduced Gradient. This technique has been tested in [11],[38].

3. Augumented Lagrangian. This algorithm solves the constrained primal problem by transforming it into an unconstrained problem. Hereto the classical Lagrangian function is augmented by a penalty term as described by Haaroff and Buys [17]. The code deals with equality constraints, so that slack variables are introduced in the formulation of the inequality constraints. (Although not in the way as described in the section on GP theory.) The unconstrained optimization uses the well known DFP method with derivatives in analytic form. The method has been tested in [35].

Another augumented Lagrangian code was also tested under the same conditions. This code [30] is able to treat inequality constraints directly without the need of slack variables. The unconstrained minimization can be executed by either the DFP method or by a self-scaled variable metric method. For both alternatives the code has the option to use a reset procedure for the Hessian.

4. THEORETICAL DIFFERENCES BETWEEN VARIOUS ALGORITHMS

Based only on the observation of the theoretical properties

of the different approaches one can make the following statement:

a) The dual program has the undeniable advantage for posynomial problems of being linearly constrained. However, this approach is bothered by a dimensionality problem. Indeed for the reduced dual, the number of variables will exceed the number of variables in the primal program as soon as the number of primal terms equals two times the number of primal variables. In practice this will very often happen. If the standard form of the dual is used, the situation is even worse for the dual. Furthermore, the local non-differentiability of the dual objective might create a problem. This is surely to be expected in these problems, where a slack variable was added to an inequality constraint, which otherwise would also have been tight at optimality.

b) By using the quadratic programming approach, one obtains a better approximation of the dual objective function but at the cost of solving a quadratic, instead of linear, program at each iteration.

c) As mentioned in [38], the transformed primal problem has the advantage of being separable and continuously differentiable to all orders. Furthermore, each variable occurs exactly once in each nonlinear function. Slackness of inequalities does not cause numerical difficulties. However, these advantages are obtained at the cost of an increased dimensionality.

d) The harmonic inequality gives a more conservative approximation for a signomial than the geometric inequality does. Furthermore, the size of the problem is reduced by condensation. On the other hand, the exponent matrix of subsequent approximations remains unchanged for the harmonic inequality approach.

e) The combination of the complementarity principle with Kelley's cutting plane technique needs the presence of bounds, which however are treated implicitly in the solution technique. Hence the method will certainly be favored by the presence of physical bounds on the variables. Due to the cutting plane technique the execution time will not be strictly proportional to the problem size. Depending on the problem this might turn out to an advantage or disadvantage. Finally, the method can handle easily loose inequalities and will also be favored by the presence of single term constraints. Indeed for such constraints no approximation is required by the computational scheme.

f) The direct primal approach is bothered by the need of slack
   variables. On the other hand, it uses a very simple computation scheme (only systems of linear equations need to
   be solved) and is favored by the dimensionality of the
   primal problem (which can be negatively influenced by the
   eventual need for slack variables). The method can thus
   be expected to work best on a problem, whose constraints
   need to be active at optimality.

5. SOURCE OF INFORMATION ON COMPUTATIONAL EVIDENCE

To draw some conclusions on the efficiency of geometric programming codes, one can rely on the following studies:

1/ Rijckaert-Martens [35]

The following set of computer codes has been examined in this
study:

Method	Code Name	Authors or Code Origin
Linear Approximation Method	LAM	M. Rijckaert, X. Martens [35]
Separable Programming	SP	M. Rijckaert, X. Martens [35]
Gradient Projection Method	VMP	R. Sargent, B. Murtagh [37]
Netwon-Raphson	NEWTGP	J. Bradley [7]
Concave Simplex (Modified)	CSGP	P. Bext [5]
Newton-Raphson for Signomial	LM	M. Rijckaert, X. Martens [35]
Lagrangian Algorithm	GOMTRY	A. Garcia, G. Hogg [23]
Marquardt	VA07AD	Harwell Library [19]
Dual Condensation	DCA	M. Rijckaert, K. Martens [35]
Complementary + Cutting plane	GGP	R. Dembo [10]
Complementary + Fletcher-Reeves for the dual	SIGNOPT	A. Templeman [39]
Use of Harmonic Inequality	GPROG	T. Jefferson (19)
Direct primal condensation	GPKTC	M. Rijckaert, X. Martens [34]
Augmented Geometric Program°	NSGP	J. McNamara [27]

| Augmented Lagrangian (Equal.) | CONMIN | Haarhoff, Buys, von Molendorf [23] |
| Augmented Lagrangian (Inequal. and Equal. Constraints)° | LPNLP | G.A. Pierre, M.J. Love [30] |

°:These codes have been studied under the same conditions but the results are not included in [35].

A set of test problems with the following characteristics was used:

Number of problems: 24

Type: posynomial and signomial, with 80 percent of them having a physical meaning attached to the optimization problem. (The others are "cooked" mathematical problems.)

Number of primal variables: ranging from 2 to 13, with an average of 7.6.

Number of primal constraints: ranging from 1 to 10, with an average of 5.4. (Bounds on the variables are not included in this figure.)

Degree of difficulty: ranting from 1 to 47, with an average of 11.2.

Characteristics of the testing procedure. All tests were performed on the same computer. (IBM 370-158 in FORTRAN IV, level H.) It is, at least to our knowledge, the only test of this size executed on the same computer. Dual posynomial codes internally computed their own starting point. For all other codes, the starting points were randomly generated and all results are based on runs from 5 different random points. Termination of the codes was controlled by the tolerance for the active constraints and for the objective function. The codes were evaluated against the following criteria: CPU-time (without input and output), robustness (number of failures), in-core storage, complexity of preparation, and implementation. The latter is, of course, a quite subjective measure.

2/ Dembo [11]

The set of computer codes tested in this study included:

Method	Code Name	Authors or Code Origin
Generalized reduced gradient	GRG	Lasdon, Waren, Jain, Ratner [24]
Generalized reduced gradient	GREG	D. Himmelblau [1]

Penalty Function	GAPF/QL	D. Himmelblau [11]
Penalty Function	COMET	D. Himmelblau [11]
Gradient Projection Method	GMP/COMNLC	J. Kreuser [22]
Complementarity + Cutting plane	GGP	R. Dembo [10]
Complementarity + Cutting plane	GEOLP	J. Dinkel, G. Lochenberger [3]
Complementarity + Fletcher-Reeves for the dual	SIGNOPT	A. Templeman [39]
Complementarity + Newton-Raphson	GEOEPS	J. Kinkel, G. Kochenberger [12]
Use of Harmonic Inequality	GPROG	T. Jefferson [19]
Direct Primal Condensation	GPKTC	M. Rijckaert, X. Martens [34]

The set of test problems had the following charaxteristics:

Number of problems: 8 (plus 5 slightly perturbed formulations.)

Type: Posynomial and signomial. About 75 percent of the problems have a physical meaning.

Number of primal variables: ranging from 5 to 16, with an average of 9.5.

Number of primal constraints (excluding bounds): ranging from 3 to 19, with an average of 8.6.

Degree of difficulty: ranging from 7 to 58, with an average of 27.4.

Characteristics of the testing procedure. The study was done in the known Colville-way. (Based on a standard timing program to compare execution times from different computers.) One starting point (a so-called educated guess) was specified for each problem. Termination was based on tolerances for the active constraints and for the objective function. The methods were evaluated against the following criteria: execution time (measured in Colville-standard time) and robustness. (Number of failures.)

3/ Smara, Martens, Reklaitis, and Rijckaert [38]

The set of computer codes tested in this study included:

Method	Code Name	Authors or Code Origin
Penalty Function	SUMT	McCormick, Mylander, Fiacco [262
Complementarity + Cutting plane	GGP	R. Dembo [10]
Transformed Geometric Program	DAP	G.V. Keklaitis [32]
Concave Simplex Method (with slacks)	CS	J.P. Van Dessel [40]
Concave Simplex Method (Modified)	MCS	P. Beck [5]

The set of test problems was the one originally proposed by Beck and Ecker [4], with the following characteristics:

Number of problems: 16 (plus 4 variations)

Type: posynomial problems with only a mathematical meaning.

Number of primal constraints (excluding bounds): ranging from 2 to 12 with an average of 4.1.

Number of primal variables: ranging from 3 to 24, with an average of 6.7.

Degree of difficulty: ranging from 2 to 26, with an average of 11.

Characteristics of the testing procedure: All tests were performed on the same computer (CDC 6500). Starting points generated by DAP, were used for the primal codes. For dual codes another starting point was generated without any relation to the primal one. Termination was based on constraint and objective function tolerances. Evaluating criteria were the CPU-time and the robustness of the different codes.

4/ McCarl [25]

This study examined the geometric inequality approach against the harmonic inequality approach for approximating a signomial by a posynomial. The posynomial program was in both cases solved by a Newton-Raphson method on the reduced dual. Both codes were written by the author of this study.

The set of test problems was characterized by:

Number of problems 20:

Type: signomial, with 50 percent of them having a physical meaning.

Number of primal variables: ranging from 1 to 9, with an

average of 3.7.

Number of primal constraints (excluding bounds): ranging from 0 to 6, with an average of 1.7.

Degree of difficulty: ranging from 1 to 12, with an average of 5.2.

Characteristics of the testing procedure: All tests were performed on the same computer. (IBM 360-67 in FORTRAN, level G.) One feasible starting point was used for all problems. Termination was based on the tolerance between the approximating primal problem and the original problem. Evaluation was based on execution times.

5/ Other studies

A few other studies have been conducted but a on a less extended basis and under less uniform conditions. Ratner et al. [31] have tested a generalized reduced gradient method by using the set of test problems mentioned in [11] and in [35]. Gochet et al. [16] have tested the generalized reduced gradient method, the modified concave simplex method and a general fixed point algorithm by using the cited Beck and Ecker test problems. However, the codes were implemented under quite different conditions and the conclusions are partially based on data taken from the literature. The same remarks apply to the study published by Bradley [9]. He examined many different approaches but the conclusions are mainly based on data taken from the literature. Therefore, codes were not tested on an identical set of test problems. Also, the termination criteria, the choice of a starting point, and the measure of effectiveness vary quite largely from one code to another.

6. GENERAL CONCLUSIONS FROM NUMERICAL COMPARISONS

In this last section, we will summarize the main conclusions drawn from the individual comparative studies. One can hardly expect that such computational comparisons might lead to a strict classification of algorithms with different level of efficiency. Indeed it would be completely unrealistic to anticipate that one code would constantly dominate all others and that in comparing two particular codes, one would outperform the other under all circumstances.

Furthermore, the results of numerical comparisons of optimization algorithms are strongly biased by several factors:

The inherent difficulty of comparing results, obtained on different computers. Several investigators have pointed out that the classical Colville approach is not perfectly satisfying in this regard and that improved procedures are needed. (For instance, the codes executed on a very fast computer seem to be disfavored in a Colville-type comparison.)

The difficulties in unifying the termination criteria for conceptually different numerical techniques. This really becomes a serious problem when comparing primal and dual codes. In fact, it is hard to translate a primal termination criterion into an equivalent dual one.

One is facing an identical problem with regard to the choice of starting points. Some codes automatically generate their own starting point; others have an optional phase-I procedure. Several codes need a very specific starting point, while others will virtually accept any point to start from. Many comparisons are based on results obtained for a single starting point for each problem. It is obvious that the choice of this point might strongly affect the results (in terms of robustness of the code as well as in terms of execution times). It is our feeling that, where possible, the results should be based on several runs initiating from randomly generated points, but with certain restrictions on the range from which points can be drawn.

The widely varying degree of sophistication of the coding will also influence the results. In the same context, one could also mention the role of the determination of certain heuristic rules and parameters.

Making the code more efficient--and hence more attractive--for the user, will often conflict with the efficiency of the code itself (especially in terms of execution time). For instance, the amount of input required and output provided by the code might create such a conflict. The question of how to provide the gradients has to be seen in this regard. (Because of the standard formulation of generalized polynomials, the derivation, if desired, can be performed on the computer.) For these reasons, the differences between codes should be at least an order of magnitude before strong conclusions can be drawn with respect to the efficiency of the numerical algorithm, of which they are the incorporation.

At this stage, it should be stressed once more, that the statements to be made are solely valid for the codes and the techniques as used in the above indicated studies.

The main conclusions, drawn by the various researchers on the basis of their experimental results, all seem to agree well. Also, in most cases, they confirm the expected (see section 3) relative efficiency of the codes based on their theoretical properties.

Dual Solution Methods for Posynomial Programs

All dual methods are severly hypothecated by their dimensionality problem and by the ill-conditioned numerical behavior for
small dual variables. The latter phenomenon seems unavoidable for
methods, needing primal slack variables when dealing with inequality constraints

The best results for this class of algorithms were obtained
with the modified convex simplex method. (The modification of the
direction-generating machinery is to be preferred above the use of
slack variables. An explanation for this observation can be found
in the previous paragraph.) Certainly not to be recommended among
this class of algorithms are the separable programming and the augmented geometric programming technique.

The rather unexpected conclusion for the posynomial methods,
described in 2.1, is that they are constantly dominated by codes
written for a more general type of problem. This means that the
disadvantages of working with the dual are not conterbalanced by
the advantageous property of the linearity of the constraint set.
Although one can possibly agree with the argument [11] that the
specific characteristics of the dual are not exploited to full extent so far, it is obvious that in the early development of geometric programming, the advantages of the dual have been greatly
overestimated.

Dual Codes for Signomial Problems

The behavior of these methods too, is completely determined by
the properties of the dual. Roughly speaking, they are no longer
robust when the size of the dual program (total number of dual
variables) exceed 50. The only positive remark, one can make about
them, is that they are easy to program. Individually, the codes
GOMTRY and DCA were the "better" ones in this class.

Primal Geometric Programming Techniques

First, there is the alternative of using the geometric or the
harmonic inequality for approximating a signomial by a posynomial
program. All results, obtained in the different studies, indicated
that the more conservative harmonic-inequality-approximation is
dominated by the geometric inequality for this purpose.

The most efficient combination with the complementarity principle is the solution of the approximating posynomial program
through condensation. Both GGP and GEOLP are based on this mathematical algorithm but GGP is doing constantly better than GEOLP.

This is an example of the influence of the internal heuristics on the efficiency of a code.

Two codes of this class (GGO and GPKTC--notice that both use the idea of condensation of posynomials--although in a completely different setting) were the most effective ones in terms of execution time and in terms of robustness among all codes used in the different experimentations. To a large extent, this is due to the smaller dimensionality of the primal program. Their relative merits and pitfalls can be summarized as follows: GPKTC is mainly bothered by the eventual need for primal slack variables. It will work best on problems for which the constraints need to be active. GGP will be favored by problems with many neutral bounds on the variables. Such bounds are needed for the operation of the algorithm and are implicitly taken care of. The absence of such bounds will raise the question of how to select them. GGP seems further to be dominated on near posynomial problems and seems to work well on problems with many monomial constraints.

General Non-linear Programming Algorithms

For the techniques considered here, one can state that globally the best geometric programming codes (see above) did better than the general codes, and this in terms of execution time and, even to a high degree, in terms of robustness. Several experiments illustrated the high sensitivity of the performance of general non-linear programming codes to certain heuristic decisions and parameters. For instance, the Augumented Lagrangian Method (LPNLP) did relatively well, when it converged, but the convergence of the code depended drastically on the initial value attributed to multipliers and parameters. One can state that the same was true for the other non-linear programming techniques, of which the penalty function approach is certainly to be less recommended than the other two for solving generalized polynomial optimization problems.

Given the present state-of-the-art, the overall conclusions concerning the solution procedures for geometric programming problems, could be that:

The best geometric programming approaches are to be recommended above the general non-linear programming techniques, because of their efficiency (execution time) and certainly because of their greater robustness (less dependent on the heuristics in the code).

An efficient geometric programming code should be a primal based code. (In which the principle of condensation can play a dominant role.)

REFERENCES

1. J. Abadie and J. Guigou, "Numerical Experiments with the GRG Method," in: J. Abadie (ed.), Integer and Nonlinear Programming, North Holland, Amsterdam, 1970.

2. M. Avriel and A.C. Williams, "Complementary Geometric Programming," SIAM Journal on Applied Mathematics, 19, 125-141, 1970.

3. M. Avriel, R. Dembo, and U. Passy, "Solution of Generalized Geometric Programs," International Journal of Numerical Methods in Engineering, 9, 149-169, 1975.

4. P.A. Beck and J.G. Ecker, "Some Computational Experience with a Modified Convex Simples Algorithm in GP." Report AFSC, 1972

5. P.A. Beck and J.G. Ecker, "A Modified Concave Simplex Algorithm for Geometric Programming," Journal of Optimization Theory and Applications, 15, 189-202, 1975.

6. G.E. Blau and D.J. Wilde, "A Lagrangian Algorithm for Equality Constrained Generalized Polynomial Optimization," AICHE Journal, 17, 235-240, 1971.

7. J. Bradley, "An Algorithm for the Numerical Solution of Prototype Geometric Programs," Report, Institute for Industrial Research and Standards, Dublin, 1973.

8. J. Bradley, "The Development of Polynomial Programming Algorithms with Applications," Dissertation, Dubline, University, Dublin, 1975.

9. J. Bradley, "Computational Aspects of Polynomial Programming, I: The Posynomial Case," Report, Central Bank of Ireland, Dublin.

10. R.S. Dembo, "The Solution of Complementary Geometric Programming Problems, Dissertation, Israel Institute of Technology, Haifa, 1972.

11. R.S. Dembo, "The Current State-of-the Art of Algorithms and Computer Software for Geometric Programming," Working Paper, 88, School of Organization and Management, Yale University, New Haven, 1976.

12. J.J. Dinkel, G.A. Kochenberger, and B. McCarl, "An Approach to the Numerical Solution of Geometric Programs," Mathematical Programming, 7, 181-190, 1974

13. R.J. Duffin, E.L. Peterson, and C. Zener, Geometric Programming, J. Wiley, New York, 1967.

14. R.J. Duffin and E.L. Peterson, "Reversed Geometric Programming Treated by Harmonic Means," Indiana University, Mathematics Journal, 22, 531-550, 1972.

504

15. R.J. Duffin and E.L. Peterson, "Geometric Programming with Signomials," Journal of Optimization Theory and Applications, 11, 3-35, 1973.

16. W. Gochet, E. Loute, and D. Solow, "Comparative Computer Results of Three Algorithms for Solving Prototype Geometric Programming Problems, Cahiers du Centre d' Etude de Recherche Operationelle, 16, 461-486, 1974.

17. P.C. Haarhoff and J.D. Buys, "A New Method for the Optimization of a Nonlinear Function Subject to Nonlinear Constraints," Computer Journal, 13 178-184, 1970.

18. Harvell Library, Theoretical Physics Division, AERE, Berkshire, 1971.

19. T.J. Jefferson, "Geometric Programming with an Application to Transportation Planning," Dissertation, Urbana Systems Engineering Center, Northwestern University, Evanston, 1972.

20. G.A. Kochenberger, "Geometric Programming: Extensions to Deal with Degrees of Difficulty and Loose Constraints," Dissertation, University of Colorado, 1969.

21. G.A. Kochenberger, R.E.D. Woolsey, and B.A. McCarl, "On the Solution of Geometric Programming via Separable Programming," Operations Research Quarterly 24, 285-296, 1973.

22. J.L. Kreuser and J.B. Rosen, "GPM/GPMNLC Extended Gradient Projection Method Nonlinear Programming Subroutines," Academic Computer Center, University of Wisconsin.

23. J.L. Kuester and J.H. Mize, Optimization with FORTRAN Programs, McGraw Hill, New York, 1973.

24. L.S. Lasdon, A. Warren, A. Jain, and M.W. Ratner, "3GRG System Documentation," Technical Memograph, Computer Information Science Department, Cleveland State University, 1975.

25. B.A. McCarl, "A Computational Study of Polynomial Geometric Programming," Dissertation, Pennsylvania State University, 1973.

26. G.P. McCormick, W.C. Mylander, and A.V. Fiacco, "Computer Program Implementing the Sequential Unconstrained Minimization Technique for Nonlinear Programming," Research Analysis Corporation, McLean, Virginia, 1967.

27. J.R. McNamara, "A Solution Procedure for Geometric Programming," Operations Research, 24, 15-25, 1976.

28. U. Passy and D.J. Wilde, "Mass Action and Polynomial Optimization," Journal of Engineering Mathematics, 3, 325-335, 1969.

29. E.L. Peterson, "Geometric Programming: A Survey," SIAM Review, 18, 1-51, 1976.

30. D.A. Oierre and M.J. Love, "Mathematical Programming via Augmented Lagrangian," Addison-Wesley, Reading, 1975.

31. M. Ratner, L.S. Lasdon, and A. Jain, "Solving Geometric Programs using GRG-Results and Comparisons," Technical Report, Systems Optimization Laboratory, Stanford University, 1976.

32. G.V. Reklaitis and D.J. Wilde, "Differential Algorithm for Posynomial Programs," Dechema Monographen, 76, 503-542, 1971.

33. M. J. Rijckaert and X.M. Martens, "Numerical Aspects of the Use of Slack Varibles," Report, Katholieke Universiteit, Leuven, 1975.

34. M. J. Rijckaert and X.M. Martens, "A Condensation Method for Generalized Geometric Programming," Mathematical Programming, 11, 89-93, 1976.

35. M.J. Rijckaert and X.M. Martens, "A Comparison of Generalized Geometric Programming Algorithms," Journal of Optimization Theory and Applications, to appear.

36. M.J. Rijckaert and X.M. Martens, "A Bibliographical Note on Geometric Programming," Journal of Optimization Theory and Applications, to appear.

37. R.W.H. Sargent and B.A. Murtagh, "Projection Methods for Nonlinear Programming," Mathematical Programming, 4, 26-28, 1973.

38. P.V.L.N. Sarma, X.M. Martens, G.V. Keklaitis, and M.J. Rijckaert, "A Comparison of Computational Strategies for Geometric Programs," Journal of Optimization Theory and Applications, to appear.

39. A.B. Templeman, "The Use of Geometric Programming Methods for Structural Optimization," Lecture Series, AGARD, Neuilly-s-Seine, France, 1974.

40. J.P. Van Dessel, "Modified Concave Simples," Katheolieke Universiteit Leuven, 1975.

41. W.I. Zangwill, Nonlinear Programming: A Unified Approach, Prentice Hall, Englewood Cliffs, 1969.

A PROPOSAL FOR THE CLASSIFICATION AND DOCUMENTATION OF TEST PROBLEMS
IN THE FIELD OF NONLINEAR PROGRAMMING

J.C.P. Bus

Department of Numerical Mathematics
Stichting Mathematish Centrum
2e Boerhaavestraat 49
Amsterdam 1005, The Netherlands

1. INTRODUCTION

In the last years there has been considerable discussion about
the evaluation of software in the field of Mathematical Programming.
In an effort to canalize these discussions the Mathematical Programming Society established the Committee on Algorithms (COAL) with the
charge to concern itself, among other things, with testing methodologies for mathematical programming algorithms (see Math. Prog.
9.1). Since a set of standard test problems is one of the basic
tools necessary for evaluating software in this field, the Dutch
Working Group on Nonlinear Programming (DWg) decided to contribute
to these discussions by creating a proposal for classification and
documentation of test problems, especially in the field of nonlinear
programming. The result of the work of this group is given in this
paper. Meanwhile, a set of about 100 test problems has been gathered
from literature and real life problems, and some members of the group
started to classify and describe these problems according to the
guidelines given in this proposal in order to have some practice.
The ultimate goal is to obtain a representative set of test problems
in the field of nonlinear programming. The classification of this
set should be suitable for testing software in this field and the
description should be given in a standardized format and in machine
readable form. Moreover, the documentation should be such that it
becomes easy to extend the set of test problems. This set may be
used, for instance, in a clearing house (cf. LOOTSMA [1976]), for
comparison, certification and validation of nonlinear programming
software. It may also be used to create standard driver programs
for testing on different computers and in various languages.
    As the DWg and the COAL feel that this proposal fits very well
into the discussion and activities of the COAL, the original

proposal (BUS [1977]) is presented here, in a revised form, as a discussion paper.

2.   CLASSIFICATION OF TEST PROBLEMS

In this proposal we will restrict ourselves to documentation guidelines for test problems of the following form:

Given: $F:R^n \to R$, $h:R^n \to R^p$, $g:R^n \to R^q$ (for some n, p, q).

Minimize $F(x)$,

subject to $h(x) = 0$,

$g(x) \geqq 0$,

where "$\geqq$" is taken element-wise.

A problem classification to be used for the classification of test problems should satisfy two general criteria. Firstly, the tester of a program should be able to choose (classes of) test problems to which the program is applicable. Moreover, he should have enough information about special properties of the test problems to be able to recognize a special behaviour of the program. Secondly, the user of the programs tested should be able to classify his real-life problems so that he can choose a program which appeared to be "best" for the class to which his problem belongs. With this in mind we consider the following special properties of nonlinear programming problems (see also LOOTSMA [1976]).

a. The type of the objective function. We may distinguish linear and quadratic functions, functions which are sums of squares, separable functions, functions with a sparse hessian, etc.

b. The type of the constraints. We may distinguish unconstrained and linearly constrained problems and problems with nonlinear constraints. The constraints may be bounds on the variables, equality constraints or inequality constraints. Furthermore, there may appear linear variables in nonlinear constraints or any linearization of the constraints may be sparse.

c. The functions (objective function and constraint functions) may be differentiable or not on the feasible region. The algorithm underlying a program to be tested should have a sound mathematical basis. Most frequently differentiability is assumed in such mathematical theory. For example, when the functions are twice continuously differentiable we may use first- and second-order theory (see FIACCO & McCORMICK [1968]) to prove optimality of some point. For non-differentiable functions optimality conditions may become very complicated.

d. The size of the problem. This includes the number of variables and the number of constraints. Computation time and memory required by a program as well as numerical stability of a program may depend on the size of the problem. An important criterion for the usefulness of a program is what size of problems can generally be solved by the program.

e. First and/or second order partial derivatives are calculated analytically or numerically (see also COLVILLE [1968]). One reason for distinguishing between analytically and numerically calculated derivatives is the fact that numerical approximation does not require the same amount of computation time as evaluation of the analytical derivatives. The ratio between these quantities depends heavily on the problem. Therefore, the efficiency of a program may be highly influenced by the way the derivatives are calculated. A second reason for this distinction is that one program may be more sensitive to errors due to approximation of the derivatives than another. And finally the program tester should be able to recognize whether a program breakdown is due to numerical approximation of the derivatives or to something else.

f. The problem is a fully analyzed theoretical problem. The functions can be calculated in almost full precision of arithmetic and the solution is also known in full precision of arithmetic. Clearly, this property is not relevant to the user, in fact his problems do not have this property. However, it is very important for practical testing to have such problems at hand for a careful examination of the program to be tested, since for real-life problems rounding errors may confuse the algorithmic aspects, to be tested.

g. The problem is convex. Some programs may take advantage of this property (FIACCO & McCORMICK [1968]). However the user will frequently be unable to prove convexity.

h. The problem functions may be generalized polynomial, posynomial or even monomial so that geometric programming techniques can be used.

i. The feasible region may be unbounded.

j. The objective function has several local minima or
other stationary points in the feasible region. In
this case, one usually cannot expect that the program
finds the global solution. Moreover, the program may
break down in the neighbourhood of a stationary point
which is not a local minimum. As an example one may
consider Box' function (BOX [1966]). As is illustrated
in BUS [1972] gradient methods sometimes break down
on this problem.

k. The hessian of the projected Lagrangian at the solution
is ill-conditioned or even singular. Usually such a
property makes a problem difficult to solve. As an
example one may consider the problem of calculating the
unconstrained minimum of Powell's function of four variables (POWELL [1962]). Numerical results with this
function are also reported in FLETCHER [1970] and
BUS [1975].

Usually, the properties a to e and h can be verified for real-life
problems. Therefore, they can be suitable as primary classification
criteria. However, the other properties may be difficult or even
impossible to verify in practice. Therefore, these properties
should not be used as primary classification criteria. We will
give them as "special properties" in the documentation so that they
can be used for testing. These properties may give an indication
for the degree of difficulty of a problem. However, one can imagine
other properties that make a problem difficult to solve by some
program. In our opinion it would be desirable to develop measures
for the degree of difficulty of a problem so that we may create
graded sets of test problems. We think that it is easy to incorporate such measures in the classification and documentation scheme
proposed here at the time they are available.

The classification scheme

The classification number of a problem has the form

OCD-KI-s,

where the letters have the following meanings:

O reflects properties of the object function:

O = S : the objective function is a sum of squares;
L : linear objective function;
Q : quadratic objective function;
G : all other functions.

C reflects properties of the constraints:

C = U : unconstrained problem;
  L : linear constraints;
  N : at least one nonlinear constraint.

D reflects the differentiability of the problem functions:

D = 2 : the problem functions are at least twice differ-
      entiable on the feasible region;
  1 : the problem functions are once differentiable
      and at least one is not twice differentiable;
  0 : at least one problem function is non-differentiable.

K denotes whether a problem is a so-called theoretical problem
or a practical problem:

K = T : "theoretical" and well-analyzed problem; in order
      to avoid ambiguity we use as a criterion that the
      solutions of the problem are given in full pre-
      cision of arithmetic;
  P : "practical" problems; all problems which are not
      theoretical in the sense given above.

I denotes which partial derivatives are available analytically
in the documentation:

I = 2 : first and second order partial derivatives are
      calculated analytically;
  1 : the first order partial derivatives are calculated
      analytically;
  0 : no partial derivatives are calculated analytically.

s gives a serial number within the class of test problems
identified by OCD-KI.

Remarks

1. The classification code is split into two groups. The first
   group gives information about the mathematical definition of
   the problem which is relevant to the tester as well as to the
   user. The second group is mainly relevant to the tester.
   This group gives information on how the problem is given in
   the test set and in the documentation.

2. Some of the properties a,b,c,e, and f are reflected in this
   classification code. The other properties are given in standard format in the heading of the problem documentation.

Example

The problem

$$\text{minimize } f(x) = 100(x_2 - x_1^2)^2 + (1 - x_1)^2$$

belongs to class SU2-T2. When its serial number within this class is 1, we denote this problem by SU2-T2-1.

3. DOCUMENTATION OF TEST PROBLEMS

Proposal

PROBLEM: OCD-KI-s

NAME: name of the problem, if it has any

SOURCE: author [year], problem/page number

NO. OF VARIABLES: N

NO. OF CONSTRAINTS:

bounds on variables	M1
linear equalities	M2
linear inequalities	M3
nonlinear equalities	M4
nonlinear inequalities	M5

(Note: if the problem is defined for fixed values of N and/or M1 to M5 then these values are specified here, otherwise they are considered as parameters; one or more may be expressed as formulas depending on the others. Specific values for these parameters are given in the block DATA AND RESULTS.)

SPECIAL PROPERTIES:

convex problem	yes/no/unkonwn
several stationary points	yes/no/unknown
generalized polynomial functions	yes/no
posynomial functions	yes/no
monomial functions	yes/no
mixed linear/nonlinear constraints	yes/no
satisfies constraint qualification	yes/no
bounded feasible region	yes/no
density of hessian	...
density of linearization of constraints	...

OBJECTIVE FUNCTION:

$$f(x) = \ldots$$

or, if $f(x)$ is a sum of squares:

$$f(x) = \sum_{i=1}^{P} [f_i(x)]^2$$

$$f_1(x) = \ldots$$

.
.
.

$$f_p(x) = \ldots$$

CONSTRAINTS:

$$1_{i_j} \leq x_{i_j} \leq u_{i_j} \quad \text{or} \quad 1_{i_j} \leq x_{i_j} \quad \text{or} \quad x_{i_j} \leq u_{i_j} \quad \text{(the total number of ine-}$$
quality signs equals M1)

$$h_j(x) = 0, \qquad j = 1,\ldots,M2$$
$$g_j(x) \geq 0, \qquad j = 1,\ldots,M3$$
$$h_j(x) = 0, \qquad j = M2+1,\ldots,M2+M4$$
$$g_j(x) \geq 0, \qquad j = M3+1,\ldots,M3+M5.$$

(Note: the objective and constraint functions may depend on quantities (parameters) whose value(s) are specified in the
block DATA AND RESULTS.)

DATA AND RESULTS:

(Note: we give here the starting point(s), the results and all
additional data necessary to define the problem uniquely.
This part of the documentation may consist of several blocks
if the problem depends on parameters (e.g.: N, M1 to M5 or
parameters in the definition of the problem function).
Then each block defines one problem. Such a problem may
have several starting points and several local solution
points and is identified by OCD-KI-s/i, where i is the
number of the block.)

BLOCK i (only if more than one block is given)

starting point(s)

a. $x^{(0)} = [\ldots]^T$ (non-feasible)

$$f(x^{(0)}) = \ldots$$

b.   .
           .
           .

precisions:

(We define tolerance values ε_1 and ε_2 which are to be regarded as input to the program to be tested. We say that the program is successful in solving the problem if the computed solution $\bar{x}$ satisfies:

$$\|\bar{x} - x^*\| \stackrel{\leq}{=} \|\bar{x}\| \, \varepsilon_1 + \varepsilon_2$$

for some solution point x^*.

We distinguish three levels of precision, which in general depend on the precision of arithmetic used and on the rounding errors in the computation of the problem functions.)

additional data:

(for example, if N is a parameter of the problem which is given the value 10)

N = 10

results:

a. $x^* = [\ldots]^T$

   $f(x^*) = \ldots$

b.   .
       .
       .

ADDITIONAL DETAILS:

A description of typical properties of the problem should be given here. We mention:

- the precision of the data;
- the precision of the calculated values of the problem functions;
- further information about other stationary points;
- further information about the condition of the hessian of the Lagrangian function or the objective function;
- the shape of the feasible region;
- appearance of linear variables that may be separated from variables that appear nonlinearly;
- nonlinearity of the problem functions.

These and other properties may be illustrated by figures and tables.

DERIVATIVES:

If the I parameter in the classification code equals 0 then

no derivatives are given;

If I = 1 then we give here

$$\frac{\partial f}{\partial x_i} \quad , \quad i = 1,\ldots,N;$$

$$\frac{\partial f_i}{\partial x_j} \quad , \quad i = 1,\ldots,P, \quad j = 1,\ldots,N, \quad \text{if } f \text{ is a sum of squares;}$$

$$\frac{\partial h_i}{\partial x_j} \quad , \quad i = 1,\ldots,M2 + M4, \quad j = 1,\ldots,N;$$

$$\frac{\partial g_i}{\partial x_j} \quad , \quad i = 1,\ldots,M3 + M5, \quad j = 1,\ldots,N.$$

If I = 2 then we also give

$$\frac{\partial^2 f}{\partial x_i \partial x_j} \quad , \quad i,j = 1,\ldots,N;$$

$$\frac{\partial^2 f_i}{\partial x_j \partial x_k} \quad , \quad i = 1,\ldots,P, \quad j,k = 1,\ldots,N, \quad \text{if } f \text{ is a sum of squares;}$$

$$\frac{\partial^2 h_i}{\partial x_j \partial x_k} \quad , \quad i = 1,\ldots,M2 + M4, \quad j,k = 1,\ldots,N;$$

$$\frac{\partial^2 g_i}{\partial x_j \partial x_k} \quad , \quad i = 1,\ldots,M3 + M5, \quad j,k = 1,\ldots,N.$$

PROGRAMS:

These programs will be given in FORTRAN, ALGOL 60 and ALGOL 68. In ALGOL 60 the parameter lists are:

```
     fun      (n,x,fx)
     funsq    (n,x,i,fx)
     dfun     (n,x,dfx)
     dfunsq   (n,x,i,dfx)
     ddfun    (n,x,ddfx)
     ddfunsq  (n,x,i,ddfx)
     constr   (n,x,j,gx)
     dconstr  (n,x,j,dgx)
     ddconstr (n,x,j,ddgx)
```

funsq, dfunsq and ddfunsq are given if the function is a sum of

squares, otherwise fun, dfun and ddfun are given. ddfun, ddfunsq
and ddconstr are only given if I = 2, dfun, dfunsq and dconstr are
only given if I = 1 or I = 2. The parameters have the following
meaning:

n : input, the number of variables;

i : input, the index of the term in the sum of squared terms
which has to be evaluated or whose derivative has to be
evaluated;

j : input, the index of the constraint function to be evaluated; these functions are given in the same order as in
the heading of the documentation;

x : input, the vector of variables;

fx : output, the value of the objective function (fun) or the
ith term of the sum of squares (funsq);

dfx : output, the gradient vector of the objective function
(dfun) or of the ith term of a sum of squares (dfunsq);

ddfx : output, the matrix of second order partial derivatives
of the objective function (ddfun) or of the ith term of
a sum of squares (ddfunsq);

gx : output, the value of the ith constraint function;

dgx : output, the gradient vector of the ith constraint function;

ddgx : output, the matrix of second order partial derivatives
of the ith constraint function.

TEST REPORTS:

Numerical experience with this problem has been reported in:

...
...

(One may refer here to papers given in literature and also to unpublished experiences given in appendices to the documentation.)

REFERENCES:

...

(end of proposal).

Remarks

1. All problems are described as minimization problems.

2. Stopping criteria have to be part of the program to be tested.

Therefore, the precision of the solution vector asked for
should be input to a program and we say that a program has
failed to solve a problem if the computed solution does not
satisfy the conditions given in the documentation. When comparing the efficiency one should judge a program by the work
that has to be done to satisfy its own stopping criteria, provided the program did not fail in the above sense.

3. Program source texts are given such that the objective function and its derivatives and the various constraint functions
are evaluated separately. This may be an inefficient way to
solve these particular test problems with a given program.

For example, some programs for unconstrained minimization only
ask for evaluation of the function and its gradient at the
same point and for some problems it may save a lot of computation time if both the function and its gradient are given in
one routine. However, if one uses computation time as a
measure for the efficiency, one should measure the time required to solve the problem minus the time required for the
evaluation of the problem functions and apart from this the
number of problem function evaluations. In this manner one
obtains a measure for the efficiency which does not depend on
the time necessary for the evaluation of the problem functions.
This is very desirable since otherwise we would also introduce
the evaluation time as a property of the problem. In our opinion, giving the source-texts as we propose will be adequate
for testing programs in the way given above or some other way
which does not use the total computation time as a measure
for the efficiency of a program.

4. The programming of the problem functions will be such that
run-time errors due to limitations of the arithmetical system
of a computer are avoided. For example, overflow/underflow,
exponential or logarithm errors will not occur. Therefore,
we need to introduce a number of machine constants, which are
assumed to be known globally. By now we confine ourselves to
refer to work done by the IFIP Working Group 2.5 on Numerical
Software, especially to FORD & SMITH [1976a, 1976b], CODY
[1976] and DEKKER [1976].

5. Our ultimate goal is to present a set of test problems in a
manual which can be upgraded from time to time. Apart from
this manual we should have available short documentation in
machine readable form. This may consist of the outlined
parts at the heads of the problem documents together with the
DATA AND RESULTS and the PROGRAMS parts. In our opinion this
will be all that is required by a driver program to test programs, so that the data for such a driver program can be obtained automatically.

518

REFERENCES

1. M.J. Box, A Comparison of Several Current Optimization Methods
    and the Use of Transformations in Constrained Problems, Comp.
    J. 9, 67-77, 1966.
2. J.C.P. Bus, Minimization of Functions of Several Variables
    (dutch), Mathematical Centre, NR 29/72, Amsterdam, 1972.
3. J.C.P. Bus, On the Convergence of a Class of Variable Metric
    Algorithms, Mathematical Centre, NW 16/75, Amsterdam, 1975.
4. J.C.P. Bus, A Proposal for the Classification and Documentation
    of Test Problems in the Field of Nonlinear Programming,
    Mathematical Centre, NN9/77, Amsterdam, 1977.
5. W.J. Cody, Machine Parameters for Numerical Analysis, Working
    paper of IFIP Working Group 2.5 on Numerical Software, 1976.
6. A.R. Colville, A Comparative Study of Nonlinear Programming
    Codes, IBM, New York Sc. Center, TR 320-2949, 1968.
7. T.J. Dekker, Machine Requirements for Reliable Portable Soft-
    ware, University of Amsterdam, Dept. of Math. Rep. 76-15, 1976.
8. A.V. Fiacco and G.P. McCormick, Nonlinear Programming:
    Sequential Unconstrained Minimization Techniques, Wiley
    Interscience, 1968.
9. R. Fletcher, A New Approach to Variable Metric Algorithms,
    Comp. J. 13, 317-322, 1970.
10. B Ford and B.T. Smith, Intrinsic Functions to Assist FORTRAN
    Portability for Numeric Computation, A Proposal to ANS FORTRAN
    Standards Committee X3J3 from IFIP WG 2.5, 1976a.
11. B. Ford and B.T. Smith, Parameters for Transportable Numerical
    Software, Working Paper of IFIP Working Group 2.5 on Numerical
    Software, 1976b.
12. F.A. Lootsma, Nonlinear Optimization in Industry and the
    Development of Optimization Programmes, Paper presented at
    the IX International Symposium on Mathematical Programming,
    Budapest, 1976 .
13. M.J.D. Powell, An Iterative Method for Finding Stationary
    Values of a Function of Several Variables, Comp. J. 5, 147-
    151, 1962.

GUIDELINES FOR REPORTING COMPUTATIONAL EXPERIMENTS IN MATHEMATICAL PROGRAMMING

H.P. Crowder,[†] R.S. Dembo,[*] and J.M. Mulvey[§]

[†]IBM Research, Yorktown Heights, New York
[*]School of Organization and Management, Yale University
[§]Graduate School of Business Administration, Harvard University

1. INTRODUCTION

A detailed examination of professional journals[1] that publish articles involving the use or development of mathematical programming shows that a high degree of mathematical competence is usually required of the authors. Unfortunately, the rigid standards that are set for mathematical exposition are invariably not applied to the reporting of computational experiments. In this regard, these journals display less concern for scientific design and reporting of experiments than do the leading journals in the social sciences. For example, very rarely can a published computational experiment in mathematical programming be completely reproduced[2]--something which is a basic criterion in scientific research. Even worse, very often important parameters of the experiment are not even reported.

Part of the problem stems from the fact that there are no published standards to guide the refereeing process. The purpose of this paper is to improve this situation by providing authors

---

1. Operations Research, Management Science, Mathematics of Operations Research, Transactions on Mathematical Software, Mathematical Programming.

2. See Section 3.2 for a precise definition of what we mean by reproduceability.

and referees with an initial set of guidelines that may be used to better write and evaluate reports of computational results.

One of the earliest computational comparisons in the mathematical programming literature was given in Hoffman et al. [1953]. It involved a comparison of three different techniques for solving linear programs. Although this experiment was carried out early in the history of computer development, when compilers and programming languages were virtually nonexistent, this paper in terms of reporting methodologies ranks among the best out of a survey of 50 mainly recent papers, in which computational comparisons of mathematical programming software are reported (Jackson and Mulvey [1977]). From this survey, one can infer that reporting methodology has not kept pace with the tremendous developments in computer technology. Very little attention has been given to the manner in which comparative tests should be carried out and to what constitutes a meaningful computational experiment. In the Hoffman et al. paper [1953], care was given to detailed reporting of tolerances used, the number of iterations as a function of tolerance, the scaling of data, input-output, and the effect of coding on the results. Only a few of the papers sampled by Jackson and Mulvey [1977] can claim to have the distinction of such a thorough analysis and reporting of results. Only 50% of the papers mentioned the programming languages used, 16% mentioned the compiler and only one paper out of 50 gives the processing time required for input-output. In a computational comparison paper written in 1968 and published in a highly respected journal, the following comment was made:

> "Since the methods were coded for different
> machines in different languages by different
> programmers, there is little point in giving
> a detailed assessment of the results, partic-
> ularly as so many of the problems were degen-
> erate. However, the results show that ..."

This quote illustrates the lack of attention paid to controlling influential parameters during the computational experiment. It is our experience that in many computational comparisons, a similar lack of understanding of careful experimental planning exists.

The plan of our paper is as follows. Section 2 takes up the issue of experimental design. We see that a careful a prior design is necessary for sound experimentation. In Section 3, we discuss why computational results are reported; we define the crucial issue of reproduceability; and we describe a method for reporting which utilizes two complementary papers, i.e., an unabridged and a summary report. The use of these guidelines within the normal referring process is taken up in Section 4, and the actual guidelines are shown in Section 5. A checklist of important points for authors and referees to consider when performing or evaluating a computational experiment appears in the Appendix. Finally, a recommendation for evolutionary improvements in the guidelines is mentioned in Section 6.

2. CONDUCTING EXPERIMENTS

This section introduces the general issue of how computational testing should be carried out. Under the heading of experimental design, the basic goals of an experiment and the means to achieve these goals are considered in Section 2.1; Section 2.2 deals with problem selection. Recommendations are made concerning pseudo-randomly generated and hand-selected examples. Performance measures for evaluating algorithms and codes are discussed in Section 2.3.

2.1 Experimental Design

A well conceived and well executed experiment begins with a careful a priori design. Establishing concrete pals, controlling influential variables, and developing a thorough experimental plan are some of the features that must be thought out beforehand.

More specifically, if statistic sampling is used for drawing inferences, there is an enormous body of literature involving statistical-based experimental design which should be consulted. One definition of good experimental planning is

> "The requirements for a good experiment are that the
> treatment comparisons should as far as possible be
> free from systematic error, that they should be made
> sufficiently precise, that the conclusions should have
> a wide range of validity, that the experimental arrange-
> ment should be as simple as possible, and finally that
> the uncertainty in the conclusions should be assess-
> able." (Anderson and Mclean [1974]).

Adhering to these objectives would go a long way towards improving the current state of computational experiments. Dembo and Mulvey [1976] and Lin and Rardin [1976] provide detailed recommendations for using statistics in comparing mathematical programming techniques.

However, the use of statistical sampling theory is almost non-existent in the mathematical programming literature. In their survey, Jackson and Mulvey [1977] found the following types of nonstatistical-based design criteria:

% of Articles	Observed Objectives
30%	understanding and predicting code behavior,
10%	determining the types of problems for which the codes were most effective,
8%	indicating possible improvements in the algorithm, and
66%	evaluating competing techniques.

It should be noted that many of these articles had multiple objectives, for instance, evaluating competing techniques and predicting code behavior. Since sampling theory was not employed, however, the conclusions drawn cannot be formally extrapolated beyond the problems which were addressed in the study. Only general trends and patterns in the code performance can be examined.

2.2 Types of Test Problems

Two basic types of test problems are available for empirical testing--pseudo-randomly generated and hand selected. The pros and cons of each category are listed in Table 1.

Table 1

Hand-Selected Problems	Randomly Generated Problems
Usually representative of real-world behavior.	Usually not representative of real-world behavior.
Expensive to collect, document and send from one researcher to another.	Problem generators can be designed to be portable and machine independent.
Population of problems from which sample problems are drawn is not usually known. Thus, generalizations based on the sample are questionable.	Population of problems is known and can be controlled. If sampling method is known, generalizations based on sample statistics can be made with a known degree of certainty.

Whichever category is selected, the following items must be considered when designing the problems for experimentation: (1) constancy of treatment effects, and (2) increased precision. Almost without exception, the <u>same</u> set of problems should be solved by each technique under investigation. Otherwise an important influential variable is left uncontrolled, causing the introduction of an unnecessary error effect.

2.3 Performance Indicators

A variety of performance indicators have been traditionally used by mathematical programmers for evaluating the efficiency of competing techniques. Jackson and Mulvey [1977] found that the following measures have been traditionally considered:

- CPU Time

    The total central processing time needed for executing the algorithm. Should include as separate items input/output, preprocessing, and starting techniques. This indicator is declining in importance due to the introduction of multi-programming.

- Numerical Accuracy

    A measurement of the algorithm's ability to compute a "correct" answer in the face of numerical instability.

- Number of Iterations (pivots)

    A simple counting of the number of steps required by the algorithm. This indicator is relatively independent of the computer used.

- Robustness

    The domain of problems which can be effectively solved by the algorithm defines its robustness.

- Number of Function Evaluations

    The number of items that the objective function subroutine or the constraint function is called during program execution.

- User Friendliness (ease of use, portability)

    A subjective measurement of a computer program's versatility. This indicator may encompass programmer

setup time, the time required to learn the program, etc. Although this indicator is obviously
difficult to measure, its importance is becoming
recognized

- Storage Requirements and/or Data Structures

  As the size of solveable problems increases and
  the usage of mini-computer and micro-processors
  accelerates, the data base requirements for
  executing the algorithm becomes crucial.

- Basic Operation Count (e.g., additions and multiplications)

  The number of items that a basic operation, such
  as an addition, is required during the execution
  of the algorithm.

It is outside the scope of this paper to make specific recommendations for which performance measure to use. In the past, certain
types of mathematical programs have been evaluated by means of a
single criteria, for example within unconstrained optimization,
the number of function evaluations. Another example is the wide-
spread use of CPU time solely for evaluating mathematical programs. This situation has occurred despite the recognition that
one performance measure is usually inadequate for a proper
evaluation.

We recommend that all measures which are applicable to a given
mathematical programming technique be taken into account when con-
ducting an experiment. As a minimum, a collection of performance
criteria--a profile--of results should be reported and the experiment should be planned accordingly. The next section takes up
the topic of reporting the results of computational experiments.

3. REPORTING OF COMPUTATIONAL RESULTS

3.1 Purposes for Reporting Computational Results

Articles appearing in scientific journals fulfill a variety of
conflicting purposes. Most papers are scanned by casual readers
who are primarily interested in keeping abreast of research trends
and significant new developments. They may only read the abstract,
the introduction, and the conclusions. For this reader, the journal should provide a concise summary of the goals of the experiment and the important conclusions. It is the referee's responsibility to decide whether the empirical evidence justifies the
stated conclusions.

A more important, and often conflicting objective for reporting results in journal publications is to provide a stepping stone for future developments. A researcher should be able to build upon and extend the results reported in a journal article. For this reader, the details are more important. Since the difference between a mediocre algorithm and an outstanding algorithm is often a minor modification, the researcher who attempts to expand previous work must be provided with all important details.[1]

A slightly different intention for reporting results in journals is to render valid comparisons with current or previous work. An article in which the primary purpose is to analyze, from empirical evidence, the effectiveness of two competing mathematical programming methods would be in this category. The emphasis in such a comparison is on the empirical evidence presented, rather than on the mathematical exposition.

The critical question of reproduceability of a computational experiment is discussed in the next section.

3.2 Reproduceability

Throughout these guidelines we refer to the criterion of reproduceability of results. Since we feel strongly that papers should be refereed according to this principle, we offer a precise statement of what we mean by reproduceability.

Computer technology is in such a rapid process of development that it has become virtually impossible to completely reproduce a computational experiment to any arbitrary order of accuracy. This is true even in the same computing environment. Compilers and operating systems change, resulting in different sequences of operations for computing the final results. These different sequences, together with the effect of numerical variations due to round-off, produce outcomes that agree only to a limited number of significant figures. Thus, when requiring reproduceability, we do not mean a precise replication of results. Rather, a set of results that agrees with the original to within a tolerance that may be reasonably attributed to changes in technology. It is this interpretation that we will use in the discussion that follows.

---

1. The journal ACM Transactions on Mathematical Software collects and distributes for a nominal charge mathematical algorithms. Complete listings of algorithms appear in "Collected Algorithms from ACM" and are available as listing card deck, and magnetic tape from ACM Algorithms Distribution Service, c/o International Mathematical and Statistical Libraries, Inc., GNB Building, Sixth Floor, 7500 Bellaire Blvd., Houston, Texas, 77036.

In many cases, it is very difficult to provide enough information in a published paper which, given sufficient time, will enable the reader to completely reproduce the stated results. For example, the results may be the output from a complicated computer program that required many man-hours of development. Nothing short of a listing of the program (which is often proprietary) and a detailed description of how to input data, will be sufficient to reproduce the computational experiment. Naturally, requiring sufficient information for reproduceability would preclude publication of valuable papers of this type. However, an absolute, reasonable, and scientifically justifiable criterion should be that the authors themselves be able to replicate their experiment. This is one of the basic principles of the scientific method and should be actively pursued in any properly conducted scientific enquiry.

To a large extent, this requirement may be too costly and time consuming to rigidly enforce. It is here where editors are required to exercise their judgment on whether sufficient evidence has been provided, to convince them that the criterion of reproduceability could be met if tested.

3.3 Method of Reporting

As mentioned in Section 2.3, a variety of performance indicators are available for evaluating mathematical programming software. If a study includes a particular indicator as a measure of performance, then we feel that there are certain points relating to that indicator which must be addressed in the journal article to make the results more meaningful. For example, if computer processing time is used as a measure of performance, then a description, a persuasive argument by the author indicating why such information is not provided would be required. The Appendix describes what we view as a minimum set of questions relating to various performance indicators which must be addressed when computational results are presented.

In some cases, it might be inappropriate to include all of this information in a report intended for journal publication. In such cases, authors should consider two versions of a report. The first version would be intended primarily for journal publication and would contain, among other things, the objectives of the study and a summary of the major results. Such a report should give readers with a moderate interest in the subject only enough detail for a good grasp of the problem statement and the major conclusions. The second, more substantive report would be more detailed about the computational experiments and address in full the measurement criteria listed in Section 2.3. This report would be intended primarily to aid referees in evaluating the work as a whole and to give more information to researchers interested in understanding and using the results for future work. It would function in a manner similar to an engineering notebook.

4. USING THE GUIDELINES

The ultimate objective of our proposal is to affect a change in the editorial policy of journals which publish computational experiments in mathematical programming. To the extent we are successful, the guidelines will function in two ways.

From the viewpoint of editors and referees, these guidelines will form the basis for an objective measure of the usefulness of computational studies submitted for publication. By introducing a formalism in reporting of experimental results, editors and referees will have a systematic method for judging the merits of a study, resulting in a more uniform evaluation process. For very extensive and detailed studies, we strongly favor authors submitting two versions of a report as mentioned in Section 3. This has two immediate advantages. First, the more expansive version of the report allows editors and referees to be privy to details of the study which might not be appropriate for journal articles, but which might offer support for the author's conclusions. Second, if the abridged version required more expansion in some areas, editors and referees could make very concrete recommendations by referring to the appropriate topics in the expanded version. (Since the expanded report should be comprehensible to referees and others interested in the details of the study, it should be written at or near a publication level.)

From the author's point of view, the guidelines will impose a discipline which will improve communications. Researchers adhering to the standards will be led naturally to a better design and execution of computational studies.

5. GUIDELINES

In this section we discuss the topics which, we believe, should be considered by designers of algorithms who conduct computational experiments and by referees who evaluate the published results of these experiments. The Appendix summarizes these issues.

5.1 Presentation of Algorithm

By algorithm, we mean the mathematical statement of the technique. An Algol-like language similar to the ACM standard could be substituted for the mathematical description provided that the essence of the technique is captured in the description and that the language is understandable by most readers.

The first required guideline states that a complete description of the algorithm is either included in the published paper or available from the references cited. Most technical journals generally adhere to this guideline today. As a second requirement, we propose that the authors identify the class of problem (estimated size and type) that the proposed algorithm is designed for. Such a statement will assist referees in evaluating whether or not the empirical evidence collaborates with their conclusions.

Three additional items are suggested for inclusion within the presentation of the algorithm. Consideration of these suggested items is discretionary.

1. An analysis of the computational complexity as measured by worst case performance. The usual criteria for an algorithm's complexity is the number of iterations as a function of a problem size. This criteria provides a worst-case bound for the algorithm's performance.

2. Convergence proofs should be provided or referenced in the article. A discussion pertaining to conditioning of non-convergence, such as cycling in the presence of degeneracy, should also be included, if appropriate.

3. Since the initial terminal rates of convergence of an algorithm often give insight into its ultimate behavior, these should be included in the article, even though computational evidence may run contrary to the theoretical rates of convergence.

5.2 Computer Implementation of Algorithms

Generally speaking, the test of an algorithm is its computational performance. Does the computer program efficiently solve problems? To properly answer this question, a number of items pertaining to the computer implementation must be provided; Section A.2 lists eight required and two suggested items. We believe that it is difficult to properly evaluate the empirical results without addressing these topics since the results are dependent on the computer implementation of the algorithm.

5.3 Experimental Design

The experimental design should be carefully spelled out in

the published report. A clear statement of the objective(s) of
the experiment should be given before the results are reported.
It is the referees' responsibility to determine if the experiment
is scientifically valid. Thus the objectives should be measurable
in the sense that the report can be evaluated in light of these
objective(s).

To facilitate cross comparisons, if a standard set of test
problems is available it should be used in addition to the
author's own set of test problems. Likewise, if a new test problem is proposed, it should be documented and a condition of its
optimality (satisfaction of Kuhn-Tucker conditions, objective
function values) furnished to the referees and other interested
parties. Occasionally, the solution of a proprietary problem
may shed light on some aspect of the algorithm which could not be
seen otherwise. Nonetheless, we believe that these problems
should be referred to in the report only under special circumstances and adequate justification.

Other aspects of the experimental design are discussed in
Section A.3.

5.4 Reporting of Results

Since it is difficult to forecast future performance indicators, we cannot provide a simple format for reporting of results.
Rather, we propose that when certain performance indicators are
used, such as CPU time, then an adequate accounting with respect
to this indicator be included. Section A.4 describes what we mean
by an adequate accounting.

5.5 Conclusions

Statements of fact and issues of speculation often appear
intermixed in the conclusions of papers reporting computational
results. Speculation is rarely labelled as such. The conclusions
should be clearly justified from the results that are presented;
again, the referees must resolve this issue. As suggested items,
directions of future research, such as possible improvements in the
algorithm, should be addressed and an attempt made to identify the
classes of problems for which the techniques were most effective
(ineffective).

6. FUTURE REFINEMENTS

Ideally, the guidelines should be periodically reviewed by
designers of algorithms, code developers and users of mathematical

programming software. Since major improvements in computer hardware technology are difficult to forecast, we believe that computational testing may take on a new and expanded role in the future
which cannot be ascertained at this time. To accommodate possible
changes in direction, the guidelines should be evolutionary.

Mathematical programming can be divided into relatively distinct subclasses, such as unconstrained optimization, networks,
linear programs, and nonlinear constrained optimization. This
paper has not attempted to develop specific guidelines for these
subclasses. As a future refinement, however, a set of specific
recommendations for one or more of these subclasses, could be put
together into handbook form. A graded collection of test problems
with known accuracy and algorithmic behavior could be included.

As a final observation, we refer to the work of the American
Society for Testing Materials. This organization's purpose is
evaluating testing methodologies and setting standards for the
usage of materials in engineering design. Although computer software has not attained the sophisticated body of commonly accepted
knowledge required to set standards such as ASTM, we should draw
useful information from their extensive experience in evaluating
and testing.

REFERENCES

1. Anderson, V.L. and R.A. Mclean, Design of Experiments: A
   Realistic Approach, M. Dekker, Inc., New York, 1974.

2. Dembo, R.S. and J.M. Mulvey, "On the Analysis and Comparison of Mathematical Programming Techniques," Proceedings of the Bicentennial Conference of Mathematical
   Programming, Gaithersberg, Maryland, 1976.

3. Hoffman, A., M. Mannose, D. Sokolowsky, and N. Weigman,
   "Computational Experience in Solving Linear Programs."
   SIAM Journal, 1, pp. 1-33, 1953.

4. Ignizio, J.P.,"On the Establishment of Standards for Comparing Algorithm Performance," Interfaces, 2, 1, November
   1971.

5. Ignizio, J.P., "Validating Claims for Algorithms Proposed
   for Publication," Operations Research, 21, 3 May 1973,
   852-854.

6. Jackson, R.H. and J.M. Mulvey, "A Critical Review of
   Methods for Comparing Mathematical Programming Algorithms
   and Software: 1951-1977," to be presented at TIMS XIII,
   Athens, July, 1977.

7. Lin, B.Y. and R.L. Rardin, "Controlled Experimental Design

for Comparison of Integer Programming Algorithms, "Georgia
Institute of Technology, Industrial and Systems Engineering, J-76-25, 1976.

APPENDIX

Checklist of Important Points to Consider
When Evaluating or Reporting a Computational Experiment

The following is a summary of important points that should be
considered when writing or evaluating a paper in which computational
results are reported. The checklist should be utilized as follows:
applicable "required" items must either be addressed or else a
justification for their omission must be included. Consideration
of "suggested" items is discretionary.

A.1.0 Presentation of Algorithms

Required: * Complete description of algorithm. Details of the
                 algorithm that are not presented should be available
                 from the references cited.

               * The class of problem (estimated size and type) for
                 which the proposed algorithm is designed.

Suggested: * Analysis of the computational complexity.

               * Convergence theorems.

               * Rate of convergence theorems (initial and terminal).

A.2.0 Computer Implementation of Algorithms

Required: * Programming Language(s) and variant used.

               * Compiler name and options used.

               * Computer environment. Manufacturer and model, op-
                 eration system and options.

               * Brief description of data input (e.g., does problem
                 have to be written in any special way, do artificial
                 variables have to added, etc).

               * Brief description of all tolerance settings.

532

* Conditions under which the code is available.

* For a user-oriented code (as opposed to test program), a user's manual must be furnished to referees.

* Description of any special data processing techniques (e.g., linked lists) that were used in the implementation.

* Description of any special tactics used in implementation, e.g., pivot strategy or starting strategy.

Suggested: * Program and test should be made available to referees free of charge.

* Experiments involving the use of proprietary programs should only be published on the basis of the presentation of a new strategy or a new theoretical development. Authors should be willing to reproduce their experiment for the referees. Where necessary, referees should exercise this right.

A.3.0 Experimental Design

Required: * A clear statement of the objective(s) of the experiment. The objectives should be measurable in the sense that the report can be evaluated by the referees with respect to whether the study met the objectives.

* Documentation of any proposed new test problems and proofs of optimality (satisfaction of Kuhn-Tucker conditions, objective function values) furnished to the referees.

* Accuracy with which solutions were obtained.

* A complete[1] description of the problem generator (unless it has been published elsewhere), if used. The rationale behind the method used to generate the problems should be justified.

* A detailed description (unless published elsehwere) of the preprocessing heuristic, if any.

---

1. Readers should be able to reproduce (in the sense of Section 3.2) the problems in the paper.

Suggested: * Employ statistical methods, such as stratified
            sampling, when applicable to reduce the costs of
            testing and to improve the accuracy of the results.

            * If a standard set of test problems is available, e.g.,
            Colville,[1] Dembo,[2] for this class of algorithms, it
            should be used.

A.4.0 Reporting of Results

Required: * Conclusions based on the data and results presented.
            Statements made without proper justification should
            clearly be labelled as speculation on the part of
            the author(s).

            * Justification for an whatever particular performance
            indicator is used (e.g., CPU time, number of itera-
            tions, robustness,... etc.) in the context of the
            desired goals of the experiment.

            * If CPU time is used as measure then:

                (i)   A precise description of how these times were
                      computed and whether they include input-out-
                      put.

                (ii) Preprocessing time, if any.

                (iii) An estimate of the variability of measured
                      CPU time due to multiprogramming (i.e.,
                      measure the CPU time for a particular prob-
                      lem at various times of the day--off-peak
                      hours, peak hours, etc).

            * Details of stopping rules. This includes all toler-
            ance level settings.

            * An analysis of the amount of work per iteration, if
            number of iterations is used as performance measure.

            * A detailed description of the way in which function
            values are counted, if number of function evaluations
            is used. The same procedure should apply to gradient
            and Hessian evaluations.

1.   A.R. Colville, "A Comparative Study on Nonlinear Programming Codes, IBM N.Y. Science Tenter, Rept. 330-2969, June 1968.

2.   R.S. Dembo, "A Set of Geometric Programming Test Problems
and Their Solutions," Mathematical Programming, 10(1976) pp. 192-213.

* The (estimated) <u>storage requirements</u> as a function of problem size. This could be done by reporting the core size required to solve the various problems whose solutions are presented in the paper.

* <u>Starting points</u>. Feasible starting points required? How were these obtained?

* For a comparison of various methods, all of the following topics:

    (1)   convergence criteria

    (2)   tolerances

    (3)   storage requirements

    (4)   starting points

    (5)   computers used (make, model, and operating system)

    (6)   methods for standardizing results across computers (e.g., standardized timers)

* The final objective function value and values for variables, if possible.

* Known problems or problem classes that the method/ code failed to solve, if any.

* Discussion and justification of statistical sampling techniques, if used. Also, a precise identification of the population from which the sampling took place.

* A discussion of why the method failed on certain problems.

Suggested: * The effect of tolerances on run times, robustness, number of iterations, etc.

* Effect of different termination criteria.

* Measurement of the variation in performance due to different internal tactics, such as different starting techniques

A.5.0 Conclusions

Required: * Conclusions justified by the results that are

presented. Any speculation on the part of the
author(s) should be clearly identified as such.

Suggested: * Direction of future research, such as possible improvements in the algorithms.

* Identification of the classes of problems for which
code/method was most effective (ineffective).

COAL SESSION SUMMARY, by R.H.F. Jackson

INTRODUCTION

The purpose of this paper is to summarize the discussion sessions organized by the Committee on Algorithms (COAL) of the Mathematical Programming Society. It should be noted that this is not a transcription; consequently, this report is inexact.

F. Lootsma opened the sessions with a status report of COAL's activities and introduced the two new candidates for membership in the European contingent of COAL: Michel Benichou (France) and Susan Powell (England). He pointed out that one of the original images of the committee, that of serving as a clearinghouse for test problems and algorithms, has been replaced by a taskforce concept, where the tasks include maintaining close contact with journals that publish algorithms and computational comparisons of algorithms, publishing sources of test problems and algorithms through a news-lletter, and developing a "circle of friends" of COAL in order to coordinate activities in these areas.

The balance of the first hour consisted of a discussion of the guidelines for publication of computational results (appearing in these proceedings). During the second hour, there was a discussion of the proposed guidelines for documentation of NLP test problems (also appearing in these proceedings).

GUIDELINES FOR COMPUTATIONAL RESULTS

After R. Dembo summarized the key points, the discussion was begun with M. Beale's prepared comments, in which he pointed out that an idea may stand apart from an author's computational exper-ience. He said that, if it is a really new idea, then, although some evidence of computational feasibility was very valuable, one should have looser standards for the amount of computational evi-dence needed, and the guidelines should make this clear. It is important, he continued, that the mathematical programming litera-ture should not be reduced to two sharply contrasting types of

papers: purely theoretical papers with no computational results,
together with papers on topics for which detailed and fully documented computational tests were feasible.

R. Jackson agreed, but said that authors should not compose
their methods with others unless they followed the guidelines.

G. Nemhauser pointed out that, at least in JORSA, there is
great inconsistency among referees as to when an author should be
asked for computational results, or even whether a program has been
written.   He bifurcated the issue into two questions: (1) when do
we ask for computational results, and (2) when we do ask for computational results, what should be their form?   He said that the
proposed guidelines answer question (2) very well, but question
(1) is still open.

W. Orchard-Hays raised another point.   He noted the dilemma
of the lag time between discovery and implementation of an idea.
Often this can be as much as two years, yet the discoverer wants
to disseminate the idea, not only for others to use, but also to
gain priority.   Further, he continued, additional delay in publication caused by use of guidelines may discourage some authors from
publishing anything.

R. Dembo replied that he felt very strongly that there are
cases, such as a new pricing strategy, whose merit is impossible
to evaluate without computational results.   Without such scrutiny
there may be a proliferation of untested ideas, which are mathematically simple variations, that could later prove useless.   In
short, there are certain ideas that are geared entirely towards
speeding up computational performance, and these must be supported
by computational evidence.

F. Lootsma suggested allowance of short papers, perhaps as
technical notes, which communicate ideas ahead of implementation.

W. Mylander commented that he liked the idea of two papers,
one short description of the idea, and the other with a detailed
accounting of the subsequent information.   He asked how the larger
paper would be handled and who would be permanently responsible for
distributing it.

R. Dembo indicated that the number of papers would be manageable, and further noted that TIMS is doing something similar now.
Therefore, perhaps the Mathematical Programming Society would do
this, and COAL would help during the initial phase.

DOCUMENTATION STANDARDS FOR TEST PROBLEMS

After J. Bus summarized the porposed scheme, H. Baier noted the absence of an important class of problems. Physical and engineering applications often use implicit functions, whose evaluation may consist of a nontrivial sequence of subproblems, such as solving a system of equations. In these cases the functions are specified by programs rather than mathematical formulae.

Bus replied that it is possible to document this in the coding scheme currently. Baier expressed apprehension that this becomes difficult to publish in a book, especially when the program is very long.

P. Gill responded that the point is, we want test problems that can be reproduced at low cost. Further, some people may not have a large computer to deal with functions represented by large problems.

M. Rijckaert raised another point by noting that several formulations of the same problem may affect an algorithm's performance. Bus replied by stating that two distinct formulations should be considered to be two test problems. H. Greenberg noted that changing scale factors is an example.

R. Dembo continued along this avenue of thought by suggesting that families of problems be specified up to a parameter with a specified range. He cited Rosenbrock's function as an example, where a coefficient could be varied to change the shape of the surface. This would, he proposed, enable one to measure impacts of certain characteristics, such as steepness of a valley, on an algorithm's performance.

Gill commented that the best thing to do is to have a standard, small number of test problems, perhaps updated every year. Greenberg objected that this promotion of a small number of problems may cause researchers to invent algorithms which work well on the test problems without necessarily performing well on unsolved problems for which they are intended. Gill emphasized that the annual update would elimininate that risk.

Rummelhard suggested an extension to the scheme to include minimax problems.

L. Dixon commented that it was his experience that authors will also quote results on their own problems, for example, to illustrate the special features of their programs.

Bus replied that such people should be encouraged to document their problems according to the proposed scheme.

NATO ASI - DESIGN AND IMPLEMENTATION OF OPTIMIZATION SOFTWARE

20 June - 2 July 1977

List of Participants

1. Jean Abadie, Lecturer
    EDF
    29 Boulevard Edgar Quinet
    Paris
    France

2. Annamaria Annicchiarico
    C.S.A.T.A.
    Via Amendola 173
    Bari
    Italy

3. Jack Anthonisse
    Mathematisch Centrum
    Tweede Boerhaavestraat 49
    Amsterdam
    Netherlands

4. Francesco Archetti
    Instituto di Matematica
    Sezione di Informatica
    Via Cicognara 7
    20129 Milano
    Italy

5. Horst Baier
    Fachgebiet Leichtbau
    Technische Hochschule
    Petersenstr. 30
    61 Darmstadt
    W. Germany

6. Michael Bastian
    Lehrstuhl fürMath. Verfahrensforschung (OR)
    und Datenverarbeitung
    Göttingen University
    Nikolausberger Weg 96
    D-34 Göttingen
    W. Germany

7. E.M.L. Beale, <u>Lecturer</u>
   Scicon Computer Services Ltd.
   Brick Close
   Kiln Farm
   <u>Milton Keynes</u> MK11 3EJ
   England

8. Colin Beeforth
   Management Sciences Dept.
   Technical Development Services
   Gold & Uranium Division
   Anglo American Corporation
   P.O. Box 20
   <u>Welkom 9460</u>
   South Africa

9. Michèl Benichou
   IBM France
   36 Avenue Raymond Poincaré
   <u>Paris</u> (16-ieme)
   France

10. Regina Benveniste
    Department of Mathematics
    Imperial College
    <u>London</u> SW7
    England

11. Hélio Bernardo Lopes
    Instituto Superior Técnico
    Rua Montepio Geral, 29, 2°-Dt
    <u>Lisboa 4</u>
    Portugal

12. Bruno Betro
    Università di Milano
    Istituto di Matematica
    Sezione di Informatica
    Via Cicognara 7
    <u>20129 Milano</u>
    Italy

13. Lucia de Biase-Archetti
    Istituto di Matematica
    Sezione di Informatica
    Via Cicognara 7
    <u>20129 Milano</u>
    Italy

14. Jacques C.P. Bus
    Mathematisch Centrum
    Tweede Boerhaavestraat 49
    Amsterdam
    Netherlands

15. Theodorus J. Dekker, Lecturer
    University of Amsterdam
    Dept. of Mathematics
    Roetersstraat 15
    Amsterdam
    Netherlands

16. Ron Dembo
    School of Organization and Management
    Yale University
    52 Hillhouse Avenue
    New Haven, Connecticut 06520
    U.S.A.

17. G. Di Lena
    Istituto Analisi Matematica
    Universita' di Bari-Palazzo Ateneo
    Via Nicolai
    70100 Bari
    Italy

18. Laurence Dixon, Lecturer
    Numerical Optimisation Centre
    The Hatfield Polytechnic
    Hatfield
    Great Britain

19. Arne Drud
    Dept. of Mathematics
    Technical University of Denmark
    DK-2800 Lyngby
    Denmark

20. Laureano F. Escudero
    IBM
    Castellana, 4
    Madrid(1)
    Spain

21. Cetin Evranos
    Marmara Research Institute
    P.O. Box 141 Kadiköy
    Istanbul
    Turkey

22. G. Galliani
    Sogesta
    Urbino PS
    Italy

23. Laura Gardini
    Sogesta
    Urbino PS
    Italy

24. David R. Gibby
    Shape Technical Centre
    P.O. Box 174
    The Hague
    Netherlands

25. Philip E. Gill, Lecturer
    Division of Numerical Analysis and Computing
    National Physical Laboratory
    Teddington MIDDX TW11 ODW
    England

26. Phyllis Martin Gilmore
    Department of Energy
    12th and Pennsylvania Avenue, N.W.
    Washington, D.C. 20461
    U.S.A.

27. Fred Glover, Lecturer
    1040 Lehigh
    Bounder, Colorado
    U.S.A.

28. Harvey J. Greenberg, Lecturer, Co-Director
    Department of Energy
    1200 Pennsylvania Avenue N.W.
    Washington, D.C. 20461
    U.S.A.

29. Stephen Hawkins
    Faculty of Commerce and Business Administration
    University of British Columbia
    2075 Wesbrook Place
    Vancouver V6T IK2, B.C.
    Canada

30. Thorkell Helgason
    University of Iceland
    Dunhagi 3
    Reykjavik
    Iceland

31. James K. Ho
     Applied Mathematics Department
     Brookhaven National Laboratory
     Upton, Long Island
     New York 11973
     U.S.A.

32. Hai-Hoc Hoang
     Ecole Polytechnique
     P.O. Box 6097 Station A
     Montreal, Quebec
     Canada

33. Gerard van der Hoek
     Econometric Institute
     Erasmus University Rotterdam
     P.O. Box 1738
     Rotterdam 3016
     Netherlands

34. Karla Hoffman
     Applied Mathematics Division - Bldg. 101 Rm. A428
     National Bureau of Standards
     Washington, D.C.   20234
     U.S.A.

35. Gunnar Holmberg
     Contract Research Group for Applied Mathematics
     Royal Institute of Technology
     Fack
     S-100 44 Stockholm
     Sweden

36. Richard H.F. Jackson
     Applied Math. Division
     National Bureau of Standards
     Boulder, Colorado 80302
     U.S.A.

37. Ellis Johnson, Lecturer
     IBM T.J. Watson Research Center
     P.O. Box 218
     Yorktown Heights, N.Y. 10598
     U.S.A.

38. Jan L. de Jong
     Onderafdeling der Wiskunde
     Technische Hogeschool
     P.O. Box 513
     Eindhoven
     Netherlands

39. Anne Kooistra
    Bilwijkerweg 111
    Stolwijk
    Netherlands

40. Janusz S. Kowalik
    Academic Services
    Washington State University
    Pullman, WA 99164
    U.S.A.

41. Dieter Kraft
    Deutsche Forschungs- und Versuchsanstalt
    für Luft- und Raumfahrt,
    Institut für Dynamik der Flugsysteme
    D-8031 Oberpfaffenhofen
    Germany

42. Leon Lasdon, Lecturer
    Department of General Business
    School of Business Administration
    University of Texas
    Austin, Texas 78712
    U.S.A.

43. Günter D. Liesegang
    Industrieseminar
    Universität Köln
    Albertus-Magnus-Platz 1
    5 Köln 41
    Germany

44. Freerk A. Lootsma, Lecturer, Director
    Department of Mathematics
    University of Technology
    Delft
    Netherlands

45. Etienne Loute
    CORE
    Université Catholique de Louvain
    Louvain-la-neuve 1348
    Belgium

46. Paul A.D. de Maine
    Dept. of Computer Science
    Whitmore Building
    Pennsylvania State University
    University Park, Pennsylvania 16802
    U.S.A.

47. Roger A. Main
    B.P. Trading Ltd.
    Britannic House
    Moor Lane
    London EC2
    England

48. Frane Marcelja
    Selenia Sp A
    Via Tiburtina Km 12.4
    Roma
    Italy

49. Istvan Maros
    Res. Inst. for Applied Computer Science (SZA'MK1)
    H-1536 Budapest Pf. 227
    Hungary

50. Hilda R. McDaniel
    Department of Energy
    1200 Pennsylvania Avenue, N.W.
    Washington, D.C. 20461
    U.S.A.

51. Michael Minkoff
    Argonne National Laboratory
    Applied Mathematics Division, Bldg. 221
    9700 S-Cass. Ave.
    Argonne, Illinois 60439
    U.S.A.

52. Frederic H. Murphy
    Department of Energy
    1200 Pennsylvania Avenue N.W.
    Washington, D.C. 20461
    U.S.A.

53. Charles Mylander
    Department of Applied Science
    U.S. Naval Academy
    Annapolis, Maryland 21402
    U.S.A.

54. George Nemhauser
    School of Operations Research
    Upson Hall
    Cornell University
    Ithaca, New York 14853
    U.S.A.

55. Susanne Norton
    College of Engineering
    University of Toledo
    Toledo, Ohio   43606
    U.S.A.

56. Richard P. O'Neill
    Department of Energy
    1200 Pennsylvania Avenue N.W.
    Washington, D.C. 20461
    U.S.A.

57. William Orchard-Hays, Lecturer
    Int. Institute for Applied System Analysis
    2361 Laxenburg
    Austria

58. Susan Powell
    Dept. of Statistics
    London School of Economics
    Houghton Street
    London WC2
    England

59. G. Ramondetta
    E.N.I. - RICOP
    Piazzale E. Mattei 1
    00144 Roma
    Italy

60. Håkan Ramsin
    The Swedish Institute of Applied Mathematics
    Box 5073
    S-10242 Stockholm
    Sweden

61. Paul H. Randolph
    Chase Manhattan Bank
    1 Chase Manhattan Plaza
    New York, New York 10015
    U.S.A.

62. Cosino Resina
    Istituto Analisi Matematica
    Universita' di Bari-Palazzo Ateneo
    Via Nicolai
    70100 Bari
    Italy

63. Marcel Rijckaert, <u>Lecturer</u>
    Instituut voor Chemie- Ingenieurstechniek
    Katholieke Universiteit Leuven
    de Croylaan 2
    <u>B-3030 Heverlee</u>
    Belgium

64. Christian Rumelhard
    Thomson C.S.F.
    33 Rue de Vouillé
    <u>75015 Paris</u>
    France

65. Klaus Schittkowski
    Institut für Angewandte Mathematik und Statistik
    Universität Würzburg
    Am Hubland
    <u>87 Würzburg</u>
    Germany

66. Piet A. Slats
    IWIS-TNO
    Koningin Marialaan 21
    <u>The Hague</u>
    Netherlands

67. Yves Smeers
    CORE
    Université Catholique de Louvain
    <u>Louvain La Neuve</u>
    Belgium

68. E. Spedicato
    CISE
    Casella postale 3986
    <u>20100 Milano</u>
    Italy

69. L. Stefanini
    Sogesta
    <u>Urbino PS</u>
    Italy

70. Jan Telgen
    Econometric Institute
    Erasmus University Rotterdam
    Burg. Oudlaan 50
    P.O. Box 1728
    <u>Rotterdam 3016</u>
    Netherlands

71. Antonio M. Vazquez-Muniz
    IBM
    Po. de la Castellana, 4
    Madrid-1
    Spain

72. Douglas Whitten
    365 Homan Avenue
    State College Pa.   16801
    U.S.A.

73. Haje Willemse (deceased)
    Afdeling der Econometrie
    R.U. Groningen
    Paddepoel
    Groningen
    Netherlands

74. Cornelis de Wit
    University of Technology
    Subdepartment of Mathematics
    Julianalaan 132
    Delft
    Netherlands

Secretary

75. Annelies Rouwenhorst
    Dept. of Mathematics
    University of Technology
    Delft
    Netherlands

Sogesta Staff

76. Clara Bottazzi (accounts)
    Via Cavour 48
    Botticino Sera
    Brescia
    Italy

77. Enrico Catani (social program)
    Sogesta
    Urbino
    Italy

78. Graziella Massi (interpreter)
    Via Corinaldise 93
    Senigallia, Ancona
    Italy

79. Valeria Rossi (travel/transport)
    Via della Rocchetta 2
    Urbino
    Italy

80. John Taylor (local study coordinator)
    Sogesta
    Urbino
    Italy